Advances in Spatial Science

For further volumes:
http://www.springer.com/series/3302

Dong-Joo Moon

Congestion-Prone Services Under Quality Competition

A Microeconomic Analysis

Springer

Ph.D. Dong-Joo Moon
Seoul National University
Institute for Environmental Planning
San 56-1 Shinlim-dong Gwanak-gu, Seoul
Korea (South)
djmoon@snu.ac.kr

Advances in Spatial Science ISSN 1430-9602
ISBN 978-3-642-20188-2 e-ISBN 978-3-642-20189-9
DOI 10.1007/978-3-642-20189-9
Springer Heidelberg Dordrecht London New York

Library of Congress Control Number: 2011944969

Printed on acid-free paper

Springer is part of Springer Science+Business Media (www.springer.com)

To My Family

Preface

This study presents new microeconomic analyses of congestion-prone services that comprise most services at the final consumption stage. This study is distinguished from other studies in that it accommodates two unique features of service markets: the importance of service quality in the decisions of both consumers and suppliers, and the difference between system throughput and physical service capacity. This study covers partial equilibrium analyses of both private and public congestion-prone services in two different circumstances: under no competition and competition among multiple options differentiated by service quality.

This monograph proposes a set of new modeling approaches for the following: consumer demands, service costs, profit-maximizing choices for firms, and policies for public services. Some of the modeling approaches proposed in this study apply and adapt existing microeconomic approaches, and others are newly proposed. The key unique feature common to all these modeling approaches is to employ service time as the variable that accommodates two important features of service markets: congestion delay and service quality competition.

The first application area of the proposed modeling approaches is to characterize the industrial structure of a service market under quality competition. Through analyses based on the modeling approaches, it is shown that interactions among consumers and suppliers endogenously determine the industrial organization type of each firm and allow the coexistence of multiple organization types in a market. Further, it is proved that a lower-quality service should charge a lower price and a lower service production cost so as to have a positive demand, and that a consumer with a larger wage tends to choose a higher-quality service.

The second application area of the new modeling approaches is to assess marketwise recourse allocation efficiency for service markets under quality competition. One important topic advocates that the diversity of service quality is an independent and indispensible criterion, in addition to Pareto optimality, to judge marketwise resource allocation efficiency for service markets. The other important topic analyzes how innovative services contribute to improving resource allocation efficiency in market economies. Further, these analytical outcomes are applied to explaining agglomeration economies of large urban areas.

The third application area is to determine the applicability of analytical outcomes from the proposed modeling approaches to economic studies dealing with practical decision-making problems. From this perspective, we analyze a number of topics that have hitherto not been considered in existing studies. For example, we introduce a new method to develop statistical models for consumer choices from among options having different service qualities. We also illustrate a cost-benefit analysis that uses user time cost that can reflect service quality. In addition, we develop optimal pricing and investment rules for a public service under the constraint of insufficient government funds.

This monograph consists of one introductory chapter, Chap. 1; 12 chapters of analyses, grouped into four parts; and one concluding chapter, Chap. 14. Chapter 1 provides a brief overview of the overall analytical approach used in this study. Each part, composed of multiple chapters, introduces and analyzes one group of decision-making problems: utility maximization problems in Part I; cost minimization problems for public and private congestion-prone services in Part II; profit maximization problems for congestion-prone private services in Part III; and social welfare maximization problems for public services in Part IV. The final chapter, Chap. 14, summarizes and concludes this work.

The four different groups of decision-making problems, introduced above, form the backbone of all the mathematical and economic analyses in this monograph. The utility maximization and cost minimization problems are used to develop consumer demand and supplier cost functions, respectively. These two functions provide inputs to profit and social welfare maximization problems. Optimality conditions for profit maximization problems are utilized to depict the market equilibrium and industrial structure of service markets. Optimality conditions for social welfare maximization problems are utilized to characterize marketwise resource efficiency for a given service type and optimal policies for a given public service.

Each part is presented according to the following plan. Firstly, each part introduces a set of postulates and their behavioral implications for the approach to model one of the four types of decision-making problems introduced above. Subsequently, it presents a number of theorems developed from optimality conditions for the specific type of decision-making problem and suggests the economic implications of the theorems. Finally, the study applies and extends the preceding analyses to explore the range of topics necessary to understand the overall structure of service markets.

Mathematically, all decision-making models proposed here are formulated as nonlinear mathematical programming problems with constraints, including stochastic programming problems. Mathematical analyses to develop theorems and corollaries from the optimization problems rely mainly on elementary optimization theory and real analysis.

This monograph will be of interest to graduate students and researchers in economics and other fields that require knowledge of microeconomics, such as urban and transportation planning as well as business administration. The monograph as a whole can serve as a self-contained book useful to readers who want to grasp the overall structure of service markets. The monograph can also be a useful reference for a number of important research themes in applied microeconomics and planning, such as consumer choice behaviors, the cost structure of public and private congestion-prone service systems, congestion pricing for public congestion-prone service systems, and agglomeration economies of large urban areas.

I am deeply grateful to Tchangho J. Kim at the University of Illinois at Urbana-Champaign for his encouragement and advice throughout this research. I also would like to take this opportunity to express gratitude to Dennis Epple at Carnegie Mellon University, who motivated me to tackle this economic study in spite of majoring in transportation planning at university. I also gratefully acknowledge the financial support of Seoul National University with funds from the BK21 Program of the Korean Government.

Finally, I greatly appreciate Barbara Fess in Springer for her kindness and cooperation in the process of publishing this monograph. I also express my deep gratitude to Julia Deems at Carnegie Mellon University and Scott Cowen from SF Creative Learning Solutions for their assistance in writing this manuscript.

Seoul, Korea Dong-Joo Moon

Contents

Part III Decisions of Congestion-Prone Service Firms

Chapter 1
Introduction: Preview of Analysis Approaches

1.1 Objectives of the Study

Congestion involves phenomena that generate service delays and/or service quality deteriorations due to crowding, and thus causes consumers to suffer economic losses. *Congestion-prone services* (services, for short) refers to the services provided by congestion-prone service systems that exhibit or have the potential to exhibit congestion due to limited capacity. Such services comprise most private services at the final consumption stage, e.g., travel, retail, dining, lodging, telecommunication, sightseeing, and entertainment services, as well as most for-pay public services or facilities, e.g., public highways, urban mass transit services, and other for-pay public facilities, such as parks, museums, and sports and convention facilities.

These congestion-prone services possess a number of distinctive features that cannot appropriately be accommodated through the application of existing microeconomic analytical methodologies. Traditional microeconomic studies typically analyze markets by employing output as a sole independent variable or vector describing the choice of consumers and suppliers. However, such an analysis framework is judged to not properly account for two distinctive features that must be explicitly included in economic analyses from which meaningful insights about real service markets can be drawn.

One important feature of congestion-prone services is congestion phenomena. For a given capacity, congestion within a service system usually causes customers or users to decrease demand for the service and/or to switch to other competing services. One way to prevent such economic losses to suppliers is to take a countermeasure to expand capacity. However, this countermeasure requires suppliers to increase costs. To accommodate this trade-off relationship, it is necessary to use an economic analysis approach that reflects congestion delay as a variable to explain consumer choices, and that separates capacity and the throughput being synonymous with demand facilitated. One example of such an analytical methodology can

D.J. Moon, *Congestion-Prone Services Under Quality Competition*,
Advances in Spatial Science, DOI 10.1007/978-3-642-20189-9_1,

be found in studies for congestion pricing such as Vickrey (1963), and Keeler and Small (1977).

The other distinctive feature is competition among options that offers the same kind of service but has different qualities. *The service quality* of an option depends on various non-monetary service quality attributes (service quality attributes, for short) that comprise not only service time, including congestion delay, but also qualitative attributes such as comfort, safety, cleanliness, beauty, etc. The importance of service quality can be found in observations of real markets, such that a higher-quality service charges a higher price. These observations appear to advocate for the use of an economic analytical methodology that designates all these service quality attributes as factors affecting the choice of consumers and suppliers.

To incorporate these two features into economic analyses, we consider an analytical methodology that employs three independent variables: price, service time, and capacity. Price and service time are independent variables explaining service demand. Service time and capacity are independent variables depicting congestion phenomena. In addition, service time is used as a variable to convey the magnitudes of qualitative attributes to consumers.

This study pursues the objective to offer a more realistic description for service markets than is currently offered by existing microeconomic studies, through the incorporation of congestion and service quality competition into economic analyses. Such economic analyses of this study cover both private and public congestion-prone services in two different circumstances: under no competition and competition among multiple options differentiated by service quality. The major themes of the economic analyses are as follows.

The first theme proposes new modeling approaches for the following decision-making problems of consumers and suppliers: Utility Maximization Problem (UMP) for consumers; Cost Minimization Problem (CMP) for public and private services; Profit Maximization Problem (PMP) for private firms; and Social Welfare Maximization Problem (SWMP) for public agencies. Each modeling approach is devised so as to account for congestion and service quality competition in the decision-making process of consumers or suppliers.

The second theme characterizes the industrial structure of service markets through analyses of the decision-making problems proposed in this study. The decision-making problems have formulations that significantly differ from the counterpart problems considered in existing studies. Therefore, the decision-making problems yield analytical outcomes that also significantly differ from the counterparts in existing studies. These analytical outcomes are utilized to demonstrate that the proposed modeling approaches are effective tools to realistically depict many aspects of service markets under quality competitions.

The third theme presents a view to assess marketwise resource allocation efficiency for the service markets considered above. One specific topic advocates that the diversity of service quality is an independent and indispensible criterion, in addition to Pareto optimality, to judge resource allocation efficiency on marketwise bases. The other important topic analyzes how innovative services contribute to improving resource allocation efficiency in market economies.

The fourth theme applies the analytical outcome from the proposed modeling approaches to other economic studies dealing with practical policy-making problems. One important topic critically reviews the following premise widely applied in benefit-cost analysis and statistical modeling for consumer choices: the value-of-time of consumers is the marginal utility of time, which is independent of service quality. Another important topic develops optimal pricing and investment rules for public services under a number of different circumstances that describe decision-making environments more realistically than depicted in previous studies for congestion pricing.

1.2 Modeling Approaches for Decision-Making Problems

The backbone of the economic analyses presented in this study consists of the four different modeling approaches introduced above for the decision-making problems of consumers and suppliers. All these modeling approaches will be presented in the following format: the mathematical decision-making problem for a consumer or a supplier; and a number of postulates for the consumer or supplier choice behaviors applied in formulating the mathematical model. The manner in which these modeling approaches accommodate the effects of congestion and service quality competition is described below, focusing on differences between the approaches of the study and those of existing studies dealing with similar decision-making problems.

Firstly, we introduce the key concern of this study in modeling consumer demands. This study explicitly accounts for service quality in analyses of consumer choices. One example that well illustrates the importance of service quality in analyses of consumer choices is three different service options commonly offered by international air carriers: economy, business, and first class seats, in the order of higher service quality and higher price. From the standpoint of a passenger who chooses one option among from the three seats in a given airplane, travel time is identical across all the available options. In this circumstance, service quality differences among the options must be considering in explaining the passenger's choice of an option charging a higher price.

On the other hand, existing studies for travel choices use the marginal utility of time, called value-of-time, as the measure of service time value per unit time (e.g., Moses and Williamson, 1963; Small, 1992). Under this approach, the implicit price of travel service is the sum of price and the multiple of service time and value-of-time. Then, the passenger considered above must choose economy class, since travel time is common to all options. However, it is clear that many actual air passengers voluntarily purchase business or first class tickets.

To account for service quality in consumer demand analyses, this study devises and applies *the service quality perception approach* (or *the perception approach*). This new approach for consumer demand modeling is an application of household production theory initiated by Becker (1965) and Lancaster (1966). The perception approach is distinguished from previous applications of household production theory in that the former explicitly quantifies differences in service quality among multiple service options.

The use of the perception approach is the most distinctive feature of this study from other microeconomic studies for service or product differentiation (e.g., Chamberlin, 1933; Lancaster, 1975; Frieman, 1983). The demand for a firm under the perception approach estimates the demand segment facilitated most economically by that firm. The most economical option is judged through comparison of implicit prices for all available options. Further, the implicit price of an option consists not only of price but also of value for various qualitative attributes. In contrast, no existing modeling approach for consumer demand explicitly quantifies differences in intangible qualitative attributes among services.

The perception approach formulates UMPs by quantifying differences in service quality among service options under the following three key postulates. First, the consumption of a service yields two kinds of commodities: one prime commodity, which refers to benefits specific to that service, and multiple hedonic commodities, each of which denotes one particular qualitative attribute such as comfort or safety. Second, consumers subjectively judge the monetary value of various qualitative attributes packed in a service. Third, the consumers' subjective perception of the consumer (or household) production of qualitative attributes is expressed as a special kind of joint homogeneous production function.

The perception approach is the theoretical keystone that enables the forthcoming economic analyses of this study to explicitly account for quality competition among multiple service options. The UMP under this approach yields the service demand function that will be applied to economic analyses throughout this study. This demand function has a number of desirable mathematical properties. For example, the criterion for consumer choices, incorporated into the demand function, reasonably explains why an air passenger chooses a business or first class ticket instead of an economy ticket and why a passenger with a higher wage prefers to a more expensive seat.

Secondly, we introduce the specific type of cost function applied to the forthcoming economic analyses. The two different cost functions that will be developed are both similar to social cost functions commonly used in transportation economics. Specifically, the social cost function of this study is almost identical to the same cost function employed in economic analyses of highway (e.g., Vickrey, 1963; Wohl, 1972; Keeler and Small, 1977) and of urban transit (e.g., Meyer et al, 1965; Mohring, 1972). The cost function for private services also has a similar functional form to the social cost function and the cost function considered in previous studies for private services (e.g., Small, 1992), but requires fundamentally different economic interpretations.

In existing studies, the social cost function for transportation services is expressed as the sum of supplier investment cost and user time cost. Moreover, the user time cost is estimated by applying the service time estimated from service time function. The service time function of a transportation system is formulated to explicitly account for the effect of congestion on user time cost. Generally, the service time estimated from service time function is decreasing in capacity but increasing in throughput.

One analytical method of developing the highway cost function depicted above is to derive it from the Social Cost Minimization Problem (SCMP), which is used to find an optimal capacity that minimizes the total cost required to facilitate a given throughput (Moon and Park 2002a). The total cost in this minimization problem is estimated under the following postulates: first, the total cost is the sum of investment cost and user time cost; second, user time cost, including user cost for congestion delay, is increasing in throughput but decreasing in capacity. Therefore, the SCMP estimates the solution of capacity through trade-off between investment cost increasing in capacity and user time cost decreasing in capacity.

We conceive that service time, especially congestion delay, is also a factor that determines supplier cost for private services, more exactly, revenue loss that can be classified as quasi-cost in a broad sense. This is because an increase in congestion delay decreases service demand and, thus, incurs revenue loss. Further, we imagine that cost function for private service can be developed from a cost minimization problem that has a formulation similar to the SCMP introduced above.

Based on the above idea, we develop *the full cost approach*, which is applied to develop cost functions for both congestion-prone public and private services. The full cost approach explicitly accounts for congestion, as does the traditional approach to develop a social cost function for highways. The full cost approach, however, differs from the existing approach in that it uses service time value estimated from the demand function under the perception approach that explicitly accounts for the qualitative attributes.

To be specific, the full cost approach develops cost functions for both public and private services from the SCMP and the Quasi-Cost Minimization Problem (QCMP), respectively. The SCMP and QCMP are constructed, respectively, as the dual of the SWMP and PMP that will be introduced subsequently. Both SCMP and QCMP have an identical formulation, with one exception. This difference is the method used to quantify time cost per unit time. The SWMP specifies time cost as user time cost per unit time estimated from the demand function under the perception approach. In contrast, the QCMP quantifies time cost as the marginal revenue loss of service time that is also estimated from the same demand function.

Thirdly, we present the approach to model the PMP for a congestion-prone private service firm. This approach differs fundamentally from the approaches considered in existing studies for industrial organization. The key distinctive feature of the approach is to describe supplier's choice behaviors more realistically than it is depicted in existing studies.

To start, we examine the nature of the PMP for congestion-prone services with an example of the choice problem for a businessman who is newly participating in the hotel business. Suppose that the businessman has predetermined the qualitative service attributes of the hotel. Then, it can be said that the key decision-making components that can be chosen by the businessman according to his will are room charge and number of guest rooms, which are synonymous with price and capacity, respectively. It can also be argued that the businessman makes the choice for price and capacity based on a judgment regarding the expected number of guests and for the desirable level of congestion to avoid severe room shortage as well as excessively large number of vacant rooms.

It is important that modeling the PMP for the businessman examined above is not straightforward. The businessman is postulated to reckon the effect of his choices for price and capacity on demand and congestion. One way to accommodate this effect could be to employ the demand function of the perception approach, which is sensitive to congestion as well as price. However, congestion is not an independent choice variable but rather an increasing function of demand; that is, congestion, the independent variable of the demand function, is sensitive to the value of demand function.

For this reason, we devise *the user equilibrium approach* that postulates the choice behaviors of a service firm as described above using the example of a hotel business. To elaborate, the core of the user equilibrium approach consists of the following two postulates: first, the directly controllable variables for a service firm consist only of price and capacity; second, the firm can understand the effect of its choice regarding the two independent variables on demand and congestion delay. In addition, it is assumed that the judgment of the firm regarding consumer demand can be formulated as the user equilibrium condition, which is an amendment of the service time function applied in the SWMP and QCMP.

An additional important postulate of the user equilibrium approach is equivalent to the ignorance of conjectural variations, which is introduced in economic analyses of congestion-free oligopoly. This study stipulates that a service firm chooses its price and service time without accounting for possible changes in the value of these choice variables for competing services. This postulate is similar to the following two different approaches for the conjectural variation in congestion-free oligopoly: the hypothesis to ignore changes in competitors' outputs in Cournot (1938); and that to neglect changes in competitors' prices in Bertrand (1883). However, the former differs from the latter in that the former additionally ignores the reaction of customers for competing services, which causes changes the service time of competing services.

The user equilibrium approach outlined above employs three independent vectors in order to characterize market equilibrium: price, service time, and capacity. Price and service time are independent vectors determining demands for service under the perception approach. Price and capacity are directly controllable choice variables for each firm under the user equilibrium approach. Further, service time is an indirectly controllable variable for each firm through the choice of directly controllable variables, and the mechanism to control service time is formulated as the user equilibrium condition.

Fourthly, we introduce a new method to assess resource allocation efficiency for congestion-prone service markets under competition. The departure point of the present study, in contrast to existing studies for resource allocation efficiency, stems from the manner in which the user equilibrium approach characterizes resource allocations in competitive service markets. To be specific, the user equilibrium approach yields the outcome such that the demand for a certain service is disjoint to those for competing services differentiated by service quality. In this circumstance, it is inevitable to include service quality diversity as well as Pareto optimality as criteria to evaluate resource allocation efficiency on marketwise bases.

One example that illustrates the validity of the above approach to judge marketwise resource allocation efficiency is a huge service market formed in metropolitan areas. One advantage of metropolitan areas in resource allocation efficiency for a particular service can be ascribed to keen competition among service firms, which generally leads to efficient resource allocations for the service. It is also obvious that metropolitan consumers receive benefit from the availability of services with diversified quality, which offers a better opportunity of purchasing services from a group of options that are more suitable to their preferences for service quality.

The reason why keen competition among services is beneficial to consumers is proved through analyses of a SWMP. This SWMP specifies the objective function as a social welfare function similar to that of previous studies such as Mohring (1970), Diamond and Mirrlees (1971), Sandmo (1973), and Moon and Park (2002b). However, the SWMP of this study differs from the same problems considered in the previous studies in the following respect: the former applies indirect utilities under the perception approach as the argument of social welfare function, whereas the latter uses indirect utilities under neoclassical consumer demand theory.

On the other hand, the key reason why service quality diversity is an indispensible and independent criterion to judge efficiency is proved through a benefit-cost analysis for the introduction of an innovative service. By definition, the innovative service reduces service production cost and/or improves service quality; that is, the introduction of this service usually enhances service quality diversity on marketwise bases. The introduction of such an innovative service triggers changes in the choices of existing firms for prices and capacities. Through analyses of these impacts, it is shown that the introduction of the innovative service improves overall resource allocation efficiency on marketwise bases.

Besides the SWMP introduced above, we test a number of other SWMPs. All the tested SWMPs are constructed by applying the user equilibrium approach that can be adapted to economic analyses of governmental decision-making problems. Further, each SWMP is designed to address one specific policy issue. One group of issues considered is resource allocation efficiency in service markets under quality competition. The other group is congestion pricing problems for a public service under a number of different circumstances, including a public service in competition with other private and/or public services.

1.3 Organization of the Study

This monograph is composed of four parts, each of which is comprised of multiple chapters. Each part introduces and analyzes one group of decision-making problems for services under quality competition: UMPs in Part I, CMPs in Part II,

PMPs in Part III, and SWMPs in Part IV. These four different groups of decision-making problems are analyzed so as to address various topics necessary to grasp the structure of service markets and to develop optimal governmental policies for public services. The organization of the analyses and the limitations of the analyses are briefly explained below.

First, for each modeling approach, we first introduce and analyze the simplest form of decision-making problems, which can apply to only one particular group of private or public services. We subsequently develop a number of variants, each of which extends to another group of services, by amending the simplest form in a fashion that reflects the peculiarity of the service group.

Second, each modeling approach is developed so that it can be applied to economic analyses of both private and public services in a consistent manner. Private firms pursue an objective that fundamentally differs from that of agencies that offer public services; the former seeks maximum profit, whereas the latter searches for maximum social welfare. Aside from this difference, there is no reason why decision-making problems for private services should be modeled differently from the problems for public services. For this reason, we devise modeling approaches for consumer demand and supplier cost functions that are uniformly applicable to both public and private services. Furthermore, we apply identical decision-making rules, except for the objective of economic activities, in formulating the choice problems of private and public agencies.

Third, the four modeling approaches are structured so that each approach constitutes a part of the whole analytical framework for various topics considered in this study, and maintains a certain consistency such that no more than one approach is applied to any analysis topic. To be specific, consumer demand and supplier cost functions are developed through analyses of UMPs and CMPs, respectively, and are applied in constructing PMPs and SWMPs. The PMPs developed in this manner are utilized to depict the equilibrium and industrial structure of service markets. On the other hand, the SWMPs are applied to analyses of marketwise resource efficiency for private services and public policies for public services.

Fourth, analyses for the four different modeling approaches include illustrations of real service markets, in order to demonstrate the efficacy of these approaches in explaining the real world circumstances. The monograph introduces some observations that cannot be explained within the context of existing approaches, and shows that these observations can be reasonably interpreted by applying the outcomes from these approaches.

Fifth, the set of modeling approaches proposed in this research pursues partial equilibrium analyses, and thus has two different kinds of limitations. The first limitation is that analyses are confined to services at the final consumption stage; that is, they exclude the case when services are inputs to the production of other goods and services. The second limitation is that analyses do not explicitly consider the case when inputs to the production of a congestion-prone service are other kinds of congestion-prone services.

Finally, the applicability of analyses in the study is confined to services in which capacity is an important choice component for the supplier of private or public services. Most, but not all, services belong to this category. Housing services constitute one typical example not included in this category. Another example not included is labor service; labor services, of course, are supplied by individuals rather than by firms.

1.4 Mathematical Notations for Decision-Making Problems

All decision-making problems analyzed in this study are formulated as constrained non-linear optimization problems, including stochastic non-linear problems. Such optimization problems are formulated in a unified manner, as defined below.

Suppose the decision-making problem of an agent is used to choose a vector $x \equiv (x_1, \cdots, x_N)$, which maximizes the objective function $f(x; a, b)$ under the constraint of $g(x; a, b) = 0$ or $g(x; a, b) \leq 0$, where both a and b are the vectors of parameters. Then, this maximization problem is expressed as the Lagrangian L:

$$L(x, \mu; a) \equiv \max \{f(x; a, b)\} + \mu g(x; a, b). \tag{1.1}$$

In the case of minimization problems, the Lagrangian is expressed by

$$L(x, \mu; a) \equiv \min \{f(x; a, b)\} - \mu g(x, a, b). \tag{1.2}$$

The function $g(x; a, b)$ is formulated so that $\mu \geq 0$, for both cases of maximization and minimization problems.

The expression that the Lagrangian L in the above includes a but not b reflects the following conventions. The saddle point of L is denoted by the vector $(\bar{x}, \bar{\mu})$ or the vector with other hat symbols, e.g., $(\hat{x}, \hat{\mu})$. Such a saddle point $(\bar{x}, \bar{\mu})$ is generally the function of parameter vectors a and b. Despite that, the use of the expression $L(x, \mu; a)$ indicates that subsequent analyses of L deal only with the image of $(\bar{x}, \bar{\mu})$ for varying values of a.

Part I
Service Demand of Consumers

Chapter 2
Service Demand of Consumer with Deterministic Perceptions

2.1 Introduction

Consumers usually choose an option from a set of available options that offer the same kind of service. Such consumer choice is affected by myriad service attributes. One example that well illustrates this aspect of consumer choice might be the choice of one travel option from among a population of available options. This choice is influenced not only by prices and service times but also by relatively subjective attributes such as comfort and privacy. Moreover, different consumers prefer different options for travel services and the same consumer makes different choices at various times. Naturally, these facts extend to the choice of other services that comprise most of our consumption activities: retail, recreation, entertainment, dining, medical clinic, hotel, housing, telecommunication, and various business services.

This chapter analyzes a consumer choice of an option from a set of available options, through the application of the perception approach newly proposed in this study. The most distinctive feature of the perception approach in contrast to other approaches to consumer demand analyses consists in its ability to explicitly incorporate service quality. The perception approach quantifies the service attributes of an option using two groups of variables: group one includes quantitative variables divided into price and service time; group two consists of all qualitative attributes such as comfort, safety, cleanliness, privacy, etc. The perception approach primarily targets the service offered by multiple options of different service attributes, termed *the qualitative choice service*, but is also applicable to the service provided by a single option.

The perception approach, an application of household production theory, adopts the following basic hypothesis of household production theory: consumer utility is the function of commodities produced through the consumption of qualitative choice services. The perception approach is, however, distinguished from previous applications of the theory in that it incorporates one additional hypothesis: each qualitative attribute packed in services constitutes an independent argument of consumer utility.

D.J. Moon, *Congestion-Prone Services Under Quality Competition*,
Advances in Spatial Science, DOI 10.1007/978-3-642-20189-9_2,

The additional hypothesis is incorporated into UMPs by employing the consumer (or household) production function developed under the two postulates that follow. First, each consumer reckons the magnitude of all qualitative attributes in an option, which generally differs from consumer to consumer. Second, each consumer judges the implicit price of each qualitative attribute, which also differs from consumer to consumer, but which is shared by that attribute for all available options.

Under the perception approach, the consumer production function incorporated into UMPs should be able to reasonably depict the jointness of consumer production. The input to consumer production for qualitative choice service should consist of multiple inputs that comprise all service options in the menu of options available to consumers. Also, the output should consist of multiple outcomes that include all qualitative attributes packed in services consumed.

By applying the perception approach outlined above, it is possible to construct the UMP that yields *the revealed preference condition* for the consumer choice of an option from among multiple options. The revealed preference condition identifies the option chosen by a consumer. The chosen option has the lowest implicit price. Also, the implicit price of an option depends on not only the magnitudes of all quantitative attributes in the option but also the implicit prices of all qualitative attributes. Further, as postulated above, *consumer perception for service quality*, which refers to the perceived magnitudes and implicit prices of qualitative attributes, differ from consumer to consumer. Therefore, it is natural that the choice of the best option differs among consumers.

The qualitative choice problem, the main target of demand analyses in this study, is a special subgroup of UMPs under the perception approach. Roughly speaking, the qualitative choice problem uses a special type of consumer production function. This type of production function, called *the joint homogeneous production function*, satisfies the following two conditions: first, production systems described by this function yield multiple outcomes from multiple inputs; second, the production function is mathematically homogeneous of degree one in both inputs and outputs.

By virtue of the homogeneity of consumer production functions, the qualitative choice problem yields the outcome that the implicit price of every qualitative attribute is a constant independent of the magnitude of quantitative attributes consumed. For this reason, the monetary value for all qualitative attributes packed in an option is also a constant. This property of the qualitative choice problem leads to the demand function of an option, which has a functional structure very similar to that of neoclassical consumer demand functions. Such a demand function for an option has the advantage of greatly simplifying analyses of its mathematical properties such as continuity and comparative statics with respect to the prices and service times of all options.

The qualitative choice problem for a certain qualitative choice service should be able to reflect the uniqueness of the service. This requirement can be fulfilled by employing a utility function and/or a consumer production function that appropriately formulates the uniqueness. We can, therefore, imagine that there are a large number of qualitative choice problems with different formulations. However, each qualitative choice problem requires demand analyses significantly different from other problems. For this reason, one specific example of qualitative choice problems is analyzed in this chapter, and other relevant choice problems are considered in the subsequent chapter.

This example of qualitative choice problems, termed *the basic choice problem*, is constructed under a number of additional simplifying conditions other than the postulates common to all qualitative choice problems. The most important condition is that the perceived magnitude of qualitative attributes is linearly proportional to the service time of options. This condition is applicable only to non-durable services such that the duration of benefit from the consumption of services is limited to a given service period. Such non-durable services include travel, communication, recreation, and entertainment services.

The perception approach of this chapter applies one additional important postulate such that the perceived magnitude of qualitative attributes is always deterministic, and therefore called *the deterministic perception approach*. The deterministic perception approach has the limitation of being unable to explain why a particular consumer makes different choices at particular times. For this reason, we will introduce an alternative approach that can accommodate the randomness of consumer choices. This approach hypothesizes that the perceived magnitude is an outcome of random processes affected by various uncertain factors such as ever-changing physical and emotional conditions. This alternative approach, called *the random perception approach*, will be introduced in Chap. 4.

This chapter develops and analyzes the basic choice problem according to the following plan. The following section presents a detailed procedure to construct the basic choice problem under the deterministic perception approach. Subsequently, Sect. 2.3 develops the revealed preference condition for the basic choice problem, and interprets economic implications of the developed revealed preference condition. This is followed by Sect. 2.4, which analyzes the mathematical property of service demand functions for the basic choice problem. That section also presents a more concrete definition of qualitative choice problems in connection with previous analyses of the basic choice problem.

2.2 Development of the Basic Choice Problem

2.2.1 Homogeneity of Consumer Production Functions

This subsection illustrates analyses of a UMP in the circumstance when each service traded in markets is offered by one option. This UMP is incorporated with a joint homogeneous production function.[1] Through analyses of this problem,

[1]The joint production function, in which all inputs are jointly used in producing multiple outputs, cannot be homogeneous of degree one in both inputs and outputs (Hall 1973; Pollak and Wachter 1975). However, there is a special group of joint homogeneous production functions in which only some inputs are jointly used in producing multiple outputs. One example of such a production functions is introduced in Moon and Kim (2002), and is applied to the basic choice problem considered in this chapter.

we illustrate that the UMP with a joint homogeneous production function satisfies *the consistency condition* such that the implicit price of commodities is independent of the amount of commodities consumed.

To begin, we introduce a UMP incorporated with a joint homogeneous production function. First, this UMP is used to find the commodity bundle $z \equiv (z_1, \cdots, z_K)$, which maximizes the value of a utility function $U(z)$. Second, the function $U(z)$ is concave and differentiable in z. Third, the commodity bundle z is the outcome of consumer production that uses inputs $x \equiv (x_1, \cdots, x_J)$, composed of goods and services traded in markets. Fourth, the purchasing cost of inputs satisfies the budget constraint such that $\bar{M} - \sum_j p_j x_j \geq 0$, where $\bar{M}$ is full income, and p_j is the price of input j. Fifth, the consumer production is a joint production, expressed by $F_k(x) - z_k = 0$, for all k, in which some, but not all, elements of x are jointly inputted. Sixth, the vector function $F \equiv (F_1, \cdots F_K)$ is homogeneous of degree one in both inputs x and outputs z.

The UMP specified above can be expressed as the Lagrangian L_1 such that

$$L_1(x, z, \mu, \eta; p) = \max \left\{ U(z) \right\} + \sum_k \mu_k \Big(F_k(x) - z_k \Big) + \left(\bar{M} - \sum_j p_j x_j \right), \quad (2.1)$$

where $\mu \equiv (\mu_1, \cdots, \mu_K) \rangle 0$ and $p \equiv (p_1, \cdots, p_J)$. This UMP is too complex to directly characterize the solution of (x, z). For this reason, this UMP is decomposed into two sub-optimization problems.

The first sub-optimization problem is used to estimate the optimal bundle of inputs x, which minimizes the input cost $\sum_j p_j x_j$ necessary for the production of an arbitrary commodity bundle z. This minimization problem, called the cost minimization problem for consumer production, is expressed by the following Lagrangian L_2:

$$L_2(x, \varphi; z, p) = \max \left\{ \sum_j p_j x_j \right\} + \sum_k \varphi_k (z_k - F_k(x)). \quad (2.2)$$

This optimization problem gives the consumer cost function $C(p; z)$ that estimates the minimum cost necessary for the production of commodity bundle z. This cost function equals $\sum_j p_j \bar{x}_j$, in which $\bar{x}_j$ is the solution of x_j to L_2.

The second sub-optimization is used to estimate the optimal bundle of z, which maximizes the utility $U(z)$, under the budget constraint $\bar{M} - C(p, z) \geq 0$. This maximization problem is expressed as the Lagrangian L_3 such that

$$L_3(z, \eta; p) = \max \left\{ U(z) \right\} + \eta \Big(\bar{M} - C(p; z) \Big). \quad (2.3)$$

This UMP depicts that the solution of z maximizes $U(z)$ value, under the premise that the optimal bundle of z is produced efficiently.

We are now ready to introduce the consistency condition for the implicit price of commodities. Let $(\bar{x}, \bar{\varphi})$ be the solution to the cost minimization problem L_2.

Then, by the envelop theorem for constrained optimization problems, the term $\bar{\varphi}_k$ represents the implicit price of commodity k. Also, the consistency of the implicit price φ_k implies that this price is independent of the value of z. This consistency is the direct consequence of the sixth assumption that the joint production function is homogeneous of degree one in both inputs and outputs, as proved below.[2]

Theorem 2.1. *The implicit price $\bar{\varphi}_k$, for all k, estimated from L_2, satisfies both the consistency condition and the equality $C(z;p) = \sum_k \bar{\varphi}_k z_k$.*

Proof. By the assumption that F is homogeneous of degree one in x, the function $Z_k(x, z_k) \equiv z_k - F_k(x)$ satisfies the following:

$$\sum_j \frac{\partial Z_k}{\partial x_j} = -\sum_j \frac{\partial \bar{F}_k}{\partial x_j} x_j = -\bar{F}_k = -z_k, \quad \text{all}\, k. \tag{2.4}$$

where $\bar{F}_k \equiv F_k(\bar{x})$. Subsequently, irrespective of homogeneity, the solution to L_2 satisfies the following first order conditions with respect to x_j:

$$\frac{\partial L_2}{\partial x_j} = p_j - \sum_k \bar{\varphi}_k \frac{\partial \bar{F}_k}{\partial x_j} = 0, \text{ all}\, j. \tag{2.5}$$

Equation (2.5) shows that the implicit price $\bar{\varphi}_k$ satisfies the consistency condition; that is, the solution of $\bar{\varphi}_k$ to (2.5) is independent of z. Finally, combining (2.4) and (2.5) gives the consumer cost function such that

$$C(p;z) = \sum_j p_j \bar{x}_j = \sum_j \sum_k \bar{\varphi}_k \frac{\partial \bar{F}_k}{\partial x_j} \bar{x}_j = \sum_k \bar{\varphi}_k \sum_j \frac{\partial \bar{F}_k}{\partial x_j} \bar{x}_j = \sum_k \bar{\varphi}_k z_k, \tag{2.6}$$

as claimed in the theorem. □

Theorem 2.1 shows that the consistency of implicit prices $\bar{\varphi}_k$, for all k, leads to the last equality of (2.6). Substituting this equality into L_3 gives

$$L_3(z, \eta; p) = \max \left\{U(z)\right\} + \eta \left(\bar{M} - \sum_k \bar{\varphi}_k z_k \right). \tag{2.7}$$

This UMP has a formulation identical to that of neoclassical utility maximization problems, with the exception that the price of the latter is replaced by the consistent implicit price $\bar{\varphi}_k$. Therefore, the solution of z can be estimated in a manner identical to that used to solve neoclassical utility maximization problems.

---

[2]The fact that the consistency condition holds, if and only if the production function incorporated into the UMP is homogeneous of degree one in both inputs and outputs is not new. See Hall (1973) and Muellbauer (1974).

2.2.2 Quantification of Service Quality

We postulate that the factor affecting the service quality of an option comprises all non-monetary service quality attributes that refer to all quantitative and qualitative attributes, excluding price. One service quality attribute is service time. This attribute is one element of quantitative attributes, and therefore can be measured objectively. The remaining attributes consist of all qualitative attributes. These attributes reflect the subjective judgment of consumers, and therefore cannot be measured objectively. The method of quantifying these qualitative attributes in the consumer production function is explained below, with an example of non-durable service.

To begin, we introduce an index system that distinguishes one option from another. An option is denoted by two integers, m and n, so as to distinguish differences in qualitative and/or quantitative attributes among options that offer the same qualitative choice service. The first index, m, designates *a heterogeneous service group* differentiated from other groups by qualitative attributes. The second index, n, distinguishes one option from the other *homogeneous service options* belonging to the same heterogeneous service group m.

One example that clearly illustrates this index system is international air passenger services. This service can be classified into three heterogeneous service groups: first ($m = 1$), business ($m = 2$), and economy classes ($m = 3$). Each option belonging to a certain heterogeneous service group can be further classified by carrier or route, using the second index, n.

Subsequently, we introduce a method of formulating consumer production that yields two groups of commodities through the consumption of a particular service. The first group consists of one commodity, which represents one special kind of benefit specific to the service, called *the prime commodity*. The second group includes multiple commodities, each of which denotes one qualitative attribute, termed *a certain hedonic com*modity. For example, the prime commodity of a passenger service option is the service that transports a traveler from one location to another, whereas the hedonic commodities comprise all relevant qualitative attributes such as comfort and safety perceived when receiving the service.

The yield of commodities in the process of consuming the service of option mn is quantified as follows. Suppose that a consumer purchases q_{mn} units of service mn, where q_{mn} represents the number of visits to purchase services from option mn. Then, the yield of the prime commodity, denoted by y_{mn}, is estimated by

$$y_{mn} = a_m \, q_{mn}, \tag{2.8}$$

where a_m is the production coefficient of service group m for the prime commodity, and is assumed to be positive. Subsequent the yield of hedonic commodity k, expressed by z_{kmn}, is quantified as follows:

$$z_{kmn} = b_{km} \, t_{mn} q_{mn}, \tag{2.9}$$

where b_{km} is the production coefficient of option mn for commodity k and can be either positive or negative, and t_{mn} is the service time of option mn.

The production coefficient a_m in (2.8) represents the yield of the prime commodity per service offered by option mn. This coefficient a_m is common to all options belonging to heterogeneous service group m, but can differ from that of other groups. For example, the prime commodity of sightseeing trips could be enjoyment achievable at the destination, and the magnitude of enjoyment usually differs from destination to destination.

The term $b_{km}t_{mn}q_{mn}$ in (2.9) estimates the number of hedonic commodity k yielded from the service of option mn, under the condition that the service is non-durable. The yield of the hedonic commodity from a non-durable service is assumed to be linearly proportional to service time; that is, the yield of commodity k is estimated by multiplying production coefficient b_{km} by total service time $t_{mn}q_{mn}$. This coefficient b_{km} is assumed to be common to all options belonging to the same group m, and to be different from that of other service groups, b_{lm}, for all $l \neq k$.

One example that clearly explains this aspect of coefficient b_{km} is air passenger services. It is certain that the coefficient perceived by a passenger differs by seat. For example, a passenger feels that a first class seat is more comfortable than is one in the economy section of the plane. Hence, first class has a larger coefficient of comfort than does economy class. But a particular seat, e.g., economy class, has an identical coefficient across all carriers or travel routes.

Finally, there is no objective way to identify relevant kinds of qualitative attributes included in demand analyses for a particular service. The kinds of qualitative attributes relevant to demand analyses for a certain qualitative choice service depend mainly on the subjective judgments of analysts. For example, one analyst may think that qualitative attributes relevant to trip demand analyses are comfort and safety only. Another analyst could argue that privacy and cleanliness should also be considered.

Fortunately, this arbitrariness in the choice of qualitative attributes does not affect subsequent demand analyses, as briefed below. The choice of an option depends only on the sum of monetary values for all service quality attributes per service, estimated by $\sum_k \bar{\varphi}_k b_{km} t_{mn}$, where $\bar{\varphi}_k$ is the implicit price of hedonic commodity k. Therefore, it is possible to analyze the demand for service mn using the summed value $\sum_k \bar{\varphi}_k b_{km} t_{mn}$, without recourse to each $\bar{\varphi}_k$ and b_{km} values for all k. Details will be explained next.

2.2.3 Consumer Production Function

We here introduce the consumer production function that will be incorporated into the basic choice problem for a certain non-durable service. This production function is formulated to fulfill the requirement that it is homogeneous in both multiple inputs and multiple outputs. The functional form of this joint homogeneous production function and the economic implications embedded in the function are presented below.

The joint production considered here yields two groups of commodities. One commodity is a prime commodity specific to a certain non-durable service, and its quantity is denoted by y. The other group consists of multiple hedonic commodities that are the byproducts of activities in which the non-durable service is consumed, and their quantities are expressed by $z \equiv (z_1, \cdots, z_K)$. Further, the hedonic commodities can be produced through substitute productions using inputs other than the non-durable service.

The production of commodities requires three groups of inputs. The first group consists of the non-durable services offered by multiple options, each of which is denoted by mn, where $m \in \langle 1, M \rangle$ and $n \in \langle 1, N_M \rangle$. The quantities purchased from the options are expressed by $q \equiv (q_{11}, \cdots, q_{MN})$. The second group is composed of goods and services traded in markets, which are the inputs to the substitute productions of hedonic commodities. Each of these inputs is denoted by $j \in \langle 1, J \rangle$, and the quantity of these inputs to the production of commodity k is expressed by $x_k \equiv (x_{k1}, \cdots, x_{kJ})$. The third group represents consumer time. The amount of time spent in consuming one unit of service mn is expressed by t_{mn}, and the amount spent in the substitute production of commodity k is denoted by t_k.

The production function specifies the relationship between the multiple inputs and multiple outputs, as described above. This production function is expressed as a set of simultaneous equation systems, each of which identifies the functional relationship of one output with multiple inputs, as presented below.

Assumption 2.1. The production function perceived by a consumer, who follows the deterministic perception approach, satisfies the following.[3]

(a) The production function of the prime commodity, denoted by Y', is

$$Y'(q; y) = y - \sum_{mn} a_m q_{mn} = 0.$$

(b) The production function of hedonic commodity k, denoted by Z'_k, is

$$Z'_k(q, x_k, t_k; z_k) = z_k - \sum_{mn} b_{km} t_{mn} q_{mn} - Z_k(x_k, t_k) = 0, \text{ all } k,$$

where Z_k is the substitute production function of k.

(c) Every substitute production Z_k is twice differentiable in (x_k, t_k), and satisfies the three following additional conditions: first, each input (x_k, t_k) is non-joint to those of other productions; second, every substitute production Z_k exhibits constant returns in its input (x_k, t_k); and third, the input (x_k, t_k) for all k is positive.

[3] A production function similar to that of $Y'(q; y)$ is introduced in Moses and Williamson (1963). In the study, the demand for work trip yield is specified by the formula $y = \Sigma_m q_m$, in order to analyze the mode choice behavior of commuters. Furthermore, a linear relationship similar to that of $Z'_k(q, x_k, t_k; z_k)$ is applied in Lancaster (1966).

The production function defined above is a joint production function; that is, the multiple inputs q are joint inputs to multiple commodities; one prime commodity y and multiple hedonic commodities z, as formulated in Assumption 2.1(a) and (b), respectively. This joint production function is structured so as to be homogeneous of degree one in its inputs and outputs, as proved below.

Lemma 2.1. *The joint production function defined in Assumption 2.1 is homogeneous of degree one in both inputs and outputs; that is,*

$$Y'(\alpha q;\alpha y)+\sum_k Z_k'(\alpha q,\alpha x_k,\alpha t_k;\alpha z_k)=\alpha Y'(q\,;y)+\alpha\sum_k Z_k'(q,x_k,t_k;z_k),$$

where α is a positive real number.

Proof. In light of Euler's theorem, the production function is homogeneous of degree one in outputs, if

$$y\frac{\partial Y'}{\partial y}+\sum_k z_k\frac{\partial Z'_k}{\partial z_k}=y+\sum_k z_k. \tag{2.10}$$

Further, this production function is homogeneous of degree one in inputs, if

$$\sum_{mn} q_{mn}\frac{\partial Y'}{\partial q_{mn}}+\sum_k\left(\sum_{mn} q_{mn}\frac{\partial Z'_k}{\partial q_{mn}}+\sum_j x_{kj}\frac{\partial Z'_k}{\partial x_{kj}}+t_k\frac{\partial Z'_k}{\partial t_k}\right)$$

$$=-y-\sum_k z_k. \tag{2.11}$$

Therefore, the proof can be completed through proof of (2.10) and (2.11).

Equation (2.10) can be shown through trite calculations. Equation (2.11) can readily be proved using the following equation:

$$\sum_j x_{kj}\frac{\partial Z'_k}{\partial x_{kj}}+t_k\frac{\partial Z'_k}{\partial t_k}=-\sum_j x_{kj}\frac{\partial Z_k}{\partial x_{kj}}-t_k\frac{\partial Z_k}{\partial t_k}=-Z_k,\ \text{all } k. \tag{2.12}$$

Here, the last equality of (2.12) follows from Assumption 2.1(c) such that the function Z exhibits constant returns in its inputs. □

Finally, we examine the mathematical and economic implications of the conditions for the production function in Assumption 2.1. Mathematically, Assumption 2.1(a) for prime commodity depicts that the yield of the prime commodity equals $\sum_{mn} a_m q_{mn}$, under the implicit assumption that there is no substitute for that service. On the other hand, Assumption 2.1(b) for hedonic commodity k expresses that the yield z_k is the sum of the production from qualitative choice services, $\sum_{mn} b_{km}t_{mn}q_{mn}$, and the substitute production, Z_k.

The three conditions for the substitute production function Z_k in Assumption 2.1(c) are the full set of mathematical devices, which reflects the following key postulate of the perception approach: the implicit price of commodity k is a constant exogenously determined, irrespective of chosen q values, as will be confirmed in Lemma 2.2. To be specific, given that the function Z_k is homogeneous of degree one, the implicit price of commodity k for this substitute production is a constant. Further, given that $Z_k \rangle 0$, this substitute production plays the role of determining the implicit price of commodity k packed in qualitative choice services, irrespective of $\sum_{mn} b_{km} t_{mn} q_{mn}$ values, as will also be proved in Lemma 2.2.

Economically, the implications of the substitute production function Z_k can be interpreted as follows. The function Z_k estimates the yield of a consumer's substitute production for hedonic commodity k, which is identical to qualitative attribute k packed in the services of all available options. Such a substitute production uses two groups of inputs: one group is goods and services traded in markets, and the other one is consumer time.

Substitute production is illustrated with the qualitative attribute of transportation services. One relevant qualitative attribute of transportation services is comfort. One way of substituting this attribute can be to spend consumer time by resting at home, which results in a feeling of comfort. If so, the substitute function for comfort, denoted by k, can be expressed as $Z_k(x_k, t_k) = a_k t_k$, where a_k is a production coefficient. Another example is safety. One substitute for enhancing the feeling of safety from accidents might be to purchase more comprehensive insurance. Then, the substitute function can be expressed as $Z_k(x_k, t_k) = b_k x_k$ under the condition of $p_k = 1$, where b_k is a production coefficient.

2.2.4 Modeling of the Basic Choice Problem

We here formulate the basic choice problem. We first introduce a set of conditions, which is sufficient to formulate the UMP under the deterministic perception approach. The only component not included is the consumer production function explained previously.

Assumption 2.2. The decision of a consumer under the deterministic perception approach satisfies the following.

(a) Consumer utility, U, is a function of a prime commodity, y, and multiple hedonic commodities, $z \equiv (z_1, \cdots, z_K)$. It is strictly concave and twice differentiable in the relevant region of its arguments.
(b) The yield of a commodity bundle,(y, z), satisfies the time constraint such that

$$t_w + \sum_{mn} t_{mn} q_{mn} + \sum_k t_k = T_o,$$

where t_w is the time spent at work, and T_o is the analysis period.
(c) The production activity satisfies the budget constraint such that

$$\sum_{mn} p_{mn} q_{mn} + \sum_{kj} p_j x_{kj} = I_o + w t_w,$$

where p_{mn} is the price of option mn, w consumer wage, p_j the price of input j, and I_o is non-labor income.
(d) The consumer can choose the amount of time, t_w, without any binding constraints.
(e) The prices of inputs other than qualitative choice services, such as I_o, w, and p_j, for all j, are fixed.

Combining the two sets of conditions in Assumptions 2.1 and 2.2 gives the basic choice problem. This choice problem, denoted by the Lagrangian L_o, is used to estimate the optimal bundle of inputs (q, x, t_w) and outputs (y, z), which maximizes the utility $U(y, z)$ under the condition that $p \equiv (p_{11}, \cdots, p_{MN})$ and $t \equiv (t_{11}, \cdots, t_{MN})$ are exogenously given:

$$L_o(q, x, t_w, y, z, \lambda, \mu, v, \eta, \phi; p, t) \equiv \max\{U(y, z)\} + \lambda\left(\sum_{mn} a_m q_{mn} - y\right)$$
$$+ \sum_k \mu_k \left(\sum_{mn} b_{km} t_{mn} q_{mn} + Z_k(x_k, t_k) - z_k\right) + v\left(T_o - t_w - \sum_{mn} t_{mn} q_m - \sum_k t_k\right)$$
$$+ \eta\left(I_o + w t_w - \sum_{mn} p_{mn} q_{mn} - \sum_{kj} p_j x_{kj}\right) + \sum_{mn} \phi_{mn} q_{mn}, \tag{2.13}$$

where $x \equiv (x_{11}, \cdots, x_{KJ}, t_1, \cdots, t_K)$ is the vector of goods and times inputted to substitute productions for K hedonic commodities, and $\lambda \rangle 0$, $\mu \equiv (\mu_1, \cdots, \mu_K) \rangle 0$, $\phi \equiv (\phi_{11}, \cdots, \phi_{MN}) \geq 0$, $v \rangle 0$, and $\eta \rangle 0$ are Lagrange multipliers. Furthermore, the term $\phi_{mn} q_{mn}$ represents the inequality constraint such that $q_{mn} \geq 0$.

Subsequently, we merge two constraints for time and budget in Assumption 2.2(b) and (c), respectively, into one constraint. The time spent at work t_w is a choice variable, as postulated in Assumption 2.1(d). Hence, it holds that

$$\frac{\partial L_o}{\partial t_w} = -v + \eta w = 0. \tag{2.14}$$

Replacing v in (2.13) with ηw and adding the two constraints in (2.13) gives *the budget constraint for the full income*:

$$\sum_{mn} (p_{mn} + w t_{mn}\, q_{mn}) + \sum_{kj} p_j x_{kj} + \sum_k w t_k = I_o + w T_o \equiv \bar{M}. \tag{2.15}$$

Here, the term $\bar{M}$ is the full income of consumers. The term v/η, which equals wage w, is called *value-of-time*.

Using the budget constraint for full income in (2.15), the basic choice problem L_o can be converted into the Lagrangian L_1 such that

$$L_1(q,x,y,z,\lambda,\mu,\eta,\phi;p,t) \equiv \max\{U(y,z)\} + \lambda\left(\sum_{mn} a_m q_{mn} - y\right)$$
$$+\sum_k \mu_k \left(\sum_{mn} b_{kmt} t_{mn} q_{mn} + Z_k(x_k,t_k) - z_k\right)$$
$$+\eta\left(\bar{M} - \sum_{mn}(p_{mn}+wt_{mn})q_{mn} - \sum_{kj} p_j x_{kj} - w\sum_k t_k\right) + \sum_{mn}\phi_{mn}q_{mn}. \quad (2.16)$$

This basic choice problem L_1 has an expression that is somewhat simpler than that of the original problem L_o. However, the problem L_1 is still too complex to perform subsequent demand analyses. For this reason, in the next section, we decompose the basic choice problem into two interrelated sub-optimization problems, and analyze these two problems.

2.3 Optimal Choice of Consumers

2.3.1 *Consistency of Implicit Prices*

The first sub-optimization problem of the basic choice problem L_1 is used to estimate the optimal input bundle that minimizes the production cost of an arbitrarily given commodity bundle. This cost minimization problem for consumer production is constructed using the production function defined in Assumption 2.1, which is homogeneous of degree one in both inputs and outputs. Because of the homogeneity, this minimization problem gives the implicit price of commodities in options, which satisfies the consistency condition, as shown below.

The cost minimization problem for consumer production, denoted by L_2, is used to search for the optimal input bundle (q,x) that gives the minimum cost required for the production of an arbitrary commodity bundle (q,x):

$$L_2(q,x,\pi,\varphi,\gamma;y,z,p,t) \equiv \min\left\{\sum_{mn}(p_{mn}+wt_{mn})q_{mn} + \sum_{kj} p_j x_{kj} + w\sum_k t_k\right\}$$
$$+\pi\left(y - \sum_{mn} a_m q_{mn}\right) + \sum_k \varphi_k\left(z_k - \sum_{mn} b_{kmt} t_{mn} q_{mn} - Z_k(x_k,t_k)\right)$$
$$-\sum_{mn}\gamma_{mn}q_{mn}, \quad (2.17)$$

where $\pi \rangle\, 0$, $\varphi \equiv (\varphi_1,\cdots,\varphi_K)\rangle\, 0$ and, $\gamma \equiv (\gamma_{11},\cdots,\gamma_{MN}) \geq 0$.

Let the vector $(\bar{q},\bar{x},\bar{\pi},\bar{\varphi},\bar{\gamma})$ be the saddle point of the Lagrangian L_2. According to the envelop theorem for constrained optimization problems, the Lagrange multiplier $\bar{\pi}$ is the implicit price of the prime commodity for services analyzed, and the

Lagrange multiplier $\bar{\varphi}_k$ for all k is the implicit price of the hedonic commodity k for these services. Below, these implicit prices are estimated under the condition that only one option mn is available.

Lemma 2.2. *When only one option mn is available, the cost minimization problem L_2 gives the following implicit prices of commodities.*

i. *The implicit price of the hedonic commodity k, $\bar{\varphi}_k$, is a constant estimated by*

$$\bar{\varphi}_k = p_j \Big/ \frac{\partial \bar{Z}_k}{\partial x_{kj}} = w \Big/ \frac{\partial \bar{Z}_k}{\partial t_k}, \quad \text{all } k,\ j.$$

ii. *The implicit price of the prime commodity for option mn, π_{mn}, is*

$$\pi_{mn}(p_{mn}, t_{mn}) = \frac{1}{a_m}(p_{mn} + v_m t_{mn}),$$

where

$$v_m = w - \sum_k \bar{\varphi}_k b_{km}.$$

iii. *Both $\bar{\varphi}_k$ and π_{mn} satisfy the consistency condition in output (y, z).*

Proof. See Appendix A.1 □

Lemma 2.2 estimates the implicit price π_{mn} and shows that this implicit price can be decomposed into three cost components: p_{mn}, wt_{mn}, and $\sum_k \bar{\varphi}_k b_{km}$. The price p_{mn} represents the money paid in purchasing one unit of service mn. The term wt_{mn} estimates the value of service time spent while consuming the service. The term $\sum_k \bar{\varphi}_k b_{km}$ quantifies the monetary value of all qualitative attributes packed in the service. The economic implications of such an implicit price π_{mn} are as below.

First, the implicit price π_{mn} differs from consumer to consumer. Of the three cost components examined above, the value of wt_{mn} is closely related to consumer wage, which usually differs from one individual to the next. Also, the value of $\sum_k \bar{\varphi}_k b_{km}$ largely depends on the subjective perception of a consumer, which is generally not identical to that of other consumers.

Second, the value of $\sum_k \bar{\varphi}_k b_{km}$ is a constant. In this term, the implicit price $\bar{\varphi}_k$ is a constant determined by the substitute production Z_k, which is independent of the consumption amount q_{mn}. Furthermore, the production coefficient b_{mk} is a constant representing the subjective consumer perception, under the deterministic perception approach.

Third, the term v_m, called *the net-value-of-time of group m*, is smaller than the value-of-time w, by the margin $\sum_k \bar{\varphi}_k b_{km}$. This margin represents the opportunity cost of K byproducts that amount to $(b_{1m}, \cdots, b_{Km})$, where b_{km} is the yield of commodity k. This margin therefore estimates cost savings accrued by the reduction in substitute productions of K hedonic commodities. Therefore, the net-value-of-time v_m is the portion of the value-of-time w, and can be sorted into the net cost required to produce one unit of the prime commodity.

Fourth, the net-value-of-time v_m has a linear relationship with value-of-time w. The net-value-of-time equals $w - \sum_k \bar{\varphi}_k b_{km}$. The implicit price $\bar{\varphi}_k$ in the v_m value equals $w/(\partial \bar{Z}_k/\partial t_k)$, and therefore is linearly proportional to w. Hence, it follows that the net-value-of-time v_m is linearly increasing in value-of-time w. This implies that a consumer having a larger wage tends to perceive a larger net-value-of-time than does a consumer with smaller wage who receives the same service, unless the values of $\partial \bar{Z}_k/\partial t_k$ and b_{km} are not significantly different among consumers.

Fifth, the term $v_m t_{mn}$, called *the net-service-time-value of option mn*, is a measure that quantifies the quality of service mn. The net-service-time-value represents the total non-monetary cost experienced in consuming one unit of service mn. This net-service-time-value becomes larger, as service time t_{mn} increases, and as the production coefficient b_{km}, for all k, decreases. Moreover, a larger service time and a smaller production coefficient imply lower service quality from the standpoint of quantitative and qualitative attributes, respectively. It can therefore be said that net-service-time-value increases as service quality decreases.

Sixth, the implicit price of a prime commodity, denoted by π_{mn} and estimated by $(p_{mn} + v_m t_{mn})/a_m$, is inversely proportional to the yield of prime commodities per service, denoted by a_m. The factor a_m expresses the quantity of prime commodities packed in option mn. Therefore, the implicit price π_{mn} represents the implicit price of a prime commodity in service mn, but not the implicit price of service mn, estimated by $p_{mn} + v_m t_m$.

Subsequently, we extend the analysis for the case when only one option is available to the case when multiple options are available. The analysis for this generalized case is presented below, focusing on characterizing the option chosen in consumer production.

Theorem 2.2. *The solution to L_2 for the case when multiple options are available satisfies the following.*

i. *The implicit price of prime commodity, $\bar{\pi}$, is*

$$\bar{\pi}(p,t) = \min_{mn} \{\pi_{mn}(p_{mn}, t_{mn})\},$$

and satisfies the consistency condition in output (y, z)

ii. *The solution $\bar{q}_{mn}$ satisfies the equality such that*

$$a_m \bar{q}_{mn} \begin{cases} = y, & \text{if } \bar{\pi} = \pi_{mn} \langle \pi_{m'n'}, \text{ all } m'n' \neq mn \\ = 0, & \text{if } \bar{\pi} \langle \pi_{mn} \\ \leqslant y, & \text{if } \bar{\pi} = \pi_{mn} = \pi_{m'n'}, \text{ some } m'n' \neq mn. \end{cases}$$

Proof. See Appendix A.1 □

Theorem 2.2 introduces a criterion for the choice of one option from among multiple options that offer the same service. This criterion can be interpreted as follows. First, the implicit price of prime commodities in Theorem 2.1.i, denoted by $\bar{\pi}$, is equal to the implicit price of the prime commodities for the option that charges the lowest implicit price. Second, Theorem 2.1.ii shows that the consumer chooses the option that requires the lowest implicit price; that is, only the option that has the lowest implicit price for its prime commodity will have a positive demand.

Finally, the consistency of π_{mn} implies that the chosen option mn has an implicit price π_{mn} that is lower than those of other available options, irrespective of (y, z) values. This consistency condition can, of course, apply to the optimal bundle that solves the original basic choice problem L_1. Therefore, the option chosen by a utility maximizer can be identified by simply comparing the implicit prices of available options, as confirmed subsequently.

2.3.2 Revealed Preference Condition

Here we consider the second sub-optimization problem of the original basic choice problem L_1, called the *reduced form of the basic choice problem* (*reduced form*, for short). This reduced form is used to estimate the optimal commodity bundle that maximizes consumer utility, which is identical that of the original basic choice problem. Using this reduced form, we determine the revealed preference condition that characterizes a decision to choose a certain option.

The first step in constructing the reduced form is to develop the consumer cost function $C(p, t; y, z)$. This estimates the minimum production cost of an arbitrary bundle (y, z):

$$C(p, t; y, z) \equiv \sum_{mn} (p_{mn} + w t_{mn})\, \bar{q}_{mn} + \sum_{kj} p_j \bar{x}_{kj} + w \sum_{k} \bar{t}_k, \tag{2.18}$$

where $\bar{q}_{mn}$, $\bar{x}_{kj}$, and $\bar{t}_k$ are the solutions to L_2. By virtue of the consistency of all implicit prices, the cost function is simplified as shown below.

Lemma 2.3. *The consumer cost function for L_2 satisfies the following equality:*

$$C(p, t; y, z) = \bar{\pi}(p, t)\, y + \sum_{k} \bar{\varphi}_k z_k.$$

Proof. This lemma is an extension of Theorem 2.1 for a simple example of joint homogeneous production functions to the production function of Assumption 2.1. The details of the proof are presented in Appendix A.2. □

Substituting the cost function in Lemma 2.3 into the basic choice problem L_1 in (2.16) gives the reduced form, denoted by L_3, such that

$$L_3(y, z, \eta; \bar{\pi}(p,t)) \equiv \max\{U(y,z)\} + \eta\left(\bar{M} - \bar{\pi}(p,t)\,y - \sum_k \bar{\varphi}_k z_k\right). \tag{2.19}$$

The solution to L_3 is identical to the solution to L_1 in (2.16), as shown below.

Lemma 2.4. *Let* $(\bar{q}, \bar{x}, \bar{y}, \bar{z}, \cdot)$ *and* $(\hat{y}, \hat{z}, \hat{\eta})$ *denote the solutions to the basic choice problem* L_1 *and its reduced form* L_3*, respectively. When the minimization problem* L_2 *takes option* mn*, it holds that*

$$(\bar{y}, \bar{z}) = (\hat{y}, \hat{z}), \text{ and } \bar{y} = a_m \bar{q}_{mn}.$$

Proof. See Appendix A.3 □

Theorem 2.2 indicates that, if option mn satisfies the inequality $\pi_{mn} \langle \pi_{m'n'}$ for an arbitrary bundle of (y, z), this option satisfies the same inequality for the entire bundle of (y, z). On the other hand, Lemma 2.4 shows that the solution of (y, z) to the original basic choice problem L_1 equals the solution to the reduced form L_3. By combining these two findings, we characterize consumer choice behaviors, as below.

Theorem 2.3. *Suppose that the cost minimization problem* L_2 *results in the choice of option* mn*. Then, the solution to the basic choice problem* L_1 *satisfies the revealed preference condition such that*

$$\bar{\pi} = \pi_{mn} \langle \pi_{m'n'} \Leftrightarrow U(\bar{y}, \bar{z}) = U(\bar{y}_{mn}, \bar{z}_{mn}) \rangle U(\bar{y}_{m'n'}, \bar{z}_{m'n'}), \text{ all } m'n' \neq mn,$$

where $(\bar{y}, \bar{z})$ *is the optimal solution of* (y, z) *when all the multiple options are available, whereas* $(\bar{y}_{mn}, \bar{z}_{mn})$ *is that of* (y, z) *when only one option* mn *is available.*

Proof. See Appendix A.4 □

Theorem 2.3 depicts the revealed preference condition of a utility maximizer as follows. "The left side implies the right" indicates that, if a consumer perceives that option mn has the lowest implicit price of a prime commodity, the choice of the option attains a higher level of the consumer utility than is attained by the choice of other options. Conversely, "the right side implies the left" shows that, if option mn chosen by a utility maximizer, the option requires the consumers to pay the minimum implicit price for the prime commodity.

2.3.3 An Illustration of Consumer Choices: Travel Choices

The previous consumer demand analyses based on the perception approach can provide plausible explanations for consumer choice behaviors that cannot be adequately explained within the context of neoclassical consumer demand theory. This advantage of demand analyses based on the perception approach is illustrated below, with travel choice problems for trip mode and destination.

To begin, we consider the following mode choice problem of a trip-maker. First, no matter what mode choice is made, the trip purpose remains the same; this means that service output a_m is common to all options, irrespective of their qualitative attributes. Second, each mode has qualitative attributes that differ from the others; in other words, each mode is designated as a different heterogeneous option $m \in \langle 1, M \rangle$. Third, each mode is assumed to have only one travel route; this implies that $N = 1$.

In this case, the production function of Assumption 2.1 can be amended as follows:

$$Y'(q; y) = y - \sum_m q_m = 0, \tag{2.20}$$

$$Z'_k(q, x_k, t_k; z_k) = z_k - \sum_m b_{km} t_m q_m - Z_k(x_k, t_k) = 0, \text{ all } k, \tag{2.21}$$

where t_m is the travel time of mode m.

The production function defined above is actually identical to the production function of Assumption 2.1, and therefore is homogeneous of degree one. Hence, it follows from Theorem 2.3 that the chosen mode m satisfies the following revealed preference condition:

$$\pi_m = p_m + v_m t_m \langle \pi_{m'} = p_{m'} + v_{m'} t_{m'}, \text{ all } m' \neq m, \tag{2.22}$$

where v_m is the net-value-of-travel-time of m, and p_m is the fare of option m.

One example that can successfully illustrate the advantage of the above mode choice criterion involves an air passenger who buys a first class ticket, rather than a business or economy class ticket on the same airplane. In this example, all options have the same travel time, denoted by t. Therefore, the full price of an option can be estimated by $p_m + wt$, whereas the implicit price of prime commodity for option m is $p_m + v_m t$.

It is certain that the full price for a first class seat is more costly than that for other options, since its price is more expensive, while their service times are identical. Therefore, there is no reason for the traveler who prefers the cheapest option when paying full price to choose a first class ticket. In contrast, the choice criterion (2.22) that compares the implicit price provides the following plausible explanation: the choice of the first class ticket is the outcome of a judgment that the additional fare does not exceed the additional value assignable to the better services.

Importantly, the above analysis can be applied to show that a consumer who receives a larger wage has a greater probability of choosing a more expensive seat when the seat offers higher-quality service. Equation (2.22) shows that the difference in the implicit price of a passenger service between a first and business class seats is equal to $p_2 - p_1 + t(v_2 - v_1)$, where 1 and 2 denote first and business class seats, respectively. Moreover, that equation implies that, if a consumer perceives this difference is positive, the consumer chooses a first class seat. In other words, if a consumer judges that $t(v_2 - v_1)$ is larger than $p_1 - p_2$, the consumer chooses a first class seat.

To be specific, the first class seat provides higher-quality service than is offered by the business class. This connotes that $v_2 - v_1$ is positive. Further, the fact that the former is more expensive implies that $p_1 - p_2$ is also positive. On the other hand, Lemma 2.2 shows that $v_2 - v_1$ equals $\sum_k \bar{\varphi}_k(b_{k1} - b_{k2})$, in which $b_{k1} - b_{k2}$ should be positive. Further, the fourth comment for Lemma 2.2 indicates that the implicit price $\bar{\varphi}_k$ tends to be greater as the consumer wage is larger. Therefore, as the wage of a consumer is larger, it is highly probable that the perceived value of $\sum_k \bar{\varphi}_k(b_{k1} - b_{k2})$ and thus of $v_2 - v_1$ is greater. Hence, it can be concluded that a consumer with a larger wage has a stronger preference for a first class seat.

Subsequently, we consider the trip destination choice problem, using the example of short-term sightseeing trips. Suppose that a traveler has already decided the trip mode and the travel period. Suppose, also, that the prime commodity of sightseeing trips is enjoyment achievable at a destination, and that the yield of the prime commodity differs by location. Suppose, however, that the yields of qualitative attributes per unit of travel time, including access and egress time, exhibit no significant difference among options.

In this special case, the production function for the prime commodity of trips must reflect the difference among options in the yield of the prime commodity, as expressed by a_m. Hence, the production function for prime commodities can be expressed by

$$Y'(q;y) = y - \sum_m a_m q_m = 0. \tag{2.23}$$

On the other hand, the production function for hedonic commodities can be constructed in such a manner that all options have the same production coefficient b_k:

$$Z'_k(q, x_k, t_k; z_k) = z_k - \sum_m b_k t_m q_m - Z_k(x_k, t_k) = 0, \text{ all } k, \tag{2.24}$$

where t_m is the sum of on-site and travel times for option m.

The production function defined above is homogeneous of degree one. Hence, it follows from Theorem 2.3 that the chosen option m satisfies the following:

$$\pi_m = \frac{1}{a_m}(p_m + v\,t_m) \langle \pi_{m'} = \frac{1}{a_{m'}}(p_{m'} + v\,t_{m'}), \text{ all } m' \neq m \tag{2.25}$$

where v is the net-value-of-time common to all options, and p_m is the sum of in-site expenditure and travel cost of option m.

The above choice criterion can be applied to explain why a traveler chooses a location more distant than other locations. The chosen option m might require higher in-site expenditure and/or a longer travel time than is required by other available options. Therefore, we cannot exclude the possibility that the full price of trip, $p_m + w\,t_m$, and/or the implicit price of trip, $p_m + v\,t_m$, are larger than those for other options. It is, however, certain that the chosen option m requires the minimum implicit cost per unit of enjoyment, estimated by $(p_m + v\,t_m)/a_m$.

Finally, the revealed preference condition of Theorem 2.3 is graphically illustrated using the following simple example of a mode choice problem. First, a shopper frequently makes trips to a certain store. Second, the decision-making components of the shopper are trip frequency and mode, and two trip modes are available: auto and transit, denoted by 1 and 2, respectively. Third, the outputs of consumer productions are composed only of two commodities: one prime commodity referred to as shopping, and one hedonic commodity defined as comfort.

In these circumstances, suppose that the consumer chooses mode 1. By the inequality on the left side of Theorem 2.3, the choice of mode 1 implies the following inequality: $\pi_1 = p_1 + v_1 t_1 \langle\ \pi_2 = p_2 + v_2\,t_2$, where p_m, t_m, and v_m are travel cost, travel time, and net-value-of-time of mode m. Here, the net-value-of-times v_1 and v_2 are distinct constants, since the qualitative attributes of the two modes differ.

We next consider the problem of graphically representing the budget constraint of the reduced form L_3 for the hypothetical case when only one mode is available. By Lemma 2.3, the cost function C_m for this hypothetical case is $C_m(y, z) = \pi_m\,y + \bar{\varphi} z$, for $m = 1, 2$, where $\bar{\varphi}$ is the implicit price of comfort. Therefore, the budget constraint of the reduced form L_3 can be expressed as $\bar{M} = \pi_m\,y + \bar{\varphi}\,z$, $m = 1, 2$. This budget line for each mode equals the production possibility frontier of y and z for consumer productions, under the condition that only that mode is available, as depicted in Fig. 2.1.

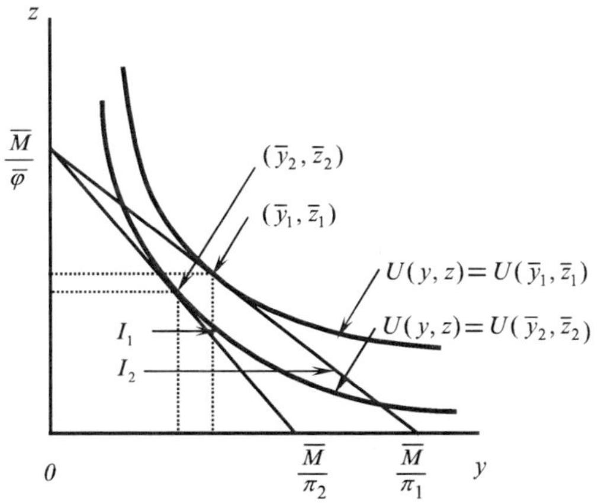

Fig. 2.1 Representation of revealed preference for the choice of a trip mode

By the inequality $\pi_1 \langle \pi_2$, the budget line for mode 1 is located atop the line for mode 2. This result leads to the right-side inequality of Theorem 2.3, such that $U(\bar{y},\bar{z}) = U(\bar{y}_1,\bar{z}_1) \rangle U(\bar{y}_2,\bar{z}_2)$, where $(\bar{y},\bar{z})$ is the solution in the case when the two modes are available, and $(\bar{y}_m,\bar{z}_m)$ is the solution in the case when only mode m is available.

2.4 Other Topics for Demand Analyses

2.4.1 *Service Demand Functions*

This subsection is concerned with the mathematical properties of demand function for option mn, denoted by $\bar{q}_{mn}$, for two independent vectors, $p \equiv (p_{11},\cdots,p_{MN})$ and $t \equiv (t_{11},\cdots,t_{MN})$. We first develop the function $\bar{q}_{mn}$ from the reduced form L_3, which has a formulation very similar to those of neoclassical utility maximization problems. We subsequently analyze the mathematical properties of $\bar{q}_{mn}$ by applying the well-known mathematical properties of neoclassical consumer demand functions.

Firstly, we develop the demand function $\bar{q}_{mn}$ from the basic choice problem L_1. The solution to the problem L_1 is the function of quantitative attribute vectors (p,t). Therefore, the basic choice problem L_1 can be expressed by the following:

$$\begin{aligned} &L_1(q(p,t),x(p,t),y(p,t),z(p,t),\lambda(p,t),\mu(p,t),\eta(p,t),\phi(p,t);p,t),\\ &\quad\equiv \max\{U(r(p,t))\} + \sum_i \kappa_i(p,t)g_i(r(p,t);p,t), \end{aligned} \tag{2.26}$$

where $r \equiv (q,x,y,z)$ and $\kappa \equiv (\lambda,\mu,\eta,\phi)$.

Under this convention, the Lagrangian of the basic choice problem L_1 at the saddle point can be expressed as follows:

$$L_1(\bar{r}(p,t),\bar{\kappa}(p,t);p,t) \equiv U(\bar{r}(p,t)) + \sum_i \bar{\kappa}_i(p,t)g_i(\bar{r}(p,t);p,t), \tag{2.27}$$

where $(\bar{r}(p,t),\bar{\kappa}(p,t))$ is the saddle point of L_1.

Theoretically, the saddle point for a certain value of (p,t) can be estimated from the Kuhn-Tucker conditions for that value. Further, it is clear that the saddle point is the function of (p,t). This means that the demand function $\bar{q}_{mn}(p,t)$, an element of $\bar{r}(p,t)$, is sensitive to the independent vector (p,t).

Secondly, we convert the expression of L_1 at the saddle point into that of the reduced form L_3. The solution of (y,z) to L_3 is a function of $\bar{\pi}(p,t)$ that equals $\min_{mn}\{\pi_{mn}(p_{mn},t_{mn})\}$, as shown in (2.19). Hence, the Lagrangian L_3 at the saddle point can be expressed as follows:

$$L_3(\hat{y}(\bar{\pi}), \hat{z}(\bar{\pi}), \hat{\eta}(\bar{\pi}); \bar{\pi}) \equiv U(\hat{y}(\bar{\pi}), \hat{z}(\bar{\pi})) + \hat{\eta}(\bar{\pi}) \left(\bar{M} - \bar{\pi}\, \hat{y}(\bar{\pi}) - \sum_k \bar{\varphi}_k \hat{z}_k(\bar{\pi}) \right). \tag{2.28}$$

This reduced form has a formulation identical to that of neoclassical utility maximization problems, except that $\bar{\pi}$ is an independent vector but the vector function of (p, t).

Thirdly, we identity the relationship between the function $\bar{q}_{mn}$ estimated from (2.27) and the function $\hat{y}(\bar{\pi})$ developed from (2.28). Functions $\bar{q}_{mn}$ and $\bar{\pi}$ have common explanatory vectors (p, t). Moreover, the two functions $\bar{q}_{mn}$ and $\hat{y}(\bar{\pi})$ satisfy the relationship presented below.

Theorem 2.4. *The solution $\bar{q}_{mn}$ to the basic choice problem L_1 and the solution $\hat{y}$ to the reduced form L_3 satisfy the following relationship:*

$$a_m \bar{q}_{mn}(p, t) \begin{cases} = \hat{y}\,(\bar{\pi}(p, t)), & \text{if } \bar{\pi} = \pi_{mn} < \pi_{m'n'}, \quad \text{all } m'n' \neq mn \\ = 0, & \text{if } \bar{\pi} < \pi_{mn} \\ \leqslant \hat{y}\,(\bar{\pi}(p, t)), & \text{if } \bar{\pi} = \pi_{mn} = \pi_{m'n'}, \quad \text{some } m'n' \neq mn. \end{cases}$$

Proof. By Lemma 2.4, it holds that $\bar{y}\,(p, t) = \hat{y}\,(\bar{\pi}(p, t))$. Substituting this equality into Theorem 2.2.ii gives the equation presented above. □

Theorem 2.4 shows that, when option mn satisfies the revealed preference condition for the choice of this option, it holds that

$$\bar{q}_{mn}(p, t) = \frac{1}{a_m} \hat{y} \left(\frac{1}{a_m} (p_{mn} + v_m\, t_{mn}) \right) \tag{2.29}$$

$$\bar{q}_{m'n'}(p, t) = 0, \text{ all } m'n' \neq mn. \tag{2.30}$$

These two equations show the following. First, the demand for option mn has a positive value only when the implicit price π_{mn} satisfies the revealed preference condition such that $\pi_{mn} \leqslant \pi_{m'n'}$, for all $m'n' \neq mn$. Second, when the demand for an option is positive, the demand for that option depends solely on the implicit price of the prime commodity, which is a function of price p_{mn} and service time t_{mn} only.

Finally, we analyze the continuity and comparative statics of demand function $\bar{q}_{mn}$ with respect to (p, t). The function $\bar{q}_{mn}$ equals $\hat{y}(\bar{\pi})/a_m$ in the range of (p, t), which satisfies the condition that $\pi_{mn} < \pi_{m'n'}$, for all $m'n' \neq mn$. On the other hand, the function $\hat{y}$ is developed from the reduced form L_3, which has a formulation identical to that of neoclassical utility maximization problems. Hence, it is possible to analyze the continuity and comparative statics of $\hat{y}$ with respect to $\bar{\pi}$ by applying the well-known properties of neoclassical consumer demand functions. Through the use of this property of $\hat{y}$, we below deduce the mathematical properties of $\bar{q}_{mn}$.

Theorem 2.5. *The demand function of prime commodity, $\hat{y}(\bar{\pi})$, and the demand function of option mn, $\bar{q}_{mn}$, satisfy the following.*

i. *The function $\hat{y}(\bar{\pi})$ is continuous in every variable of (p,t). However, the function $\bar{q}_{mn}$ is not continuous at the point where*

$$\bar{\pi}(p,t) = \pi_{mn}(p_{mn}, t_{mn}) = \pi_{m'n'}(p_{m'n'}, t_{m'n'}), \quad \text{some } m'n' \neq mn.$$

ii. *Suppose that the function $\bar{q}_{mn}$ is positive and continuous at a certain point (p,t). Then, the function has the following comparative statics at that point:*

$$\frac{\partial \bar{q}_{mn}(p,t)}{\partial p_{mn}} = \frac{1}{v_m}\frac{\partial \bar{q}_{mn}(p,t)}{\partial t_{mn}} = \frac{\partial \hat{y}(\bar{\pi}(p,t))}{\partial \pi_{mn}} \langle 0 \tag{2.31}$$

$$\frac{\partial \bar{q}_{mn}(p,t)}{\partial p_{m'n'}} = \frac{1}{v_{m'}}\frac{\partial \bar{q}_{mn}(p,t)}{\partial t_{m'n'}} = 0, \text{ all } m'n' \neq mn. \tag{2.32}$$

iii. *Suppose now that the function $\bar{q}_{mn}$ is not continuous at a certain point (p,t), and that $\pi_{mn}(p_{mn}, t_{mn}) = \pi_{m'n'}(p_{m'n'}, t_{m'n'})$, for some $m'n' \neq mn$. Then, it holds that*

$$\frac{\partial \bar{q}_{mn}(p,t)}{\partial p_{mn}} = \frac{1}{v_m}\frac{\partial \bar{q}_{mn}(p,t)}{\partial t_{mn}} = -\infty \tag{2.33}$$

$$\frac{\partial \bar{q}_{mn}(p,t)}{\partial p_{m'n'}} = \frac{1}{v_{m'}}\frac{\partial \bar{q}_{mn}(p,t)}{\partial t_{m'n'}} = \infty. \tag{2.34}$$

Proof. See Appendix A.5

Theorem 2.5 shows the following. First, the demand function of option mn is continuous and decreasing in p_{mn} and t_{mn} in the range of (p,t), on which the demand for this option is positive. Second, the demand function of option mn is discontinuous at the implicit price of that option, which equals that of some other options but is less than those of other remaining options.

It should be emphasized that the comparative statics estimated in the above theorem have one critical shortcoming: they cannot properly quantify substitutability among options. In general, a change in price or service time of an option causes a demand shift to competing options, and the shifted demand is finite. Contrary to this, the partial derivative $\partial\bar{q}_{mn}/\partial p_{m'n'}$ is zero at the point (p,t) where $\bar{q}_{mn}$ is continuous, whereas the term $\partial\bar{q}_{mn}/\partial p_{m'n'}$ is infinitely large at the point where $\bar{q}_{mn}$ is not continuous.

2.4.2 Mathematical Properties of Qualitative Choice Problems

Qualitative choice problems are the main target for forthcoming demand analyses of this monograph. Qualitative choice problems refer to a subgroup of UMPs under the perception approach. These choice problems should take a reduced form similar to neoclassical utility maximization problems, as does the basic choice problem. Below, we present the implications of this requirement for qualitative choice problems and the advantage of qualitative choice problems over other UMPs under the perception approach.

To begin, we consider the requirement that qualitative choice problems should take a reduced form similar to neoclassical utility maximizations. This requirement implies that the reduced form of qualitative choice problems should have an expression identical or almost identical to the reduced form of the basic choice problem in (2.19). Moreover, the implicit price of commodities in the budget constraint for the reduced form should possess certain mathematical regularities that can greatly simplify forthcoming demand analyses. This aspect of qualitative choice problems is illustrated with the basic choice problem, an example of qualitative choice problems.

One distinctive feature of the reduced form in (2.19) is that the implicit price of all commodities fulfills two different consistency conditions that follow. First, the implicit price π_{mn} satisfies the consistency condition such that this implicit price is independent of commodity bundles (y, z). Second, the net-value-of-time v_m in π_{mn} fulfills the consistency condition such that the net-value-of-time is independent not only of commodity bundles (y, z) but also of quantitative attribute vectors (p, t).

As illustrated above with an example, all qualitative choice problems should have a reduced form that fulfills the two different consistency conditions: the consistency of implicit prices of all commodities; and that of net-value-of-time or equivalent terms representing the monetary value of qualitative attributes packed in a service. The first consistency for implicit price is fulfilled when the consumer production function of a UMP is homogeneous in both inputs and outputs, as shown in Theorem 2.1. However; it is not straightforward to identify the condition under which a UMP satisfies the second consistency for net-value-of-time. This issue will be explored in detail in the following chapter

Subsequently, we introduce the advantages of qualitative choice problems over other UMPs under the perception approach. The advantages of qualitative choice problems consist in that only these choice problems can yield analytical outcomes that are crucial inputs to forthcoming economic analyses of service markets in this study. These advantages, all of which stem from the two different kinds of consistency introduced above, are as below.

First, only qualitative choice problems have their stochastic versions for the random perception approach considered in Chaps. 4 and 5. Mathematically, only a parameter in optimization problems can be designated as a random variable, but a function cannot be. On the other hand, the random perception approach hypothesizes that a net-value-of-time is a random variable that reflects uncertainty for the yield of hedonic commodities in consumer production. For this reason, the hypothesis of randomness can apply only to the net-value-of-time that satisfies the second consistency condition such that it is independent of q and (p, t).

Second, only qualitative choice problems yield the demand functions $\bar{q}_{mn}$ and $\bar{y}$ for which comparative statistics with respect to (p, t) can be estimated through relatively simple analyses. Since qualitative choice problems take net-value-times satisfying the consistency requirement, it is feasible to identify the relationship between $\bar{q}_{mn}/\partial p_{mn}$ and $\bar{q}_{mn}/\partial t_{mn}$ and between $\bar{q}_{mn}/\partial p_{m'n'}$ and $\bar{q}_{mn}/\partial t_{m'n'}$ in a manner shown in (2.31)~(2.34). Such a property of qualitative choice problems greatly simplifies analyses of comparative statistics, the main theme of Chap. 5.

We illustrate such an advantage of qualitative choice problems with an example. Suppose that a UMP under the perception approach gives the outcome that satisfies the equality of Theorem 2.4, but that gives the v_m value sensitive to (p_m, t_m). Then, (2.31) can be amended as follows:

$$\begin{aligned}\frac{\partial \bar{q}_{mn}(p,t)}{\partial p_{mn}} &= \frac{\partial \hat{y}(\bar{\pi}(p,t))}{\partial \pi_{mn}} \frac{\partial \pi_{mn}}{\partial p_{mn}} = \frac{\partial \hat{y}(\bar{\pi}(p,t))}{\partial \pi_{mn}} \left(1 + \frac{\partial v_{mn}}{\partial p_{mn}} t_{mn}\right) \\ &\neq \frac{1}{v_m} \frac{\partial \bar{q}_{mn}(p,t)}{\partial t_{mn}} = \frac{1}{v_m} \frac{\partial \hat{y}(\bar{\pi}(p,t))}{\partial \pi_{mn}} \left(1 + \frac{\partial v_{mn}}{\partial t_{mn}} t_{mn}\right).\end{aligned} \tag{2.35}$$

This equation shows that $v_m \bar{q}_{mn}/\partial p_{mn} \neq \bar{q}_{mn}/\partial t_{mn}$. This means that it is not simple to identify the relationship between $\bar{q}_{mn}/\partial p_{mn}$ and $\bar{q}_{mn}/\partial t_{mn}$, which is a very important input to the forthcoming analyses of this study. Two choice problems similar to this example will be introduced in Sect. 3.4.

Third, qualitative choice problems can provide the revealed preference condition amenable to statistical estimations. The revealed preference condition that identifies chosen options compares implicit prices π_m for all mn. On the other hand, in statistical estimations of the revealed preference condition, the variables unknown to statistical analysts are confined to v_m values for all m. These v_m values are statistically identifiable only when they are independent of dependent variables q and explanatory variables (p, t); the v_m values should fulfill the consistency condition.

It should be noted that statistical estimations of $v_m (= w - \sum_k \bar{\varphi}_k b_{km})$ values are free from the choice of qualitative attributes included in the formulation of qualitative choice problems. As noted in Subsect. 2.2.2, it is impossible to objectively identify all relevant qualitative attributes included in consumer production functions for a particular service. However, statistical estimations of v_m values target the summed value of $\sum_k \bar{\varphi}_k b_{km}$, but not the value of $\bar{\varphi}_k b_{km}$ for each commodity k. For this reason, the difficulty of objectively identifying relevant qualitative attributes does not cause any bias or error in statistical estimations.

Chapter 3
Extensions and Limitations of the Perception Approach

3.1 Introduction

The perception approach can be applied to modeling the UMP of consumers for various qualitative choice services under quality competition, in addition to the non-durable service examined in the previous chapter. In modeling of a UMP for a certain service, the perception approach has the advantage of reasonably reflecting the uniqueness of the service. Therefore, the UMP for a particular service generally has an expression different from that for other services. Such a UMP for a particular service can be sorted into two categories: *qualitative choice problems* defined in Sect. 2.4.2, and *non-qualitative choice problems* that refer to UMPs under the perception approach other than qualitative choice problems.

This chapter analyzes a number of qualitative and non-qualitative choice problems in a manner analogous to that of the basic choice problem. Analyses of these choice problems pursue three specific objectives that follow. First, we illustrate that the choice problem of consumers for large groups of services under quality competition can be approximated as qualitative choice problems. Second, we show that qualitative choice problems yield analysis outcomes very similar to those of the basic choice problem for non-durable service. Third, we compare and contrast qualitative and non-qualitative choice problems in the mathematical properties of revealed preference condition and service demand function.

One critical concern of analyses presented in this chapter is whether a UMP is a qualitative choice problem. As defined in Subsect. 2.4.2, qualitative choice problems must take a reduced form similar to neoclassical utility maximization problems. Moreover, the reduced form of qualitative choice problems must fulfill the additional requirement of two consistency conditions: consistency for implicit prices such that the implicit prices of all commodities must be independent of the amount of inputs to commodities and the yield of commodities; consistency condition for net-value-of-times such that terms that quantify the monetary values of qualitative attributes packed in a service must be independent of the price and service time of all inputs as well as the yield of commodities.

D.J. Moon, *Congestion-Prone Services Under Quality Competition*, Advances in Spatial Science, DOI 10.1007/978-3-642-20189-9_3,

However, being able to judge whether a UMP fulfills these two different kinds of consistency requires analyses to estimate the implicit prices of all commodities produced through consumer productions. Moreover, an estimation of the implicit prices requires relatively complex analyses of cost minimization problems for consumer productions, as illustrated with the basic choice problem in Subsect. 2.3.1. Therefore, we introduce a simpler method that can be used to judge qualitative choice problems without estimation of the implicit prices.

The alternative method to judge qualitative choice problems can be stated as follows: first, the consumer production function must be homogeneous of degree one in both multiple inputs and outputs; second, the output of consumer productions must comprise more than one kind of prime commodity, in addition to more than one kind of hedonic commodity. Among these two requirements, the first requirement implies that qualitative choice problems must yield the consistent implicit price of prime commodities, as proved in Theorem 2.1. However, it is difficult to confirm that the second requirement is sufficient to ensure that the estimated implicit monetary value of qualitative attributes satisfies the consistency condition.

For this reason, this study presents analyses to confirm that UMPs, which satisfy the two requirements introduced above, are indeed qualitative choice problems, by testing several examples. The test covers not only qualitative choice problems, which satisfy these two requirements, but also non-qualitative choice problems, which fail to fulfill one of the two requirements. This test of UMPs is divided into three different types, as explained below.

The first type of test, presented in Sect. 3.2, illustrates the applicability of demand analyses for the basic choice problem to other qualitative choice problems that fulfill the following two conditions: first, each qualitative choice problem deals with consumer production that yields only one type of prime commodity, as is the case in the basic choice problem; second, each qualitative choice problem replaces or releases some of several restrictive assumptions applied to the basic choice problem. Further, the second condition is accommodated by simply amending the consumer production function for non-durable services given in Assumption 2.1. Thus, we develop and analyze four different qualitative choice problems, each of which is applicable to a certain group of qualitative choice services different from the services analyzed in other problems.

The second type of test, introduced in Sect. 3.3, demonstrates the extendibility of demand analyses for the basic choice problem to qualitative choice problems for the case when consumer productions yield multiple types of prime commodities. Qualitative choice problems for this type of test are constructed by modifying both the production function described in Assumption 2.1 and the utility function described in Assumption 2.2. One qualitative choice problem covers the decision to choose a set of multiple options, each of which offers a particular non-durable service that differs from the services of other chosen options. Another qualitative choice problem is the choice problem for a service within which multiple types of prime commodities are packed.

The third type of test in Sect. 3.4 illustrates demand analyses of non-qualitative choice problems with two examples. The first example is the location choice problem of shopping trips, which uses a non-homogeneous production function. This production function is designed to reflect that the yield of prime commodities per trip exhibits decreasing returns in purchasing amount per trip. The second example is the mode choice problem of work trips, which uses a joint homogeneous production function but does not yield any prime commodity.

So far, we have described three groups of UMPs that will be tested in this chapter. The UMPs belonging to the first two groups are qualitative choice problems applicable to subsequent market analyses of this monograph. These UMPs are selected so as to demonstrate that the consumer choice problem for quite large families of service under quality competition can be modeled as qualitative choice problems. The two UMPs in the third group are not qualitative choice problems. Both UMPs have the advantage of more realistically depicting the decision-making environment of consumers. They are formulated so as to confirm that qualitative choice problems must be modeled to fulfill two requirements: the homogeneity of the consumer production function, and the inclusion of prime commodities in the utility function.

3.2 Qualitative Choice Problems for One Prime Commodity

3.2.1 Choice of Service Times

The time period during which a certain service will be received is an important choice component for a consumer. Usually, most consumers prefer a particular hour of the day, a particular day of the week, and/or a particular month of the year. Such a preference of consumers for a particular time period causes peaking phenomena. Naturally, during a peak period consumers are commonly required to accept a service delay and/or higher service charge. How to model such a decision-making problem as a qualitative choice problem is explained below.

We consider a hypothetical case where a consumer makes a choice decision regarding service time-period, under the condition that only one service system is available and that the arrival rate of demands differs by period. In this case, one way to define the option is to divide the whole analysis time-period into T periods according to demand intensity, and then designate each period as an independent option denoted by $t \in \langle 1, T \rangle$. Under this convention, each option can have an arbitrary duration $\delta_t \rangle 0$, but should satisfy the condition that $\sum_t \delta_t = 1$. Further, the demand for option t is expressed by $\delta_t q_t$, so as to quantify the difference in demand intensity among periods through the use of q_t.

It is postulated that the prime commodity of this choice problem is enjoyment achievable in the service system, and that the yield of prime commodities per service, denoted by a_t, can differ by time-period. This postulate implies that the user of a service system perceives the magnitude of enjoyment, which differs from period to period. Further, it is assumed that the service of each option t is usually distinguished not only by quantitative attributes, p_t and t_t, but also qualitative attributes perceived, b_{kt}, for some k. This assumption about b_{kt} reflects consumer perception such that the relative importance of some qualitative attributes differs from period to period.

Under the conditions specified above, the production function of a consumer can be expressed as the simultaneous equation systems similar to the production function of Assumption 2.1:

$$Y'(q;y) = y - \sum_t \delta_t a_t q_t = 0, \tag{3.1}$$

$$Z'_k(q, x_k, t_k; z_k) = z_k - \sum_t \delta_t b_{kt} t_t q_t - Z_k(x_k, t_k) = 0, \text{ all } k. \tag{3.2}$$

The UMP for the production function of (3.1) and (3.2) has an expression identical to that of the basic choice problem, with the exception that the term $\delta_t q_t$ replaces the demand q_{mn} in the latter. Therefore, this UMP is a qualitative choice problem, and yields an outcome identical to Theorems 2.2–2.5 for the basic choice problem, except for a number of minor amendments.

For example, the revealed preference condition for the choice problem of service time period t, which is developed by amending that of Theorem 2.2, is

$$\pi_t = \frac{1}{a_t}(p_t + v_t t_t) \langle \pi_{t'} = \frac{1}{a_{t'}}(p_{t'} + v_{t'} t_{t'}), \text{ all } \quad t' \neq t, \tag{3.3}$$

where $v_t = w - \sum_k \bar{\varphi}_k b_{kt}$. Here, the implicit price π_t satisfies the consistency condition with respect to the output (y, z). Moreover, the net-value-of-time v_t in the implicit price fulfills the consistency condition with respect to prices $p \equiv (p_1, \cdots, p_T)$ and service times $t \equiv (t_1, \cdots, t_T)$.

The revealed preference condition (3.3) can help explain the decision made by a traveler who visits a resort area during the busiest period, denoted by t. At a resort, the busiest period often entails larger in-site service charges and longer access travel times than are required during other time-periods. Therefore, it is highly probable that the full price of option t, estimated by $p_t + wt_t$, is larger than that for other time-periods, and that the implicit price of option t, estimated by $p_t + v_t t_t$, is also larger. However, it can be argued that the busiest time-period gives the traveler a larger amount of enjoyment, which is defined as the prime commodity in this choice problem. Thus, the decision to choose period t can be justified on the grounds that the implicit price per enjoyment, estimated by $(p_t + v_t t_t)/a_t$, is less than that for other periods.

3.2.2 Choice of Durable Goods and Service Options

Here we consider the qualitative choice problem for retail services that sell durable goods such as autos, clothes, and home appliances, or for durable services such as clinics and various business services. The qualitative choice problem for durable goods or services should take account of the fact that the duration during which consumers receive benefit from them is significantly longer than the service time required for their purchase. Further, the qualitative choice problem must reflect another fact: the decision to choose one option from among multiple options generally depends not only on the quantitative and qualitative attributes of durable goods or services but also on those of the shop selling those goods or services.

We formulate a qualitative choice problem for durable goods or services under the following conditions. First, the analysis period of the qualitative choice problem is identical to the duration that the goods or services continue to contribute to consumer utility. Second, the analysis period is significantly longer than the service time of sales services. Third, the transportation cost for the purchase of services can be ignored.

Further, we construct the consumer production function under the following postulates. First, the production quantity of the prime commodity is linearly proportional to the consumption amount of durable goods or services, but independent of sales service quality and time. Second, various hedonic commodities come from two sources: the durable goods or services themselves, and non-durable services offered by the sales service system for those durable goods or services.

Under these postulates, the consumer production function can be formulated as the following amendment of the function in Assumption 2.1:

$$Y'(q;y) = y - \sum_{mn} a_m q_{mn} = 0, \tag{3.4}$$

$$Z'_k(q, x_k, t_k; z_k) = z_k - \sum_{mn} \left(b^d_{km} + \sum_{mn} b_{km} t_{mn} \right) q_{mn} - Z_k(x_k, t_k) = 0, \text{ all } k, \tag{3.5}$$

where b^d_{km} is the production coefficient of option mn for commodity k per unit of durable goods or services, b_{km} the production coefficient of mn for k per in-site service time, and t_{mn} the in-site service time of mn.

The production function of (3.4) and (3.5) is homogeneous of degree one in both input (x, q) and output (y, z), where $x \equiv (x_{11}, \cdots, x_{KJ}, t_1, \cdots, t_K)$, as can be proved in a manner almost identical to that of Lemma 2.1. Hence, the UMP for this production function can be identified as a qualitative choice problem. Therefore, this choice problem characterizes consumer choice behaviors, as they are characterized in Theorems 2.2–2.5 for the basic choice problem.

To be specific, the UMP for the production function of (3.4) and (3.5) gives the revealed preference condition for the choice of option mn, such that

$$\pi_{mn} = \frac{1}{a_m}(p_{mn} - r_m + v_m t_{mn})$$
$$\langle \pi_{m'n'} = \frac{1}{a_{m'}}(p_{m'n'} - r_{m'} + v_{m'} t_{m'n'}), \text{ all } m'n' \neq mn, \tag{3.6}$$

where $r_m = \sum_k \bar{\varphi}_k b^d_{km}$ is the sum of monetary values of hedonic commodities packed in durable goods or services in heterogeneous service group m, and $v_m = w - \sum_m \bar{\varphi}_k b_{km}$ is the net-value-of-time for in-site retail services offered by option mn.

The above implicit price π_{mn} confirms that the choice problem for the production function in (3.4) and (3.5) satisfies the two different consistency conditions. First, the price π_{mn} is independent of (y, z). Second, two terms, r_m and v_m, which quantify the implicit monetary values of qualitative attributes in the durable and non-durable portions of services, respectively, are both independent of p_{mn} and t_{mn}. Further, the implicit price $a_m\pi_{mn}$ represents a portion of full cost $p_{mn} + wt_{mn}$, and this portion represents the monetary value assignable to the net cost of a prime commodity that refers to a particular kind of benefit from goods and services mn.

One example to which the choice criterion (3.6) can be applied involves the decision of a shopper who chooses a certain brand of personal computer from multiple options, denoted by $m \in \langle 1, M \rangle$. For simplicity, suppose that each brand is sold at one retail shop. Suppose also that the shopper plans to purchase a predetermined type of personal computer with specific functionality; that is, all options have an identical value for a_m. In these circumstances, the term r_m reflects the cost savings accrued from the qualitative attributes of computers, e.g., after-services, the value of good design, etc. The term $\sum_k \bar{\varphi}_k b_{km}$ estimates the monetary value per unit service time, which is assignable to the qualitative attributes of sales service, e.g., the helpfulness and professional knowledge of salesmen, facility cleanliness, etc.

Another example might occur when a consumer seeks the best medical clinic for the treatment of a certain disease. In this case, it might be reasonable to assume that all options offer the service yielding the same amount of prime commodities; that is, the term a_m is identical across all options. It is also natural to hypothesize that all options offer heterogeneous services in terms of quality of medical service. Specifically, the quality of medical service can be sorted into two categories: first, unobservable long-run qualitative attributes such as confidence in medical service quality, reflected in r_m; and second, observable short-run attributes that depend primarily on the quality of facility and supporting services, such as comfort, cleanliness, etc., quantified in $v_{mn}t_{mn}$.

3.2.3 *Location Choice of Non-durable Service Options*

The location choice problem of a consumer is commonly affected not only by the service quality of a destination but also by transportation cost incurred in reaching the destination. This location choice problem must employ a production function that can accommodate the condition that the hedonic commodities are generated from two sources: destination and transportation service. Below, we illustrate this location choice problem using examples of non-durable qualitative services such as groceries, entertainment, recreation, hotel, and dining services.

The location choice problem considered here uses index mm to identify an option. In this index, the number m designates a particular group distinguished by a combination of destination and access trip mode. This convention accommodates the fact that each trip mode as well as each destination has different qualitative attributes from those of other trip modes. On the other hand, the number n represents a particular trip route for service group. The number n accommodates the situation when multiple routes are available to a certain combination of destination and trip mode.

We next consider the problem of constructing a production function being homogeneous of degree one. One component of the production function for the prime commodity can be expressed as (3.4). The other component for hedonic commodities can be formulated as follows:

$$Z_k'(q, x_k, t_k; z_k) = z_k - \sum_{mn} \left(b_{km}^s t_{mn}^s + b_{km}^a t_{mn}^a\right) q_{mn} - Z_k(x_k, t_k) = 0, \text{ all } k, \tag{3.7}$$

where t_{mn}^s and t_{mn}^a are the in-site service and travel times of option mn, respectively, and b_{km}^s and b_{km}^a are the production coefficients of the in-site service and travel time for commodity k, respectively.

The above production function is homogeneous of degree one in input (x, q) and output (y, z), as can be shown in a manner analogous to that used to prove Lemma 2.1. Therefore, the UMP for this production function is a qualitative choice problem. Further, this production function gives the revealed preference condition for the choice of option mn, such that

$$\begin{aligned} \pi_{mn} &= \frac{1}{a_m}\left(p_{mn}^s + v_m^s t_{mn}^s + p_{mn}^a + v_m^a t_{mn}^a\right) \\ &\langle\, \pi_{m'n'} = \frac{1}{a_{m'}}\left(p_{m'n'}^s + v_{m'}^s t_{m'n'}^s + p_{m'n'}^a + v_{m'}^a t_{m'n'}^a\right), \text{ all } m'n' \neq mn, \end{aligned} \tag{3.8}$$

where p_{mn}^s is the in-site service charge of mn, p_{mn}^a the transportation cost of mn, $v_m^s = w - \sum_k \bar{\varphi}_k b_{km}^s$ net-value-of-time for on-site service time, and $v_m^a = w - \sum_k \bar{\varphi}_k b_{km}^a$ net-value-of-time for travel time.

We apply the above choice criterion to the location choice for a trip having the goal of purchasing a predetermined amount of non-durable goods such as groceries. Suppose that there are two options: one is a shop at a suburban shopping mall, denoted by 1, and the other is a nearby shop, denoted by 2. Suppose, also, that a shopper plans to purchase the same quantity of goods, irrespective of the location choice; that is, $a_m = 1$. Suppose, further, that the shopper chooses option 1, which is located a greater distance from home than option 2.

For this case, the choice criterion (3.8) is simplified as below:

$$\pi_1 = p_1^s + v_1^s t_1^s + p_1^a + v_1^a t_1^a \,\langle\, \pi_2 = p_2^s + v_2^s t_2^s + p_2^a + v_2^a t_2^a. \tag{3.9}$$

This formula connotes that the price of goods at the shopping mall must be significantly lower than that at the nearby shop in order for this difference to compensate for higher travel cost and longer travel time.

3.2.4 Choice for Services Having Substitutes

Certain kinds of qualitative choice service are provided by close substitutes. For example, one can substitute a visit to retailers for household items with at-home shopping. A substitute for a movie currently playing at a cinema could be a TV movie or DVD viewed at home. A substitute for a meal available at a restaurant could be a meal made at home. Similarly, a substitute for a business trip to visit customers and colleagues could be achieving the same objective via telecommunication media. For such services, we here construct and analyze a qualitative choice problem.

Suppose that a consumer can achieve a certain prime commodity by consuming two different services: a qualitative choice service, which is the target of demand analyses, and its substitute service. Suppose, also, that the qualitative choice service is offered by M multiple options differentiated by qualitative attributes, whereas its substitute service has only one option. Suppose, furthermore, that the consumer's decision follows all the conditions introduced in Assumptions 2.1 and 2.2, except for the functional form of the consumer production function.

The production function must be constructed so that it is homogeneous of degree one in both its inputs and outputs. To meet this requirement, the production function for the prime commodity is formulated as the Cobb-Douglas production function such that

$$Y'(g, q; y) = y - g^{\alpha}\left(\sum_m q_m\right)^{1-\alpha} = 0, \tag{3.10}$$

where $q \equiv (q_1, \cdots, q_M)$ is the vector of demands for qualitative choice services, g the demand for substitute service, and α a positive constant less than one. On the other hand, the production function for hedonic commodities, under the assumption that the substitute service also generates the same kinds of hedonic commodities, is expressed as follows:

$$Z'_k(g, q, x_k, t_k; z_k) = z_k - b_k t_o g - \sum_m b_{km} t_m q_m - Z_k(x_k, t_k) = 0, \text{ all } k, \tag{3.11}$$

where t_o and t_m are the service times of the substitute service and service m, respectively, and b_k is the production coefficient of the substitute service for commodity k.

For the production function defined in (3.10) and (3.11), the cost minimization problem, denoted by L_2, is

$$\begin{aligned} L_2 \equiv \min & \left\{ (p_o + wt_o)g + \sum_m (p_m + wt_m)\, q_m + \sum_{kj} p_j x_{kj} + w \sum_k t_k \right\} \\ & + \pi \left(y - g^{\alpha}(\sum_m q_m)^{1-\alpha} \right) + \sum_k \varphi_k \left(z_k - b_k t_o g - \sum_m b_{km} t_m q_m - Z_k(x_k, t_k) \right) \\ & - \sum_m \gamma_m q_m, \end{aligned} \tag{3.12}$$

where p_o and p_m are the prices of the substitute and service m, respectively. Through analyses of L_2, the functional structure of the implicit price π is characterized as below.

Theorem 3.1. *The solution* $(\bar{g}, \bar{q}, \bar{x}, \bar{\pi}, \bar{\varphi}, \bar{y})$ *to* L_2 *satisfies the following.*

i. *Under the condition when only one option* m *is available, there is a function* ψ *such that*

$$\pi_m(p_o, t_o, p_m, t_m) = \psi(r_o,\ r_m), \tag{3.13}$$

$$\frac{\partial \psi(r_o, r_m)}{\partial p_m} = (1-\alpha)\frac{r_o}{\det\{J\}} > 0. \tag{3.14}$$

where $r_o = p_o + v_o t_o$, $r_m = p_m + v_m t_m$, $v_o = w - \sum_k \bar{\varphi}_k b_k$, $v_m = w - \sum_k \bar{\varphi}_k\ b_{km}$, *and* $\det\{J\} = (1-\alpha)^2 r_o \bar{g} + \alpha^2 r_m \bar{q}_m > 0$.

ii. *When option* m *is chosen from* M *options, it holds that*

$$p_m + v_m t_m < p_{m'} + v_{m'} t_{m'} \text{ and } \pi_m < \pi_{m'},\ \text{all } m' \neq m. \tag{3.15}$$

Proof. The proof of Theorem 3.1.i is presented in Appendix A.6. The proof of Theorem 3.1.ii is as follows. (i) If option m is chosen, it holds that $p_m + v_m t_m < p_{m'} + v_{m'} t_{m'}$, for all $m' \neq m$, as can be shown in a manner identical to that used to prove Lemma 2.1, through the use of first order conditions for L_2 in (3.12). (ii) Equation (3.14) implies that ψ is increasing in $p_m + v_m t_m$. By (i) and (ii), it follows that $\pi_m = \psi(r_o, r_m) < \pi_{m'} = \psi(r_o, r_{m'})$. □

Theorem 3.1 shows that the choice problem for the production function in (3.10) and (3.11) is a qualitative choice problem, as explained below. First, the implicit price π_m is independent of commodity bundle (y, z), as shown in (3.13) and (3.14). This result is the direct consequence of the fact that the production function is homogeneous in both input (x, g, q) and output (y, z). Second, the net-value-of-time v_m in π_m satisfies the consistency condition such that it is independent of (y, z) and (p, t).

Subsequently, the inequality of Theorem 3.1.ii and the consistency of the implicit price π_m imply that the consumer choice of option m satisfies the following revealed preference condition:

$$p_m + v_m t_m < p_{m'} + v_{m'} t_{m'} \Leftrightarrow U(\bar{y}, \bar{z}) = U(\bar{y}_m, \bar{z}_m) > U(\bar{y}_{m'}, \bar{z}_{m'}),\ \text{all } m' \neq m, \tag{3.16}$$

where $(\bar{y}, \bar{z})$ is the solution of (y, z) when multiple options are available, whereas $(\bar{y}_m, \bar{z}_m)$ is that of (y, z) when only one option m is available.

Furthermore, owing to the consistency of the implicit price ψ_m, the original UMP takes the following reduced form:

$$L_3(y, z, \eta) \equiv \max\{U(y, z)\} + \eta\left(\bar{M} - \psi(r_o, r)\, y - \sum_k \bar{\varphi}_k z_k\right), \tag{3.17}$$

where $r \equiv (r_1, \cdots, r_M)$ and $\psi(r_o, r) = \min_m\{\psi_m(r_o, r_m)\}$. This reduced form gives the demand function $\hat{y}$, which has a structure similar to neoclassical consumer demand functions.

Using the solution $\hat{y}$, we can estimate the utility-maximizing choices of q_m and g, denoted by $\hat{q}_m$ and $\hat{g}$, respectively. Under the condition that $\hat{q}_m \rangle 0$ or $\pi_m = \bar{\pi}$, one input necessary to estimate $\hat{q}_m$ and $\hat{g}$ is the production function such that

$$\hat{g}^{\alpha}\, \hat{q}_m{}^{1-\alpha} = \hat{y}. \tag{3.18}$$

Another input is the implicit price π_m, estimated from first order conditions for L_2, such that

$$\pi_m = \frac{r_o}{\alpha(\hat{g})^{\alpha-1}(\hat{q}_m)^{1-\alpha}} = \frac{r_m}{(1-\alpha)(\hat{g})^{\alpha}(\hat{q}_m)^{-\alpha}}. \tag{3.19}$$

Given the solution $\hat{y}$, the optimal choices $\hat{q}_m$ and $\hat{g}$ are the solutions to the simultaneous equation system composed of (3.18) and (3.19) .

Finally, we estimate $\partial\hat{q}_m/\partial p_m$ and $\partial\hat{q}_m/\partial t_m$ under the condition of $\bar{q}_m \rangle 0$. Differentiating (3.18) and (3.19) with respect to r_m, and estimating $\partial\hat{q}_m/\partial p_m$ and $\partial\hat{q}_m/\partial t_m$ from the preceding outcomes gives

$$\frac{\partial\,\hat{q}_m}{\partial\, p_m} = \frac{1}{v_m}\frac{\partial\,\hat{q}_m}{\partial\, t_m} = \frac{1}{\det\{J\}}\left((1-\alpha)\,r_o\frac{\partial\hat{y}(\psi)}{\partial r_m} - \alpha^2(\hat{g})^{\alpha-1}(\hat{q}_m)^{2-\alpha}\right) \langle\, 0, \tag{3.20}$$

as shown in Appendix A.6. Here, the first equality follows from the fact that the net-value-of-time v_{mn} satisfies the consistency condition.

In summary, the qualitative choice problem analyzed above uses the Cobb-Douglas production function, which is homogeneous of degree one, as the production function of prime commodities. The use of the Cobb-Douglas production function purports to accommodate the presence of a substitute to the multiple options of a qualitative choice service. This use yields the implicit price of prime commodities, which has a functional form that fundamentally differs from that of the implicit price for the basic choice problem. Nonetheless, the revealed preference condition for this choice problem has an expression identical to that of the basic choice problem, and is thus independent of the service quality of substitutes, as shown in (3.15).

3.3 Qualitative Choice Problems for Multiple Prime Commodities

3.3.1 The Basic Choice Problem for Multiple Kinds of Services

We here introduce an extension of the basic choice problem for the case when the choice set of a consumer is composed of multiple kinds of non-durable services.

This choice problem involves the decision of a consumer who simultaneously chooses a bundle of multiple optimal options in which each option offers one specific kind of qualitative choice service. This choice problem has a more complex expression than the basic choice problem for the case when the choice set is composed of options all of which provide the same kind of service. Nonetheless, the revealed preference condition for a particular kind of service is identical to that of the basic choice problem, irrespective of the choice for other kinds of services, as shown below.

Firstly, we construct the UMP. Suppose that the choice set of a consumer is composed of L kinds of qualitative choice services, each denoted by $l \in \langle 1, L \rangle$. Suppose, also, that each kind of qualitative service yields only one kind of prime commodity, which differs from that of the others. Suppose, further, that the qualitative attributes of all L services have in common K hedonic commodities, each denoted by $k \in \langle 1, K \rangle$. Then, the choice problem for multiple kinds of services, denoted by LM_1, can be formulated as follows:

$$
\begin{aligned}
LM_1(q,x,y,z,\lambda,\mu,\phi,\eta;p,t) &\equiv \max\{U(y,z)\} + \sum_l \lambda_l \left(\sum_{mn} a_{lm} q_{lmn} - y_l \right) \\
&+ \mu_k \left(\sum_{lmn} b_{klm} t_{lmn} q_{lmn} + Z_k(x_k, t_k) - z_k \right) \\
&+ \eta \left(\bar{M} - \sum_{lmn} (p_{lmn} + w t_{lmn}) q_{lmn} - \sum_{kj} p_j x_{kj} - w \sum_k t_k \right) + \sum_{lmn} \phi_{lmn} q_{lmn}, \qquad (3.21)
\end{aligned}
$$

where y_l is the number of prime commodity l, and q_{lmn} is the demand for service lmn. Also, the vectors in this problem represent the following: $q \equiv (q_{111}, \cdots, q_{LMN})$, $x \equiv (x_{11}, \cdots, x_{KJ}, t_1, \cdots t_K)$, $y \equiv (y_1, \cdots, y_L)$, $z \equiv (z_1, \cdots, z_K)$, $p \equiv (p_{111}, \cdots, p_{LMN})$, $t \equiv (t_{111}, \cdots, t_{LMN})$, $\lambda \equiv (\lambda_1, \cdots, \lambda_L) \rangle 0$, and $\phi \equiv (\phi_{111}, \cdots, \phi_{LMN}) \geq 0$.

Secondly, we construct the cost minimization problem for the above LM_1 in a manner analogous to that of the basic choice problem in (2.17). This cost minimization problem, denoted by LM_2, is

$$
\begin{aligned}
LM_2 \equiv \min &\left\{ \sum_{lmn} (p_{lmn} + w t_{lmn}) q_{lmn} + \sum_{kj} p_j x_{kj} + w \sum_k t_k \right\} \\
&+ \sum_l \pi_l \left(y_l - \sum_{mn} a_{lm} q_{lmn} \right) + \sum_k \varphi_k \left(z_k - \sum_{lmn} b_{klm} t_{lmn} q_{lmn} - Z_k(x_k, t_k) \right) \\
&- \sum_{lmn} \gamma_{lmn} q_{lmn}, \qquad (3.22)
\end{aligned}
$$

where $\pi \equiv (\pi_1, \cdots, \pi_L) \rangle 0$, and $\gamma \equiv (\gamma_{111}, \cdots, \gamma_{LMN}) \geq 0$.

Suppose, now, that each service l is provided by only one option lmn. Then the above cost minimization problem yields the implicit price of prime commodity l, π_{lmn}, which is identical to that of Lemma 2.2:

$$
\pi_{lmn}(p_{lmn}, t_{lmn}) = \frac{1}{a_{lm}} (p_{lmn} + v_{lm} t_{lmn}), \qquad (3.23)
$$

where $v_{lm} = w - \sum_k \bar{\varphi}_k b_{klm}$. Here, the solution $\bar{\varphi}_k$ is the implicit price of commodity k, which is identical to the one in Lemma 2.2.

The above analysis for implicit prices confirms that LM_2 is a qualitative choice problem; that is, the production function of LM_2 is homogeneous of degree one in both inputs and outputs. Therefore, the implicit price π_{lmn} satisfies both kinds of consistency; that is, the implicit price π_{lmn} is independent of output (y, z), and the net-value-of-time v_{lm} in π_{lmn} is free from the value of quantitative variables (p, t).

Suppose, next, that every service l is offered by more than one option. Then, through analyses analogous to that used to prove Theorem 2.2, it can be shown that the choice of option lmn satisfies the inequality such that

$$\bar{\pi}_l(p_l, t_l) = \pi_{lmn}(p_{lmn}, t_{lmn}) \langle \pi_{lm'n'}(p_{lm'n'}, t_{lm'n'}), \text{ all } m'n' \neq mn, \tag{3.24}$$

where $p_l \equiv (p_{l11}, \cdots, p_{lMN})$, $t_l \equiv (t_{l11}, \cdots, t_{lMN})$, and $\bar{\pi}_l$ is the implicit price of service group l.

All the implicit prices in (3.24) are independent of outputs (y, z), including the solution $(\bar{y}, \bar{z})$ to LM_1. Hence, this equation implies that the choice of option mn satisfies the revealed preference condition such that

$$\bar{\pi}_l = \pi_{lmn} \langle \pi_{lm'n'} \Leftrightarrow U(\bar{y}, \bar{z}) = U(\bar{y}_{mn}, \bar{z}_{mn}) \rangle U(\bar{y}_{m'n'}, \bar{z}_{m'n'}), \text{ all } lm'n' \neq lmn, \tag{3.25}$$

where $(\bar{y}, \bar{z})$ is the solution of (y, z) to LM_1 under the condition that all L services have multiple options, whereas $(\bar{y}_{mn}, \bar{z}_{mn})$ is the solution to LM_1 under the condition that each of the L services is offered by the single option chosen from LM_2.

Thirdly, we analyze the mathematical properties of service demand functions. By virtue of consistent implicit prices, the qualitative choice problem LM_1 can be converted into the reduced form LM_3 such that

$$LM_3(y, z, \eta; \bar{\pi}) \equiv \max\{U(y, z)\} + \eta \left(\bar{M} - \sum_l \bar{\pi}_l(p_l, t_l)\, y_l - \sum_k \bar{\varphi}_k z_k \right), \tag{3.26}$$

where $\bar{\pi} \equiv (\bar{\pi}_1(p_1, t_1), \cdots, \bar{\pi}_L(p_L, t_L))$. This reduced form is very similar to neoclassical utility maximization problems. The choice components of the reduced form are prime commodities $y \equiv (y_1, \cdots, y_L)$ and hedonic commodities $z \equiv (z_1, \cdots z_K)$. Moreover, the implicit prices of these prime and hedonic commodities are independent of one another; that is, all elements of $\bar{\pi} \equiv (\bar{\pi}_1, \cdots, \bar{\pi}_L)$ are independent of one another, and all elements of $\bar{\varphi} \equiv (\bar{\varphi}_1, \cdots, \bar{\varphi}_K)$ are assumed to be constant.

The reduced form LM_3 gives the demand function $\hat{y}(\bar{\pi})$, which equals the demand function $\bar{y}$, estimated from LM_1. Hence,

$$a_{lm}\bar{q}_{lmn}(p, t) = \begin{cases} \hat{y}_l\,(\bar{\pi}(p, t)), & \text{if } \bar{\pi}_l = \pi_{lmn} \langle \pi_{lm'n'}, \text{ all } lm'n' \neq lmn \\ 0, & \text{if } \bar{\pi}_l \langle \pi_{lmn} \\ \leqslant \hat{y}_l\,(\bar{\pi}(p, t)), & \text{if } \bar{\pi}_l = \pi_{lmn} = \pi_{lm'n'}, \text{ some } lm'n' \neq lmn, \end{cases} \tag{3.27}$$

as can be shown in a manner analogous to the proof of Theorem 2.4. This equation shows that the functional structure of $\bar{q}_{mnl}$ is identical to that of $\bar{q}_{mn}$ for the basic choice problem, with the exception that the former depends on the vector of implicit price, $\bar{\pi}(\equiv(\bar{\pi}_1,\cdots\bar{\pi}_L))$.

In summary, the above analyses of consumer choice show that the important analysis outcomes for a single kind of service can be applied to the case of multiple kinds, without any fundamental amendment. Specifically, first, the choice of an option from a set of multiple options that offer a particular kind of service is not affected by the choice for other kinds of service. Therefore, the revealed preference condition for multiple kinds in (3.25) has an expression identical to the same condition of the basic choice problem for one kind. Second, the reduced form for multiple kinds in (3.26) has an expression identical to that for a single kind, except for one difference in the number of prime commodities. Therefore, the demand function of an option for multiple kinds in (3.27) has a functional structure almost identical to that for a single kind.

3.3.2 Housing Location Choice

The housing location choice of a household depends not only on the price and quality of houses but also on the transportation costs incurred by household members. To analyze this location choice under the perception approach, the UMP should be constructed so as to be able to accommodate the case in which the choice of an option yields multiple prime commodities: one prime commodity that reflects the dwelling service of a house, and other prime commodities that induce multiple kinds of trip demands grouped by purpose. The UMP that reflects this requirement is modeled as a qualitative choice problem, and the developed qualitative choice problem is analyzed in a manner similar to that of the basic choice problem, as presented below.

Firstly, we present the approach to construct the household production function. House prices differ by location, even when physical dimensions such as lot size and floor space are identical. Each housing location is differentiated from other locations by qualitative attributes such as safety, landscape, prestige, etc. Therefore, each candidate location can be designated by a heterogeneous service option, denoted by m. The price of a house in location m is expressed as $p_m q_m$, where p_m is the price per unit of physical dimension such as floor space, and q_m is the size of the house in that unit.

A house is a joint input to the production of multiple prime and multiple hedonic commodities, which collectively comprise all the outcomes related to activities inside the house as well as those related to activities leading to various trips away from the house. It is postulated that activities inside the house yield one prime commodity that refers to dwelling services, and that activities outside the house involve multiple kinds of trips differentiated by purpose such as work, school, shopping, etc. In addition, it is assumed that both inside and outside activities yield K different hedonic commodities.

Prior to the presentation of the production function, we introduce a fictitious function $\delta_m(q_m)$, called the delta function, defined by

$$\delta_m(q_m) = \lim_{N\to\infty} (q_m)^{1/N} = \begin{cases} 1, & \text{if } q_m \rangle 0 \\ 0, & \text{if } q_m = 0, \end{cases} \tag{3.28}$$

so as to accommodate the fact that the trip demand generated from location l can be positive only when option l is chosen. One important property of this fictitious function is

$$\frac{\partial \delta_m(q_m)}{\partial q_m} = \lim_{N\to\infty} \frac{1}{N}(q_m)^{1/N-1} = 0, \tag{3.29}$$

irrespective of the value of q_m. Using this fictitious function, we construct the homogeneous production function below.

The production function for dwelling service is formulated under the assumption that the yield of this prime commodity, denoted by y_1, is linearly proportional to the house's physical size only:

$$Y_1'(q; y_1) = y_1 - \sum_m q_m \delta_m(q_m) = 0, \tag{3.30}$$

where $q \equiv (q_1, \cdots, q_M)$.

The production function for other prime commodities, each of which refers to a certain trip purpose and is denoted by $l \in \langle 2, L \rangle$, is constructed under the following two conditions: first, all household members use the same mode, irrespective of trip purposes; second, the yield of trips for purpose l, denoted by y_l, is equal to the number of trips from the chosen housing location m to the predetermined destination for trips for purpose l, represented by g_{lm}. Thus we have

$$Y_l'(g, q; y_l) = y_l - \sum_m g_{lm}\, \delta_m(q_m) = 0, \;\; \text{all } l \in \langle 2, L \rangle, \tag{3.31}$$

where $g \equiv (g_{21}, \cdots, g_{LM})$. Here, the function $\delta_m(q_m)$ assigns a positive trip demand to only one location as chosen by the household.

On the other hand, the production function for hedonic commodities is constructed under the premise that the house is a durable good but that all trips are non-durable services. Therefore,

$$Z_k'(q, x_k, t_k; z_k) = z_k - \sum_m b_{km} q_m - \sum_{lm} b_k^a t_{lm}^a\, g_{lm} - Z_k(x_k, t_k) = 0, \;\; \text{all } k, \tag{3.32}$$

where b_{km} is the production coefficient of location m for commodity k, b_k^a the production coefficient of all trips for commodity k, and t_{lm}^a the travel time between location m and destination of trips l.

The production function, expressed as the system of (3.30)–(3.32), is homogeneous in both inputs and outputs, as explained below. In the case when only one location is available, the proof of the homogeneity can be worked out in a manner almost identical to the proof of Lemma 2.1 for the basic choice problem. In the case where multiple locations are available, by virtue of the property of the delta function $\delta_m(q_m)$, the production function for multiple options is simplified to the function for a single output; that is, provided that option m is chosen, $\sum_{m'} q_{m'}\delta_{m'}(q_{m'})$ in (3.30) and $\sum_{m'} g_{lm'}\delta_{m'}(q_{m'})$ in (3.31) are simplified to q_m and g_{lm}, respectively. Hence, the production function for the multiple options is also homogeneous.

Secondly, we analyze the choice behavior of households. To this end, we first construct the choice problem, denoted by L_1:

$$
\begin{aligned}
&L_1(g,q,x,y,z,\lambda,\mu,\eta,\phi,\chi;p,p^a,t^a)\equiv\max\{U(y,z)\}+\lambda_1\left(\sum_m q_m\delta_m(q_m)-y_1\right)\\
&+\sum_{l\geqslant 2}\lambda_l\left(\sum_m g_{lm}\delta_m(q_m)-y_l\right)+\sum_k\mu_k\left(\sum_m b_{km}q_m+\sum_{lm} b^a_k t^a_{lm} g_{lm}+Z_k(x_k,t_k)-z_k\right)\\
&+\eta\left(\bar{M}-\sum_m p_m q_m-\sum_m (p^a_{lm}+wt^a_{lm})g_{lm}-\sum_{kj} p_j x_{kj}-w\sum_k t_k\right)\\
&+\sum_m \phi_m q_m+\sum_{lm}\chi_{lm} g_{lm},
\end{aligned}
\tag{3.33}
$$

where $y\equiv(y_1,\cdots,y_L)$, $p\equiv(p_1,\cdots,p_M)$, $p^a\equiv(p^a_{21},\cdots,p^a_{LM})$, and $t^a\equiv(t^a_{21},\cdots,t^a_{LM})$.

The cost minimization problem for the above UMP, L_2, is used to find the optimal inputs (x,g,q) for the arbitrarily given outputs (y,z):

$$
\begin{aligned}
L_2\equiv\ &\min\left\{\sum_m p_m q_m+\sum_{lm}(p^a_{lm}+wt^a_{lm})g_{lm}+\sum_{kj} p_j x_{kj}+w\sum_k t_k\right\}\\
&+\pi_1\left(y_1-\sum_m q_m\delta_m(q_m)\right)+\sum_{l\geqslant 2}\pi_l\left(y_l-\sum_m g_{lm}\delta_m(q_m)\right)\\
&+\sum_k\varphi_k\left(z_k-\sum_m b_{km}q_m-\sum_{lm} b^a_k t^a_{lm} g_{lm}-Z_k(x_k,t_k)\right)\\
&-\sum_m \gamma_m q_m-\sum_{lm}\tau_{lm} g_{lm}.
\end{aligned}
\tag{3.34}
$$

Through analyses of this cost minimization problem, we below develop two kinds of outcomes useful in understanding consumer choice behaviors.

The first outcome of the analyses is the implicit price of various prime commodities, which is estimated under the condition when only one option m is available:

$$\pi_{1m}=p_m-r_m, \tag{3.35}$$

$$\pi_{lm}=p^a_{lm}+v^a t^a_{lm},\quad \text{all}\quad l\geq 2, \tag{3.36}$$

where $r_m = \sum_k \bar{\varphi}_k b_{km}$ and $v^a = w - \sum_k \bar{\varphi}_k b_k^a$, as shown in Appendix A.7.

The above implicit prices can be interpreted as follows. The implicit price π_{1m} represents the implicit house price per physical unit for a house in location m, which can be assigned to the dwelling service of the house. This implicit price equals the market price of the house per physical unit, expressed by p_m, minus the value for the qualitative attributes of the house per physical unit, denoted by r_m. The implicit price π_{lm} for $l \geq 2$, in contrast, estimates the net implicit price per trip to achieve purpose l for location m. This implicit price equals the total transportation cost per trip, minus the value of qualitative attributes packed in one unit of trip.

The second outcome of the analyses is a criterion to identify the chosen option. To develop this criterion, we proceed with analyses to construct the consumer cost function for the cost minimization problem in (3.34) in a manner analogous to that used in estimating the cost function for the basic choice problem in Lemma 2.3. Thus, we show that this consumer cost function C, under the condition where location m is selected, satisfies the following choice criterion:

$$C(p, p^a, t^a; y, z) = \sum_l \pi_{lm} y_l + \sum_k \varphi_k z_k$$
$$\langle \sum_l \pi_{lm'} y_l + \sum_k \varphi_k z_k, \text{ all } m' \neq m, \tag{3.37}$$

as shown in Appendix A.7.

It is important to remember that the housing location choice problem for the production function defined in (3.30)–(3.32) is a qualitative choice problem that satisfies two different kinds of consistency. First, the implicit prices π_{lm} for all l are independent of commodities (y, z). This confirms that the production function is homogeneous. Second, the terms r_m and v_a are both independent of (y, z) and (p, p^a, t^a), as shown in (3.35) and (3.36).

The choice criterion in (3.37) for the cost minimization problem L_2 is applicable to arbitrary output bundles (y, z), including the bundle $(\bar{y}, \bar{z})$ estimated from L_1. Therefore, the solution to L_1 satisfies the revealed preference condition presented below.

Theorem 3.2. *Suppose that the cost minimization problem (3.34) results in the choice of option m. Then, the qualitative choice problem (3.33) yields the revealed preference condition for the choice of option m, such that*

$$\sum_l \bar{\pi}_l \bar{y}_l = \sum_l \pi_{lm} \bar{y}_{lm} \langle \sum_l \pi_{lm'} \bar{y}_{lm'} \Leftrightarrow U(\bar{y}, \bar{z}) = U(\bar{y}_m, \bar{z}_m) \rangle\, U(\bar{y}_{m'}, \bar{z}_{m'}), \text{ all } m' \neq m,$$

where $(\bar{y}, \bar{z})$ is the solution of (y, z) when all multiple options are available, whereas $(\bar{y}_m, \bar{z}_m)$ is the solution when only one option m is available.

Proof. The proof can be worked out in a manner analogous to that used to prove Theorem 2.3. □

Theorem 3.2 shows that the chosen location has the smallest total implicit cost required to produce an arbitrary bundle of prime commodities y, estimated by $\sum_l \pi_{lm} y_l$, but independent of costs related to the production of hedonic commodities. This revealed preference condition indicates that it is impossible to identify the chosen option by simply comparing only the implicit prices of one particular prime commodity for all options. For example, the implicit price of dwelling service for the chosen option m, denoted by π_{1m}, is not required to be smaller than $\pi_{1m'}$, for all $m' \neq m$. Such a result is plausible in our economic sense, considering that neither house price nor transportation cost can be the sole factor determining housing location.

The revealed preference condition shows that the choice of an option from among multiple options depends on the quantities of various prime commodities. For example, the total implicit cost of a household that desires a larger dwelling space is likely more sensitive to the implicit price of dwelling services. For this reason, a household that desires a larger dwelling space may make a choice that differs from that made by another household that wants a smaller space, even when the two households have similar tastes for qualitative attributes and disposable incomes.

Thirdly, we develop and analyze the demand function $\bar{q}_m$ for L_1 in (3.33). To this end, we first construct the reduced form of L_1, denoted by L_3:

$$L_3(y,z,\eta) \equiv \max\{U(y,z)\} + \eta\left(\overline{M} - \sum_l \bar{\pi}_l(p,t)\, y_l - \sum_k \bar{\varphi}_k z_k\right). \tag{3.38}$$

This UMP has a formulation very similar to that of neoclassical utility maximization problems, as is the case for the basic choice problem.

The original optimization problem L_1 and the combination of its two sub-optimization problems L_2 and L_3 have identical solutions of inputs (g,q,x) and outputs (y,z). Hence,

$$\bar{q}_m(p,p^a,t^a) = \begin{cases} \hat{y}_1(\bar{\pi}), & \text{if } m \text{ is chosen} \\ 0, & \text{otherwise}, \end{cases} \tag{3.39}$$

where $\bar{\pi} \equiv (\pi_1, \cdots, \pi_L) \rangle 0$. Here, the function $\hat{y}_1(\bar{\pi})$ is the solution of y_1 to the reduced form L_3.

The mathematical property of $\bar{q}_m$ can readily be deduced from that of $\hat{y}_1(\bar{\pi})$, as explained below. The reduced form L_3 has a formulation identical to that of neoclassical utility maximization problems. This implies that the function $\hat{y}_1(\bar{\pi})$ is continuous in $\bar{\pi}$, and thus in (p,p^a,t^a). Therefore, the function $\bar{q}_m$ is continuous in (p,p^a,t^a), except at the point where $\sum_l \pi_{lm}\hat{y}_{lm} = \sum_l \pi_{lm'}\hat{y}_{lm'}$, for some $m' \neq m$. Moreover, the function $\hat{y}_1(\bar{\pi})$ has comparative statics for $\bar{\pi}$, which resemble those of neoclassical consumer demand functions. Therefore, we can estimate the comparative statics of $\bar{q}_m$ by applying (2.31)–(2.34).

3.4 Non-Qualitative Choice Problems

3.4.1 Decreasing Returns in Prime Commodity Production

We here illustrate demand analyses for the UMP with a non-homogeneous production function, which is a variant of the production function in the location choice problem in Subsect. 3.2.3. We construct this variant by applying an alternative condition: here the purchasing amount of a consumer per visit is not a predetermined constant but an important decision-making variable. We focus analyses of this UMP on showing the following: the revealed preference condition can plausibly explain consumer choice behaviors, but the net-value-of-time for each option cannot satisfy the consistency requirement due to the inconsistent implicit price of services.

In general, by increasing the quantity purchased per visit, a shopper can decrease the number of shopping trips required to purchase the given total amount of a qualitative choice service. However, such a decision accompanies the risk of a potentially bigger economic loss caused by maintaining a larger inventory. For example, an excessively large purchase of fresh groceries per trip would result in an economic loss due to spoilage, and this economic loss can outweigh transportation cost savings. Similarly, an excessively large purchase of fashionable clothes per trip carries a risk of economic loss caused by changes in fashion, and this loss can exceed the savings gained by the reduction of transportation costs.

A similar argument can be applied to recreational activities and the consumption of entertainment services. It can be said that the prime commodity of these services is enjoyment, and that the marginal yield of this prime commodity per visit diminishes as duration of stay per visit increases beyond a certain limit. For example, the marginal increase in the yield of enjoyment perceived by a vacationer of a resort area usually diminishes over the length of a vacationer's stay, when the length of stay per visit exceeds a certain limit. For this reason, if the transportation cost to visit a site were negligible, the consumer would choose a strategy to increase the number of visits but decrease the duration of stay per visit.

Firstly, we construct the production function for prime commodity, which can accommodate diminishing returns-to-scale in purchasing quantity per visit. Under the assumptions introduced above, the production function for the prime commodity can be expressed as follows:

$$Y'(g,q;y) = y - \sum_m Y(g_m)q_m = 0, \tag{3.40}$$

where y is the yield of prime commodity, g_m the purchasing quantity per visit to location m, and q_m the number of visits to m. The function $Y(g_m)$ is non-decreasing and concave in g_m, and satisfies the condition $Y(0) = 0$.

On the other hand, the production function for hedonic commodities can be formulated as follows:

$$Z'_k(g,q,x_k,t_k;z_k) = z_k - \sum_m \left(b^s_{km}t^s_m g_m + b^a_{km}t^a_m\right) q_m - Z_k(x_k,t_k)$$
$$= 0, \text{ all } k, \tag{3.41}$$

where t^s_m and t^a_m are in-site service and travel times, respectively, and b^s_{km} and b^a_{km} are the production coefficients of in-site service and travel times for commodity k, respectively.

Secondly, we analyze the choice of a consumer, who has the production function defined above. For that production function, the cost minimization problem L_2 is

$$L_2 \equiv \min\left\{\sum_m (p^s_m + wt^s_m)g_m q_m + \sum_m (p^a_m + wt^a_m)q_m + \sum_{kj} p_j x_{kj} + w\sum_k t_k\right\}$$
$$+\pi\left(y - \sum_m Y(g_m)q_m\right)$$
$$+\sum_k \varphi_k\left(z_k - \sum_m \left(b^s_{km}t^s_m g_m + b^a_{km}t^a_m\right) q_m - Z_k(x_k,t_k)\right) - \sum_m \gamma_m q_m. \tag{3.42}$$

Here, the first term of the objective function estimates the total purchasing cost of qualitative choice service, and the second term expresses the total transportation cost.

In the case when only option m is available, first-order conditions for the above cost minimization problem with respect to g_m and q_m, respectively, are arranged as follows:

$$\pi_m(p_m,t_m;y) = (p^s_m + v^s_m t^s_m) \Big/ \frac{\partial Y(\bar{g}_m)}{\partial g_m} \tag{3.43}$$

$$= \frac{1}{Y(\bar{g}_m)}\left((p^s_m + v^s_m t^s_m)\bar{g}_m + (p^a_m + v^a_m t^a_m)\right), \text{ all } m, \tag{3.44}$$

where $p_m \equiv (p^s_m, p^a_m)$, $t_m \equiv (t^s_m, t^a_m)$, $v^s_m = w - \sum_k \bar{\varphi}_k b^s_{km}$ and $v^a_m = w - \sum_k \bar{\varphi}_k b^a_{km}$.

The above implicit price π_m is the function of y, $p^s_m + v^s_m t^s_m$ and $p^a_m + v^a_m t^a_m$. Moreover, there is a function ψ such that

$$\pi_m(p_m,t_m;y) = \psi(y, p^s_m + v^s_m t^s_m, p^a_m + v^a_m t^a_m), \text{ all } m. \tag{3.45}$$

The proof is as follows. By the implicit function theorem, the equality of production function in (3.40) and the equality between (3.43) and (3.44) give the outcome that the solutions $\bar{g}_m$ and $\bar{q}_m$ are the function of y, $p^s_m + v^s_m t^s_m$ and $p^a_m + v^a_m t^a_m$. This implies the existence of ψ defined above.

The economic implication of the implicit price π_m is illustrated with an example of shopping trips to purchase groceries. In this example, the yield of prime commodities is the quantity of groceries actually consumed by the shopper, excluding the number of those lost due to spoilage. This yield per visit equals $Y(\bar{g}_m)$ and is usually smaller than the quantity purchased $\bar{g}_m$. Also, the total implicit cost necessary for the purchase of quantity $\bar{g}_m$ equals the sum of the implicit cost of groceries $(p^s_m + v^s_m t^s_m)\bar{g}_m$ and the implicit transportations cost $p^a_m + v^a_m t^a_m$. Therefore, the implicit price of the prime commodity, π_m, is estimated by dividing the sum of $(p^s_m + v^s_m t^s_m)\bar{g}_m$ and $p^a_m + v^a_m t^a_m$ by the quantity actually consumed $Y(\bar{g}_m)$, as depicted in (3.44).

In the case when multiple options are available, the cost minimization problem (3.42) gives the following revealed preference condition for the choice of option m:

$$\bar{\pi}(p, t; y) = \pi_m(p_m, t_m; y) \langle \pi_{m'}(p_{m'}, t_{m'}; y), \text{ all } m' \neq m, \tag{3.46}$$

where $p \equiv (p^s_1, \cdots, p^s_M, p^a_1, \cdots, p^a_M)$ and $t \equiv (t^s_1, \cdots, t^s_M, t^a_1, \cdots, t^a_M)$. This inequality can readily be proved in a manner analogous to that used to show the same assertion for the basic choice problem. Also, this inequality holds for every value of y, including the optimal solution to the UMP.

However, this implicit price π_m in the revealed preference condition (3.46) does not fulfill the consistency condition, as shown in (3.45); that is, the choice of an option depends on output y. We illustrate this dependence of optimal choices on the y value with the choice problem of a shopper who has two options of locations at which to purchase groceries: a nearby shop, and a shop in a relatively distant shopping mall. If the purchasing quantity y is small, the optimal decision could be to choose a nearby shop, since the transportation cost savings would outweigh the additional purchasing cost of groceries. In contrast, if the y value is large, the optimal decision would be to switch to the other option, wherein the purchasing cost reduction would exceed the additional transportation cost.

Thirdly, we analyze the sensitivities of $\bar{q}_m$ with respect to p_m and t_m. The cost minimization problem in (3.42) yields the cost function C such that

$$C(p, t; y, z) = \bar{\pi}(p, t; y)\, y + \sum_k \bar{\varphi}_k z_k. \tag{3.47}$$

This cost function can be developed using the first order condition in (3.44) in a manner similar to that used to prove Lemma 2.3.

For the above cost function, the reduced form of the UMP, denoted by L_3, is

$$L_3(y, z, \eta; \bar{\pi}) = \max\{U(y, z)\} + \eta \left(\bar{M} - \bar{\pi}(p, t; y)\, y - \sum_k \bar{\varphi}_k z_k \right). \tag{3.48}$$

This reduced form fundamentally differs from that of the basic choice problem in that the implicit price $\bar{\pi}$ depends on y, as depicted in (3.45).

Because of this dependency, it is infeasible to develop the demand function $\bar{q}_m$, which has a functional structure identical to that of the demand function for the basic choice problem in Theorem 2.5. To confirm this, we examine the following first order condition for L_3:

$$\frac{\partial L_3}{\partial y} = \frac{\partial U(\hat{y}, \hat{z})}{\partial y} - \eta \left(\frac{\partial \bar{\pi}(p, t, \hat{y})}{\partial y} \hat{y} + \bar{\pi} \right) = 0, \tag{3.49}$$

where $\hat{y}$ and $\hat{z}$ are the solutions of y and $\hat{z}$ to L_3, respectively. In this equation, due to the dependency of $\bar{\pi}$ on y, it holds that $\partial\bar{\pi}/\partial y \neq 0$. Hence, it is impossible to characterize the sensitivity of $\bar{q}_m$ in a manner analogous to that for the basic choice problem in Theorem 2.5.

In summary, the choice problem analyzed in this subsection is actually identical to the choice problem considered in Subsect. 3.2.3, with the exception that the consumer production function is not homogeneous. This non-homogeneous production function in (3.40) depicts decision-making environments more realistically than does the homogeneous function in (3.4). For this reason, the revealed preference conditions for the non-homogeneous production function in (3.46) can more reasonably depict consumer choice behaviors than does the condition for the homogeneous function in (3.8). However, the reduced form for this non-qualitative choice problem fundamentally differs from that for the basic choice problem, as shown in (3.49).

3.4.2 *Mode Choice of Work Trips*

We here analyze the choice of trip mode for commuting to/from work. This trip mode choice problem shares a similarity with qualitative choice problems in that it uses a homogeneous production function. However, the mode choice problem differs from all the qualitative choice problems analyzed previously in the following respect: a commuting activity affects only disposable incomes and the amount of hedonic commodities consumed, without yielding any prime commodity. This critical difference results in the inconsistent net-value-of-time, and thereby leads to the inevitable conclusion that this choice problem is not a qualitative choice problem, as explained below.

Firstly, we construct the UMP of a commuter who makes a trip mode choice under the following conditions. First, the worker decides the number of work days, which determines commute demands. Second, the worker earns a predetermined hourly wage, w, and works a certain number of fixed hours per day, t_w. Third, the commuter has M modes available, each of which is denoted by $m \in \langle 1, M \rangle$. Fourth, daily production, which determines daily labor income, is identical, irrespective of mode choice decision.

In addition, we apply the following two conditions, which are required to construct the UMP under the perception approach. First, the work trip is the sole variable determining monetary labor income; that is, labor income is estimated by $\sum_m wt_w q_m$. Second, the work trip does not yield any prime commodity, unlike qualitative choice problems; that is, the utility function is expressed by $U(z)$. Third, the work trip yields K hedonic commodities, and the production function of these commodities is identical to that of the basic choice problem.

Incorporating a series of assumptions identified above into the basic choice problem in (2.13) gives the UMP for the commuter, denoted by L_o, such that

$$L_o(q,x,z,\mu,v,\eta,\phi;p,t)=\max\{U(z)\}+\sum_k \mu_k\left(\sum_m b_{km}t_m q_m+Z_k(x_k,t_k)-z_k\right)$$
$$+v\left(T_o-\sum_m (t_w+t_m)q_m-\sum_k t_k\right)$$
$$+\eta\left(I_o+\sum_m (wt_w-p_m)q_m-\sum_{kj} p_j x_{kj}\right)+\sum_m \phi_m q_m. \tag{3.50}$$

One but critical difference of this UMP from the basic choice problem is that the argument of the utility function U is composed only of the vector z.

For the UMP in (3.50), it is not straightforward to merge the two constraints for time and monetary income into one constraint for full income. The reason is as follows. Differentiation of L_o in (3.50) with respect to q_m, which is equivalent to the differentiation with respect to t_w for the basic choice problem in (2.13), does not lead to the equality $v = \eta w$. Therefore, we apply an alternative method of merging the two constraints, as introduced next.

Secondly, we find the relationship between the Lagrange multipliers of the two constraints for time and monetary income. To this end, we consider the special case when only one option m is available to a commuter. For this case, we estimate the relationship between $\bar{v}_m$ and $\bar{\eta}_m$ under the convention that the saddle point of L_o is $(\bar{q}_m, \bar{x}_m, \bar{z}_m, \bar{\mu}_m, \bar{v}_m, \bar{\eta}_m)$.

To be specific, we estimate the term w_m, which satisfies the equality $\bar{v}_m = \bar{\eta}_m w_m$. One expression of this term, as shown in Appendix A.8, is as follows:

$$w_m \equiv \frac{\bar{v}_m}{\bar{\eta}_m} = \frac{w\,t_w - p_m + \sum_k \bar{\varphi}_k b_{km} t_m}{t_w + t_m}, \text{ all } m, \tag{3.51}$$

where

$$\bar{\varphi}_k = \frac{\bar{\mu}_{km}}{\bar{\eta}_m} = p_j \bigg/ \frac{\partial \bar{Z}_k}{\partial x_{kj}}, \text{ all } k. \tag{3.52}$$

Equation (3.51) shows that the w_m value is sensitive not only to the implicit price $\bar{\varphi}_k$ but also to p_m and t_m values. This implies that the w_m value is affected by consumer's mode choice. It is also relevant to note that the implicit price $\bar{\varphi}_k$ is determined by substitute productions, as is true of qualitative choice problems.

Economically, the term w_m represents the net wage after the payment of transportation cost, when the commuter chooses trip mode m. The right side of (3.51) depicts that the net wage equals actual wage minus transportation cost assignable to one hour actually worked. Specifically, the numerator on the right side estimates net monetary income per day after paying net monetary travel cost assignable to commutes, whereas the denominator is gross working hours, which is the sum of the number of daily working hours and commuting hours.

Thirdly, we merge the two constraints of L_o under the condition that only one mode m is available. Substituting (3.51) into (3.50) yields an amendment, denoted by L_m, such that

$$L_m(q_m,x,z,\mu_m,v_m,\eta_m;p_m,t_m)=\max\{U(z)\}+\sum_k \mu_{km}\left(b_{km}t_m q_m+Z_k(x_k,t_k)-z_k\right)$$

$$+\eta_m\left(I_o+w_m T_o-(p_m+w_m t_m)q_m-(w_m-w)t_w q_m-\sum_{kj} p_j x_{kj}-w_m\sum_k t_k\right). \quad (3.53)$$

This trip mode choice problem gives the following.

Theorem 3.3. *The trip mode choice problem L_m satisfies the following:*

$$\pi_m(p_m,t_m)=p_m+v_m t_m=t_w(w-w_m), \quad (3.54)$$

where

$$v_m=w_m-\sum_k \bar{\varphi}_k b_{km}. \quad (3.55)$$

Proof. The proof is worked out by arranging first order conditions for L_m, as shown in Appendix A.8. □

Theorem 3.3 shows that the net-value-of-time v_m depends on p_m and t_m values, as can be deduced from (3.51). This implies that the net-value-of-time v_m in (3.55) does not meet the consistency requirement. Therefore, the trip mode choice problem for a commuter is not a qualitative choice problem, in spite that its production function is homogeneous in both inputs and outputs.

Fourthly, we develop the revealed preference condition. Let the solution of L_m be $(\bar{q}_m,\bar{x},\bar{z},\bar{\mu}_m,\bar{v}_m,\bar{\eta}_m)$. For this solution, all the constraints of L_m can be merged into one equation such that

$$\bar{M}_m\equiv I_o+w_m T_o=\sum_k \varphi_k\bar{z}_k,\ \text{all } m, \quad (3.56)$$

where $\bar{M}_m$ is the net full income after paying transportation cost, as proved in Appendix A.8. Using this equation, the choice of trip mode m can be characterized as below.

Theorem 3.4. *Suppose that the trip mode choice problem L_o leads to the choice of trip mode m. Then, it holds that*

$$\pi_m \langle \pi_{m'} \Leftrightarrow w_m \rangle w_{m'} \Leftrightarrow \bar{M}_m \rangle \bar{M}_{m'} \Leftrightarrow U(\bar{z}_m) \rangle U(\bar{z}_{m'}), \; all \; m' \neq m.$$

Proof. First, equation (3.54) implies that $w_m \rangle w_{m'} \Leftrightarrow \pi_m \langle \pi_{m'}$. Second, the first equality of (3.56) shows that $w_m \rangle w_{m'} \Leftrightarrow \bar{M}_m \rangle \bar{M}_{m'}$ Third, the second equality of (3.56) connotes that all the constraints of L_m can be merged into one constraint for full income: $\bar{M}_m - \sum_k \bar{\varphi}_k z_k = 0$. Hence, it follows that $\bar{M}_m \rangle \bar{M}_{m'} \Leftrightarrow U(\bar{z}_m) \rangle U(\bar{z}_{m'})$.□

Theorem 3.3 introduces three criteria for the choice of trip mode m. The first criterion $\pi_m \langle \pi_{m'}$ depicts that the commuter always chooses the trip mode that charges the lowest implicit price of trip for net wage. The second criterion $w_m \rangle w_{m'}$ shows that the choice of the least implicit price mode m gives the maximum net wage to the commuter. The third inequality $M_m \rangle M_{m'}$ indicates that the choice of the least implicit price mode m results in the maximum net full income after the payment of transportation cost, and thereby the maximum utility.

The choice criterion $\pi_m \langle \pi_{m'}$ in the theorem can lead to the mode choice differing from the mode choice by the criterion used to compare $p_m + wt_m$ with $p_{m'} + wt_{m''}$, for all $m' \neq m$. To illustrate this, we consider a special case when two modes of auto and bus have the identical value of $p_m + wt_m$. In this circumstance, the expression of w_m in (3.51) implies that auto mode gives the net wage w_m, which is larger than that for bus, since the bus is slower but cheaper. Hence, by Theorem 3.3, it follows that auto mode has a smaller value of π_m. Therefore, we can deduce from Theorem 3.4 that the chosen mode is auto.

Finally, we analyze the mathematical property of trip demand function $\bar{q}_m$. The mode choice problem L_o has a production function that yields no prime commodity. For this reason, the reduced form, denoted by L_3, can be expressed as follows:

$$L_3(z;p,t) \equiv \max\{U(z)\} + \eta\left(I_o + \hat{w}_m T_o - \sum_k \hat{\varphi}_{km} z_k\right). \tag{3.57}$$

However, from this reduced form, it is infeasible to develop the demand function $\bar{q}_m$. To clarify this, a set of simultaneous equation systems, from which the sensitivity of $\bar{q}_m$ can be estimated, is presented in Appendix A.8.

In summary, the production function for the trip mode choice problem analyzed in this subsection is homogeneous in both inputs and outputs, but does not yield any prime commodity. Therefore, the trip mode choice problem is not a qualitative choice problem. This trip mode choice problem yields the implicit price of service, which is independent of output, but does not give the net-value-of-time, which is independent of the price and service time of travel services, as shown in (3.51). Such a trip mode choice problem gives revealed preference conditions that can reasonably depict consumer choice behavior, but does not yield the trip demand function that has a functional structure identical to neoclassical consumer demand functions.

Chapter 4
Service Demand of Consumers with Random Perceptions

4.1 Introduction

The previous two chapters have analyzed qualitative choice problems constructed under the condition that consumers have deterministic perception for qualitative attributes packed in a given service. Under this assumption, qualitative choice problems give the revealed preference condition that deterministically identifies the option chosen by consumers; that is, the chosen option does not vary as long as the values of quantitative variables such as price and service time do not change. Contrary to this assumption, actual consumers, in real life situations, change their choices of options for a particular service from time to time, even though the values of quantitative variables do not change.

One way to accommodate consumers' ever-changing choice behaviors is to apply the random perception approach. The random perception approach is identical to the deterministic perception approach, except that the method used to quantify the yield of hedonic commodities reflects the subjective perceptions of consumers. The random perception approach postulates that the yield of hedonic commodities is not a deterministic number but rather random numbers. This randomness connotes that the yield of hedonic commodities varies from time to time, and that the varying perceptions can cause changes in the selection of options for a certain qualitative choice service.

We model UMPs that follow the random perception approach by applying the hypothesis that the production coefficient of hedonic commodities in consumer production functions is an outcome of a random process. This hypothesis can apply to all UMPs that follow the deterministic perception approach. For example, the application of this hypothesis to the Deterministic Basic Choice Problem (DBCP) analyzed in Chap. 2 yields the basic choice problem under the random perception approach, called the Stochastic Basic Choice Problem (SBCP).

The objective of this chapter is to develop the demand function of an option through analyses of the Stochastic Qualitative Choice Problem (SQCP), which refers to the qualitative choice problem under the random perception approach.

D.J. Moon, *Congestion-Prone Services Under Quality Competition*, Advances in Spatial Science, DOI 10.1007/978-3-642-20189-9_4,

To this end, this chapter details demand analyses for an example of the SBCP that has been developed from the DBCP. Subsequently, this chapter extends the demand analyses for the SBCP to the SQCPs for other Deterministic Qualitative Choice Problems (DQCPs) analyzed in Chap. 3.

The structure of the SBCP analyzed here is as follows. Its objective function is the expected value of the utility function with respect to the random outcomes of hedonic commodities with a certain distribution. The constraints are identical to those of the DBCP, except that the yields of hedonic commodities are specified as random outcomes. The solution to the SBCP should attain maximum expected utility under point-wise constraints such that consumer choice for each realization of random variables should satisfy the deterministic budget constraint for that realization.

The SBCP gives the demand function of an option for the vector of independent variables that comprise the prices and service times of all available options. This demand function is the expected value of demands for that option with respect to the random variable for hedonic commodities. Such an expected demand function of an option can be expressed as a multiple integral of the deterministic demand function for that option with respect to random variables for hedonic commodities. However, the expected demand function with respect to random variables for hedonic commodities is insufficiently specified to identify the functional form and behavioral implication of the expected demand function.

For this reason, we develop the stochastic version of the deterministic demand function for the reduced form of the DBCP. To this end, we utilize the point-wise Kuhn-Tucker conditions for stochastic optimization problems in Rockafellar and Wets (1978), which correspond to the stochastic version of the Kuhn-Tucker conditions for deterministic optimization problems. Thus, we develop the expected demand function for the reduced form of the SBCP, which is expressed as a multiple integral with respect to random variables for net-value-of-times.

The expected demand function of an option for random net-value-of-times is the main output of demand analyses in this chapter. This demand function will be used as the input to subsequent economic analyses in Parts II, III and IV of this study. For this demand function, we in this chapter thoroughly explore its functional form and behavioral implication, leaving the sensitivity analysis with respect to prices and service times in the next chapter.

Moreover, it should be noted that the demand analyses presented in this chapter can apply only to qualitative choice problems. These UMPs under the deterministic perception approach satisfy two different kinds of consistency, as pointed out in Subsect. 2.4.2. For this reason, these UMPs have the reduced form in which net-value-of-times are constants that can be designated as the outcome of random variables, as also explained in that subsection. In contrast, non-qualitative choice problems that do not satisfy the two consistency requirements yield net-value-of-times that cannot be designated as the outcome of random variables.

The material in this chapter unfolds as follows. Sect. 4.2 constructs the SBCP by incorporating the uncertainty about consumer production into the DBCP. Subsequently, Sect. 4.3 converts the previously developed SBCP into its reduced form, and then develops the expected demand function of an option from the reduced form. Finally, Sect. 4.4 extends the demand analysis for the SBCP to two other SQCPs, and assesses the applicability of demand functions under the random perception approach to the formulation of choice probabilities for statistical estimations.

4.2 The Stochastic Basic Choice Problem

4.2.1 Consumer Production Function under Uncertainty

The SBCP is identical to the DBCP except that the former incorporates uncertainty into the consumer production function for hedonic commodities. This production function of the DBCP is constructed under the postulate that the yield of hedonic commodities is the outcome of deterministic production processes. In contrast, the production function of the SBCP is formulated under the postulate that the future yield of hedonic commodities is an outcome of random processes. Below we present the process used to convert the production function of the DBCP to that of the SBCP.

To begin, we introduce several examples that support the postulate that the magnitude of qualitative service attributes is the outcome of a random process affected by various uncertain factors. One example is the magnitude of comfort perceived in the process to receive services. A key factor that affects consumer perception for the quantity of comfort is a consumer's physical and mental condition. When a consumer is in good physical condition, he might not perceive a large or important difference between a more comfortable service option and a less comfortable one. In contrast, when this same consumer's physical condition worsens, he might very well perceive a big, even crucial, difference.

Another example is found in the perception of safety. One important factor that affects the perceived importance of safety could be an accident recently experienced by a consumer, or a consumer's relatives, friends, etc. Such an accident, by its nature, cannot be controlled by consumer will. Yet, randomly occurring accidents can lead consumers to perceive a big difference in the perceived amount of safety between options offering relatively less or more safe services.

The other example comes from the perceived importance of aesthetic values or attractiveness in the choice of meeting places or restaurants. An event that calls for this choice usually involves various interactions among people. Additionally, the type of event that takes place at a certain time in the future could be regarded as the outcome of a random process over a relatively long time span. Further, the type of event might be a key factor that influences the importance of psychic attributes affecting the choice of an option. When a consumer has a meeting with an important business guest, he is likely to be more sensitive to the different service attributes of available options than he is likely to be when he plans to meet a close friend.

Subsequently, we introduce a method for incorporating uncertainty about the magnitude of qualitative attributes into the deterministic production function of hedonic commodities. This method involves amending the production function of hedonic commodity k in Assumption 2.1 as follows:

$$z_k - \sum_{mn} \beta_{km} t_{mn} q_{mn} - Z_k(x_k, t_k) = 0, \text{ all } k, \tag{4.1}$$

where β_{km} is the random production coefficient of option mn for commodity k, and the other terms are identical to their counterparts in Assumption 2.1(b). One way of quantifying the random production coefficient β_{km} is as below.

Assumption 4.1. The perception of a consumer for the production coefficient $\beta \equiv (\beta_{11}, \cdots, \beta_{KM})$ is the outcome of the following random process.

(a) Each event β is an outcome of a continuous random variable $\mathrm{B} \equiv (\mathrm{B}_{11}, \cdots, \mathrm{B}_{KM})$ with a joint distribution G defined on the sample space $RB \in \mathbf{R}^{\mathrm{KM}}$, where B_{km} is a coordinate variable such that $\mathrm{B}_{km}(\beta_{km}) = \beta_{km}$
(b) The distribution function G is absolutely continuous in β, and the sample space RB is convex.

Assumption 4.1 depicts that the distribution of the random vector β is only information about the yield of hedonic commodities; such information is available to an analyst of consumer behaviors, including the consumer himself. This assumption characterizes the mathematical properties of the distribution in a format that is as generalized as possible. This mathematical description embeds a number of behavioral implications, as explained below.

First, randomness implies that outcome β, which will be realized in the future, is not certain at the moment the qualitative choice problem is analyzed. At that moment, the only knowledge available to an analyst is the distribution function $G(\beta)$. Furthermore, the distribution of β for a future period of analysis is independent of the value realized in previous periods.

Second, the joint distribution function $G(\beta)$ does not exclude the case when a certain random term β_{km} has a correlation with other terms β_{in}, for every $in \neq km$. Such a specification of $G(\beta)$ can accommodate the case when a random event accompanies simultaneous changes in the perceived quantity of a certain hedonic commodity across multiple options. For example, one can imagine a situation when a traveler's poor physical condition simultaneously influences his perceived quantity of comfort for various trip options.

Third, a random variable B_m is common to all options belonging to heterogeneous service group m and is independent of other random variables B_i, for all $i \neq m$. This means that the β_{km} value perceived by a consumer at a certain instance is identical to all the options belonging to a heterogeneous service group m, but generally differs from the β_{ki} value of other groups, for all $i \neq m$.

Note that we will express the expected value of a summable function u with respect to the random variable B as follows:

$$E\{u(\beta); RB)\} = \int_{RB} u(\beta) d\lambda_G, \tag{4.2}$$

where E is the expectation operator with respect to random outcomes β, and λ_G is the probability measure of B with the distribution G on the sample space RB. Note, also, that the term $E\{u(\beta; RB)\}$ will sometimes be expressed as $E\{u(\beta)\}$.

4.2.2 Modeling of the Stochastic Basic Choice Problem

Here we construct the SBCP by amending the DBCP into a decision-making model compatible with Assumption 4.1. To this end, we first develop the SBCP by replacing the deterministic production function in the DBCP with the stochastic production function in (4.1). We next introduce the behavioral implication embodied in the SBCP, focusing on how this implication differs from that for the DBCP.

To start, we reintroduce the structure of the DBCP as an optimization problem, in order to facilitate forthcoming discussions. The DBCP is used to estimate the solution of production inputs, $q \equiv (q_{11}, \cdots, q_{MN})$ and $x \equiv (x_1, \cdots, x_K, t_1, \cdots, t_K)$; and production outputs, y and $z \equiv (z_1, \cdots, z_K)$, so as to maximize the utility $U(y, z)$, under the constraints for the productions of y and z, and for the available budget $\bar{M}$.

We next consider the problem of converting the DBCP to the SBCP. Both DBCP and SBCP have identical choice variables, q, x, y, and z. The solution of these choice variables to the DBCP are affected by the parameters in the optimization problem: not only price vector p and service time vector t but also production coefficients for consumer production, denoted by $b \equiv (b_{11}, \cdots, b_{KM})$. Likewise, the solution of the choice variables to the SBCP are influenced not only by the vectors p and t but also production coefficient vector $\beta \equiv (\beta_{11}, \cdots, \beta_{KM})$. However, the parameter vector b is a deterministic term, whereas the vector β is the outcome of a random variable. Hence, the choice vectors of the latter, q, x, y, and z, are represented as $q(\beta,p,t)$, $x(\beta,p,t)$, $y(\beta,p,t)$, and $z(\beta,p,t)$, respectively, so as to explicitly reflect that the solution for the choice vectors is affected by realized β values. Under this convention, the SBCP can be formulated as below.

Assumption 4.2. The SBCP is used to search for the optimal values of $q(\beta,p,t)$, $x(\beta,p,t)$, $y(\beta,p,t)$, and $z(\beta,p,t)$ that satisfy the following conditions.

(a) The output bundle of $y(\beta,p,t)$ and $z(\beta,p,t)$ maximizes the expected utility $E\{U\}$, defined by

$$E\{U(y(\beta,p,t), z(\beta,p,t))\} = \int_{RB} U(y(\beta,p,t), z(\beta,p,t))\, d\lambda_G,$$

where U is twice differentiable and strictly concave on the relevant region of (y, z).

(b) The input bundle of $q(\beta,p,t)$ and $x(\beta,p,t)$ satisfies the point-wise technical constraints:

$$y(\beta,p,t) = \sum_{mn} a_m q_{mn}(\beta,p,t), \text{ all } \beta,$$

$$z_k(\beta,p,t) = \sum_{mn} \beta_{km} t_{mn} q_{mn}(\beta,p,t) + Z_k(x_k(\beta,p,t), t_k(\beta,p,t)), \text{ all } \beta, k,$$

where $Z_k(x_k, t_k)$ exhibits constant returns in non-joint inputs $(x_k, t_k) \rangle 0$.

(c) The input bundle fulfills the point-wise budget constraint for full income:

$$\sum_{mn} (p_{mn} + wt_{mn})\, q_{mn}(\beta,p,t) + \sum_{kj} p_j x_{kj}(\beta,p,t) + \sum_k wt_k(\beta,p,t) \le \bar{M}, \text{ all } \beta.$$

(d) The wage w, the price p_j for all j, and the time t_k for all k are fixed.

The SBCP defined above is constructed by incorporating uncertainty about the value of β into the DBCP of (2.16). Therefore, the behavioral implication of the SBCP can be interpreted in a manner identical to that for (2.16), except for the addition of comments associated with the random production coefficient of hedonic commodities. These additional comments, which are useful to our understanding of the nature of the decision-making mechanism embodied in the SBCP, are introduced below.

First, the SBCP formulates the UMP under the condition that perfect information about the production coefficients is not available to the analyst. This SBCP is applicable, while the production coefficients are still uncertain, to the forecast of a decision to be made in a relatively distant future, e.g., next week or next month. In contrast, the DBCP is applicable to the analysis of a decision to be made in a relatively near future, e.g., this week or this month, when the decision environment affecting the perception about the production coefficients is certain.

Second, the random vector β is assumed to be realized at the beginning point of an analysis period. Further, the value realized at that point does not vary afterward. That is, from this point, the future choice of independent variables will be made under the assumption that the random vector takes a deterministic value. Therefore, the UMP that a consumer will face becomes the DBCP for the parameter vector β that was realized.

Third, the solution to the SBCP should maximize the expected utility, which is expressed by $E\{u(y,z)\}$, with respect to the random vector β under a set of point-wise constraints for each β value. The point-wise constraints for each β value imply that the consumer choice for inputs (q,x) and outputs (y,z) should surely fulfill the constraints under the condition that random vector β will be realized.

4.2.3 Development of Point-Wise Kuhn-Tucker Conditions

The demand function of option mn, denoted by $Q_{mn}(p,t)$, is the solution of demand for the option to the SBCP, when the price and service time vector consumers face is (p,t). This demand function can be developed from optimality conditions for the SBCP in a manner analogous to that used to develop the demand function from optimality conditions for the DBCP in Chap. 2. The procedure for developing the demand function is presented below.

To start, we present the procedure to construct the Lagrangian of the SBCP. First, the Lagrangian for a fixed value of (β,p,t) is formulated. This Lagrangian, which has a formulation identical to the Lagrangian L_1 of (2.26) and denoted by J_1, is expressed in the following:

$$J_1(r(\beta,p,t),\kappa(\beta,p,t);\beta,p,t) \equiv \max\ U(r(\beta,p,t)) + \sum_i \kappa_i(\beta,p,t)g_i(r(\beta,p,t);\beta,p,t), \tag{4.3}$$

where $r \equiv (q,x,y,z)$ and $\kappa \equiv (\lambda,\mu,\phi,\eta)$. Second, the expected value of J_1 is estimated with respect to β:

$$E\{J_1\} \equiv \int_{RB} J_1(\,r(\beta,p,t),\ \kappa(\beta,p,t);\beta,p,t)\,d\lambda_G. \tag{4.4}$$

Using the Lagrangian $E\{J_1\}$, we characterize the solution of $r(\beta,p,t)$ as below.

Lemma 4.1. *Necessary and sufficient conditions for the solution, ($\bar{r}(\beta,p,t)$ and $\bar{\kappa}(\beta,p,t)$), to $E\{J_1\}$ are the point-wise Kuhn-Tucker conditions for the solution, such that the solution to J_1 for each β value satisfies the Kuhn-Tucker conditions for J_1 with the deterministic parameter vector of this β value.*[1]

Proof. The solution of $r(\beta,p,t)$ to the SBCP for every realization of β should satisfy the point-wise constraints that $g_i(\cdot) = 0$ or ≥ 0, for all i. (i) This point-wise constraints require that, for each β value, the solution of $r(\beta,p,t)$ should maximize the j_1 value, so that the expected utility $E\{U(y(\beta,p,t),z(\beta,p,t))\}$ has the maximum value. On the other hand, for each β value, the DBCP with the parameter β satisfies the convexity condition for optimization problems. (ii) Hence, for each β value, the Kuhn-Tucker conditions for the solution to the DBCP with the parameter β are necessary and sufficient conditions for the solution to the DBCP. By (i) and (ii), it follows the assertion in the lemma. □

[1] The SUMP is an application of the optimal recourse problem in Rockafellar and Wets (1978), which is a multi-period optimization problem under both equality and inequality constraints.

Lemma 4.1 depicts optimality conditions for the SBCP using the point-wise Kuhn-Tucker conditions. Here, the term "point-wise" comes from the point-wise constraints in Assumption 4.2(b) and 4.2(c). These point-wise constraints imply that the optimal choice of $r \equiv (q, x, y, z)$ for each β value should satisfy the constraints under the condition that that β value will be realized. Therefore, the point-wise Kuhn-Tucker conditions imply that the optimal choice of r for each β value, which satisfies the point-wise Kuhn-Tucker conditions, is the solution to Kuhn-Tucker conditions for the DBCP with the parameter vector (β, p, t).

We are now ready to introduce the definition of the demand function of an option. The demand function of option mn for the independent vector (p, t) is defined as the solution of q_{mn} to the SBCP in which the (p, t) value is incorporated as a parameter. Hence, by Lemma 4.1, this demand function of option mn, denoted by $Q_{mn}(p, t)$, is the expected value of $\bar{q}_{mn}(\beta, p, t)$ with respect to the random vector β having distribution G:

$$Q_{mn}(p, t) = E\{\, \bar{q}_{mn}(\beta, p, t)\} = \int_{RB} \bar{q}_{mn}(\beta, p, t)\; d\lambda_G, \text{ all } mn. \tag{4.5}$$

Here, $\bar{q}_{mn}(\beta, p, t)$ is one element of the vector $r(\beta, p, t)$, which is the solution to the point-wise Kuhn-Tucker conditions. Further, the function Q_{mn} is called *the expected demand function of option mn for hedonic commodities.*

The economic implication of Q_{mn} can be interpreted as follows. In a future analysis period, the consumer will make a consumption decision that optimizes the DBCP with the parameter vector β that will already have been realized. However, the specific value of random outcome β remains unrealized. Instead, the only knowledge available to the analyst is the distribution of the parameter vector. In such a circumstance, the analyst's best guess about the demand of option mn is the expected value of $\bar{q}_{mn}$ with respect to random vector β having a known distribution, as expressed by the right side of (4.5).

However, the above expression of Q_{mn} is too abstract to evaluate the advantage of the random perception approach. Specifically, the expression provides no hint about the consumer choice behavior. Furthermore, the expression is not specific enough so that one can evaluate its mathematical properties, such as continuity or comparative statics with respect to p and t.

4.3 Expected Demand Functions

4.3.1 Revealed Preference Condition under Uncertainty

Point-wise Kuhn-Tucker conditions for the SBCP in Lemma 4.1 imply that the optimal decision to be made in the future is actually identical to the solution to the DBCP with a parameter vector β that will be realized. Using this relationship, we present below the revealed preference condition for the situation in which a certain value of β will be realized in a future analysis period.

Suppose that a certain β value will be realized in a future analysis period. By Lemma 4.1, the solution of all the choice variables to the SBCP for this β value is identical to that of the DBCP for this β value. Hence, by Lemma 2.2, the SBCP gives the implicit price of a prime commodity for option mn, denoted by $\hat{\pi}_{mn}$, such that

$$\hat{\pi}_{mm}(\xi_m, p_m, t_m) = \frac{1}{a_m}(p_{mn} + \xi_m t_{mn}), \text{ all } mn. \tag{4.6}$$

Here, ξ_m is the random net-value-of-time of service group m for the realized β value, estimated by

$$\xi_m = w - \sum_k \hat{\varphi}_k \beta_{km}, \text{ all } m, \tag{4.7}$$

and the term $\hat{\varphi}_k$ is the price of hedonic commodity k, estimated by

$$\hat{\varphi}_k = p_j \bigg/ \frac{\partial \bar{Z}_k}{\partial x_{kj}} = w \bigg/ \frac{\partial \bar{Z}_k}{\partial t_k}, \text{ all } k, j, \tag{4.8}$$

where $\bar{Z}_k \equiv Z_k(\bar{x}_k(\beta,p,t), \bar{t}_k(\beta,p,t))$. Furthermore, the implicit price $\hat{\varphi}_k$ is a constant, irrespective of β values, as shown in Lemma 2.2.

Subsequently, by Theorem 2.2, the implicit price of the prime commodity for the chosen option, denoted by $\hat{\pi}$, is

$$\hat{\pi}(\xi, p, t) = \min_{mn} \{\hat{\pi}_{mm}(\xi_m, p_{mm}, t_{mn})\}, \tag{4.9}$$

where $\xi \equiv (\xi_1, \cdots, \xi_M)$. This equation implies that the consumer chooses the option that will charge the lowest implicit price for the prime commodity. Hence, the consumer choice satisfies the relationship presented below, as also shown in Theorem 2.2.

Theorem 4.1. *The solution to the SBCP for all β values satisfies the choice criterion under uncertainty, such that*

$$a_m \bar{q}_{mn}(\beta,p,t) \begin{cases} = \bar{y}(\beta,p,t), & \text{if } \hat{\pi} = \hat{\pi}_{mn} \langle \hat{\pi}_{m'n'}, \quad \text{all} \quad m'n' \neq mn \\ = 0, & \text{if } \hat{\pi} \langle \hat{\pi}_{mn} \\ \leq \bar{y}(\beta,p,t), & \text{if } \hat{\pi} = \hat{\pi}_{mn} \langle \hat{\pi}_{m'n'}, \quad \text{some} \quad m'n' \neq mn. \end{cases}$$

The above criterion for the choice of an option satisfies the consistency condition such that the implicit price $\hat{\pi}_{mn}$, for all mn, is independent of outputs (y,z). Therefore, this choice criterion can apply to any value of (y,z), including the solution to the SBCP for a certain parameter vector β. Hence, the revealed preference condition that identifies the chosen option for the realization of a certain β value can be characterized in a manner identical to that of Theorem 2.3.

Theorem 4.2. *The solution to the SBCP for all β values satisfies the revealed preference condition under uncertainty, such that*

$$\hat{\pi} = \hat{\pi}_{mn} \leq \hat{\pi}_{m'n'} \Leftrightarrow U(\bar{y}, \bar{z})) = U(\bar{y}_{mn}, \bar{z}_{mn}) \geq U(\bar{y}_{m'n'}, \bar{z}_{m'n'}), \text{ all } m'n' \neq mn,$$

where $(\bar{y}, \bar{z})$ is the solution of (y, z) to the SBCP when all the multiple options are available, whereas $(\bar{y}_{mn}, \bar{z}_{mn})$ is the solution when only option mn is available.

Theorem 4.2 depicts the revealed preference condition for a future decision under the condition that a particular β value will be realized. "The left side implies the right" indicates that the future decision to choose option mn, which has the lowest implicit price for the future realization of a particular β value, will attain a higher utility than would the choice of other options. Conversely, "the right side implies the left" shows that option mn, which will be chosen by a utility maximizer, will have the lowest implicit price for the realized outcome of β values.

4.3.2 The Reduced Form for Random Net-Value-of-Times

The reduced form of the SBCP is a stochastic version of the reduced form of the DBCP. This reduced form of the SBCP is identical to the reduced form of the DBCP, except that the deterministic net-value-of-time $v \equiv (v_1, \cdots, v_M)$ is replaced by the random net-value-of-time $\xi \equiv (\xi_1, \cdots, \xi_M)$, as defined in (4.7). This reduced form is the stochastic optimization problem used to find the solution that maximizes an expected utility with respect to random vector ξ. The reduced form gives a solution identical to that of the SBCP specified in Assumptions 4.1 and 4.2, as shown below.

Firstly, we develop a new random variable for net-value-of-time $\Xi \equiv (\Xi_1, \cdots, \Xi_M)$ from the random variable $\mathrm{B} \equiv (\mathrm{B}_{11}, \cdots, \mathrm{B}_{KM})$ by applying a linear relationship (4.7):

$$\xi = w - \hat{\varphi}\beta, \text{ or} \tag{4.10}$$

$$\begin{pmatrix} \xi_1 \\ \vdots \\ \xi_M \end{pmatrix} = \begin{pmatrix} w \\ \vdots \\ w \end{pmatrix} - \begin{pmatrix} \beta_{11} & \cdots & \beta_{K1} \\ \vdots & \ddots & \vdots \\ \beta_{1M} & \cdots & \beta_{KM} \end{pmatrix} \begin{pmatrix} \hat{\varphi}_1 \\ \vdots \\ \hat{\varphi}_K \end{pmatrix}. \tag{4.11}$$

This new random variable Ξ can be characterized, as below.

Lemma 4.2. *Suppose that $\xi = w - \hat{\varphi}\beta$, and that two arbitrary continuous functions $\bar{u}(\beta)$ and $\hat{u}(\xi)$ satisfy the condition such that*

$$\bar{u}(\beta) = \hat{u}(\xi).$$

i. *Then, there is the random variable Ξ, which has a uniquely defined distribution function H and satisfies the following equality:*

$$E\{\bar{u}(\beta; RB)\} = E\{\hat{u}(\beta; RV)\},$$

where

$$E\{\hat{u}(\xi); RV\} = \int_{RV} \hat{u}(\xi) d\mu_H,$$

Ξ_m *is a coordinate variable such that* $\Xi_m(\xi_m) = \xi_m$, *RV is a set in* $\mathbf{R}^{\mathrm{M}}$, *and* μ_H *is a probability measure on RV.*

ii. *The distribution function H is absolutely continuous in ξ, and the sample space RV is convex.*

Proof. See Appendix A.9 □

Lemma 4.2 describes the structure of the measure μ_H constructed by projecting the original measure μ_G on $\mathbf{R}^{\mathrm{KM}}$ into the reduced space $\mathbf{R}^{\mathrm{M}}$ through the linear transformation $\xi = w - \hat{\varphi}\beta$. The lemma shows that there exists a uniquely defined measure μ_H that satisfies the equality such that $E\{\bar{u}(\beta)\} = E\{\hat{u}(\xi)\}$. It also shows that the distribution function H and its domain RV have mathematical properties identical to that of function G and its domain RB, as stipulated in Assumption 4.1.

Secondly, we construct the reduced form of the SBCP in a manner analogous to that by which the DBCP in (2.16) was converted into the reduced form in (2.28). To this end, we first set up the Lagrangian for a given value of $\hat{\pi}$, denoted by J_3, such that

$$J_3(y(\hat{\pi}(\xi,\cdot)), z(\hat{\pi}(\xi,\cdot)), \eta(\hat{\pi}(\xi,\cdot)); (\hat{\pi}(\xi,\cdot)) \equiv \max \{U(y(\hat{\pi}(\xi,\cdot)), z(\hat{\pi}(\xi,\cdot)))\}$$
$$+ \eta(\hat{\pi}(\xi,\cdot)) \left(\overline{M} - \hat{\pi}(\xi,\cdot) y(\hat{\pi}(\xi,\cdot)) - \sum_k \hat{\varphi}_k z_k(\hat{\pi}(\xi,\cdot))\right), \tag{4.12}$$

where $\hat{\pi}(\xi,\cdot) \equiv \hat{\pi}(\xi, p, t)$. We subsequently estimate the expected value of J_3 with respect to ξ:

$$E\{J_3\} \equiv \int_{RV} J_3(y(\hat{\pi}(\xi,\cdot)), z(\hat{\pi}(\xi,\cdot)), \eta(\hat{\pi}(\xi,\cdot)); (\hat{\pi}(\xi,\cdot)) d\mu_H. \tag{4.13}$$

This Lagrangian $E\{J_3\}$ has the solution as characterized below.

Lemma 4.3. *Necessary and sufficient conditions for the solution,* $(\hat{y}(\hat{\pi}(\xi,p,t)),$ $\hat{z}(\hat{\pi}(\xi,p,t)),$ *and* $\hat{\eta}(\hat{\pi}(\xi,p,t))),$ *to* $E\{J_3\}$ *are the point-wise Kuhn-Tucker conditions for* $E\{J_3\}$ *for all* ξ *values, such that the solution to* J_3 *for each* ξ *value satisfies the Kuhn-Tucker conditions of* J_3 *with the parameter vector of this* ξ *value.*

Proof. The reduced form J_3 for a given ξ value is the optimization problem satisfying the convexity condition, as in the case of the Lagrangian J_1. Hence, necessary and sufficient conditions for the Lagrangian $E\{J_3\}$ can be characterized by analogy to those conditions for the Lagrangian $E\{J_1\}$, as depicted in this lemma. □

Thirdly, we analyze the relationship between solutions to the SBCP and its reduced form. The SBCP gives solutions that are the functions of (β,p,t), whereas its reduced form yields solutions that are the functions of (ξ,p,t). The relationship between these two sets of solutions is prescribed in the two theorems presented below.

Theorem 4.3. *Under the condition that* $\xi = w - \hat{\varphi}\beta$, *the solution* $(\bar{y},\bar{z})$ *to the SBCP and the solution* $(\hat{y}(\hat{\pi}),\hat{z}(\hat{\pi}))$ *to its reduced form satisfy the following:*

$$\bar{y}\,(\beta,p,t) = \hat{y}\,(\hat{\pi}(\xi,p,t)), \quad \text{and} \quad \bar{z}_k\,(\beta,p,t) = \hat{z}_k\,(\hat{\pi}(\xi,p,t)), \text{ all } k, \tag{4.14}$$

and $\bar{y}$ *and* $\hat{y}(\hat{\pi})$ *are continuous in* (β,p,t) *and* (ξ,p,t), *respectively.*

Proof. First, the following three facts lead to the equality $\bar{y} = \hat{y}\,(\hat{\pi})$. (i) If $\xi = w - \hat{\varphi}\beta$, the solution of y to L_1 is equal to the solution of y to L_3, as shown in Theorem 2.4. (ii) By Lemma 4.1, the solution of y to L_1 for a certain β value is equal to the solution $\bar{y}$ to J_1 for that β value. (iii) By Lemma 4.3, the solution of y to L_3 for a certain ξ value is equal to the solution $\hat{y}$ to J_3 for that ξ value. Subsequently, the equality $\bar{z}_k = \hat{z}_k\,(\hat{\pi})$ can be proved in the same way by proving $\bar{y} = \hat{y}\,(\hat{\pi})$.

Second, the following three facts imply the continuity of $\hat{y}(\hat{\pi})$. (i) The solution of y to L_1 for a certain β value equals the solution $\bar{y}$ to J_1 for that β value, as indicated above. (ii) By Theorem 2.5, the solution of y to L_1 is continuous in $\hat{\pi}$. (iii) The function $\hat{\pi}(\xi,p,t)$, defined in (4.9), is continuous in ξ as well as (p,t); this can be proved in a manner analogous to that demonstrating the continuity of $\hat{\pi}$ in (p,t) in Appendix A.5. □

Theorem 4.4. *It follows from Theorem 4.3 that the solutions of* (y,z) *to the SBCP and its reduced form satisfy the following relationships:*

$$E\{\bar{y}\,(\beta,p,t)\} = E\{\hat{y}\,(\hat{\pi}(\xi,p,t))\}, \tag{4.15}$$

$$E\{\,U(\bar{y}\,(\beta,p,t),\bar{z}(\beta,p,t))\} = E\{\,U(\hat{y}\,(\hat{\pi}(\xi,p,t)),\hat{z}(\hat{\pi}(\xi,p,t)))\}. \tag{4.16}$$

Proof. First, under the condition $\bar{y} = \hat{y}\,(\hat{\pi})$ in Theorem 4.3, the equality that $E\{\bar{y}\} = E\{\hat{y}\,(\hat{\pi})\}$ can readily be proved using Lemma 4.2. That is, replacing $\bar{u}$ and $\hat{u}$ in Lemma 4.2 with $\bar{y}$ and $\hat{y}(\hat{\pi})$, respectively, leads to the equality.

Second, the proof of (4.16) is as follows. By Theorem 4.3, it holds that $U(\bar{y}, \bar{z}) = U(\hat{y}(\hat{\pi}), \hat{z}(\hat{\pi}))$ for every pair of (β, ξ). Hence, by Lemma 4.2, (4.16) follows. □

Theorems 4.3 and 4.4 depict that the SBCP and its reduced form have identical solutions for (y, z), in three different ways. Equation (4.14) shows that, for each pair (β, ξ) such that $\xi = w - \hat{\varphi}\beta$, the solution $(\bar{y}, \bar{z})$ to the SBCP is identical to the solution $(\hat{y}, \hat{z})$ to the reduced form. Equation (4.15) indicates that the expected value of $(\bar{y}, \bar{z})$ with respect to β is identical to the expected value of $(\hat{y}, \hat{z})$ with respect to ξ. Finally, (4.16) describes that the maximum expected utility for the SBCP $E\{U(\bar{y}, \bar{z})\}$ equals the maximum expected utility for its reduced form $E\{\, U(\hat{y}\,(\hat{\pi}), \hat{z}(\hat{\pi}))\}$.

4.3.3 Development of Expected Demand Functions

In the previous subsection, it was shown that the solution to the Lagrangian $E\{J_1\}$ for a certain random vector β equals the solution to the Lagrangian $E\{J_3\}$ for the random vector ξ. Using this relationship, in this subsection we estimate the expected demand function of an option with respect to random net-value-of-times ξ. Analyses for this expected demand function focus on developing its expression that will be utilized in subsequent analyses to deduce behavioral implications in the following subsection and mathematical properties such as continuity and sensitivity in the next chapter.

Firstly, we introduce an alternative expression of the integral domain for the expected demand function Q_{mn}, called *the catchment domain* of option mn, denoted by D_{mn}, such that

$$D_{mn}(p, t) = \{\, \xi \in RV |\ \hat{\pi}_{mn} \leq\ \hat{\pi}_{m'n'},\ \text{all } m'n' \neq mn \,\}. \tag{4.17}$$

This catchment domain D_{mn} estimates the range of β or $\xi(= w - \hat{\varphi}\beta)$, which satisfies the inequality such that $\hat{\pi}_{mn} \leq \hat{\pi}_{m'n'}$, for all $m'n' \neq mn$.

By Theorem 4.1, this inequality implies that the set D_{mn} is a subset of RV, in which $\bar{q}_{mn} \rangle\ 0$. Hence, it follows that

$$Q_{mn}(p, t) = \int_{RV} \bar{q}_{mn}(\beta, p, t) d\lambda_G = \int_{D_{mn}} \bar{q}_{mn}(\beta, p, t) d\lambda_G. \tag{4.18}$$

This equation implies that the integral domain of Q_{mn} can be replaced by D_{mn}. This catchment domain D_{mn} has the geometry explained below.

Lemma 4.4. *The catchment domain D_{mn} is a convex set in* $\mathbf{R}^{\mathrm{M}}$.

Proof. The set D_{mn} can alternatively be expressed as follows:

$$D_{mn}(p,t) = RV \bigcap \left(\bigcap_{m'n' \neq mn} HS_{m'n'}(p,t) \right),$$

where $HS_{m'n'}(p,t) \equiv \{\xi \in RV \,|a_m^{-1}(p_{mn} + \xi_m t_{mn}) \leq a_{m'}^{-1}(p_{m'n'} + \xi_{m'} t_{m'n'})\}$ is a half space in $\mathbf{R}^{\mathrm{M}}$. This equation implies that D_{mn} is an intersection of the convex set $RV$and the polyhedron formed by $M-1$ half spaces. Since the intersection of convex sets is also a convex set, the set D_{mn} is convex. Note that if the set RV is not convex, it is possible that some of D_{mn} are neither convex sets nor connected sets. □

Secondly, we introduce three cases of the relationship between D_{mn} and $D_{m'n'}$, for all $m'n' \neq mn$. The first case occurs when the two sets are spatially separated. In this case, it holds that $\mu_H(D_{mn} \cap D_{m'n'}) = 0$; that is, the probability of $\xi \in D_{mn} \cap D_{m'n'}$, expressed by $\mu_H(D_{mn} \cap D_{m'n'})$, is zero. The second case occurs when the two sets are tangent to each other, but do not overlap. This case also gives the result that $\mu_H(D_{mn} \cap D_{m'n'}) = 0$, since the set $D_{mn} \cap D_{m'n'}$ belongs to $\mathbf{R}^{\mathrm{M}-1}$. The third case occurs when the two sets completely overlap. This case gives the result that $\mu_H(D_{mn} \cap D_{m'n'}) \neq 0$. However, there does not exist a partially overlapped set $D_{m'n'}$ such that $\mu_H(D_{mn} \cap D_{m'n'}) \neq 0$, as proved next.

Lemma 4.5. *The interior of D_{mn} is either completely disjoint or completely overlaps with the interior of $D_{m'n'}$, for all $m'n' \neq mn$; that is, it holds that*

$$\mu_H(D_{mn}(p,t) \cap D_{m'n'}(p,t)) \begin{cases} > 0, & \textit{if } D_{mn}(p,t) = D_{m'n'}(p,t)\,,\ \textit{some } m'n' \neq mn \\ = 0, & \textit{otherwise}. \end{cases}$$

Proof. The proof is worked out by showing that, unless the sets D_{mn} and $D_{m'n'}$ completely overlap each other, it holds that $\mu_H(D_{mn} \cap D_{m'n'}) \neq 0$; that is, $\mu_H(D_{mn} \cap D_{m'n'}) \neq 0$, unless $(p_{mn}, t_{mn}) = (p_{m'n'}, t_{m'n'})$ and $\Xi_m = \Xi_{m'}$. Suppose, first, that $(p_{mn}, t_{mn}) \neq (p_{m'n'}, t_{m'n'})$ and $\Xi_m = \Xi_{m'}$. Then, all the points satisfying the equality $\hat{\pi}_{mn} = \hat{\pi}_{m'n'}$ are located only on the tangent plane $D_{mn} \cap D_{m'n'}$ belonging to $\mathbf{R}^{\mathrm{M}-1}$. Hence, $\mu_H(D_{mn} \cap D_{m'n'}) = 0$. Suppose, second, that $(p_{mn}, t_{mn}) = (p_{m'n'}, t_{m'n'})$ and $\Xi_m \neq \Xi_{m'}$. These two conditions also lead to the outcome that the equality $\hat{\pi}_{mn} = \hat{\pi}_{m'n'}$ holds only on the tangent plane $D_{mn} \cap D_{m'n'}$; that is, $\mu_H(D_{mn} \cap D_{m'n'}) = 0$.[2] □

---

[2] The first and the second cases correspond to the cases of quantitative and qualitative competition that will be thoroughly examined in Sects. 5.2 and 5.3, respectively. Further, the precise meanings of the proofs presented here will pictorially be illustrated in those sections.

Thirdly, we clarify the relationship between the two functions $\bar{q}_{mn}$ and $\bar{y}$ in Theorem 4.1, in connection with the two cases identified in Lemma 4.5. In the case of $\mu_H(D_{mn} \cap D_{m'n'}) = 0$ for all $m'n' \neq mn$, the relationship of Theorem 4.1 implies that

$$a_m\, \bar{q}_{mn}(\beta, p, t) = \begin{cases} \bar{y}(\beta, p, t), & \text{if} \quad \xi \in D_{mn}(p, t) \\ 0, & \text{otherwise.} \end{cases} \tag{4.19}$$

On the other hand, in the case of $\mu_H(D_{mn} \cap D_{m'n'}) \neq 0$ for some $m'n' \neq mn$, the relationship indicates that

$$\sum_{m'n' \in I_{mn}} a_m\, \bar{q}_{m'n'}(\beta, p, t) = \begin{cases} \bar{y}(\beta, p, t), & \text{if} \quad \xi \in D_{mn}(p, t) \\ 0, & \text{otherwise,} \end{cases} \tag{4.20}$$

where $I_{mn} = \{m'n' \mid \hat{\pi}_{mn} = \hat{\pi}_{mn'}, \text{ all } m'n' \neq mn\}$.

Fourthly, we consider the problem of searching for an appropriate surrogate to the integrand $\bar{q}_{mn}(\beta, p, t)$ in the second and third terms of (4.18). One possible candidate is the function $\hat{y}\,(\hat{\pi}(\xi, p, t))$, which has the same value as the function $\bar{y}(\beta, p, t)$ under the condition $\xi = w - \hat{\varphi}\beta$. However, this candidate function has an expression too complex to use frequently throughout this study. We therefore introduce an abbreviated expression of the function $\hat{y}\,(\hat{\pi}(\xi, p, t))$, and also analyze the mathematical properties of the function.

Lemma 4.6. *Let function f_m be defined by*

$$f_m(p_{mn} + \xi_m\, t_{mn}) = \frac{1}{a_m}\hat{y}\left(\frac{1}{a_m}(p_{mn} + \xi_m\, t_{mn})\right). \tag{4.21}$$

Under the condition $\xi = w - \hat{\varphi}\beta$, it holds that

$$\sum_{m'n' \in I_{mn}} \bar{q}_{m'n'}(\beta, p, t) = f_m(p_{mn} + \xi_m\, t_{mn}), \text{ all } m. \tag{4.22}$$

Also, the function f_m is continuous in (ξ_m, p_{mn}, t_{mn}) within D_{mn}.

Proof. The equality between $\bar{q}_{mn}$ (or $\sum_{m'n'} \bar{q}_{m'n'}$) and f_m follows from (4.14) and (4.19). On the other hand, the continuity of f_m is none other than the continuity of $\hat{y}$, which was proved in Theorem 4.3. □

We are now ready to formulate an alternative expression of Q_{mn} in which the integral domain is D_{mn} instead of RV, and the integrand is f_m instead of $\bar{q}_{mn}$. This alternative expression, called *the expected demand function for random net-value-of-times*, is developed by taking the expected values of both sides of (4.19) or (4.20), as presented below.

Theorem 4.5. *The expected demand function Q_{mn} in (4.5) can be expressed as follows.*

i. *Suppose that $\mu_H(D_{mn} \cap D_{m'n'}) = 0$, for all $m'n' \neq mn$. Then, the expected demand function for random net-value-of-times is expressed as a Riemann integral such that*

$$Q_{mn}(p,t) = \int_{D_{mn}} f_m\,(p_{mn} + \xi_m\, t_{mn}) h\,(\xi)\, d\mu, \tag{4.23}$$

where h is the probability density function of ξ, and μ is the ordinary product measure on the sample space RV.

ii. *Suppose that $\mu_H(D_{mn} \cap D_{mn'}) \rangle\, 0$ for some $m'n' \neq mn$. Then, the demand function for random net-value-of-times becomes*

$$\sum_{m'n' \in I_{mn}} Q_{m'n'}(p,t) = \int_{D_{mn}} f_m(p_{mn} + \xi_m\, t_{mn})\, h\,(\xi)\, d\mu. \tag{4.24}$$

Proof. The following three facts lead to the equality of Theorem 4.5.i. (i) Equation (4.19) implies that $E\{\, a_m \bar{q}_{mn}|\, w - \hat{\varphi}\beta \in D_{mn}\} = E\{\,\bar{y}|\, w-\ \hat{\varphi}\beta \in D_{mn}\}$. (ii) By Lemma 4.2, it follows that $E\{\,\bar{y}\,|\, w - \hat{\varphi}\beta \in D_{mn}\} = E\{\,\hat{y}\,(\hat{\pi})|\ \xi \in D_{mn}\}$. (iii) By the definition of f_m in Lemma 4.6, it holds that $E\{\hat{y}(\hat{\pi})|\xi \in D_{mn}\} = E\{a_m f_m|\xi \in D_{mn}\}$. Subsequently, Theorem 4.5.ii can be proved in a manner identical to that which led to Theorem 4.5.i. □

4.3.4 Economic Implications of Expected Demand Functions

The expected service demand function for random net-value-of-times has a formulation from which one can readily deduce its precise economic implications. This aspect is demonstrated below, focusing on interpreting the relationship between deterministic and expected demand functions for net-value-of-times

First, the catchment domain D_{mn} for a consumer corresponds to the revealed preference condition for the SBCP; that is, the set D_{mn} estimates the range of random vectors ξ, within which option mn is chosen by the consumer, as explained below. The integral domain D_{mn} is the range of ξ, within which option mn gives the lowest implicit price of a prime commodity, as depicted in (4.17). On this range D_{mn}, the demand for option mn can be positive, whereas the demand for other options for all $m'n' \neq mn$ is zero, as shown in (4.19) and (4.20).

Second, the catchment domain D_{mn} estimates the range of random vectors ξ, within which option mn satisfies the condition such that

$$D_{mn}(p,t) = \{\ \xi \in RV \mid U(\bar{y}_{mn}, \bar{z}_{mn}) \geq U(\bar{y}_{m'n'}, \bar{z}_{m'n'}),\ \text{all } m'n' \neq mn\}. \qquad (4.25)$$

That is, the set D_{mn} depicts the range of ξ, within which the choice of option mn attains a higher utility than can be achieved by the choice of other options, as shown in Theorem 4.2.

Third, the value of the integrand f_m for a certain value of $\xi \in D_{mn}$ estimates the solution $\bar{q}_{mn}$ to the DBCP for the parameter vector β such that it satisfies the linear relationship $\xi = w - \hat{\varphi}\beta$, as depicted in (4.22). To be specific, if $\xi \in D_{mn}(p,t)$ and $\xi = w - \hat{\varphi}\beta$, the value of $\bar{q}_{mn}(\beta, p, t)$ is positive and equals the value of $f_m(p_{mn} + \xi_m t_{mn})$. In contrast, if $\xi \notin D_{mn}$, the value of $\bar{q}_{mn}$ equals zero, but the value of $f_m(p_{mn} + \xi_m t_{mn})$ is positive.

Fourth, the fact that the function Q_{mn} estimates the expected value of demand for option mn can be more clearly explained using the following alternative expression of the integral in Theorem 4.5:

$$Q_{mn}(p,t) = \inf_{PD_l} \sum_l v_l \mu_H(PD_l),\ \text{all } mn, \qquad (4.26)$$

where $v_l = \sup\{f_m \mid \xi \in PD_l\}$, and $\mu_H(PD_l)$ is the probability of $\xi \in PD_l$. Here, the set PD_l for all $l \in \mathbf{N}$ is a partition of D_{mn}, where $\mathbf{N}$ is the index set of countably many positive integers.[3]

Equation (4.26) can be explained as follows. The term $\mu_H(PD_l)$ is the probability that a certain realization of net-value-of-time vector, denoted by ξ, belongs to a set PD_l, subset of RV. The term v_l is the supremum of f_m on PD_l. Under the condition that the volume of PD_l is very small, the value of Q_{mn} equals the sum of $f_m \times \mu_H(PD_l)$ for all l.

Finally, Theorem 4.5 introduces two different formulas that estimate demands for two different groups of options, respectively. The first group consists of all options mn that satisfy the condition $D_{mn}(p,t) \neq D_{m'n'}(p,t)$, for all $m'n' \neq mn$. By Lemma 4.5, this condition implies that $(p_{mn}, t_{mn}) \neq (p_{m'n'}, t_{m'n'})$ and/or $\Xi_m \neq \Xi_{m'}$. The second group refers to all options mn that fulfill the condition $D_{mn}(p,t) = D_{m'n'}(p,t)$, for some $m'n' \neq mn$. Lemma 4.5 shows that this condition holds when $(p_{mn}, t_{mn}) = (p_{m'n'}, t_{m'n'})$ and $\Xi_m = \Xi_{m'}$.

Every option belonging to the first group can be distinguished from the others by one or more than one element of quantitative and qualitative attributes. The expected demand for this group of options has a definite value estimated by the integral in (4.23). In contrast, an option in the second group has one or more than one competing option having identical qualitative and quantitative attributes. The only available information about demand for this group is the sum of demands for all the options in the group, as depicted in (4.24).

[3] A partition of a nonempty set D_{mn} is a family of nonempty subsets of D_{mn} that are pair-wise disjoint with one another and whose union is D_{mn}, as introduced in many books for real analysis, such as Kolmogorov and Fomin (1970).

4.4 Extensions and Applications of the Stochastic Basic Choice Problem

4.4.1 Extension to Choices for Durable Services

In this chapter, we have developed the expected demand function of a non-durable service option for the reduced form of the SBCP in Theorem 4.5. Importantly, other SQCPs take the expected demand function that has a functional form similar to that of the demand function for the reduced form of the SBCP. This property of SQCPs is illustrated with an example of the SQCP for durable services (or goods), a stochastic counterpart of the DQCP analyzed in Subsect. 3.2.2.

To begin, we develop the consumer production function for hedonic commodities packed in durable service under uncertainly for the magnitude of these commodities. This consumer production function under uncertainty can readily be formulated by amending the deterministic production function for the DQCP in (3.5):

$$\begin{aligned} Z_k'(q, x_k, t_k; z_k) &= z_k - \sum_{mn} \left(\beta_{km}^d + \sum\nolimits_{mn} \beta_{km} t_{mn}\right) q_{mn} - Z_k(x_k, t_k) \\ &= 0, \text{ all } k, \end{aligned} \tag{4.27}$$

where β_{km}^d is the random production coefficient of option mn for commodity k per unit of durable service, and β_{km} is the random production coefficient of mn for k per in-site service time.

Equation (4.27) indicates that the SQCP for durable services can be formulated as a stochastic optimization problem for two random variables. These two random variables, denote by $\mathrm{B}^d \equiv (\mathrm{B}_{11}^d, \cdots, \mathrm{B}_{KM}^d)$ and $\mathrm{B} \equiv (\mathrm{B}_{11}, \cdots, \mathrm{B}_{KM})$, have the following properties: first, the terms β_{km}^d and β_{km} are the realizations of B^d and B, respectively; second, B^d and B are independent of each other. The solution to the SQCP for these two random variables can be characterized by the point-wise Kuhn-Tucker conditions in a manner identical to that used to describe the solution for the SBCP with one random variable in Lemma 4.1.

Through analyses of the point-wise Kuhn-Tucker conditions for the SQCP, we can readily develop the revealed preference condition similar to that of Theorem 4.2 for the SBCP. The developed revealed preference condition for the choice of option mn, which is a stochastic version of (3.6), is

$$\begin{aligned} \hat{\pi}_{mn} &= \frac{1}{a_m}\left(p_{mn} - \xi_m^d + \xi_m t_{mn}\right) \\ \langle\, \hat{\pi}_{m'n'} &= \frac{1}{a_{m'}}(p_{m'n'} - \xi_{m'}^d + \xi_{m'} t_{m'n'}), \text{ all } m'n' \neq mn, \end{aligned} \tag{4.28}$$

where

$$\xi_m^d = \sum_k \hat{\varphi}_k \beta_{km}^d, \quad \text{and} \quad \xi_m = w - \sum_k \hat{\varphi}_k \beta_{km}. \tag{4.29}$$

Here, one random term ξ_m^d is the sum of the monetary values of hedonic commodities packed in the durable portion of service for service group m, and the other random term ξ_m is the net-value-of-time for the non-durable portion.

The two random terms ξ_m^d and ξ_m satisfy the consistency requirement with respect to (p,t), as shown with the DQCP for durable service. Hence, it is feasible to construct two independent linear transformations that convert the random vectors β^d and β into other random vectors ξ^d and ξ, respectively, using linear equation systems similar to that of (4.11). These two linear transformations yield random variables Ξ^d and Ξ with absolutely continuous distribution functions H^d and H, respectively, as can be shown by applying Lemma 4.2.

Subsequently, we analyze the relationship between the solution of $\bar{q}_{mn}$ for the SQCP and that of $\hat{y}(\pi_m)$ for the reduced form. By the revealed preference condition (4.28), the solutions $\bar{q}_{mn}$ and $\hat{y}(\pi_m)$ satisfy the condition, equivalent to that of Theorem 4.4, such that

$$a_m\bar{q}_{mn}(\beta,p,t) = \begin{cases} \hat{y}(\hat{\pi}_m(p,t)), & \text{if } \hat{\pi}_{mn} \le \hat{\pi}_{m'n'}, \text{ all } m'n' \ne mn \\ 0, & \text{otherwise.} \end{cases} \tag{4.30}$$

This equation implies that the catchment domain of option mn, D_{mn}, within which that option has a positive demand, can be expressed as follows:

$$D_{mn}(p,t) = \left\{\xi^d \in RV^d,\ \xi \in RV \middle|\ \hat{\pi}_{mn} \le \hat{\pi}_{m'n'}, \text{ all } m'n' \ne mn\right\}, \tag{4.31}$$

where RV^d and RV are the sample spaces of β^d and β, respectively.

Combining (4.30) and (4.31) gives the expected demand function of durable service option mn, denoted by Q_{mn}, which is similar to the expected demand function estimated in Theorem 4.5:

$$Q_{mn}(p,t) = \int_{D_{mn}} f_m\,(p_{mn} + \xi_m^d + \xi_m\, t_{mn})d\mu_{H^d} \otimes \mu_H, \tag{4.32}$$

where $f_m = (1/a_m)\hat{y}$, and $\mu_{H^d} \otimes \mu_H$ is the product measure of μ_{H^d} and μ_H. The functional form of Q_{mn} on the right side of (4.32) is almost identical to that of the QBCP except for one major difference of using the product measure $\mu_{H^d} \otimes \mu_H$.

Finally, note that the demand function for the other DQCPs introduced in Sect. 3.2 can be readily developed by applying the previous demand analyses for the SBCP and SQCP in this chapter. It was shown in Sect. 3.2 that all DQCPs satisfy the two different kinds of consistency condition. Hence, it is possible to construct the SQCP that takes a reduced form for random variables developed through a linear transformation similar to the one in (4.11). Moreover, the solutions for the SQCP and its reduced form satisfy the equality similar to one in Theorem 4.4 or (4.30). Therefore, we can have the expected demand function that has a functional form similar to the one in Theorem 4.5 or (4.32).

4.4.2 Extension to Choices for Multiple Kinds of Services

Here, we extend the demand analysis of the SBCP for a special case when only one kind of service is available to the case of multiple kinds are available, considered in Sect. 3.3.1. This SQCP differs from the SBCP in that the structure of the random variable for net-value-of-times is more complex, since the choice set of consumers is composed of multiple types of services. Nonetheless, the demand function of an option has a functional form identical to that of Theorem 4.5 with the exception that the structure of the random variable for net-value-of-times slightly differs, as shown below.

For this case, the deterministic production function for hedonic commodities in the choice problem (3.21) can be converted into the following stochastic form:

$$z_k(\beta, p, t) = \sum_{mnl} \beta_{klm} t_{lmn} q_{lmn} + Z_k(x_k, t_k), \text{ all } k, \tag{4.33}$$

where β_{klm} is the random production coefficient of option lmn for commodity k.

It is assumed that the production coefficient β_{klm} is the outcome of a random variable specified in a manner similar to the random variable of Assumption 4.1; specifically, the random vector $\beta \equiv (\beta_{111}, \cdots, \beta_{KLM})$ is the outcome of a continuous random variable $\mathrm{B} \equiv (\mathrm{B}_{111}, \cdots, \mathrm{B}_{KLM})$ with joint distribution $G(\beta)$ that is absolutely continuous in β on a convex sample space RB. It is also postulated that the SQCP for random vector B is identical to the SBCP of Assumption 4.2, except that the extended choice variables $q \equiv (q_{111}, \cdots, q_{LMN})$ and $y \equiv (y_1, \cdots, y_L)$ are incorporated.

Then, we can construct the Lagrangian of the SQCP for multiple kinds of non-durable service, in a manner analogous to that leading to the Lagrangian $E\{J_1\}$ in (4.4). This SQCP gives the expected demand function of an option, which has a functional form identical to that of the demand function in Theorem 4.5. The development of this expected demand function is described below.

Firstly, the point-wise Kuhn-Tucker conditions for the SQCP give the revealed preference condition for the choice of option lmn, such that

$$\hat{\pi}_{lmn}(\xi_{lm}, p_{lmn}, t_{lmn}) \langle \hat{\pi}_{lm'n'}(\xi_{lm'}, p_{lm'n'}, t_{lm'n'}), \text{ all } mn \neq m'n', \tag{4.34}$$

where

$$\hat{\pi}_{lmn}(\xi_{lm}, p_{lmn}, t_{lmn}) = \frac{1}{a_{lm}}(p_{lmn} + \xi_{lm} t_{lmn}) \tag{4.35}$$

$$\xi_{lm} = w - \sum_k \hat{\varphi}_k \beta_{klm}. \tag{4.36}$$

This revealed preference condition for an arbitrary service group l holds, irrespective of the choice for other service groups, for all $l' \neq l$.

Subsequently, we develop the random variable for realization $\xi \equiv (\xi_{11}, \cdots, \xi_{LM})$ in (4.36). All the elements of ξ satisfy the consistency condition such that they are independent of (p, t). Hence, it is feasible to construct the random variable $\Xi \equiv (\Xi_{11}, \cdots, \Xi_{LM})$ through the linear transformation of $\mathrm{B} \equiv (\mathrm{B}_{111}, \cdots, \mathrm{B}_{KLM})$ such that

$$\xi = w - \hat{\varphi}\beta, \text{ or} \tag{4.37}$$

$$\begin{pmatrix} \xi_{11} \\ \vdots \\ \xi_{LM} \end{pmatrix} = \begin{pmatrix} w \\ \vdots \\ w \end{pmatrix} - \begin{pmatrix} \beta_{111} & \cdots & \beta_{K11} \\ \vdots & \ddots & \vdots \\ \beta_{1LM} & \cdots & \beta_{KLM} \end{pmatrix} \begin{pmatrix} \hat{\varphi}_1 \\ \vdots \\ \hat{\varphi}_K \end{pmatrix}. \tag{4.38}$$

This linear transformation also converts the distribution function G for β into the distribution function H for ξ.

Using the random variable Ξ, we next construct the Lagrangian for the reduced form of the SQCP in a formulation similar to that of the SBCP in (4.13). By the revealed preference condition (4.34), the solution of $q_{lmn}(\beta, p, t)$ to the SQCP and the solution of $y_l(\beta, p, t)$ to the reduced form fulfill the equality, equivalent to that of Theorem 4.4, such that

$$a_{lm}\bar{q}_{lmn}(\beta, p, t) = \begin{cases} \bar{y}_l(\hat{\pi}(p, t)), & \text{if } \hat{\pi}_{lmn} \leq \hat{\pi}_{lm'n'}, \text{ all } m'n' \neq mn \\ 0, & \text{otherwise,} \end{cases} \tag{4.39}$$

where $p \equiv (p_{111}, \cdots, p_{LMN})$, $t \equiv (t_{111}, \cdots, t_{LMN})$, and $\hat{\pi} \equiv (\hat{\pi}_1, \cdots, \hat{\pi}_L)$. This implies that the catchment domain of option mn, D_{mn}, within which that option has a positive demand, can be expressed as follows:

$$D_{lmn}(p, t) = \{\xi \in RV \mid \hat{\pi}_{lmn} \leq \hat{\pi}_{lm'n'}, \text{ all } m'n' \neq mn\}. \tag{4.40}$$

Here, the range of D_{mn} includes all the values of $\xi_{m'}$ for all $m' \neq m$, since it is independent of the $\hat{\pi}_{l'}$ value, for all $l' \neq l$.

Finally, taking the expectation of both sides of (4.39) gives the expected demand function of option lmn, Q_{lmn}, equivalent to the demand function of Theorem 4.5:

$$Q_{lmn}(p, t) = \int_{D_{lmn}} f_{lm}\left(p_{lmn} + \xi_{lm}t_{lmn}\right) h\left(\xi\right) d\mu, \tag{4.41}$$

where $f_{lm} = (1/a_{lm})\hat{y}_l$, and h is the density function of ξ. This equation confirms that the functional form of Q_{lmn} is actually identical to that of the demand function for the SBCP, except for one difference: ξ and μ belong to $\mathbf{R}^{\mathrm{LM}}$.

4.4.3 Comparison with Random Utility Theory

Qualitative choice models such as logit and probit models have proven quite effective econometric tools, honed to statistically estimate the choice behavior of consumers for qualitative choice services using disaggregated data. The microeconomic foundation of these qualitative choice models has mainly relied on random utility theory. Another plausible microeconomic rationale is the random perception approach introduced in this chapter. Given this potential, similarities and dissimilarities between the two approaches are articulated below.[4]

First, the target of demand analyses differs between the two approaches in one fundamental way. Random utility theory is concerned only with choice probability for a particular option, neglecting total demand for the option. In contrast, the random perception approach estimates total expected demand for a particular option. In spite of such a difference, the two approaches yield similar expressions to estimate the choice probability of an option.

Specifically, under random utility theory, a qualitative choice model postulates that the probability function for the choice of option mn, denoted by P_{mn}, is expressed as follows:

$$P_{mn}(p,t) = \Pr\left\{U_{mn}(p,t) + \varepsilon_{mn} \geq U_{m'n'}(p,t) + \varepsilon_{m'n'},\ \text{all } m'n' \neq mn\right\}, \quad (4.42)$$

where U_{mn} is the systematic portion of the indirect utility achievable by choosing option mn, and ε_{mn} is the random portion of the indirect utility.

On the other hand, the demand function of option mn under the random perception approach estimates the expected demand. This demand function can be converted to a choice probability function similar to that of (4.42) if total demand, the sum of demands for all options, is insensitive with respect to changes in their prices and service times. Under this restrictive condition, the integrand of the expected demand function in Theorem 4.5 becomes a constant. Therefore, the probability of choosing option mn can be expressed as follows:

$$P_{mn}(p,t) = \frac{\mu_H(D_{mn})}{\sum_{m'n'} \mu_H(D_{m'n'})} = \mu_H(D_{mn}), \quad (4.43)$$

where μ_H is the probability measure of random vector ξ with the distribution function H. Note that $\sum_{m'n'} \mu_H(D_{m'n'}) = \mu_H(RV) = 1.0$.

[4] The argument for random utility theory in this section is largely based on the discussion in McFadden (1973) and (1998), Domencich and McFadden (1975), and Kockelman (2001). Other important references that share the same vein with these articles are Ben Akiva (1974), Manski (1977), and De Palma et al. (1994).

The above probability function can alternatively be expressed as follows:

$$P_{mn}(p,t) = \Pr\{\ \xi \in D_{mn}(p.t)\ \} \tag{4.44}$$

$$= \Pr\{\ \hat{\pi}_{mn}(\xi,p,t) \leqslant \hat{\pi}_{m'n'}(\xi,p,t),\ \text{all}\ m'n' \neq mn\ \} \tag{4.45}$$

$$= \Pr\{\ U(\bar{y}_{mn},\bar{z}_{mn}) \geqslant U(\bar{y}_{m'n'},\bar{z}_{m'n'}),\ \text{all}\ m'n' \neq mn\ \}. \tag{4.46}$$

Here, (4.44) is an alternative expression of (4.43). Subsequently, (4.45) and (4.46) come from (4.17) and (4.25), respectively. Additionally, (4.46) has an expression very similar to (4.42), as claimed above.

Second, the two approaches have different specifications for the revealed preference condition targeted by statistical estimations. The revealed preference condition for random utility theory postulates that the option chosen by a consumer attains the largest indirect utility, as depicted in (4.42). Such a random utility theory has a critical shortcoming in that it is unable to provide any hint about the appropriate functional form of indirect utilities. On the other hand, the same condition for the random perception approach characterizes the chosen option by employing two different criteria that are nonetheless equivalent to each other: one criterion for indirect utility in (4.46), and the other one for the implicit price of prime commodities in (4.45). Moreover, the choice criterion in (4.45) has advantages explained next.

The use of the implicit price of a prime commodity for statistical estimations of choice behaviors has a number of advantages, as demonstrated in Chaps. 2 and 3. First, the implicit price can be directly estimated from a deterministic cost minimization problem for consumers. Such a minimization problem requires relatively less complex analyses than is required by a UMP for this minimization problem. Second, the production function incorporated in the cost minimization problem can be formulated in such a manner that it can reasonably approximate decision-making environments specific to an analyzed choice problem. In addition, it is easy to judge whether the production function yields the implicit price such that it is amenable to statistical estimations, as discussed fully in Subsect. 2.4.2.

Third, the two approaches differently define randomness in the modeling of statistical choice problems. Randomness under random utility theory refers to the irregularity of choice behaviors among consumers under certainty, which stems from their heterogeneous preferences for service quality. In contrast, the randomness under the random perception approach is caused by uncertainty, which affects consumer preference at a certain place and time and is itself directly linked to their choice behaviors.

Under random utility theory, the random term ε_{mn} in the indirect utility of (4.42) represents the discrepancy between the indirect utility of a representative consumer and the indirect utilities of the consumers sampled. The indirect utility of a representative consumer, called the systematic portion, is the target of statistical estimations, whereas the indirect utility of each consumer, which is the sum of systematic portion and random term, represents the deterministic outcome of the decision under certainty. Hence, statistical estimations involve calibrating the parameters of the indirect utility function of representative consumers.

In contrast, under the random perception approach, the random net-value-of-time ξ_m in the implicit price of (4.45) is not a deterministic term, but rather the outcome of a random process uncontrollable by consumers. Furthermore, this random term is assumed to have a distribution given exogenously. Such a distribution of random net-value-of-times is the key factor that determines the choice probability of an option. It is therefore conceived that the statistical test of choice behavior should focus on estimating the distribution of the random term. However, this estimation issue requires an analysis that fundamentally differs from that described in this study.

Chapter 5
Comparative Statics and Elasticity of Expected Demand Functions

5.1 Introduction

In Chap. 4, we have developed the expected demand function (the demand function, for short) of an option for a number of SQCPs under the random perception approach. This individual demand function for SQCPs estimates the expected value of the demand for a particular option with respect to the vector of independent variables composed of the prices and service times of all options in a market. The individual demand function is expressed as a Riemann multiple integral with respect to the random net-value-of-times of all heterogeneous service groups. For this individual demand function, the market demand function of an option can be developed by simply adding the integrands of multiple integrals for all consumers.

This chapter analyzes the sensitivity of market demand functions for the SBCP, one example of SQCPs, with respect to its independent variables (here, the price and service times of all options in competition). This analysis, which can be extended to the case of the demand function for other SQCPs without any fundamental modification, covers two different but interrelated topics. These two topics and the approaches used for their analysis are presented below.

One main topic involves estimating the comparative statics of the market demand function of an option with respect to independent variables. The input of this analysis is the expected demand function, usually expressed as a multiple integral. However, the demand function in the functional form of a multiple integral cannot be used to estimate its comparative statics. For this reason, as the first step of the analysis, we convert the multiple integral into an iterated indefinite integral. Subsequently, we estimate the partial derivative of the iterated indefinite integral with respect to its independent variables.

In this analysis, the generalized expression of an expected demand function in a multiple integral requires a series of lengthy and complex computations. In particular, the conversion of the multiple integral into an iterated indefinite integral calls for a quite complex calculation to formulate the integral domain, called the

D.J. Moon, *Congestion-Prone Services Under Quality Competition*,
Advances in Spatial Science, DOI 10.1007/978-3-642-20189-9_5,

catchment domain. Further, the outcome of sensitivity analyses is very lengthy and complex, and thus its economic implications are difficult to deduce.

For this reason, we begin with analyses for two special cases where the catchment domain of the demand function for an option has a simple geometry that can be easily formulated. The first case is *quantitative (or horizontal) competition*. The services of all options in this competition are homogeneous from the standpoint of qualitative attributes, and are thereby differentiated only by quantitative attributes: prices and service times. The second case is *qualitative (or vertical) competition*. The services of all options in this competition have different qualitative attributes such as safety and comfort. Analyses for these two special cases are extended to a generalized case of *mixed competition* that refers to a mixed form of qualitative and quantitative competition.

Another topic involves identifying a full set of necessary conditions for an option to have *perfectly elastic demand*; this refers to demand with either very large but bounded or infinitely large elasticity. The elasticity of expected demand for an option under competition usually has an approximately inverse relationship to the thickness of a catchment domain for that option. To be specific, an option that facilitates perfectly elastic demand must have either a thin catchment domain or a catchment domain overlapping those of other options. Additionally, the option holding a thin catchment domain has substitutes that offer the same kind of service at close implicit prices; whereas the option having an overlapping catchment domain has perfect substitutes that provide services at the same implicit price.

For this reason, the analysis that identifies the necessary conditions for an option to have perfectly elastic demands should consider the circumstance under which its catchment domain is thin. This analysis needs to separately assess two different kinds competition: quantitative and qualitative competition. In the case of quantitative competition, the implicit service prices perceived by consumers are distributed along a line that represents random net-value-of-times common to all options. For this reason, it is relatively simple to estimate the thickness of catchment domains and to identify the necessary conditions for thin catchment domains. In the case of qualitative competition the implicit prices are distributed in space $\mathbf{R}^{M}$, where M is the number of heterogeneous services. Therefore, it is not straightforward to calculate thickness. Moreover, it is infeasible to define necessary conditions for thin catchment domains without introducing an additional condition.

This additional necessary condition for an option in qualitative competition to have perfectly elastic demand is called the *identical ordering condition*. Roughly speaking, the identical ordering condition implies that all consumers rank heterogeneous services in the same order of preference under the assumption that their prices are free. For example, this condition implies that all consumers prefer a first class ticket for air services rather than a business or economy class ticket, when they ignore ticket price.

We proceed with the sensitivity analysis of demand functions according to the following sequence: the cases of quantitative competition, qualitative competition, qualitative competition under the identical ordering condition, and finally mixed competition. For each case, we first estimate the comparative statics of the demand function of an option with respect to the price and service times for all options. Subsequently, we identify the necessary conditions for an option to have perfectly elastic demands with respect to price. Finally, the last section on mixed competition summarizes all the important finding of this chapter, which will be inputs for subsequent analyses in this chapter.

5.2 Quantitative Competition

5.2.1 Conversion into Indefinite Integrals

Here we convert the demand function into an indefinite integral for the case of quantitative competition specified as follows. First, there are N options, all of which offer the same service in terms of qualitative attributes. Second, each option for all $n \in \langle 1, N \rangle$ charges price p_n and service time t_n, one or both of which can be equal to the price or service time, respectively, of other options for some $k \neq n$. Third, all options have the identical yield of a prime commodity per service; that is, $a = 1$.

To begin, we develop the formula that estimates the implicit price of an option in quantitative competition. All options in quantitative competition have a common random net-value-of-time ξ, estimated by $\xi = w - \sum_k \hat{\varphi}_k \beta_k$. By the assumption that $a = 1$, option n has the implicit price of the prime commodity, $\hat{\pi}_n$, estimated by

$$\hat{\pi}_n(\xi, p_n, t_n) = p_n + \xi t_n, \quad \text{all } n, \tag{5.1}$$

as shown in (4.6). On the other hand, the implicit price of the prime commodity, denoted by $\hat{\pi}$, equals the implicit price of the option chosen by consumers, estimated by $\min_n\{\hat{\pi}_n(p_n, t_n)\}$, as shown in (4.9).

We next estimate the catchment domain of option n, denoted by D_n. Substituting the implicit price in (5.1) to the catchment domain in (4.17) gives a specific expression of D_n, such that

$$D_n(p, t) = \{\xi \in RV \mid p_n + \xi t_n \leq p_k + \xi t_k, \text{ all } k \neq n\}, \tag{5.2}$$

where $p \equiv (p_1, \cdots, p_N)$, $t \equiv (t_1, \cdots, t_N)$, and RV is the domain of ξ. By Lemma 4.4, the set D_n is convex in ξ; it is a closed interval in $\mathbf{R}$, denoted by $[l_n, u_n]$.

Lemma 5.1. *The catchment domain D_n has the following properties.*

i. *Suppose that all the options satisfy the strong trade-off condition such that*

$$p_1 \langle \cdots \langle p_N \quad \text{and} \quad t_1 \rangle \cdots \rangle t_N.$$

Then, it follows that $\mu(D_n(p,t)) = [\, l_n(p,t), u_n(p,t)\,] \neq 0$*, for all n, where*

$$l_n(p,t) = \frac{p_n - p_{n-1}}{t_{n-1} - t_n} \quad \textit{and} \quad u_n(p,t) = \frac{p_{n+1} - p_n}{t_n - t_{n+1}}.$$

ii. *Suppose next that option n fulfills the weak trade-off condition with other options, for some* $k \neq n$*, e.g.,* $n+1$*, such that*

$$p_1 \rangle \cdots \langle p_n = p_{n+1} \langle \cdots \langle p_N \quad \textit{but} \quad t_1 \rangle \cdots \rangle t_n = t_{n+1} \rangle \cdots \rangle t_N.$$

Then it follows that $\mu(D_n(p,t)) = \mu(D_{n+1}(p,t)) \neq 0$.

iii. *Suppose finally that option n does not fulfill the trade-off condition; that is,*

$$p_n \geq p_k \quad \textit{and} \quad t_n \rangle t_k, \quad \textit{some } k \neq n.$$

Then, it follows that $\mu(D_n(p,t)) = 0$.

Proof. Firstly, we estimate the range of D_n in Lemma 5.1.i. The lower boundary l_n is the intersection point of $p_{n-1} + \xi t_{n-1}$ and $p_n + \xi t_n$, which can be estimated through simple calculations. Also, the upper boundary u_n can be computed in an identical manner (refer to $n = 1, 2, 3$ of Fig. 5.1).

Subsequently, we prove Lemma 5.1.ii and 5.1.iii. If $p_n \rangle p_k$ and $t_n \rangle t_k$, no value of $\xi \in RV$ satisfies the condition in the definition of D_n in (5.2). Hence, $D_n(p,t) = \emptyset$ and thus $\mu(D_n(p,t)) = 0$ (e.g., $n = 4$ of Fig. 5.1). This implies lemma. Note that we use the expression $\mu(D_n(p,t)) \neq 0$, instead of $D_n(p,t) \neq \emptyset$, in order to exclude the case when D_n is a singleton. □

Lemma 5.1 estimates the set D_n for one variable of net-value-of-time ξ common to all options in competition. This estimation result is schematically illustrated in

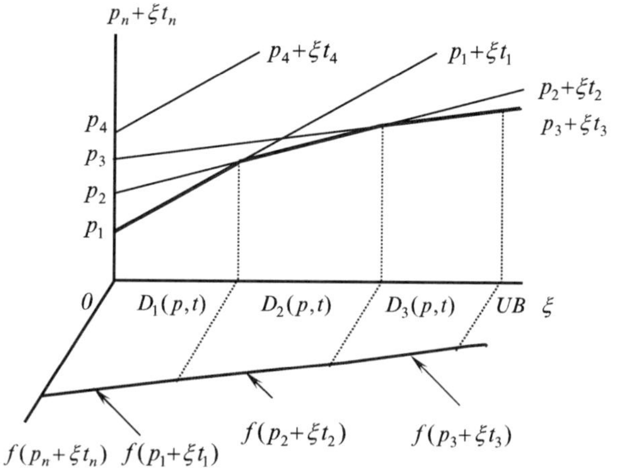

Fig. 5.1 Representation of D_n and f under quantitative competition

the upper part of Fig. 5.1 for the varying value of ξ. This figure depicts that each option, for $n = 1, 2, 3$, satisfies the strong trade-off condition with other options. Hence, the set D_n for $n = 1, 2, 3$ is the range of ξ, in which the corresponding option has the lowest implicit price. The figure also illustrates that option 4, which does not fulfill the trade-off condition over the first three options, has an empty catchment domain.

Lemma 5.1 introduces another important property of D_n. If option n satisfies the strong trade-off condition, the set D_n has a non-empty interior that does not overlap those of other options. On the other hand, if option n fulfills the weak trade-off condition with some other options, e.g., option $n + 1$, the set D_n has a non-empty interior that overlaps D_{n+1}. Using these properties, we estimate the indefinite integral of demand function Q_n, as presented below.

Lemma 5.2. *The demand function Q_n can be expressed as the following indefinite integral.*

i. *Suppose that option n satisfies the strong trade-off condition with all the other options. Then, the demand function Q_n is expressed by*

$$Q_n(p,t) = \int_{l_n}^{u_n} f(p_n + \xi t_n) h(\xi) d\xi. \tag{5.3}$$

ii. *Suppose that option n satisfies the weak trade-off condition with some others, e.g., $n + 1$. Then, the functions $Q_n(p,t)$ and $Q_{n+1}(p,t)$ satisfy the following:*

$$Q_n(p,t) + Q_{n+1}(p,t) = \int_{l_n}^{u_n} f(p_n + \xi t_n) h(\xi) d\xi. \tag{5.4}$$

Proof. Applying Lemmas 5.1.i and 5.1.ii to Theorems 4.5.1 and 4.5.ii, respectively, gives the expressions of Q_n in Lemmas 5.2.i and 5.2.ii, respectively. □

The indefinite integral in Lemma 5.2.i is schematically illustrated in Figs. 5.1 and 5.2. The lower part of Fig. 5.1 graphically depicts the integrand $f(p_n + \xi t_n)$, which refers to the deterministic demand function for varying ξ values. On the other hand, the lower part of Fig. 5.2 pictorially represents the integrand $f(p_n + \xi t_n)h(\xi)$ in which h is the probability density function of random term ξ. The figure shows that the value of $Q_n(p,t)$, for $n = 1, 2, 3$, is represented by the area estimated by integrating $f(p_n + \xi t_n)h(\xi)$ with respect to ξ from $\xi = l_n$ to $\xi = u_n$.

The graph of $f(p_n + \xi t_n)$ in Fig. 5.1 reflects the following. First, the value of f on D_n, for $n = 1, 2, 3$, depends only on $\hat{\pi}_n \equiv p_n + \xi t_n$, as shown in Theorem 4.5. Second, the function f is continuous and decreasing in $p_n + \xi t_n$, and therefore in $\xi \in D_n$, as proved in Lemma 4.6. Third, it holds that $f(p_n + u_n t_n) = f(p_{n+1} + l_{n+1} t_{n+1})$ at $\xi \in D_n \cap D_{n+1}$, for $n = 1, 2$, since $p_n + u_n t_n = p_{n+1} + l_{n+1} t_{n+1}$.

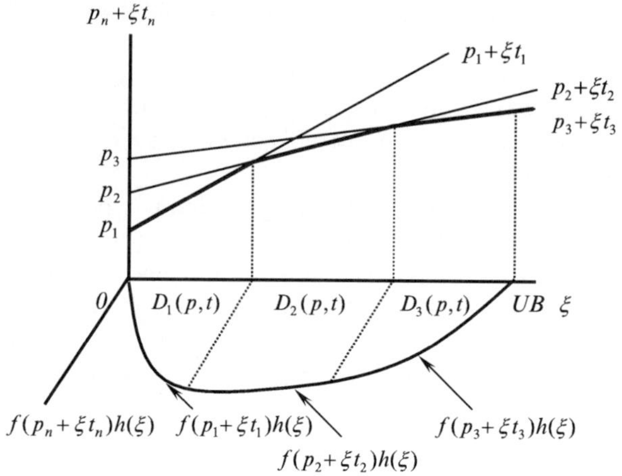

Fig. 5.2 Representation of Q_n under quantitative competition

Finally, we evaluate the continuity of Q_n by applying the following theorem for the continuity of indefinite integrals: the function F such that

$$F(x) = \int_0^x f(w)dw \tag{5.5}$$

is continuous in $x \in \mathbf{R}$ if the integrand f is summable.

Theorem 5.1. *The function Q_n is continuous in (p,t), except at the point (p_n, t_n) that satisfies the following weak trade-off condition:*

$$\mu(D_n(p,t)) \neq 0 \quad \textit{and} \quad (p_n, t_n) = (p_k, t_k), \ \textit{some } k \neq n.$$

Proof. The following two facts imply the continuity of Q_n in (p,t), except at the point defined in the theorem. First, by the above theorem for the indefinite integral in (5.5), the function Q_n is continuous in l_n and u_n. Second, the functions l_n and u_n defined in Lemma 5.1 are continuous in (p,t), except at $(p_n, t_n) = (p_k, t_k)$, for some $k \neq n$. On the other hand, the discontinuity of Q_n at the point defined in the theorem is the consequence of Lemma 5.2.ii such that the function Q_n has a degenerate value at $(p_n, t_n) = (p_k, t_k)$. □

5.2.2 Comparative Statics of Expected Demand Functions

We here show that the comparative statics of Q_n with respect to (p,t) exhibit certain regularities that are acceptable to our economic sense. These properties of the partial derivatives are as follows: the gross substitutability, characterized by $\partial Q_n/\partial p_n \langle 0$ but $\partial Q_k/\partial p_n \geq 0$, for all $k \neq n$; and the diagonal dominance, expressed by $|\partial Q_n/\partial p_n|\rangle \sum_{k\neq n}|\partial Q_k/\partial p_n|$.

To show these two properties, we estimate the partial derivatives of Q_n with respect to each element of (p, t) by applying the following theorem: if f is continuous in t,

$$\frac{d}{dx}\int_a^x f(t)dt = f(x). \tag{5.6}$$

Using this theorem, it is shown below that the partial derivatives of Q_n possess the two properties.

Theorem 5.2. *At a point (p, t) where the functions Q_k for $k = n-1,\ n,\ n+1$ are continuous, the partial derivatives $\partial Q_n/\partial p_k$ (and $\partial Q_n/\partial t_k$) satisfy the gross substitute condition such that*

$$\frac{\partial Q_n(p,t)}{\partial p_{n-1}} = \frac{\partial Q_{n-1}(p,t)}{\partial p_n} = f(p_n + l_n t_n)\, h(l_n)\, \frac{\partial l_n(p,r)}{\partial p_n} \rangle\, 0 \tag{5.7}$$

$$\frac{\partial Q_n(p,t)}{\partial p_{n+1}} = \frac{\partial Q_{n+1}(p,t)}{\partial p_n} = f(p_n + u_n t_n)\, h(u_n)\, \frac{\partial u_n(p,r)}{\partial p_n} \rangle\, 0 \tag{5.8}$$

$$\frac{\partial Q_n(p,t)}{\partial p_n} = \int_{l_n}^{u_n} \frac{\partial f(p_n + \xi t_n)}{\partial p_n} h(\xi)d\xi - \frac{\partial Q_n(p,t)}{\partial p_{n-1}} - \frac{\partial Q_n(p,t)}{\partial p_{n+1}} \langle\, 0. \tag{5.9}$$

Proof. Note that there is no difference in expressions between $\partial Q_m/\partial t_k$ and $\partial Q_m/\partial p_k$, except that ∂p_k is replaced by ∂t_k. The proof of the theorem for the case of $\partial Q_m/\partial p_k$ is presented in Appendix A.10. □

Theorem 5.3. *If Q_n is continuous at a point (p, t), its partial derivatives $\partial Q_n/\partial p_k$ (and $\partial Q_n/\partial t_k$), for all k, satisfy the diagonal dominance condition such that*

$$\left|\frac{\partial Q_n(p,t)}{\partial p_n}\right| \rangle \sum_{k\neq n}\left|\frac{\partial Q_n(p,t)}{\partial p_k}\right| = \sum_{k\neq n}\frac{\partial Q_n(p,t)}{\partial p_k}.$$

Proof. It can generally be assumed that the deterministic demand function f satisfies the condition $\partial f(p_n + \xi t_n)/\partial p_n \langle\, 0$. Hence, all the terms of $\partial Q_n/\partial p_n$ in (5.9) are negative. Therefore, the above inequalities hold. □

The partial derivatives $\partial Q_n/\partial p_2$ and $\partial Q_n/\partial t_2$, estimated in Theorem 5.2, are schematically illustrated in Figs. 5.3 and 5.4, respectively, with the example considered in Figs. 5.1 and 5.2. Fig. 5.3 depicts that a marginal price increase dp_2 causes two different kinds of impacts on the integral that estimates the Q_2 value. First, the marginal price increase dp_2 raises the implicit price of prime commodities for option 2 from $p_2 + \xi t_2$ to $p_2 + dp_2 + \xi t_2$ on $D_2(p, t)$, and thus decreases in the integrand from $f(p_2 + \xi t_2)h(\xi)$ to $f(p_2 + dp_2 + \xi t_2)h(\xi)$. Second, the marginal

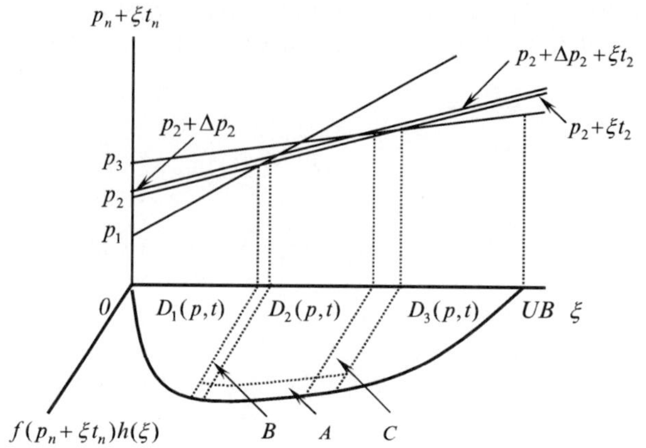

Fig. 5.3 Representation of $\partial Q_2/\partial p_2$ under quantitative competition

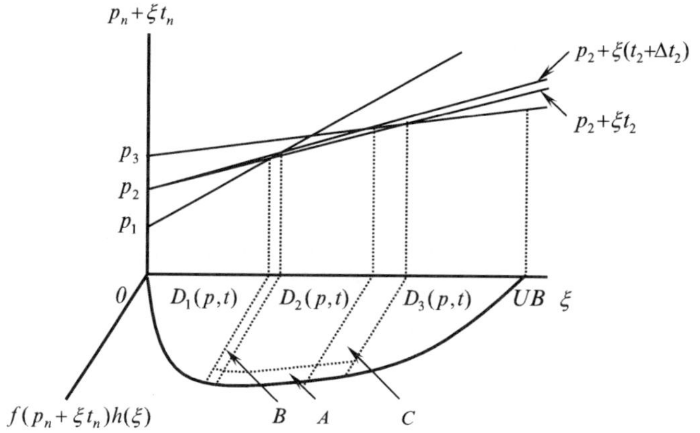

Fig. 5.4 Representation of $\partial Q_2/\partial t_2$ under quantitative competition

price increase dp_2 causes a decrease in D_2, which is brought by an increase in l_2 and a decrease in u_2. On the other hand, Fig. 5.4 illustrates the impact of an increase dt_2 in a manner analogous to that depicted in Fig. 5.3.

The two different types of impacts identified above satisfy the diagonal dominance condition characterized in Theorem 5.3, as explained below. First, the decrease in $f(p_2 + \xi t_2)$ causes a net decrease in demand itself, which is represented by area A in the figure. Second, the decrease of D_2 causes demand shifts to competing options $n-1$ and $n+1$. These demand shifts are estimated by the values of $\partial Q_{n-1}/\partial p_n$ and $\partial Q_{n+1}/\partial p_n$, which are equal to $\partial Q_n/\partial p_{n-1}$ and $\partial Q_n/\partial p_{n+1}$, respectively, and are represented by areas B and C, respectively. Third, the absolute value of $\partial Q_2/\partial p_2$ is larger than the sum of the absolute values of $\partial Q_2/\partial p_1$ and $\partial Q_2/\partial p_3$ by margin A. This means that the comparative statics of Q_n satisfy the diagonal dominance condition.

5.2.3 Characterization of Perfectly Elastic Demands

In this study, *perfectly elastic demand* for an option in quantitative competition consists of two groups. The first group of perfectly elastic demand for an option is the demand that has infinitely large elasticity with respect to the price of that option, whereas the second group includes the demand has very large but finitely bounded elasticity. However, the second group of perfectly elastic demand can hardly be defined in an objective way by applying a particular elasticity value. For this reason, we propose below a qualitative method for characterizing perfectly elastic demand.

Firstly, we present a formula that expresses perfectly elastic demand for an option with respect to the price of that option. Let $E(Q_n(p,t))$ be the demand elasticity of option n. Then, the formula that option n has perfectly elastic demand is expressed by

$$E(Q_n(p,t)) \equiv -\frac{\partial Q_n(p,t)}{\partial p_n} \bigg/ \frac{Q_n(p,t)}{p_n} \rangle K, \tag{5.10}$$

where K is a very large positive value. Here, if $E(Q_n(p,t)) \rangle K$, it is said that the demand Q_n is perfectly elastic, whereas if $E(Q_n(p,t)) \leq K$, the demand Q_n is imperfectly elastic.

Secondly, we introduce a set of necessary conditions, under which demand for an option has elasticity sufficiently large to judge that the demand is perfectly elastic. These necessary conditions, which can only be expressed as qualitative criteria for the judgment, are defined below.

Lemma 5.3. *Under quantitative competition, option n having perfectly elastic demand satisfies one of the following two conditions.*

i. *Option n has perfect substitutes. Such substitutes satisfy the weak trade-off condition with the option and thus lead to the outcome that $E(Q_n(p,t)) = \infty$.*
ii. *Option n has close substitutes. Such substitutes lead to the outcome that thickness of D_n, estimated by $\theta_n \equiv u_n - l_n$, is small and thus $E(Q_n(p,t))$ is large but finite.*

Proof. Lemma 5.3.i deals with the case when option n satisfies the weak trade-off condition with other options. If option n fulfills this condition with option $n+1$, the function Q_n is not continuous at $(p_n, t_n) = (p_{n+1}, t_{n+1})$. At this point of discontinuity, the elasticity of Q_n is infinitely large, since Q_n is non-increasing in p_n.

Subsequently, Lemma 5.3.ii covers the case when option n satisfies the strong trade-off condition with other options. In this case, the condition that the thickness $\theta_n \equiv u_n - l_n$ is small implies that

$$Q_n(p,t) \cong \theta_n(f(p_n + l_n t_n)h(l_n) \cong \theta_n f(p_n + u_n t_n)h(u_n). \tag{5.11}$$

Hence,

$$\frac{\partial Q_n}{\partial p_n} \cong \frac{\partial \theta_n}{\partial p_n} f(p_n + l_n t_n) h(l_n) + \theta_n \frac{\partial f(p_n + l_n t_n)}{\partial p_n} h(l_n)$$

$$\langle \left(\frac{1}{t_{n+1} - t_n} + \frac{1}{t_n - t_{n-1}} \right) f(p_n + l_n t_n) h(l_n) \langle 0. \tag{5.12}$$

By (5.11) and (5.12), the elasticity of Q_n satisfies the following inequality:

$$E(Q_n(p,t)) \rangle \left(\frac{1}{t_n - t_{n+1}} + \frac{1}{t_{n-1} - t_n} \right) \frac{p_n}{(u_n - l_n)} \rangle K. \tag{5.13}$$

The proof of the second inequality in (5.13) is as follows: first, the two terms in the parenthesis are both positive and sufficiently larger than zero; second, the term $\theta_n \equiv u_n - l_n$ is very small. □

Lemma 5.3.i depicts that an option that has perfect substitutes faces infinitely large demand elasticity. Perfect substitutes for option n have catchment domains that completely overlap catchment domain D_n. For this reason, all consumers perceive that the implicit prices of option n, estimated by $p_n + \xi\, t_n$, are identical to that of perfect substitutes, irrespective of ξ values perceived by the consumers. In this circumstance, even a small price increase Δp_n makes all the customers of option n judge that the implicit price $p_n + \Delta p_n + \xi\, t_n$ is greater than the implicit prices of perfect substitutes. Hence, mathematically, this increase Δp_n causes the complete loss of demand for option n.

Lemma 5.3.ii depicts that an option that has close substitutes serves demands with very large but finite elasticity. Close substitutes for option n have catchment domains tangent to D_n (e.g., options $n - 1$ and $n + 1$ in Fig. 5.1). Hence, if the thickness of D_n is small, all consumers perceive that the implicit price, $p_n + \xi\, t_n$, is lower than the implicit prices of close substitutes only by a small margin, as can be deduced from Fig. 5.1. In this circumstance, even a small price increase Δp_n makes a large portion of customers for option n perceives that the resulting implicit price $p_n + \Delta p_n + \xi\, t_n$ is greater than the implicit prices of close substitutes. Therefore, this increase shifts a large portion of demands for option n to close substitutes.

Thirdly, by applying Lemma 5.3, we devise a method to distinguish *perfectly elastic* and *imperfectly elastic demands* under the random perception approach. Perfectly and imperfectly elastic demands used in forthcoming analyses are actually qualitative terms. This set of dichotomous qualitative terms, perfectly and imperfectly elastic demands, is characterized by employing another set of dichotomous qualitative terms, *thin* and *thick* catchment domains.

We use the symbol "ε" as the upper boundary for the thickness of a catchment domain, which leads to perfectly elastic demand for an option. The number ε qualitatively represents a positive value that is small but sufficiently larger than zero. Using this number, the catchment domain of option n that has perfectly elastic demand is expressed as $\theta_n \cong \varepsilon$, rather than $\theta_n \cong 0$. This expression is adopted so as to distinguish between the following two cases:

$$\int_{D_n} d\xi \rangle 0 \quad \text{if} \quad \theta_n \cong \varepsilon, \quad \text{but} \quad \int_{D_n} d\xi \cong 0 \quad \text{if} \quad \theta_n \cong 0. \tag{5.14}$$

The other expression $\theta_n \rangle \varepsilon$ is applied when the demand for option n is imperfectly elastic.

Furthermore, we employ the symbol "δ" as the upper boundary for the average value of the integrand $f(p_n + \xi\, t_n)\, h(\xi)$ on D_n, denoted by F_n, called *the average demand intensity function*. The number δ also qualitatively represents a positive value that is small but sufficiently larger than zero. Using the number δ, the condition that the value of F_n is small but significantly larger than zero is expressed as follows:

$$F_n(p,t) = \frac{Q_n(p,t)}{\mu(D_n)} = \int_{D_n} f(p_n + \xi t_n) d\xi \bigg/ \int_{D_n} d\xi \cong \delta. \tag{5.15}$$

For reference, the F_1 value of option 1 in Fig. 5.2 is the average height of $f(p_1 + \xi\, t_1)\, h(\xi)$ on D_1.

Fourthly, we introduce an approach to categorize the demand function of an option by the geometry of an integral that estimates the demand for the option under the following conditions. First, it holds that the term $\sum_n \theta_n \equiv [0, RV]$ is a large positive value. Second, the average demand intensity for the interval $[0, RV]$, estimated by $\sum_n \theta_n F_n / RV$, is also a large positive value. Under these conditions, we can identify three different types of demands for options.

The first type satisfies the following two conditions: (i) $\theta_n \cong \varepsilon$ and (ii) $F_n \rangle \delta$. The first condition depicts that the integral domain D_n is thin. Therefore, the demand for this integral domain is perfectly elastic. The second condition expresses that the average value F_n is significantly larger than zero. This condition indicates that the demand for option n is a positive value sufficiently larger than zero, in spite of the fact that the integral domain θ_n is thin. Therefore, an option that satisfies these two conditions has a perfectly elastic demand that shares a very small portion of total market demand that equals $\sum_n \theta_n F_n$.

The second type fulfills two conditions such that (i) $\theta_n \rangle \varepsilon$ and (ii) $F_n \cong \delta$. The first condition implies that the set D_n is thick and, thereby, that the demand is imperfectly elastic. The second condition indicates that the integrand $f(p_n + \xi\, t_n)\, h(\xi)$ has very small values for D_n. Hence, under the first condition, the second condition leads to the demand for option n, which shares a very small portion of total market demand. This implies that this type has imperfectly elastic demand, though its market share is quite small.

The third type consists of option n that fulfills the following: (i) $\theta_n \rangle \varepsilon$ and (ii) $F_n \rangle \delta$. The condition $\theta_n \rangle \varepsilon$ is identical to its counterpart condition of the second type, whereas the condition $F_n \rangle \delta$ is identical to the counterpart condition of the first type. Therefore, the demand for an option that satisfies the two conditions is so large that its market share is significantly larger than zero. Furthermore, by the first condition, the demand for the option is, of course, imperfectly elastic.

It should be noted that we ignore the case in which $\theta_n \cong \varepsilon$ and $F_n \cong \delta$. In this case, (5.14) and (5.15) indicate that the integral domain and integrand of the integral Q_n are both negligibly small. Hence, the value of Q_n is approximately equal to zero. For this reason, we can ignore the demand for option n in analyzing real service markets.

5.2.4 *Necessary Conditions for Perfectly Elastic Demand*

Lemma 5.3 indicates that, if the thickness of a catchment domain for an option is thin, the option has perfectly elastic demand, whereas if its catchment domain is thick, the option has imperfectly elastic demand. As a sequel to that lemma, we present a set of necessary conditions under which a service option will have perfectly elastic demand.

Theorem 5.4. *Option n in quantitative competition has close substitutes that lead to the outcome* $\theta_n \equiv u_n(p,t) - l_n(p,t) \cong \varepsilon$, *if the option provides services under the following circumstances.*

(a) *The total number N is very large, and it holds that* $Q_k(p,t) \rangle 0$, *for all* $k \in \langle 1, N \rangle$.
(b) *The market share of option n is negligible but sufficiently larger than zero.*
(c) *The demand function* Q_n *satisfies the condition* $F_n \rangle \delta$.

Proof. Without loss of generality, it can be assumed that all options satisfy the strong trade-off condition. In this case, it follows that $\sum_k \theta_k = UB \langle \infty$. Then, the market share of option n, denoted by B_n, can be expressed as follows:

$$B_n \equiv Q_n / \sum_k Q_k = \theta_n F_n / A \sum_k \theta_k = \theta_n F_n / A \times UB, \tag{5.16}$$

where

$$A = \sum_k Q_k / \sum_k \theta_k = \sum_k \theta_k F_k / \sum_k \theta_k.$$

Subsequently, we evaluate the magnitude of all terms in (5.16). It follows from condition (a) that all options belong to one of the three types identified in the previous subsection; that is, $\theta_k \rangle 0$, for all $k \in \langle 1, N \rangle$, and $F_k \rangle \delta$ for some k. (i) Hence, the number A is a positive value sufficiently larger than zero, since $\sum_k \theta_k F_k = A \times UB = \sum_k Q_k \langle \infty$. (ii) By condition (b), the market share B_n is a positive number that is very small but sufficiently larger than zero. (iii) Condition (c) implies that $F_n \rangle \delta$. By (i)~(iii), the last term of (5.16) implies that $\theta_n \cong \varepsilon$. □

Theorem 5.4 identifies three necessary conditions under which demand for option n is perfectly elastic with respect to price p_n. Among them, conditions (a) and (b) are the requirements commonly employed in characterizing perfectly elastic demands. In contrast, condition (c) is the requirement specific to demand functions under the random perception approach.

The necessity of introducing condition (c) can readily be deduced from the second type introduced in the previous subsection, which satisfies the conditions such that $\theta_n \rangle \varepsilon$ and $F_n \cong \delta$. These two conditions connote that demand for option n has net-value-of-times distributed over a wide range, in spite of the fact that the volume of this demand is small. An example of an option with this type of demand can be found in a service firm in the following circumstances: first, it has a few competitors; second, the total market demand is small; and third, the market demand has much diversified net-value-of-times.

In contrast, perfectly elastic demand is characterized by two conditions opposite to the conditions for the imperfectly elastic demand examined above; these conditions are $\theta_n \cong \varepsilon$ and $F_n \rangle \delta$, as depicted in the previous subsection. The first condition $\theta_n \cong \varepsilon$ implies that all demands for option n have very similar net-value-of-times that reflect customer perception for the magnitude of qualitative service attributes. On the other hand, the second condition $F_n \rangle \delta$ connotes that the demand belonging to a small range of net-value-of-times for option n is quite large.

So far, we have sorted demands for options into two dichotomous groups: perfectly and imperfectly elastic demands. However, this classification does not mean that the demand function under the random perception approach can be objectively sorted into two groups. Actually, the elasticity of demand differs from option to option, because the thickness of catchment domains cannot be uniform across all options in competition, as depicted in Fig. 5.2. Moreover, we cannot exclude the possibility that the demand elasticity of an option has a median value that that cannot be placed in either of the two categories: perfectly and imperfectly elastic demands.

5.3 Qualitative Competition

5.3.1 Conversion into Iterated Indefinite Integrals

Here, we convert the multiple integral that estimates demand for an option in qualitative competition, as denoted by m or k. The implicit price of an option in qualitative competition must be estimated using its specific random net-value-of-times that differ from those of other options. Moreover, the demand function of an option in that competition is expressed as a multiple integral with respect to the vector of M random net-value-of-times, in which M is the number of options for that competition. Such a multiple integral is converted into an indefinite integral as below.

To begin, we develop a specific expression of the multiple integral that estimates the demand for option m in qualitative competition. The random net-value-of-time specific to option m is estimated by $\xi_m = w - \sum_k \hat{\varphi}_k \beta_{km}$. For this random net-value-of-time, the implicit price of the prime commodity for option m is

$$\hat{\pi}_m(p_m, t_m) = \frac{1}{a_m}(p_m + \xi_m t_m). \tag{5.17}$$

Moreover, the implicit price of the prime commodity for the option chosen by a consumer is estimated by $\hat{\pi}(p,t) = \min_m\{\hat{\pi}_m(p_m, t_m)\}$, where $p \equiv (p_1, \cdots, p_M)$ and $t \equiv (t_1, \cdots, t_M)$.

Subsequently, by (4.17), the catchment domain D_m is expressed by

$$D_m(p,t) = \{\xi \in RV \mid \hat{\pi}_m \leq \hat{\pi}_k, \text{ all } k \neq m\}, \tag{5.18}$$

where RV is the domain of $\xi \equiv (\xi_1, \cdots, \xi_M)$ in $\mathbf{R}^{\mathrm{M}}$. Without loss of generality, this domain RV can be defined as follows:

$$RV = \prod_m [0, UB_m], \tag{5.19}$$

where UB_m is the maximum value of ξ_m in RV. Then, the set D_m is a polyhedron in $\mathbf{R}^{\mathrm{M}}$. Also, a cross-section of D_m on the $\xi_m - \xi_k$ plane can be depicted as Fig. 5.5.

Moreover, under qualitative competition, every net-value-of-time ξ_m is independent of ξ_k, for all $k \neq m$. Hence, by Lemma 4.5,

$$\mu(D_m(p,t) \cap D_k(p,t)) = 0, \text{ all } k \neq m, \tag{5.20}$$

where μ is the ordinary product measure in $\mathbf{R}^{\mathrm{M}}$. Therefore, by Theorem 4.5, it follows that

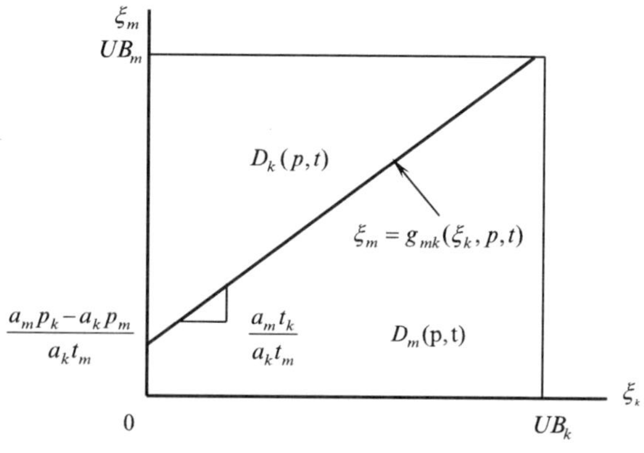

Fig. 5.5 Representation of D_m under qualitative competition

$$Q_m(p,t) = \frac{1}{a_m}\int_{D_m} f\left(\frac{1}{a_m}(p_m + \xi_m t_m)\right) h(\xi) d\mu \tag{5.21}$$

$$\equiv \int_{D_m} f_m\,(p_m + \xi_m t_m)\, h(\xi)\, d\mu, \tag{5.22}$$

where f is the demand function for the prime commodity. This equation depicts that the value of Q_m is the volume of the epigraph of $f_m(p_m + \xi_m t_m)h(\xi)$ on D_m in $\mathbf{R}^{\mathrm{M}}$.

The multiple integral introduced above is not suitable for the analysis of its mathematical properties, such as continuity and partial derivatives. We therefore convert it into an iterated indefinite integral. However, there are many ways to express it as an iterated indefinite integral, in terms of the ordering of iterated integrals with respect to multiple random terms. Moreover, the complexity of analyses of the mathematical properties depends on the ordering of iterated integrals. We therefore must carefully consider the most desirable ordering of iterated integrals. The first step in the construction of this iterated indefinite integral is to construct an alternative expression of D_m, as below.

Lemma 5.4. *Let $SD_{mk}(p,t)$ be a subset of $D_m(p,t)$, defined by*

$$SD_{mk}(p,t) = \left\{\xi \in RV \mid \hat{\pi}_m \leq \hat{\pi}_k \leq \hat{\pi}_j, \text{ all } j \neq m, k\right\}.$$

Then, it holds that

$$\mu(D_m(p,t)) = \sum_{k \neq m} \mu(SD_{mk}(p,t)).$$

Proof. By definition of SD_{mk}, the interior of SD_{mk} is disjoint to the interior of SD_{mj}, for all $j \neq m, k$. Hence, it follows that $\mu(SD_{mk} \cap SD_{mj}) = 0$. Therefore,

$$\mu(D_m(p,t)) = \mu\left(\bigcup_{k \neq m} SD_{mk}(p,t)\right) = \sum_{k \neq m} \mu(SD_{mk}(p,t)). \qquad \square$$

The next step is used to construct the function SQ_{mk} on the integral domain SD_{mk}:

$$SQ_{mk}(p,t) = \int_{SD_{mk}} f_m(p_m + \xi_m t_m)h(\xi)d\mu. \tag{5.23}$$

Then, by Lemma 5.4, it follows that

$$Q_m(p,t) = \sum_{k \neq m} SQ_{mk}(p,t). \tag{5.24}$$

The multiple integral SQ_{mk} is converted into an iterated indefinite integral, as shown below.

Lemma 5.5. *The function $SQ_{mk}(p,t)$ can be converted into the following iterated and indefinite integral:*

$$SQ_{mk}(p,t) = \int_{SD^o_{mk}} \int_0^{g_{mk}} f_m(p_m + \xi_m t_m) h(\xi)\, d\xi_m\, d\mu^o_m,$$

where

$$g_{mk}(\xi_k, p, t) = \max\left\{0,\ \frac{a_m p_k - a_k p_m}{a_k t_m} + \xi_k \frac{a_m t_k}{a_k t_m}\right\}$$

$$SD^o_{mk}(\xi_m, p, t) = \{\xi^o_m \in RV^o_m \,|\xi_m = \xi'_m,\ (\xi'_m, \xi^o_m) \in SD_{mk}(p,t)\}$$

$$\xi^o_m = \xi \backslash \{\xi_m\},^1\ RV^o_m = \prod_{k \neq m} [0, UB_k], \text{ and } \mu^o_m = \prod_{k \neq m} \mu_k.$$

Proof. By Lemma 4.6, the integrand f_m is continuous. Therefore, by Fubini's theorem, the multiple integral in (5.23) can be converted into an iterated integral. In this iterated integral, the function g_{mk}, which is the upper boundary of the first iterated integral with respect to ξ_m, is estimated from the following inequality:

$$\frac{1}{a_m}(p_m + g_{mk}(\xi_k, p, t) t_m) \leq \frac{1}{a_k}(p_k + \xi_k t_k).$$

The second iterated integral is a multiple integral with respect to the product measure μ^o_m on the integral domain SD^o_{mk}, which is a cross-section of SD_{mk} for a given value of ξ_m in the integrand. To clarify this relationship, the range of SD^o_{mk} is expressed by (ξ'_m, ξ^o_m) under the condition $\xi_m = \xi'_m$. □

5.3.2 Comparative Statics of Expected Demand Functions

Lemma 5.5 expresses the function Q_m as the sum of iterated and indefinite integrals SQ_{mk}, for all $k \neq m$. Using this alternative expression of Q_m, we estimate the comparative statics of Q_m with respect to p and t. We also show that these partial derivatives satisfy the gross substitutability and diagonal dominance conditions, as in the case of demand functions for quantitative competition.

To start, we estimate $\partial Q_m / \partial p_k$(and $\partial Q_m / \partial t_k$) under the condition that D_m is tangent to D_k, for some $k \neq m$. The integrand f_m of Q_m in (5.23) is not sensitive with respect to a marginal change in p_k. In contrast, the integral domain D_m is directly

[1] The symbol "\" expresses that $(a,b,c)\backslash\{a\} = (a,b)$. Hence, $\xi\backslash\{\xi_m\} = (\xi_1, \cdots, \xi_{m-1}, \xi_{m+1}, \cdots, \xi_M)$.

affected by the marginal price change dp_k; the marginal price increase dp_k enlarges the volume of D_m, due to the outward movements of its tangent plane $D_m \cap D_k$. Hence, the estimation of $\partial Q_m/\partial p_k$ must consider the impact of dp_k on the range of D_m only.

We next estimate $\partial Q_m/\partial p_m$ (and $\partial Q_m/\partial t_m$). In this estimation, we must include the effect of a marginal price increase dp_m on the integrand of Q_m as well as on the integral domain D_m. To be specific, the marginal price increase dp_m decreases the integrand f_m. Moreover, this marginal price increase accompanies a decrease in the volume of D_m, which is caused by the inward movements of tangent planes $D_m \cap D_k$, for all $k \neq m$. Summing these two effects gives an estimation of $\partial Q_m/\partial p_m$.

Theorem 5.5. *The partial derivatives $\partial Q_m/\partial p_k$ (and $\partial Q_m/\partial t_k$), for all $k \neq m$, satisfy the gross substitute condition such that*

$$\frac{\partial Q_m(p,t)}{\partial p_k} = \frac{\partial SQ_{mk}(p,t)}{\partial p_k} = \frac{a_k}{t_m} \int_{D_m \cap D_k} f_k(p_k + \xi_k t_k)\, h(\xi) \frac{\partial \hat{\pi}_k}{\partial p_k} d\mu^o_m \geq 0 \tag{5.25}$$

$$\frac{\partial Q_m(p,t)}{\partial p_k} = \frac{\partial Q_k(p,t)}{\partial p_m} = \frac{a_m}{t_k} \int_{D_m \cap D_k} f_m(p_m + \xi_m t_m)\, h(\xi) \frac{\partial \hat{\pi}_m}{\partial p_m} d\mu^o_k \geq 0 \tag{5.26}$$

$$\frac{\partial Q_m(p,t)}{\partial p_m} = \int_{D_m} \frac{\partial f_m(p_m + \xi_m t_m)}{\partial p_m} h(\xi) d\mu - \sum_{k \neq m} \frac{\partial Q_m(p,t)}{\partial p_k} \langle 0, \tag{5.27}$$

where

$$D_m \cap D_k = \left\{ \xi^o_m \in RV^o_m \,|\hat{\pi}_m = \hat{\pi}_k, \text{ and } \hat{\pi}_m \leq \hat{\pi}_j, \text{ for all } j \neq m,\ k \right\}.$$

Proof. See Appendix A.11. □

The partial derivative $\partial Q_m/\partial p_k$ (and $\partial Q_m/\partial t_k$) estimates the increase in the value of Q_m, which is caused by a marginal movement of the tangent plane $D_m \cap D_k$ in the outward direction of D_m due to a marginal price increase dp_k. Equation (5.25) shows that this partial derivative can be expressed as a kind of line integral. In this integral, the integral domain is the tangent plane $D_m \cap D_k$ in $\mathbf{R}^{M-1}$ that satisfies the condition $\hat{\pi}_m = \hat{\pi}_k$ on the $\xi_k - \xi_m$ plane. The integrand is the image of $f_k(p_k + \xi_k t_k)h(\xi)$ along the border line $\hat{\pi}_m = \hat{\pi}_k$. This border line is expressed as the function g_{mk}, which is estimated from $\hat{\pi}_m = \hat{\pi}_k$.

Equation (5.26) shows that $\partial Q_m/\partial p_k = \partial Q_k/\partial p_m$, for all $k \neq m$. This equality holds, even in the case of $a_m \neq a_k$. To confirm the equality, we consider the case when $a_m = 1$ but $a_k \neq 1$. Suppose, first, that price p_m increases by Δp unit, and that this price increase results in the Δy unit of demand shift for the prime commodity from option m to k. This demand shift for the prime commodity causes the $\Delta y/a_k$

unit increase in demand for service k, since $(1/a_k)f = f_k$ on $D_m \cap D_k$; that is $\partial Q_k/\partial p_m = \Delta y/a_k$. Suppose, next, that price p_k increases by Δp unit. This increase Δp raises the value of $\hat{\pi}_k$ by $\Delta p/a_k$ unit. This implicit price increase shifts the $\Delta y/a_k$ unit of demand for the prime commodity from option k to m, since $f = f_m$ on $D_m \cap D_k$. Hence, the demand shift from option k to m is also by the $\Delta y/a_k$ unit; that is, $\partial Q_m/\partial p_k = \Delta y/a_k$.

The partial derivative $\partial Q_m/\partial p_m$ in (5.27) is composed of two terms. The first term, $\partial f_m/\partial p_m$, estimates a net decrease in demand for service itself, whereas the second term, $-\sum_k \partial Q_m/\partial p_k$, represents a demand shift from option m to other competing options, due to the inward movement of tangent planes $D_m \cap D_k$, for all $k \neq m$. These two different types of effects under the assumption of $a_m = a_k = 1$ are schematically depicted in Fig. 5.6. The upper part of the figure represents the reduction in D_m, whereas the lower part shows the change in integrand from $f_m(p_m + \xi_m t_m)\, h(\xi)$ to $f_k(p_k + dp_k + \xi_k t_k)\, h(\xi)$ across cross-section $H - H$.

The partial derivative $\partial Q_m/\partial p_m$ in (5.27) satisfies the diagonal dominance condition, as graphically illustrated in the lower part of Fig. 5.6. The first term on the right side of the equation, represented by area A, depicts a net decrease in demand for the service. One element of the second term, $\partial Q_k/\partial p_m$, denoted by area B_k, estimates a demand shift to competing option k. These two different impacts of the marginal price increase dp_m can be characterized as below.

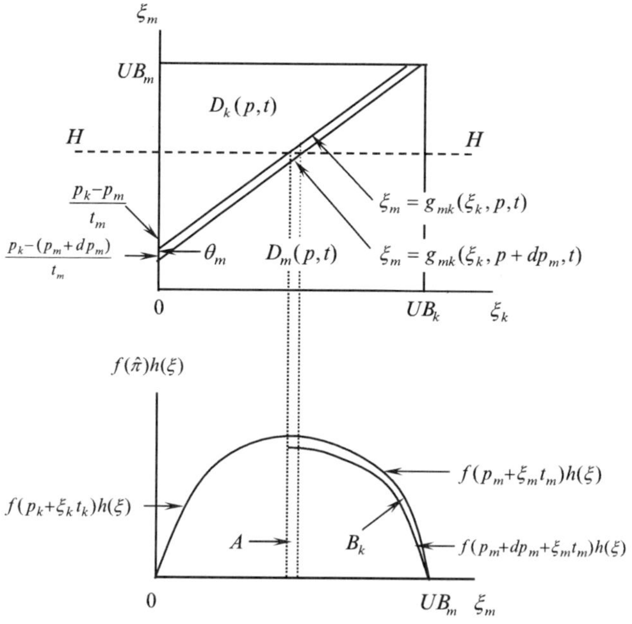

Fig. 5.6 Representation of $\partial Q_m/\partial p_m$ under qualitative competition

Theorem 5.6. *The partial derivatives $\partial Q_m/\partial p_k$ (and $\partial Q_m/\partial t_k$), for all $k \neq m$, satisfy the diagonal dominance condition such that*

$$\left|\frac{\partial Q_m(p,t)}{\partial p_m}\right| \rangle \sum_{k\neq m}\left|\frac{\partial Q_m(p,t)}{\partial p_k}\right| = \sum_{k\neq m}\frac{\partial Q_m(p,t)}{\partial p_k}.$$

Proof. This can be proved in a manner analogous to that of Theorem 5.3. □

5.3.3 Characterization of Perfectly Elastic Demand

We here show that the demand function of some options in qualitative competition can be imperfectly elastic, even though the number of firms in competition is very large. To show this, we first introduce an intuitive explanation for this assertion. We subsequently develop a formula to support this assertion. Finally, we draw the necessary condition for a firm to have perfectly elastic demands from the formula developed in the previous step.

To begin, using Fig. 5.6, we explain the reason why the demand Q_m, for some m, can be imperfectly elastic with respect to p_m, even though the number of competing options is very large. A marginal price increase Δp_m moves the tangent plane $D_m \cap D_k$, for all $k \neq m$, in the inward direction of D_m. This movement reduces the thickness of D_m on the ξ_m axis, as depicted in the upper part of Fig. 5.6. However, this marginal change in thickness is significantly smaller than the average thickness of D_m on the ξ_m axis. Therefore, this marginal change usually results in a decrease in demand for option m, which can be significantly smaller than the demand Q_m, as can be deduced from the lower part of the figure. This implies that the elasticity of Q_m with respect to p_m is not always infinitely large.

Subsequently, we develop a formula that approximates the elasticity of Q_m with respect to p_m, in order to show that the elasticity is not always infinitely large. We develop this formula under the simplifying assumption that $a_m = 1$ for all m. As the first step in developing the formula, we identify the relationship between $\partial Q_m/\partial p_k$ and SQ_{mk} defined in Lemma 5.5.

Lemma 5.6. *If $SQ_{mk}(p,t) \rangle 0$, there is a unique value of $\psi_{mk} \rangle 0$ such that*

$$SQ_{mk}(p,t) = \psi_{mk}\frac{\partial\, Q_m(p,t)}{\partial p_k} = \frac{\psi_{mk}}{t_m}\int_{D_m\cap D_k} f_k(p_k + \xi_k t_k)\, h(\xi) d\mu_m^o.$$

Proof. The function SQ_{mk} is the integral of f_m on SD_m, a subset of D_m, which has a tangent plane $D_m \cap D_k$, as depicted in Lemma 5.5. The second equality follows from (5.25). Therefore, the proof can be completed by showing that there exists a unique ψ_{mk} value.

The integral on the last term is the line integral of f_k on the integral domain $D_m \cap D_k$ in $\mathbf{R}^{M-1}$, as described in the previous comment for (5.25). The integrand of this line integral, $f_k(p_k + \xi_k t_k)h(\xi)$, requires the first iterated integral with respect to $d\xi_k$ on the $\xi_m - \xi_k$ plane depicted in Fig. 5.5. Hence, the factor ψ_{mk}/t_m in the last term can be interpreted as the average band width on the ξ_m axis, which equates the first and third terms of the above equation. Also, the existence of a unique ψ_{mk}/t_m value follows from the mean value theorem for integrals. □

By Lemma 5.6, (5.24) can be amended as follows:

$$Q_m(p,t) = \sum_{k \neq m} \psi_{mk} \frac{\partial Q_m(p,t)}{\partial p_k}. \tag{5.28}$$

On the other hand, it follows from (5.27) that

$$-\frac{\partial Q_m(p,t)}{\partial p_m} \rangle \sum_{k \neq m} \frac{\partial Q_m(p,t)}{\partial p_k}. \tag{5.29}$$

Substituting (5.28) and (5.29) into (5.10) gives

$$E(Q_m(p,t)) \rangle\, p_m \sum_{k \neq m} \frac{\partial Q_m(p,t)}{\partial p_k} \Bigg/ \left(\sum_{k \neq m} \psi_{mk} \frac{\partial Q_m(p,t)}{\partial p_k} \right). \tag{5.30}$$

Here, all the terms on the right sides of (5.30) are usually finite. Therefore, we cannot exclude the possibility that the demand Q_m is imperfectly elastic with respect to p_m, irrespective of numbers of options in competition.

Finally, we consider the necessary condition under which the demand estimated by Q_m is perfectly elastic. By analogy to the analysis for an option with perfectly elastic demand under quantitative competition, it can be said that the demand elasticity estimated in (5.30) is large, if

$$\psi_{mk} \cong \varepsilon, \text{ all } k. \tag{5.31}$$

Here, the number ε qualitatively represents a value that is small but significantly larger than zero.

The condition (5.31) is equivalent to the condition that $\theta_n \equiv u_n - l_n \cong \varepsilon$ in Lemma 5.3.ii for quantitative competition. This condition implies that option m has a close substitute k such that all the customers of option m perceive that the implicit price $\hat{\pi}_m$ is lower than the price $\hat{\pi}_k$ by a very small margin. Furthermore, this strange condition appears to be fulfilled by many kinds of qualitative services. All these aspects of qualitative competition are closely analyzed in the next section.

5.4 Qualitative Competition under Identical Ordering Condition

5.4.1 Identical Ordering Condition

It has been shown in the previous section that the demand function of an option, which satisfies the condition in (5.31), is perfectly elastic. However, that condition has a shortcoming in that it is a pure mathematical expression from which its economic implications cannot easily be deduced. For this reason, we devise *the identical ordering condition*, as one necessary condition for a firm to have perfectly elastic demand. The definition and economic implications of this condition are presented below.

The identical ordering condition implies that all consumers have an identical ordering relationship for preference among various heterogeneous service options under the condition that the prices of all options are free. This identical ordering condition implies that all consumers i in the market satisfy an identical preference ordering expressed by

$$\frac{\xi_1^i t_1}{a_1} \rangle \cdots \rangle \frac{\xi_m^i t_m}{a_m} \rangle \cdots \rangle \frac{\xi_M^i t_M}{a_M}. \tag{5.32}$$

Here, each term expresses the net-service-time-value of option m for consumer i per one unit of prime commodity. Additionally, the inequalities represent the ordering of net-service-time-values, which is assumed to hold across all consumers.

Firstly, we present the supplementary interpretation of the identical ordering condition, focusing on the mathematical implications of the formula in (5.32). First, the term $\xi_m^i t_m / a_m$ estimates the implicit price of the prime commodity for option m under the condition that $p_m = 0$. Second, all consumers identically order the values $\xi_m^i t_m / a_m$ across all options. Third, such a preference ordering remains unaffected by ever-changing perceptions; that is, the value of $\xi_m^i t_m / a_m$ may differ in a situation that affects a consumer perception about the amount of hedonic commodities, but the preference ordering is always identical.

Secondly, we interpret economic implications of the identical ordering condition through the application of the fifth comment for Lemma 2.2. The net-service-time-value of an option is the non-monetary portion of the implicit price for that option. This non-monetary portion reflects the monetary value of service quality attributes packed in that option. This monetary value of an option is larger than that of its competing option if consumers perceive that the service quality of the former is lower than the latter. Therefore, the identical ordering condition implies that all consumers identically judge the ordering of service qualities among all options.

This aspect of the identical ordering condition is illustrated using an example that follows. Suppose that two hotels are available, and that Hotel 1 offers service with a lower level of qualitative attributes than is offered by Hotel 2. Suppose, also, that total service time, including the delay at the front desk, is almost identical; that is $t_1 \cong t_2$. Furthermore, it can be said that $a_1 = a_2 = 1$.

Then, the identical ordering condition implies that the net-value-of-times of the two options satisfy the following inequality: $\xi_1^i = w^i - \sum_k \hat{\pi}_k \beta_{k1} \rangle \xi_2^i = w^i - \sum_k \hat{\pi}_k \beta_{k2}$, for all i. This implies that Hotel 1, a lower quality option, requires that all guests consume a larger portion of value-of-time w^i, due to smaller quantities of hedonic commodities received in the process of lodging service, estimated by $\sum_k \hat{\pi}_k \beta_{k1}$.

Thirdly, we show that the identical ordering condition can apply to many kinds of services. We can apply, without hesitation, this condition to qualitative choice services such that the capacity cost necessary to provide one unit of capacity is a dominant factor that determines service quality in terms of qualitative attributes. One typical example is a hotel service such as that examined above. Another example is found in international air passenger service, where three options (economy, business, and first class seats) are generally available. We can also apply this condition to retail stores, sport facilities, etc.

However, it is difficult to apply this condition to a certain service option that targets a specific group of customers endowed with cultural and aesthetic tastes that differ from other groups. One example can be a Korean restaurant in a Western city. The restaurant targets a certain group of customers that has a stronger preference for Korean dishes than do the majority of consumers, who satisfies the identical ordering condition for other typical services. Another example can be resort areas each of which has a unique climate, natural scenes, and/or entertainment facilities. In this case, the ordering of preferences for these options having different types of attractiveness differs from consumer to consumer. Therefore, it is impossible to construct the representative identical ordering condition applicable to the general population.

It should be noted that that we proceed with forthcoming analyses, for the time being, under the restrictive condition that all options satisfy the condition, in order to simplify the presentation of the analysis. The prime purpose of forthcoming analyses is to identify the condition under which an option in qualitative competition has perfectly elastic demand. To be specific, consider the case when only some options in qualitative competition satisfy the identical ordering condition one another; these options do not satisfy the condition with remaining options in the same competition. In this case, the options satisfying the identical ordering condition have perfectly elastic demand if the number of these options is large, irrespective of the presence of other options. Nonetheless, we present analyses, for the time being, under the condition that all options satisfy the condition.

5.4.2 *Demand Functions under Identical Ordering Condition*

Mathematically, the identical ordering condition has the effect of reducing the catchment domain but does not change the integrand of multiple integrals estimating expected demands. For this reason, the demand function of an option under this condition can have a thin catchment domain that leads to large elasticity with respect to price. Nonetheless, the comparative statics of the demand function has expressions identical to those of the demand function examined in the previous section, with a few minor exceptions. These aspects of the demand function under the identical ordering condition are explained below.

To begin, we show that, under the identical ordering condition, the price of an option in qualitative competition must satisfy a certain requirement so that the option has a positive demand. This requirement, called the trade-off condition under qualitative competition, is similar to the same condition under quantitative competition in Lemma 5.1. This requirement is presented below.

Lemma 5.7. *Suppose that all consumers preferentially order options in qualitative competition according to the identical ranking, expressed by (5.32).*

i. *It holds that $\mu(D_m(p,t)) \neq 0$, for all m, if the following trade-off condition is fulfilled:*

$$\frac{p_1}{a_1} \langle \frac{p_2}{a_2} \langle \cdots \langle \frac{p_M}{a_M}.$$

ii. *In contrast, it holds that $\mu(D_m(p,t)) = 0$, for some m, if price p_m does not satisfy the trade-off condition with some other options; e.g.,*

$$\frac{p_{m-1}}{a_{m-1}} \langle \frac{p_{m+1}}{a_{m+1}} \langle \frac{p_m}{a_m} \langle \frac{p_{m+2}}{a_{m+2}}.$$

Proof. If Lemma 5.7.ii holds, Lemma 5.7.i follows automatically. Hence, the proof of the lemma can be completed by proving Lemma 5.7.ii through contradiction. Suppose that p_m leads to a non-empty D_m. (i) Then, all the ξ values in D_m satisfy the following: $a_m^{-1}(p_m + \xi_m t_m) \langle a_{m+1}^{-1}(p_{m+1} + \xi_{m+1} t_{m+1})$. (ii) Suppose, however, that the price p_m also fulfills the inequality in Lemma 5.7.ii. Then, by (i) and (ii), it should hold that $\xi_m t_m / a_m \langle \xi_{m+1} t_{m+1} / a_{m+1}$. However, this inequality contradicts the identical ordering condition in (5.32). □

The trade-off condition describes the requirement for the price of an option to have a positive demand. It shows that an option in qualitative competition can have positive demand only when the service quality of the option in terms of qualitative attributes must be superior to competing options that charge lower prices. For example, if an airliner charges a higher fare for an economy seat than that charged for first class, this pricing policy will certainly result in zero demand for economy seat.

Lemma 5.7 implies that the identical ordering condition has the effect of reducing the range of D_m. This can readily be confirmed from the amendment of Lemma 5.4 under the identical ordering condition, such that

$$\mu(D_m(p,t)) = \sum_{k \neq m} \mu\left(ED_{mk}(p,t)\right), \tag{5.33}$$

where

$$ED_{mk}(p,t) = SD_{mk}(p,t) \cap OD(t), \text{ all } k \neq m,$$

$$OD(t) = \{\xi \mid \xi_1 t_1/a_1 \rangle \xi_2 t_2/a_2 \rangle \cdots \rangle \xi_M t_M/a_M\}.$$

Here, it always holds that $ED_{mk} \subset SD_{mk}$, due to the presence of OD. This implies that the identical ordering condition reduces the range of D_m. The geometry of the reduced range is closely examined below.

Lemma 5.8. *Under the identical ordering condition, the image of ED_{mk} on the $\xi_k - \xi_m$ plane, denoted by CD_{mk}, and the thickness of ED_{mk} on the ξ_m axis, denoted by ψ_{mk}, are as follows:*

$$CD_{mk}(p,t) = \{(\xi_m, \xi_k) \mid r_{mk}(\xi_k, p, t) \leq \xi_m \leq g_{mk}(\xi_k, p, t)\}, \tag{5.34}$$

$$\frac{\psi_{mk}}{t_m} = \theta_k \equiv \frac{a_m}{a_{m+1}} \frac{p_{m+1}}{t_m} - \frac{p_m}{t_m}, \ \textit{all } k \neq m, \tag{5.35}$$

where

$$r_{mk}(\xi_{mk}, p, t) = \max\left\{ 0, \ \frac{a_m}{t_m}\left(\frac{p_k}{a_k} - \frac{p_{m+1}}{a_{m+1}}\right) + \xi_k \frac{a_m t_k}{a_k t_m} \right\}.$$

Proof. See Appendix A.12 □

Lemma 5.8 depicts the geometry of D_m under the identical ordering condition. In the lemma, equation (5.34) presents the formula that estimates the range of $D_m \cap D_k$ on the $\xi_k - \xi_m$ plane. On the other hand, equation (5.35) shows that the thickness of $D_m \cap D_k$ on the ξ_m axis is a constant θ_m, and that this thickness depends only on the values of p_m, p_{m+1}, t_m, a_m, and a_{m+1}. This result connotes that the thickness θ_m is independent of implicit prices $\hat{\pi}_k$, for all $k \neq m, \ m+1$.

To better understand Lemma 5.8, we consider a special case when $a_k = 1$, for all k. In this case, the range of $CD_{m(m+1)}$ on the $\xi_{m+1} - \xi_m$ plane is estimated by solving the following two equalities: $p_m + \xi_m t_m \leq p_{m+1} + \xi_{m+1} t_{m+1}$, and $\xi_m t_m \geq \xi_{m+1} t_{m+1}$. The range estimated in this manner is graphically illustrated in the upper part of Fig. 5.7. Subsequently, the range of CD_{mk} on the $\xi_k - \xi_m$ plane, for all $k \neq m, \ m+1$, is estimated from the following two inequalities: $p_m + \xi_m t_m \leq p_k + \xi_k t_k$, and $p_k + \xi_k t_k \leq p_{m+1} + \xi_m t_m$. Here, the second inequality is obtained by combining one condition of SD_{mk}, such that $p_k + \xi_k t_k \leq p_{m+1} + \xi_{m+1} t_{m+1}$, and the identical ordering condition such that $\xi_m t_m \geq \xi_{m+1} t_{m+1}$. The estimated range of CD_{mk} for $k \leq m$ is illustrated in the lower part of Fig. 5.7.

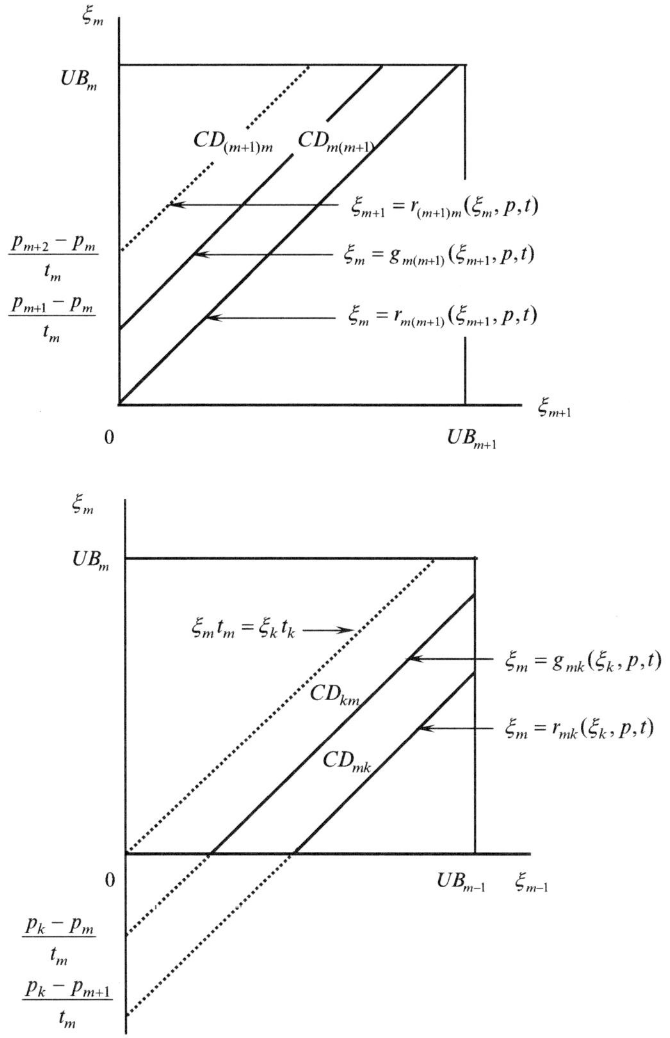

Fig. 5.7 Representation of $CD_{m(m+1)}$ and $CD(p, t)$

Option $m + 1$, which delineates the thickness θ_m, is called *the closest superior substitute* for option m regarding service quality, as explained below. First, the term $\xi_m t_m$ is the net-service-time-value of option m, which represents the total non-monetary cost experienced in consuming one unit of service m. Second, as the service quality of option m is higher, the net-service-time-value of the option is smaller. Hence, the identical ordering condition connotes that option $m + 1$ offers a service superior to option m but inferior to other superior options, for all $k \rangle m + 1$.

Using Lemma 5.8, the expected demand function Q_{mn} can be converted into an iterated indefinite integral such that

$$Q_{mn}(p,t) = \sum_{k \neq m} SQ_{mk}(p,t), \tag{5.36}$$

where

$$SQ_{mk}(p,t) = \int_{ED^o_{mk}} \int_{r_{mk}}^{g_{mk}} f_m(p_m + \xi_m t_m) h(\xi)\, d\xi_m\, d\mu^o_m.$$

Using (5.36), we estimate the comparative statics of Q_m with respect to (p,t), as shown below.

Theorem 5.7. *Under the identical ordering condition, the sensitivities $\partial Q_m / \partial p_k$ (and $\partial Q_m / \partial t_k$), for all $k \neq m$, fulfill the gross substitute condition such that*

$$\frac{\partial Q_m(p,t)}{\partial p_k} = \frac{\partial SQ_{mk}(p,t)}{\partial p_k} = \frac{\partial Q_k(p,t)}{\partial p_m} \rangle\ 0 \tag{5.37}$$

$$\frac{\partial Q_m(p,t)}{\partial p_m} = \int_{D_m} \frac{\partial f_m(p_m + \xi_m t_m)}{\partial p_m} h(\xi)\, d\mu - \sum_{k \neq m} \frac{\partial Q_m(p,t)}{\partial p_k} \langle\ 0. \tag{5.38}$$

Proof. This theorem is proved in a manner identical to that which showed Theorem 5.5, except that the proof of this theorem reflects the following difference: a marginal price increase dp_m (and dt_m) moves the location of the lower boundary r_{mk} in the integral of (5.36) as well as the upper boundary g_{mk}. □

Theorem 5.7 shows the signs of $\partial Q_m / \partial p_k$, for all $k \neq m$, are identical to those of the demand function of option m in Theorem 5.5. These $\partial Q_m / \partial p_k$ values satisfy the diagonal dominance condition, as does the demand for option m that does not satisfy the identical ordering condition.

Theorem 5.8. *The sensitivities $\partial Q_m / \partial p_k$ (and $\partial Q_m / \partial t_k$), estimated in Theorem 5.7, satisfy the diagonal dominance condition such that*

$$\left| \frac{\partial Q_m(p,t)}{\partial p_m} \right| \rangle \sum_{k \neq m} \left| \frac{\partial Q_m(p,t)}{\partial p_k} \right|.$$

Proof. This theorem is a direct consequence of Theorem 5.7. □

5.4.3 Necessary Conditions for Perfectly Elastic Demand

Under the identical ordering condition, an option in qualitative competition can have a thin catchment domain. Of more importance, the thin catchment domain is a decisive indication that the option has perfectly elastic demand, as is the case of perfectly elastic demand under quantitative competition. This aspect of qualitative competition is confirmed below, under the innocuous assumption that $a_k = 1$, for all k.

Firstly, we introduce a formula that estimates the thickness of D_m under the identical ordering condition. Fig. 5.7 depicts that the thickness of D_m is $(p_{m+1} - p_m)/t_m$, irrespective of the number of options that satisfy the identical ordering condition. This finding can be extended to option m, which satisfies the identical ordering condition with some options but not all options in qualitative competition, as explained below.

Lemma 5.9. *Suppose that option m in qualitative competition is a member of L options, which satisfy the identical ordering condition, and which do not fulfill the condition with other members of M options, for all $k \in \{L+1, \cdots, M\}$. Then, the thickness of D_m on the ξ_m axis in the $\xi_m - \xi_k$ plane, denoted by ψ_{mk}, is*

$$\frac{\psi_{mk}}{t_m} = \theta_m = \frac{p_{m+1} - p_m}{t_m}, \quad all\ k \neq m.$$

Proof. Lemma 5.8 shows that the above equalities hold, if option $k \in \langle 1, L \rangle$. The above equalities for options $k \in \{L+1, \cdots, M\}$ can also be proved in a manner identical to that for the proof for options $k \in \langle 1, L \rangle$. □

Lemma 5.9 shows that option m has the set D_m that has a common thickness, estimated by $(p_{m+1} - p_m)/t_m$, on the $\xi_m - \xi_k$ planes for all $k \neq m$, even though some competing options do not satisfy the identical ordering condition. On the other hand, (5.30) shows that the elasticity of demand for option m has an approximately inverse relationship with the thickness of D_m. Combining these two facts, the condition under which an option in qualitative competition has perfectly elastic demand can be characterized as below.

Lemma 5.10. *Suppose that option $m+1$ is the closest superior substitute under the identical ordering condition. Then, the demand for option m is perfectly elastic, if*

$$\theta_m = \frac{p_{m+1} - p_m}{t_m} \cong \varepsilon,$$

where ε is small but sufficiently larger than zero.

Proof. First, (5.24) shows that $Q_m = \sum_{k \neq m} SQ_{mk}$. Second, Lemma 5.9 indicates that the thickness of SD_{mk} on the $\xi_m - \xi_k$ plane, for all $k \neq m$, equals θ_m. Incorporating these two facts into (3.30) gives

$$E(Q_m(p,t))\rangle p_m \sum_{k \neq m} \frac{\partial Q_m(p,t)}{\partial p_k} \Big/ \theta_m t_m \sum_{k \neq m} \frac{\partial Q_m(p,t)}{\partial p_k} \cong \infty. \tag{5.39}$$

Here, the last approximation is the direct consequence of $\theta_m \cong \varepsilon$. □

An economic reasoning why the function Q_m with a small θ_m value is perfectly elastic is as below. Consumer i, who chooses option m, perceives that $0 \le \xi^i_m t_m - \xi^i_{m+1} t_{m+1} \le \theta_m t_m (= p_{m+1} - p_m)$ equivalent to $p_m + \xi^i_m t_m \le p_{m+1} + \xi^i_{m+1} t_{m+1}$. Hence, the condition that θ_m is small implies that the price difference $p_{m+1} - p_m (= \theta_m t_m)$, which is positive and fulfill the condition that $p_m + \xi^i_m t_m \le p_{m+1} + \xi^i_{m+1} t_{m+1}$, is also small. In this circumstance, even a small price increase Δp_m causes a large portion of consumers, who have been demanding option m, to feel that the resulting implicit price $p_m + \Delta p_m + \xi^i_m t_m$ is greater than $p_{m+1} + \xi^i_{m+1} t_{m+1}$. Therefore, this price increase shifts a large portion of the demand for option m to substitutes, for some $k \neq m$.

Secondly, we identify all necessary conditions for option m to fulfill the requirement that $\theta_m \cong \varepsilon$. One necessary condition to meet this requirement is as follows: option m must satisfy the identical ordering condition with a large number of options in qualitative competition, irrespective of the presence of options that do not fulfill the identical ordering condition with option m. The reason why this necessary condition must be included is explained below.

Suppose that L options, a subgroup of M options in qualitative competition, satisfy both the identical ordering condition in (5.32) and the trade-off condition in Lemma 5.7. Then, the sum of $\theta_m t_m$, for all $m \in \langle 1, L-1 \rangle$, is

$$\sum_{m \in \langle 1, L-1 \rangle} \theta_m t_m = \sum_{m \in \langle 1, L-1 \rangle} p_{m+1} - p_m \,\langle\, p_L - p_1 \,\langle\, \infty. \tag{5.40}$$

This equation implies that, if L is sufficiently large, some options $m \in \langle 1, L-1 \rangle$ have the high potential of $\theta_m \cong \varepsilon$.

However, the condition that the number L is very large is not sufficient for the outcome that option $m \in \langle 1, L-1 \rangle$ fulfills the requirement of $\theta_m \cong \varepsilon$. For example, some options m in qualitative competition do not fulfill the requirement, irrespective of their market shares, if their demand functions have a small value of F_m as defined by

$$F_m(p,t) = \frac{Q_m(p,t)}{\mu(D_m(p,t))}. \tag{5.41}$$

The function F_m estimates the average of integrand $f_m(p_m + \xi_m t_m)\, h(\xi)$ on integral domain D_m. This function is introduced so as to characterize perfectly elastic demands in a manner analogous to that used to define perfectly elastic demands for options under quantitative competition with the use of F_n defined in (5.15).

Thirdly, we introduce conventions that will be used to describe the geometry of a multiple integral that estimates the Q_m value. These conventions, which are almost identical to the ones introduced in Subsect. 5.2.3, are as follows. First, the thin and thick catchment domains are expressed by $\theta_m \cong \varepsilon$ and $\theta_m \rangle\ \varepsilon$, respectively. Under this convention, the equality $\theta_m \cong \varepsilon$ implies that $p_{m+1} - p_m$ is negligibly smaller than $p_L - p_1$, as can be deduced from (5.40). Second, the small and large values of F_m are expressed by $F_m \cong \delta$ and $F_m \rangle\ \delta$, respectively. Therefore, the equality $F_m \cong \delta$ implies that F_m is quite a bit smaller than the average of F_k for all $k \in \langle 1, L \rangle$, as estimated by $\sum_{k \in \langle 1,L \rangle} (Q_k / \mu(D_k))$.

Using the above conventions, we identify three types of demand functions for options $m \in \langle 1, L-1 \rangle$, in a manner analogous to that used to sort demand functions under quantitative competition. The first type fulfills the following two conditions: (i) $\theta_m \cong \varepsilon$, and (ii) $F_m \rangle\ \delta$. The demand in this type is perfectly elastic, and is negligibly smaller than total market demand. The second type satisfies the conditions that (i) $\theta_m \rangle\ \varepsilon$ and (ii) $F_m \cong \delta$. This type is imperfectly elastic, in spite of the fact that its share of total market demand is very small. The third type fulfills the two conditions that (i) $\theta_m \rangle\ \varepsilon$ and (ii) $F_m \rangle\ \delta$. This demand is imperfectly elastic, and its ratio to total market demand is significantly larger than zero.

We are now ready to present the full set of necessary conditions for an option in qualitative competition to have perfectly elastic demand. Using the conventions introduced above, we specify these necessary conditions as below.

Theorem 5.9. *Option m satisfies the condition such that $\theta_m \cong \varepsilon$, and thereby has perfectly elastic demand, if the option satisfies all the following conditions.*

(a) *Option m is a member of L options that constitute a subset of M options in quantitative competition and that consist only of options satisfying the identical ordering condition.*
(b) *Option m has more than one superior substitute that belongs to L options and L is a very large number.*
(c) *It holds that $Q_k(p,t) \rangle\ 0$, for all $k \in \langle 1, M \rangle$.*
(d) *The market share of option m is negligible but sufficiently larger than zero.*
(e) *The demand function of option m satisfies the condition that $F_m \rangle\ \delta$.*

Proof. The proof can be worked out in a manner analogous to the proof of Theorem 5.4 for quantitative competition, as shown in Appendix A.13. □

Finally, we analyze the elasticity of demand function for option $m \notin \langle 1, L-1 \rangle$, which does not have a superior substitute that satisfies the identical ordering condition. In this case, the range of CD_{mk} on the $\xi_k - \xi_m$ plane, for all $k \neq m$, can be estimated by solving only one inequality: $p_m + \xi_m t_m \leq p_k + \xi_k t_k$. Therefore, the thickness of D_m with respect to ξ_m mainly depends on the upper limit UB_m instead of the price of a superior substitute, as depicted in Fig. 5.5. For this reason, the set D_m is usually thick, irrespective of numbers of competing options. Therefore, the demand Q_m is imperfectly elastic, irrespective of its market share.

5.5 Mixed Competition

5.5.1 *Conversion into Iterated Indefinite Integrals*

In this subsection, we develop iterated indefinite integrals that estimate the market demand function of an option under a mixed form of qualitative and quantitative competition. For an option under mixed competition, the multiple integral that estimates demand for the option can be decomposed into three different groups of integrals. Each group of integrals has a functional form similar to that of one of the three previously analyzed, respectively, in Sects. 5.2~5.4. It is therefore feasible to convert the multiple integral for mixed competition into the sum of iterated indefinite integrals developed by combining previous analyses to convert multiple integrals into indefinite integrals, as demonstrated below.

In the case of mixed competition, the catchment domain D_{mn} can be expressed by

$$D_{mn}(p,t) = \{ \xi \in RV \mid \hat{\pi}_{mn} \le \hat{\pi}_{m'n'}, \text{ all } m'n' \neq mn \}. \tag{5.42}$$

This set D_{mn} can be decomposed into a number of subsets, $SD_{m'n}$, such that[2]

$$SD_{m'n'}(p,t) = \left\{ \xi \in RV \left| \begin{matrix} \hat{\pi}_{mn} \le \hat{\pi}_{m'n'}, \text{ all } m'n' \neq mn \\ \text{and all } m''n'' \neq mn,\ m'n' \end{matrix} \right. \right\}. \tag{5.43}$$

The subset $SD_{m'n'}$ satisfies the relationship similar to the one in Lemma 5.4, such that

$$\mu(SD_{m'n'}(p,t)) = \begin{cases} \rangle\, 0, & \text{if } D_{mn} \cap D_{m'n'} \neq \emptyset \\ = 0, & \text{if } D_{mn} \cap D_{m'n'} = \emptyset \end{cases} \tag{5.44}$$

$$\mu(D_{mn}(p,t)) = \sum_{m'n' \neq mn} \mu(SD_{m'n'}(p,t)). \tag{5.45}$$

as can be proved in a manner analogous to the proof of Lemma 5.4

By (5.45), it follows that

$$Q_{mn}(p,t) = \sum_{m'n' \neq mn} SQ_{m'n'}(p,t), \tag{5.46}$$

[2] In this section, we use an index system $m'n'$, instead of $mn, m'n'$, in order to simplify expressions. Therefore, the expression $SD_{m'n'}$, in (5.43) is equivalent to $SD_{mn,m'n'}$ under the index system used previously.

where

$$SQ_{m'n'}(p,t) = \int_{SD_{m'n'}} f_m\ (p_{mn} + \xi_m\, t_{mn}) h(\xi)\, d\mu. \tag{5.47}$$

For a multiple integral $SQ_{m'n'}$ such that $SD_{m'n'} \neq \emptyset$, the method to convert the multiple integral into an indefinite integral depends on the type of competition between options mn and $m'n'$, which can be sorted into three types.

The first type of competition between options mn and $m'n'$ is quantitative competition. The integrals $SQ_{m'n'}$ belonging to this type of competition are $SQ_{m(n-1)}$ and $SQ_{m(n+1)}$. For this type, the indefinite integral of $SQ_{m'n'}$ can be formulated in a manner almost identical to that used to convert SQ_{mk} in Lemma 5.5. The key difference is the method to estimate the lower boundary of the first iterated integral; that is, the lower boundary is estimated in a manner identical to that used for quantitative competition in Lemma 5.2.

For example, the indefinite integral of $SQ_{m(n-1)}$ can be formulated as follows:

$$SQ_{m(n-1)}(p,t) = \int_{SD^o_{m(n-1)}} \int_{l_{m(n-1)}}^{g_{m'n'}} f_m\ (p_{mn} + \xi_m t_{mn})\, h(\xi)\, d\xi_m\, d\mu^o_m, \tag{5.48}$$

where

$$SD^o_{m(n-1)}(\xi_m, p, t) = \left\{\xi^o_m \in RV^o_m \,\middle|\, \xi_m = \xi'_m,\ (\xi'_m, \xi^o_m) \in SD_{m(n-1)}(p,t)\right\}.$$

This indefinite integral has a functional form similar to that of the integral in Lemma 5.5. In this integral, the upper boundary $g_{m'n'}$ is estimated from equation $\hat{\pi}_{m(n-1)} = \hat{\pi}_{m'n'}$, in which $\hat{\pi}_{m'n'}$ should satisfy the condition such that $\hat{\pi}_{mn} \leq \hat{\pi}_{m(n-1)} \leq \hat{\pi}_{m'n'} \leq \hat{\pi}_{m''n''}$, for all $m'' \neq m$ and n''. On the other hand, the lower boundary $l_{m(n-1)}$ is estimated in a manner identical to that used to calculate the lower boundary l_n in Lemma 5.2.

The second type of competition is qualitative competition that does not satisfy the identical ordering condition. The indefinite integral of $SQ_{m'n'}$ for this type can also be formulated in a manner identical to that used to convert SQ_{mk} in Lemma 5.5:

$$SQ_{m'n'}(p,t) = \int_{SD^o_{m'n'}} \int_0^{g_{m'n'}} f_m\ (p_{mn} + \xi_m t_{mn})\, h(\xi)\, d\xi_m\, d\mu^o_m. \tag{5.49}$$

Here, the set $SD^o_{m'n'}$ and the function $g_{m'n'}$ are estimated in the same manner as that presented in Lemma 5.5.

The third type of competition is qualitative competition under the identical ordering condition. For this type of competition, Lemma 5.8 shows that the indefinite integral of $SQ_{m'n'}$, for all $m' \neq m$ and n' can be constructed in a manner identical to that used to estimate the iterated integral of SQ_{mk} in (5.36):

$$SQ_{m'n'}(p,t) = \int_{ED^o_{m'n'}} \int_{r_{m'n'}}^{g_{m'n'}} f_m(p_m + \xi_m t_m) h(\xi)\, d\xi_m\, d\mu^o_m. \tag{5.50}$$

Here, the set $ED^o_{m'n'}$ and the functions $g_{m'n'}$ and $r_{m'n'}$ are estimated in the manner presented in Lemma 5.8.

Finally, we evaluate the continuity of Q_{mn} with respect to (p,t). The function Q_{mn} is continuous in (p,t), except at the point where Q_{mn} has a catchment domain that overlaps that of demand functions for other options, as can be deduced from Theorem 5.1. Therefore, we can characterize the continuity of Q_{mn} as below.

Theorem 5.10. *The demand function Q_{mn} is continuous in (p,t), except at the point (p_{mn}, t_{mn}) such that*

$$\mu\left(D_{mn}(p,t)\right) \neq 0, \quad \textit{and} \quad (p_{mn}, t_{mn}) = (p_{mn'}, t_{mn'}), \ \textit{some } n' \neq n.$$

Proof. Equation (5.46) indicates that the continuity of Q_{mn} can be evaluated by analyzing, respectively, that of $SQ_{m'n'}$ in (5.48)~(5.50). The continuity of an indefinite integral for the first category in (5.48) can be characterized in the same manner used to prove the continuity of an indefinite integral for quantitative competition in the proof of Theorem 5.1. The continuity for the second and third categories in (5.49) and (5.50) can also be proved in the same manner used to show the continuity of the first category. □

5.5.2 Comparative Statics of Expected Demand Functions

In this subsection, we show that the comparative statics of the market demand function for an option in mixed competition also satisfies the gross substitute and diagonal dominance conditions. We work out the proof of these properties in a manner analogous to that used to show these properties of demand functions under quantitative and qualitative competition. We proceed with the proof of the properties using the iterated indefinite integral estimated in the previous subsection.

The partial derivative $\partial Q_{mn}/\partial p_{mn}$ (or $\partial Q_{mn}/\partial t_{mn}$) can be decomposed into two components, as in the case of $\partial Q_n/\partial p_n$ and $\partial Q_m/\partial p_m$. The first component is a change caused by decreases in the value of integrand $f_m(p_m + \xi_m t_{mn})$:

$$\int_{D_{mn}} \frac{\partial f_m(p_{mn} + \xi_m t_{mn})}{\partial p_{mn}} h(\xi)\, d\mu \, \langle\, 0. \tag{5.51}$$

This integral estimates a net decrease in service demand itself, as explained in the comments for Theorems 5.2 and 5.5.

The second component is a decrease caused by reductions in the volume of the integral domain D_{mn}. A marginal price increase dp (or dt) moves all the tangent planes of $D_{mn} \cap D_{m'n'}$, for some $m'n' \neq mn$, in the inward direction of D_{mn}. This movement of $D_{mn} \cap D_{m'n'}$ causes a decrease in the volume of D_{mn}, which equals an increase in the volume of $D_{m'n'}$. Moreover, on $D_{mn} \cap D_{m'n'}$, the value of f_{mn} equals that of $f_{m'n'}$.

Hence, the impact of the movement of $D_{mn} \cap D_{m'n'}$ on Q_{mn} values can be expressed as a kind of line integral, such that

$$\begin{aligned}\frac{\partial Q_{mn}(p,t)}{\partial p_{m'n'}} &= \frac{\partial SQ_{m'n'}(p,t)}{\partial p_{m'n'}} \\ &= \frac{1}{t_m}\int_{D_{mn}\cap D_{m'n'}} f_{m'n'}(p_{m'n'} + \xi_{m'} t_{m'n'})\; h(\xi)\; d\mu_m^o \;\geq\; 0.\end{aligned} \tag{5.52}$$

This formula for the movement of $D_{mn} \cap D_{m'n'}$ estimates the demand shift of option mn to other options for some $m'n' \neq mn$, as explained in the comments for Theorems 5.2 and 5.5.

The partial derivative $\partial Q_{mn}/\partial p_{mn}$ is the sum of two different impacts that are estimated in (5.51) and (5.52), respectively. This partial derivative satisfies the gross substitute and diagonal dominance conditions. These properties can be proved in a manner analogous to that used to show the properties for the three special cases of competition, as analyzed previously.

Theorem 5.11. *Whether or not option mn satisfies the identical ordering condition with other options in qualitative competition, a marginal price increase dp_{mn} (and dt_{mn}) brings about change in Q_{mn} and $Q_{m'n'}$ values, for some $m'n' \neq mn$, which satisfies the gross substitutability condition such that*

$$\frac{\partial Q_{mn}(p,t)}{\partial p_{m'n'}} = \frac{\partial Q_{m'n'}(p,t)}{\partial p_{mn}} \geq 0$$

$$\frac{\partial Q_{mn}(p,t)}{\partial p_{mn}} = \int_{D_{mn}} \frac{\partial f_m(p_{mn} + \xi_m t_{mn})}{\partial p_{mn}} h(\xi)\; d\mu - \sum_{m'n' \neq mn} \frac{\partial Q_{mn}(p,t)}{\partial p_{m'n'}} \langle\; 0.$$

Proof. The first equation for $\partial Q_{mn}/\partial p_{m'n'}$ can be proved in a manner identical to the proof of (5.25) in Appendix A.11. The second equation for $\partial Q_{mn}/\partial p_{mn}$ is a direct consequence of (5.51) and (5.52). □

Theorem 5.12. *The partial derivative $\partial Q_{mn}/\partial p_{m'n'}$ (and $\partial Q_{mn}/\partial t_{m'n'}$), for all $m'n' \neq mn$, satisfies the diagonal dominance condition such that*

$$\left|\frac{\partial Q_{mn}(p,t)}{\partial p_{mn}}\right| \;\rangle\; \sum_{m'n' \neq mn} \left|\frac{\partial Q_{mn}(p,t)}{\partial p_{m'n'}}\right| = \sum_{m'n' \neq mn} \frac{\partial Q_{mn}(p,t)}{\partial p_{m'n'}}.$$

Proof. It is clear from the two equations in Theorem 5.11. □

5.5.3 Necessary Conditions for Perfectly Elastic Demand

Here we confirm that previous analyses for perfectly elastic demands under quantitative and qualitative competition can be readily extended to the case of mixed competition. We focus these analyses on showing that, if an option satisfies either a set of necessary conditions for perfectly elastic demand in Theorems 5.4 or 5.9, then demand for the option is perfectly elastic. We work out the proof, under the simplifying assumption that $a_m = 1$, for all m.

To start, we enumerate all the cases in which demand for an option is perfectly elastic. Lemmas 5.3 and 5.9 identify all the cases in which an option has perfectly elastic demands under quantitative and qualitative competition, respectively. By combining the analytical outcome of the two lemmas, we below present all possible cases for perfectly elastic demands under mixed competition.

Theorem 5.13. *Option mn in mixed competition has perfectly elastic demand, if it satisfies one of three conditions:*

i. *Option mn has more than one perfect substitute such that catchment domain D_{mn} overlaps their catchment domains.*
ii. *Option mn has two close substitutes in quantitative competition, denoted by $m(n-1)$ and $m(n+1)$, which leads to an outcome such that the thickness of D_{mn} between $D_{mn} \cap D_{m(n-1)}$ and $D_{mn} \cap D_{m(n+1)}$, denoted by θ^n_{mn}, is small:*

$$\theta^n_{mn} \equiv u_{mn}(p,t) - l_{mn}(p,t) \cong \varepsilon. \tag{5.53}$$

iii. *Option mn has a close superior substitute in qualitative competition, denoted by $(m+1)n'$, which leads to an outcome that the thickness of D_{mn} on the ξ_m axis, denoted by θ^m_{mn}, is small:*

$$\theta^m_{mn} = \frac{p_{(m+1)n'} - p_{mn}}{t_{mn}} \cong \varepsilon. \tag{5.54}$$

Proof. Firstly, we prove Theorem 5.13.i for option mn that has perfect substitutes. Options mn and mn', for some $n' \neq n$, are perfect substitutes each others when they satisfy the condition that $(p_{mn}, t_{mn}) = (p_{mn'}, t_{mn'})$. At the point that fulfills the condition of perfect substitutes, the function Q_{mn} is not continuous, as shown in Theorem 5.10. Hence, the elasticity of Q_{mn} at that point is infinitely large, as can be shown in a manner similar to that used to prove Lemma 5.3.i.

Secondly, we present a formula that approximates the elasticity of demand for option mn that has a thin catchment domain and thus has perfectly elastic demands. The fact that option mn with a thin catchment domain has perfectly elastic demands is proved using the following equation:

$$E(Q_{mn}) \cong -\frac{\partial \mu(D_{mn})}{\partial p_{mn}} \bigg/ \frac{\mu(D_{mn})}{p_{mn}}. \tag{5.55}$$

This approximation for demand elasticity is developed by applying the fact that the value of $f_{mn}(p_{mn} + \xi_{mn}t_{mn})$ is almost identical for all the ξ_m values within a thin catchment domain, as explained in the proof of Lemmas 5.3 and 5.9.

Thirdly, we prove Theorem 5.13.ii for option mn that has a thin catchment domain due to keen quantitative competition. For options of this type, the smallest thickness of D_{mn} is determined by the catchment domains of two close substitutes in the same service group m, denoted by $m(n-1)$ and $m(n+1)$.

In this circumstance, the right side of (5.55) can be expressed as follows:

$$E(Q_{mn}))\rangle \frac{\partial\theta^n_{mn}}{\partial p_{mn}}\Big/\frac{\theta^n_{mn}}{p_{mn}} = \left(\frac{1}{t_m - t_{m\,(n+1)}} + \frac{1}{t_{m(n-1)} - t_{mn}}\right)\frac{p_{mn}}{u_{mn} - l_{mn}} \cong \infty. \tag{5.56}$$

This equation is proved below, through analyses for two different components that constitute the marginal change of $\partial\mu(D_{mn})/\partial p_{mn}$ in (5.55).

The first component is a decrease, which is caused by the inward movement of $D_{mn} \cap D_{m(n-1)}$ and $D_{mn} \cap D_{m(n+1)}$, due to an increase dp_{mn}, whereas the second component results from the inward movement of tangent planes $D_{mn} \cap D_{m'n'}$, for some $m' \neq m$ and n'. Moreover, it is assumed that thickness between $D_{mn} \cap D_{m(n-1)}$ and $D_{mn} \cap D_{m(n+1)}$ on the $\xi_m - \xi_{m'}$ plane, estimated by $u_{mn}(p,t) - l_{mn}(p,t)$, is very small, while the thickness for $D_{mn} \cap D_{m'n'}$ on the same plane is thick. Hence, an increase dp_{mn} results in an outcome such that the first component is significantly larger than the second component. Therefore, the first component plays the dominant role in determining the value of $E(Q_{mn})$; that is, (5.55) can be approximated by (5.56), which only reflects the first component.

Fourthly, we present the proof of Theorem 5.13. iii for option mn that has a thin catchment domain ascribable to quantitative competition satisfying the identical ordering condition. In this case, the smallest thickness of D_{mn} is determined by the price of the closest superior service group $m+1$, as shown in (5.54). Moreover, the change in $\mu(D_{mn})$ in (5.55) for an increase dp_{mn} can be reasonably approximated by counting only the impact of the change for the decrease of the smallest thickness.

Therefore, the approximation of $E(Q_{mn})$ for the smallest thickness of D_{mn} can be estimated as follows:

$$E(Q_{mn})\,\rangle \frac{\partial\theta^m_{mn}}{\partial p_{mn}}\Big/\frac{\theta^n_{mn}}{p_{mn}} = \frac{p_{mn}}{p_{(m+1)n'} - p_{mn}} \cong \infty. \tag{5.57}$$

The second and third terms of this equation approximates the elasticity for the inward movement of tangent planes $D_{mn} \cap D_{m'n'}$ for all $m' \neq m$ and n'. The third term shows that the elasticity is very large, given that $(p_{(m+1)n'} - p_{mn}) \cong \varepsilon$. Further, the first inequality of the equation reflects that the elasticity is the sum of the second term and an additional decrease caused by the inward movement of $D_{mn} \cap D_{m(n-1)}$ and $D_{mn} \cap D_{m(n+1)}$. □

Theorem 5.13 depicts that option *mn* with a thin catchment domain has perfectly elastic demand. It also proves that option *mn* has a thin catchment domain if the option faces either keen quantitative or keen qualitative competition under the identical ordering condition. Therefore, a set of necessary conditions for option *mn* to have perfectly elastic demands can be described as below.

Theorem 5.14. *Option mn in mixed competition has perfectly elastic demands, if it satisfies one of the following two conditions:*

(a) *Option mn and other options in the same group m fulfill the three necessary conditions for keen quantitative competition in Theorem 5.4.*
(b) *Option mn and other options, all of which have differentiated qualitative attributes from one another, fulfill the five conditions for keen qualitative competition in Theorem 5.9.*

Proof. The proof of why condition (a) or (b) leads to a thin catchment domain can be worked out in a manner analogous to the proof of Theorems 5.4 or 5.9, respectively. □

From Theorem 5.14, we can deduce that the key features of necessary conditions required for option *mn* to have perfectly elastic demand are as follows. First, option *mn* must have a very large number of competing options in either quantitative or qualitative competition under the identical ordering condition. Second, the demand function of option *mn* in either quantitative or qualitative competition must have a large average for demand intensity on the catchment domain of that option. Third, option *mn* in qualitative competition must have more than one superior substitute that satisfies the identical ordering condition for the option.

Part II
Cost Analyses for Congestion-Prone Service Systems

Chapter 6
Cost Analyses for the Basic Service System

6.1 Introduction

Congestion-prone service systems (or simply, *service systems*) refer to service production systems that exhibit or have the potential to exhibit congestion causing economic losses to its customers due to limited service capacity. While such congestion causes economic loss to customers, the decision to avoid congestion sometimes leads to excess capacity. Excess capacity, of course, brings its own adverse effects, including uneconomical investments and excessive operating costs to suppliers. It can therefore be said that service time, congestion in particular, is an important factor that affects both supplier and consumer choice, even though service time itself is not a factor contributing to supplier monetary costs.

Congestion has been an important consideration in previous studies for cost analyses of public transportation service, especially highway service (Mohring and Harwitz 1962; Wohl 1972; Keeler and Small 1977; Moon and Park 2002a). In those studies, congestion is a critical component of social cost paid by users. Such a social cost for congestion, called as user time time, is linearly proportional to total service time, including congestion delay. Further, user time cost is estimated by applying the assumption that value-of-travel-time is equal to the value-of-time referring to the marginal utility of time.

However, the existing approach for public transportation service is not directly applicable to forthcoming economic analyses of this study for both private and public services. First, user time cost is not a relevant component of cost functions for private service. Second, the use of value-of-time does not reflect the value of qualitative attributes packed in public service. Third, all previous studies estimate congestion delay by employing a service time function specific to the congestion-prone service system analyzed in those studies. Therefore, those studies are not applicable to cost analyses for other service systems.

The objective of this chapter is to develop the cost function of congestion-prone service systems through the application of a new modeling approach for the cost of a congestion-prone service system, termed *the full cost approach*. This proposed

D.J. Moon, *Congestion-Prone Services Under Quality Competition*, Advances in Spatial Science, DOI 10.1007/978-3-642-20189-9_6,

approach is an adaptation from the existing cost analysis approach for congestion-prone public transportation service. This adaptation is made so that the proposed approach can explicitly reflect differences not only in the level of congestion but also in the magnitude of qualitative attributes among service systems.

The full cost approach develops the cost function of both public and private service systems from cost minimization problems. It is important to note that cost minimization problems for public and private services are very similar. The only difference between the two cost minimization problems is the method used to quantify the value for unit service time. We below briefly describe the structure of these cost minimization problems, focusing on the approach used to accommodate congestion and qualitative attributes.

First, the full cost approach separates *throughput* from *capacity*, as does the existing approach for congestion-prone public transportation service. Throughput refers to the demand facilitated by a service system, whereas capacity represents the upper limit of throughput that can be facilitated by the system. This distinction is indispensible to accommodate congestion delay, which is decreasing in capacity but increasing in throughput.

Second, the cost function for the independent variable of throughput is developed from cost minimization problem, which estimates optimal capacity. Optimal capacity minimizes the total cost of public or private service systems. The total cost of public service systems is expressed as the sum of supplier monetary cost (monetary cost, for short) and user time cost, whereas the total cost of private service systems is formulated as the sum of monetary cost and revenue loss caused by congestion delay.

Third, the congestion delay of service systems is estimated by employing service time functions that are formulated so as to be as generalized as possible, in order to enhance their applicability to real service systems. According to queuing theory, the service time of congestion-prone service systems generally is increasing in throughput but decreasing in capacity. Moreover, the service time is affected by many factors such as service procedures and pattern of random arrivals at service systems. However, there is no universal service time function that can explicitly reflect differences in all these factors among service systems, as one can readily imagine. For this reason, this study devises and utilizes two different generalized formulas, each of which approximates service time for one of the two typical queuing systems most described in literature for queuing theory.

Fourth, the full cost approach estimates economic loss for congestion delay by applying *the value-of-service-time* estimated from the market demand function under the perception approach. This value-of-service-time for public service is the ratio of the marginal consumer benefit loss of service time to the same loss of price for the market demand function. This ratio for public service, called *the social value-of-service-time*, is equal to the mean net-value-of-time of total demands composed of individual demands with different net-value-of-times. On the other hand, the value-of-service-time for private service is the ratio of marginal revenue loss of service time to same loss of price for the market demand function. This ratio for private service, called *the private value-of-service-time*, is a kind of weighted average for the net-value-of-times of total demands.

Fifth, the cost minimization problem for public service and the same problem for private service are constructed, respectively, as the dual problems of a SWMP and PMP introduced later in this study. These two dual problems for a particular service system have an identical formulation, except for one difference in the method used to quantify the value-of-service-time between public and private services. Further, both social and private value-of-service-times are estimated from the optimal demands for the SWMP and PMP, respectively. Such a dual relationship for public service and the same relationship for private service will be explored in detail in Chaps. 11 and 8, respectively.

Sixth, the cost minimization problem for a service system explicitly reflects the consumer perception about the monetary value of qualitative attributes packed in the service of the system. Under the full cost approach, economic loss for service time is expressed as the multiple of service time and social or private value-of-service-time. Both social and private value-of-service-times are two different kinds of averages for the net-value-of-times of all users. Further, the net-value-of-time for a consumer reflects the consumer perception for the monetary value of qualitative attributes. Therefore, it is clear that the quality of a service system influences the cost of the system. This aspect of the full cost approach will be analyzed in great detail separately in Chap. 10.

In short, the full cost approach outlined above estimates the cost function of a service system for the independent variable of throughput from a well defined cost minimization problem for a public or private service system. This cost minimization problem is designed so that it is compatible with the choice problems analyzed in other parts of this study: utility, profit and social welfare maximization problems in Parts I, II and IV, respectively. Such a cost minimization problem for a public service system is called the Social Cost Minimization Problem (SCMP), and the counterpart problem for private service system is termed the Quasi-Cost Minimization Problem (QCMP).

Cost analyses in this chapter are confined to a special kind of congestion-prone service system, called *the basic service system*, which satisfies the following three restrictive conditions. First, the random arrival of demands forms a stable flow that has a constant mean arrival rate of demands throughout the entire analysis period. Second, supplier cost is composed only of capacity cost, which refers to the long-run costs necessary to construct a service system with a certain capacity. Third, supplier can optimally adjust capacity as well as price, so as to minimize total social cost or total quasi-cost.

This chapter is organized as follows. Section 6.2 introduces two different types of generalized service time functions and the SCMP for the basic service system, called the Basic Social Cost Minimization Problem (BSCMP). Section 6.3 develops various forms of marginal cost functions for the BSCMP and examines their economic implications. It is followed by Sect. 6.4, which extends the preceding analyses for the BSCMP to the QCMP for the private basic service system, termed the Basic Quasi-Cost Minimization Problem (BQCMP). That section also compares and contrasts social and private value-of-service-times.

6.2 Development of the Basic Social Cost Minimization Problem

6.2.1 Two Different Types of Service Time Functions

In queuing theory, the service time of a queuing system is defined as the expected value of the duration of service, from commencement to completion, which is common to all customers receiving services. This service time is generally composed of net service time and delay time due to congestion. Delay time usually refers to the time a customer spends in a queue before receiving service at facilities such as transportation terminals, retail shops, restaurants, theaters, etc. Delay time also includes additional time due to slow movement caused by excessive number of users at facilities such as highways, museums, etc.

Congestion delay is usually caused by two different types of randomness: randomness of service time required to facilitate each arrival, and that of time gaps between arrivals. These two different kinds of randomness generally result in congestion delays, even in those cases when mean arrival rate is less than capacity throughout the entire analysis period. Such a congestion delay is affected by the service procedure of service systems, termed *service technology* in this study, such as service priority, number of service channels, and distribution of service times consumed when facilitating individual customer. Moreover, congestion delay is influenced by the pattern of random arrivals, especially differences in the mean rate of random arrivals for various service periods.

On the other hand, service time functions estimate the service time of a service system for two independent variables: capacity and throughput. Service time functions considered in this study are categorized by types of service technologies, without explicitly accounting for differences in the arrival pattern of demands. One group of service technologies facilitates customers under a first-come-first-served policy, whereas the other one offers batch (or shuttle) services with vessels (or vehicles) operated in accordance with a predetermined schedule. The service time functions for these two different types of service systems, which will be applied in subsequent cost analyses, are presented below.

Assumption 6.1. Under the condition that the random arrival of demands forms a steady demand flow, the basic service system has a service time function, denoted by T, which can be expressed as one of the following two groups of formula.

(a) One group of service time functions is *homogeneous of degree zero* in mean arrival rate and capacity, denoted by s and c respectively, and is expressed by

$$t = T(s/c) = t^o + T^d(s/c),$$

where t is total service time per customer, t^o net service time, and T^d delay time function homogeneous of degree zero.

(b) Another group is *non-homogeneous* in mean arrival rate and capacity, and is expressed by

$$T(s,c) = t^o + \frac{1}{2y} T^d(s/c),$$

where T^d is the delay time function homogeneous of degree zero, c the service frequency of a service system analyzed, and y the sum of frequencies for all systems in competition, including the one analyzed.

(c) The functions T^d is positive, convex and twice differentiable in and c. It is also monotonically increasing in s, but decreasing in c.

The two service time functions in Assumption 6.1 are not formula specific to particular service systems, but rather generalized expressions applicable to a large group of service systems. They accommodate the effect of congestion on service time, through inclusion of delay time functions that are increasing in throughput but decreasing in capacity. Such a modeling approach is thought to reasonably approximate the service time functions of queuing systems analyzed in existing literature for queuing theory, such as Cinlar (1975).

Assumption 6.1 presents two different types of service time functions. The service time function in Assumption 6.1(a) is homogeneous of degree zero in both throughput and capacity. This service time function can be an approximation for service systems that provide individual services on a first-in-first-served basis. The second service time function in Assumption 6.1(b) includes an additional term $1/2y$, which leads to the non-homogeneity of the service time function. This service time function approximates the service time of systems that serve customers with vehicles operated under a predetermined schedule that can be controlled by the system operator.

Examples of the two different service systems examined above are as follows. The first-in-first-served service system comprises most congestion-prone service systems such as highway, seaport, retail store, personal communication media, clinics, entertainment facilities, etc. The examples of non-homogeneous service systems, which facilitate customers with vehicles operated under predetermined schedules, include various transportation services such as urban public transportation service, interurban and international passenger services, etc.[1]

Subsequently, the key feature of service time functions in Assumption 6.1 is the homogeneity of delay time function T^d, which leads to the following equality:

$$T^d(s/c) = T^d(\alpha s/\alpha c) \quad \text{and} \quad \frac{\partial T^d(s/c)}{\partial s} = -\frac{c}{s}\frac{\partial T^d(s/c)}{\partial c}, \tag{6.1}$$

[1] The queue length of this queuing system is estimated in Boudreau, Griffin, and Mark Kac (1962). The estimated queue length is not a closed-form solution.

where α is a positive constant. This condition implies that delay time depends only on the system utilization ratio, estimated by s/c, irrespective of the values of s and c.

Finally, we clarify the difference between expressions $T(s/c)$ and $T(s, c)$, which will be used in the forthcoming discussion. The expression $T(s/c)$ is applied only when it is necessary to include the distinction that the service time function is homogeneous. By the same token, the expression $T^d(s/c)$ is used in order to ensure that this delay time function is homogeneous. In contrast, the expression $T(s, c)$ applies not only to the case when function T is non-homogeneous but also to the case when it is not necessary to distinguish between whether it is homogenous or not.

6.2.2 Examples of Service Time Functions

The two different types of service time functions in Assumption 6.1 are formulated in expressions as generalized as possible, so as to maximize their applicability to real congestion-prone service systems. For this reason, these expressions are not sufficiently precise to reflect the uniqueness of certain service systems. Therefore, we introduce below a number of examples of these two functions, each of which is applicable to a specific type of service system.

One specific example of homogeneous service time functions is an approximation formula such that

$$T(s/c) = t^o + t^d \frac{Js/c}{1 - s/c}, \tag{6.2}$$

where $0 \langle J \langle 1$ is a parameter characterizing the queuing system.[2] This formula for the case of $J = 1$ becomes the exact solution to the system that facilitates random arrivals with a single channel, under the condition that both service time and time gap between arrivals have negative exponential distributions. Also, the formula generally has a smaller J value as the number of channels increases. The graphic representation of the formula for various J values is illustrated in Fig. 6.1.

An amendment of (6.2), which reflects that J is a function of capacity, does not satisfy the requirement of homogeneity. Such an amendment could have the advantage of reflecting that J has a smaller value, as the number of service channels increases. However, if the term J is not constant but rather a function of capacity, the service time function (6.2) is not homogeneous of degree zero. This implies that the homogeneity assumption for service time functions can only be applied to the case when the choice range of capacity is not very large.

Another example of homogeneous service time functions is the approximation formula for highway systems that facilitate peaking demands:

---

[2] The approximation formula, known as the Davidson formula, is available in many books dealing with transportation planning such as Manheim (1982).

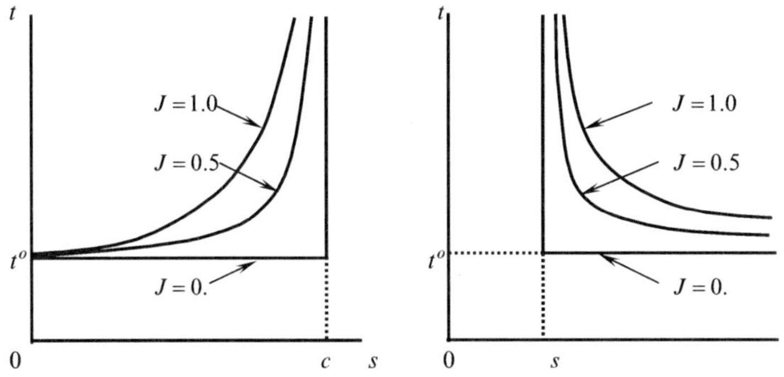

Fig. 6.1 A graphic representation of homogeneous service time functions

$$T(s/c) = t^o + t^d\left(\frac{s}{c}\right)^{\alpha}, \tag{6.3}$$

where $4.0 \leq \alpha \leq 6.0$ (Highway Capacity Manual, 1999). This service time function has a structure that can accommodate the case when mean flow rate exceeds capacity at a peak period; in contrast, the function of (6.2) cannot accommodate such a case.

Subsequently, the service time function in Assumption 6.1(b) is one special example of non-homogeneous service time functions for scheduled transportation services. The service time function of scheduled transportation services generally does not have a closed-form solution. For this reason, this study employs an approximation formula $T(s, c)$ that is more generalized than those commonly used in transportation systems analyses. In this formulation, the term $(2y)^{-1}T^d(s/c)$ estimates mean waiting time before finding an available seat.

One specific example of the approximation formula $T(s, c)$ is the following service time function for urban public transit not requiring seat reservations:

$$T(s, c) = t^o + \frac{1}{2c}\left(1 + \frac{Js/\tau c}{1 - s/\tau c}\right), \tag{6.4}$$

where τ is the seat capacity per vehicle and is a constant, as introduced in many books for transportation planning (e.g., Manheim, 1982). Here, the term $1/2c$ estimates the mean waiting time under the condition that a passenger can board the first vehicle that arrives, and the remaining term estimates waiting time caused by not boarding full vehicles.

Finally, the service time function of a service system that provides services under a fixed schedule that is not directly controlled by its operators can be approximated as a homogeneous service time function. Movies, live theater, and other performances are typical examples of this kind. For this kind of service, a plausible approximation of service time function could be the formula (6.4) in which service duration c is an uncontrollable parameter but seat capacity τ is the choice variable of the system operator. Under this alternative specification, the formula (6.4) is homogeneous of degree zero in τ and s.

6.2.3 Modeling of the Social Cost Minimization Problem

As pointed out in Sect. 6.1, the BSCMP is the SCMP for the basic service system that satisfies the following three restrictive conditions: steadiness of demand flows, no variable cost, and no restriction on choices for optimal capacity. The BSCMP for this special kind of congestion-prone service system is used to find an optimal capacity and its input, so as to minimize total social cost consumed to facilitate a certain throughput.

The BSCMP is constructed under the conventions that follow. First, the service system facilitates an arbitrarily given demand, expressed by the vector of individualistic throughput vector $S \equiv (s^1, \cdots, s^I)$, in which s^i is the demand of consumer i. Second, the net-value-of-times perceived by I consumers are $V \equiv (v^1, \cdots, v^I)$, where v^i is the deterministic net-value-of-time of consumer i. Third, the demand of I consumers forms a steady flow of random arrivals to the service system with a mean rate of $s \equiv \sum_i s^i$, under the condition that the analysis period is one unit of time. Hence, the mean arrival rate s equals the throughput of the service system. Under these conventions, the BSCMP of the supplier can be modeled as below.

Assumption 6.2. The BSCMP is used to estimate the capacity c and its input $x = (x_1, \cdots, x_J)$, so as to minimize total social cost, which refers to the sum of user time cost and capacity cost defined below.

(a) User time cost represents the monetary value of service time experienced by users, and is estimated by

$$User\ Time\ Cost = t \sum_i v^i s^i = t\bar{v}s.$$

Here, the term t, estimated by $T(s, c)$, represents the service time of a service system, whereas the term $\bar{v}$, estimated by $\bar{v} = \sum_i v^i s^i / s$, is a parameter that denotes the mean net-value-of-time for aggregated throughputs $s \equiv \sum_i s^i$.

(b) The capacity cost equals the monetary cost of inputs to capacity c and is estimated by

$$Capacity\ Cost = \sum_j p_j x_j,$$

where p_j is the price of input j, which is equal to the social cost. Also, the input vector x and capacity c satisfy the constraint such that $c \leq F(x)$, where the production function F is increasing and twice differentiable in x.

The BSCMP is constructed under a number of unrealistic conditions that are introduced to simplify the forthcoming cost analyses. However, some restrictive conditions can readily be replaced by more realistic ones that do not call for a fundamental change in cost analyses. We explain below these restrictive conditions and amendments to make them more realistic.

First, the condition that the net-value-of-time of a consumer is deterministic is not applicable to a consumer who follows the random perception approach. To accommodate uncertainty, the only necessary amendment is to replace the net-value-of-time v^i for a deterministic term s^i with the expected value of net-value-of-times with a certain distribution, estimated by $E\{v^i s^i(v^i)\}/E\{s^i(v^i)\}$. Therefore, the cost analysis of this chapter can be applied to the case for uncertainty without any further amendment, as will be addressed in Sect. 6.4.

Second, it is assumed that the variable cost of a supplier for throughput is zero. That is, supplier cost is defined as equal to capacity cost. This assumption is not applicable to most congestion-prone service systems. This assumption can be more realistically amended by adding variable cost to the total cost estimated in Assumption 6.1. Moreover, such an amendment does not require fundamentally different analyses to estimate various marginal costs, which are the key concern of cost analyses in this study, as will be shown in the next chapter.

Third, the condition that random arrival forms a steady demand flow implies that the mean arrival rate does not vary by period. Here, steady flow does not mean that the time gap between every arrival and its subsequent arrival is uniform, but rather that the average arrival rate does not vary by period. Such a steady flow allows the system operator to select the capacity so as to be constant throughout the entire analysis period, and thus greatly simplifies cost analyses. However, this condition is unrealistic in some cases of service systems. For this reason, the next chapter will demonstrate that analyses of a single-period problem considered in this chapter can readily be extended to analyses of a multi-period problem that accommodates the unsteady flow of random arrivals.

6.3 Cost Functions for the Basic Social Cost Minimization Problem

6.3.1 Optimality Conditions

The BSCMP is used to choose the capacity that minimizes total social cost. This solution for a specific capacity is the outcome of a trade-off between user time and capacity costs. When a chosen capacity is smaller than optimal, the additional user cost caused by increased congestion delays exceeds savings from the reduction in capacity cost. One method to estimate the optimal capacity for the BSCMP is presented below.

The BSCMP of Assumptions 6.1 and 6.2 is used to find the solution of (x, c, t), so as to minimize the social cost necessary to facilitate a given throughput s. The Lagrangian of this minimization problem, denoted by Z^o, is

$$Z^o(x,c,t,\kappa,\tau;s,V) \equiv \min\left\{\sum_j p_j x_j + t\sum_i v^i s^i\right\} \\ + \kappa(c - F(x)) + \tau(T(s,c) - t), \tag{6.5}$$

where $\kappa \rangle 0$ and $\tau \rangle 0$ are Lagrange multipliers. Note that the service time function $T(s, c)$ can be either homogeneous or non-homogeneous in both s and c.

The above BSCMP is incorporated with two constraints: the first constraint for the production of capacity, and the second one for the effect of chosen capacity on service time. For this reason, it is not straightforward to characterize optimality conditions for the BSCMP. We therefore decompose the BSCMP into two sub-optimization problems, each of which contains one constraint.

The first sub-optimization problem, denoted by Z^1, is used to find the solution for inputs x, so as to minimize the supplier cost required to construct an arbitrary capacity c under the constraint $c \le F(x)$:

$$Z^1(x,\kappa;c) \equiv \min\left\{\sum_j p_j x_j\right\} + \kappa(c - F(x)). \tag{6.6}$$

Here, the solution of κ is not equal to that of κ to Z^o, unless the above c value equals the solution of c to Z^o.

Let $(\hat{x}, \hat{\kappa})$ be the solution to Z^1. Then *the capacity cost function* of the service system, denoted by KC, which estimates the minimum supplier cost required to construct of an arbitrary capacity c, has the following expression:

$$KC(c) = Z^1(\hat{x}, \hat{\kappa}; c) = \sum_j p_j \hat{x}_j. \tag{6.7}$$

This capacity cost function has the mathematical property characterized below.

Lemma 6.1. *The marginal capacity cost, denoted by MKC, satisfies the following:*

$$MKC(c) \equiv \frac{\partial KC(c)}{\partial c} = \hat{\kappa} = p_j \Big/ \frac{\partial F(\hat{x})}{\partial x_j}, \text{ all } j.$$

Proof. (i) By the envelop theorem for constrained optimization problems, it follows that $MKC(c) \equiv \partial Z^1(\hat{x}(c), \hat{\kappa}(c))/\partial c = \hat{\kappa}$. (ii) The first order condition for Z^1 with respect to x_j gives the outcome such that $\hat{\kappa} = p_j/(\partial F(\hat{x})/\partial x_j)$. By (i) and (ii), it follows that $MKC(c) = p_j/(\partial F(\hat{x})/\partial x_j)$. □

The second sub-optimization problem is developed by substituting KC into Z^o. This sub-optimization problem, denoted by Z^2, is used to find the solution of (c, t), so as to minimize the total social cost under the constraint of $T(s, c) = t$:

$$Z^2(c, t, \tau; s, V) \equiv \min \left\{ KC(c) + t \sum_i v^i s^i \right\} + \tau(T(s, c) - t). \quad (6.8)$$

Here, the solution of (c, t, τ) is equal to that of the same unknown of Z^o, as will be shown later in this subsection.

Let $(\bar{c}, \bar{t}, \bar{\tau})$ be the solution to Z^2. Then, the term $Z^2(\bar{c}, \bar{t}, \bar{\tau}; s, V)$ represents *the total social cost function*, denoted by $TSC(s; V)$, such that

$$TSC(s; V) \equiv Z^2(\bar{c}, \bar{t}, \bar{\tau}; s, V) = KC(\bar{c}) + \bar{t} \sum_i v^i s^i. \quad (6.9)$$

This total cost function estimates the minimum total social cost required to facilitate an arbitrary amount of throughputs $\sum_i s^i$, under the constraint $T(s, c) = t$.

The differentiation of TSC with respect to t, called *the marginal social cost of service time*, estimates an increase in total social costs, which results from a one-unit increase in service time. This marginal cost of service time is estimated as below.

Lemma 6.2. *The marginal social cost of service time for Z^2 satisfies the following equalities:*

$$\frac{\partial TSC(s; V)}{\partial t} = \bar{\tau} = \sum_i v^i s^i = \bar{v}s.$$

Proof. The proof can be provided in a manner analogous to that proving Lemma 6.1. □

The decision-making problem Z^2 characterizes the optimal capacity of a public service system as below. A certain choice of capacity automatically determines service time through the constraint $T(s, c) = t$. The service time estimated by this constraint decreases in capacity. For this reason, the optimal choice of capacity is an outcome of the trade-off between the following two different effects of capacity increase: first, a capacity increase raises capacity cost in the objective function of Z^2; second, this increase has the opposite effect of decreasing user time cost. Such an optimal capacity can be characterized, as below.

Lemma 6.3. *The solution $\bar{c}$ to Z^2 satisfies the following:*

$$MKC(\bar{c}) = -\bar{\tau} \frac{\partial T(s, \bar{c})}{\partial c}.$$

Proof. Substituting the optimality condition in Lemma 6.2 into the first order condition for Z^2 with respect to c yields the above optimality condition. □

The optimality condition in Lemma 6.3 can be interpreted as follows. The term $\bar{\tau}$ represents the marginal social cost of service time, as shown in Lemma 6.2, whereas the term $\partial T/\partial c$ estimates the service time decrease caused by a one-unit increase in capacity. Hence, the right side of the optimality condition estimates the decrease in user time costs, which results from a one-unit increase in capacity. Therefore, the optimal capacity estimated from Lemma 6.3 equates the marginal capacity cost to the marginal user cost saving of capacity.

So far, we have analyzed the two sub-optimization problems Z^1 and Z^2, which are developed by decomposing the problem Z^o. Importantly, the solution to the combined problem of Z^1 and Z^2 is identical to the solution to Z^o, as shown below.

Theorem 6.1. *The solution* $(\bar{x}, \bar{c}, \bar{t}, \bar{\kappa}, \bar{\tau})$ *to* Z^o *equals the solution to the combination of two sub-optimization problems in* (6.7) *and* (6.10)*, and thereby satisfies the optimality conditions in Lemmas 6.1~6.3.*

Proof. The Kuhn-Tucker conditions for Z^o are identical to the combinations of the same conditions for Z^1 and Z^2. This implies the assertion. □

The three optimality conditions in Lemmas 6.1~6.3 are sufficient to estimate all the unknowns of Z^o, as explained below. The number of unknowns $(\bar{x}, \bar{c}, \bar{t}, \bar{\kappa}, \bar{\tau})$ in Z^o is $J+4$, where J is the number of variables in a vector x. Also, the number of equations available for estimating these unknowns is $J+4$: J equations from Lemma 6.1, two equations from Lemmas 6.2 and 6.3, and two remaining equations from the two constraints in Z^1 and Z^2.

6.3.2 The Social Marginal Cost of Throughput

The social marginal cost of throughput for a congestion-prone service system refers to the additional social cost required to facilitate one additional unit of throughput, under the condition that the service system efficiently serves throughput. In this subsection, we first estimate the social marginal cost through the differentiation of the total social cost function of (6.9) with respect to throughput. We subsequently estimate the same social marginal cost in two different forms both of which will be used in forthcoming cost analyses.

Firstly, we estimate the social marginal cost of throughput s^i for the *TSC* of (6.9). This social marginal cost, denoted by SMC^i, equals $\partial TSC/\partial s^i$, and can be characterized as below.

Theorem 6.2. *The social marginal cost SMC^i satisfies the following:*

$$SMC^i(s;V) = MUC^i(s;V) + SMCC(s;V) \tag{6.10}$$

$$MUC^i(s;V) = v^i T(s,\bar{c}) \tag{6.11}$$

$$SMCC(s;V) = \bar{v}\, s\frac{\partial T(s,c=\bar{c})}{\partial s} \equiv \bar{v}\, s\frac{\partial T(s,c)}{\partial s}\bigg|_{c=\bar{c}(s)} \tag{6.12}$$

Proof. By the dentition of SMC^i, it follows that

$$SMC^i = \frac{\partial TSC}{\partial s^i} = \frac{\partial \bar{Z}^o}{\partial s^i} = \frac{\partial \bar{Z}^2}{\partial s^i}, \tag{6.13}$$

where $\bar{Z}^o \equiv Z^o(\bar{x},\bar{c},\bar{t},\bar{\kappa},\bar{\tau};s,V)$ and $\bar{Z}^2 \equiv Z^2(\bar{c},\bar{t},\bar{\tau};s,V)$. Applying the envelop theorem to Z^o or Z^2 gives

$$\frac{\partial Z^o}{\partial s^i} = v^i\bar{t} + \bar{\tau}\frac{\partial T(s,c=\bar{c})}{\partial s}. \tag{6.14}$$

Substituting $\bar{\tau} = \bar{v}s$ into the above equation gives the equalities of the theorem. □

The cost function SMC^i estimates an increase in total social costs, as is required when increasing throughput from s^i to $s^i + 1$. This cost function can be decomposed into two functions, MUC^i and $SMCC$. The two functions in common quantify the effect of a marginal increase in throughput on user time cost at optimal capacity, but reflect two different kinds of effects, as detailed below.

One function MUC^i represents *the marginal user cost of throughput*. This marginal cost estimates an increase in total social costs, which is caused by a one-unit increase in throughput s^i with a net-value-of-time v^i, under the condition that the capacity adjustment to facilitate one additional throughput will not change service time. This marginal social cost equals the product of the net-value-of-time v^i specific to consumer i and the service time $T(s,\bar{c})$ common to all consumers, as depicted in (6.11). It is important that this marginal cost equals the average user time cost per visit of consumer i to the service system.

The other function $SMCC$ refers to *the social marginal congestion cost of throughput*, a synonym of *the marginal congestion cost of throughput for public service* . This marginal cost estimates an increase in total social cost, which is caused by a one-unit increase in service time, under the condition that capacity c is fixed to the optimum $\bar{c}$. This social marginal cost is expressed as the multiple of the following two terms: the social marginal cost of service time, estimated by $\bar{v}s$; and the increase in service time for a one-unit increase in throughput s^i, estimated by $\partial T(s,c=\bar{c})/\partial s$.

Moreover, the formula in (6.12) reflects two important aspect of the cost function $SMCC$. First, the expression $\partial T(s,c=\bar{c})/\partial s$ represents the increase in service time due to a one-unit increase in aggregated throughput s, under the condition that capacity is fixed to $\bar{c}$. Second, the expression $\bar{v}s\partial T(s, c = \bar{c})/\partial s$, in which s is a variable, implies that facilitation of one additional random arrival increases the service time cost of the additional customer as well as all existing customers.

Secondly, we estimate the social marginal cost from an amendment of the BSCMP for an aggregated throughput $s \equiv \sum_i s^i$, instead of individualistic throughputs $S \equiv (s^1, \cdots, s^I)$. This amendment, denoted by Z^3, specifies user time cost as $t\bar{v}s$, instead of $t\sum_i v^i s^i$, in which $\bar{v}$ represents social value-of-service-time:

$$Z^3(x, c, t, \kappa, \tau; s, \bar{v}) \equiv \min\left\{\sum_j p_j x_j + t\bar{v}s\right\} + \kappa\left(c - F(x)\right) + \tau(T(s, c) - t). \tag{6.15}$$

Let $\bar{Z}^3$ denote the Lagrangian Z^3 at the saddle point. Then, the differentiation $\partial\bar{Z}^3/\partial s$ gives the social marginal cost for aggregated throughput s, denoted by SMC. The relationship between SMC and SMC^i is analyzed below.

Theorem 6.3. *The functions SMC and SMC^i satisfy the following:*

$$SMC(s; \bar{v}) = MUC(s; \bar{v}) + SMCC(s; \bar{v}) = \frac{1}{s}\sum_i s^i SMC^i(s; V) \tag{6.16}$$

$$MUC(s; \bar{v}) = \bar{v}T(s, \bar{c}) = \frac{1}{s}\sum_i s^i MUC^i(s; V) \tag{6.17}$$

$$SMCC(s; \bar{v}) = \bar{v}s\frac{\partial T(s, c = \bar{c})}{\partial s} = SMCC(s; V). \tag{6.18}$$

Proof. The first equalities of (6.16)~(6.18) can be proved in a manner identical to the proof of Theorem 6.2. The second equalities of the three equations can readily be confirmed using the formulas in Theorem 6.2. □

Thirdly, we introduce another method that estimates the social marginal cost through two step analyses. The first step of this method estimates the optimal capacity $\bar{c}$ by solving the equation of Lemma 6.3. The second step develops the social marginal cost from an amendment of Z^3 (or Z^2), in which the capacity is a fixed term $\bar{c}$, called the short-run social cost minimization problem (SRSCMP).

The SRSCMP, denoted by Z^4, can be expressed as follows:

$$Z^4(t, \tau; s, \bar{c}, \bar{v}) \equiv \min\left\{KC(\bar{c}) + t\bar{v}s\right\} + \tau(T(s, \bar{c}) - t). \tag{6.19}$$

Let $\bar{Z}^4$ be the Lagrangian Z^4 at the saddle point. The differentiation $\partial\bar{Z}^4/\partial s$ represents the short-run social marginal cost function, denoted by $SRSMC$, which has the following property.

Theorem 6.4. *The function SRSMC satisfies the following equalities:*

$$SRSMC(s;\bar{c},\bar{v}) = SRMUC(s;\bar{c},\bar{v}) + SRSMCC(s;\bar{c},\bar{v}) = SMC(s;\bar{v}) \quad (6.20)$$

where

$$SRMUC(s;\bar{c},\bar{v}) = MUC(s;\bar{v}) \quad (6.21)$$

$$SRSMCC(s;\bar{c},\bar{v}) = SMCC(s;\bar{v}). \quad (6.22)$$

Proof. It suffices to show that $\partial \bar{Z}^4/\partial s = SMC(s;\bar{v})$. The differentiation $\partial Z^4/\partial t$ gives the optimality condition $\bar{\tau} = \bar{v}s$. Substituting $\bar{\tau} = \bar{v}s$ into the result of $\partial \bar{Z}^4/\partial s$ yields the outcome that confirms $\partial \bar{Z}^4/\partial s = SMC(s;\bar{v})$. □

Theorem 6.4 introduces the following three facts. First, the short-run cost of *SRSMC* for the exogenously given optimal capacity $\bar{c}$ that satisfies Lemma 6.3 is equal to the long-run cost of *SMC* for the SCMP that endogenously estimates optimal capacity. Second, the short-run cost of *SRSMC* can be decomposed into short-run marginal user cost, *SRMUC*, and short-run social marginal congestion cost, *SRSMCC*. Third, the two short-run costs, *SRMUC* and *SRSMCC*, for the given capacity $\bar{c}$ are equal to the two long-run costs *MUC* and *SMCC* respectively.

Finally, it should be noted that the functions $TSC(s;\bar{v})$ and $SMC(s;\bar{v})$ cannot estimate exact total social and social marginal costs, respectively, for the arbitrary value of aggregated throughput s, under the condition that the $\bar{v}$ value is fixed. The reasoning is as below. The term $\bar{v}$ is the mean net-value-of-time for a specific s value. It is also clear that, as the aggregated throughput s varies, the composition of individual throughputs s^i for all i also changes. Therefore, the average $\bar{v}$ is not constant unless one of the following two restrictive conditions holds: first, all throughputs s^i have an identical net-value-of-time; second, the ratio of s^i to s, for all i is constant for all s values.

The dependency of $\bar{v}$ values on throughput s does not mean that the application of $TSC(s;\bar{v})$ and $SMC(s;\bar{v})$ to analyses of the SWMP in Part IV will lead to erroneous or fallacious outcomes for costs, as explained below. The SCMP under the full cost approach is the dual of a SWMP. Moreover, the SCMP is constructed by applying the solution of demand to the SWMP. Therefore, the cost function estimated from the SCMP certainly estimates the exact values of $TSC(s;\bar{v})$ and $SMC(s;\bar{v})$ for the SWMP analyzed.

6.3.3 The Social Marginal Full Cost of Throughput

The social marginal cost of throughput, estimated in the previous subsection, does not contain any term that reflects the monetary cost paid by supplier. For this reason, the previous analysis of social marginal cost alone is not sufficient to draw conclusions about how the social marginal cost is related to marginal supplier's monetary cost. To identify the relationship between these two marginal costs, we introduce another kind of social marginal cost of throughput, termed *the social marginal full cost of throughput*. The definition of this marginal cost, the procedure to develop this cost, and the economic implications of this cost are presented below.

The social marginal full cost of throughput is similar to the social marginal cost of throughput. Both of the two different marginal costs estimate the additional social cost necessary to facilitate one additional throughput. However, the two marginal costs differ in the following respect: the additional user time cost for the social marginal full cost consists of the additional user time cost for existing users only, excluding one additional user; in contrast, the same cost for the social marginal cost contains the additional user time costs for all users, where "all users" consists of all existing users and one additional user.

The first step to estimate social marginal full cost constructs the Full Cost Minimization Problem (FCMP) for a public service system that facilitates an original throughput s with an optimal capacity $\hat{c}$. This FCMP is used to estimate a new optimal capacity that minimizes the additional social cost required to facilitate an arbitrary additional throughput e that can be either positive or negative. This additional social cost is estimated as the sum of the additional monetary cost AMC and the additional user time cost ATC.

The FCMP defined above, denoted by Z^5, can be expressed as follows:

$$Z^5(c; s+e, \bar{v}) \equiv \min\{AMC(c; s+e, \bar{v}) + ATC(c; s+e, \bar{v})\}, \tag{6.23}$$

where

$$AMC(c; s+e, \bar{v}) \equiv KC(c(s+e)) - KC(\hat{c}), \tag{6.24}$$

$$ATC(c; s+e, \bar{v}) \equiv \bar{v}s\,T(s+e, c(s+e)) - \bar{v}sT(s, \hat{c}), \tag{6.25}$$

$\bar{v}$ is the social value-of-service-time specific to the original throughput s, and $c(s+e)$ estimates the capacity used in facilitating total throughput $s+e$. Here, it should be noted that ATC estimates the change in the time cost experienced by existing users only.[3]

The second step estimates the optimal capacity that minimizes the additional social cost, the sum of AMC and ATC. To this end, we differentiate the unconstrained maximization problem Z^5 with respect to c:

[3] Assume that ATC is supposed to include the time cost of additional throughput e. Then, (6.25) would be amended as follows: $\bar{v}(s+e)\,T(s+e, c(s+e)) - \bar{v}sT(s, \hat{c})$. For this amended cost function, the marginal full cost is equal to the social marginal cost. This confirms that the social marginal cost estimates the additional time cost of all users, including one additional user.

$$\frac{\partial Z^5(c; s+e, \bar{v})}{\partial c} = MKC(\bar{c}(s+e)) + \bar{v}s\frac{\partial T(s+e, \bar{c}(s+e))}{\partial c} = 0, \tag{6.26}$$

where $\bar{c}$ is the function that estimates the solution of c to (6.26) for an arbitrarily given e value. This optimality condition is identical to that of Lemma 6.3, except that the social value-of-service-time applied is a constant $\bar{v}$, irrespective of e values.

The third step develops the social full cost function for throughput $s+e$, denoted by *SFC*, which estimates the minimum additional full cost for variable e. This cost function *SFC* equals the sum of *AMC* and *ATC* for the optimal capacity $\bar{c}$:

$$\begin{aligned} AFC\,(\bar{c}\,(s+e); s+e, \bar{v}) &= AMC\,(\bar{c}\,(s+e); s+e, \bar{v}) \\ &\quad + ATC\,(\bar{c}\,(s+e); s+e, \bar{v}). \end{aligned} \tag{6.27}$$

The final step estimates the social marginal full cost of throughput, denoted by *SMFC*. This marginal full cost is estimated by

$$SMFC(s; \bar{v}) = \left.\frac{\partial AFC\,(\bar{c}\,(s+e); s+e, \bar{v})}{\partial e}\right|_{e=0}. \tag{6.28}$$

This equation depicts that the marginal full cost represents the minimum additional cost, which is required to facilitate a one-unit increase in throughput from s.

The marginal full cost defined above can be decomposed into two components. The first cost component is *the marginal monetary cost*, denoted by *MMC*, such that

$$\begin{aligned} MMC(s; \bar{v}) &= \left.\frac{\partial AMC\,(\bar{c}\,(s+e); s+e, \bar{v})}{\partial e}\right|_{e=0} \\ &\quad - MKC\,(\hat{c})\frac{\partial \bar{c}(s)}{\partial s}. \end{aligned} \tag{6.29}$$

The second component is *the marginal time cost of existing users*, denoted by *MTC*:

$$\begin{aligned} MTC(s; \bar{v}) &= \left.\frac{\partial ATC\,(\bar{c}\,(s+e); s+e, \bar{v})}{\partial e}\right|_{e=0} \\ &= \bar{v}s\frac{\partial T(s, \bar{c}(s))}{\partial s}. \end{aligned} \tag{6.30}$$

These marginal costs satisfy the relationships presented below.

Theorem 6.5. *The social marginal full cost of throughput satisfies the following equalities:*

$$SMFC(s; \bar{v}) = MMC(s; \bar{v}) + MTC(s; \bar{v}) = SMCC(s; \bar{v}).$$

Proof. By (6.28), it follows that

$$\left.\frac{\partial SFC(\cdot)}{\partial e}\right|_{e=0} = MKC(\hat{c})\frac{\partial \bar{c}(s)}{\partial s} + \bar{v}s\frac{\partial T(s,\hat{c})}{\partial s} + \bar{v}s\frac{\partial T(s,\hat{c})}{\partial c}\frac{\partial \bar{c}(s)}{\partial s} \tag{6.31}$$

$$= \bar{v}s\frac{\partial T(s,\hat{c})}{\partial s}. \tag{6.32}$$

Equation (6.31) is none other than the sum of (6.29) and (6.30). Equation (6.32) is obtained by substituting (6.26) into (6.31). Also equations (6.31) and (6.62) imply the first and second equalities of the equation in theorem, respectively. □

We first examine the implication of the equality $SMFC = MMC + MTC$ in the above theorem. In this equation, the function MMC estimates the minimum monetary cost required to adjust an original optimal capacity to a new optimal, in response to a one-unit change in s, as shown in (6.29). The other function MTC estimates the change in the time cost of existing users, due to the supplier action to optimally adjust capacity, as depicted in (6.30). Therefore, the cost estimated by $SMFC$ refers to the sum of the marginal monetary cost of suppliers and the marginal time cost of existing users, under the condition that capacity is optimally adjusted in response to a one-unit increase in throughput s.

We next interpret the equality $SMFC = SMCC$ in the theorem. The function $SMCC$ in Theorems 6.2 and 6.3 estimates the additional user cost, which results from an increase in t due to a one-unit increase in s, under the condition that the supplier does not further invest to adjust the originally optimal $\bar{c}$. Therefore, the equality that $SMFC = SMCC$ implies that the social marginal full cost incurred under the condition that the supplier optimally adjusts capacity in response to a one-unit increase in s is equal to the change in social congestion cost for a one-unit increase in s under the condition that the supplier does not pay any cost to adjust an original optimal capacity.

6.3.4 Graphical Methods of Developing Various Social Costs

We here present graphical methods of developing various social cost functions for the independent variable of aggregated throughput, under the condition that all consumers have an identical net-value-of-time. The condition of identical net-value-of-time among consumers is certainly unrealistic. Instead, this condition allows the tangible form of various social cost functions to be developed through relatively simple graphical analyses, as presented below.

Firstly, we introduce a graphical method of developing the total social cost function $TSC(s;\bar{v})$, where $\bar{v}$ is the net-value-of-time common to all throughputs. The first step estimates the capacity cost function $KC(c)$ through application of Lemma 6.1. The second step draws a social cost function, denoted by $TC(s;c,\bar{v})$,

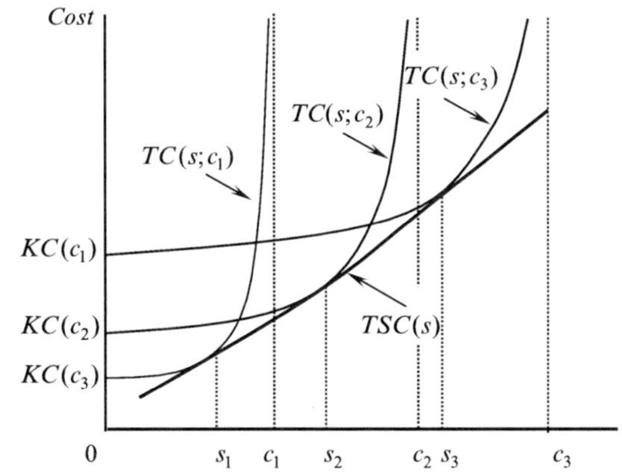

Fig. 6.2 Procedure to develop the total social cost function

that estimates the value of $KC(c) + \bar{v}sT(s,c)$ for varying throughput s under the condition of an arbitrarily given capacity c. For example, Fig. 6.2 depicts the graphs of $TC(s;c,\bar{v})$ for three different capacities: c_1, c_2 and c_3. The third step develops the function $TSC(s;\bar{v})$ for each s value, estimated by $\min_c\{TC(s,c;\bar{v})\}$, as defined in (6.9). The function $TSC(s;\bar{v})$ estimated in this manner is represented as a curve that forms the lower boundary for the collection of curves depicting the values of $TC(s;c,\bar{v})$ for all capacities, as illustrated in Fig. 6.2.

As a supplementary analysis, we introduce another graphical method that develops the graph of $TSC(s_1;\bar{v})$ from $TC(s;c_1,\bar{v})$. The first step calculates the optimal capacity c_1 for the given throughput s_1 by solving the optimality condition in Lemma 6.3. The second step draws the function $TC(s;c_1,\bar{v})$, which is monotonically increasing and convex in s, as stipulated in Assumption 6.1. Then, the value of $TC(s_1;c_1,\bar{v})$ is smaller than the value of $TC(s_1;c,\bar{v})$ for all other c values, as can be deduced from Theorem 6.4.

Secondly, we develop the social marginal cost function $SMC(s;\bar{v})$ for the example analyzed above. One graphical method of estimating $SMC(s;\bar{v})$ involves differentiating the graph of $TSC(s;\bar{v})$ in Fig. 6.2 with respect to s. However, this method has a shortcoming in that it does not allow for the decomposition of $SMC(s;\bar{v})$ into $MUC(s;\bar{v})$ and $MCC(s;\bar{v})$. For this reason, we estimate $MUC(s;\bar{v})$ and $SMCC(s;\bar{v})$ for each s value by applying optimality conditions in (6.20)–(6.22) for the SRSCMP, as explained below.

Suppose that facilitation of throughput s_3 requires optimal capacity c_3. Then, the value of *SRSMC* for the fixed capacity c_3 can be estimated by differentiating $TC(s;c_3,\bar{v})$ $(= KC(c_3) + \bar{v}\,sT(s;c_3,\bar{v}))$ with respect to s. This differentiation, which is estimated in (6.20), yields the function *SRSMC*, expressed by $\bar{v}T(s;c_3,\bar{v})$ $+\bar{v}s\partial T(s;c_3,\bar{v})/\partial s$. This shows that the graph of *SRSMC* should be located above the graph of *SRMUC*, estimated by $\bar{v}T(s;c_3,\bar{v})$, since $\bar{v}T(s,c_3,\bar{v})$ is increasing and concave in s, as depicted in Fig. 6.3. Furthermore, (6.21) and (6.22) indicate, respectively, that $\bar{v}T(s_3;c_3,\bar{v}) = MUC(s_3;\bar{v})$ and $\bar{v}s\partial T(s_3;c_3,\bar{v})/\partial s = MCC(s_3;\bar{v})$, as also depicted in Fig. 6.3.

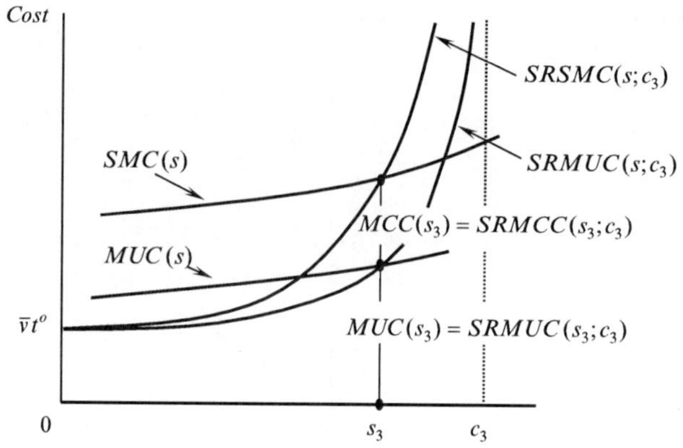

Fig. 6.3 Representation of social marginal cost functions

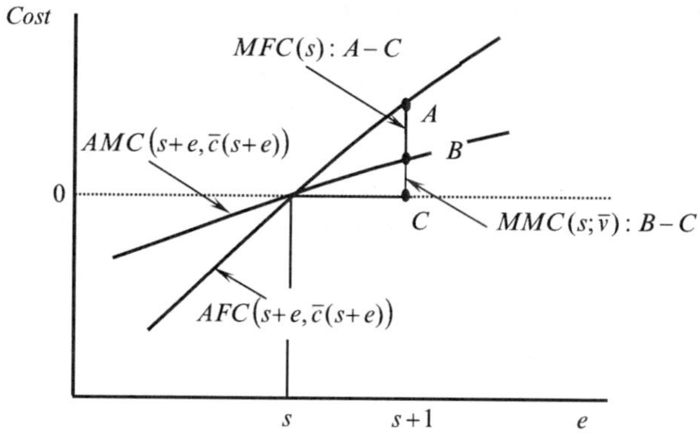

Fig. 6.4 Relationship between *MFC* and *MMC*

Thirdly, we schematically illustrate the relationship between *MMC* and *SMFC* in (6.29) and (6.28), respectively. We first draw the functions *AMC* and *SFC*, which satisfy the relationship in (6.27). The graphs of *AMC* and *SFC* are drawn so that they satisfy the following two requirements, as illustrated in Fig. 6.4: $AMC(s,\hat{c};\bar{v}) = SFC(s,\hat{c};\bar{v}) = 0$; and $AMC(s+e,\bar{c}(s+e);\bar{v}) \neq SFC(s+e, \bar{c}(s+e);\bar{v})$, for all $e \neq 0$, unless $T(s+e,\bar{c}(s+e)) - T(s,\hat{c}) = 0$.

The values of $MMC(s;\bar{v})$ and $SMFC(s;\bar{v})$ at a certain throughput s are the slopes of $AMC(s+e,\bar{c}(s+e);\bar{v})$ and $SFC(s+e,\bar{c}(s+e);\bar{v})$, respectively, at $e = 0$, as depicted in the figure. It usually holds that $MMC(s;\bar{v}) \neq SMFC(s;\bar{v})$, except for a special case of $AMC(s+e,\bar{c}(s+e);\bar{v}) = SFC(s+e,\bar{c}(s+e);\bar{v})$ for all $e \neq s$. It should also be noted that, in order to estimate the value of *MMC* and *SMFC* for another throughput $s' \neq s$, it is required to newly construct $AMC(s'+e, \bar{c}(s'+e);\bar{v}')$ and $AFC(s'+e,\bar{c}(s'+e);\bar{v}')$, in which $\bar{v}'$ is the social value-of-service-time for s'. Finally, note that the condition under which the value of

$MMC(s;\bar{v})$ is larger or smaller than that of $SMFC(s;\bar{v})$ will be considered in Sect. 7.1.

6.4 Extensions to the Basic Quasi-Cost Minimization Problem

6.4.1 Modeling of the Quasi-Cost Minimization Problem

It would be logical and usual to introduce a dual problem after presenting a primal optimization problem. In this chapter, however, we first introduce the BQCMP that will be proved to be a dual of the PMP for a congestion-prone service system analyzed in Part III. This BQCMP has a formulation almost identical to that of the BSCMP, even though the economic implication of these two cost minimization problems are fundamentally different, as explained below.

Firstly, we introduce an approach to model the BQCMP for a private service firm. The BQCMP is modeled in a formulation identical to that of the BSCMP in Assumption 6.1, except for one difference made to the method used to estimate value-of-service-time for private service, termed private value-of-service-time. The specification of such a BQCMP is presented below, highlighting the difference between this and that of the BSCMP in Assumption 6.2.

Assumption 6.3. The BQCMP is used to estimate the solution of capacity c and input $x = (x_1, \cdots, x_J)$, so as to minimize total quasi-cost, which refers to the sum of quasi-cost for service time and capacity cost defined below:

(a) Quasi-cost for service time estimates the implicit revenue loss ascribable to service time t and is estimated by

$$\textit{Quasi-Cost for Service Time} = \breve{v}\, ts.$$

Here, $\breve{v}$ is the private value-of-service-time defined by

$$\breve{v} = \frac{\partial \bar{q}(p,t)}{\partial t} \Big/ \frac{\partial \bar{q}(p,t)}{\partial p},$$

where $\bar{q}$ is the demand function under the deterministic perception approach, and satisfies the equality that $\bar{q} = \sum_i \bar{q}^i \equiv \sum_i s^i = s$

(b) The capacity cost for input x to capacity c is estimated by

$$\textit{Capacity Cost} = \sum_j p_j x_j,$$

where p_j is the market price of j. Also, input x and capacity c satisfy the constraint such that $c \leqslant F(x)$.

Secondly, we present the reasoning why the objective function of the BQCMP comprises the quasi-cost for service time, estimated by $\breve{v}ts$. This quasi-cost reflects the implicit revenue loss, which is caused by demand decrease due to service time increase. At first glance, it is unclear why the implicit revenue loss term is included, given that customer service time does not directly affect supplier's monetary cost. Upon reflection, however, one sees that it is infeasible to properly characterize the optimal choice of a supplier selling congestion-prone services without including a term that reflects the effect of service time change on supplier cost, as explained below.

Suppose that the service time experienced by users is determined by the service time function in Assumption 6.1. If we ignore the effect of service time on supplier cost, the cost minimization problem of a service system, denoted by Z', would be

$$Z'(c,t,\mu,\varphi;s) \equiv \min\{KC(c)\} + \mu(T(s,c)-t) + \varphi(s-c), \tag{6.33}$$

where $\varphi(s-c)$ depicts the constraint that the domain of $T(s,c)$ is generally confined to $c \geqslant s$, as schematically illustrated in Fig. 6.1.

This optimization problem has the solution of c, which approaches throughput s, and the solution of t, which approaches infinity. Therefore, the service demand under the perception approach, which is sensitive to service time, approaches zero; that is, a positive value of s is not compatible with the solution to Z'. This examination of the logic behind the improper cost minimization problem indicates that service time must certainly include congestion delays as an important cost factor for private congestion-prone service systems.

Thirdly, we examine the precise economic implication of the quasi-cost $\breve{v}ts$ in the BQCMP. This quasi-cost has an expression identical to the counterpart cost $\bar{v}ts$ in the BSCMP. However the method used to estimate private value-of-service-time $\breve{v}$ fundamentally differs from that of the counterpart term $\bar{v}$. This difference leads to the different economic implication of $\breve{v}ts$ from that of $\bar{v}ts$, as explained next.

The net-value-of-time v^i in the BSCMP is estimated from optimality conditions for the utility maximization problem under the deterministic perception approach. Theorem 2.5 for the net-value-of-time indicates that the demand of consumer i, denoted by $\bar{q}^i$, satisfies the following optimality condition:

$$v^i = \frac{\partial U^i(\bar{y}^i,\bar{z}^i)}{\partial t} \bigg/ \frac{\partial U^i(\bar{y}^i,\bar{z}^i)}{\partial p} \tag{6.34}$$

$$= \frac{\partial \bar{q}^i}{\partial t} \bigg/ \frac{\partial \bar{q}^i}{\partial p}, \tag{6.35}$$

where $\bar{y}^i(= a\,\bar{q}^i)$ is demand for a prime commodity, and $\bar{z}^i(\equiv (z_1^i,\cdots z_K^i))$ is demand for hedonic commodities.

Equation (6.34) indicates that the net-value-of-time v^i is the ratio of a change in consumer utility for a one-unit increase in service time to a change in utility for a one-unit increase in price. It can therefore be argued that the user time cost $t\bar{v}s$ represents the monetary value of consumer benefits for service time t. Further, it can be said the term $\bar{v}$, called the social value-of-service-time, represents the mean net-value-time for aggregated throughput s.

On the other hand, Assumption 6.3 depicts that the private value-of-service-time $\breve{v}$ is equal to the ratio of $\partial\bar{q}/\partial t$ to $\partial\bar{q}/\partial p$. This ratio is equivalent to the ratio of $p\partial\bar{q}/\partial t$ to $p\partial\bar{q}/\partial p$. Here, the term $p\partial\bar{q}/\partial t$ estimates the revenue loss, which results from a demand decrease due to a marginal service time increase dt, whereas the term $p\partial\bar{q}/\partial p$ represents the revenue loss for a marginal price increase dp.

Therefore, it can be said the private value-of-service-time $\breve{v}$ is the ratio of revenue changes for a marginal service time increases to revenue changes for a marginal price increase. In other words, the revenue loss for a one-unit increase in service time equals the revenue loss for a price increase in $\breve{v}$ monetary units. Therefore, the term $\breve{v}\,ts$ can be interpreted as the equivalent of total service time ts to a revenue loss experienced by service system operators, including public agencies.

6.4.2 The Marginal Quasi-Cost of Throughput

The BQCMP of Assumption 6.3 has a Lagrangian identical to that of the BSCMP for aggregated throughput, except that private value-of-service-time replaces the social value. For this reason, it is not necessary to iterate the mathematical analysis that develops the formulas equivalent to the ones presented in the previous section. However, the economic implications of the formulas for the BQCMP fundamentally differ from those of the previous section. We therefore reintroduce some formulas that will be referred to in subsequent analyses of this study and interpret the economic implications of these formulas.

The BQCMP for aggregated throughput in Assumption 6.3 has the Lagrangian Z^6, which has an expression almost identical to that of (6.15):

$$Z^6\left(x, c, t, \kappa, \tau; s, \breve{v}\right) \equiv \min\left\{\sum_j p_j x_j + t\breve{v}s\right\} + \kappa\,(c - F(x)) + \tau(T(s,c) - t). \tag{6.36}$$

The only single difference between (6.36) and (6.15) is the replacement of $\bar{v}$ with $\breve{v}$. Hence, under that convention that the solution of Z^6 is $(\bar{x}, \bar{c}, \bar{t}, \bar{\kappa}, \bar{\tau})$, the optimality condition for this BQCMP, which is equivalent to that of Lemmas 6.1 and 6.2 for the BSCMP, can be expressed, as below.

Lemma 6.4. *The solution $\bar{\kappa}$ to Z^6 equals the marginal capacity cost MKC, and satisfies the following:*

$$MKC(\bar{c}) \equiv \frac{\partial KC(\bar{c})}{\partial c} = \bar{\kappa} = p_j \Big/ \frac{\partial F(\bar{x})}{\partial x_j}, \quad all\ j.$$

Lemma 6.5. *The solution $\bar{\tau}$ to Z^6, termed the marginal revenue loss of service time, satisfies the following equality: $\bar{\tau} = \breve{v}s$.*

Lemma 6.4 indicates that a one-unit increase in service time, which is caused by congestion, leads to a revenue reduction, as estimated by $\breve{v}s$. This implies that a profit maximizer must recognize the effect on congestion delay when making a choice regarding capacity. For example, the choice of a smaller capacity than would be optimal leads to a revenue loss due to a decrease in demand, which exceeds reduction in capacity cost.

Next, we present the optimality condition for the choice of capacity, which has the same expression as that of Lemma 6.3.

Lemma 6.6. *The solution $\bar{c}$ to Z^6 satisfies the following:*

$$MKC(\bar{c}) = -\breve{v}s\frac{\partial T(s,\bar{c})}{\partial c}.$$

The right side of the equation in Lemma 6.5 is the product of the following two terms: the term $-\bar{\tau}(= -\breve{v}s)$ that represents the marginal revenue increase by a one-unit decrease in service time; and the term $\partial T/\partial c$ that estimates the marginal decrease in service time due to a one-unit expansion of capacity. Hence, the right side of the equation represents the marginal increase in revenue, brought about by a one-unit increase in capacity. Therefore, Lemma 6.6 implies that the marginal capacity cost at optimal capacity should be equal to the marginal increase in revenue, which is accrued by a decrease in service time due to a one-unit increase in capacity.

Finally, we estimate the marginal quasi-cost of aggregated throughput s, denoted by MQC. The marginal quasi-cost refers to the additional quasi-cost required to facilitate one additional throughput under the condition that the service system efficiently facilitates throughput. This marginal cost, estimated by $\partial \bar{Z}^6/\partial s$, has an expression very similar to that of Theorem 6.3, as presented below.

Theorem 6.6. *The function $MQC(s;\breve{v})$ satisfies the following:*

$$MQC(s;\breve{v}) = MRL(s;\breve{v}) + MCC(s;\breve{v}) \tag{6.37}$$

$$MRL(s;\breve{v}) = \breve{v}\,T(s,\bar{c}) \tag{6.38}$$

$$MCC(s;\breve{v}) = \breve{v}\,s\frac{\partial T(s,c=\bar{c})}{\partial s}. \tag{6.39}$$

The function *MRL* estimates *the marginal revenue loss of throughput for service time*, under the condition that facilitation of one additional unit of throughput does not change service time. This marginal revenue loss estimates the revenue loss for the service-time consumed in facilitating one additional unit of throughput under the condition of "fixed service time". Hence, this marginal revenue loss equals the product of the private value-of-service-time, $\breve{v}$, and the service time per throughput, estimated by $T(s, \bar{c})$, as depicted in (6.38).

The other function *MCC* refers to *the marginal congestion cost of throughput for private service* (*marginal congestion cost of throughput,* for short). This marginal congestion cost, a kind of marginal quasi-cost, represents the revenue loss that results from an "additional increase in service time" due to a one-unit increase in throughput under the condition that capacity c is fixed to an original optimal capacity $\bar{c}$. Equation (6.39) shows that the marginal congestion cost equals the multiple of the marginal revenue loss of service time, $\breve{v}s$, and the increase in service time for a marginal increase in throughput, $\partial T(s, c = \bar{c})/\partial s$.

6.4.3 The Marginal Full Cost of Throughput

The marginal full cost of throughput for private service systems represents the additional quasi-cost required to adjust an original optimal capacity to a new optimum in response to a one-unit increase in throughput. This marginal full cost of private service systems can be developed in a manner identical to that of public service systems. However, its economic implication fundamentally differs from the marginal full cost for public service systems. Focusing on this difference, we analyze the marginal full cost of private service systems in a manner analogous to that of public service systems.

To start, we develop the FCMP for a private basic service system. This FCMP for private service is the counterpart of the FCMP for public service in (6.23). This cost minimization problem, denoted by Z^7, is

$$Z^7(c; s+e, \breve{v}) \equiv \min\left\{AMC(c;\ s+e, \breve{v}) + ATC(c; s+e, \breve{v})\right\}, \tag{6.40}$$

where

$$AMC(c; s+e, \breve{v}) \equiv KC(c(s+e)) - KC(\hat{c})$$

$$ATC(c\,; s+e, \breve{v}) \equiv \breve{v}sT(s+e, c(s+e)) - \breve{v}sT(s, \hat{c}).$$

The function *AMC* estimates the additional capacity cost spent in the process to adjust capacity. The function *ATC* represents the additional revenue change that is incurred by a service time change due to capacity adjustment.

Proceeding with analyses with Z^7 in a manner identical to that which led from Z^5 to (6.27) gives the full cost function for a variable e, denoted by FC, as shown below.

$$FC\left(\bar{c}\left(s+e\right);s+e,\breve{v}\right) = AMC\left(\bar{c}\left(s+e\right);s+e,\breve{v}\right) + ATC\left(\bar{c}\left(s+e\right);s+e,\breve{v}\right). \tag{6.41}$$

Differentiating FC with respect to e yields the marginal full cost, denoted by MFC. This marginal cost satisfies the relationship identical to that of Theorem 6.5.

Theorem 6.7. *The solution to the BQCMP satisfies the following:*

$$MFC(s;\breve{v}) = MMC(s;\breve{v}) + MTC(s;\breve{v}) = MCC(s;\breve{v}),$$

where

$$MMC(s;\breve{v}) = MKC(\hat{c})\frac{\partial\bar{c}(s)}{\partial s}$$

$$MTC(s;\breve{v}) = \breve{v}s\frac{\partial T(s,\hat{c})}{\partial s}.$$

The equality $MFC = MMC + MTC$ can be interpreted as below. The function MMC estimates the marginal monetary cost required to adjust an original optimal capacity for throughput s to a new optimum in response to a one-unit increase in throughput. The function MTC calculates the revenue loss, which is brought about by a service time change due to a supplier action to optimally adjust capacity. Therefore, the function MFC estimates a change in the sum of monetary cost and revenue change for service time change, both of which are incurred in the process of adjusting an original optimal capacity to a new optimal.

Therefore, the equality $MFC = MCC$ can be interpreted as follows. The function MCC estimates a marginal reduction in revenue, which is caused by a change in t due to a one-unit increase in s, under the condition that the supplier does not invest further to adjust the original optimal capacity. Hence, the equality that $MFC = MCC$ implies the following: the additional quasi-cost incurred by a supplier action to optimally adjust capacity in response to a one-unit increase in s is equal to the revenue loss caused by a decision to maintain the original optimal capacity without further investment.

6.4.4 Comparison Between Social and Private Value-of-Service-Times

Both social and private value-of-service-times for a service system are the average of different net-value-of-times for all throughputs. However, the methods used to estimate these two different averages fundamentally differ. In spite of this difference, in the case of deterministic demands, if all throughputs have an identical net-value-of-time, these two different averages become identical. In the case of expected demands, if demands for the system are very elastic but finite, these two averages are approximately identical. These facts are proved below.

To begin, we reintroduce the definition of social value-of-service-time and estimate the range of this value for the demand of a service system under the deterministic perception approach. Under this approach, the social value-of-service-time equals the mean net-value-of-time of total demands and satisfies the following relationship:

$$\bar{v} = \sum_i v^i \bar{q}^i \Big/ \sum_i \bar{q}^i \in \left[\min_i \{v^i\},\ \max_i \{v^i\}\right]. \tag{6.42}$$

Here, the relationship "$\in$" is the consequence of $\bar{q}^i \rangle 0$ for all i.

We next present the definition of private value-of-service-time and estimate the range of this value in a manner similar to that used in (6.42). Using (6.35), the private value-of-service-time defined in Assumption 6.3 can alternatively be expressed as follows:

$$\breve{v} = \sum_i v^i \frac{\partial \bar{q}^i}{\partial p} \Big/ \sum_i \frac{\partial \bar{q}^i}{\partial p} \in \left[\min_i \{v^i\},\ \max_i \{v^i\}\right]. \tag{6.43}$$

Here, the relationship "$\in$" holds, because $\partial \bar{q}^i / \partial p \ \langle\ 0$ for all i.

Equations (6.42) and (6.43) show that both social and private value-of-service-times depend on the net-value-of-times of individual users. Moreover, each net-value-of-time v^i reflects the perceived value of a user for the qualitative attributes of service systems. It can therefore be argued that the service quality of a service system affects both social and private value-of-service-times and, thereby, the total and marginal full costs of throughput for both public and private services.[4]

We next analyze the relationship between the social and private value-of-service-times. Equations (6.42) and (6.43) show that social and private value-of-service-times are both averages for the different net-value-of-times of users, although the methods used to estimate averages differ. To be specific, the social value-of-service-time $\bar{v}$ is the arithmetic average of $v^i s^i$ values, whereas the private value $\breve{v}$ is the average of v^i values for the weight factor $\partial \bar{q}^i / \partial p$. These two different value-of-service-times satisfy the following relationship.

---

[4] From (6.41) and (6.42), we readily deduce the following: an improvement in service quality has the effect of reducing various costs affected by the social or private value-of-time. However, this does not mean that a service system with a higher quality has a smaller marginal full cost. These aspects of the full cost approach will be thoroughly explored in Sect. 10.4.

Theorem 6.8. *Under the deterministic perception approach, if net-value-of-times v^i for all i are identical, it holds that $\bar{v} = \breve{v}$.*

Proof. Let v be the net-value-of-time common to all consumers. Then, it follows from (6.42) to (6.43) that $\bar{v} = \breve{v} = v$. □

Subsequently, we extend the previous analysis for demands under the deterministic perception approach to expected demands under the random perception approach. Let service system mn under competition have the expected market demand Q_{mn}. For this market demand, the social value-of-service-time $\bar{\xi}_{mn}$ can be estimated by

$$\bar{\xi}_{mn} = \int_{D_{mn}} \xi_m f_{mn}(p_{mn} + \xi_m t_{mn})\, h(\xi)\, d\mu \Big/ \int_{D_{mn}} f_m(p_{mn} + \xi_m t_{mn})\, h(\xi)\, d\mu. \quad (6.44)$$

On the other hand, Theorem 5.11 shows that the private value-of-service-time $\breve{\xi}_{mn}$ $(= (\partial Q_{mn}/\partial t_{mn})/\partial Q_{mn}/\partial p_{mn})$ can be approximated by

$$\breve{\xi}_{mn} \cong \int_{D^c_{mn}} \xi_m f_{mn}(p_{mn} + \xi_m t_{mn})\, h(\xi) d\mu \Big/ \int_{D^c_{mn}} f_m(p_{mn} + \xi_m t_{mn})\, h(\xi) d\mu, \quad (6.45)$$

where $D^c_{mn} = \sum_{m'n' \neq mn} D_{mn} \cap D_{m'n'}$.

Equation (6.45) is an approximation of formulas for $\partial Q_{mn}/\partial p_{mn}$ and $\partial Q_{mn}/\partial t_{mn}$ in Theorem 5.11, which is developed by applying the following assumption:

$$\int_{D_{mn}} \frac{\partial f_m(p_{mn} + \xi_m t_{mn})}{\partial p_{mn}} h(\xi)\, d\mu \Big/ \frac{\partial Q_{mn}(p,t)}{\partial p_{mn}} \cong 0. \quad (6.46)$$

This assumption connotes that the net decrease in service demand, which equals the numerator, is negligibly smaller than the demand shift to competing services, which equals the denominator minus the numerator.

Equations (6.44) and (6.45) introduce the formulas that estimate the social and private value-of-service-times under the random perception approach, denoted by $\bar{\xi}_{mn}$ and $\breve{\xi}_{mn}$, respectively. These two formulas for $\bar{\xi}_{mn}$ and $\breve{\xi}_{mn}$ values have expressions very similar to the ones for the deterministic perception approach in (6.42) and (6.43), respectively. The one single difference between them is that the former uses integrals in defining the social and private value-of-service times, whereas the latter applies summations. Therefore, it can be said that the service quality of a service system affects the social and private value-of-service times and, thereby, the total and marginal full costs for both public and private services.

The $\bar{\xi}_{mn}$ and $\breve{\xi}_{mn}$ values belong to the common range of net-value-of-times for all throughputs. This property of the $\bar{\xi}_{mn}$ and $\breve{\xi}_{mn}$ values can be characterized in a manner analogous to that of (6.42) and (6.43) for the deterministic demand function, respectively, as presented below.

Theorem 6.9. *The two different averages $\bar{\xi}_{mn}$ and $\breve{\xi}_{mn}$ satisfy the following:*

$$\bar{\xi}_{mn} \text{ and } \breve{\xi}_{mn} \in L_{mn}(p,t),$$

where

$$\begin{aligned} L_{mn}(p,t) &= \left\{\xi_m \,|\xi \in D_{mn}(p_{mn}, t_{mn}; p^o_{mn}, t^o_{mn})\right\} \\ &= \left[\min\left\{L_{mn}(\xi_m)\right\},\ \max\{L_{mn}(\xi_m)\right]. \end{aligned}$$

Proof. This theorem is an extension of analyses for the deterministic demand function in (6.42) and (6.43) to the expected demand function. The theorem holds, even in the case when the restrictive condition of (6.46) is not applied. Such a theorem is proved in Appendix B.1 by applying the mean value theorem for integrals. □

Theorem 6.9 connotes that, if the interval $\left[\min\ L_{mn},\ \max L_{mn}\right]$ is very small, it follows that $\bar{\xi}_{mn} \cong \breve{\xi}_{mn}$. The condition that the interval is short is similar to the condition that thickness of D_{mn} on the ξ_m axis is very small.[5] This latter is fulfilled when the demand Q_{mn} is very elastic but finite, as shown in Theorems 5.13 and 5.14. Also, the condition leads to the relationship in (6.46), as explained in the proof of Theorem 6.13. Furthermore, the condition yields the analytical outcome that $\bar{\xi}_{mn} \cong \breve{\xi}_{mn}$, as proved below.

Theorem 6.10. *If service system mn faces either the keen quantitative competition characterized in Theorem 5.13.ii or the keen qualitative competition depicted in Theorem 5.13.iii, it holds that $\bar{\xi}_{mn} \cong \breve{\xi}_{mn}$.*

Proof. See Appendix B.2 □

[5] In the case of quantitative competition, the fact that the interval $\left[\min\ L_{mn},\ \max L_{mn}\right]$ is "short" implies that the thickness of D_{mn} is small, as can be deduced from Fig. 5.1. In contrast, in the case of qualitative competition, the interval can be large even though the thickness is small, as shown in Fig. 5.7.

Chapter 7
Extensions of Cost Analyses for the Basic Service System

7.1 Introduction

Chapter 6 introduced the full cost approach that estimates various cost functions of public and private congestion-prone service systems. That chapter illustrated analyses to develop the cost functions using an example of the basic service system. The cost analyses showed that a certain cost function for both public and private services has an identical expression, except for one difference in value-of-service-times that reflect consumer perception about the value of qualitative attributes packed in a service. The cost functions for a public service use the social value-of-service-time, which estimates the decrease in consumer utilities for a one-unit increase in service time as a unit of money. The cost functions for private service, in contrast, apply the private value-of-service-time, which reflects the revenue loss for each unit increase in service time.

As a sequel, this chapter covers two groups of further topics for the full cost approach. The first group of topics analyzes the structure of marginal full cost for the basic service system in order to develop inputs for subsequent economic analyses presented in Parts III and IV. The second group extends analyses for the basic service system to other service systems in order to demonstrate the applicability of the full cost approach to a large group of real service systems. These two groups of topics, which provide identical analytical outcomes for both public and private service systems, are presented below.

One topic belonging to the first group, covered in Sect. 7.2, converts the marginal full cost of the basic service system, estimated in the previous chapter, into an alternative formulation suitable to determine its economic implications. The marginal full cost of a congestion-prone service system is the cost that plays the same role in analyses of pricing decision as is played by the marginal cost in analyses of a congestion-free production system. However, the marginal full cost developed in the previous chapter has a formulation independent of monetary cost; that is, the marginal full cost is defined using service time function. It is therefore impossible to understand how monetary cost is related to marginal full cost. For this

D.J. Moon, *Congestion-Prone Services Under Quality Competition*, Advances in Spatial Science, DOI 10.1007/978-3-642-20189-9_7,

reason, we develop an alternative formulation of marginal full cost by replacing service time function with marginal capacity cost function.

Another topic in the first group, also examined in Sect. 7.2, evaluates the returns-to-scale of the basic service system in throughput through analyses of marginal full cost. The returns-to-scale of a service system operated by a firm is a decisive factor that determines the industrial organization type of the firm, an important theme of Part III. Such returns-to-scale of a service system is judged from the differential of marginal full cost with respect to throughput.

Subsequently, one topic included in the second group, covered in Sect. 7.3, extends analyses to estimate marginal full cost for the basic service system to other service systems. The social cost or quasi-cost minimization problem for each service system analyzed in that section is constructed by replacing one of the following three restrictive conditions for the basic service system with more realistic ones: no short-run variable cost, no restriction on the choice of optimal capacity, and no variation of demand flow rates over the entire analysis period. For example, one quasi-cost minimization problem analyzed has an identical formulation with the quasi-cost minimization problem for the basic service system except for one difference that variable cost is added to supplier cost.

Another topic in the second group, analyzed in Sect. 7.4, illustrates developing the marginal full cost function of a particular service system for which the specific expressions of service time and capacity cost functions are available. Three examples are selected so as to illustrate estimating the marginal full cost function for the following three combinations of demand arrival pattern and service technology: the combination of steady demand flow and service technology with a homogeneous service time function, termed homogeneous service technology; steady demand flow and non-homogeneous service technology; and unsteady demand flow and homogeneous service technology.

7.2 The Returns-to-Scale of the Basic Service System

7.2.1 Relationship between Marginal Full and Marginal Capacity Costs

Analyses of the BSCMP and BQCMP in the previous chapter show that the marginal full cost of throughput equals the marginal congestion cost of the same variable, irrespective of the ownership of service systems. The formulation of the marginal full cost, developed in that chapter, includes a service time function that has no direct relationship to monetary cost. For this reason, below we replace the service time function in the marginal full cost function with the marginal capacity cost function that reflects monetary cost paid by supplier.

The marginal full cost of throughput for the basic service system, as estimated in Chap. 6, has an expression $vs\partial T/\partial s$ that is applicable to both homogeneous and non-homogeneous service time functions. In contrast, an alternative formulation of marginal full cost, which replaces the service time function with the marginal capacity cost function, differs by the type of service technology. To demonstrate this, we first present an alternative expression of the marginal full cost for the case of the private basic service system with a homogeneous service technology.

Theorem 7.1. *In the case of the basic service system with a homogeneous service technology defined in Assumption 6.1(a), the marginal full and marginal capacity costs for the BQCMP satisfy the following relationships:*

$$MFC(s;\breve{v}) = \frac{\bar{c}}{s} MKC(\bar{c}) \tag{7.1}$$

$$MMC(s;\breve{v}) = \frac{\partial \bar{c}}{\partial s} MKC(\bar{c}) \tag{7.2}$$

$$MTC(s;\breve{v}) = \left(\frac{\bar{c}}{s} - \frac{\partial \bar{c}}{\partial s}\right) MKC(\bar{c}). \tag{7.3}$$

where $\bar{c}$ is an abbreviation of $\bar{c}(s)$ and $\bar{c}$ is the function that estimates the solution of c to the BQCMP.

Proof. Prove first (7.1). Theorem 6.7 shows that $MFC = MCC$. Substituting (6.1) and Lemma 6.6 into the expression of MCC in the theorem in sequence gives the following:

$$MFC(s;\breve{v}) = \breve{v}\frac{\bar{c}}{s}\left(-s\frac{\partial T(s/\bar{c})}{\partial c}\right) = \frac{\bar{c}}{s}\frac{\partial KC(\bar{c})}{\partial c}. \tag{7.4}$$

Subsequently, (7.2) is none other than the specific expression of MMC introduced in Theorem 6.7. Finally, (7.3) is given by substituting (7.1) and (7.2) into $MFC = MMC + MTC$ in Theorem 6.7. □

Theorem 7.1 presents alternative formulations of the three marginal costs introduced in Theorem 6.7. All alternative formulations depict, in common, the relationships with marginal capacity cost. These formulations have the following two advantages over the formulations that use service time function: first, the use of marginal capacity cost conveys more specific information about the cost structure of service systems than is conveyed by the use of service time function; second, econometric estimations of the former are easier and more reliable from the standpoint of input data collection.

Specifically, the expression of MFC in Theorem 7.1, which is the most important input for subsequent economic analyses, has the two advantages that follow. First, the implication of the formulation for marginal full cost is clear; it shows that the marginal full cost equals the product of the marginal capacity cost and the inverse of system utilization ratio, as expressed by $\bar{c}/s$. Second, the formulation uses terms that are either all directly observable or statistically estimable: s, c and y are observable, while MKC and $\breve{v}$ are statistically estimable.

Theorem 7.2. *In the case of non-homogeneous service technology defined in Assumption 6.1(b), the three relationships in Theorem 7.1 can be amended as follows:*

$$MFC(s;\breve{v}) = \frac{\bar{c}}{s}\left(MKC(\bar{c}) - MWT(s,\bar{c};\breve{v})\right) \tag{7.5}$$

$$MMC(s;\breve{v}) = \frac{\partial \bar{c}}{\partial s} MKC(\bar{c}) \tag{7.6}$$

$$MTC(s;\breve{v}) = \left(\frac{\bar{c}}{s} - \frac{\partial \bar{c}}{\partial s}\right) MKC(\bar{c}) - \frac{\bar{c}}{s} MWT(s,\bar{c};\breve{v}) \tag{7.7}$$

where

$$MWT(s,\bar{c};\breve{v}) = \frac{\breve{v}\, s}{2\,\bar{y}^2} T^d(s/\bar{c}) \ \geq 0.$$

Proof. It suffices to prove (7.5) only; that is, if (7.5) holds, Theorem 6.7 implies that (7.6) and (7.7) also hold. The delay function T^d of Assumption 6.1(b) is homogeneous. Hence, by (6.1), it follows that

$$\frac{\partial T(s,c)}{\partial s} = -\frac{1}{2y}\frac{c}{s}\frac{\partial T^d(s/c)}{\partial c}. \tag{7.8}$$

Using (7.8), the optimality condition in Lemma 6.6 can be restated as below:

$$\begin{aligned} MKC(\bar{c}) &= \breve{v}\, s\left(\frac{1}{2\,\bar{y}^2} T^d(s/\bar{c}) - \frac{1}{2\,\bar{y}}\frac{\partial T^d(s/\bar{c})}{\partial c}\right) \\ &= \frac{\breve{v}s}{2\,\bar{y}^2} T^d(s/\bar{c}) + \breve{v}\, s \frac{s}{\bar{c}} \frac{\partial T(s,c;\, c=\bar{c})}{\partial s} \\ &= \frac{\breve{v}\, s}{2\,\bar{y}^2} T^d(s/\bar{c}) + \frac{s}{\bar{c}} MCC(s;\breve{v}). \end{aligned} \tag{7.9}$$

Arranging (7.9) gives (7.5). □

The only single difference between Theorems 7.1 and 7.2 is that *MFC* and *MTC* for non-homogenous service technology have one additional term, *MWT*. The term *MWT* represents the marginal waiting time cost of throughput for service frequency. This marginal cost function estimates the decrease in waiting time cost, which results from a service frequency increase made in response to a one-unit increase in throughput. This marginal cost function is decreasing in $y(\equiv a + c)$, in which a is a constant that represents the sum of service frequencies offered by other service firms.

To be specific, growth in throughput s accompanies increases in marketwise service frequency y. Also, as frequency y grows, the mean waiting time of all customers, which is linearly proportional to $1/2y$, monotonically decreases. Therefore, this marginal decrease in waiting time is monotonically decreasing in throughput s. Further, when frequency y is very large, the contribution of one additional passenger to the decrease in y is negligible and, thereby, the value of MWT is approximately zero.

Finally, it is important to clarify differences in the analytical outcome of Theorems 7.1 and 7.2. In the case of homogeneous service technology, Theorem 7.1 is applicable, irrespective of the functional form of service time function T. In other words, the theorem holds, as long as the function T is homogeneous of degree zero. In contrast, Theorem 7.2 is the outcome for a specific non-homogeneous service time function defined in Assumption 6.1. Therefore, the theorem is not directly applicable to those service systems that require the use of different non-homogeneous service time functions.

7.2.2 *Returns-to-Scale for Homogeneous Service Technology*

We here present two different analyses for the private basic service system with a homogeneous service technology. The first analysis involves characterizing the returns-to-scale of the whole service system in throughput. The second analysis develops, from the outcome of the first analysis, the following: the sensitivity of system utility ratio and service time with respect to throughput; and the relative magnitude between marginal full and marginal monetary costs.

The returns-to-scale of a congestion-prone service system can be judged from the slope of the marginal full cost with respect to throughput; if the slope is positive (or negative), the service system exhibits decreasing (or increasing) returns in throughput. This slope is estimated from the differentiation of MFC ($= MCC$) with respect to throughput s:

$$\frac{\partial MFC(s;\breve{v})}{\partial s} = \left(\frac{1}{s}MFC(s;\breve{v}) + \breve{v}s\frac{\partial^2 T^d}{\partial s^2}\right)\left(1 - \frac{s}{c}\frac{\partial \bar{c}}{\partial s}\right), \tag{7.10}$$

as shown in Appendix B.3. Through analyses of (7.10), the returns-to-scale of the basic service system is characterized, as below.

Theorem 7.3. *The returns-to-scale of the basic service system with a homogeneous service technology can be characterized as follows:*

$$\frac{\partial MFC(s;\breve{v})}{\partial s} \gtrless 0, \quad \textit{if} \quad \frac{\partial^2 KC(\bar{c})}{\partial c^2} \gtrless 0.$$

Proof. Equation (7.10) shows that the sign of $\partial MFC/\partial s$ entirely depends on the sign of $1-(s/\bar{c})\partial\bar{c}/\partial s$, since the convexity of T in s implies that both $\partial T^d/\partial s$ and $\partial^2 T^d/\partial s^2$ are always positive. To find the sign of $1-(s/\bar{c})\partial\bar{c}/\partial s$, we reorganize the differentiation of the investment rule in Lemma 6.6 with respect to s, as follows:

$$\frac{s}{\bar{c}}\frac{\partial\bar{c}}{\partial s}=\left(2\frac{\partial KC(\bar{c})}{\partial c}+\breve{v}\frac{s^3}{\bar{c}}\frac{\partial^2\bar{T}}{\partial s^2}\right)\Big/\left(\bar{c}\frac{\partial^2 KC(\bar{c})}{\partial c^2}+2\frac{\partial KC(\bar{c})}{\partial c}+\breve{v}\frac{s^3}{\bar{c}}\frac{\partial^2\bar{T}}{\partial s^2}\right)\rangle\ 0, \tag{7.11}$$

as shown in Appendix B.3. Here, the function MKC is expressed as $\partial KC/\partial c$ in order to clarify the relationship with $\partial^2 KC/\partial c^2$.

The sign of $1-(s/\bar{c})\partial\bar{c}/\partial s$ is equal to the sign of $\partial^2 KC/\partial c^2$ in the denominator of (7.11), as explained below. The denominator of (7.11) has an additional term $\partial^2 KC/\partial c^2$ not found in the numerator. Further, the two terms in the numerator are both positive. Therefore, it follows that, if $\partial^2 KC/\partial c^2$ is positive (or negative), the term $(s/\bar{c})\partial\bar{c}/\partial s$ is smaller (or larger) than 1.0; that is, the term $1-(s/\bar{c})\partial\bar{c}/\partial s$ is positive (or negative). Hence, it follows the theorem. □

Theorem 7.3 depicts the relationship between returns-to-scale in throughput, judged by the sign of $\partial MFC/\partial s$, and returns-to-scale in capacity, assessed by $\partial^2 KC/\partial c^2$. The theorem shows that the sign of $\partial MFC/\partial s$ is determined solely by the sign of $\partial^2 KC/\partial c^2$. For example, suppose that $\partial^2 KC/\partial c^2\ \rangle\ 0$; that is, the production technology for capacity exhibits decreasing returns in capacity. Then, the returns-to-scale of the whole queuing system with a homogeneous service technology exhibits decreasing returns in throughput. That is, as the production system exhibits decreasing returns in capacity, the marginal full cost increases as throughput increases.

A corollary to Theorem 7.3 is that the sign of $\partial MFC/\partial s$ is independent of the functional form of service time function, as long as the service time function is homogeneous. This implies that, irrespective of the specific functional from of $T(s/c)$, the sign of $\partial MFC/\partial s$ entirely depends on the sign of $\partial^2 KC/\partial c^2$. However, this does not mean that the value of $\partial MFC/\partial s$ is also independent of the functional form of $T(s/c)$, as can be deduced from (7.10) and (7.11).

Theorem 7.3 can be used to generate a quick statistical judgment for the returns-to-scale of the entire service system. The theorem implies that the returns-to-scale of the entire service system can be judged through statistical estimation of the sign of $\partial^2 KC/\partial c^2$, which is thought to be easier than estimation of the sign of $\partial MFC/\partial s$. However, this does not mean that the value of $\partial MFC/\partial s$ equals or is linearly proportional to the value of $\partial MKC/\partial c$, as can be deduced from (7.10).

Subsequently, by applying the above analysis for the sign of $1-(s/\bar{c})\partial\bar{c}/\partial s$, below we assess other performance indexes of the basic service system with a homogeneous service technology.

Theorem 7.4. *The basic service system with a homogeneous service technology satisfies the following:*

$$MFC(s;\breve{v}) \gtreqless MMC(s;\breve{v}) \quad \frac{\partial \bar{\rho}(s;\breve{v})}{\partial s} \gtreqless 0, \quad and \quad \frac{\partial \bar{t}(s;\breve{v})}{\partial s} \gtreqless 0, \quad if \quad \frac{\partial^2 KC(\bar{c})}{\partial c^2} \gtreqless 0.$$

Proof. Prove first the sign of $MFC - MMC$. By Theorem 7.1, it follows that

$$MFC(s;\breve{v}) - MMC(s;\breve{v}) = MTC(s;\breve{v}) = \frac{\bar{c}}{s}\left(1 - \frac{s}{\bar{c}}\frac{\partial \bar{c}}{\partial s}\right) MKC(\bar{c}). \tag{7.12}$$

Hence, the sign of $MFC - MMC$ is identical to that of $1 - (s/\bar{c})\partial\bar{c}/\partial s$.

Prove next the signs of $\partial\bar{\rho}/\partial s$ and $\partial\bar{t}/\partial s (\equiv \partial\bar{T}/\partial s)$ using the following:

$$\frac{\partial \bar{\rho}(s;\breve{v})}{\partial s} = \frac{\partial}{\partial s}\left(\frac{s}{\bar{c}}\right) = \frac{1}{\bar{c}}\left(1 - \frac{s}{\bar{c}}\frac{\partial \bar{c}}{\partial s}\right) \tag{7.13}$$

$$\frac{\partial T(s/\bar{c})}{\partial s} = \frac{\partial \bar{T}}{\partial s}\left(1 - \frac{s}{\bar{c}}\frac{\partial \bar{c}}{\partial s}\right). \tag{7.14}$$

Hence, the signs of $\partial\bar{\rho}/\partial s$ and $\partial\bar{t}/\partial s$ are also equal to that of $1 - (s/\bar{c})\partial\bar{c}/\partial s$. □

The three inequalities of Theorem 7.4 can be interpreted as below. First, the sign of $MFC - MMC$ implies that, if the production technology exhibits decreasing (or increasing) returns in capacity, MFC is larger (or smaller) than MMC, as illustrated in Fig. 6.4. Second, the sign of $\partial\bar{\rho}/\partial s$ indicates that, if the production technology exhibits decreasing (or increasing) returns in capacity, the optimal utilization ratio of the service system is increasing (decreasing) in throughput s. Third, the sign of $\partial\bar{t}/\partial s$ shows that, if $\partial^2 KC/\partial c^2$ is positive (or negative), the optimal congestion delay is increasing (decreasing) in s.

7.2.3 *Returns-to-Scale for Non-homogeneous Service Technology*

Here we extend the analysis of the previous subsection for the basic service system with a homogeneous service technology to the system with a non-homogeneous service technology. We proceed with analyses≡ in a manner identical to that used to analyze the system with a homogeneous service technology.

To begin, we estimate $\partial MFC/\partial s$ for non-homogeneous service time function in Assumption 6.1, in a manner analogous to that used to estimate the same term for homogeneous service time function in (7.10):

$$\frac{\partial MFC(s;\breve{v})}{\partial s} = \left(\frac{1}{s}MFC(s;\breve{v}) + \frac{\breve{v}s}{2y}\frac{\partial^2 T^d}{\partial s^2}\right)\left(1 - \frac{s}{c}\frac{\partial \bar{c}}{\partial s}\right) - \frac{1}{y}MFC(s;\breve{v})\frac{\partial \bar{c}}{\partial s}. \tag{7.15}$$

Using this equation, we below develop the following theorem.

Theorem 7.5. *The returns-to-scale of the basic service system with a non-homogeneous service technology can be characterized as follows:*

$$\frac{\partial MFC(s;\breve{v})}{\partial s} + \frac{1}{y} MFC(s;\breve{v}) \frac{\partial \bar{c}}{\partial s} \gtrless 0, \quad \textit{if} \quad \frac{\partial^2 KC(\bar{c})}{\partial c^2} \gtrless Y,$$

where

$$Y = c\frac{\partial^2 KC(c)}{\partial^2 c} + \left(1 + 2\frac{c}{y}\right)\frac{\partial KC(\bar{c})}{\partial c} - \frac{s}{\bar{c}}\left(\frac{1}{c} - \frac{1}{y}\right) MFC(s;\breve{v}).$$

Proof. We analyze the sign of $1 - (s/\bar{c})\partial\bar{c}/\partial s$ in a manner analogous to that used to assess the sign for homogeneous service technology. To this end, we differentiate the investment rule in Lemma 6.6 with respect to s and generate the following:

$$\begin{aligned}\frac{s}{\bar{c}}\frac{\partial \bar{c}}{\partial s} &= \left(\left(\frac{s}{c} - \frac{s}{y}\right) MFC(s;\breve{v}) + \frac{\partial KC(c)}{\partial c} + \frac{\breve{v}s^3}{2yc}\frac{\partial^2 T^d}{\partial s^2}\right) \Big/ \left(c\frac{\partial^2 KC(c)}{\partial^2 c}\right.\\ &\left. +2\left(1 + \frac{c}{y}\right)\frac{\partial KC(c)}{\partial c} + \frac{\breve{v}s^3}{2yc}\frac{\partial^2 T^d}{\partial s^2}\right).\end{aligned} \tag{7.16}$$

Using this equation, we characterize the sign of $1 - (s/\bar{c})\partial\bar{c}/\partial s$ in a manner identical to that used to determine the sign for homogeneous service technology. Details of the proof of (7.16) are presented in Appendix B.4. □

Theorem 7.5 depicts the relationship between returns-to-scale in throughput and returns-to-scale in capacity in a manner similar to that used for homogeneous service technology. The theorem indicates that the sign of $\partial MFC/\partial s$ can be positive, even though the sign of $\partial^2 KC/\partial c^2$ is non-positive. To be specific, if y is a very large value, (7.17) becomes identical to (7.11) for homogeneous service technology. However, if y is a small value, the possibility that the sign of $\partial MFC/\partial s$ can be positive is large.

To illustrate this, we consider the special case of $c = y$. In this case, the value of Y is simplified as follows:

$$Y = c\frac{\partial^2 KC(c)}{\partial^2 c} + 3\frac{\partial KC(\bar{c})}{\partial c}. \tag{7.17}$$

This equation shows that the sign of $1 - (s/\bar{c})\partial\bar{c}/\partial s$ is usually positive. Therefore, from the theorem, we can deduce that the sign of $\partial MFC/\partial s + (1/y)MFC$ is also usually positive.

The fact that the sign of $\partial MFC/\partial s$ can be positive, even when that of $\partial^2 KC/\partial c^2$ is non-negative, connotes the following: a non-homogeneous service technology affects the returns-to-scale of entire service systems, whereas a homogenous one is neutral in determining the returns-to-scale. Specifically, in the case of the service system analyzed here, the non-homogeneous service technology has the effect of decreasing the returns-to-scale of the entire service system. However, this example does not mean that other non-homogenous service technologies also always have the effect of decreasing the returns-of-scale of entire service systems.

Subsequently, we analyze the sign of $\partial\bar{p}/\partial s$ for non-homogeneous service technology in a manner analogous to that used to judge the sign of a homogeneous service technology. The analysis of $\partial\bar{p}/\partial s$ shows that

$$\frac{\partial\bar{p}(s;\breve{v})}{\partial s}=\frac{1}{\bar{c}}\left(1-\frac{s}{\bar{c}}\frac{\partial\bar{c}}{\partial s}\right)\ \substack{\rangle\\ =\\ \langle}\ 0,\quad \text{if}\quad Y(s;\breve{v})\ \substack{\rangle\\ =\\ \langle}\ 0. \tag{7.18}$$

Hence, the sign of $\partial\bar{p}/\partial s$ can be characterized in a manner identical to that of $\partial MFC/\partial s$ using the term Y. This means that $\partial\bar{p}/\partial s$ is usually positive.

Finally, we evaluate the signs of $MFC - MMC$ and $\partial t/\partial s$ through analyses of the following:

$$MFC(s;\breve{v})-MMC(s;\breve{v})=\left(\frac{\bar{c}}{s}-\frac{\partial\bar{c}}{\partial s}\right)MKC(\bar{c})-\frac{\bar{c}}{s}MWT(\bar{c};\breve{v}) \tag{7.19}$$

$$\frac{\partial\bar{t}}{\partial s}=\frac{1}{\breve{v}s}MTC(s;\breve{v})=\frac{1}{\breve{v}s}\left(\left(\frac{\bar{c}}{s}-\frac{\partial\bar{c}}{\partial s}\right)MKC(\bar{c})-\frac{\bar{c}}{s}MWT(\bar{c};\breve{v})\right). \tag{7.20}$$

Equation (7.20) is provided using the following two relationships in Theorem 6.7: $MTC = \breve{v}\,s\partial T/\partial s$ and $MTC = MFC - MMC$.

Equations (7.19) and (7.20) show that the sign of $MFC - MMC$ is identical to that of $\partial\bar{t}/\partial s$. Moreover, the sign of $MFC - MMC$ and $\partial\bar{t}/\partial s$ depends mainly on the first term on the right side of (7.19) or (7.20). Further, this first term is usually positive, since $1-(s/c)\partial c/\partial s$ is mostly positive. Therefore, it can be concluded that the sign of $MFC - MMC$ and $\partial\bar{t}/\partial s$ is usually positive.

7.3 Cost Functions of Other Service Systems

7.3.1 The Service System with a Fixed Capacity

Frequently, a congestion-prone service system is operated under conditions by which capacity is not optimally adjusted. To reflect this reality, we here analyze the effect of an under- or over-sized capacity on the marginal quasi-cost of throughput with an example of the private basic service system. To be specific, we compare the marginal quasi-cost for a private service system having an arbitrary capacity with that cost for a service system with an optimal capacity.

The capacity of service systems is the long-run choice variable of the BQCMP. Therefore, the marginal quasi-cost estimated in the previous chapter, under the condition that capacity is optimally adjusted to changes in throughput, is by its very nature the long-run marginal cost. On the other hand, the marginal quasi-cost of a service system with a fixed capacity quantifies only the revenue loss from a service time increase due to a marginal increase in throughput. This marginal quasi-cost can therefore be defined as a short-run marginal cost.

The short-run marginal quasi-cost is developed from the Short-Run Quasi-Cost Minimization Problem (SRQCMP) under the condition that the capacity is a fixed value c_o. This SRQCMP, denoted by *SRZ*, has an expression identical to the short-run problem Z^4 for public service in (6.19) except for a difference that the fixed capacity c_o is not optimal:

$$SRZ(t, \tau ; s, c_o, \breve{v}) \equiv \min \left\{ KC(c_o) + t\breve{v}s \right\} + \tau(T(s, c_o) - t). \qquad (7.21)$$

For the optimization problem *SRZ*, the short-run marginal quasi-cost, *SRMQC*, is

$$\begin{aligned} SRMQC\,(s; c_o, \breve{v}) &= \frac{\partial SRZ(\bar{t}, \bar{\tau}; s, c_o, \breve{v})}{\partial s} \\ &= SRMRL(s; c_o, \breve{v}) + SRMCC(s; c_o, \breve{v}), \end{aligned} \qquad (7.22)$$

where $SRMRL(s; c_o, \breve{v}) = \breve{v}\,T(s, c_o)$, and $SRMCC\,(s; c_o, \breve{v}) = \breve{v}s \times \partial T(s, c_o)/\partial s$.

The function *SRMQC* estimates the short-run implicit marginal revenue loss of throughput for a service system with a fixed capacity c_o, and is the sum of *SRMRL* and *SRMCC*. The one function *SRMRL* estimates the implicit revenue loss for the service time consumed in facilitating one additional throughput under the condition that service time is fixed. The other function *SRMCC*, termed the short-run marginal congestion cost function, estimates the additional implicit revenue loss for the service system, which results from an increase in service time due to a one-unit increase in throughput under the condition that capacity is fixed.

Both *SRMRL* and *SRMCC* are positive and monotonically increasing in s. This property of *SRMRL* follows from the fact that T is monotonically increasing and convex in s. The same assertion for *SRMCC* results from the fact that $\partial T/\partial s$ is also monotonically increasing in s. These two short-run marginal costs fulfill the following relationship with their counterparts for long-run marginal costs.

Theorem 7.6. *Let c_o be an arbitrary capacity, and $\bar{c}$ be the solution of c to a hypothetical long-run problem for the basic service system in (6.36) for an aggregated throughput $\bar{s}$ with the private value-of-service-time $\breve{v}$. Then, it holds that*

$$SRMQC(\bar{s}; c_o, \breve{v}) \overset{<}{\underset{>}{=}} MQC(\bar{s}; \breve{v}) = SRMQC(\bar{s}; \bar{c}, \breve{v}), \quad \text{if} \quad c_o \overset{>}{\underset{<}{=}} \bar{c}.$$

Specifically, it holds that

$$SRMRL(\bar{s}; c_o, \breve{v}) \underset{>}{\overset{<}{-}} MRL(\bar{s}; \breve{v}) = SRMRL(\bar{s}; \bar{c}, \breve{v}),$$

$$SRMCC(\bar{s}; c_o, \breve{v}) \underset{>}{\overset{<}{-}} MCC(\bar{s}; \breve{v}) = SRMCC(\bar{s}; \bar{c}, \breve{v}), \quad \textit{if} \quad c_o \underset{<}{\overset{>}{-}} \bar{c}.$$

Proof. The equalities $MRL(\bar{s};\breve{v}) = SRMRL(\bar{s};\bar{c},\breve{v})$ and $MCC(\bar{s};\breve{v}) = SRMCC(\bar{s};\bar{c},\breve{v})$ are proved in Theorem 6.4 for the public basic service system. The inequality between $SRMRL(\bar{s};c_o,\breve{v})$ and $SRMRL(\bar{s};\bar{c},\breve{v})$ follows from the fact that T is decreasing in c. Likewise, the inequality between $SRMCC(\bar{s};c_o,\breve{v})$ and $SRMCC(\bar{s};\bar{c},\breve{v})$ results from the fact that $\partial T/\partial s$ is also decreasing in c. □.

Theorem 7.6 depicts the finding that, when the previously paid capacity cost is ignored, the short-run marginal quasi-cost of an under-sized (or over-sized) service system is larger (or smaller) than that of a service system in operation under optimal capacity. To be specific, the inequality between *SRMRL* and *MRL* indicates that the revenue loss of an under-sized (or over-sized) service system, which is linearly proportional to the service time experienced by customers, is greater than a service system in operation under optimal capacity. On the other hand, the inequality between *SRMCC* and *MCC* depicts that the revenue loss of an under-sized (or over-sized) system, which quantifies the loss for the additional increase in service time due to a marginal increase in throughput, is greater (or lesser) than the system with optimal capacity.

Finally, it should be emphasized that the function *SRMCC* does not have a counterpart equivalent to the function *MFC* that equals *MCC*. To be specific, both *SRMCC* and *MCC* estimate the marginal quasi-cost of throughput under the condition that capacity is fixed. It is therefore feasible to estimate marginal congestion cost whether or not capacity is optimal. This implies that we can define the function *SRMCC* as well as the function *MCC*. In contrast, the function *MFC* estimates the marginal quasi-cost of throughput, which is incurred by the investment of adjusting the original optimal capacity to a new optimum. Therefore, marginal full cost can be defined only when capacity is a choice variable that can be adjusted optimally. This means that we cannot define the marginal cost equivalent to the marginal full cost if capacity is not a variable but rather a fixed value.

7.3.2 The Service System with Variable Costs

Congestion-prone service systems usually consume not only capacity cost, which is independent of throughput, but also variable cost, which is sensitive to throughput. Indeed, almost all private congestion-prone services share this property. We illustrate here how this property can be incorporated into analyses for the marginal full cost of the basic service system, through depiction of a system providing private service.

Firstly, we construct the QCMP for a service system with variable costs. To accommodate variable costs, we introduce two different kinds of production functions. One is the production function for capacity, which is identical to that of the basic service system, and is expressed here as follows:

$$c \leq F^l(x^l), \tag{7.23}$$

where $x^l \equiv (x_1^l, \cdots, x_J^l)$. The other is the production function for throughput, expressed by

$$s \leq F^s(x^l, x^s), \tag{7.24}$$

where $x^s \equiv (x_1^s, \cdots, x_J^s)$. Here, x_j^l is the quantity of goods or services j inputted in constructing long-run choice component c, whereas x_j^s is the amount of the same goods or services j consumed in processing short-run throughput s. Also, it is assumed that the functions F^s and F^l are increasing and differentiable in their variables.

The structures of the capacity function F^l and the throughput function F^s are illustrated with an example of a retail shop. The function F^l is increasing in number of long-run inputs x^l that are required to maintain a certain capacity determined by various factors such as floor display space, merchandise storage space, etc. On the other hand, the function F^s is increasing not only in long-run inputs x^l but also in short-run inputs x^s. This means that these two different kinds of inputs, x^l and x^s, are substitutable for one another in delivering a given amount of throughput.

The substitutability of the two different kinds of inputs reflects that a retail shop with a fixed capacity can facilitate a larger amount of throughput by inputting more short-run variables such as manpower. Furthermore, this substitutability implies that a service system with a bigger capacity yields the same amount of throughput with a smaller amount of short-run inputs. An example can be found in the trade-off relationship between the short-run cost for transporting merchandise and long-run investment cost for storage facilities; a shop with a larger storage capacity can usually reduce transportation cost by purchasing a larger quantity of merchandise per order.

Incorporating (7.23) and (7.24) into the BQCMP in (6.36) gives a QCMP, denoted by Z^8, such that

$$Z^8(x^l, x^s, c, t, \kappa^l, \kappa^s, \tau; s, \breve{v}) \equiv \min\left\{\sum_j p_j(x_j^l + x_j^s) + t\breve{v}s\right\} + \kappa^l\left(c - F^l(x^l)\right) + \kappa^s\left(s - F^s(x^l, x^s)\right) + \tau(T(s,c) - t). \tag{7.25}$$

This QCMP is identical to the BQCMP, except for two differences: inclusion of the variable cost $\sum_j p_j x_j^s$ into the objective function and the incorporation of one additional constraint for the production of throughput.

Secondly, we develop a number of relevant optimality conditions for Z^8. Let $(\bar{x}^l, \bar{x}^s, \bar{c}, \bar{t}, \bar{\kappa}^l, \bar{\kappa}^s, \bar{\tau})$ be the solution to Z^8. Proceeding with the analysis of Z^8 in a manner analogous to that leading to Lemmas 6.4–6.6 gives

$$\bar{\tau} = \breve{v}s \tag{7.26}$$

$$MVC(s;\breve{v}) = \bar{\kappa}^s = p_j \Big/ \frac{\partial \bar{F}^s}{\partial x_j^s} \rangle\ 0, \quad \text{all} \quad j \tag{7.27}$$

$$MKC(s;\breve{v}) = \bar{\kappa}^l = p_j \left(1 - \frac{\partial \bar{F}^s}{\partial x_j^l} \Big/ \frac{\partial \bar{F}^s}{\partial x_j^s}\right) \Big/ \frac{\partial \bar{F}^l}{\partial x_j^l} \rangle\ 0, \quad \text{all} \quad j \tag{7.28}$$

$$MKC(s,\breve{v}) = -\breve{v}s \frac{\partial T(s,\bar{c})}{\partial c}, \tag{7.29}$$

where $\bar{F}^l \equiv F^l(\bar{x}^l)$, $\bar{F}^s \equiv F^s(\bar{x}^l, \bar{x}^s)$, and MVC stands for the marginal variable cost. Note that $\bar{c} - \bar{F}^l = 0$, and $s - \bar{F}^s = 0$.

The marginal capacity cost MKC for the service system with variable costs in (7.28) is less than the marginal capacity cost for long-run inputs, expressed as $p_j/(\partial \bar{F}^l/\partial x_j^l)$, by the value of the parentheses. The term $(\partial \bar{F}^s/\partial x_j^l)/(\partial \bar{F}^s/\partial x_j^s)$ in the parentheses represents the marginal rate of technical substitution of x_j^l for x_j^s to the production of short-run throughput s. As this substitution rate is larger, the value of MKC becomes smaller; that is, as the substitution effect of x_j^l for x_j^s is larger, the value of MKC decreases. This substitution rate should be less than one so that $\bar{\kappa}^l \rangle\ 0$; otherwise, the cost-minimizing choice would be $\bar{x}_j^l \rangle\ 0$ and $\bar{x}_j^s = 0$, for all j, since the use of x_j^l could be more economical than the use of x_j^s in facilitating a given amount of throughput s.

Thirdly, we estimate the marginal quasi-cost of throughput for Z^8, denoted by MQC. Applying the envelop theorem to Z^8 gives

$$MQC(s;\breve{v}) = MRL(s;\breve{v}) + MCC(s;\breve{v}) + MVC(s;\breve{v}). \tag{7.30}$$

Here, MQC, MRL, and MCC have expressions identical to the same marginal costs for the basic service system in Theorem 6.6.

Fourthly, we estimate the marginal full cost of throughput. This marginal full cost represents the minimum of additional quasi-costs incurred in the process of expanding the original optimal capacity to the new optimum in response to a one-unit increase in throughput. We estimate this marginal full cost for the QCMP of (7.25) just as we did in Sect. 6.4.3 for the BQCMP.

The first step in estimating the marginal full cost constructs the FCMP similar to Z^7 in (6.40). This FCMP is used to find the solution of (x^l, x^s, c) that minimizes the sum of additional monetary cost, ASC, and additional revenue loss due to changes in service time, *ATC*, for the system that facilitates an additional throughput e together with an original throughput s. Under the convention that the solution of (x^l, x^s, c) to Z^8 for s is $(\hat{x}^l, \hat{x}^s, \hat{c})$, the FCMP, denoted by Z^9, is

$$Z^9(x^l, x^s, c, \kappa^l, \kappa^s;\, s+e, \breve{v}) \equiv \min\Big\{ ASC(x^l, x^s, c; s+e, \breve{v}) + ATC(c\,; s+e, \breve{v})\Big\} + \kappa^l\big(c - F^l(x^l)\big) + \kappa^s\big(s+e - F^s(x^l, x^s)\big), \tag{7.31}$$

where

$$ASC(x^l, x^s, c; s+e, \breve{v}) = \sum_j p_j(x_j^l + x_j^s) - \sum_j p_j(\hat{x}_j^l + \hat{x}_j^s) \tag{7.32}$$

$$ATC(c; s+e, \breve{v}) = \breve{v}s(T(s+e, c)) - T(s, \hat{c})). \tag{7.33}$$

The second step develops optimality conditions for the minimization problem Z^9. To simplify analyses, we first decompose the minimization problem Z^9 into two sub-optimization problems. We next present optimality conditions for these two sub-optimization problems, which constitute optimality conditions for Z^9, under the convention that the vector function $(\bar{x}^l, \bar{x}^s, \bar{c}, \bar{\kappa}^l, \bar{\kappa}^s)$ estimates the solution to Z^9 for an arbitrary value of e.

The first sub-optimization problem, denoted by Z^{10}, is used to estimate the solution of (x^l, x^s), which minimizes the additional monetary cost for an arbitrary capacity c, expressed by *ASC*:

$$Z^{10}(x^l, x^s, \kappa^l, \kappa^s;\, s+e, c, \breve{v}) \equiv \min\Big\{ ASC(x^l, x^s; c\,, s+e, \breve{v}) \Big\} + \kappa^l\big(c - F^l(x^l)\big) + \kappa^s\big(s+e - F^s(x^l, x^s)\big). \tag{7.34}$$

Let $(\widetilde{x}^l, \widetilde{x}^s)$ be the solution to Z^9, and let $AMC(c;\,\cdot)$ denote $ASC(\widetilde{x}^l, \widetilde{x}^s; c,\,\cdot)$. Substituting *AMC* into Z^9 gives the second sub-optimization problem, Z^{11}, such that

$$Z^{11}(c\,;\, s+e, \breve{v}) \equiv \min\Big\{ AMC(c; s+e, \breve{v}) + ATC(c\,; s+e, \breve{v})\Big\}. \tag{7.35}$$

The combined optimization problem of Z^{10} and Z^{11} has the solution identical to the solution for Z^9. Therefore, first, the solution $(\widetilde{x}^l, \widetilde{x}^s, \widetilde{\kappa}^l, \widetilde{\kappa}^s)$ to Z^9 for the given value $\bar{c}$ satisfies first order conditions for Z^{10} with respect to x^l and x^s, which are identical to (7.27) and (7.28), respectively, except that $s+e$ replaces s. Second, the solution $\bar{c}$ to Z^9 also satisfies the first order condition for Z^{11} with respect to c, which is identical to (7.29), except that $s+e$ replaces s.

The third step estimates the marginal full cost function *MFC*. Substituting the solution $(\bar{x}^l, \bar{x}^s, \bar{c})$, as estimated through analyses of two sub-optimization problems, into Z^9 gives the full cost function FC that estimates the minimum of additional quasi-costs:

$$FC(\bar{c}; s+e, \breve{v}) = AMC(\bar{c}\,; s+e, \breve{v}) + ATC(\bar{c}\,; s+e, \breve{v}), \tag{7.36}$$

Then, the marginal full cost MFC is estimated by

$$MFC(s; \breve{v}) = \left.\frac{\partial FC(\bar{c}; s+e, \breve{v})}{\partial e}\right|_{e=s} = MMC(s; \breve{v}) + MTC(s; \breve{v}), \tag{7.37}$$

where

$$MMC(s) = \left.\frac{\partial AMC(\cdot)}{\partial e}\right|_{e=s}, \quad \text{and} \quad MTC(s; \breve{v}) = \left.\frac{\partial ATC(\cdot)}{\partial e}\right|_{e=s}. \tag{7.38}$$

This marginal full cost satisfies the relationship presented below.

Theorem 7.7. *The solution* $(\bar{x}^l, \bar{x}^s, \bar{c}, \bar{\kappa}^l, \bar{\kappa}^s)$ *to* Z^9 *satisfies the following equality:*

$$MMC(s; \breve{v}) = MKC(\bar{c}; s, \breve{v})\frac{\partial \bar{c}}{\partial s} + MVC(s; \breve{v}) \tag{7.39}$$

$$MCC(s; \breve{v}) = MKC(\bar{c}; s, \breve{v})\frac{\partial \bar{c}}{\partial s} + MTC(s; \breve{v}) \tag{7.40}$$

$$MFC(s; \breve{v}) = MCC(s; \breve{v}) + MVC(s; \breve{v}). \tag{7.41}$$

Proof. Firstly, prove (7.39). By the definition of MMC in (7.38), it follows that

$$MMC(s; \breve{v}) = \left.\frac{\partial AMC(\cdot)}{\partial e}\right|_{e=s} = \sum_j p_j \left(\frac{\partial \bar{x}^l_j}{\partial s} + \frac{\partial \bar{x}^s_j}{\partial s}\right) + \bar{\kappa}^l \left(\frac{\partial \bar{c}}{\partial s} - \sum_j \frac{\partial \bar{F}^l}{\partial x^l_j}\frac{\partial \bar{x}^l_j}{\partial s}\right)$$
$$+ \bar{\kappa}^s \left(1 - \sum_j \frac{\partial \bar{F}^s}{\partial x^l_j}\frac{\partial \bar{x}^l_j}{\partial s} - \sum_j \frac{\partial \bar{F}^s}{\partial x^s_j}\frac{\partial \bar{x}^s_j}{\partial s}\right).$$

The solution to Z^9 satisfies the optimality conditions of (7.27)∼(7.29), as pointed out in analyses of two sub-optimization problems. Substituting these optimality conditions of (7.27) and (7.28) into the above equation gives (7.39).

Secondly, prove (7.40) and (7.41). By the definition of MTC in (7.38) and Lemma 6.6, it follows that

$$MTC(s; \breve{v}) = \breve{v}s\frac{\partial T(s, \bar{c})}{\partial s} = \breve{v}s\frac{\partial T(s, \hat{c})}{\partial s} - MKC(\hat{c}; s, \breve{v})\frac{\partial \bar{c}}{\partial s}. \tag{7.42}$$

This implies (7.40). Finally, substituting (7.39) and (7.42) sequentially into (7.37) gives (7.41). □

Theorem 7.7 for a service system with variable costs can be interpreted as below. Equation (7.39) depicts that the marginal monetary cost is the sum of the marginal capacity cost for the action that optimally adjusts capacity and the marginal variable cost that is independent of cost for capacity adjustment. Equation (7.40) indicates that the marginal congestion cost is equal to the sum of the marginal capacity cost for optimal capacity adjustment and the implicit marginal revenue change due to the service time change caused by capacity adjustment. Equation (7.41) shows that the marginal full cost is the sum of the marginal congestion cost and the marginal variable cost.

Equations (7.40) and (7.41) characterize the difference between marginal congestion and marginal full costs for the service system with variable costs as below. Equation (7.40) is identical to the first equality of Theorem 6.7 for the basic service system, It can therefore be interpreted in the same manner as the marginal congestion cost for the basic service system; the marginal congestion cost for additional congestion delay under the condition that capacity is fixed to optimal capacity is equal to the minimum additional quasi-cost for the action to optimally adjust capacity. Equation (7.41) depicts that the marginal full cost estimates the minimum additional total quasi-cost, including variable cost, necessary to facilitate one unit of additional throughput. Such a marginal full cost is the sum of marginal quasi-cost for the action to adjust capacity and marginal variable cost free from the action to adjust capacity.

7.3.3 The Service System Serving Unsteady Demand Flows

Here we extend cost analyses for the public basic service system to a public service system that facilitates the random arrivals of demands whose flow rates vary by time period. This public service system facilitates the random arrival of demands with mean flow rates that differ by period $t \in \langle 1, T \rangle$. The duration of the tth period is $\delta_t \rangle 0$ for all t and satisfies the condition that $\sum_t \delta_t = 1.0$, under the convention that the analysis period is one unit of time. Each period t has a mean arrival rate of demands per unit time, denoted by s_t. Also the capacity of the tth period, denoted by c_t, represents the maximum throughput of the service system per unit time.

Firstly, we construct a SCMP under the convention introduced above. Capacity c_t is the outcome of an investment decision of a supplier and satisfies the constraint for the production technology F, such that

$$c_t \leqslant F(x_o, x_t), \text{all } t, \tag{7.43}$$

where $x_o \equiv (x_{o1}, \cdots, x_{oJ})$ is an input vector that affects the capacity of all the periods simultaneously, whereas $x_t \equiv (x_{t1}, \cdots, x_{tJ})$ is an input vector that exerts the effect only on the capacity of the tth period.

The variables x_{oj} and x_{tj} denote in common the quantities of good or service j, but express the quantities in different usages. The variable x_{oj}, termed *the long-run capacity variable*, represents the amount of good or service j consumed during the construction of sub-systems operated throughout all periods. On the other hand, the variable x_{tj}, termed *the short-run capacity variable*, refers to the quantity of j inputted to the operation to maintain a predetermined capacity during the tth period only. Using these two groups of variables, the total monetary cost can be expressed by

$$Monetary\ Cost = \sum_j p_j \left(x_{oj} + \sum_t \delta_t x_{tj} \right), \tag{7.44}$$

where $\delta_t x_{tj}$ is the actual amount of input j consumed at the tth period.

Service time differs by period t but is common to all users for each period. The service time of the tth period, denoted by t_t, is estimated by

$$t_t = T_t(s_t, c_t), \text{all } t. \tag{7.45}$$

Then, the user time cost of the service system is estimated by

$$User\ Time\ Cost = \sum_{it} \delta_t t_t v_t^i s_t^i = \sum_t \delta_t t_t \bar{v}_t s_t, \tag{7.46}$$

where v_t^i is the net-value-of-time perceived by consumer i during the tth period, and $\bar{v}_t \equiv \sum_i v_t^i s_t^i / s_t$ is the mean net-value-of-time for all demands during the tth period.

By combining (7.43)~(7.46), we construct a Multi-Period Social Cost Minimization Problem (MPSCMP) for aggregated throughputs $s \equiv (s_1, \cdots, s_T)$, denoted by MPZ^3, such that

$$\begin{aligned} MPZ^3(x, c, t, \kappa, \tau; s, \bar{v}) \equiv \min \left\{ \sum_j p_j \left(x_{oj} + \sum_t \delta_t x_{tj} \right) + \sum_t \delta_t t_t \bar{v}_t s_t \right\} \\ + \sum_t \delta_t \kappa_t (c_t - F(x_o, x_t)) + \sum_t \delta_t \tau_t (T_t(s_t, c_t) - t_t), \end{aligned} \tag{7.47}$$

where $x \equiv (x_o, x_1, \cdots, x_T)$, $c \equiv (c_1, \cdots, c_T)$, $\bar{v} \equiv (\bar{v}_1, \cdots, \bar{v}_T)$, $\kappa \equiv (\kappa_1, \cdots, \kappa_T) \rangle\ 0$, and $\tau \equiv (\tau_1, \cdots, \tau_T) \rangle\ 0$.

Secondly, we develop optimality conditions for MPZ^3, which are similar to those of Lemmas 6.1–6.3 for Z^3, under the convention that $(\bar{x}, \bar{c}, \bar{t}, \bar{\kappa}, \bar{\tau})$ is the solution to MPZ^3. The optimality condition for the choice of x, which is equivalent to that of Lemma 6.1, gives the following capacity cost function KC:

$$KC(c) = \sum_j p_j \left(\bar{x}_{oj} + \sum_t \delta_t \bar{x}_{tj} \right). \tag{7.48}$$

In addition, the solution $\bar{x}_{oj}$ satisfies the production efficiency condition such that

$$\sum_t \delta_t MKC_t(\bar{c}) \frac{\partial \bar{F}}{\partial x_{oj}} = p_j, \text{ all } j, \tag{7.49}$$

where $\bar{F} \equiv F(\bar{x}_o, \bar{x}_t)$. The solution $\bar{x}_{tj}$ fulfills the condition such that

$$MKC_t(\bar{c}) = \frac{\partial KC(\bar{c})}{\partial \delta_t c_t} = \bar{\kappa}_t = p_j \Big/ \frac{\partial \bar{F}}{\partial x_{tj}}, \text{ all } t, j. \tag{7.50}$$

Here, $\delta_t c_t$ is the upper limit of throughput yieldable at the tth period.

The optimality condition for the solution $\bar{\tau}_t$, which is equivalent to that of Lemma 6.2, is as follows:

$$\bar{\tau}_t = \bar{v}_t s_t, \text{ all } t. \tag{7.51}$$

On the other hand, the optimality condition for the choice of c, which is equivalent to that of Lemma 6.3, is as below:

$$\begin{aligned} MKC_t(\bar{c}) &= -\delta_t \bar{v}_t s_t \frac{\partial T_t(s_t, \bar{c}_t)}{\partial \delta_t c_t} \\ &= -\bar{v}_t s_t \frac{\partial T_t(s_t, \bar{c}_t)}{\partial c_t}, \text{ all } t. \end{aligned} \tag{7.52}$$

This equation depicts that the optimal capacity $\bar{c}_t$ must equate the marginal capacity cost estimated in (7.50) to the additional user cost saving accrued in facilitating throughput $\delta_t s_t$ through an action to increase one unit of c_t.

Thirdly, we estimate the marginal social cost of throughput s_t for MPZ^3. By the envelop theorem, this marginal quasi-cost SMC_t is

$$SMC_t(s; \bar{v}) = MUC_t(s; \bar{v}) + SMCC_t(s; \bar{v}), \text{ all } t, \tag{7.53}$$

where

$$MUC_t(s; \bar{v}) = \bar{v}_t T_t(s_t, \bar{c}_t), \text{ and } SMCC_t(s_t; \bar{v}) = \bar{v}_t s_t \frac{\partial T_t(s_t, c_t = \bar{c}_t)}{\partial s_t^i}. \tag{7.54}$$

This equation shows that the cost SMC_t has an expression identical to that of the basic service system in Theorem 6.3, except for the incorporation of subscript t.

Fourthly, we estimate the marginal full cost of aggregated throughput s_t. To this end, we develop the social full cost function that estimates the minimum additional social cost necessary to facilitate additional throughput $e \equiv (e_1, \cdots, e_T)$ through the adjustment of the original optimal capacity $\hat{c} \equiv (\hat{c}_1, \cdots, \hat{c}_T)$ for $s \equiv (s_1, \cdots, s_T)$ to the new optimal capacity $\bar{c} \equiv (\bar{c}_1, \cdots, \bar{c}_T)$ for $s + e \equiv (s_1 + e_1, \cdots, s_T + e_T)$.

Proceeding with analyses analogous to that used to from the QCMP in (7.31) to the full cost function in (7.36) for a service system with variable costs gives the social full cost function for the MPSCMP in (7.27):

$$SFC(\bar{c};s+e,\bar{v}) \equiv AMC(\bar{c};s+e,\bar{v}) + ATC(\bar{c};s+e,\bar{v}), \tag{7.55}$$

where

$$AMC(\bar{c};s+e,\bar{v}) = \sum_j p_j\left(\bar{x}_{oj} + \sum_t \delta_t \bar{x}_{tj}\right) - \sum_j p_j\left(\hat{x}_{oj} + \sum_t \delta_t \hat{x}_{tj}\right) \tag{7.56}$$

$$ATC(\bar{c};\ s+e,\bar{v}) = \sum_t \delta_t \bar{v}_t s_t T_t(s_t+e_t,\bar{c}_t) - \sum_t \delta_t \bar{v}_t s_t T_t(s_t,\hat{c}_t). \tag{7.57}$$

Here, the solution $(\bar{x}^l,\bar{c})$ satisfies the optimality conditions for MPZ^3 in (7.49), (7.50), and (7.52).

Then, the social marginal full cost of the tth period, $SMFC_t$, is estimated by

$$SMFC_t(s;\bar{v}) = \left.\frac{\partial SFC(\cdot)}{\partial e_t}\right|_{e_t=s_t} = MMC_t(s;\bar{v}) + MTC_t(s;\bar{v}), \tag{7.58}$$

where

$$MMC_t(s;\breve{v}) = \left.\frac{\partial AMC(\cdot)}{\partial e_t}\right|_{e=s} = \sum_k MKC_k(\bar{c})\frac{\partial \bar{c}_k}{\partial s_t} \tag{7.59}$$

$$MTC_t(s;\breve{v}) = \left.\frac{\partial ATC(\cdot)}{\partial e_t}\right|_{e=s} = \sum_k \bar{v}_k s_k \frac{\partial T_k(s_k,\bar{c}_k)}{\partial s_t}. \tag{7.60}$$

Here, (7.59) is proved using (7.49) and (7.50). These marginal costs satisfy the relationships shown below.

Theorem 7.8. *The function $SMFC_t$, estimated in (7.58), satisfies the following:*

$$SMFC_t(s;\bar{v}) = SMCC_t(s;\bar{v}), \quad all \quad t.$$

Proof. It can be proved in a manner analogous to the proof of Theorem 7.7. □

Fifthly, we identify the relationship between $SMFC_t$ and MKC_t in a manner analogous to the relationship in Theorems 7.1 and 7.2. In the case of homogeneous service technology, this relationship is

$$SMFC_t(s;\bar{v}) = \frac{\bar{c}_t}{s_t}MKC_t(\bar{c}),\ \text{all } t, \tag{7.61}$$

as can be confirmed in the manner used to prove Theorem 7.1. In the case of non-homogeneous service technology, the relationship is

$$SMFC_t(s;\bar{v}) = \frac{\bar{c}_t}{s_t}(MKC_t(\bar{c}) - MWT_t(\bar{c};\bar{v})), \text{ all } t, \tag{7.62}$$

where

$$MWT_t(\bar{c};\bar{v}) = \frac{\bar{v}_t\, s_t}{2\,(\bar{y}_t)^2} T_1^d(s_t/\bar{c}_t), \tag{7.63}$$

and $\bar{y}_t$ is the sum of the total service frequencies of all service systems available to consumers during the tth period, including the frequency of the service system analyzed.

7.4 Examples of Cost Analyses

7.4.1 Homogeneous Service Technology Serving Steady Demand Flows

The service time function of (6.2) is an approximation applicable to many congestion-prone service systems that offer services on the first-in-first-out basis. Using this service time function, we here illustrate the procedure to estimate various marginal cost functions for Z^3 in (6.15) under the condition that net-value-of-time is identical across all consumers.

The SCMP analyzed here, which is developed by substituting the service time function in (6.2) into (6.15), is

$$Z^3(c,t,\tau;s,\bar{v}) \equiv \min\{KC(c) + \bar{v}ts\} + \tau\left(t^o + t^d\frac{Js/c}{1-s/c} - t\right), \tag{7.64}$$

where $\bar{v}$ is the net-value-of-time common to all consumers. By Theorems 6.3 and 6.5, the function *SMC* for this SCMP satisfies the following relationship:

$$SMC(s;\bar{v}) = MUC(s;\bar{v}) + SMFC(s;\bar{v}). \tag{7.65}$$

The solutions of *SMC*, *MUC*, and *SMFC* are estimated below.

To start, we estimate the capacity function $\bar{c}(s)$ that estimates optimal capacities for varying s values. For the cost minimization problem (7.64), the optimality investment rule in Lemma 6.3 has the expression such that

$$MKC(\bar{c}) = \bar{v}J\left(\frac{s/\bar{c}}{1-s/\bar{c}}\right)^2. \tag{7.66}$$

The above equation gives

$$\bar{c}(s) = \left(1 + \frac{1}{\sqrt{\theta(s)}}\right)s. \tag{7.67}$$

where

$$\theta(s) = \frac{MKC(\bar{c})}{\bar{v}J}.$$

Equation (7.67) depicts that the optimal capacity $\bar{c}(s)$ should be larger than the throughput s by a ratio $(1 + 1/\sqrt{\theta})$, which is larger than 1.0.

The formula (7.67) implies the following. First, the ratio $(1 + 1/\sqrt{\theta})$ becomes smaller as the value of $MKC(\bar{c})$ is larger. Therefore, the service system with a larger value of $MKC(\bar{c})$ should maintain a higher level of system utilization ratio, $\bar{\rho}(\equiv s/\bar{c})$. Second, the ratio $(1 + 1/\sqrt{\theta})$ becomes larger as the $\bar{v}$ value increases. Therefore, the service system that serves customers having larger net-value-of-times should maintain a lower system utilization ratio.

Subsequently, we estimate the specific expressions of *MUC* and *SMFC* in (7.65). By (7.67), the function *MUC* is

$$\begin{aligned} MUC(s) &= \bar{v}t^o + \bar{v}t^d J\frac{s/\bar{c}}{1-s/\bar{c}} \\ &= \bar{v}t^o + t^d\sqrt{\bar{v}J\,MKC(\bar{c})}. \end{aligned} \tag{7.68}$$

The function *SMFC*, which is estimated by substituting (7.67) into (7.1), is

$$\begin{aligned} SMFC(s) &= \frac{\bar{c}}{s}MKC(\bar{c}) \\ &= MKC(\bar{c}) + \sqrt{\bar{v}J\,MKC(\bar{c})}. \end{aligned} \tag{7.69}$$

The above analysis shows that, if the function $MKC(c)$ is known, the functions $SMC(s)$, $MUC(s)$, and $SMFC(s)$ can readily be estimated. For example, suppose that the function $MKC(c)$ is a constant for all c values. Then, all three of the functions $SMC(s)$, $MUC(s)$, and $SMFC(s)$ are also constant for all s values. Suppose, next, that the function $MKC(c)$ is increasing in c. Then, the three functions are also increasing in s. Suppose, further, that the function $MKC(c)$ is convex (or concave) in c. Then, the three functions are also convex in c, since $\sqrt{SMC(s)}$ is convex (or concave).

7.4.2 Non-homogeneous Service Technology Serving Steady Demand Flows

The service time function in (6.4) is a plausible approximation of urban public transit services in no competition on a certain corridor. This service time function is not homogeneous of degree zero in s and c, due to the presence of the term $1/2c$. For this service time function, we develop various marginal cost functions in a manner analogous to the analyses for homogeneous service time function in the Sect. 7.4.1.

For service time function (6.4), the SCMP is

$$Z^3(c,t,\tau;s,\bar{v}) \equiv \min\{KC(c) + \bar{v}ts\} + \tau\left(t^o + \frac{1}{2c}\left(1 + T^d(s/\tau c)\right) - t\right), \quad (7.70)$$

where

$$T^d(s/\tau c) = \frac{Js/\tau c}{1 - s/\tau c} = \frac{J\rho}{1-\rho},$$

and $\bar{v}$ is the net-value-of-time common to all consumers. Here, J is a positive value significantly smaller than 1.0, as explained in the comment for (6.2). It is also assumed that the capacity cost function KC is

$$KC(c) = \alpha + \beta c, \quad (7.71)$$

where $\alpha \geqslant 0$, and $\beta \rangle 0$, in order to simplify the analysis.

The SCMP of (7.70) yields the social marginal function that satisfies the equality such that $SMC = MUC + SMFC$ in (7.65). Also, the solutions of SMC, MUC, and $SMFC$ are estimated from the optimal investment rule in Lemma 6.3 for the minimization problem (7.70), such that

$$MKC(\bar{c}) = \beta = \bar{v}s\left(\frac{1}{2\bar{c}^2}\left(1 + T^d(s/\tau\bar{c})\right) - \frac{1}{2\bar{c}}\frac{\partial T^d(s/\tau\bar{c})}{\partial c}\right). \quad (7.72)$$

The solution $\bar{c}$ to the optimality condition (7.72) is a useful input to estimate various marginal cost functions, as illustrated in the previous subsection. However, this optimality condition in the form of an ordinary differential equation that estimates the capacity $\bar{c}$ is so complex that it is infeasible to estimate a closed-form solution. We therefore rely on an approach to determine the functional forms of various social cost functions in a piecemeal manner, and thus develop Fig. 7.1. The inputs necessary to develop the figure are presented below.

First, the term $\partial\bar{\rho}/\partial s$ satisfies the inequality such that

$$\frac{\partial\bar{\rho}}{\partial s} = \frac{\partial}{\partial s}\left(\frac{s}{\tau\bar{c}}\right) \geq 0, \quad (7.73)$$

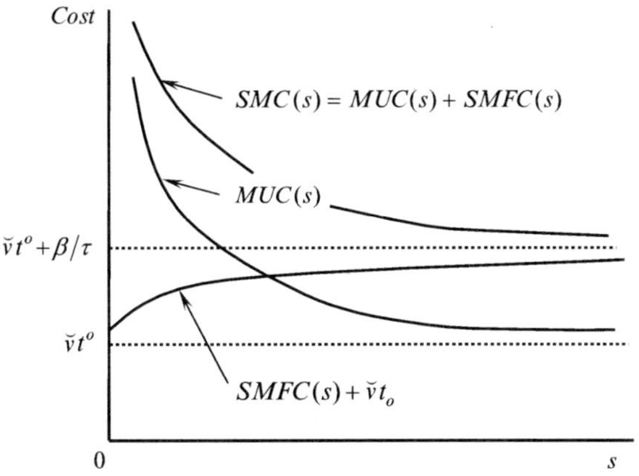

Fig. 7.1 Marginal cost function for non-homogeneous service technology

as can be proved by substituting $\partial^2 KC/\partial c^2 = 0$ and $y = s$ into Y in (7.17). This equation implies that the ratio $\bar{\rho}$ is increasing in s and that it approaches 1.0 as s grows infinitely; that is, optimal capacity $\tau\bar{c}$ approaches throughput s as throughput s increases infinitely.

Second, by (7.5), it follows that

$$SMCC(s;\bar{v}) = SMFC(s;\bar{v}) \leq \frac{\beta\bar{c}}{s} = \frac{\beta}{\tau\bar{\rho}}, \tag{7.74}$$

where $\beta = MKC(c)$. This implies that the social marginal full cost is smaller than the long-run average supplier cost of throughput, estimated by $\beta/\tau\bar{\rho}$.

Third, a special solution of $\bar{c}\,(s)$ to the differential equation in (7.72), which is applicable only to very small s values, gives

$$\lim_{s\to+0} MUC(s;\bar{v}) = \infty, \quad \text{and} \quad \lim_{s\to+0} SMFC(s;\bar{v}) = \frac{J\beta}{\tau}, \tag{7.75}$$

as proved in Appendix B.5. Here, a very large value of MUC for a very small s value reasonably reflects that the waiting time of passengers is very large when the small service frequency is very small. Also, the function $SMFC$ indicates that, if s is very small, the marginal full cost is smaller than the long-run average supplier cost per seat, β/τ, since $0 \langle J \langle 1.0$.

Fourth, a special solution of $c\,(s)$ to the differential equation in (7.72), which is applicable only to very large s values, leads to

$$\lim_{s\to\infty} MUC(s;\bar{v}) = \bar{v}t_o, \quad \text{and} \quad \lim_{s\to\infty} SMFC(s;\bar{v}) = \frac{\beta}{\tau}, \tag{7.76}$$

as also shown in Appendix B.5. The first equation for MUC indicates that, if s is very large, the waiting time is negligibly small, due to very large service frequency.

The second equation for *SMFC* implies that, if s is very large, the ratio $\bar{\rho}$ is 1.0, and thus that the social marginal full cost equals the long-run average supplier cost per seat, β/τ.

Fifth, it holds that

$$\frac{\partial MUC(s;\bar{v})}{\partial s} \langle\ 0, \tag{7.77}$$

$$\frac{\partial SMFC(s;\bar{v})}{\partial s} \rangle\ 0, \tag{7.78}$$

as shown in Appendix B.5. Hence, combining (7.77) with the first equalities of (7.75) and (7.66) yields the monotonically decreasing and convex curve of *MUC*, as depicted in Fig. 7.1. Likewise, merging (7.78) with the second equalities of (7.75) and (7.76) yields the monotonically increasing and concave curve of *SMFC*, as illustrated in the figure.

7.4.3 Homogeneous Service Technology Serving Peaking Demands

Here we illustrate analyses of a MPSCMP with an example of a highway link facilitating peaking demands. Analyses focus on estimating approximate optimal capacities and approximate marginal social costs for peak and off-peak periods, respectively, under the following conditions. First, mean flow rate varies by period. Second, capacity is constant throughout the entire analysis period. Third, service time function is expressed as (6.2), which is common to all periods. Fourth, highway is a divisible facility; that is, capacity is a continuous variable.

The second condition implies that the function *KC* has a single explanatory variable c common to all periods. Substituting this function *KC* into the MPSCMP in (7.47) yields a SCMP such that

$$MPZ^3(x,c,t,\tau;s,\bar{v}) \equiv \min\left\{KC(c) + \sum_t \delta_t \bar{v}_t t_t s_t\right\} + \sum_t \delta_t \tau_t \left(t^o + T^d(s_t/c) - t_t\right), \tag{7.79}$$

where $T^d(s_t/c) = t^d(s_t/c)^\alpha$.

In addition, we introduce the following three conditions, which are acceptable in cost analyses of highways. First, the pth period exhibiting peaking phenomena has a flow rate that is significantly larger than other periods; in other words,

$$s_p \rangle\ s_t, \text{ all } t \neq p. \tag{7.80}$$

Second, the coefficient α in T^d is larger than 4, as reported in Highway Capacity Manual (1999). Third, the ratio δ_p is not negligibly smaller than $1 - \delta_p$.

We next analyze the cost function of highways. As a first step, we develop the optimality condition for capacity. Differentiating MPZ^3 with respect to c gives

$$\begin{aligned} MKC(\bar{c}) &= -\sum_t \delta_t \bar{v}_t s_t \frac{\partial T^d(s_t/\bar{c})}{\partial c} \\ &= \sum_t \delta_t \bar{v}_t \frac{(s_t)^2}{\bar{c}} \frac{\partial T^d(s_t/c\,;c=\bar{c})}{\partial s_t}. \end{aligned} \tag{7.81}$$

This equation is none other than a special version of (7.52), which is applicable only to the case where capacity is constant throughout all periods.

Subsequently, differentiating MPZ^3 in (7.9) with respect to $\delta_t s_t$ and simplifying the previous result in a manner similar to that of (7.53) gives

$$SMC_t(s;\bar{v}) = MUC_t(s;\bar{v}) + SMCC_t(s;\bar{v}), \text{ all } t, \tag{7.82}$$

where MUC_t and $SMCC_t$ are identical to the same functions defined in (7.54). Substituting $SMCC_t$ in (7.54) into (7.81) gives

$$MKC(\bar{c}) = \frac{1}{\bar{c}} \sum_t \delta_t s_t SMCC_t(s). \tag{7.83}$$

Substituting $T^d(s_t/c) = t^d(s_t/c)^\alpha$ into the right side of (7.83) yields

$$MKC(\bar{c}) = \sum_t \delta_t\, t^d \alpha\, (s_t/\bar{c})^{\alpha+1}. \tag{7.84}$$

Then, under the condition (7.80), (7.84) is simplified as follows:

$$MKC\,(\bar{c}) \cong \delta_p t^d \alpha\, (s_p/\bar{c})^{\alpha+1}. \tag{7.85}$$

On applying an additional condition that $MKC(c)$ is approximately constant irrespective of the c value on the relevant region, it is possible to estimate the approximate solution of the optimal capacity $\bar{c}$ from the above equation:

$$\bar{c}(s) \cong \left(\delta_p t^d \alpha / MKC(\bar{c})\right)^{1/(\alpha+1)} s_p. \tag{7.86}$$

This equation shows that the optimal capacity $\bar{c}$ mainly depends upon the flow rate and duration of the peak period together with the marginal capacity cost.

Finally, substituting (7.86) into MUC_t and MCC_t in (7.54) gives the approximations of MUC_t and MFC_t, respectively:

$$MUC_t(s;\bar{v}) \cong \begin{cases} \bar{v}_t\left(t^o + \dfrac{\bar{c}MKC(\bar{c})}{\alpha\delta_t s_t}\right), & \text{when } t = p \\ \bar{v}_t t^o, & \text{when } t \neq p \end{cases} \tag{7.87}$$

$$SMFC_t(s;\bar{v}) \cong \begin{cases} \dfrac{\bar{c}MKC(\bar{c})}{\delta^t s^t}, & \text{when } t = p \\ 0, & \text{when } t \neq p. \end{cases} \tag{7.88}$$

Note that the relationship $\delta_t s_t SMFC_t(s) \cong \bar{c}MKC(\bar{c})$ in (7.87) is equivalent to the relationship $s\,SMFC(s) = \bar{c}MKC(\bar{c})$ for the single-period problem in Theorem 7.1.

Part III
Decisions of Congestion-Prone Service Firms

Chapter 8
The Equilibrium of Monopoly Service Markets

8.1 Introduction

A service firm usually facilitates demands below the capacity of the service system operated. For such a service firm, called *the congestion-prone service firm* (*service firm* or *firm*, for short), the actual choice component consists only of price and capacity. After the firm chooses its price and capacity, its customers play the role of finalizing the demand and service time of the service system operated. For example, if the service system is congested, some customers stop using the system, and, thus, the demand and service time of the system are both reduced.

In order to account for the effect of congestion on profit, the PMP for service firms must be modeled so that it can reflect the following three aspects of decision-making problems faced by service firms. First, demand for a service is sensitive to service time as well as price. Second, the directly controllable variables of the firm consist only of price and capacity. Third, consumers themselves determine the service time they experience in receiving services.

However, modeling the PMP for a service firm that fulfills the three requirements specified above is not simple. The difficulty exists because of the interdependency between the service time and demand function of a congestion-prone service system; service time is an independent variable of the demand function and, simultaneously, the dependent variable of the service time function, which is increasing in demand but decreasing in capacity. This interdependency makes it difficult to properly model the PMP as an optimization problem in which either service time or demand must be designated as the independent choice variable of decision-makers.

The user equilibrium approach proposed in this chapter is a modeling approach for the PMP of a service firm. This approach designates service time as the choice variable of the firm. To model the PMP in that manner, we hypothesize that a firm comprehends and utilizes the service time and demand resulting from consumer reaction to a certain choice of the firm for its directly controllable variables: price and capacity. Mathematically, this hypothesis

D.J. Moon, *Congestion-Prone Services Under Quality Competition*, Advances in Spatial Science, DOI 10.1007/978-3-642-20189-9_8,

implies that service time is also the choice variable that can be indirectly controlled through the choice of directly controllable variables.

The term *user equilibrium* depicts consumer reaction to the choice of a service firm regarding its directly controllable variables. This term was originally introduced in a study by Beckmann et al. (1955) examining the traffic volume forecast of a highway network composed of multiple links with predetermined capacities. In that study, user equilibrium was used to refer to the state at which no traveler could shorten travel time by changing their travel route. In this study, in contrast, the term represents the state at which no consumer is willing to change service demand for firms or to alter the service time of congestion-prone service systems by changing the demand, in the circumstance that firms have already made the choice regarding their directly controllable variables.

The user equilibrium approach is synonymous with the modeling approach for the PMP of a firm under the following leader-and-follower game. First, the firm, the leader of the game, pursues maximum profit through its choices of price and capacity. Second, consumers, the followers of the game, are willing to maximize utility through the optimal choice of service demand and time. Third, a certain choice of the firm for price and capacity is followed by consumer reaction to reach user equilibrium for the choice. Fourth, the firm utilizes knowledge of consumer reaction in choosing its price and capacity.

The knowledge of a service firm for consumer reaction is formulated as the *user equilibrium condition,* which constitutes a constraint for the PMP. The user equilibrium condition is designed to estimate service time at user equilibrium for an arbitrary choice of price and capacity.[1] The user equilibrium condition has a formulation identical to that of the service time function used in the cost analysis of Part II, except that throughput is replaced by the service demand function.

In addition, the PMP under the user equilibrium approach is constructed by applying the modeling approaches for consumer demands and supplier costs from Parts I and II, respectively. The demand function incorporated into the PMP is the market demand function under the perception approach, which is sensitive to service time as well as price. The supplier cost is characterized from a dual of the PMP, which is expressed as a QCMP for congestion-prone services under the full cost approach.

This chapter illustrates analyses of service market equilibrium under the user equilibrium approach outlined above. One objective of these analyses is to introduce

[1] The approach of Beckmann et al. (1955) estimates travel time at user equilibrium from a minimization problem with constraints, and have been extensively studied for its application to traffic forecasts (Scheffi, 1985) and optimal highway design (Boyce, 1984 and 1987). This minimization problem is not formulated in such a way that it can be incorporated into PMPs as a constraint. In contrast, the user equilibrium condition of this study is formulated as one equation from which service time at user equilibrium is estimated. This user equilibrium condition cannot apply to analyses that estimate the travel time forecast of a highway network composed of multiple links, as is true of the approach of Beckman et al. Instead, this condition can be a useful tool for economic analyses at an abstract level, as illustrated with social welfare maximization problems in Moon and Park (2002b).

the overall approach to modeling the PMP that applies not only to monopolistic but also to competitive firms. Another objective is to illustrate analyses for the equilibrium of service markets with an example of monopoly markets.

The following section presents the overall approach to modeling the PMP applicable to all congestion-prone service firms, irrespective of types of competition the firm faces. First, we introduce the method for adapting the demand and cost analyses presented in Parts I and II, respectively, to PMPs under the user equilibrium approach. Subsequently, we present a specific expression of the user equilibrium condition and the implication of the expression. Finally, we introduce the PMP for monopolists under the user equilibrium approach in the simplest form, called *the basic form of PMPs*.

This is followed by Sect. 8.3, which presents analyses for the basic form of PMPs. The first topic of analyses shows that the PMP has a dual problem identical to the BQCMP considered in Sect. 6.4. The second topic develops the pricing and investment rules of the service firm, and compares and contrasts these rules with the same rules of congestion-free firms. The third topic characterizes market equilibrium in the context of leader-and-follower games.

In Sect. 8.4, we extend the analysis of the previous sections for a special case of congestion-prone service systems to other service systems considered in Chap. 7. One problem analyzes service systems with fixed capacities that are not optimal. Another problem covers service systems that consume variable costs in serving demands. A third problem analyzes service systems that facilitate unsteady demand flows.

8.2 Development of Profit Maximization Problems

8.2.1 Types of Congestion-Prone Services

Congestion-prone services refer to all services for which congestion must be addressed in economic analyses. To be specific, congestion-prone services are the target of cost analyses under the full cost approach. Further, congestion-prone services constitute a large subset of qualitative choice services considered in service demand analyses under the perception approach. Such congestion-prone services comprise most private services at the final consumption stage, as identified below.

To begin, we identify congestion-prone services to which the forthcoming economic analyses of this study can apply. First, congestion-prone services are offered by service systems that exhibit congestion caused by limited capacities. Second, increases in capacity reduce congestion and thus improve service quality but require larger supplier investment. Third, the supplier of congestion-prone services facilitates all the random arrivals of demands for the services, without rejecting any arrival.

We can categorize most services at the final consumption stage into the congestion-prone services defined above. In a narrow sense, congestion-prone services comprise all services that exhibit the observable form of congestion. In a broad sense, congestion-prone services encompass all services such that their limited capacity causes or has the potential to cause economic losses to customers.

The observable form of congestion that occurs in service systems can be further divided into two types. One type of observable congestion is service delays that force customers to queue before receiving service. Service systems that exhibit this type are found in retail shops, restaurants, theaters, medical clinics, banks, telecommunication facilities, etc. The other type arises from crowding phenomena that cause customers to spend additional time and/or to experience discomfort in the process of receiving services. The service systems that cause this type include recreation facilities, resort complexes, etc.

Furthermore, the unobservable form of congestion that exerts economic loss to customers can be grouped into two types. One type of such congestion includes reservation delays, which makes it impossible for customers to receive services at the most opportune time. This type of congestion may force customers to switch to other options or to postpone using a certain service system. Typical examples of this type are those experienced in reserving hotel rooms and airline tickets. The other type of unobservable congestion involves service delay or service quality deterioration due to capacity shortage. Examples of services exhibiting this type include construction services and various business services offered by law, advertising, engineering, and management consulting firms.

It should be noted that all congestion-prone services have a certain service component that can be classified as non-durable, as long as capacity is an important decision-making component of the firm. This assertion, of course, applies to all services that can be sorted into non-durable services such as travel, hotel, communication, and entertainment services. Less obviously, this assertion applies to durable but congestion-prone services offered in clinic, retail, construction, and business service environments. For example, service in a clinic is a typical durable service, but the service process certainly involves congestion.

Subsequently, we distinguish congestion-prone services from qualitative choice services. Qualitative choice services refer to services that are offered by multiple options differentiated by various service quality attributes. These service quality attributes comprise not only congestion that constitutes a part of service time but also other qualitative attributes such as comfort and safety. Therefore, all congestion-prone services under competition can be sorted into qualitative choice services. However, some qualitative choice services cannot be categorized as congestion-prone services.

We can imagine that some qualitative choice services do not fulfill the three restrictive conditions defining the congestion-prone service, as described in the beginning of this subsection. One group of such qualitative services does not require the use of approaches that account for congestion or capacity shortage in economic studies. Examples include the labor supply of workers and housing services. Another group includes services not open to the public. Typical examples of this type include the education service provided by all universities and private high schools.

The education service offered at such schools can differ both quantitatively and qualitatively. Further, the service systems of schools have the potential such that having a limit on capacity can cause economic losses to students. However, schools not open to the general public have selection processes, as service providers, to choose customers from among all those demanding their service. Therefore, it is difficult to apply the demand function under the perception approach to analyses of the supplier's decision-making problem using the user equilibrium approach.

8.2.2 Decision-Making Components of Service Firms

The market analysis of this monograph is a kind of abstraction of the real world, as, of course, are all other economic studies. Naturally, one important factor that delineates the effectiveness of the analysis is how fully and appropriately the decision-making model of a firm considers important decision-making components. Associated with this issue, we discuss here how the PMP under the user equilibrium approach reflects all the important decision-making components of a firm that plans to offer a certain congestion-prone service.

The decision-making components of a service firm can be sorted into two categories under the framework used to distinguish a service option in demand analyses. The first category includes all decision-making components that determine the qualitative attributes of service. The second category, predictably, consists of all directly controllable variables that determine the value of quantitative attributes in the demand function.

The first category includes all the decision-making components that affect the qualitative attributes of service. The choice of these components plays the role of determining a service group differentiated by qualitative attributes under the demand analysis framework of the perception approach. Moreover, mathematically, the decision of entrepreneurs in this category can be incorporated into the net-value-of-time of the demand function under the perception approach.

One specific choice component of this qualitative category is the specialization of service. An example here might be the choice of an entrepreneur who contracts to choose the best manufacturing brand to operate a franchise shop. A rather different example involves specialization of service areas, such as the type of dishes served by restaurants, disease specialization at particular hospitals, groups of customers targeted by legal firms or other business service firms, and the particular specialization area chosen by construction companies.

Another choice component could be the choice of service facilities and employees, which play important roles in determining levels of service diversification and quality. Examples of choice components that affect service diversification are variety of facilities installed by resort complexes, types of medical equipment owned by hospitals, diversity of menu offerings at restaurants, etc. Rather different examples are the quality of interior design of retail stores, and the experience and knowledge of hospital staff.

The second category naturally contains all choice components that determine the two quantitative attributes of service demand: price and service time. Furthermore, the choice components that affect service time can be sorted into two groups. The first group comprises all choice variables that determine the capacity of service systems, whereas the second group includes all the choice components related to the service process of service systems.

These choice components for quantitative attributes, except for service time, can be sorted into *directly controllable variables* that can be determined solely by the firm, and are integrated into the PMP in the following manner. First, price is incorporated into the demand function as an independent variable. Second, capacity is employed as a sole independent variable that determines the cost of service systems. Third, capacity and service process are reflected in the service time function that constitutes a constraint of PMPs.

The service time function employed in PMPs is constructed through an amendment of the original service time function in Assumption 6.1. This amendment replaces exogenously given throughput in the original function with the service demand function under the perception approach. This amended service time function plays the role of determining service time, one remaining choice component of firms for quantitative attributes.

Importantly, the service time estimated from the service time function is sensitive to the choice of firms for price and capacity, as explained below. The service time function gives a larger service time as demand increases and as capacity decreases. On the other hand, demand decreases as price increases. Hence, the service time function gives a larger service time as price and capacity decrease. This implies that service time is a function of two directly controllable variables: price and capacity.

The incorporation of the service time function into PMPs as a constraint reflects the postulate that service time is *an indirectly controllable choice variable* for a service firm. This postulate connotes that the firm makes a choice regarding prices and capacities with the prior expectation that the choice will lead to a certain amount of demand, and thus achieve a certain service time. The process of estimating service time in this postulate is explained in the following two subsections.

8.2.3 Representation of Service Time

Service demand functions under the perception approach and service time functions under the full cost approach are the key components that constitute PMPs under the user equilibrium approach. All demand functions in PMPs have in common a functional form identical or similar to that developed from the basic choice problem for non-durable services. On the other hand, all service time functions are identical or close to that applied in the basic service system for non-durable services. The process of representing service time in these demand and service time functions used in PMPs under the user equilibrium approach is presented below.

The PMP for congestion-prone services under the user equilibrium approach includes demand and service time functions, both of which are sensitive to service time. This variable of service time should be measured using a common basis applicable to both demand and service time functions. This common service time should be separated from total service time, so that it can fulfill the following requirements: first, the entire service time must have a uniform net-value-of-time; second, it should reflect the congestion delay of the service system due to limited capacity.

The rationale for introducing the two requirements is as follows. The net-value-of-time is a factor that determines the implicit price of services in demand function under the perception approach. Importantly, the net-value-of-time of congestion delay sometimes differs from that of net service times. Moreover, congestion delay is sensitive to demand and capacity, while net service time is usually insensitive. For example, the net-value-of-time of waiting time for public transit is larger than that of in-vehicle time, since waiting time is usually more exhausting than in-vehicle time. Furthermore, the waiting time usually increases as service frequency decreases, whereas in-vehicle time is commonly less sensitive or insensitive to these two variables.

The method of representing the service time, which fulfills these two requirements, depends on the characteristics of congestion exhibited by the system. Consider a service system that forms either observable or unobservable queues. For this service system, this service time can be represented by service delay time, excluding net service time. Consider next a service system that shows crowding phenomena. For this system, the service time can be measured by applying total service time.

Moreover, all service demand functions under the percept approach can be changed to the demand function for the basic choice problem analyzed in Chap. 2. For example, suppose that the implicit price of prime commodities in the demand function of consumer i for a certain service is expressed by

$$\pi^i(p, t^n, t^d) = \frac{1}{a}\left(p + v^{ni}\, t^n + v^{di}\, t^d\right), \tag{8.1}$$

where t^n is net service time, t^d delay time, v^{ni} the net-value-of-time for net service time, and v^{di} the net-value-of-time for delay time. This implicit price function can be amended as follows:

$$\pi^i(p, t^n, t^d) = \frac{1}{a}\left(p + v^{di}\, t^d + \alpha^i\right), \tag{8.2}$$

where $\alpha^i = v^{ni} t^n$ is a constant. This implicit price has a functional form identical to that of the demand function for the basic service system, except for the inclusion of a constant α^i.

Finally, we consider the case of services composed of multiple service components. For example, the PMP for a resort complex should include an access/egress service as well as in-site service, both of which are susceptible to congestion. In this case, it might be appropriate to designate in-site service time inside the complex as the sole choice variable for service time in the PMP. In other words, it is recommended that in-site service time be assumed to be sensitive to demand and capacity, but that access/egress service time be assumed to be insensitive.

8.2.4 User Equilibrium Condition

Suppose that a firm has chosen a price and capacity that are not necessarily the solutions to the PMP. In this circumstance, the motivation of consumers who are willing to maximize utility plays the role of determining their demand for the service together with the service time experienced in the service system. Moreover, consumer reaction always leads to unique values for demand and service time, as shown below.

User equilibrium in a monopolistic service market can be characterized in a manner analogous to the equilibrium of a perfectly competitive market for a single good or service free from congestion. Under this analogy, the service time of the market is equivalent to the price of a perfectly competitive market. Further, the demand and service time functions of the monopolist are equivalent to the demand and supply functions of the perfectly competitive market, respectively.

Under the analogy introduced above, the supply side is represented by the service time function introduced in Assumption 6.1:

$$t = T(s, c). \tag{8.3}$$

The function T is increasing and convex in throughput s. Hence, the function can be depicted in the manner illustrated in Fig. 8.1.

On the other hand, the demand side of the market is expressed as the demand function of a monopolist. This demand function is constructed in accordance with the deterministic perception approach. Thus, the relationship between the throughput facilitated and the demand function can be expressed as follows:

$$s = \bar{q}(p, t) = \sum_i \bar{q}^i(p, t), \tag{8.4}$$

where

$$\bar{q}^i = \frac{1}{a}\hat{y}^i\left(\frac{1}{a}(p + v^i t)\right).$$

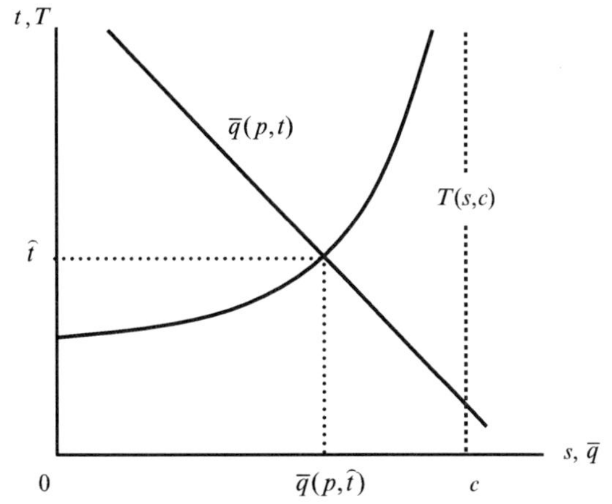

Fig. 8.1 Representation of user equilibrium condition

Here, the market demand function $\bar{q}$ is a simplified version of the demand function in Theorem 2.4 for the case when only one service option is available. By Theorem 2.5, this demand function $\bar{q}$ is decreasing and differentiable in service time t, as schematically illustrated in Fig. 8.1.

User equilibrium refers to the state when the service time estimated from the service time function equals the service time in the demand function. The service time at user equilibrium can be estimated by solving the simultaneous equation system composed of (8.3) and (8.4) for the two unknowns of service time t and throughput s. Therefore, at that state, the demand estimated by the demand function equals the throughput in the service time function.

One alternative way of formulating user equilibrium is to merge (8.3) and (8.4) into one equation. The outcome of this merge, called *the user equilibrium condition*, is as follows:

$$t = T(\bar{q}(p, t), c). \tag{8.5}$$

This user equilibrium condition has an expression identical to the constraint for service times in the QCMP of Assumption 6.3, except that the throughput s of the latter is replaced by the demand function $\bar{q}$.

Mathematically, the user equilibrium condition is sufficient to estimate the service time at user equilibrium, denoted by $\hat{t}$, and the market demand at equilibrium, estimated by $\bar{q}(p, \hat{t})$. Specifically, the service time $\hat{t}$ can be estimated by solving (8.5), which has only one unknown t. Subsequently, substituting the estimated solution $\hat{t}$ into the demand function $\bar{q}$ gives the market demand at user equilibrium. These outcomes $\hat{t}$ and $\bar{q}(p, \hat{t})$ are equal to the solutions of t and s for the simultaneous equation system composed of (8.3) and (8.4), respectively.

Behaviorally, the demand $\bar{q}(p, \hat{t})$ is the outcome of consumer decisions such that no consumer i can be better off by changing the demand q^i. This implies that the service time t currently predicted to achieve the utility-maximizing choice of q^i

should be equal to the service time actually experienced afterward; otherwise, the chosen value of q^i differs from the value that maximizes the utility. This requirement of the user equilibrium condition is well reflected in (8.5). That is, the service time in the demand function of (8.5) represents the service time predicted before visiting the service system, whereas the service time on the left side of (8.5) estimates the service time actually experienced.

Another important aspect of user equilibrium is that the solution of service time t to (8.5) is unique. This uniqueness is the direct consequence of the following: first, the function $\bar{q}$ is continuous and decreasing in service time t; second, the function T is continuous and increasing in throughput s, as illustrated in Fig. 8.1. This uniqueness of service time leads to the uniqueness of the demand for the service.

Theorem 8.1. *Suppose that a monopolist has chosen arbitrary values for price p and capacity c. Then, consumer reaction reaches the user equilibrium such that the solution of t to (8.5) is unique.*

Proof. It suffices to show that the Jacobian of $t - T(\bar{q}, c) = 0$ with respect to t, denoted by $J(t)$, is always positive for every value of $t \geq t^o$:

$$J(t) = 1 - \frac{\partial T\,(\bar{q}, c)}{\partial \bar{q}} \frac{\partial \bar{q}}{\partial t} \rangle\ 0. \tag{8.6}$$

Here, by Assumption 6.1, it holds that $\partial T / \partial \bar{q} \rangle\ 0$. Also, by Theorem 2.5, it follows that $\partial\, \bar{q} / \partial t \ \langle\ 0$. Therefore, the Jacobian $J(t)$ is always positive for every $t \geq t^o$. □

8.2.5 *Modeling of the Basic Form of Profit Maximization Problems*

We here formulate the basic form of PMPs for a monopoly under the user equilibrium approach. This PMP is none other than the decision-making problem of the monopolist who plays leader-and-follower games in which the monopolist is the leader and consumers are followers.

The rule of the leader-and-follower game can be depicted as follows. First, the monopolist should maximize profit through optimal choice for its directly controllable variables: price and capacity. Second, consumers are willing to maximize utility by optimizing service demands. Third, the utility-maximizing choice of consumers always reaches a unique service time at user equilibrium in response to supplier choice regarding directly controllable variables. Fourth, the monopolist has access to and utilizes complete knowledge of consumer reaction for the service time at user equilibrium. Under these four conditions, the decision-making problem of the firm can be expressed as below.

Assumption 8.1. The monopolist maximizes profit through the operation of a congestion-prone service system under the following conditions.

(a) Profit is the function of control variables that comprise price p, service time t, capacity c, and capacity inputs $x = (x_1, \cdots, x_J)$, and is estimated by

$$p\,\bar{q}(p,t) - \sum_j p_j x_j,$$

where $\bar{q}$ is the market demand function constructed under Assumptions 2.1 and 2.2.

(b) The choice for control variables is made by utilizing complete knowledge of consumer reactions formulated by the user equilibrium condition such that

$$t = T(\bar{q}(p,t), c),$$

where T is either a homogeneous or non-homogeneous service time function defined in Assumption 6.1.

(c) The production of capacity satisfies the constraint such that

$$c \leq F(x),$$

where F is increasing, concave and twice differentiable on the relevant region of x.

The above PMP accommodates the hypothesis that the monopolist is the leader of leader-and-follower games through the introduction of Assumption 8.1(b), which reflects the following two postulates for leader-and-follower games. First, the monopolist predicts the service time at user equilibrium from the user equilibrium condition that depicts consumer reactions to the choice of directly controllable choice variables. Second, the monopolist utilizes knowledge of consumer reactions for service time and demand in making the choice of directly controllable choice variables. In short, this assumption implies that the monopolist indirectly controls t and $\bar{q}$ though choices for p and c.

Moreover, the PMP is constructed by integrating three interrelated components, each of which is the outcome of the modeling approach proposed in this study. These three components are as follows: the service demand function $\bar{q}$ under the deterministic perception approach in Assumptions 2.1 and 2.2; the service time function T under the full cost approach in Assumption 6.1; and the leader-and-follower game approach introduced in Assumption 8.1(b).

Finally, the service system exhibits increasing returns in throughput synonymous with demand, as stipulated in Assumption 8.1(c). The returns-to-scale of a service system is delineated by the production function F, as pointed out in Theorems 7.3 and 7.5 for homogeneous and non-homogeneous service technologies, respectively. These theorems show that, if the function F is concave in x, the service system usually exhibits increasing returns in capacity, and thus in throughput.[2] Therefore, Assumption 8.1(c) implies that the service system operated by monopolists exhibits increasing returns in throughput. This aspect of the service market will be thoroughly explored in Chap. 10.

8.3 Optimality Conditions for the Basic Form of Profit Maximization Problems

8.3.1 Development of Optimality Conditions

We here analyze the PMP of Assumption 8.1, focusing on the mathematical presentation of optimality conditions. One key theme of analyses determines the marginal full cost for the PMP from the dual problem formulated as the QCMP of Assumption 6.3. The other theme develops a set of optimality conditions that are useful in understanding the decision of the monopolist and its customers at the equilibrium of leader-and-follower games.

Firstly, we formulate the PMP of Assumption 8.1 as a Lagrangian, denoted by Π^o:

$$\Pi^o(x,p,c,t,\kappa,\tau) \equiv \max \left\{ p\,\bar{q}(p,t) - \sum_j p_j x_j \right\} \\ + \kappa\,(F(x) - c) + \tau\,(t - T(\bar{q}(p,t),c)), \tag{8.7}$$

where $\kappa \rangle 0$ and $\tau \rangle 0$ are Lagrange multipliers.

The above PMP has two constraints: one for the production of capacity, and the other for the user equilibrium condition. This PMP can readily be converted into the problem with one constraint for the user equilibrium condition, denoted by Π^1, in a manner analogous to that used to simplify the SCMP with two constraints in (6.5) to the problem with one constraint in (6.8):

$$\Pi^1(p,c,t,\tau) = \max\, \{p\,\bar{q}(p,t) - KC(c)\} + \tau(\,t - T(\bar{q}(p,t),c)), \tag{8.8}$$

where

$$KC(c) = \sum_j p_j \hat{x}_j(c). \tag{8.9}$$

---

[2] The condition "usually" reflects an exceptional outcome such that the service system with a non-homogeneous service technology can exhibit decreasing returns in throughput, even though it shows non-decreasing returns in capacity, as pointed out in the comment for Theorem 7.5. In spite of this exception, Assumption 8.1(c) can apply to forthcoming analyses without any amendment. This aspect of the assumption will be proved in Subsect. 10.3.4.

The function $\hat{x}_j$ estimates the solution of x_j to the optimality condition for Π^o with respect to x_j under the condition that a value of c is arbitrarily given.

The PMP Π^1 usually has a nontrivial solution of (p, c, t). To confirm this property, it suffices to show that Π^1 has a nontrivial solution of (p, c), since substitution of this solution to the constraint $t - T(\bar{q}(p, t), c) = 0$ gives a nontrivial value of t. The existence of a nontrivial solution of (p, c) follows from the fact that the profit function $p\bar{q}(p, t) - KC(c)$ has a bell shape on the $p - c$ plane, as shown below: first, for each value of c, it is clear that the profit function usually has a bell shape with respect to p on its relevant range; second, for each value of p, the profit function has a bell shape with respect to c on its relevant range, as explained below.

Capacity is a choice variable that simultaneously affects revenue and capacity cost. By the user equilibrium condition, an excessive small capacity causes a severe congestion delay. This in turn leads to an excessive decrease in demand and thus in revenue. Furthermore, this revenue loss is usually larger than the capacity cost reduction. In contrast, an excessive expansion of capacity beyond a certain limit causes a steady increase in capacity cost, while an increase in demand due to a decrease in congestion delay gradually. Hence, the profit function also usually has a bell shape.

Secondly, we develop first order conditions for the maximization problem Π^1 with respect to p, t, and c:

$$\frac{\partial \Pi^1}{\partial p} = \breve{q} + \breve{p}\frac{\partial \breve{q}}{\partial p} - \breve{\tau}\frac{\partial \breve{T}}{\partial \bar{q}}\frac{\partial \breve{q}}{\partial p} = 0 \tag{8.10}$$

$$\frac{\partial \Pi^1}{\partial t} = \breve{p}\frac{\partial \breve{q}}{\partial t} + \breve{\tau}\left(1 - \frac{\partial \breve{T}}{\partial \bar{q}}\frac{\partial \breve{q}}{\partial t}\right) = 0 \tag{8.11}$$

$$\frac{\partial \Pi^1}{\partial c} = -MKC(\breve{c}) - \breve{\tau}\frac{\partial \breve{T}}{\partial c} = 0. \tag{8.12}$$

where $\breve{q} \equiv \bar{q}(\breve{p}, \breve{t})$, and $\breve{T} \equiv T(\breve{q}, \breve{c})$.

The term $\breve{\tau}$ in the above first order conditions represents the marginal revenue loss of service time for Π^1. This marginal revenue loss estimates the revenue loss that results from a one-unit increase in service time as actually experienced by consumers, as will be clarified in the next subsection. This marginal revenue loss satisfies the equality in Lemma 6.5 for the BQCMP of Assumption 6.3, as shown below.

Lemma 8.1. *The solution* $(\breve{p}, \breve{c}, \breve{t}, \breve{\tau})$ *to* Π^1 *satisfies the following:*

$$\breve{\tau} = \breve{v}\breve{q} \quad \textit{and} \quad \breve{v} \in RV = [0, UB],$$

where $\breve{v}$ is the private value-of-service-time, estimated by

$$\breve{v} = \frac{\partial \breve{q}}{\partial t} \Big/ \frac{\partial \breve{q}}{\partial p},$$

and RV is the range of v^i, which is common to all i.

Proof. The relationship $\breve{v} \in RV = [0, UB]$ is proved in (6.42). Hence the proof can be completed by showing that $\breve{\tau} = \breve{v}\breve{q}$. This proof is as follows: (i) multiplying $\breve{v}$ defined in the lemma to (8.10), and (ii) subtracting the result of the previous step from (8.11) yields the asserted equality. □

Thirdly, we analyze the dual problem of the PMP Π^1, from which the marginal full cost embedded in the PMP will be estimated. Suppose that the PMP yields the solution such that the throughput is $\breve{q}$ and that the private value-of-service-time for the throughput is $\breve{v}$. In this circumstance, the dual of the PMP, denoted by Z^1, can be expressed as follows:

$$Z^1(c, t, \tau; \breve{q}, \breve{v}) \equiv \min \left\{ KC(c) + t\breve{v}\breve{q} \right\} + \tau\Big(T(\breve{q}, c) - t\Big). \quad (8.13)$$

This QCMP, which is identical to the BQCMP of Assumption 6.3, has the following property.

Theorem 8.2. *The BQCMP Z^1 is the dual of Π^1; that is, the solution $(\breve{c}, \breve{t}, \breve{\tau})$ to Π^1 and the solution $(\bar{c}, \bar{t}, \bar{\tau})$ to Z^1 satisfy the following equality:*

$$(\breve{c}, \breve{t}, \breve{\tau}) = (\bar{c}, \bar{t}, \bar{\tau}).$$

Proof. It holds that $\bar{\tau} = \breve{v}\breve{q}$, as shown in Lemma 6.5. By this equality and Lemma 8.1, it follows that $\breve{\tau} = \bar{\tau}$. Under the condition that $\breve{\tau} = \bar{\tau}$, the two problems Z^1 and Π^1 have identical first order conditions with respect to c and t, as can readily be confirmed. This implies that $(\breve{c}, \breve{t}) = (\bar{c}, \bar{t})$. □

The BQCMP Z^1 has a formulation identical to Z^6 in (6.36). Therefore, by Theorem 6.7, it holds that

$$MFC(\breve{q}) = MCC(\breve{q}) = \breve{v}\breve{q}\frac{\partial \breve{T}}{\partial q}. \quad (8.14)$$

Here, the marginal congestion cost $\breve{v}\breve{q}\partial\breve{T}/\partial q$ equals $\breve{\tau}\partial\breve{T}/\partial q$ in (8.10). Hence, it follows that $\breve{\tau}\partial\breve{T}/\partial q$ equals the marginal full cost $MFC(\breve{q}; \breve{v})$. Note also that we use $MFC(\breve{q})$ and $MCC(\breve{q})$ instead of $MFC(\breve{q}; \breve{v})$ and $MCC(\breve{q}; \breve{v})$, respectively, in order to simplify expression, since it is possible to estimate $\breve{v}$ from $\breve{q}$.

Fourthly, we develop the optimality conditions that will be used in characterizing the market equilibrium attained by the solution $(\breve{c}, \breve{t}, \breve{\tau})$ to Π^1.

Substituting Lemma 8.1 and (8.14) into the first order conditions in (8.10)~(8.12) for Π^1 gives the optimality conditions presented below.

Theorem 8.3. *The solution* $(\breve{p}, \breve{c}, \breve{t})$ *to* Π^1 *simultaneously satisfies the following three conditions.*

i. *The user equilibrium condition:*

$$\breve{t} = T(\breve{q}, \breve{c}).$$

ii. *The pricing rule:*

$$MR(\breve{q}) \equiv \breve{p}\left(1 - \frac{1}{E(\breve{q})}\right) = MFC(\breve{q}).$$

iii. *The investment rule for the choice of capacity:*

$$MKC(\breve{c}) = -\breve{v}\breve{q}\frac{\partial T(\breve{q}, \breve{c})}{\partial c}.$$

Proof. First, the solution $(\breve{p}, \breve{c}, \breve{t})$ should satisfy the constraint of the user equilibrium condition in Theorem 8.3.i. Second, substituting $\breve{v}\breve{q}\partial T/\partial q = MFC(\breve{q})$ of (8.14) into (8.10), and arranging the resulting equation gives the above pricing rule in Theorem 8.3.ii. Note that $E(q)$ in this pricing rule is the elasticity of q with respect to p, as defined in (5.10). Third, substituting $\breve{\tau} = \breve{v}\breve{q}$ into (8.12), and arranging the preceding result gives the above investment rule in Theorem 8.3.iii. □

Mathematically, one important feature of Theorem 8.3 is that the optimal price $\breve{p}$, estimated from the pricing rule, is assumed to be positive, as can be deduced from (8.10). This assumption implies that the elasticity $E(\breve{q})$ must be larger than one. This condition for demand elasticity is equivalent to the idea that the price $\breve{p}$ must be larger than the marginal full cost $MFC(\breve{q})$. It should also be noted that this condition must apply to the PMP for a firm under competition.

Finally, the optimality conditions of Theorem 8.3 are sufficient to estimate the solution of (p, c, t) to Π^1. That is, mathematically, the three unknowns (p, c, t) can be estimated by solving the three simultaneous equation systems composed of three optimality conditions in Theorem 8.3. For this reason, it is feasible to characterize the equilibrium of monopoly markets through analyses of the three optimality conditions of the theorem, without recourse to the first order conditions of (8.10)~(8.12).

8.3.2 Implications of the Marginal Revenue Loss of Service Time

We presumed in the previous subsection that the term $\breve{\tau}$ represents the marginal revenue loss of service time. We also showed in Lemma 8.1 that this marginal value

$\breve{\tau}$ equals $\breve{v}\breve{q}$. However, this relationship in the lemma is not sufficient to prove that the term $\breve{\tau}$ indeed represents the marginal revenue loss of service time. For this reason, we directly deduce the exact implication of the term $\breve{\tau}$ from the first order condition with respect to service time in (8.11). Thus, we show that the term $\breve{\tau}$ is the marginal revenue loss for the service time consumers actually experience.

Equation (8.11) can be rearranged as follows:

$$\breve{\tau} = -\frac{1}{1-\alpha}\breve{p}\frac{\partial \breve{q}}{\partial t}, \tag{8.15}$$

where $\alpha = \partial \breve{T}/\partial \bar{q} \times \partial \breve{q}/\partial t \langle 0$. In this equation, the term $-p\partial \breve{q}/\partial t$ appears to represent the marginal revenue loss of service time. Then, one immediate question is what the additional term $1/(1-\alpha)$ implies.

The implication of denominator $1-\alpha$ can be explained using Fig. 8.2. Suppose that the solution (p_1, c_1, t_1) to Π^1 leads to the demand $q_1(=\bar{q}(p_1, t_1))$ and the service time $t_1(=T(q_1, c_1))$. Suppose also that an exogenous impact to increase service time by Δt unit reduces demand from q_1 to $q_2(\equiv \bar{q}(p_1, t_1+\Delta t))$. For this new demand q_2, the service time that satisfies the user equilibrium condition is not $t_1+\Delta t$ but rather $t_2(=T(q_2, c_1))$. Then, the new user equilibrium (t_2, q_2) is the solution to the following two simultaneous equations: $t = T(s, c_1)$ and $s = \bar{q}(p_1, t+t_1+\Delta t - t_2)$, as can readily be deduced from the figure.

We next show that $t_1+\Delta t - t_2$ is approximately equals to $(1-\alpha)\Delta t$ representing $(1 - \partial \breve{T}/\partial q \times \partial \breve{q}/\partial t)\,\Delta t$. The Δt unit increase of service time decreases the demand by $\partial \breve{q}/\partial t \times \Delta t$, while a one-unit decrease in demand reduces service time by $\partial \breve{T}/\partial q$. Therefore, it can be said that a Δt unit increase of service time has the secondary effect of reducing service time by $\partial \breve{T}/\partial \bar{q} \times \partial \breve{q}/\partial t \times \Delta t$. This decrease $\partial \breve{T}/\partial \bar{q} \times \partial \breve{q}/\partial t \times \Delta t$ is approximately equal to $t_2 - t_1$, which is negative. Hence, the term $t_1 + \Delta t - t_2$ approximately equals $(1-\alpha)\Delta t$.

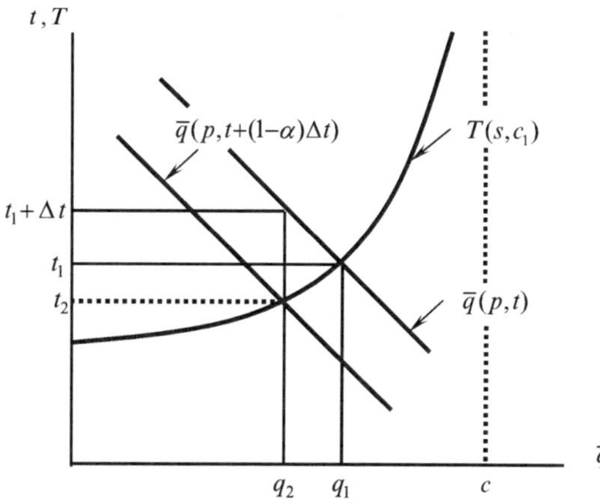

Fig. 8.2 Estimation of marginal revenue loss of service time

The above analysis implies the following:

$$\frac{1}{1-\alpha}\frac{\partial \bar{q}(\breve{p}, \breve{t})}{\partial t} = \lim_{\Delta t \to 0} \frac{\bar{q}\left(\breve{p},\ \breve{t} + \Delta t\right) - \breve{q}}{\breve{t} + \Delta t - T\left(\bar{q}(\breve{p},\ \breve{t} + \Delta t), c\right)}, \tag{8.16}$$

since

$$1 - \alpha = \lim_{\Delta t \to 0} \frac{\breve{t} + \Delta t - T\left(\bar{q}(\breve{p},\ \breve{t} + \Delta t), c\right)}{\Delta t}. \tag{8.17}$$

Here the term $\breve{t} - T(\bar{q}(\breve{p},\ \breve{t} + \Delta t), c))$ represents the secondary effect represented by $t_1 - t_2$ in Fig. 8.2. Hence, the term $\breve{t} + \Delta t - T(\bar{q}(\breve{p},\ \breve{t} + \Delta t), c))$ equals the actual service time change experienced by customers at the new user equilibrium reached by an exogenous impact to increase the Δt unit of service time.

Based on the above analysis, (8.15) can be interpreted as follows. The factor $1 - \alpha$ is the ratio of an actual service time change under the constraint of the user equilibrium condition to a marginal service time change under the condition of no constraint. Therefore, the term $1/(1-\alpha) \times \partial\bar{q}/\partial t$ estimates the decrease in demand $\bar{q}$ brought about by a marginal increase in the service time actually experienced by customers under the user equilibrium constraint. This implies the term $\breve{\tau}$ can be interpreted as the marginal revenue loss of actual service time under the user equilibrium constraint.

8.3.3 *Characterization of Market Equilibrium*

The equilibrium of a monopolistic service market represents the state at which no player of leader-and-follower games can be better off by changing his or her choice. To show this aspect, we first convert each of the three optimality conditions in Theorem 8.3 into two simultaneous equations that yield the solution of one unknown, under the condition that the solutions of the two remaining unknowns have already been estimated. We next show that the solution of the one unknown to these two simultaneous equations represents the state in which the firm or its customers attains the maximum profit or utilities, respectively. This aspect of the three optimality conditions is explained below.

First, the user equilibrium condition in Theorem 8.3 depicts the service time determined by consumers who are willing to maximize utility, in the circumstance where the optimal price $\breve{p}$ and capacity $\breve{c}$ have already been chosen by the firm. In this circumstance, the service time at user equilibrium can be formulated as the solution of the following two simultaneous equations: $t = T(s, \breve{c})$ and $s = \bar{q}(\breve{p}, t)$. These two equations can be graphically depicted as in Fig. 8.1. These two equations have the solution $(\breve{t}, \breve{s})$ at which the two curves intersect. This solution is none other than the service time $\breve{t}$ and the demand $\breve{s}$ at user equilibrium for the given value $(\breve{p}, \breve{c})$.

The service time at user equilibrium can be interpreted as the following outcome of leader-and-follower games. The firm, the leader of the game, makes the choices $\breve{p}$ and $\breve{c}$, so as to attain maximum profit. These choices of the firm are the outcome of judgment that consumers will reach the user equilibrium characterized by $\breve{t}$ and $\breve{q}\,(\equiv \bar{q}(\breve{p}, \breve{t}))$. In response to this choice, consumers, the followers of the game, make the decisions that coincide with the supplier's expectation. Such a consumer reaction is the outcome of their search process to reach maximum utility, as explained in Subsect. 8.2.4. Therefore, no agent in the market can be better off by changing his or her choices that fulfill the user equilibrium condition.

Second, the optimality condition for the pricing rule in Theorem 8.3 estimates the optimal price $\breve{p}$ that maximizes profit, under the hypothetical circumstance that the firm would have knowledge of the $\breve{t}$ and $\breve{c}$ values. In this situation, the pricing rule in the theorem is identical to that of a monopolist in a market free from congestion. Moreover, the pricing rule of the service firm can be interpreted in a manner analogous to that of the pricing rule of the monopolist in a congestion-free market.

To be specific, the optimal price $\breve{p}$ is the intersection point of two curves, as depicted in Fig. 8.3, which is drawn in the following manner. Under the condition that the service time $\breve{t}$ is known, we can estimate the demand $\bar{q}(p, \breve{t})$ for the varying values of p. This demand $\bar{q}(p, \breve{t})$ decreases in price p, as depicted in the figure. For that demand $\bar{q}(p, \breve{t})$, the marginal revenue $MR(\bar{q})$ is the multiple of $1 - 1/E(\bar{q})$ and $\bar{q}(p, \breve{t})$. For each $\bar{q}$ value, the marginal revenue $MR(\bar{q})$ is smaller than the value of p due to the multiplier $1 - 1/E(\bar{q})$, which is assumed to be positive but less than one. On the other hand, the marginal full cost function $MFC(s)$ is decreasing in its independent variable s equivalent to demand q. The downward slope of the marginal full cost on the relevant region of s reflects that the service system of the monopolist exhibits increasing returns in s, as explained in the comment for Assumption 8.1(c).

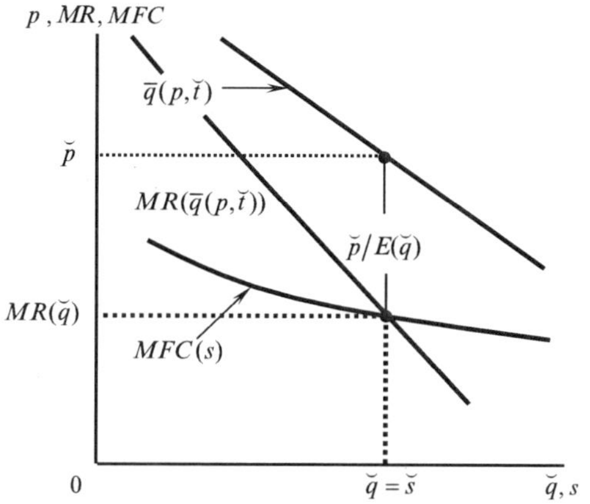

Fig. 8.3 Representation of optimal price

Fig. 8.3 depicts that the demand at market equilibrium equals $\breve{q}$ at which point the two curves $MR(\bar{q})$ and $MFC(s)$ intersect. It also shows that, if the demand for a certain value of p is smaller (or larger) than $\breve{q}$, the marginal revenue of demand is greater (or less) than the marginal full cost of throughput. This implies that the price $\breve{p}$ achieves maximum profit.

Third, the investment rule for capacity in Theorem 8.3 characterizes the optimal capacity $\breve{c}$ under the condition that the $\breve{p}$ and $\breve{t}$ values are known. The optimal capacity $\breve{c}$ is represented as the intersection point of two curves, as depicted in Fig. 8.4. One curve represents the marginal capacity cost function $MKC(c)$. This function is depicted as a downward curve with respect to capacity c, in order to reflect Assumption 8.1(c) such that this function of monopolists is decreasing in c. Another curve represents the function $-\breve{v}\breve{q}\partial T(\breve{q}, c)/\partial c$. This function is decreasing in capacity c, since T is decreasing and convex in c, as illustrated in Fig. 6.1.

The function $-\breve{v}\breve{q}\partial T(\breve{q}, c)/\partial c$ estimates the revenue increase caused by a one-unit increase in capacity, as explained below. The function is the product of the following two terms: one term $-\bar{\tau}(= -\breve{v}\breve{q})$ that represents s the revenue increase accrued by a one-unit decrease in service time; the other term $\partial T/\partial c$ that estimates the service time decrease caused by a one-unit expansion of capacity. Hence, the function estimates the marginal revenue increase brought about by a service time decrease due to a one-unit increase in capacity.

Fig. 8.4 depicts that the two curves intersect at the optimal capacity $\breve{c}$. It also shows that, on the left side of the point $\breve{c}$, the graph of $MKC(c)$ is located beneath the graph of $-\breve{v}\breve{q}\partial T(\breve{q}, c)/\partial c$. This representation of the two curves depicts that the firm cannot increase profit by choosing a capacity larger than $\breve{c}$. This implies that capacity should be increased to the point where the marginal capacity cost is equal to the marginal revenue increase of capacity due to a decrease in service time.

Finally, the capacity cost $KC(\breve{c})$ estimates the minimum cost necessary to construct the optimal capacity $\breve{c}$. The minimum capacity cost can be attained by choosing the optimal input $\breve{x}$, which satisfies the production efficiency condition in Lemma 6.4. This efficiency condition implies that the supplier should construct

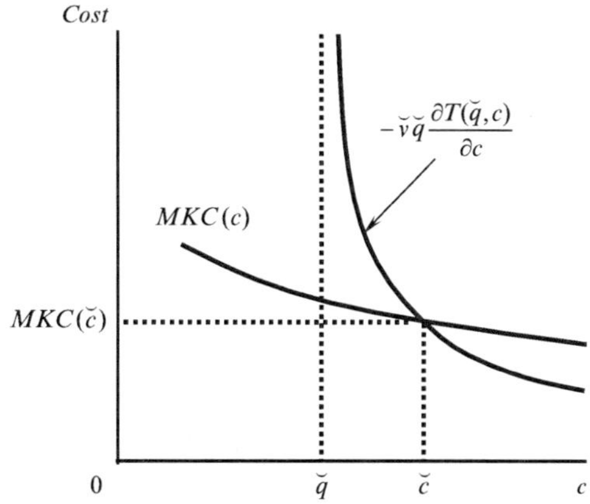

Fig. 8.4 Representation of optimal capacity

a congestion-prone service system as efficiently as possible, without taking into consideration the effect of capacity on revenue.

8.4 Extensions to Other Service Systems

8.4.1 *Optimal Price under Short-Run Adjustments*

So far, we have analyzed the PMP for a monopolist who supplies a congestion-prone service under the premise that the supplier makes a decision to simultaneously adjust price and capacity, a type of judgment called a long-run decision. It might however be more common that the supplier adjusts price only without changing capacity. This situation is called a short-run price adjustment. We concern ourselves here with the short-run price adjustment made by the supplier.

Firstly, we explain the reason that firms frequently make only short-run price adjustments. Consider a hypothetical PMP that simultaneously estimates optimal capacity and price, under the condition that the capacity cost previously spent could be recovered without experiencing any economic loss. In such a case, it is certain that the supplier would always adjust price and capacity simultaneously. Also the additional cost necessary for the capacity adjustment from an existing capacity c_o to a new optimal capacity for the hypothetical PMP, denoted by $\breve{c}$, would amount to $KC(\breve{c}) - KC(c_o)$. However, in reality, the additional cost consumed in capacity adjustment is usually larger than this difference in capacity cost. Therefore, a firm can take advantage of the option to adjust price only without changing capacity.

Secondly, we consider the problem of how to model the Short-Run Profit Maximization Problem (SRPMP) for a monopolist under the condition that capacity is fixed to a constant c_o. Consumers always reach a unique service time at user equilibrium, irrespective of the values of capacity and price, as shown in Lemma 8.1. Further, the monopolist is postulated to have complete knowledge of the unique service time reached by consumer reaction to the choice made by the firm. Therefore, the SRPMP should incorporate the user equilibrium constraint as a constraint, as is true of the long-run problem.

Hence, under the condition that the capacity cost $KC(c_o)$ previously paid is a sunk cost, the SRPMP for monopolists, denoted by Π^s, can be expressed by

$$\Pi^s(p,t,\tau,c_o) \equiv \max\ \{p\,\bar{q}(p,t) - KC(c_o)\} + \tau(t - T(\bar{q}(p,t),c_o)). \tag{8.18}$$

This short-run problem Π^s has a formulation identical to that of the long-run problem Π^1, with the exception that the capacity cost $K(c_o)$ is assumed as a constant. This problem Π^s generally has a nontrivial solution, denoted by $(\tilde{p},\tilde{t},\tilde{\tau})$ and, therefore, has a non-trivial optimal demand $\bar{q}(\tilde{p},\tilde{t})$, expressed by $\tilde{q}$, as is true of Π^1.

Thirdly, we estimate the pricing formula in a manner analogous to that used to develop the formula for long-run adjustment in Theorem 8.3. Differentiating Π^s with respect to p and t, and arranging these first order conditions in a manner identical to that leading to Lemma 8.1 gives the marginal revenue loss of service time, $\tilde{\mu}$, such that

$$\tilde{\mu} = \tilde{v}\,\tilde{q}, \tag{8.19}$$

where $\tilde{v}$ is the private value-of-service-time $\tilde{v}$, estimated by $(\partial\tilde{q}/\partial t)/(\partial\tilde{q}/\partial p)$.

Substituting (8.19) into the first order condition for Π^s with respect to p gives the pricing rule such that

$$MR(\tilde{q}) \equiv \tilde{p}\left(1 - \frac{1}{E(\tilde{q})}\right) = SRMCC\,(\tilde{q}\,; c_o), \tag{8.20}$$

where

$$SRMCC(\tilde{q}\,; c_o) = \tilde{v}\,\tilde{q}\frac{\partial T(\tilde{q}, c_o)}{\partial \bar{q}}, \tag{8.21}$$

and *SRMCC* is the short-run marginal congestion cost, as defined in Subsect. 7.3.1.

The optimal price $\tilde{p}$, estimated in (8.20), is graphically illustrated under the conditions that $c_o \langle \breve{c}$ in Fig. 8.5. In the figure, first, the demand function $\bar{q}(p, \tilde{t})$ and the marginal revenue function $MR(\bar{q}(p, \tilde{t}))$ are drawn in a manner identical to that used to depict the functions $\bar{q}(p, \breve{t})$ and $MR(\bar{q}(p, \breve{t}))$ in Fig. 8.3, respectively. Second, the value of *SRMCC* $(s; c_o, \tilde{v})$ is depicted so as to meet the requirement that the function T is monotonically increasing and convex in throughput s, as

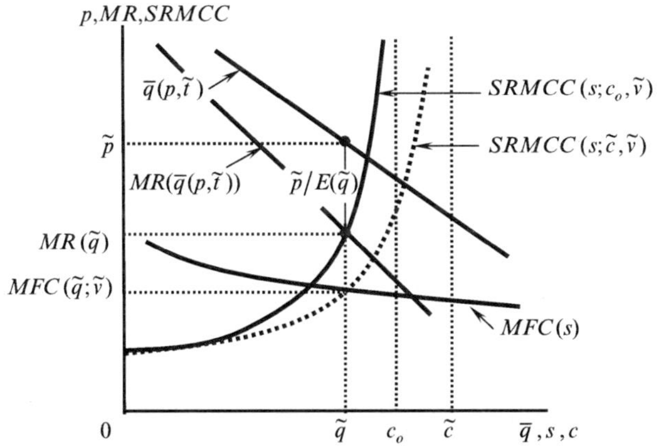

Fig. 8.5 Representation of optimal price under short-run price adjustment

postulated in Assumption 6.1 Third, the optimal price $\tilde{p}$ is positioned so that $MR(\tilde{q})$ equals $SRMCC\,(\tilde{q};\ c_o)$ at that price, as shown in (8.20).

Fourthly, we compare relative magnitudes between $\tilde{q}$ and $\breve{q}$, $\tilde{p}$ and $\breve{p}$, and $\tilde{t}$ and $\breve{t}$. For these comparisons, we assume that

$$\tilde{v} \cong \breve{v} \quad \text{and} \quad \frac{\partial E(\bar{q})}{\partial p} \cong 0. \tag{8.22}$$

The first equation implies that the $\tilde{v}$ value of the demand $\tilde{q}$ is approximately equal to that of $\breve{q}$. The second equation postulates that the demand elasticity $E(\bar{q})$ is approximately constant on the relevant region of p.

Theorem 8.4. *Under the condition (8.22), the solution $(\tilde{p}, \tilde{t})$ to the short-run problem Π^s and the solution $(\breve{p}, \breve{t}, \breve{c})$ to the hypothetical long-run problem Π^1 satisfy the following:*

$$\tilde{q} \equiv \bar{q}(\tilde{p}, \tilde{t}) \underset{\rangle}{\overset{\langle}{-}} \breve{q} \equiv (\breve{p}, \breve{t}),\ \tilde{p} \underset{\langle}{\overset{\rangle}{-}} \breve{p}, \quad \textit{and} \quad \tilde{t} \underset{\langle}{\overset{\rangle}{-}} \breve{t}, \quad \textit{if} \quad c_o \underset{\rangle}{\overset{\langle}{-}} \breve{c}.$$

Proof. See Appendix C.1. Note that, if the service system exhibits decreasing returns, the above inequalities for price and service times do not always hold. □

In addition, we provide the a proof of Theorem 8.4, which complements the proof in the appendix, in order to facilitate understanding of the theorem through the use of Fig. 8.5. First, under the condition of $c_o \langle \breve{c}$ and $\tilde{v} \cong \breve{v}$, it holds that $SRMCC\,(s;\ c_o, \tilde{v}\,)\rangle\ SRMCC\,(s;\ \breve{c}, \tilde{v}\,)$ for all s, since $SRMCC$ is decreasing in c. Second, under the condition that $c_o \langle \breve{c}$ and $\partial E(\bar{q})/\partial p \cong 0$, it holds that $MR\,(\bar{q}(p, \tilde{t}))\ \langle\ MR\,(\bar{q}(p, \breve{t}))$ for all p, because of the following two facts: $\bar{q}$ and thus MR for each p are decreasing in $t (= T(s, c)$; and T is decreasing in c. Third, the first and second facts lead to the outcome that $\tilde{q} \langle \breve{q}$; that is, the demand $\tilde{q}$, the intersection point of $SRMCC\,(s;\ c_o, \tilde{v}\,)$ and $MR\,(\bar{q}(p, \tilde{t}))$, must be smaller than the demand $\breve{q}$, the intersection point of $SRMCC\,(s;\ \breve{c}, \tilde{v}\,)$ and $MR\,(\bar{q}(p, \breve{t}))$, as can be deduced from the figure. Fourth, the inequality $\tilde{q} \langle \breve{q}$ implies that $\tilde{p} \langle \breve{p}$ by the following three conditions: (i) $\partial E(\bar{q})/\partial p \cong 0$; (ii) the decrease of MFC in s; and (iii) $SRMCC\,(\tilde{q};\ c_o)\ \rangle MFC\,(\tilde{q})$.

The proof of (iii) is as below. First, the long-run cost $MFC(\tilde{q})$ equals the short-run cost $SRMCC(\tilde{q}; \tilde{c})$ for the capacity $\tilde{c}$ satisfying the investment rule $MKC(\tilde{c}) = -\tilde{v}\tilde{q}\partial T(\tilde{q}, \tilde{c})/\partial c$, as shown in Theorem 6.4. Second, under the condition that $\tilde{v} \cong \breve{v}$, the assumption $c_o \langle \breve{c}$ implies the inequality $c_o \langle \tilde{c}$. Third, under the condition that $c_o \langle \tilde{c}$, it holds that $SRMCC\,(s;\ c_o, \tilde{v}\,)\ \rangle SRMCC\,(s;\ \tilde{c}, \tilde{v}\,)$, for all s, since $SRMCC$ is decreasing in c. By the first and third facts, it follows that $SRMCC\,(\tilde{q};\ c_o)\ \rangle MFC\,(\tilde{q}\,)$, as claimed.

Theorem 8.4 characterizes the effect of capacity shortage (or excess capacity) on demand and implicit price. According to the theorem, if the fixed capacity c_o is smaller than the optimal capacity $\breve{c}$ for the hypothetical long-run problem, the demand after short-run price adjustment, denoted by $\tilde{q}$, is smaller (or larger) than the demand for hypothetical long-run adjustment, expressed by $\breve{q}$. Moreover, the short-run adjustment price $\tilde{p}$ and service time $\tilde{t}$ are larger (or smaller) than the hypothetical long-run adjustment price $\breve{p}$ and service time $\breve{t}$, respectively.

8.4.2 The Service System with Variable Costs

Here we extend analyses of the basic form of PMPs to the PMP for firms that consume variable costs in facilitating customers. This PMP is constructed by incorporating the QCMP for systems with variable costs in (7.25) into the basic form in (8.7). The PMP for these firms has a formulation that differs significantly from the basic form. Nonetheless, the pricing and investment rules are very similar to those of the basic form in Theorem 8.3, as shown below.

The PMP for service systems with variable costs, Π^2, constructed in the manner explained above, is as follows:

$$\Pi^2(x^l, x^s, p, c, t, \kappa^l, \kappa^s, \tau) = \max \left\{ p\,\bar{q}(p,t) - \sum_j p_j(x_j^l + x_j^s) \right\}$$
$$+ \kappa^l\left(F^l(x^l) - c\right) + \kappa^s\left(F^s(x^l, x^s) - \bar{q}(p,t)\right) + \tau\left(t - T(\bar{q}(p,t), c)\right). \quad (8.23)$$

This problem Π^2 can be decomposed into two sub-optimization problems.

The first sub-optimization problem is a cost minimization problem, Z^2, which is used to estimate the solution of inputs (x^l, x^s) for the production of an arbitrary pair of throughput s and capacity c:

$$Z^2(x^l, x^s, \kappa^l, \kappa^s; s, c) \equiv \min \sum_j p_j(x_j^l + x_j^s)$$
$$+ \kappa^l\left(c - F^l(x^l)\right) + \kappa^s\left(s - F^s(x^l, x^s)\right). \quad (8.24)$$

This cost minimization problem is constructed by replacing the demand function $\bar{q}$ with the variable s.

Let $(\bar{x}^l, \bar{x}^s, \bar{\kappa}^l, \bar{\kappa}^s)$ be the solution for Z^2. Then, the total supplier's monetary cost function for independent variables (s, c), denoted by $TMC(s, c)$, equals $Z^2(\bar{x}^l, \bar{x}^s, \bar{\kappa}^l, \bar{\kappa}^s; s, c)$. Moreover, by the envelop theorem, first order conditions for $Z^2(\bar{x}^l, \bar{x}^s, \bar{\kappa}^l, \bar{\kappa}^s; s, c)$ with respect to x_j^s and x_j^l give the marginal variable cost for throughput, *MVC*, and the marginal capacity cost for capacity, *MKC*, respectively. These marginal costs *MVC* and *MKC* are identical to the same marginal costs in (7.27) and (7.28), respectively.

The second sub-optimization problem is developed in the following sequences: first, replace s in *TMC* with $\bar{q}(p,t)$; second, substitute $TMC(\bar{q}(p,t), c)$ into Π^2

in (8.23). This optimization problem, denoted by Π^3, is used to determine the solutions of (p, c, t), which maximize the profit of the firm:

$$\Pi^3(p, c, t, \tau) \equiv \max \{ p\bar{q}(p,t) - TMC(\bar{q}(p,t), c)) \} \\ + \tau\,(t - T(\bar{q}(p,t), c)), \tag{8.25}$$

where

$$TMC(\cdot) = Z^2(\hat{x}^l(\cdot), \hat{x}^s(\cdot), \hat{\kappa}^l(\cdot), \hat{\kappa}^s(\cdot)).$$

Proceeding with the analysis of Π^3 in a manner analogous to that leading to Theorem 8.3 gives the following.

Theorem 8.5. *The solution $(\breve{p}, \breve{c}, \breve{t})$ to the PMP Π^3 satisfies the following pricing and investment rules.*

$$MR(\breve{q}) \equiv \breve{p}\left(1 - \frac{1}{E(\breve{q})}\right) = MFC(\breve{q}) \tag{8.26}$$

$$= MCC(\breve{q}) + MVC(\breve{q}) \tag{8.27}$$

$$MKC(\breve{q}) = -\breve{v}\breve{q}\frac{\partial \breve{T}}{\partial c}, \tag{8.28}$$

where MVC and MKC represent the marginal variable cost in (7.27) and the marginal capacity cost in (7.28), respectively.

Proof. Prove first (8.26) and (8.27). The first step of the proof shows that $\breve{\tau} = \breve{v}\breve{q}$ through analyses of Π^3. This equality can be proved in a manner analogous to the proof of Lemma 8.1. The second step develops and rearranges the first order condition Π^3 with respect to p; that is,

$$\frac{\partial \Pi^4}{\partial p} = \breve{q} + \breve{p}\frac{\partial \breve{q}}{\partial p} - \frac{\partial TMC(\breve{q}, \breve{c})}{\partial q}\frac{\partial \breve{q}}{\partial p} - \breve{v}\breve{q}\frac{\partial \breve{T}}{\partial q}\frac{\partial \breve{q}}{\partial p}$$

$$= \breve{q} + \breve{p}\frac{\partial \breve{q}}{\partial p} - MVC(\breve{q})\frac{\partial \breve{q}}{\partial p} - MCC(\breve{q})\frac{\partial \breve{q}}{\partial p} \tag{8.29}$$

$$= \breve{q} + \breve{p}\frac{\partial \breve{q}}{\partial p} - MFC(\breve{q})\frac{\partial \breve{q}}{\partial p}. \tag{8.30}$$

Here the equality $\partial TMC/\partial q = MVC$ in (8.29) follows from the fact that this equality is equivalent to $\partial Z^2(\hat{x}^l, \hat{x}^s, \hat{\kappa}^l, \hat{\kappa}^s; s, c)/\partial s = MVC$. The equality

$MVC + MCC = MFC$ in (8.30) follows from Theorem 7.7. Finally, reorganizing (8.30) gives the pricing formulas in the theorem.

Finally, proof of (8.28) is worked out in the following sequences: (i) differentiate Π^3 with respect to c; (ii) substitute $\partial TSC/\partial c = MKC$ and $\breve{\tau} = \breve{v}\breve{q}$ into the outcome of the first step; and (iii) arrange the outcome of the previous step. This gives (8.28). □

Theorem 8.5 shows that the pricing and investment rules for a congestion-prone service firm with variable costs are identical to those for the firm without variable costs, except for the following two differences. First, the marginal full cost in the pricing rule for a service system with variable costs is the sum of marginal variable cost and marginal full cost for the same system without variable costs. Second, the marginal capacity cost in the investment rule is smaller than the marginal capacity cost for long-run inputs $\breve{x}^l$ by a ratio of less than one. This ratio reflects the substitution effect of the long-run input $\breve{x}^l$ for the short-run input $\breve{x}^s$, which leads to a reduction of $\breve{x}^s$ in producing the throughput $\breve{q}$, as explained in detail in the comment to (7.28).

8.4.3 The Service System with Peaking Demands

Here we analyze the PMP for a monopolist that facilitates unsteady demand flows. We first construct the PMP as a Multi-Period Profit Maximization Problem (MPPMP). Through analyses of this MPPMP, we subsequently develop pricing and investment rules for the system in a manner similar to that used to derive the rules for the basic form.

First, we construct the demand function for a certain period under the random perception approach. This demand function for a certain period is formulated as the expected demand function for the deterministic demand function developed for analyses of service period choices in Subsect. 3.2.1. To be specific, the demand function of the tth period, Q_t, is expressed as the expected demand function under qualitative competition that satisfies the identical ordering condition among multiple service periods. Therefore, the demand function Q_t has a functional structure identical to the one analyzed in Sect. 5.4.

Then, the demand function Q_t, which is structured to estimate the demand flow rate of the tth period, is expressed as follows:

$$Q_t(p,t) = \frac{1}{\delta_t} \int_{D_t} f_t(p_t + \xi_t t_t) h(\xi) d\xi, \tag{8.31}$$

where

$$f_t(p_t + \xi_t t_t) = \frac{1}{a_t} f\left(\frac{1}{a_t}(p_t + \xi_t t_t)\right) h(\xi).$$

Here the factor $1/\delta_t$ converts the actual demand of the tth period into the demand flow rate of that period.

The identical ordering condition applied to the demand function Q_t implies that

$$\xi^i_1 t_1 \langle \cdots \langle \xi^i_T t_T, \text{ all } i. \tag{8.32}$$

This identical ordering condition connotes that all consumers most prefer the first period, next the second period, and so on sequentially. This condition is thought to be acceptable in most cases. It is also relevant to clarify that the first period in (8.32) does not refer to the beginning period but rather the period most preferred.

In addition, it is assumed that the catchment domain D_t, for all t, is thin on the ξ_t axis. This condition connotes that the service offered during the tth period is a superior close substitute to the service for the $t+1$th periods. Under this condition, it holds that

$$\frac{\partial \breve{Q}_t}{\partial t_t} \bigg/ \frac{\partial \breve{Q}_t}{\partial p_t} \cong \frac{\partial \breve{Q}_{t\pm 1}}{\partial t_t} \bigg/ \frac{\partial \breve{Q}_{t\pm 1}}{\partial p_t}, \text{ all } t \in \langle 2,\ T-1 \rangle. \tag{8.33}$$

The reason is as follows. If the set D_t is thin, (6.45) implies that

$$\breve{\xi}_t = \frac{\partial \breve{Q}_t}{\partial t_t} \bigg/ \frac{\partial \breve{Q}_t}{\partial p_t} \cong \frac{1}{2}\left(\frac{\partial \breve{Q}_{t-1}}{\partial t_t} \bigg/ \frac{\partial \breve{Q}_{t-1}}{\partial p_t} + \frac{\partial \breve{Q}_{t\pm 1}}{\partial t_t} \bigg/ \frac{\partial \breve{Q}_{t\pm 1}}{\partial p_t} \right), \quad \text{all } t \in \langle 2, T-1 \rangle.$$

Further, if the set D_t is thin, the two terms in the parenthesis on the right side are approximately equal to each other. Hence, (8.33) follows.

Second, we construct the capacity cost function under the convention applied in the cost analyses of service systems for unsteady demand flows in Subsect. 7.3.3. The capacity cost function is developed from the cost minimization problem, denoted by Z^3, such that

$$Z^3(x, \kappa; c) \equiv \min \left\{ \sum_j p_j \left(x_{oj} + \sum_t \delta_t x_{tj} \right) \right\} + \sum_t \delta_t \kappa_t (c_t - F(x_o, x_t)). \tag{8.34}$$

This cost minimization problem gives the capacity cost function KC, which is equal to $Z^3(\bar{x}, \bar{\kappa}; c)$, in which $(\bar{x}, \bar{\kappa}; c)$ is the solution to Z^3. This cost function KC is identical to the same function of (7.48) for the MPSCMP of (7.47), except that $\breve{v}$ replaces $\bar{v}$.

Third, we construct the MPPMP for a service system that serves peaking demands. We model this MPPMP, denoted by Π^4, by modifying the basic form of PMPs:

$$\begin{aligned} \Pi^4(p, c, t, \tau) \equiv \max &\left\{ \sum_t \delta_t p_t Q_t(p, t) - KC(c) \right\} \\ &+ \sum_t \delta_t \tau_t (t_t - T_t(Q_t(p, t), c_t)), \end{aligned} \tag{8.35}$$

where p, c, t, and τ are the vectors of T variables, e.g., $p \equiv (p_1, \cdots, p_T)$.

Fourth, we develop first order conditions for Π^4 with respect to p_t, t_t, and c_t:

$$\frac{\partial \Pi^4}{\partial p_t} = \delta_t \breve{Q}_t + \sum_k \delta_k \breve{p}_k \frac{\partial \breve{Q}_k}{\partial p_t} - \sum_k \delta_k \breve{\tau}_k \frac{\partial \breve{T}_k}{\partial Q_k} \frac{\partial \breve{Q}_k}{\partial p_t} = 0 \tag{8.36}$$

$$\frac{\partial \Pi^4}{\partial t_t} = \sum_k \delta_k \breve{p}_k \frac{\partial \breve{Q}_k}{\partial t_t} + \delta_t \breve{\tau}_t - \sum_k \delta_k \breve{\tau}_k \frac{\partial \breve{T}_k}{\partial Q_k} \frac{\partial \breve{Q}_k}{\partial t_t} = 0 \tag{8.37}$$

$$\frac{\partial \Pi^4}{\partial c_t} = -MKC_t(\breve{c}) - \delta_t \breve{\tau}_t \frac{\partial \breve{T}_t}{\partial c_t} = 0, \text{ all } t, \tag{8.38}$$

where $\breve{Q}_t \equiv Q_t(\breve{p}, \breve{t})$, and $\breve{T}_t \equiv T_t(\breve{Q}_t, \breve{c}_t)$. Here, by the identical ordering condition, it holds that

$$\frac{\partial \breve{Q}_t}{\partial p_k} = \frac{\partial \breve{Q}_t}{\partial t_k} \cong 0, \quad \text{if} \quad k \neq t,\ t+1,$$

as explained in the proof of Theorem 5.7.

Fifth, we show that, under the condition of (8.33), first order conditions in (8.36) and (8.37) give the relationship similar to $\breve{\tau} = \breve{v}\breve{q}$ in Lemma 8.1.

Lemma 8.2. *Under the condition (8.33), the solution $(\breve{p}, \breve{c}, \breve{t}, \breve{\tau})$ to Π^4 satisfies the following:*

$$\breve{\tau}_t \cong \breve{\xi}_t \breve{Q}_t \quad \textit{and} \quad \breve{\xi}_t \in L_t(p, t), \ \textit{all } t.$$

Proof. (i) Multiplying $\breve{\xi}_t (= (\partial \breve{Q}_t / \partial t_t)/(\partial \breve{Q}_t / \partial p_t))$ to (8.36), (ii) subtracting the result of the previous step from (8.37), and (iii) simplifying the result of the previous step by applying (8.33) gives the above equality. □

Sixth, we show that the term $\breve{\tau}_t \partial \breve{T}_t / \partial Q_t$ in (8.36) and (8.37) equals the marginal full cost of the tth period. To show that, we first construct the dual problem of Π^4 by amending the MPZ^3 of (7.47); that is, replacing $\bar{v}_t s_t$ of MPZ^3 with $\breve{\xi}_t \breve{Q}_t\ (= \breve{\tau}_t)$ gives the dual of Π^4. This dual yields the outcome such that

$$MFC_t(\breve{Q}) = MCC_t(\breve{Q}) \cong \breve{\xi}_t \breve{Q}_t \frac{\partial T_t(\breve{Q}_t, \breve{c}_t)}{\partial Q_t}, \text{ all } t, \tag{8.39}$$

where $\breve{Q} \equiv (\breve{Q}_1, \cdots, \breve{Q}_T)$ and $\breve{\xi} \equiv (\breve{\xi}_1, \cdots, \breve{\xi}_T)$, as shown Theorem 7.8.

Seventh, we develop the pricing and investment rules for the MPPMP by combining the analytical outcomes of the previous steps.

Theorem 8.6. *Under the condition (8.33), the solution $(\breve{p}, \breve{c}, \breve{t})$ to Π^4 satisfies the following pricing and investment rules:*

$$\begin{pmatrix} \breve{p}_1 - MFC_1(\breve{Q}) \\ \vdots \\ \breve{p}_T - MFC_T(\breve{Q}) \end{pmatrix} \cong - \begin{pmatrix} a_{11} & \cdots & a_{1T} \\ \vdots & \ddots & \vdots \\ a_{T1} & \cdots & a_{TT} \end{pmatrix}^{-1} \begin{pmatrix} \delta_1 \breve{Q}_1 \\ \vdots \\ \delta_T \breve{Q}_T \end{pmatrix} \tag{8.40}$$

$$MKC_t(\breve{c}) \cong -\breve{\xi}_t \breve{Q}_t \frac{\partial \breve{T}_t}{\partial c_t}, \text{ all } t, \tag{8.41}$$

where $a_{mn} = \delta_n \times \partial \breve{Q}_n / \partial p_m$.

Proof. Substituting Lemma 8.2 and (8.39) into (8.36) and arranging the result of the previous step gives (8.40). Substituting Lemma 8.2 into (8.38) and arranging the result of the previous step gives (8.41). □

Finally, we examine the structure of the optimal price $\breve{p}_t$ in (8.40) for the case of $T = 2$. In this special case, the identical ordering condition in (8.32) implies $\breve{p}_1 \geq \breve{p}_2$; otherwise, $\breve{Q}_2 = 0$, since the thickness of D_2 would be zero, as shown in Lemma 5.7. Furthermore, the optimal $\breve{p}_t$, for $t = 1, 2$, is always greater than the marginal full cost $MFC_t(\breve{Q})$. The explanation is as below.

By Cramer's rule, the solution $\breve{p}_1$ to (8.40) is

$$\breve{p}_1 \cong MFC_1(\breve{Q}; \breve{v}) - \left(\breve{Q}_1 \frac{\partial \breve{Q}_2}{\partial p_2} - \breve{Q}_2 \frac{\partial \breve{Q}_2}{\partial p_1} \right) \Big/ \left(\frac{\partial \breve{Q}_1}{\partial p_1} \frac{\partial \breve{Q}_2}{\partial p_2} - \frac{\partial \breve{Q}_1}{\partial p_2} \frac{\partial \breve{Q}_2}{\partial p_1} \right). \tag{8.42}$$

This equation shows that the price $\breve{p}_t$, for $t = 1, 2$, is always greater than the marginal full cost $MFC_t(\breve{Q})$ by the margin that equals the last term of the equation. This margin is always positive; that is, by the inequalities in Theorem 5.7, the numerator and denominator of the last term are both positive.

Chapter 9
The Equilibrium of Competitive Service Markets

9.1 Introduction

This chapter extends analyses presented in the previous chapter for service markets in monopoly to service markets in forms of quantitative and qualitative competition among multiple firms. Analyses in the previous chapter are extended through the application of the user equilibrium approach for competitive service markets, a more generalized version of the same approach for service markets in monopoly. This user equilibrium approach for competitive markets fundamentally differs from existing approaches for congestion-free firms in two respects.

One key difference involves the modeling approach for consumer demands. Existing approaches for congestion-free markets commonly assume that each firm captures a certain portion of homogeneous market demands. In contrast, the user equilibrium approach for competitive service markets uses a consumer demand function under the random perception approach in order to explicitly account for heterogeneity in preference for service quality among consumers. Under the random perception approach, consumers, who have unique preferences for service quality, should choose the most economical option among all available options that are distinguished from one another by service quality. For this reason, each firm in competition facilitates a certain demand segment the particular firm most economically serves.

The other difference is the approach for modeling the PMP. Traditional approaches for analyses of market equilibrium commonly presume that multiple firms in a market belong to one identical type of industrial organization. Moreover, the PMP under existing approaches for a certain industrial organization type generally differs from those for other types. In contrast, the user equilibrium approach for competitive markets models the PMP of a firm in a unified formulation, irrespective of its industrial organization type. Instead, the industrial organization type of a service firm in competitive markets is identified through the posterior evaluation of analysis outcomes for market equilibrium, as will be explored in the next chapter.

D.J. Moon, *Congestion-Prone Services Under Quality Competition*, Advances in Spatial Science, DOI 10.1007/978-3-642-20189-9_9,

Subsequently, we compare and contrast the user equilibrium approach for competitive markets with the same approach for markets in monopoly. The former postulates that a service firm plays leader-and-follower games with consumers, as does the latter. However, the former applies an additional postulate that each service firm plays non-cooperative games against competitors in order to maximize profit. The two hypotheses applied in the former are explained in detail below.

The hypothesis that a service firm in competition plays non-cooperative games resembles the rule of non-cooperative games for congestion-free Cournot oligopolies, called *the hypothesis of zero conjectural variation*. The hypothesis for a congestion-prone service firm is identical to the hypothesis for congestion-free firms in that every service firm is assumed to make a choice regarding its directly controllable variables, ignoring the reaction of other agents in the market to this choice. The former, however, differs from the latter in that the former applies the zero conjectural variation to all the quantitative and qualitative service attributes of competitors.

The target of the zero conjectural variation for competitive service firms comprises not only the price but also the service time of competitors. The application of this postulate to the price charged by competitors implies that a firm ignores the reaction of competitors in making profit-maximizing choices. On the other hand, its application to the service time implies that a firm neglects not only the possible capacity adjustment made by competitors but also the reaction of competitors' customers who play the role of finalizing the service time of service systems operated by the competitors.

The other postulate that a service firm in competition plays leader-and-follower games resembles the key postulate applied to monopolists. This postulate implies that every firm forecasts and utilizes knowledge of consumer reaction in making profit-maximizing choices. This postulate connotes that a firm in competitive markets also indirectly controls its service time through the choice of its directly controllable price and capacity, as is true of the monopolist.

Importantly, the combination of the two postulates introduced above implies that a service firm plays leader-and-follower games with its customers on the basis of *incomplete knowledge of consumer reaction*. The zero conjectural variation connotes that the knowledge used in forecasting the reaction of its customers does not consider the impact on competitor price or competitor service time. Such knowledge as is acquired under the zero conjectural variation is certainly incomplete. Further, the use of incomplete knowledge requires completely different analyses of market equilibrium than are required for analyses for a monopoly market, as explained below.

Suppose that a service firm in a competitive market makes a change in price and/or capacity. This action is followed by reactions not only by competitors but also by consumers. The reactions by consumers are realized through the adjustment of demands for all service firms in the market. This adjustment of demands accompanies changes in demands and service times for all firms, including the firm that makes the change. The adjustment continues until it reaches the state at which no consumer is willing to change demand for all service firms in competition.

This state, which is characterized by a set of service times and demands for all firms, is called *marketwise user equilibrium* for competitive markets, which is synonymous with user equilibrium for a monopoly market.

Contrary to the actual consumer reaction explained above, the service firm under the hypothesis of zero conjectural variation ignores changes in competitor service times and competitor demands. Therefore, the consumer reaction as judged by the firm can be formulated as a simplified version of the marketwise user equilibrium condition, in which competitor service times as well as prices are fixed as constants. Such a hypothetical user equilibrium condition based on incomplete knowledge is called *the incomplete user equilibrium condition*, which has a formulation identical to that of the same condition for monopolists.

The use of the incomplete user equilibrium condition leads to the choice of a firm regarding price and capacity, which usually differs from the values of these two choice variables at market equilibrium. For this reason, the choice of a firm usually triggers the reaction of consumers and competitors so as to maximize utility and profit, respectively. Such adjustment of consumers and competitors continues until their adjustments reach the state of market equilibrium, such that no consumer or service firm can increase utility and profit through changes in their choices.

The user equilibrium approach outlined above requires that the reaction functions of consumers as well as service firms be developed, in order to characterize market equilibrium, as will be explained in Sect. 9.2. The reaction function of consumers estimates the service time of all service firms at marketwise user equilibrium for the independent variables that comprise the prices and capacities of all service firms. This will be detailed in Sect. 9.3. The reaction function of each service firm calculates the price and capacity that maximize profit for the independent variables composed of prices and service times for all competitors. This will be developed in Sect. 9.4. The analysis to prove the existence of market equilibrium requires showing the existence of a fixed point of the mapping that consists of all the reaction functions of consumers and suppliers. This proof will be presented in Sect. 9.5.

9.2 Approaches to Market Equilibrium Analysis

9.2.1 The Basic Form of Profit Maximization Problems Under Competition

Here, we present the PMP applicable to a service firm in a competitive service market, irrespective of industrial organization type. Firstly, we model the PMP of a firm in a competitive market, in accordance with the user equilibrium approach outlined in the previous section. Subsequently, we compare and contrast the mathematical structure of the PMP of a competitive firm with that of a monopolist.

The PMP presented here targets firm *mn* in a competitive service market, which is synonymous with option *mn* in demand analyses of Sect. 2.2. The PMP for option

mn is identical to the same problem for monopolists in Assumption 8.1, except that the former has a number of additional clauses that accommodate competition faced by the firm.

Assumption 9.1. Every firm mn in a competitive market is used to maximize profit through the operation of a service system under the following conditions.

(a) The profit of firm mn is the function of its control variables that comprise price p_{mn}, capacity c_{mn}, and service time t_{mn}, and is estimated by

$$p_{mn}\,Q_{mn}(p,t) - KC_{mn}(c_{mn}),$$

where $Q_{mn}(p,t)$ is the market demand function constructed under Assumptions 4.1 and 4.2, and KC_{mn} is the capacity cost function defined in Lemma 6.1.

(b) The choices for the control variables are made under the condition of zero conjectural variation for the service quality of competitors, such that

$$\frac{\partial(p^o_{mn}, t^o_{mn})}{\partial(p_{mn}, c_{mn}, t_{mn})} = 0, \quad \text{or} \quad \frac{\partial(p^o_{mn}, t^o_{mn})}{\partial e_{mn}} = 0,$$

where $e_{mn} \equiv (p_{mn}, c_{mn}, t_{mn})$, $p^o_{mn} \equiv p\backslash\{\ p_{mn}\}$ and $t^o_{mn} \equiv t\backslash\{\ t_{mn}\}$.

(c) The choices are made by utilizing incomplete knowledge of consumer reactions, as is expressed by the incomplete user equilibrium condition such that

$$t_{mn} = T_{mn}(Q_{mn}(p,t), c_{mn}),$$

where T is either a homogeneous or non-homogeneous service time function as defined in Assumption 6.1.

(d) The capacity cost function KC_{mn} is increasing and twice differentiable in c_{mn}, and either concave or convex on the relevant region of c_{mn}.

(e) The value of (p^o_{mn}, t^o_{mn}) in the incomplete user equilibrium condition is the observed value at the moment when the choices are made.

The most important difference between the PMP in Assumption 9.1 and the same problem in Assumption 8.1 is the addition of the zero conjectural variation condition in Assumption 9.1(b). This condition postulates that the prices and service times of competitors, expressed by (p^o_{mn}, t^o_{mn}), are constants not affected by the choices of firm mn, denoted by e_{mn} $(\equiv (p_{mn}, c_{mn}, t_{mn}))$. By virtue of this condition, the unknowns of the PMP are reduced to the three variables constituting the vector e_{mn}. Further, the marketwise user equilibrium condition is simplified to the incomplete user equilibrium condition in Assumption 9.1(c), as explained below.

One way of formulating the marketwise user equilibrium condition is as follows:

$$t_{m'n'} = T_{m'n'}(Q_{m'n'}(p,t), c_{m'n'}), \ \text{all}\ m'n', \tag{9.1}$$

in which $p_{m'n'}$ and $t_{m'n'}$ for all $m'n'$ are variables. However, under the zero conjectural variation condition, the values of $p_{m'n'}$ and $t_{m'n'}$, for all $m'n' \neq mn$, are constant. Therefore, the marketwise user equilibrium condition is simplified to the incomplete user equilibrium condition in Assumption 9.1(c).

In addition, the PMP of Assumption 9.1 expresses supplier cost as the capacity cost KC_{mn}, rather than the cost of inputs to capacity, $\Sigma_j p_j x_j$, as in the case of the PMP in (8.8) for monopolists. The use of KC_{mn} has the effect of reducing explanatory variables for market analyses from $(p_{mn}, c_{mn}, t_{mn}, x_{mn})$ to (p_{mn}, c_{mn}, t_{mn}). This reduction of explanatory variables will greatly simplify analyses that characterize market equilibrium without loss of generality.

Finally, the PMP of Assumption 9.1 has a mathematical structure identical to that of (8.8) for monopolists, as a constrained optimization problem. The PMP has only three unknown variables $e_{mn} \equiv (p_{mn}, c_{mn}, t_{mn})$, as is true for the PMP under monopoly. Further, the functional structures of the profit function and the constraint of the partial user equilibrium condition are identical to those for the PMP under monopoly. For these reasons, the PMP has a nontrivial solution for its directly controllable variables p_{mn} and c_{mn} unless it gives a negative profit, as is true for monopolists.

9.2.2 Implications of the Profit Maximization Problem

We here present the economic implications embodied in the PMP of Assumption 9.1, focusing on the differences between Assumption 9.1 for competitive firms and Assumption 8.1 for monopolists. To this end, we first introduce the differences between the two, and subsequently present the economic implications of these differences.

First, as indicated in Assumption 9.1(a), the demand for option mn is estimated by applying the expected demand function under the random perception approach, rather than the demand function under the deterministic perception approach. The deterministic demand function has a critical shortcoming in that it is unable to properly quantify demand shifts among firms in competition, which are caused by changes in price and service times, as pointed out in the comment for Theorem 2.5. In contrast, the expected demand function reasonably quantifies demand shifts, as demonstrated throughout Chap. 5.

Second, the zero conjectural variation condition in Assumption 9.1(b) formulates that firm mn makes the choice for the vector $e_{mn} \equiv (p_{mn}, c_{mn}, t_{mn})$, as if the vector (p^o_{mn}, t^o_{mn}) in the expected demand function Q_{mn} were constant. This condition connotes that the firm ignores not only competitor reactions but also those of consumers. To be specific, the inclusion of p^o_{mn} to the condition indicates that the firm overlooks the reaction of competitors, whereas the inclusion of t^o_{mn} to the condition implies that firm mn neglects the reaction not only of competitors for the choice of capacity but also of their customers for the choice of demands.

Third, the incomplete user equilibrium condition in Assumption 9.1(c) postulates that the firm has incomplete knowledge of the reaction of competitors and consumers to its choice regarding price and capacity. In contrast, one possible alternative approach to employing the marketwise user equilibrium condition reflects that the firm has complete knowledge. In this regard, it is conceived that the former more reasonably specifies the scope of actual knowledge the firm can acquire.

Fourth, Assumption 9.1(d) about the configuration of the capacity cost function KC_{mn} connotes that the PMP can apply to all service firms, irrespective of industrial organization type. Whether the function KC_{mn} is concave or not in capacity c_{mm} is a critical factor that determines the returns-to-scale of the service system for throughput s_{mn}, as shown in Theorems 7.3 and 7.5. Further, the returns-to-scale of KC_{mn} plays a crucial role in determining the industrial organization type of firm mn, as will be confirmed in the following chapter. Therefore the assumption that the capacity cost function can be either convex or not implies that the PMP can be applicable to all types of industrial organization.

Fifth, Assumption 9.1(e) regarding the value of vector (p^o_{mn}, t^o_{mn}) in the demand function is a device used to reflect a feedback process regarding the decisions made by all firms and consumers. The zero conjectural variation indicates that the value of (p^o_{mn}, t^o_{mn}) should be fixed, but does not give any guideline about how to determine the value of this vector. In this circumstance, if a firm uses an arbitrary value for the vector, a new choice made by the firm would not be linked to previous decisions made by other firms and consumers. In contrast, if a firm uses the observed value at the moment it makes the choice, such problem disappears.

Finally, the PMP of service firm mn estimates the reaction of the firm, which usually differs from the choice of the firm at market equilibrium. This discrepancy stems from the use of the incomplete user equilibrium condition in which the (p^o_{mn}, t^o_{mn}) value is the value observed when making the choice of e_{mn}. However, the observed value of (p^o_{mn}, t^o_{mn}) at a certain instance usually not equal to the value at market equilibrium. For this reason, the solution of e_{mn} is usually also not equal to the value at market equilibrium. Therefore, the action of firm mn to implement the optimal solution usually triggers subsequent reactions from consumers and competitors.

The use of the incomplete user equilibrium condition usually leads to a profit that differs from the one expected by the firms at the moment they chose price and capacity. Such incomplete knowledge of firms can cause a deficit leading to bankruptcy; this is obviously contrary to the expectation of the firm. It can therefore be said that the introduction of the incomplete user equilibrium condition makes it possible to accommodate one important aspect of real service markets: the bankruptcy of firms that must make rational choices.

9.2.3 Types and Variables of Reaction Functions

It was pointed out above that the implementation of the solution to the PMP of Assumption 9.1 usually triggers reactions by consumers and competitors. These reactions can be formulated by their reaction functions, which are the key units of analyses used to characterize the equilibrium of a competitive service market. Prior to detailed equilibrium analyses, we here brief the basic structure of these reaction functions, so as to facilitate an understanding of the forthcoming analyses for market equilibrium in this chapter.

To start, we define the competitive market that will be analyzed. Suppose that all firms in the market have already determined the qualitative attributes of the service systems they operate. Suppose, also, that all firms can be sorted into M differentiated service groups, each of which is denoted by $m \in \langle 1, M \rangle$. Suppose, further, that each differentiated service is sometimes offered by more than one firm, each of which is expressed by $n \in \langle 1, N_m \rangle$, and that the total number of firms is assumed to be $NT(= \Sigma_m N_m)$.

Given all the above, the number of variables necessary for describing all the reaction functions defined above is as follows. The independent variables in the demand function of all firms under the perception approach are prices $p \equiv (p, \cdots, p_{MN})$ and service times $t \equiv (t, \cdots, t_{MN})$; the demand side introduces the $2NT$ variables. On the other hand, each firm mn determines both the price p_{mn} and the capacity c_{mn} of its service system; the supply side brings the $2NT$ variables of $p \equiv (p, \cdots, p_{MN})$ and $c \equiv (c_{11}, \cdots, c_{MN})$. Therefore, the description of all the reactions calls for the use of $3NT$ variables, denoted by (p, c, t).

Now we can consider the reaction function of consumers. Consumers are motivated by their desire to maximize utilities. Consumer reactions are triggered by changes in the choices firms make about the vector of their directly controllable variables, (p, c). Consumer reactions reach the state of marketwise user equilibrium, such that no consumer can be better off by changing demand given all firms available. This marketwise user equilibrium is formulated by the marketwise user equilibrium condition in (9.1), from which one can estimate the service time vector t at marketwise user equilibrium.

Based on the above discussion, the reaction function of consumers can be expressed in an abbreviated form using a multi-valued mapping Γ^u such that

$$\Gamma^u : (p, c) \rightarrow t. \tag{9.2}$$

The mapping Γ^u estimates the service time t, which satisfies the marketwise user equilibrium condition for the arbitrary values of (p, c). However, the service time estimated from Γ^u usually differs from the service time estimated from the incomplete user equilibrium condition in Assumption 9.1(c).

We next consider the reaction function of firms. The choice of firm mn regarding directly controllable variables (p_{mn}, c_{mn}) is the solution to the PMP of Assumption 9.1. This choice usually changes the decision-making environment for competitors. For example, firm $m'n'$ faces a demand function in which the $(p^o_{m'n'}, t^o_{m'n'})$ value differs from the value observed in making its previous choice of $(p_{m'n'}, c_{m'n'})$. The reaction to adjust the choice of $(p_{m'n'}, c_{m'n'})$ therefore follows, so as to maximize profit under the changed decision-making environment.

Such a reaction of every firm mn can be expressed as the multi-valued mapping Γ^s_{mn} such that

$$\Gamma^s_{mn} : (p^o_{mn}, t^o_{mn}) \to (p_{mn}, c_{mn}), \text{ all } mn. \tag{9.3}$$

This mapping Γ^s_{mn} estimates the solution of (p_{mn}, c_{mn}) to the PMP for the given value of (p^o_{mn}, t^o_{mn}). Also, the reaction function of all firms, denoted by Γ^s, can be expressed by the Cartesian product of Γ^s_{mn}, for all mn:

$$\Gamma^s = \prod_{mn} \Gamma^s_{mn} : (p, t) \to (p, c). \tag{9.4}$$

Here the input variables of Γ^s are $\bigcup_{mn} (p^o_{mn}, t^o_{mn}) = (p, t)$.

The two mappings Γ^u and Γ^s have different functional structures and behavioral implications. The mapping Γ^u is expressed as the simultaneous equation system that estimates all the values of $t \equiv (t_{11}, \cdots, t_{MN})$, as shown in (9.1). This formulation of Γ^u is indispensible to any effort to reflect the interdependency of demands and service times among firms. In contrast, the mapping Γ^s is expressed as the Cartesian product of mappings Γ^s_{mn}, for all mn. This Cartesian product depicts that each mapping Γ^s_{mn} estimates its image (p_{mn}, c_{mn}) independent of other mappings $\Gamma^s_{m'n'}$, for all $m'n' \neq mn$. Such a formulation reflects that each firm mn chooses (p_{mn}, c_{mn}) independent of its competitor decisions under the zero conjectural variation condition.

Finally, we consider the problem of how to characterize market equilibrium using the mappings Γ^u and Γ^s. The market equilibrium is characterized by the fixed point of the Cartesian product of reaction functions Γ^s and Γ^s. Roughly speaking, the fixed point is the solution of (p, c, t) to the simultaneous equation system composed of the mappings Γ^s and Γ^s. Further, the existence of market equilibrium implies that the Cartesian product of the two reaction functions has a fixed point.

The market equilibrium characterized above represents the state when no agency in a service market is willing to change its choice so as to increase utility or profit, as explained below. First, the service times calculated from the incomplete user equilibrium conditions of all firms at market equilibrium are equal to the service times estimated from the marketwise user equilibrium condition. This implies that the service times forecast by firms equal the service times later determined by consumers. Second, the prices and service times of competitors, which are observed by a firm in choosing optimal price and capacity, are equal to those values at market equilibrium. This indicates that the optimal choice of each firm at market equilibrium does not trigger any further reaction from competitors.

9.2.4 Degeneracy of Service Demand Functions

The demand function of a service firm under the random perception approach is discontinuous in its explanatory variables at certain points, as shown in Chap. 5. Unfortunately, this discontinuity may appear to make it infeasible to properly characterize the marketwise user equilibrium condition and the optimality condition for the PMP of firms. Given this possibility, a number of issues that must be carefully analyzed are presented below.

To begin, we reintroduce the condition for the discontinuity of the demand function Q_{mn} in Theorems 5.1 and 5.10. Suppose that the demand functions of firms mn and $m(n+1)$ satisfy *the degeneracy condition* such that

$$p_{mn} = p_{m(n+1)} \quad \text{and} \quad t_{mn} = t_{m(n+1)}. \tag{9.5}$$

Then, the demand functions Q_{mn} and $Q_{m(n+1)}$ share a common catchment domain D_{mn} and satisfy the equality such that

$$Q_{mn}(p,t) + Q_{m(n+1)}(p,t) = \int_{D_{mn}} f_m(p_{mn} + \xi_m t_{mn})\, h(\xi) d\mu. \tag{9.6}$$

Hence, the functions Q_{mn} and $Q_{m(n+1)}$ have degenerate values at the point that satisfies the degeneracy condition and are thereby not continuous at that point.

At first glance, it appears that the degeneracy of Q_{mn} makes it infeasible to properly formulate the marketwise user equilibrium. To be specific, suppose that firm mn makes the choice of (p_{mn}, c_{mn}), which would lead to the degeneracy of Q_{mn}. Then, the degenerate value of Q_{mn} would yield the solution of t_{mn} to the marketwise user equilibrium condition, which is also a degenerate value, as can be inferred from (9.1). This means, by Assumption 9.1(e), that the parameter of the demand function faced by other firms, for all $m'n' \neq mn$, would be the degenerate value of t_{mn}. Such a degeneracy of the t_{mn} value would make it impossible to properly construct the PMP of options for all $m'n' \neq mn$.

However, in reality, such a problem does not occur. In fact, any choice of (p_{mn}, c_{mn}) values always leads to a unique value of Q_m at marketwise user equilibrium; that is, there is a unique solution of t to the marketwise user equilibrium condition. Further, the estimated demand for every firm at the user equilibrium is always a definite value. This assertion, of course, holds even in the case when the resulting user equilibrium satisfies the degeneracy condition, as will be proved in the following section.

Another conceivable problem caused by the degeneracy of Q_{mn} is the difficulty of properly characterizing optimality conditions for the PMP. The discontinuity of Q_{mn} implies that the PMP has the objective function of Assumption 9.1(a) and constraint functions of Assumption 9.1(c), both of which are discontinuous at a certain point of (p_{mn}, t_{mn}). Therefore, if the solution of (p_{mn}, t_{mn}) to the PMP satisfies the degeneracy condition of (9.5), it would be infeasible to properly characterize optimality conditions.

Fortunately, we do not need to worry about such a possibility. The value of the function Q_{mn} in the PMP is continuous along the locus of (p_{mn}, c_{mn}, t_{mn}), in which t_{mn} is the solution to the constraint of the incomplete user equilibrium condition for the varying value of (p_{mn}, c_{mn}). For this reason, it is possible to properly characterize the optimality conditions at the point that satisfies the degeneracy condition, as will be proved in Sect. 9.4.

9.3 Reaction by Consumers

9.3.1 User Equilibrium under the Non-degeneracy Condition

The mapping Γ^u in (9.2), termed the marketwise user equilibrium condition, has been tentatively expressed as a set of conditions in (9.1), which is developed by analogy to the user equilibrium condition of the monopoly market. It is shown below that (9.1) is applicable without any amendment, as long as the demand functions of all firms in a market do not violate the degeneracy condition of (9.5).

Suppose that all firms in a market have determined the values of (p, c), which are not necessarily the solutions to their PMPs. Suppose, also, that the prices of all firms in each service group m differ from one another; that is, $p_{mn} \neq p_{mn'}$, for all m and $n' \neq n$. In light of (9.5), this condition implies that demands for all firms do not violate the degeneracy condition.

In these circumstances, one method of formulating marketwise user equilibrium involves depicting the equilibrium in a manner analogous to that of a neoclassical market under perfect competition, as in the case of a monopoly market. Under this analogy, the user equilibrium can be expressed as the solution of the following equation systems:

$$t_{mn} = T_{mn}(s_{mn}, c_{mn}) \tag{9.7}$$

$$s_{mn} = Q_{mn}(p, t), \text{ all } mn. \tag{9.8}$$

Here the demand function Q_{mn} is decreasing in t_{mn} and non-decreasing in $t_{m'n'}$ for all $m'n' \neq mn$, as shown in Theorem 5.11. On the other hand, the service time function T_{mn} is increasing in throughput s_{mn}, as depicted in Assumption 6.1.

The service time t plays a role equivalent to that of price in a neoclassical market: it determines the demand of all consumers and the throughput of all service systems at marketwise user equilibrium. In this analogy, the demand function Q_{mn} corresponds to the market demand function of a certain good traded in a neoclassical market. This demand function is sensitive only to service times t, since prices p are assumed to be fixed. On the other hand, the service time function T_{mn} is equivalent to the supply function of a certain good. In addition, the service time t_{mn}, estimated from T_{mn}, is sensitive only to throughput s_{mn}, since the capacity c_{mn} is predetermined.

The marketwise user equilibrium can be represented as the solution of service times $t \equiv (t_{11}, \cdots, t_{MN})$ and throughputs $s \equiv (s_{11}, \cdots, s_{MN})$ to the $2NT$ simultaneous equations in (9.7) and (9.8). These $2NT$ equations can be merged into NT

equations, called the marketwise user equilibrium condition, through the substitution of (9.8) into (9.7):

$$\hat{t}_{mn} = T_{mn}(Q_{mn}(p, \hat{t}), c_{mn}), \text{ all } mn. \tag{9.9}$$

where $\hat{t} \equiv (\hat{t}_{11}, \cdots, \hat{t}_{MN})$ is the service time at marketwise user equilibrium.

Mathematically, the marketwise user equilibrium condition is sufficient to estimate the service time at equilibrium, denoted by $\hat{t}$, and the demand of all firms at equilibrium, estimated by $Q_{mn}(p, \hat{t})$, for all mn. To be specific, the NT simultaneous equations (9.9) give a unique solution $\hat{t}$, as will be proved later in this section. Substituting the solution $\hat{t}$ to the function Q_{mn} yields a unique value of the market demand for firm mn at equilibrium, estimated by $Q_{mn}(p, \hat{t})$.

Behaviorally, (9.9) well depicts that the demand $Q_{mn}(p, \hat{t})$ is the outcome of consumer decisions such that no single individual is better off by changing demand. To be specific, the service time in the demand function of (9.9) represents the service time predicted at the moment one makes the utility-maximizing decision, whereas the service time on the left of (9.9) estimates the service time actually experienced afterward. Also, the user equilibrium condition of (9.9) depicts that the service time, predicted before visiting the service system, should be equal to the service time actually experienced.

Finally, marketwise user equilibrium can be interpreted as the outcome of the search process in which consumers is used to find the most economical service option. It is certain that every consumer who is willing to maximize utility surely chooses the most economical firm. Further, the demand function Q_{mn} is incorporated with the revealed preference condition that reflects such a search process; its integral domain D_{mn} formulates the revealed preference condition under the random perception approach, as pointed out in Sect. 4.3. Therefore, the service time $\hat{t}$ and the demand $Q_{mn}(p, \hat{t})$ at equilibrium represent the final outcome of the search process.

9.3.2 User Equilibrium under the Degeneracy Condition

The consumer process to search out the most economical firm always results in a new set of unique service times for all firms at marketwise user equilibrium, whether or not the prices and service times of some firms fulfill the degeneracy condition of (9.5). This implies that the demand actually served by a firm is not a degenerate value, but rather a definite value, even in the case when its price service time satisfies the degeneracy condition. The marketwise user equilibrium condition that can explicitly reflect this aspect is constructed below.

To begin, we introduce a more inclusive condition for the degeneracy of Q_{mn} than that of (9.5). This more inclusive condition characterizes the degeneracy using only one variable p_{mn}, instead of two variables, p_{mn} and t_{mn}, as shown below.

Lemma 9.1. *Let I_{mn} be the index set defined by*

$$I_{mn} = \{ mn' \mid p_{mn'} = p_{mn}, \text{ all } mn' \}.$$

If the demands of firm mn and some other firms $mn' \in I_{mn}$ are not zero at marketwise user equilibrium, these firms have a service time $\widehat{t}_{mn}$ that is common to all of them.

Proof. The proof can readily be worked out by applying the weak trade-off condition of Lemma 5.1. By the weak trade-off condition, firms mn and mn', both of which have positive demands under the condition $p_{mn'} = p_{mn}$, must fulfill another condition such that $t_{mn'} = t_{mn}$. Therefore, the condition $p_{mn'} = p_{mn}$ is sufficient to characterize the degeneracy condition of (9.5). □

Next, we consider the main problem of estimating the demand of firm mn, which violates the degeneracy condition. For the group of firms that belong to I_{mn}, the simultaneous equations (9.7) and (9.8) can be amended as follows:

$$t_{mn} = T_{mn'}(s_{mn'}, c_{mn'}), \text{ all } mn' \in I_{mn} \tag{9.10}$$

$$\sum_{mn' \in I_{mn}} s_{mn'} = \int_{D_{mn}} f_m(p_{mn} + \xi_m t_{mn})\, h(\xi)\, d\mu. \tag{9.11}$$

This simultaneous equation system is composed of $N_{mn} + 1$ equations, where N_{mn} is the number of firms in I_{mn}; that is, (9.10) gives N_{mn} equations, and (9.11) gives one equation. Also, the number of unknowns is $N_{mn} + 1$; one unknown t_{mn} and N_{mn} unknowns $s_{mn'}$, for all $mn' \in I_{mn}$. Therefore, it is feasible to solve the above simultaneous equation system.

To solve the above equation system, we first develop the inverse function of T_{mn}, denoted by Φ_{mn}. This inverse function Φ_{mn} estimates the throughput s_{mn} for the arbitrarily given values of time t_{mn} and capacity c_{mn}, as shown below.

Lemma 9.2. *The throughput function Φ_{mn}, defined by*

$$\Phi_{mn}(t_{mn}, c_{mn}) = \{ s_{mn} \mid t_{mn} = T_{mn}(s_{mn}, c_{mn})\}, \text{ all } mn,$$

is concave, increasing, and differentiable in both of t_{mn}, and c_{mn}.

Proof. The function T_{mn} is differentiable in s_{mn} and satisfies the condition that $\partial T_{mn}/\partial s_{mn} \rangle\ 0$ for all s_{mn}. Hence, by the implicit function theorem, there exists Φ_{mn} that replaces s in $t_{mn} = T_{mn}(s_{mn}, c_{mn})$ and thus satisfies the following equality: $t_{mn} = T_{mn}(\Phi_{mn}(t_{mn}, c_{mn}), c_{mn})$.

Differentiating $t_{mn} = T_{mn}(\Phi_{mn}(t_{mn}, c_{mn}), c_{mn})$ with respect to t_{mn} gives

$$\frac{\partial \Phi_{mn}}{\partial t_{mn}} = 1 \Big/ \frac{\partial T_{mn}}{\partial s_{mn}} \rangle\ 0. \tag{9.12}$$

Here, $\partial T_{mn}/\partial s_{mn}$ is positive and monotonically increasing in s_{mn}, since T_{mn} is convex and increasing. Hence, it follows that $\partial \Phi_{mn}/\partial t_{mn}$ is positive and monotonically decreasing; that is, Φ_{mn} is concave and increasing in t_{mn}.

Next, differentiating $t_{mn} = T_{mn}(\Phi_{mn}(t_{mn}, c_{mn}), c_{mn})$ with respect to c_{mn} yields

$$\frac{\partial \Phi_{mn}}{\partial c_{mn}} = -\frac{\partial T_{mn}}{\partial c_{mn}} \Big/ \frac{\partial T_{mn}}{\partial s_{mn}} \rangle\ 0. \tag{9.13}$$

In the case of homogeneous service technology, by (6.1), the above equation leads to $\partial \Phi_{mn}/\partial c_{mn} = c_{mn}/s_{mn}$. This implies that Φ_{mn} has a linear relationship with c_{mn}; that is, Φ_{mn} is weakly concave in c_{mn}. In the case of non-homogeneous service technology, the term $\partial \Phi_{mn}/\partial c_{mn}$ is positive and decreasing in c_{mn}, and asymptotically approaches a constant, as can be proved using (7.8) and (7.9). Hence, the function Φ_{mn} is concave and increasing in c_{mn}. □

Subsequently, substituting the function Φ_{mn} into (9.11) gives

$$\sum_{mn' \in I_{mn}} \Phi_{mn'}(t_{mn}, c_{mn'}) = \int_{D_{mn}} f_m(p_{mn} + \xi_m t_{mn})\, h(\xi) d\mu. \tag{9.14}$$

Here, the function $\Phi_{mn'}$ is increasing in service time t_{mn}, which is common to all firms $mn \in I_{mn}$, as shown in Lemma 9.1, whereas the integral on the right side estimates the sum of demands facilitated by all firms $mn \in I_{mn}$ and decreases in t_{mn}.

Therefore, there exists the service time $\widehat{t}_{mn}$, for which both sides of (9.11) are equal. The solution $\widehat{t}_{mn}$ is the service time that satisfies the user equilibrium condition characterized in (9.10) and (9.11). Also, the demand of firm mn at equilibrium is $\Phi_{mn}(\widehat{t}_{mn}, c_{mn})$. Using these facts, we deduce the following.

Lemma 9.3. *Suppose that the demand of firm mn is positive at marketwise user equilibrium characterized by (9.10) and (9.11). Then, the demand for firm mn at user equilibrium, denoted by* Q^u_{mn}, *is*

$$Q^u_{mn}(\widehat{t}; p, c_m) = \int_{D_{mn}} f_m(p_{mn} + \xi_m \widehat{t}_{mn})\, h(\xi) d\mu \frac{\Phi_{mn}(\widehat{t}_{mn}, c_{mn})}{\sum_{mn' \in I_{mn}} \Phi_{mn'}(\widehat{t}_{mn}, c_{mn'})},$$

where c_m *is the vector composed of* $c_{mn'}$ *for all* $mn' \in I_{mn}$.

Proof. It suffices to show that $Q^u_{mn}(\widehat{t};\ \cdot)$ is the solution of s_{mn} to the simultaneous equation system composed of (9.10) and (9.11). Firstly, this solution satisfies the equality of (9.11); that is,

$$\sum_{mn' \in I_{mn}} Q^u_{mn}(\widehat{t}; p, c_m) = \int_{D_{mn}} f_m(p_{mn} + \xi_m \widehat{t}_{mn})\, h(\xi) d\mu. \tag{9.15}$$

Secondly, the proof that this solution fulfills the equality of (9.10) is as below. Substituting (9.14) into the right side of the equation in the lemma gives

$$Q^u_{mn}(\hat{t};p,c_m) = \Phi_{mn}(\hat{t}_{mn},c_{mn}). \tag{9.16}$$

Here, Φ_{mn} is the implicit function of s_{mn} in (9.10). Hence, the function Q^u_{mn} satisfies (9.10). □

9.3.3 *Uniqueness of User Equilibrium*

Here we prove that, for any choice of firms regarding prices and capacities, the utility-maximizing choice of consumers always results in unique service times and demands for all firms at marketwise user equilibrium. The proof of this uniqueness is worked out under a generalized condition given that multiple subgroups satisfy the degeneracy condition of Lemma 9.1.

To start, we sort N_m options for all $m \in \langle 1, M \rangle$ into a number of subgroups, each of which, as denoted by I_{ml}, simultaneously fulfills the following conditions:

$$\begin{aligned} &I_{ml} = \{\ mn\ |p_{mn} = p_{ml},\ for\ all\ \ n\} \\ &I_{ml} \bigcap I_{mn'} = \varnothing, \quad for\ all \quad n' \neq l \\ &\bigcup_l I_{ml} = \langle 1, N_m \rangle. \end{aligned} \tag{9.17}$$

Under the index system defined above, group I_{ml} consists of all options that simultaneously fulfill the following two requirements: first the member offers service m; second, the member charges the same price with option ml. The index system also accommodates the case when one group contains only one element. In addition, the representative firm of group I_{ml} refers to firm ml that satisfies the inequality such that

$$t^o_{ml} \leq t^o_{mn},\ \text{all}\ mn \in I_{ml}, \tag{9.18}$$

where t^o_{mn} is the net service time. Such a representative option ml has a positive demand, as long as the total demand for all the options belonging to group I_{ml} is positive. The reason is as follows: first, the function Φ_{mn} is increasing in t_{mn}; second, therefore, if $t_{mn} \rangle\ t^o_{mn}$, it holds that $\Phi_{mn}(t_{mn},c_{mn}) \rangle\ 0$.

By utilizing the above index system, we can amend the marketwise user equilibrium condition in (9.1), as follows:

$$\widehat{t}_{ml} = T_{ml}\left(Q^u_{ml}(\widehat{t};p,c_m),c_{ml}\right), \text{ all } ml \tag{9.19}$$

$$\widehat{t}_{mn} = \begin{cases} \widehat{t}_{ml}, & \text{if } \Phi_{mn}(\widehat{t}_{ml},c_{mn}) \rangle\ 0, \\ t^o_{mn}, & \text{otherwise,} \end{cases} \quad \text{all } mn \in I_{ml}\backslash\{ml\}. \tag{9.20}$$

These equation systems have a unique solution of service time t, as shown below.

Theorem 9.1. *Under the condition that all firms have already determined the values of* (p,c), *the utility-maximizing choices of consumers always lead to a unique service time* $\widehat{t} \equiv (\widehat{t}_{11},\cdots,\widehat{t}_{MN})$ *and a unique throughput* $\Phi_{mn}(\widehat{t}_{mn},c_{mn})$, *for all* mn, *both of which collectively satisfy the marketwise user equilibrium condition specified in* (9.19) *and* (9.20).

Proof. The proof that the service time $\widehat{t} \equiv (\widehat{t}_{11},\cdots,\widehat{t}_{MN})$ is unique is presented in Appendix C.2. The uniqueness of $\widehat{t} \equiv (\widehat{t}_{11},\cdots,\widehat{t}_{MN})$ implies that $\Phi_{m'n'}(\widehat{t}_{mn'},c_{mn'})$ in Lemma 9.2, for all $m'n'$, is single-valued. This implies that, by (9.16), $Q^u_{mn}(\widehat{t};p,c_m)$ in Lemma 9.3 is also single-valued. □

9.4 Reaction of Service Firms

9.4.1 Virtual Demand under the Non-degeneracy Condition

Virtual demand functions refer to the demand functions judged by service firms under decision-making rules depicted in Assumption 9.1. In this subsection, we first introduce two different kinds of virtual demand functions. Subsequently, we analyze the mathematical properties of these two different kinds of virtual demand function, under the non-degeneracy condition of Lemma 9.1.

The first kind of virtual demand function has a functional structure expressed by $Q^s_{mn}(p_{mn},t_{mn};p^o_{mn},t^o_{mn})$. This virtual demand function of firms is developed from the demand function under the random perception approach, $Q_{mn}(p,t)$, through the incorporation of the two conditions of Assumption 9.1 that follow: the zero conjectural variation condition in Assumption 9.1(b), and the use of observed (p^o_{mn},t^o_{mn}) values at marketwise user equilibrium in 9.1(e). The relationship between the two demand functions Q^s_{mn} and Q_{mn} is presented below.

Lemma 9.4. *For all values of* (p,t), *the virtual demand function* Q^s_{mn} *and the real demand function* Q_{mn} *satisfy the following relationship:*

$$Q^s_{mn}(p_{mn},t_{mn};p^o_{mn},t^o_{mn}) = \begin{cases} Q_{mn}(p,t), & \textit{if } p_{mn} \neq p_{mn'}, \textit{ all } n' \neq n \\ \Phi_{mn}(t_{mn},c_{mn}), & \textit{otherwise.} \end{cases}$$

Proof. Assumption 9.1(e) implies that the value of (p^o_{mn}, t^o_{mn}) in Q^s_{mn} equals that of Q_{mn}. (i) Hence, it holds that $Q^s_{mn} = Q_{mn}$ unless Q_{mn} has a degenerate value. (ii) Lemma 9.1 shows that Q_{mn} does not have a degenerate value if $p_{mn} \neq p_{mn'}$, for all $n' \neq n$. (iii) Furthermore, Theorem 9.1 shows that Q^s_{mn} equals Φ_{mn}, even in the case when Q_{mn} has a degenerate value. These three facts imply the lemma. □

The second kind of virtual demand function has a functional structure expressed by $Q^{ue}_{mn}(p_{mn}, c_{mn}; p^o_{mn}, t^o_{mn})$ and is developed by merging the incomplete user equilibrium condition of Assumption 9.1(c) into $Q^s_{mn}(p_{mn}, t_{mn}; p^o_{mn}, t^o_{mn})$. We below introduce the procedure to develop the virtual demand function Q^{uc}_{mn}, under the condition that $p_{mn} \neq p_{mn'}$, for all $n' \neq n$.

The first step constructs the function T^{ue}_{mn} such that

$$T^{ue}_{mn}(p_{mn}, c_{mn}) = \{ t_{mn} \mid t_{mn} = T_{mn}(Q^s_{mn}(p_{mn}, t_{mn};\ \cdot), c_{mn})\}. \tag{9.21}$$

This function T^{ue}_{mn} estimates the service time t_{mn}, which satisfies the incomplete user equilibrium condition of firm mn, and therefore satisfies the equality such that

$$T^{ue}_{mn}(p_{mn}, c_{mn}) = T_{mn}(Q^s_{mn}(p_{mn}, T^{ue}_{mn}(p_{mn}, c_{mn});\ \cdot), c_{mn}). \tag{9.22}$$

The second step constructs the function Q^{uc}_{mn} by replacing the variable t_{mn} in the function Q^s_{mn} with the function T^{uc}_{mn}:

$$Q^{ue}_{mn}(p_{mn}, c_{mn};\ p^o_{mn}, t^o_{mn}) = Q^s_{mn}(p_{mn}, T^{ue}_{mn}(p_{mn}, c_{mn});\ p^o_{mn}, t^o_{mn}\ ). \tag{9.23}$$

The function Q^{uc}_{mn} has a functional structure such that its explanatory variables are composed only of directly controllable variables, p_{mn} and c_{mn}. Finally, we analyze the continuity and differentiability of T^{uc}_{mn} and Q^{uc}_{mn}, for the case when $p_{mn} \neq p_{mn'}$, for all $n' \neq n$.

Lemma 9.5. *The functions T^{ue}_{mn} and Q^{uc}_{mn} are both continuous and differentiable in (p_{mn}, c_{mn}) at the point that $p_{mn} \neq p_{mn'}$, for all $n' \neq n$. Moreover, if $Q^{uc}_{mn}(p, t) \rangle\ 0$ at that point, it holds that*

$$\frac{\partial \breve{T}^{ue}_{mn}}{\partial p_{mn}} = \frac{\partial \breve{T}_{mn}}{\partial Q_{mn}} \frac{\partial \breve{Q}^s_{mn}}{\partial p_{mn}} \Bigg/ \left(1 - \frac{\partial \breve{T}_{mn}}{\partial Q_{mn}} \frac{\partial \breve{Q}^s_{mn}}{\partial t_{mn}}\right) \langle\ 0 \tag{9.24}$$

$$\frac{\partial \breve{Q}^{ue}_{mn}}{\partial p_{mn}} = \frac{\partial \breve{Q}^s_{mn}}{\partial p_{mn}} \Bigg/ \left(1 - \frac{\partial \breve{Q}^s_{mn}}{\partial t_{mn}} \frac{\partial \breve{T}_{mn}}{\partial Q_{mn}}\right) \langle\ 0. \tag{9.25}$$

Proof. The differentiability of T^{ue}_{mn} can readily be proved by applying the implicit function theorem to (9.22). The differentiability of T^{ue}_{mn} implies that the composite function $Q^{uc}_{mn}(p_{mn}, T_{mn})$, defined in (9.23), is also differentiable. Further, the differentiability of T^{ue}_{mn} and Q^{uc}_{mn} implies that (9.24) and (9.25) can be estimated in the following manner: (i) differentiating (9.22) and (9.23) with respect to p_{mn}, respectively; and (ii) arranging the results of the previous step, giving the partial derivatives in the lemma. □

9.4.2 *Virtual Demand under the Degeneracy Condition*

Here we analyze the continuity and differentiability of T^{ue}_{mn} and Q^{uc}_{mn} at the point (p_{mn}, c_{mn}) such that $p_{mn} = p_{mn'}$, for some $n' \neq n$. At that point, the function Q^{s}_{mn} is not continuous. Hence, it impossible to deduce the mathematical properties of T^{ue}_{mn} and Q^{uc}_{mn} at the point by applying the implicit function theorem to formulas in (9.22) and (9.23), respectively. For this reason, we below analyze the mathematical properties, without using the implicit function theorem.

Lemma 9.6. *The functions T^{ue}_{mn} and Q^{uc}_{mn} are both continuous but not differentiable at the point (p_{mn}, c_{mn}) such that $p_{mn} = p_{mn'}$, for some $n' \neq n$. At that point, it also holds that*

$$\lim_{p_{mn} \to p_{mn'}} Q^{ue}_{mn}(p_{mn}, c_{mn}; p^{o}_{mn}, t^{o}_{mn}) = \Phi_{mn}(t_{mn'}, c_{mn}). \tag{9.26}$$

Proof. Firstly, prove the continuity of T^{ue}_{mn} at $p_{mn} = p_{mn'}$. Without loss of generality, the proof can be worked out for a special case when

$$p_{mn} = p_{m(n+1)} \neq p_{mn'}, \text{ all } \quad n' \neq n, \ n+1. \tag{9.27}$$

For this case, the proof of the continuity is provided using Fig. 9.1, which depicts the locus of (p_{mn}, T^{uc}_{mn}) on the $p_{mn} - t_{mn}$ plane.

Lemma 9.5 indicates that the locus of (p_{mn}, T^{uc}_{mn}) is continuous in p_{mn}, except for the point $p_{mn} = p_{m(n+1)}$. Furthermore, (9.24) implies that the locus has a downward slope with respect to p_{mn}. In these circumstances, the proof of the fact that T^{uc}_{mn} is continuous at every point of p_{mn} can be completed by showing that the locus of (p_{mn}, T^{uc}_{mn}) must pass point B in Fig. 9.1.

The proof of the above assertion is as follows. The two blocks, which include either point A or C, satisfy the condition that both p_{mn} and t_{mn} are neither simultaneously larger nor smaller than $p_{m(n+1)}$ and $t_{m(n+1)}$, respectively. Therefore, by the trade-off condition in Lemma 5.1, the demands of firms mn and $m(n+1)$ are both positive, as depicted in the figure. In contrast, the two blocks, which contain neither A nor C, represent the case when demands for the two firms do not satisfy the trade-off condition for each other. Hence, only one firm has a positive demand, as indicted in the figure. However, such an outcome cannot occur, as evidenced by the contradiction described below.

Suppose that the locus of (p_{mn}, T^{ue}_{mn}), which starts from point A, can reach point $D \equiv (p_{m(n+1)}, t^{d}_{mn})$, where $t^{d}_{mn} \rangle\ t_{m(n+1)}$. By the strong trade-off condition of

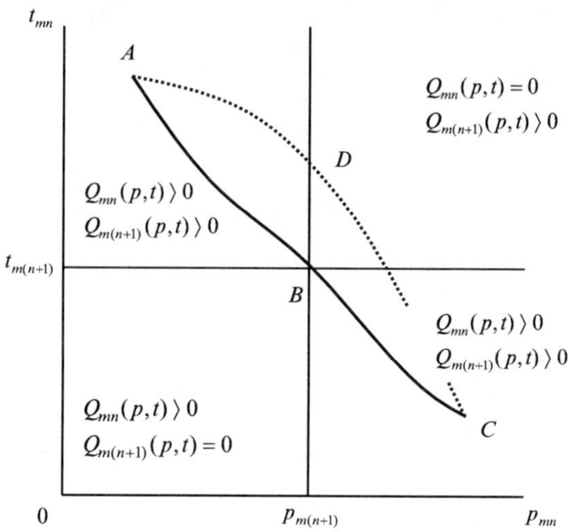

Fig. 9.1 Graphic representation of continuity of T^{ue}_{mn}

Lemma 5.1, this possibility implies that, as p_{mn} approaches $p_{m(n+1)}$ from the left, it would follow that

$$\lim_{p_{mn}\uparrow p_{m(n+1)}} Q^{uc}_{mn}(p_{mn}, T^{uc}_{mn};\ \cdot) = 0. \tag{9.28}$$

Then, it would hold that

$$\lim_{p_{mn}\uparrow p_{m(n+1)}} T_{mn}(Q^{uc}_{mn}(p_{mn}, T^{uc}_{mn};\ \cdot), c_{mn}) \,\langle\, t_{m(n+1)}, \tag{9.29}$$

because of the following: (i) T_{mn} is continuous and increasing in Q^{uc}_{mn}; (ii) there is a unique value of $Q_{mn} \rangle\, 0$ at point B. However, (9.29) contradicts the assumption of $t^{d}_{mn} \rangle\, t_{m(n+1)}$. Hence, the locus of (p_{mn}, T^{ue}_{mn}) must pass through point B.

Subsequently, prove that Q^{ue}_{mn} is continuous at $p_{mn} = p_{mn'}$. It follows from (9.16) and (9.23) that

$$\Phi_{mn}(T^{ue}_{mn}(p_{mn}, c_{mn};\ \cdot), c_{mn}) = Q^{s}_{mn}(p_{mn}, T^{ue}_{mn};\ \cdot) = Q^{ue}_{mn}(p_{mn}, c_{mn};\ \cdot), \tag{9.30}$$

for all values of (p_{mn}, c_{mn}). Hence, by the continuity of Φ_{mn} in (t_{mn}, c_{mn}) and of T^{ue}_{mn} in p_{mn}, the continuity of Q^{ue}_{mn} in (p_{mn}, c_{mn}) follows. Moreover,

$$\lim_{p_{mn}\to p_{m(n+1)}} Q^{ue}_{mn}(p_{mn}, c_{mn};\ \cdot) = \lim_{p_{mn}\to p_{m(n+1)}} \Phi_{mn}(T^{ue}_{mn}(p_{mn}, c_{mn}), c_{mn}) = \Phi_{mn}(t_{m(n+1)}, c_{mn}).$$

This equation implies (9.26). □

The continuity of $Q^{ue}_{mn}(p_{mn}, c_{mn};\ \cdot)$ in p_{mn} can be interpreted as follows. The function $Q^{s}_{mn}(p_{mn}, t_{mn};\ \cdot)$ is not continuous in all directions of t_{mn}. However, the function $Q^s_{mn}(p_{mn}, t_{mn};\ \cdot)$ is continuous along the line $(p_{mn}, T^{ue}_{mn}(p_{mn}, c_{mn}))$, which can be depicted in the fashion shown in Fig. 9.1. This continuity of $Q^s_{mn}(p_{mn}, T^s_{mn};\ \cdot)$ in p_{mn} implies that the decrease in the value of the function T^{ue}_{mn}, due to increases in p_{mn}, changes the range of the integral domain $D_{mn}(p_{mn}, T^{ue}_{mn};\ \cdot)$. As a result, the multiple integral $Q^s_{mn}(p_{mn}, T^{ue}_{mn})$ defined on $D_{mn}(p_{mn}, T^{ue}_{mn};\ \cdot)$ is continuous in p_{mn}.

However, the function Q^{ue}_{mn} is not differentiable at $p_{mn} = p_{mn'}$, for some $n' \neq n$. This implies that the left and right directional derivatives of Q^{ue}_{mn} at that point are both finite but differ from one another. To illustrate this property, we first introduce the definition of the directional derivatives of Q^{ue}_{mn} with respect to p_{mn}. The left directional derivative of Q^s_{mn} with respect to p_{mn} is defined by

$$\frac{\partial Q^{ue}_{mn}(-\lambda p_{mn}; p_{mn}, c_{mn})}{\partial p_{mn}} = -\lim_{\lambda \downarrow 0} \frac{Q^{ue}_{mn}(p_{mn} - \lambda p_{mn}, \cdot) - Q^{ue}_{mn}(p_{mn}, \cdot)}{\lambda}, \tag{9.31}$$

and the right directional derivative is estimated by

$$\frac{\partial Q^{ue}_{mn}(\lambda p_{mn}; p_{mn}, c_{mn})}{\partial p_{mn}} = \lim_{\lambda \downarrow 0} \frac{Q^{ue}_{mn}(p_{mn} + \lambda p_{mn}, \cdot) - Q^{ue}_{mn}(p_{mn}, \cdot)}{\lambda}, \tag{9.32}$$

where $\lambda \downarrow 0$ implies that λ approaches zero from the right.

We schematically illustrate the left directional derivative of Q^s_n at $p_n = p_{n+1}$ in Fig. 9.2. This figure is developed by amending Fig. 5.3 that illustrates the partial derivative of the differentiable demand function. The figure depicts that the catchment domain D_n for the limiting value of p_n is expressed by

$$\lim_{p_n \uparrow p_{n+1}} D_n(p_n, T^{ue}_n; p^o_n, t^o_n) = [l_{n+1}, U^{ue}_n], \tag{9.33}$$

where $l_{n+1} = (p_{n+1} - p_{n-1})/(t_{n-1} - t_{n+1})$. The figure also shows that the directional derivative is represented by the sum of three areas: area A representing net decrease in demand, and areas B and C depicting demand shifts to firms $n-1$ and $n+1$, respectively.

In the figure, the set D_n for the limiting value of p_n has the lower boundary estimated by $l_{n+1} = (p_{n+1} - p_{n-1})/(t_{n-1} - t_{n+1})$, as depicted in (9.33). The limiting value of U^{ue}_n, on the other hand, is estimated by

$$U^{ue}_n = \lim_{p_n \uparrow p_{n+1}} \frac{p_{n+1} - p_n}{T^{ue}_n(p_n, c_n) - t_{n+1}}. \tag{9.34}$$

Here, both numerator and denominator of the right side approach zero, as p_n approaches p_{n+1} from the left. This does not mean that the limiting value of U^{ue}_n is degenerate. Instead, (9.26) shows that there is a unique upper limit U^{ue}_n such that

$$\Phi_n(t_{n+1}, c_n) = \lim_{p_n \uparrow p_{n+1}} Q^s_n(p_{mn}, T^{ue}_{mn};\ \cdot) = \int_{l_{n+1}}^{U^{ue}_n} f(p_{n+1} + \xi t_{n+1}) h(\xi) d\xi. \tag{9.35}$$

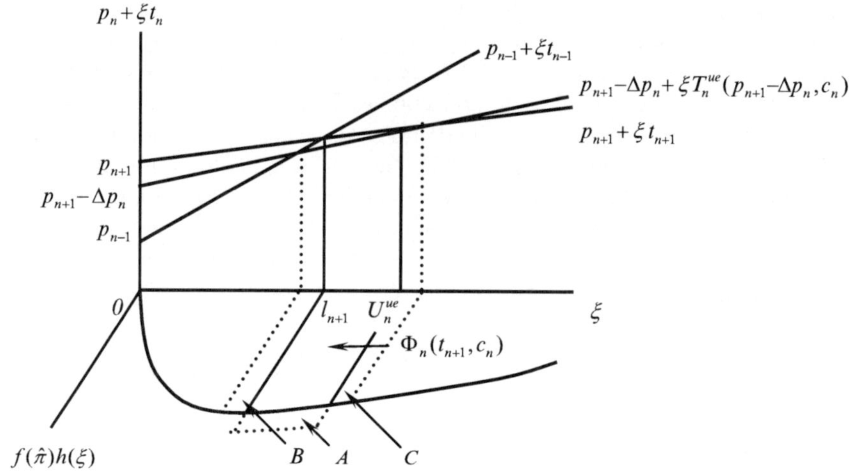

Fig. 9.2 Representation of the left directional derivative of Q_n^{ue}

That is, this unique upper limit U_n^{ue} satisfies the condition such that the integral of $f\,h$ on the interval $[\,l_{n+1}, U_n^{ue}]$, called *the net catchment domain* of firm n, equals $\Phi_n(t_{n+1}, c_n)$.

The right directional derivative of Q_n^s at $p_n = p_{n+1}$ can be graphically represented in a manner similar to Fig. 9.2. The figure for the right directional derivative should be able to pictorially depict the following:

$$\Phi_n(t_{n+1}, c_n) = \lim_{p_n \downarrow p_{n+1}} Q_n^s(p_n, T_n^{ue};\, \cdot) = \int_{L_n^{ue}}^{u_{n+1}} f(p_{n+1} + \xi t_{n+1})h(\xi)d\xi, \tag{9.36}$$

where

$$L_n^{ue} = \lim_{p_n \downarrow p_{n+1}} \frac{p_n - p_{n-1}}{t_{n-1} - T_n^{ue}(p_n; c_n)}, \tag{9.37}$$

and $u_{n+1} = (p_{n+2} - p_{n+1})/(t_{n+1} - t_{n+2})$. Here, the upper boundary of integral u_{n+1} is a constant. Also, the lower boundary L_n^{ue} is a unique value that satisfies the requirement such that the integral of $f\,h$ on the net catchment domain $[L_n^{ue}, u_{n+1}]$ equals $\Phi_n(t_{n+1}, c_n)$.

We conclude by explaining why the left and right directional derivatives of Q_n at $p_n = p_{n+1}$ differ from one another. We can imagine a figure that depicts the right directional derivative a manner similar to Fig. 9.2 for the left directional derivative. On comparing the two figures, it is obvious that areas A, B, and C in Fig. 9.2 differ from their counterpart areas for the figure that represents the right directional derivative. Hence, the two directional derivatives differ.

9.4.3 Reaction of Firms under the Non-degeneracy Condition

The PMP of Assumption 9.1 is used to estimate the solution of the choice vector $e_{mn}(\equiv (p_{mn}, c_{mn}, t_{mn}))$, which yields the maximum profit of firm mn under the condition that the firm faces a certain value of the vector (p^o_{mn}, t^o_{mn}). This PMP has optimality conditions that can be formulated in a manner identical to those conditions for monopolists in Theorem 8.3. These optimality conditions are developed here, for the case when the demand function of firm mn does not violate the degeneracy condition of Lemma 9.1.

To start, we formulate the PMP of firm mn under Assumption 9.1. By Assumption 9.1(b) and 9.1(e), the demand function of firm mn is the virtual demand function Q^s_{mn}, estimated in Lemma 9.4. Therefore, the PMP of firm mn, denoted by Π^1_{mn}, can be expressed as follows:

$$\Pi^1_{mn}(e_{mn}, \tau_{mn}; p^o_{mn}, t^o_{mn}) = \max \left\{ p_{mn} Q^s_{mn}(p_{mn}, t_{mn}; p^o_{mn}, t^o_{mn}) - KC_{mn}(c_{mn}) \right\}$$
$$+ \tau_{mn}(t_{mn} - T_{mn}(Q^s_{mn}(p_{mn}, t_{mn}; p^o_{mn}, t^o_{mn}), c_{mn})). \tag{9.38}$$

This PMP has a formulation identical to that of monopolists in (8.8). Hence, we can characterize the marginal revenue of service time, $\breve{\tau}_{mn}$, in a manner identical to the formula for monopolists in Lemma 8.1.

Theorem 9.2. *Let $(\breve{e}_{mn}, \breve{\tau}_{mn})$ denote the solution to Π^1_{mn}. Suppose also that $\breve{p}_{mn} \neq p_{mn'}$, for all $n' \neq n$. Then, it holds that*

$$\breve{\mu}_{mn} = \breve{\xi}_{mn} \breve{Q}^s_{mn},$$

$$\breve{\xi}_{mn} = \frac{\partial \breve{Q}^s_{mn}}{\partial t_{mn}} \Big/ \frac{\partial \breve{Q}^s_{mn}}{\partial t_{mn}} \in L_{mn} = \left\{ \xi_m \,|\xi \in D_{mn}(\breve{p}_{mn}, t_{mn}; p^o_{mn}, t^o_{mn}) \right\}.$$

Proof. The proof of $\breve{\mu}_{mn} = \breve{\xi}_{mn} \breve{Q}^s_{mn}$ can be worked in a manner identical to that of Lemma 8.1, and the relationship $\xi_{mn} \in L_{mn}$ follows from Theorem 6.9. □

By applying Theorem 9.2, we can readily construct a dual cost minimization problem in a manner analogous to that of the monopolist in (8.13). Proceeding with analyses of this dual analogous to that which led to (8.14) gives

$$MFC_{mn}(\breve{Q}^s_{mn}) = MCC_{mn}(\breve{Q}^s_{mn}) = \breve{\xi}_{mn} \breve{Q}^s_{mn} \frac{\partial \breve{T}_{mn}}{\partial Q_{mn}}. \tag{9.39}$$

Finally, we develop optimality conditions for Π^1_{mn} in a manner analogous to those conditions for the problem of monopolists in Theorem 8.3. We present these optimality conditions below, omitting the proof.

Theorem 9.3. *Under the condition that $\breve{p}_{mn} \neq p_{mn'}$, for all $n' \neq n$, the solution of e_m to Π^1_{mn} satisfies the following three conditions.*

i. *The incomplete user equilibrium condition:*

$$\breve{t}_{mn} = \breve{T}_{mn}. \tag{9.40}$$

ii. *The pricing rule: marginal revenue for competitive firm*

$$MR_{mn}(\breve{Q}^s_{mn}) \equiv \breve{p}_{mn}\left(1 - \frac{1}{E(\breve{Q}^s_{mn})}\right) = MFC_{mn}(\breve{Q}^s_{mn}). \tag{9.41}$$

iii. *The investment rule for the choice of capacity:*

$$MKC_{mn}(\breve{c}_{mn}) = -\breve{\xi}_{mn}\breve{Q}^s_{mn}\frac{\partial \breve{T}_{mn}}{\partial c_{mn}}. \tag{9.42}$$

Theorem 9.3 shows that optimality conditions for the PMP of competitive firms have expressions identical to those of monopolists in Theorem 8.3, except here the virtual demand function $\breve{Q}^s_{mn}$ is used. Therefore, the functional relationship in the theorem can be interpreted in a manner identical to that of optimality conditions for monopolists, except for an additional interpretation associated with the use of the virtual demand function $\breve{Q}^s_{mn}$. This additional interpretation is as follows: the solution $(\breve{p}_{mn}, \breve{c}_{mn}, \breve{t}_{mn})$ for a given value of (p^o_{mn}, t^o_{mn}) usually differs from the choice of (p_{mn}, c_{mn}, t_{mn}) at market equilibrium, since the (p^o_{mn}, t^o_{mn}) value in $\breve{Q}^s_{mn}$ usually differs from that value at market equilibrium.

9.4.4 Reaction of Firms under the Degeneracy Condition

We here introduce optimality conditions for Π^1_{mn} in (9.38) for the case when the problem Π^1_{mn} has a solution such that $\breve{p}_{mn} = p_{mn'}$, for some $n' \neq n$. In this case, the function Q^{ue}_{mn} is continuous but not differentiable at $\breve{p}_{mn}$. For this reason, optimality conditions for Π^1_{mn} cannot be formulated using partial derivatives. Nonetheless, optimality conditions for this case can still be expressed as formulas similar to those of Theorem 9.3, as shown below.

Suppose that the maximization problem Π^1_{mn} in (9.38) satisfies the following two conditions: first, the revenue function $p_{mn}Q^s_{mn}$ attains the global maxima at $(\breve{p}_{mn}, \breve{t}_{mn})$; second, the demand function Q^s_{mn} at $(\breve{p}_{mn}, \breve{t}_{mn})$ satisfies the degeneracy condition. The first condition, which connotes that the revenue function is concave in (p_{mn}, t_{mn}), implies that

$$\frac{\partial \breve{Q}^s_{mn}(-\lambda p_{mn})}{\partial p_{mn}} \rangle \frac{\partial \breve{Q}^s_{mn}(\lambda p_{mn})}{\partial p_{mn}} \quad \text{and} \quad \frac{\partial \breve{Q}^s_{mn}(-\lambda t_{mn})}{\partial t_{mn}} \rangle \frac{\partial \breve{Q}^s_{mn}(\lambda t_{mn})}{\partial t_{mn}}, \tag{9.43}$$

where $\breve{Q}^s_{mn}(\cdot) \equiv Q^s_{mn}(\cdot\,; \breve{p}_{mn}, \breve{t}_{mn})$. On the other hand, by Lemma 9.6, the second condition implies that the locus of (p_{mn}, T^{uc}_{mn}) is continuous and passes the point $(\breve{p}_{mn}, \breve{t}_{mn})$ on the $p_{mn} - t_{mn}$ plane, as depicted in Fig. 9.1.

Given the above two conditions, there exist unique sub-differentials of Q^s_{mn} with respect to p_{mn} and t_{mn} at $(\breve{p}_{mn}, \breve{t}_{mn})$, denoted by $Y(\breve{p}_{mn})$ and $Y(\breve{t}_{mn})$ respectively, which satisfy first order conditions such that[1]

$$\frac{\partial \Pi^1_{mn}}{\partial p_{mn}} = \breve{Q}^s_{mn} + \breve{p}_{mn} Y(\breve{p}_{mn}) - \breve{\mu}_{mn} \frac{\partial \breve{T}_{mn}}{\partial Q^s_{mn}} Y(\breve{p}_{mn}) = 0 \tag{9.44}$$

$$\frac{\partial \Pi^1_{mn}}{\partial t_{mn}} = \breve{p}_{mn} Y(\breve{t}_{mn}) + \breve{\mu}_{mn} \left(1 - \frac{\partial \breve{T}_{mn}}{\partial Q^s_{mn}} Y(\breve{t}_{mn})\right) = 0 \tag{9.45}$$

where

$$Y(\breve{p}_{mn}) \in \left[\frac{\partial \breve{Q}^s_{mn}(\lambda p_{mn})}{\partial p_{mn}}, \frac{\partial \breve{Q}^s_{mn}(-\lambda p_{mn})}{\partial p_{mn}}\right] \tag{9.46}$$

$$Y(\breve{t}_{mn}) \in \left[\frac{\partial \breve{Q}^s_{mn}(\lambda t_{mn})}{\partial t_{mn}}, \frac{\partial \breve{Q}^s_{mn}(-\lambda t_{mn})}{\partial t_{mn}}\right] \tag{9.47}$$

as shown in Rockafellar (1970). From these two first order conditions, we estimate the marginal revenue loss of service time, $\breve{\mu}_{mn}$, as shown below.

Theorem 9.4. *Suppose that $\breve{p}_{mn} = p_{mn'}$, for some $n' \neq n$, and that the profit of firm mn attains the global maxima at $(\breve{p}_{mn}, \breve{t}_{mn})$. Then, it holds that*

$$\breve{\mu}_{mn} = \breve{\xi}_{mn} \breve{Q}^s_{mn} = Y(\breve{t}_{mn})/Y(p_{mn}) \tag{9.48}$$

$$\breve{\xi}_{mn} \in [L_1, L_2] \tag{9.49}$$

$$[L_1, L_2] \subset L_{mn} = \{\xi_m | \xi \in D_{mm}(\breve{p}_{mn}, \breve{t}_{mn}; p^o_{mn}, t^o_{mn})\}, \tag{9.50}$$

[1] The sub-differential of a concave function f at a point x refers to the set of $\hat{x}$ such that $f(z) \leq f(x) + \langle \hat{x}, z - x \rangle$, for all z, where $\langle a, b \rangle$ denotes the inner product of a and b (Rockafellar 1970).

where

$$L_1 = \frac{\partial \breve{Q}^s_{mn}(\lambda t_{mn})}{\partial t_{mn}} \Bigg/ \frac{\partial \breve{Q}^s_{mn}(-\lambda p_{mn})}{\partial p_{mn}}$$

$$L_2 = \frac{\partial \breve{Q}^s_{mn}(-\lambda t_{mn})}{\partial t_{mn}} \Bigg/ \frac{\partial \breve{Q}^s_{mn}(\lambda p_{mn})}{\partial p_{mn}}.$$

Proof. Firstly, the proof of (9.48) can readily be provided in a fashion identical to that used to show the counterpart equality of Theorem 9.2. Subsequently, the proof of (9.49) is as follows. (i) The condition that $(\breve{p}_{mn}, \breve{t}_{mn})$ is the global solution implies the two inequalities of (9.43). (ii) By Lemma 9.6, the locus of (p_{mn}, T^{uc}_{mn}) is continuous and passes the point $(\breve{p}_{mn}, \breve{t}_{mn})$ on the $p_{mn} - t_{mn}$ plane, as depicted in Fig. 9.1. The facts (i) and (ii) imply that $\xi_{mn} \in [L_1, L_2]$. Here the term L_1 is the private value-of-service-time of the demand Q^s_{mn} for the (p_{mn}, T^{uc}_{mn}) value, which approaches from point A to point B in Fig. 9.1, whereas the term L_2 is the private value-of-service-time of Q^s_{mn} for the value (p_{mn}, T^{uc}_{mn}), which approaches from point C to point B. Finally, the proof of (9.50) is as follows. (iii) It holds that $L_1 \in L_{mn}$, as can be deduced from Fig. 9.2; Specifically, the value of L_1 equals the average of net-value-of-times for demands that belong to areas A, B, and C in Fig. 9.2. (iv) Likewise, it holds that $L_2 \in L_{mn}$. Hence, from the facts (iii) and (iv), (9.50) follows. □

Finally, we develop optimality conditions for Π^1_{mn} for the case when Q^s_{mn} is not differentiable at the optimal price $\breve{p}_{mn}$. These optimality conditions, which are formulated in a manner analogous to that of Theorem 9.3, are presented below.

Theorem 9.5. *The solution* $(\breve{e}_{mn}, \breve{\tau}_{mn})$ *to* Π^1_{mn} *and the demand for this solution,* $\breve{\Phi}_{mn}(\equiv \Phi_{mn}(\breve{t}_{mn}, \breve{c}_{mn}))$, *satisfies the following:*

$$\breve{t}_{mn} = T_{mn}(\breve{\Phi}_{mn}, \breve{c}_{mn}) \tag{9.51}$$

$$MR_{mn}(\breve{\Phi}_{mn}) \equiv \breve{p}_{mn}\left(1 + Y(\breve{p}_{mn}) \Bigg/ \frac{\breve{\Phi}_{mn}}{\breve{p}_{mn}}\right) = MFC_{mn}(\breve{\Phi}_{mn}) \tag{9.52}$$

$$MKC_{mn}(\breve{c}_{mn}) = -\breve{\xi}_{mn}\breve{\Phi}_{mn}\frac{\partial T_{mn}(\breve{\Phi}_{mn}, \breve{c}_{mn})}{\partial c_{mn}}. \tag{9.53}$$

Proof. Equation (9.51) is none other than the incomplete user equilibrium for the option that satisfies the degeneracy condition. Equation (9.52) is developed by arranging (9.44) and (9.45). Equation (9.53) is estimated from the first order condition for Π^1_{mn} with respect to c_{mn}. □

Theorem 9.5 depicts the pricing and investment rules of a firm that faces a kinked demand function at optimal price, in a format identical to those of

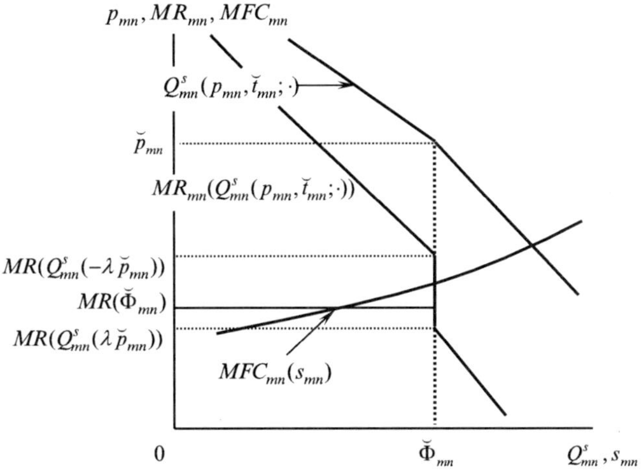

Fig. 9.3 Representation of optimal price for kinked demand function

Theorem 9.3. The key difference between the former and the latter is the pricing rule in which the marginal revenue is formulated using the sub-differential $Y(\breve{p}_{mn})$ that belongs to the interval defined in (9.46). This pricing formula resembles that of congestion-free goods with kinked demand functions in Sweezy (1939). The implication of this pricing formula is described in detail below.

Suppose that the function $Q^s_{mn}(p_{mn}, T_{mn};\ \cdot)$ is kinked at optimal price $\breve{p}_{mn}$, as illustrated in Fig. 9.3. Then, the marginal revenue function for the kinked demand function is not continuous at $\breve{p}_{mn}$. Nonetheless, the marginal revenue $MR_{mn}(\breve{\Phi}_{mn})$ is uniquely defined and satisfies the following condition:

$$MR_{mn}(\breve{\Phi}_{mn}) \in [MR(\breve{Q}^{ue}_{mn}(\lambda p_{mn})),\ MR(\breve{Q}^{ue}_{mn}(-\lambda p_{mn}))], \tag{9.54}$$

where

$$MR\left(\breve{Q}^{s}_{mn}(\lambda p_{mn})\right) = \breve{p}_{mn}\left(1 + \frac{\partial \breve{Q}^{s}_{mn}(\lambda p_{mn})}{\partial p_{mn}} \Big/ \frac{\breve{\Phi}_{mn}}{\breve{p}_{mn}}\right)$$

$$MR\left(Q^{s}_{mn}(-\lambda p_{mn})\right) = \breve{p}_{mn}\left(1 + \frac{\partial \breve{Q}^{s}_{mn}(-\lambda p_{mn})}{\partial p_{mn}} \Big/ \frac{\breve{\Phi}_{mn}}{\breve{p}_{mn}}\right),$$

as depicted in the figure. Here, the terms $-\left(\partial Q^s_{mn}/\partial p_{mn}\right)\big/\left(\breve{\Phi}_{mn}\big/\breve{p}_{mn}\right)$ and $-\left(\partial Q^s_{mn}(-\lambda p_{mn})/\partial p_{mn}\right)\big/\left(\breve{\Phi}_{mn}\big/\breve{p}_{mn}\right)$ represent demand elasticity for right and left directional derivatives with respect to p_{mn}, respectively.

The figure shows that optimal price $\breve{p}_{mn}$ is insensitive with respect to a small change in marginal full costs, estimated by $MFC(\breve{\Phi}_{mn}; \xi_{mn})$. Specifically, it shows that firm mn chooses price $\breve{p}_{mn}$, as long as the marginal full cost belongs to the range of marginal revenues, as estimated in (9.54). Further, the lower and upper boundaries of this range are marginal revenues for right and left directional derivatives, respectively. Hence, a small change in the cost structure of the firm does not bring price changes, as long as the marginal full cost belongs to the range estimated in (9.54).

From the figure, we can also deduce the following: the range of marginal revenues becomes smaller given that the virtual demand function Q^s_{mn} has larger elasticity for directional derivatives at price $\breve{p}_{mn}$. This implies that the range of marginal revenues, such that firm mn can absorb changes in cost without adjusting price, becomes narrower, as the function Q^s_{mn} becomes flatter with respect to price. One extreme case is that the function Q^s_{mn} is perfectly elastic. In this case, theoretically, the range defined in (9.54) is not an interval but rather a point $\breve{p}_{mn}$. Therefore, the price set by the firm equals the marginal full cost, as in the case of perfectly competitive firms free from congestion.

9.5 Characterization of Market Equilibrium

9.5.1 *Reaction Function of Consumers*

This subsection presents two different analyses inputted to subsequent analyses to prove the existence of market equilibrium. Both analyses address consumer reactions made in response to choices firms make regarding directly controllable variables (p, c). The first analysis shows that the reaction function of consumers, Γ^u defined in (9.2), is continuous in (p, c). The second analysis proves that the virtual demand function Q^{ue}_{mn} defined in (9.23) is continuous in its arguments (p_{mn}, c_{mn}) and (p^o_{mn}, t^o_{mn}).

To begin, we develop the specific expression of the mapping $\Gamma^u : (p, c) \to t$ in (9.2). The mapping Γ^u should be formulated using a set of marketwise user equilibrium conditions for all mn in (9.19) and (9.20), so as to accommodate the case of degeneracy defined in Lemma 9.1. The mapping Γ^u that satisfies this requirement is

$$\Gamma^u(p, c) = \left\{ t \mid t_{mn} - T_{mn}(Q^u_{mn}(p, t, c_m), c_{mn}) = 0, \;\; \text{all } mn \right\}, \tag{9.55}$$

where Q^u_{mn} equals that used in Lemma 9.3. The mapping Γ^u is single-valued and continuous in (p, c). Below, this property of Γ^u is proved in a manner analogous to the proof of Lemmas 9.5 and 9.6 for the continuity of T^{uc}_{mn}.

Lemma 9.7. *The mapping $\Gamma^u : (p, c) \to t$, defined in (9.55), is single-valued and continuous in (p, c).*

Proof. Firstly, prove the continuity of Γ^u at the point (p,c) that satisfies the condition of $p_{mn} \neq p_{mn'}$, for all mn. In this case, the marketwise user equilibrium condition defined in (9.55) is expressed by NT simultaneous equations. Hence, the continuity of Γ^u can be proved by showing that this equation system have the Jacobian with respect to t, which is positively definite, as is true for the proof of Lemma 9.5. The proof for the Jacobian is shown in Appendix C.2.

Secondly, show the continuity of Γ^u at the point that $p_{mn} = p_{mn'}$, for some $n' \neq n$. In this case, the continuity of Γ^u at that point can be proved in a manner very similar to the proof of the continuity of T^{uc}_{mn} in Lemma 9.6. The detail of the proof is presented in Appendix C.3. □

Subsequently, we analyze the continuity of the virtual demand function Q^{ue}_{mn} defined in (9.23). By Lemmas 9.4, the virtual demand function Q^{ue}_{mn} satisfies the following relationship with the real demand function Q_{mn}:

$$Q^{ue}_{mn}(p_{mn}, c_{mn}; \cdot) = \begin{cases} Q_{mn}(p_{mn}, T^{ue}_{mn}(p_{mn}, c_{mn}); ,), & \text{if } p_{mn} \neq p_{mn'}, \text{ all } n' \neq n \\ \Phi_{mn}(T^{ue}_{mn}(p_{mn}, c_{mn}), c_{mn}; \cdot), & \text{otherwise.} \end{cases} \tag{9.56}$$

Through analyses of the right side of (9.56), it is shown below that the function Q^{ue}_{mn} is continuous not only in (p_{mn}, c_{mn}) but also in (p^o_{mn}, t^o_{mn}).

Lemma 9.8. *The virtual demand function $Q^{ue}_{mn}(p_{mn}, c_{mn}, p^o_{mn}, t^o_{mn})$ is single-valued and continuous not only in (p_{mn}, c_{mn}) but also in (p^o_{mn}, t^o_{mn}).*

Proof. Since the value of Φ_{mn} in Lemma 9.2 is equal to that of Q^{ue}_{mn} in (9.23), it follows that

$$\Phi_{mn}(T^{ue}_{mn}(p_{mn}, c_{mn};\ p^o_{mn}, t^o_{mn}), c_{mn}) = Q^{ue}_{mn}(p_{mn}, c_{mn};\ p^o_{mn}, t^o_{mn}).$$

The function Φ_{mn} is continuous in (t_{mn}, c_{mn}), as shown in Lemma 9.2. Also, the function T^{ue}_{mn} is continuous in (p_{mn}, c_{mn}) and (p^o_{mn}, t^o_{mn}), as shown in Lemma 9.7. These two facts imply that Q^{ue}_{mn} is continuous in (p_{mn}, c_{mn}) and (p^o_{mn}, t^o_{mn}). □

9.5.2 *Reaction Function of Service Firms*

The prime concern of analyses in this subsection is to show that the reaction function of firm mn, $\Gamma^s_{mn} : (p^o_{mn}, t^o_{mn}) \to (p_{mn}, c_{mn})$ in (9.3), is upper semi-continuous in (p^o_{mn}, t^o_{mn}) under the concavity condition of revenue function. To this end, we first develop the PMP without constraint through the use of the virtual demand function Q^{ue}_{mn}. Subsequently, we estimate the mapping Γ^s_{mn}, which calculates the reaction of firm mn, from the PMP without constraint. Finally, we show that the image of

Γ^s_{mn} satisfies the three optimality conditions for the PMP with constraint in Theorems 9.3 or 9.5.

The first step of the analysis converts the optimization problem Π^1_{mn} in (9.38) into the problem without constraint. To this end, we construct the profit function X_{mn} using the virtual demand function Q^{ue}_{mn}:

$$X_{mn}(p_{mn}, c_{mn}; p^o_{mn}, t^o_{mn}) = p_{mn}\, Q^{ue}_{mn}(p_{mn}, c_{mn}; p^o_{mn}, t^o_{mn}) - KC_{mn}(c_{mn}). \tag{9.57}$$

The function X_{mn} estimates the profit of firm mn for an arbitrary value of (p_{mn}, c_{mn}), without recourse to the incomplete user equilibrium condition. By Lemma 9.8, this function X_{mn} is continuous in (p^o_{mn}, t^o_{mn}).

The second step constructs the convexified form of X_{mn}. The function X_{mn} is generally not concave in (p_{mn}, c_{mn}) for all (p^o_{mn}, t^o_{mn}). We therefore modify the function X_{mn} to the convexified form, denoted by $\bar{X}_{mn}$, in the following fashion:

$$\begin{aligned}\bar{X}_{mn}(p_{mn}, c_{mn}; p^o_{mn}, t^o_{mn}) &= \max\{\theta_{mn}(p^o_{mn}, t^o_{mn}) | (p_{mn}, c_{mn}, \theta_{mn}(p^o_{mn}, t^o_{mn}))\\ &\subseteq conv\ \Psi_{mn}(p_{mn}, c_{mn}, X_{mn}(p_{mn}, c_{mn}; p^o_{mn}, t^o_{mn}))\},\end{aligned} \tag{9.58}$$

where $\Psi_{mn}(\cdot)$ is the epigraph of X_{mn}, and $conv\ \Psi_{mn}$ refers to the convex hull of Ψ_{mn}.

The third step develops the reaction function Γ^s_{mn} from the profit function $\bar{X}_{mn}$. Define the function M, which estimates the maximum profit under the condition that the profit is non-negative, as follows:

$$M(p^o_{mn}, t^o_{mn}) = \max\ \{0, \bar{X}_{mn}(p_{mn}, c_{mn}; p^o_{mn}, t^o_{mn})\}. \tag{9.59}$$

Then, the mapping Γ^s_{mn} is given by

$$\Gamma^s_{mn}(p^o_{mn}, t^o_{mn}) = \{\ (p_{mn}, c_{mn}) |\ M(p^o_{mn}, t^o_{mn}) - \bar{X}_{mn}(p_{mn}, c_{mn}; p^o_{mn}, t^o_{mn}) \leqslant 0\ \}. \tag{9.60}$$

The image of Γ^s_{mn} for each (p^o_{mn}, t^o_{mn}) is the level set of $\bar{X}_{mn}$ for that point, which includes all the values of (p_{mn}, c_{mn}) that give a profit equal to $M(p^o_{mn}, t^o_{mn})$. The mathematical properties of Γ^s_{mn} are analyzed below.

Lemma 9.9. *The mapping Γ^s_{mn}, defined in (9.60), is upper semi-continuous in (p^o_{mn}, t^o_{mn}) and has an image that is convex in (p_{mn}, c_{mn}) for all (p^o_{mn}, t^o_{mn}).*

Proof. The profit function $\bar{X}_{mn}$, which is concave in (p_{mn}, c_{mn}) for each (p^o_{mn}, t^o_{mn}), is certainly continuous in $(p_{mn}, c_{mn}, p^o_{mn}, t^o_{mn})$ and concave in (p_{mn}, c_{mn}) for all (p^o_{mn}, t^o_{mn}). Therefore, the image of Γ^s_{mn}, which is the level set of $\bar{X}_{mn}$ for each (p^o_{mn}, t^o_{mn}), is upper semi-continuous in (p^o_{mn}, t^o_{mn}) and convex in (p_{mn}, c_{mn}) for all (p^o_{mn}, t^o_{mn}), as shown in Berge (1963). □

We next consider the mapping $\Gamma^s(\equiv \prod_{mn}\Gamma^s_{mn})$, which depicts the reactions of all firms in a competitive market. Using Lemma 9.9, the mathematical properties of this Cartesian product Γ^s are characterized below.

Lemma 9.10. *The mapping $\Gamma^s(\equiv \prod_{mn}\Gamma^s_{mn})$ is upper semi-continuous in (p,t), and its image is convex in (p,c) for each (p,t).*

Proof. The mapping Γ^s, which is the Cartesian product of upper semi-continuous mappings, is also upper semi-continuous in (p,c), and thus has the convex image in (p,c), as shown in Berge (1963). □

Finally, we show that the image of Γ^s_{mn} is equivalent to the three optimality conditions for the PMP Π^1_{mn} in Theorem 9.3 or 9.5. Specifically, the image of Γ^s_{mn} satisfies the three optimality conditions in Theorem 9.3 or 9.5 under the strong convexity condition of X_{mn}, as shown below.

Theorem 9.6. *Suppose that the image of the mapping Γ^s_{mn}, expressed by $(\breve{p}_{mn}, \breve{c}_{mn})$, is unique. Then, the image of Γ^s_{mn} satisfies the following.*

i. *If $\breve{Q}^{ue}_{mn}$ is differentiable at $(\breve{p}_{mn}, \breve{c}_{mn})$, the point $(\breve{p}_{mn}, \breve{c}_{mn})$ satisfies the three optimality conditions of Theorem 9.3.*
ii. *If $\breve{Q}^{ue}_{mn}$ is not differentiable, the point $(\breve{p}_{mn}, \breve{c}_{mn})$ satisfies the three optimality conditions of Theorem 9.5.*

Proof. The demand function $\breve{Q}^{ue}_{mn}$, which is applied in formulating X_{mn}, estimates the demand of firm mn, which satisfies the incomplete user equilibrium condition; that is, the solution $(\breve{p}_{mn}, \breve{c}_{mn})$ automatically satisfies either (9.40) or (9.49). Subsequently, first order conditions for X_{mn} with respect to p_{mn} and c_{mn} can be rearranged into the optimality conditions in either (9.41) and (9.42) or (9.50) and (9.51), respectively, as shown in Appendix C.4. □

9.5.3 Existence of Market Equilibrium

Here we prove the existence of market equilibrium by showing that the Cartesian product of the reaction functions of all consumers and firms have a fixed point. To this end, we construct a mapping composed of the reaction functions of all consumers and firms in the market. This mapping, denoted by Γ, is expressed by the Cartesian production of Γ^u and Γ^s, such that

$$\Gamma = \Gamma^u \times \Gamma^s : (p,c,t) \rightarrow (p,c,t). \tag{9.61}$$

This mapping Γ has a fixed point. This implies the existence of market equilibrium. The proof of the existence of such a fixed point is presented below.

Theorem 9.7. *The mapping* Γ*, defined in (9.61), has a fixed point* $(\breve{p}, \breve{c}, \breve{t})$ *such that* $(\breve{p}, \breve{c}, \breve{t}) \in \Gamma(\breve{p}, \breve{c}, \breve{t})$.

Proof. The image of $\Gamma^u : (p, c) \rightarrow t$ is single-valued and continuous in (p, c), as shown in Lemma 9.7. The image of $\Gamma^s : (p, c, t) \rightarrow (p, c)$ is upper semi-continuous in (p, c, t) and convex in (p, c) for each (p, c, t), as shown in Lemma 9.10. Hence, the Cartesian product Γ of these two mappings has the image that is upper semi-continuous in (p, c, t) and convex in (p, c, t) for each (p, c, t). Therefore, by Kakutani's fixed point theorem, there is the fixed point $(\breve{p}, \breve{c}, \breve{t})$ characterized as above. □

The existence of market equilibrium is expressed by $(\breve{p}, \breve{c}, \breve{t}) \in \Gamma(\breve{p}, \breve{c}, \breve{t})$ in Theorem 9.7. The expression $(\breve{p}, \breve{c}, \breve{t}) \in \Gamma(\breve{p}, \breve{c}, \breve{t})$ implies that the fixed point $(\breve{p}, \breve{c}, \breve{t})$ belongs to the image of the product mapping Γ for that fixed point. However, the existence of the fixed point does not mean that the fixed point is unique; that is, it does not always hold that $(\breve{p}, \breve{c}, \breve{t}) = \Gamma(\breve{p}, \breve{c}, \breve{t})$. For example, if the profit function X_{mn} is weakly concave in (p_{mn}, c_{mn}), it is possible that the solution $(\breve{p}_{mn}, \breve{c}_{mn})$ is a certain convex set that includes multiple values of (p_{mn}, c_{mn}).

The outcome that satisfies the equality $(\breve{p}, \breve{c}, \breve{t}) = \Gamma(\breve{p}, \breve{c}, \breve{t})$ can be characterized as follows. This equality holds only when the profit function X_{mn} of (9.57), for all mn, is strictly concave at the point $(\breve{p}_{mn}, \breve{c}_{mn})$. In this case, the service time $\breve{t}$ is a unique solution to the simultaneous equation system Γ^u in (9.55); that is, the solution is the unique service time at marketwise user equilibrium as characterized in Theorem 9.1. Further, the fixed point $(\breve{p}_{mn}, \breve{c}_{mn}, \breve{t}_{mn})$, for all mn, simultaneously satisfies the three optimality conditions in Theorems 9.3 or 9.5, as can be deduced from Theorem 9.6.

Chapter 10
The Industrial Structure of Service Markets

10.1 Introduction

Existing approaches for analyses of market equilibrium generally postulate that all firms in a given market have a single, exogenously predetermined type of industrial organization. Examples include oligopoly, perfect competition, or any one of other traditional organizational types. Furthermore, such approaches characterize market equilibrium through analyses of a decision-making problem specific to each industrial organization type. In contrast, the user equilibrium approach introduced in the previous chapter characterizes market equilibrium without imposing any restrictions on the industrial organization type of firms in competitive markets. Instead, the approach depicts market equilibrium through analyses of a PMP common to all types of industrial organization under the following two implicit premises.

First, the industrial organization type of a firm in competitive markets is not predetermined exogenously, but rather determined endogenously through interaction among consumers and firms. Under the user equilibrium approach, the demand segment served by a firm is represented as the integral on an integral domain, called the catchment domain. The catchment domain for a firm represents the range of net-value-of-times, on which the firm has smaller implicit prices than do other options. Further, the thickness of the catchment domain has an inverse relationship with demand elasticity for the firm. Such a catchment domain for a firm is endogenously determined through interaction between all consumers and all firms in a market. Therefore, it can be said that the industrial organization type of affirm, which is delineated by the elasticity of demand for a firm, is endogenously determined.

Second, a competitive service market can have multiple industrial organization types coexisting within the given market. A firm in competition facilitates demands on its catchment domain that has a thickness generally differs from those of other options. Therefore, each firm in a competitive market usually has demand elasticity that differs from other firms. Moreover, each firm has a unique cost structure, which usually differs from those of others. For these reasons, we cannot exclude the

D.J. Moon, *Congestion-Prone Services Under Quality Competition*, Advances in Spatial Science, DOI 10.1007/978-3-642-20189-9_10,

possibility that a service market comprises multiple types of industrial organization, each characterized by a unique combination of demand elasticity and cost structure; e.g., firms in perfect competition serve perfectly elastic demands through the use of production systems that exhibit non-increasing returns.

This chapter analyzes how interactions between consumers and firms lead to a market manifesting a certain *industrial structure*. Here, the industrial structure of a market refers to the collection of various industrial organization types that coexist within the market. Analyses of industrial structure in this chapter largely address two issues: first, the causalities between the industrial organization type of a firm in a competitive market and its exogenous factors such as returns-to-scale of service systems and relevant socioeconomic variables; second, the effect that service quality competition among firms has on the industrial structure, as explained in detail below.

The first step of the analyses, presented in Sect. 10.2, develops the taxonomy of all industrial organization types under the user equilibrium approach. The taxonomy categorizes the industrial organization type of a firm by combining each of two dichotomous circumstances: first, when demand for a firm is or is not perfectly elastic; second, when the demand elasticity of a firm is dominated by either quantitative or qualitative competition. Thus, we identify five different industrial organization types: true monopoly; pure and differentiated oligopolistic firms; and perfectly and differentiated (or monopolistically) competitive firms.

We also show in Sect. 10.2 that the industrial organization type of a firm can be identified through a posterior evaluation of its demand at market equilibrium. Under the random perception approach, the demand for a firm is expressed as a multiple integral with respect to the vector of random net-value-of-times. Further, the geometry of the multiple integral contains all information sufficient to judge the demand elasticity of the firm and the dominant type of competition. Using this property of the multiple integral, we identify the five different types of industrial organization, as introduced above.

The second step of the analyses, conducted in Sect. 10.3, examines the causality between the industrial organization type of a firm and its exogenous determinants. The taxonomy of Sect. 10.2 distinguishes the industrial organization type of a firm by its demand at market equilibrium. This demand is an endogenous outcome of interactions between consumers and firms. Further, that endogenous outcome is influenced by various exogenous factors; such factors include the returns-to-scale of service systems, diversity of consumer perceptions regarding service quality, etc.

We analyze the causality for a particular industrial organization type by employing two exogenous determinants: the returns-to-scale of a service system operated by the firm, as examined in Chap. 7, and the average intensity of demands for a firm, as introduced in Chap. 5. Using these two determinants, we develop a criterion to judge whether demand for a firm, as endogenously determined, is perfectly or imperfectly elastic at market equilibrium.

The third step of the analyses, offered in Sect. 10.4, presents a number of findings useful to our understanding of the industrial structure of a service market under quality competition. The accommodation of diversified consumer perceptions for service quality is the most important feature that distinguishes analyses of industrial structure under the user equilibrium approach from those of existing studies. This distinct feature of the user equilibrium approach allows the industrial structure of real service markets to be more realistically depicted than is possible using the approaches utilized by existing studies.

To demonstrate this advantage, we analyze three topics related to service quality competition. The first topic considers the trade-off between price and service quality among services in quantitative and qualitative competitions, respectively. The next topic shows that, under the trade-off relationship introduced above, consumers with higher wages tend to choose higher-quality services. The subsequent topic shows that lower quality services should require smaller marginal full costs so as to fulfill the trade-off relationship between price and service quality.

The fourth step in the analyses, presented in Sect. 10.5, considers two topics that cover a high-level view of all the analyses provided in this chapter. The first topic develops a comprehensive picture that explains the causality between all possible types of industrial organization and their exogenous determinants. The causality is identified by incorporating a number of exogenous socioeconomic variables for consumers into the following two previous outcomes: the industrial organization type, as identified in Sect. 10.2; and the relationship between returns-to-scale and pricing rule, as analyzed in Sect. 10.3.

The second topic illustrates the applicability of the preceding analyses to interpreting real service markets with two examples of service markets: freight market in quantitative competition, and lodging service market in qualitative competition. The analysis of these two examples focuses on the following topics that cannot be accommodated by applying existing approaches for industrial organization: (i) the distinction of low- and high-quality services in a competitive market; (ii) the difference in socioeconomic characteristics of customers between low- and high-quality services; (iii) the relationship among price, marginal full cost, and service quality; and (iv) the coexistence of multiple industrial organization types within a market.

Finally, it should be recognized that this chapter covers only static analyses of industrial structure. The analyses in this chapter are confined to the choices made by firms regarding prices and capacities, under the premise that the firms have already made a choice regarding technologies that delineate cost structure and service quality. Contrary to this premise, firms continuously introduce innovative technologies in order to increase profit. Importantly, the introduction of innovative technologies changes the industrial structure of the market. This dynamic aspect of service markets will be explored separately in Chap. 13.

10.2 The Taxonomy of Industrial Organization Types

10.2.1 Geometric Representation of Equilibrium Demands

This study has presented analyses that are advantageous when determining the geometry of demands for a service firm. We first briefly describe these relevant analyses in the order so as to be most helpful to the understanding of the geometry of the demand. Subsequently, by integrating the analyses, we extrapolate figures that illustrate the geometries of demands for firms in quantitative and qualitative competitions, respectively. To simplify the discussion, we present the analyses for non-durable services under an innocuous assumption that all heterogeneous service groups have an identical yield of prime commodities per service: $a_m = 1$, for all $m \in \langle 1, M \rangle$.

Firstly, we reintroduce a formula that estimates the market demand function of firm *mn* under mixed competition. Theorem 4.5 shows that, if firm *mn* satisfies the non-degeneracy condition of Lemma 9.1, its demand function Q_{mn} can be expressed as a multiple integral such that

$$Q_{mn}(p,t) = \int_{D_{mn}} f(p_{mn} + \xi_m t_m)\, h(\xi)\, d\mu, \tag{10.1}$$

where $D_{mn}(p,t) = \{\xi \in RV | \hat{\pi}_{mn} \leq \hat{\pi}_{m'n'}, \text{for all } m'n' \neq mn\}$.

Equation (10.1) depicts that the value of Q_{mn} equals the volume of the set $\{(\xi, x) \in \mathrm{R}_{+}^{\mathrm{M}+1} | \xi \in D_{mn},\ x \in \mathrm{R}_{+},\ x \leq fh\}$, called the epigraph of *fh* on D_{mn}. Here, the vector $\xi \equiv (\xi_1, \cdots, \xi_M)$ represents the net-value-of-times of *M* heterogeneous service groups in the market. The integral domain D_{mn} is a polyhedron in $\mathbf{R}^{\mathrm{M}}$, which is the intersection of half spaces estimated by $\hat{\pi}_{mn} \leq \hat{\pi}_{m'n'}$, for all $m'n' \neq mn$. The integrand *fh* forms the surface of the epigraph.

Equation (10.1) also shows that the function Q_{mn} estimates the portion of total market demand that can be most economically served by firm *mn*, as explained below. The catchment domain D_{mn} represents the range of ξ on which firm *mn* is the most economical service option. One function in the integrand, *f*, is the deterministic demand function for ξ values belonging to D_{mn}, and the other function, *h*, is the probability density function of ξ in $\mathbf{R}^{\mathrm{M}}$.

Secondly, we introduce the user equilibrium condition that depicts the following: the demand Q_{mn} at market equilibrium is the outcome of consumer reaction to the profit-maximizing choice of price p_{mn} and capacity c_{mn}. Theorem 9.1 shows that the consumer desire to search for the most economical option leads to the marketwise user equilibrium condition such that

$$\breve{t}_{mn} = T_{mn}(Q_{mn}(\breve{p}, \breve{t}), c_{mn}), \text{ all } mn. \tag{10.2}$$

This equation reflects that the demand $Q_{mn}(\breve{p}, \breve{t})$ and service time $\breve{t}$ are finalized by consumers who pursue maximum utility.

Theorem 9.1 also indicates that the demand for firm *mn* fulfills the following:

$$Q_{mn}(\breve{p}, \breve{t}) = \Phi_{mn}(\breve{t}_{mn}, \breve{c}_{mn}), \text{ all } mn, \tag{10.3}$$

where Φ_{mn} is the throughput function of firm mn, as introduced in Lemma 9.2. The function Φ_{mn} is a kind of inverse function of T_{mn}. Therefore, the above two equations depict the same relationship in two different ways.

Thirdly, we consider the problem of locating catchment domains for all firms in the space representing ξ values in $\mathbf{R}^{\mathrm{M}}$. One critical input necessary to solve this problem is the trade-off condition. This condition specifies the range of prices and service times for all firms, which leads to positive demands for all firms at market equilibrium. This condition differs by competition type: quantitative or qualitative.

The trade-off condition for firms in quantitative competition, as introduced in Lemma 5.1, is

$$p_1 \langle \cdots \langle p_N, \quad \text{if } t_1 \rangle \cdots \rangle t_N. \tag{10.4}$$

The same condition for firms in qualitative competition under the identical ordering condition, as presented in Lemma 5.7, is

$$p_1 \langle \cdots \langle p_M, \quad \text{if } \xi_1^i t_1 \rangle \cdots \rangle \xi_M^i t_M, \text{ all } i, \tag{10.5}$$

where ξ_m^i is the net-value-of-time of consumer i for firm m.

Fourthly, in Fig. 10.1, we pictorially illustrate the integral that estimates the demand for firms in a quantitatively competitive market. This figure is developed in a manner analogous to draw Fig. 5.2 by applying Lemma 5.1. This figure shows that firms, for all $n \in \langle 1, l-1 \rangle$, satisfy the strong trade-off condition in (10.4), whereas firms, for all $n \in \langle l, N \rangle$, fulfill the weak trade-off condition such that they have the same prices and service times.

Fig. 10.1 represents the demand for a firm in the following manner. Firstly, firms, for all $n \in \langle 1, l-1 \rangle$, have a catchment domain D_n, estimated by

$$D_n(p,t) = \left\{ \xi \mid \frac{p_n - p_{n-1}}{t_{n-1} - t_n} \le \xi \le \frac{p_{n+1} - p_n}{t_n - t_{n+1}} \right\}. \tag{10.6}$$

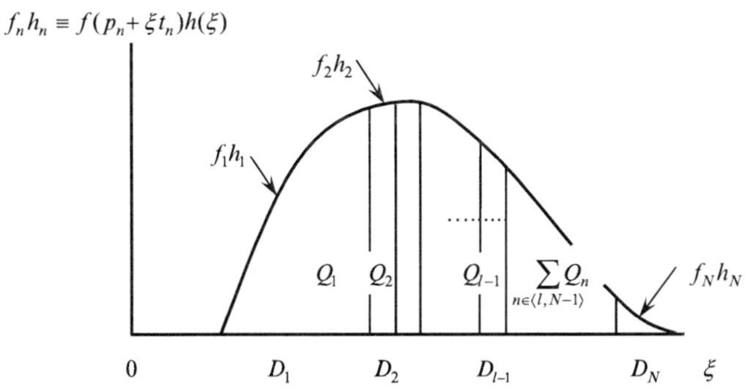

Fig. 10.1 Representation of demands for firms in quantitative competition

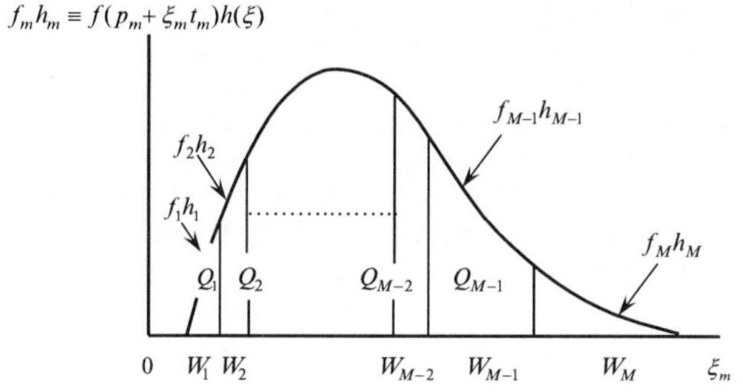

Fig. 10.2 Representation of demands for firms in qualitative competition

Further, the demand for these firms is depicted as the area that represents the integral of $f(p_n + \xi t_n)\,h(\xi)$ with respect to ξ on D_n. In contrast, the other firms, for all $n \in \langle l, N\rangle$, share a common catchment domain. Hence, the sum of their demands equals the integral of $f(p_n + \xi t_n)\,h(\xi)$ on the common catchment domain, as shown in Lemma 9.3. Further, the demand for each firm with a common catchment domain must be estimated using (10.3); the demand for firm n equals the throughput $\Phi_n(t_n, c_n)$.

Finally, we graphically illustrate in Fig. 10.2 the integrals that estimate the demands of firms for all $n \in \langle 1, M\rangle$ in qualitative competition under the identical ordering condition. This figure differs from Fig. 10.1 in that it does not depict the M dimensional volume of D_m in $\mathbf{R}^{\mathrm{M}}$, but rather shows the thickness of D_m with respect to ξ_m. Likewise, the figure does not represent the actual volume of the integral defined on $\mathbf{R}^{\mathrm{M}}$, but, instead illustrates a cross-section of the epigraph of the integrand $f(p_m + \xi_m t_m)$ on the ξ_m axis.

The width W_m in the figure represents the thickness of D_m with respect to ξ_m. This width under the trade-off condition in (10.5), as estimated Lemma 5.9, is

$$W_m(p,t) = \left\{ \xi_m | v_m \leq \xi_m \leq \frac{p_{m+1} - p_m}{t_m} + v_m \frac{t_{m+1}}{t_m} \right\}, \tag{10.7}$$

where

$$v_2 = v_1 \frac{t_1}{t_2}, \qquad \text{if } m = 1$$

$$v_m = v_1 + \sum_{k=1}^{m-1} \frac{p_{k+1} - p_k}{t_k}, \qquad \text{if } m \geq 2.$$

Here, v_1 represents a certain net-value-of-time of ξ_1 and is commonly positive.

10.2.2 Approximation of Demand Elasticity for Firms

Under the random perception approach, the market demand for a service firm is expressed as a multiple integral defined on its catchment domain. Importantly, the geometry of the catchment domain contains information sufficient to approximate the demand elasticity of a firm with respect to price, and the dominant type of competition for the firm. This property of a catchment domain is explored below.

Firstly, we introduce a formula that approximates the demand elasticity of a firm in keen competition. A firm in keen competition has a thin catchment domain, as shown in Theorem 5.13. For this reason, the range of $f(p_{mn} + \xi_m t_{mn})\, h(\xi)$ values for the varying values of ξ_m within this thin catchment domain is not large. Hence, the elasticity of demand for change in price, $E(Q_{mn})$, can be approximated by

$$E(Q_{mn}) \cong -\frac{\partial \mu(D_{mn})}{\partial p_{mn}} \Big/ \frac{\mu(D_{mn})}{p_{mn}}, \tag{10.8}$$

where $\mu(D_{mn})$ is the volume of D_{mn} in $\mathbf{R}^{\mathrm{M}}$, and $\partial \mu(D_{mn})/\partial p_{mn}$ is the changed value of $\mu(D_{mn})$, which is brought about by a marginal price increase dp_{mn}.

Secondly, we apply (10.8) to show that, if firm n in quantitative competition has a thin (or thick) catchment domain, demand for the firm is perfectly elastic (or imperfectly elastic). Under this competition, the term $\mu(D_n)$ equals the thickness of D_n with respect to ξ. This thickness equals $u_n - l_n$, as estimated in (10.6).

Hence, (10.8) becomes

$$E(Q_n(p,t)) \cong \left(\frac{1}{t_{n-1} - t_n} + \frac{1}{t_n - t_{n+1}}\right) \frac{p_n}{(u_n - l_n)}, \tag{10.9}$$

as shown in Lemma 5.3. This equation shows that the elasticity $E(Q_n)$ is inversely proportional to the thickness. This implies that the demand Q_n is perfectly elastic (or imperfectly elastic), if the thickness of D_n is small (or large).

Thirdly, by applying (10.8), we show that, if firm m in qualitative competition under the identical ordering condition has a thin (or thick) catchment domain, the demand for the firm is perfectly elastic (or imperfectly elastic). Suppose that firm m faces keen qualitative competition from its superior substitute $m + 1$ under the identical ordering condition with that firm. Then, the thickness of D_m is $(p_{m+1} - p_m)/t_m$, as shown in Lemma 5.9.

Hence, (10.8) becomes

$$E(Q_m) \cong \frac{p_m}{p_{m+1} - p_m}. \tag{10.10}$$

This equation also confirms that the elasticity $E(Q_m)$ is inversely proportional to the thickness of D_m.

Fourthly, we extend the above analyses for quantitative and qualitative competition to mixed competition in which quantitative competition plays a dominant role

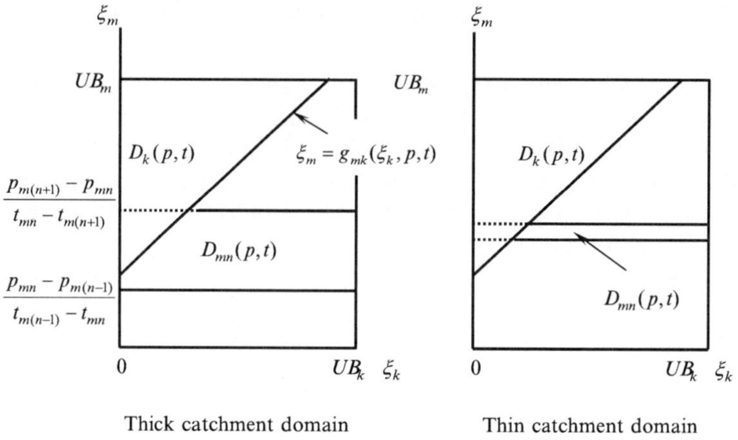

Fig. 10.3 Mixed competition dominated by quantitative competition

in determining demand elasticity. The catchment domain for firm mn in this type of mixed competition can be depicted as on the right side of Fig. 10.3. The figure shows that the thickness of D_{mn} between $D_{m(n-1)}$ and $D_{m(n+1)}$ is significantly smaller than the thickness formed by D_{kl}, for all $k \neq m$ and l.

In the above circumstance, a decrease in the volume of D_{mn} due to a marginal price increase Δp_{mn} can be decomposed into two components. The first component is the shrinkage caused by the marginal movement of tangent planes to $D_{m(n-1)}$ and $D_{m(n+1)}$, whereas the second component is the decrease by the shift of tangent planes to D_{kl} for some $k \neq m$ and l. For a fixed value of Δp_{mn}, the first and second components of marginal changes in the elasticity $E(Q_{mn})$ can be approximated using (10.9) and (10.10), respectively. From these two equations, we can deduce that the contribution of the first component to the elasticity $E(Q_{mn})$ is greatly larger than that of the second. It can therefore be said that the demand elasticity of firm mn is dominated by quantitative competition from firms $m(n-1)$ and $m(n+1)$.

Fifthly, we extend the above analyses to mixed competition under the dominance of qualitative competition satisfying the identical ordering condition. In this case, the catchment domain D_{mn} can be represented as on the right side of Fig. 10.4. As shown in the figure, the thickness of D_{mn} on the ξ_m axis, which is determined by qualitative competition from its superior substitute $m+1$, is significantly smaller than the thickness determined by quantitative competition from firms $m(n-1)$ and $m(n+1)$. Therefore, a marginal price increase Δp_{mn} gives impacts such that the shift of D_{mn} for a change Δp_{mn} to $D_{(m+1)l}$, for some l is quite larger than the shift to both $D_{m(n-1)}$ and $D_{m(n+1)}$ This implies that the demand elasticity of firm mn is dominated by qualitative competition from firm $m+1$.

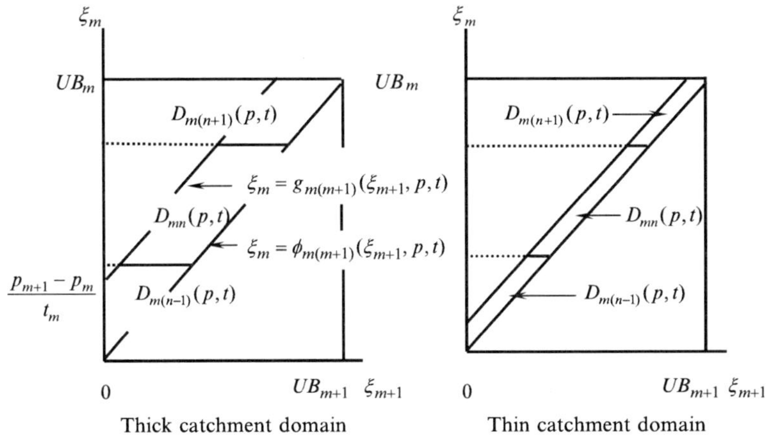

Fig. 10.4 Mixed competition dominated by qualitative competition

10.2.3 Characterization of Perfectly Elastic Demands

It has been shown that the thickness of catchment domains can be a simple but effective criterion to judge the degree of elasticity of demands for firms in competition. Based on that finding, we apply one set of dichotomous qualitative terms, thin and thick catchment domains, to defining another set of dichotomous qualitative terms, perfectly and imperfectly elastic demands, respectively. Below we present the implication of this classification criterion for perfectly and imperfectly elastic demands.

From the standpoint of individual firms, the firm with a thin catchment domain has close substitutes that offer services at implicit service prices identical or similar to the implicit service price of that firm. For this reason, a small increase in the price of a firm leads to the outcome that a large portion of its catchment domain changes into the catchment domain of its close substitutes. This implies that even a small increase in the price of the firm causes most of its demand to switch to close substitutes; that is, demand for the firm is very elastic.

Importantly, the firm with a thin catchment domain must be a participant in a market that satisfies the set of necessary conditions identified in Theorem 5.4 or 5.9 for quantitative and qualitative competitions, respectively. Among those necessary conditions, the two conditions common to both types of competition are as follows: first, a firm that is considered should face competition from a sufficiently large number of firms; second, the market share of the firm should be negligible. In addition, another necessary condition for a thin catchment domain, specific to qualitative competition, is that the firm must have superior substitutes that satisfy the identical ordering condition.

We can deduce from Figs. 10.1 and 10.2 that a market should fulfill the two common necessary conditions identified above, in order for a firm to have a thin catchment domain. Both figures illustrate markets within which a large number of firms compete against one another. Both figures also show that some firms in the market have thin catchment domains and thus have small market shares; that is, the area that represents the demand of these firms shares a small portion of total area that depicts total market demand. Examples are firms $n \in \langle 2, l-1 \rangle$ in Fig. 10.1, and firms $m \in \langle 1, M-2 \rangle$ in Fig. 10.2.

However, the necessary conditions identified above are not sufficient to ensure the thin catchment domain that causes very large demand elasticity. Such a limitation of these necessary conditions is schematically illustrated with the demand of firm M in both Figs. 10.1 and 10.2. The figures depict that these two firms have in common a negligible market share, but also in common have thick catchment domains. To exclude this case both Theorems 5.4 and 5.9 introduce an additional necessary condition.

This additional necessary condition is that the perfectly elastic demand of a firm must have high average demand intensity. The average demand intensity of firm mn represents the average of fh on D_{mn}, estimated by

$$\text{Average Demand Intensity} = \int_{D_{mn}} f(p_{mn} + \xi_m t_{mn}) h(\xi) d\mu \Big/ \int_{D_{mn}} d\mu, \tag{10.11}$$

where $\int_{D_{mn}} d\mu = \mu(D_{mn})$ (see Theorems 5.4(c) and 5.9(e)).

Figure 10.5 graphically illustrates low and high average demand intensity with the demands of two firms in quantitative competition. The demands on both sides of the figure are roughly identical and satisfy the condition that their market shares are very small. However, the two demands represent two different cases: low average demand intensity on the left side of the figure, and high average demand intensity on the right. Accordingly, the demand on the left side of the figure has a thick catchment domain, whereas the demand on the right has a thin catchment domain. Hence, the demand on the left side is very imperfectly elastic with respect to price, whereas the demand on the right is very elastic.

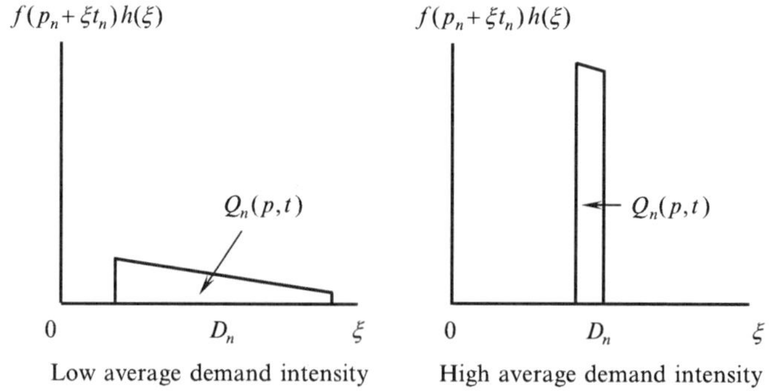

Fig. 10.5 Low and high demand intensities under quantitative competition condition

Finally, we consider a firm that has an overlapping catchment domain with other firms in quantitative competition, e.g., firms $n \in \langle l, M-1 \rangle$ in Fig. 10.1. The demand for a firm, which overlaps the others, has infinitely large elasticity, when the elasticity is estimated directly from the demand function under the random perception approach, as shown in Lemma 5.3. In contrast, the elasticity is not always infinitely large, when the elasticity is estimated under the constraint that the demand of the firm must satisfy the user equilibrium condition in (10.3). Given these two methods, the second method gives, of course, the elasticity applicable to analyses for industrial organization type, as shown in Theorem 9.5.

Theorem 9.5 shows that a firm with an overlapping catchment domain has a kinked demand function, which is continuous but not differentiable at optimal price. It also indicates that the elasticity of demand at the kinked point must be estimated by applying the sub-differential at equilibrium price. This elasticity is larger than elasticity for the right directional derivative but smaller than elasticity for the left directional derivative. Also, the catchment domain applied in estimating right or left directional derivative is not the total catchment domain common to other firms, but rather the net catchment domain on which the integral of $f\,h$ equals the value of Φ_{mn} in (10.3), as explained in the comments for (9.35) and (9.36).

The above discussion indicates that the net catchment domain should be substituted into (10.8) to estimate the approximate elasticity of demands for a firm with an overlapping catchment domain. Such a net catchment domain of a firm in quantitative competition is always smaller than that of the catchment domain common to other firms. Moreover, irrespective of the thickness of common catchment domains, the demand for a firm with a thin net catchment domain is very elastic.

10.2.4 Classification of Industrial Organization Types

Under the user equilibrium approach, the industrial organization type of a certain firm is classified according to the two different kinds of dichotomous criteria. The first criterion reflects the magnitude of demand elasticity a firm faces, classified into perfect and imperfect demand elasticity; the second criterion accommodates the type of dominant competition for a firm, sorted into quantitative and qualitative competition. By applying these two criteria, we identify the five different types of industrial organization in Table 10.1.

Table 10.1 Types of industrial organization under the user equilibrium approach

	Demand elasticity	
Type of dominant competition	Imperfect elasticity	Perfect elasticity
No competition	Monopoly	–
Quantitative competition	Pure oligopoly	Perfect competition
Qualitative competition	Differentiated oligopoly	Differentiated competition

The monopolist here refers to a sole firm that provides a certain kind of service in monopoly. Under the random perception approach, the demand function of a monopolist can also be expressed as an integral with respect to a single net-value-of-time. In this circumstance, the catchment domain of a monopolist is equal to the range of the net-value-of-times for all consumers.

The pure oligopolistic firm comprises firms that have a thick catchment domain under quantitative competition (e.g. firms 1 and N in Fig. 10.1) or mixed competition dominated by quantitative competition (e.g., firm mn on the left side of Fig. 10.3). A firm in pure oligopolistic competition shares the following similarities with a congestion-free firm in pure oligopoly: both firms serve imperfectly elastic demands. However, a pure oligopolistic firm in congestion-prone service markets differs from its congestion-free counterpart in the following respect: the market share of the former can be either significantly larger than zero (e.g., some firms 1 in Fig. 10.1) or negligible (e.g., firm N in the same figure), whereas the share of the latter must be large enough to exert the power to control its market price.

The demand function of a firm in pure oligopolistic competition has a thick catchment domain that can be sorted into one of the following two kinds: a thick catchment domain that does not overlap those of competitors (e.g., firms 1 and N in Fig. 10.1); or a thick net catchment domain that is a part of the total catchment domain common to other firms offering an identical service (e.g., some firms $n \in \langle l, N-1 \rangle$ in the same figure). However, average demand intensity can be either high (e.g., firm 1) or low (e.g., firm N).

The differentiated oligopolistic firm has a thick catchment domain under qualitative competition (e.g. firms $M-1$ and M in Fig. 10.2) or mixed competition dominated by qualitative competition (e.g., firm mn on the left side of Fig. 10.4). A firm in this category is similar to a congestion-free firm in differentiated oligopoly in two respects: first, qualitative competition plays the dominant role in determining demand elasticity; second, both firms serve imperfectly elastic demand. However, the congestion-prone service firm differs from the congestion-free firm in the following manner: the market share of the former can be either significantly larger than zero (e.g., firm $M-1$ in Fig. 10.2) or very small (e.g., firm M in the same figure). In contrast, the share of the latter must be large enough to control its market price.

A firm in differentiated oligopolistic competition can be subdivided into two groups. The first group consists of firms that do not satisfy the identical ordering condition. This group has a catchment domain that is generally thick, irrespective of the number of firms in qualitative competition. The second group comprises firms that face competition from other firms that satisfy the identical ordering condition with these firms. In addition, the demand for firms in this kind of imperfect competition can have either high or low average demand intensity, as noted above.

The perfectly competitive firm represents any firm that either has a thin catchment domain led by quantitative competition (e.g., firms $n \in \langle 2,\ l-1 \rangle$in Fig. 10.1) or mixed competition under the dominance of quantitative competition (e.g., firm mn on the right side of Fig. 10.3). A firm in this category resembles a congestion-free firm in a perfectly competitive market in the following respect: both firms face very keen competition from a very large number of firms in the same service group.

A firm in perfect competition has a thin catchment domain that belongs to one of the two following kinds: either a thin catchment domain that does not overlap those of competitors (e.g., some firms $n \in \langle 2, l-1 \rangle$ in Fig. 10.1) or a thin net catchment domain, which constitutes a part of the total catchment domain common to its competitors (e.g., some firms $n \in \langle l, M-1 \rangle$ in the same figure). Further, the firm should have high average demand intensity, whether or not the catchment domain overlaps those of others.

The differentiated competitive firm confronts competition that forces the firm to have a thin catchment domain led by qualitative competition (e.g., firms $m \in \langle 1, M-2 \rangle$ in Fig. 10.2) or mixed competition dominated by qualitative competition (e.g., firm mn on the right side of Fig. 10.4). This congestion-prone service firm resembles a congestion-free firm in differentiated (or monopolistic) competition in the following respect: both firms confront very keen qualitative competition, resulting in perfectly elastic demands.

A firm in differentiated competition has a thin catchment domain and a large average demand intensity (e.g., firms $m \in \langle 1, M-2 \rangle$ in Fig. 10.2), as does a firm in perfect competition. However, a firm in differentiated competition has two critical dissimilarities to a firm in perfect competition. First, the demand elasticity of the former depends mainly on the difference between the price of that firm and that of its closest superior substitute, as depicted in (10.10), whereas the elasticity of the latter is affected by many factors, including the prices and service times of that firm and of its two close substitutes, as shown in (10.9). Second, the former has a wide range of net-value-of-times, as shown in Fig. 10.4. In contrast, the latter has a very small range, as depicted in Fig. 10.3.

10.3 The Relationship between Prices and Their Determinants

10.3.1 Determinants of Price Choices: Homogeneous Service Technology

The industrial organization type of a firm, as classified in the previous section, can be merged into two categories according to the pricing formula chosen by the firm: one formula for imperfectly elastic demand, and the other for perfectly elastic demand. Further, the choice of a particular pricing formula is influenced by many exogenous determinants that can be sorted into two groups: the cost structure of the service system operated by the firm and the socioeconomic variables of consumers. The pricing rule that identifies this relationship between the chosen pricing formula and its determinants can be summarized as shown in Table 10.2. Below, the content of the pricing rule depicted in the table is explained using an example of firms that have homogenous service technologies.

To begin, we introduce the pricing formula for firms that face imperfectly elastic demand, under the condition that firms have homogeneous service technologies. This pricing formula in an abbreviated form is

Table 10.2 Relationship between pricing rule and its determinants

Pricing rule by demand elasticity	Determinant of pricing rule Returns-to-scale in capacity	Average demand intensity
(*A*) Imperfect elasticity	Increasing	Either low or high
(*B*) Perfect elasticity	Non-increasing	High
(*C*) Imperfect elasticity	Non-increasing	Low

$$\breve{p}\left(1-\frac{1}{E(\breve{Q})}\right)=MFC(\breve{s};\breve{\xi})=\frac{\breve{c}}{\breve{s}}MKC(\breve{c}), \tag{10.12}$$

where $\breve{s}$ is the throughput at market equilibrium and is equal to $\breve{Q}$. The first and second equality of this equation comes from Theorem 9.3 (or 9.5) and Theorem 7.1, respectively.

We next present the amendment of the above pricing formula for perfectly elastic demands. Substituting the condition $E(\breve{Q})\cong\infty$ into (10.12) gives

$$\breve{p}=MFC(\breve{s};\breve{\xi})=\frac{\breve{c}}{\breve{s}}MKC(\breve{c}). \tag{10.13}$$

This equation is identical to (10.12), except that the elasticity term is deleted.

These two pricing formulas both resemble pricing formulas for congestion-free firms that face similar competition. To be specific, the pricing formula for imperfectly elastic demand in (10.12) is quite similar to the formula for congestion-free firms in imperfect competition. The other pricing formula for perfectly elastic demand in (10.13) has an expression that resembles the formula for congestion-free firms in perfect competition. The choice of one formula from these two pricing formulas can be characterized by employing two groups of exogenous determinants.

The first group of exogenous factors that delineate the choice of a firm regarding its pricing formula involves the cost structure of the service system the firm operates. This group of factors determines the marginal full cost on the right side of (10.12) and (10.13). Further, the factors that decide the structure of marginal full cost can be characterized by employing two different technologies: production technology for capacity and service technology for throughput, as shown in Sect. 7.2. Among these two different technologies, the technology for capacity is a dominant factor, as will be shown through forthcoming analyses in this section.

The production technology for capacity can be characterized by the returns-to-scale of a service system for capacity. In the case of homogeneous service technology, a service system with increasing (or decreasing) returns in capacity exhibits increasing (or decreasing) returns in throughput, as shown in Theorem 7.3. This returns-to-scale in capacity can be an effective criterion by which to determine the pricing formula that a firm should choose, as depicted in Table 10.2.

Table 10.2 shows that the pricing rule for a congestion-prone service firm significantly differs from that of existing approaches for a congestion-free firm.

The two different pricing rules are similar in the following respect: a service system exhibiting increasing returns must serve imperfectly elastic demand, as presumed in analyses of pricing rule for a congestion-free firm with increasing returns. However, the two rules are dissimilar in the following respect: a congestion-prone service firm with non-increasing returns can facilitate either perfectly or imperfectly elastic demand, while the congestion-free counterpart must have perfectly elastic demand. Such a difference is more closely examined next.

The second group of exogenous determinants consists of various socioeconomic variables. This group influences the value of demand elasticity on the left side of (10.12) and (10.13). This group comprises many variables, as one can imagine: for example, diversity of consumer perceptions for service quality, income distribution of consumers, total populations in a market, etc. In this section, we however represent this group of determinants as a single dichotomous variable: low and high average demand intensities. This convention is introduced so as to facilitate forthcoming analyses of this section for the relationship between a particular pricing formula and its determinants. Instead, the effect of more specific socioeconomic variables on the industrial structure of a market will be separately explored in detail in the following two sections.

The average demand intensity of a firm has significance in that it is an exogenous variable that influences the demand elasticity of the firm in a manner independent of the returns-to-scale of service systems. To be specific, the elasticity of demand for a firm at market equilibrium can be either perfectly or imperfectly elastic when the service system exhibits non-increasing returns, as shown in Table 10.2. The approach taken in the present study for demand elasticity differs from other existing approaches for industrial organization, which presuppose that a firm with non-increasing (or increasing) returns must face perfectly (or imperfectly) elastic demand.

To show that average demand intensity is a variable independent of returns-to-scale, we consider the case when a firm catches a demand segment that has a small market share but has low demand intensity, as schematically illustrated on the left side of Fig. 10.5. In this case, the demand for the firm at market equilibrium is imperfectly elastic, irrespective of the returns-to-scale of the service system. Such a firm therefore can enjoy imposing a price larger than marginal full cost, even in the case when the service system exhibits non-increasing returns, as depicted in (10.12).

In summary, the pricing rule a congestion-prone service firm should follow can be expressed as Table 10.2. The pricing rule shows that the pricing formula chosen by a firm can be expressed as one of two formulas: the one for imperfectly elastic demand in (10.12), and the other one for perfectly elastic demand in (10.13). Further, the pricing rule shows that the choice of one formula from among the two is delineated by the two exogenous factors: returns-to-scale and average demand intensity. Such a pricing rule is proved in the following two subsections.

10.3.2 Effect of Returns-to-Scale on Price Choices

This subsection develops a simple and effective criterion to determine which pricing rule a firm should choose one from the two pricing formulas given in (10.12) and (10.13), respectively. This criterion is estimated from an unconstrained PMP for a firm that operates the basic service system with homogeneous service technology. This PMP, called the PMP for throughput, is constructed so as to fulfill the following two requirements: first, the choice variable of a firm is composed only of throughput; second, this PMP must be able to yield the pricing formula identical to that of (10.12), under the premise that a certain throughput is the solution to the optimality conditions of Theorem 9.3.

Firstly, we reintroduce the full cost function for a private service system in (6.41). This full cost function FC can be expressed as follows:

$$FC\left(\bar{c}\left(\breve{s}+e\right);\breve{s}+e,\breve{\xi}\right) = AMC\left(\bar{c}\left(\breve{s}+e\right);\breve{s}+e,\breve{\xi}\right) + ATC\left(\bar{c}\left(\breve{s}+e\right);\breve{s}+e,\breve{\xi}\right), \tag{10.14}$$

where e is additional throughput, and $\bar{c}$ is the function that estimates the solution of c to the optimality condition for the QCMP in Lemma 6.6. Differentiation of FC with respect to e gives the marginal full cost function MFCsuch that

$$MFC(\breve{s};\breve{\xi}) = \left.\frac{\partial FC(\bar{c}(\breve{s}+e);\breve{s}+e,\breve{\xi})}{\partial e}\right|_{e=0} \tag{10.15}$$

In addition, a specific expression of MFC is presented in Theorem 6.7.

The function FC estimates the minimum additional full cost necessary for the service system to facilitate throughput e in addition to existing throughput $\breve{s}$. This function is the sum of two functions. The first function AMC estimates the additional capacity cost spent in optimally adjusting capacity in response to a change in throughput from $\breve{s}$ to $\breve{s}+e$. The second function ATC quantifies the additional revenue change, which is incurred by a service time change due to capacity adjustment.

Secondly, we construct the PMP for the sole independent variable e. This PMP, denoted by Z_h, can be expressed as follows:

$$Z_h(e) = \max\{\Pi_h(\breve{s}+e)\} \geq 0, \tag{10.16}$$

where

$$\Pi_h(s+e) = \bar{p}(s+e)(s+e) - \bar{p}(s)s - FC\left(\bar{c}(s+e);\, s+e,\breve{\xi}\right).$$

Here, the price function $\bar{p}(s+e)$ is the inverse of the virtual demand function $\breve{Q}(p,t)$, defined in Lemma 9.4, under the condition that t_{mn} is fixed as $\breve{t}_{mn}$. This profit function $\bar{p}$ has only one explanatory variable e, because, by the definition of virtual demand functions, the prices and service times of other firms are fixed.

The above PMP is an exact formulation of additional profits for the independent variable e, except for the inclusion of a minor error caused by the application of the fixed value-of-service-time ξ, as explained below. First, the revenue function $\bar{p}(\breve{s}+e)\times(\breve{s}+e)$ is structured so that it reflects the effect of changes in price on demands. Second, the full cost $FC\,(\bar{c}(s+e);\, s+e, \breve{\xi})$ is formulated to accommodate changes not only in capacity costs but also in revenue losses due to changes in service time.

Thirdly, we develop the optimal pricing rule for the PMP in (10.16) under the premise that the solution of e is zero; that is, the optimal throughput is $\breve{s}$. This premise of $e = 0$ implies that

$$\left.\frac{dZ_h(e)}{de}\right|_{e=0} = \left.\frac{d\Pi_h(\breve{s}+e)}{de}\right|_{e=0} = 0. \tag{10.17}$$

This equation gives

$$\bar{p}(\breve{s}) = \frac{\breve{c}}{\breve{s}} MKC\,(\breve{c}) + \breve{s}X, \tag{10.18}$$

where $\breve{c} = \bar{c}(\breve{s})$ and $X = -\partial\bar{p}/\partial e = -1/(\,\partial\breve{Q}/\partial p) \rangle\; 0$. The pricing rule of (10.18) is identical to that of (10.12), as expected.

We are now ready to introduce a criterion for the choice of one from two formulas of (10.12) and (10.13). Equation (10.18) shows that the revenue of the firm. $\bar{p}(\breve{s})\,\breve{s}$ is

$$\bar{p}(\breve{s})\,\breve{s} = \breve{c}\,MKC(\breve{c}) + \breve{s}^2X. \tag{10.19}$$

Here, the term $\breve{s}^2X$ represents the revenue ascribable to the imperfect elasticity of demands; if the demand $\breve{Q}$ is perfectly elastic, the revenue becomes $\bar{c}(\breve{s})MKC(\breve{c})$.

On the other hand, the revenue estimated in (10.19) should be not less than the monetary cost, estimated by $KC(\bar{c}(\breve{s}))$. Therefore, one minimum requirement to gain a non-negative profit is

$$X \equiv -1 \bigg/ \frac{\partial\breve{Q}}{\partial p} = \begin{cases} \rangle\; 0, & \text{if } \breve{c}\,MKC(\breve{c}) - KC(\breve{c}) \;\langle\; 0 \\ = 0, & \text{if } \breve{c}\,MKC(\breve{c}) - KC(\breve{c}) \geq 0. \end{cases} \tag{10.20}$$

Equation (10.20) indicates that, if the term $\breve{c}\,MKC(\breve{c}) - KC(\breve{c})$ is negative, the firm should choose the pricing formula for imperfectly elastic demand in (10.12); otherwise, the firm will surely experience a deficit. In contrast, if the term is non-negative, the firm can choose the pricing formula for perfectly elastic demand in (10.13). However, this does not mean that the firm must choose this pricing rule, because the demand elasticity of a firm is sometimes exogenously determined by average demand intensity, as pointed out in the previous subsection.

10.3.3 Causality between Price Choices and their Determinants

Here we analyze the causality between the chosen pricing rule and its two exogenous determinants for three different cases identified in Table 10.2. Specifically, it is shown that the choice of one pricing formula from the two of (10.12) and (10.13) must follow the decision-making rule in the table that employs two exogenous determinants: returns-to-scale and average demand intensity. The key input for this analysis is the criterion for the choice of pricing formula in (10.20).

Firstly, we consider the pricing rule for Group A classified in Table 10.2. This group has the production technology for capacity, which exhibits increasing returns in capacity; that is, $\partial^2 KC(c)/\partial c^2 \rangle 0$ on the relevant region of capacity c. This group must choose the pricing formula for imperfectly elastic demand in (10.12), irrespective of average demand intensity value.

Specifically, a firm in this group should be able to capture imperfectly elastic demand, whether the average intensity of the demand segment served by the firm is low or high, as will be proved subsequently. Therefore, the price chosen by the firm is larger than marginal full cost by a margin $\breve{s}X \rangle 0$, as indicated in (10.19). For this price, the revenue of the firm is equal to $\breve{s}^2X + \breve{c}MKC(\breve{c})$. This revenue should not be less than the monetary cost, estimated by $KC(\breve{c})$.

The explanation for why a firm in Group A should choose the pricing formula for imperfectly elastic demand is as below. This group has the cost function KC, which is increasing and strongly concave on the relevant region of c, as graphically illustrated in Fig. 10.6. This concave cost function does not have a capacity that satisfies the condition that $c\,MKC(c) - KC(c) \rangle 0$. Hence, if the choice of the firm

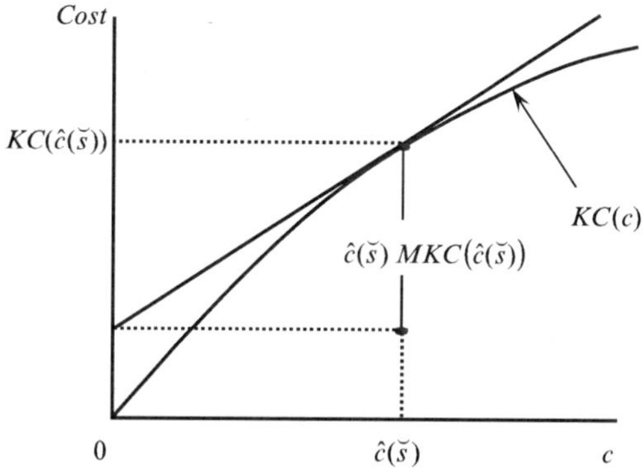

Fig. 10.6 Representation of supplier costs for Group A

for price were the marginal full cost $(\breve{c}/\breve{s})MKC(\breve{c})$, the firm would certainly experience a deficit. For this reason, the firm should be able to capture imperfectly elastic demand that allows the choice of a price larger than marginal full cost, as depicted in (10.20).

A firm in Group *A* resembles a congestion-free firm in natural monopoly in two respects: first, this group has a service system that exhibits increasing returns in throughput; second, it serves imperfectly elastic demand. However, the former differs from the latter in that it allows for the coexistence of other firms. This difference can be ascribed to the diversified tastes of consumers for qualitative attributes, as will be discussed in Subsect. 10.5.1.

It should also be noted that a firm in Group *A* does not have a catchment domain that overlaps that of competitors. Under the random perception approach, multiple firms have a catchment domain in common only when they offer an exactly identical service in terms not only of quantitative but also of qualitative attributes. However, the coexistence of multiple firms offering an identical service contradicts that the given firm has increasing returns.

Secondly, we analyze the pricing rule for Group *B* defined in Table 10.2. The two conditions for this group imply the following. The first condition, decreasing returns in capacity, indicates that $\partial^2 KC(c)/\partial c^2 \geq 0$. Given the first condition, the second condition, high average demand intensity, connotes that the firm faces perfectly elastic demand. Therefore, the firm should choose a price equal to marginal full cost, and hence will experience zero profit, as proved below.

This choice of the firm for price is proven, under two innocuous premises that follow. First, newcomers face no entry barrier. Second, when the demand segment of a firm in Group *B* has high average demand intensity, the other demand segments adjacent to that of the firm do not have abruptly low average demand intensity.

We, first, show that that one feasible choice for the firm regarding price is the price equal to marginal full cost, and that this choice satisfies the requirement of zero profit. The first condition implies that the cost function *KC* is concave, including weakly concave. Hence, there is a capacity c_o such that $KC(c_o) = c_o MKC(c_o)$, as depicted in Fig. 10.7. On the other hand, the second condition

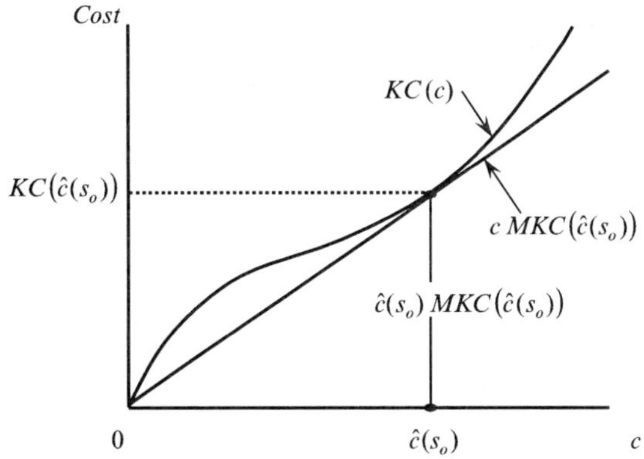

Fig. 10.7 Representation of supplier costs for Group *B*

implies that the demand with a thin catchment domain can be sufficiently large to give a non-negative profit to the firm. Such a demand is very elastic, and therefore forces the firm to choose the price equal to the marginal full cost $(c_o/s_o)MKC(c_o)$. This price satisfies the zero profit condition such that $c_o MKC(c_o) = KC(c_o)$.

We, next, show that the price that equals $(c_o/s_o)MKC(c_o)$ is actually only one possible choice of the firm under the two premises introduced above. Suppose that the optimal throughput and capacity are $\breve{s}$ and $\breve{c}$, respectively. Suppose also that $\breve{s}$ and $\breve{c}$ differ, respectively, from s_o and c_o that result in zero profit. This difference implies that the collective choice $\breve{s}$ and $\breve{c}$ should be able to give a positive profit; otherwise the firm chooses s_o and c_o. However, this positive profit contradicts the two innocuous premises introduced above.

The reasoning is as follows. The positive profit of the firm considered certainly invites the entry of newcomers who offer perfect and/or close substitutes to the service of the firm. Further, the newcomers can capture sufficient demands on the catchment domain that is adjacent to that of the firm and therefore has high demand intensity. Moreover, the entry of newcomers will continue, until the firm gains no profit.

Thirdly, we analyze the pricing rule for a firm belonging to Group C. This group satisfies the condition of $\partial^2 KC(c)/\partial c^2 \geq 0$, as does Group B, but serves a demand segment that has low average demand intensity, unlike Group B. By the first condition, a firm in this group can make a non-negative profit by charging a price that equals marginal full cost. Nonetheless, by the second condition, the firm serves demand with low elasticity. This demand has a thick catchment domain, even though the market share of the firm is small, and therefore allows the choice of a price larger than marginal full cost[1].

The combination of these two conditions imply that a firm in Group C can make a positive profit through the choice of a price larger than marginal full cost, in spite of the fact that the service system of the firm has non-increasing returns. Such a pricing rule differs from that of existing studies, which indicate that a firm with non-increasing returns generally serves perfectly elastic demand and thus earns zero profit. The mechanism of this pricing rule is illustrated below, by considering two different circumstances.

Suppose, first, that the throughput $\breve{s}$ is smaller than s_o, due to the insufficiency of demands that can be captured by the firm given that the firm captures the demand on a catchment domain with low average demand intensity. In this case, the first condition implies that the throughput $\breve{s}$ gives the outcome $\breve{c}\, MKC(\breve{c}) - KC(\breve{c}) \langle\, 0$, as can be deduced from Fig. 10.7. This connotes that the price equal to marginal full cost would yield the revenue $\breve{c}\, MKC(\breve{c})$ smaller than the cost $KC(\breve{c})$. On the other

[1] Mathematically, the demand segment, which satisfies the two conditions of low average demand intensity and thin catchment domain, is approximately zero, as pointed out in analyses of Case. A. Behaviorally, these two conditions reflect that the service firm, which targets a demand segment with low average demand intensity, cannot capture a demand sufficient to achieve non-negative profit.

hand, the second condition indicates that the firm can charge a price larger than marginal full cost by a positive margin $\breve{s}X$. This price must be able to yield a non-negative profit; otherwise, the firm would experience a deficit due to insufficient demand.

Suppose next that, for reasons explained subsequently, the throughput $\breve{s}$ is larger than s_o. By the convexity of KC, the throughput $\breve{s}$ certainly gives the outcome such that $\breve{c}\,MKC(\breve{c}) - KC(\breve{c}) \geq 0$. Therefore, the price equal to marginal full cost can give non-negative profit. Nonetheless, the firm can catch imperfectly elastic demand. Hence, the firm can choose a price larger than marginal full cost by a margin $\breve{s}X$, and therefore certainly earn a positive profit.

The decision-making environment of a firm that chooses a throughput $\breve{s}$ larger than the output s_o can be depicted as follows. Under the condition of costless entry, the choice of a price that gives a positive profit has the potential to attract a newcomer. However, the demand segment that can be served most economically by the firm is too small to attract a newcomer that offers an identical service or close substitute. Therefore, the firm can enjoy charging a price larger than marginal full cost.

10.3.4 Extensions to the Case of Non-homogeneous Service Technology

Here, we extend a series of previous analyses for firms with homogeneous service technology to firms with non-homogeneous ones, as defined in Assumption 6.1. We analyze the pricing rule for the firm under the premise that only a small number of heterogeneous service groups are available to consumers. Analyses presented here can be applied to a competitive transportation market within which every carrier operates vehicles on a particular corridor according to a predetermined schedule, as is true of intercity airlines, intercity buses and rail systems, and international airlines and container liners.

To begin, we restate the necessary conditions for a carrier to have perfectly elastic demand. It was pointed out in Sect. 10.2.3 that the two necessary conditions for perfectly elastic demand are as follows: the demand for a firm should be sufficiently larger than zero, but share a negligible portion of total market demand. For the case of transportation markets introduced above, these necessary conditions are amended as follows: the service frequency of an analyzed carrier, denoted by c, is significantly larger than zero, but negligibly smaller than the marketwise total service frequency of all carriers, estimated by $y \equiv \sum_l c_{ml}$, where m is the index of a heterogeneous service group to which the carrier belongs.

For the transportation market characterized above, firstly, we present the pricing formula for a carrier serving imperfectly elastic demand in the format of (10.12). Substituting the marginal full cost of the carrier in Theorem 7.2 into the pricing formula of Theorem 9.3 gives

$$\breve{p}\left(1-\frac{1}{E(\breve{Q})}\right)=MFC(\breve{s};\breve{\xi})=\frac{\breve{c}}{\breve{s}}(MKC(\breve{c})-MWT(\breve{c};\breve{\xi})), \tag{10.21}$$

where

$$MWT(\breve{c};\breve{\xi})=\frac{\breve{\xi}\,\breve{s}}{2\,\breve{y}^2}T_1^d(\breve{s}/\breve{c}).$$

where $\breve{y}$ is the marketwise service frequency at market equilibrium. In this equation, when the analyzed carrier operates a monopoly, $\breve{c}$ equals $\breve{y}$, whereas when the carrier competes with others, $\breve{c}$ is smaller than $\breve{y}$.

The pricing formula for perfectly elastic demand is developed by amending the above formula for imperfectly elastic demand. One necessary condition for perfectly elastic demand is $\breve{c}/\breve{y}\cong 0$, as indicated above. Since it always holds that $\breve{s}/\breve{c}\leq 1$, this necessary condition implies that $\breve{s}/\breve{y}\cong 0$. Substituting $\breve{s}/\breve{y}\cong 0$ and $E(\breve{Q})\cong\infty$ into (10.21) yields the approximate pricing formula such that

$$\breve{p}=MFC(\breve{s};\breve{\xi})=\frac{\breve{c}}{\breve{s}}MKC(\breve{c}). \tag{10.22}$$

It is important that this price is identical to that of (10.13) for homogeneous service technology.

Secondly, we develop the criterion for the choice of a pricing formula from the two formulas of (10.21) and (10.22). To this end, we construct the profit function for a single independent variable s using (10.21) in a manner analogous to the same function for homogenous service technology in (10.16). This profit function, denoted by Π_n, is

$$\begin{aligned}\Pi_n(s)&=\bar{p}(\breve{s})\,\breve{s}-KC(\breve{c})\\&=\breve{c}\,MKC(\breve{c})+\breve{s}^2X-\breve{c}\,MWT(\breve{c};\breve{\xi})-KC(\breve{c}).\end{aligned} \tag{10.23}$$

Note that, if the demand $\breve{Q}$ is perfectly elastic, this profit function is simplified to $\breve{c}\,MKC(\breve{c})-KC(\breve{c})$, as is true in the case of homogeneous service technology.

Fourthly, we show that the relationship depicted in Table 10.2 can be applied to carriers with non-homogenous service technologies. Theorem 7.5 shows that a firm with a non-homogeneous service technology has returns-to-scale in capacity, which may not equal that for throughput, unlike a firm with homogeneous service technology. In spite of this difference, we can characterize the relationship between the chosen pricing rule and its determinants in a manner identical to that for the firm with homogeneous service technology, as shown below.

Group A satisfies the condition that $\partial^2KC(c)/\partial c^2\,\langle\,0$. This condition implies that $\breve{c}MKC(\breve{c})-KC(\breve{c})\,\langle\,0$, as is true for the case of homogeneous service technology. Moreover, term $\breve{c}\,MWT(\breve{c};\breve{\xi})$ is non-negative. Hence, the profit estimated in (10.23) is automatically negative. Therefore, in order to earn non-negative profit, the carrier in this group should follow the pricing rule to choose the formula for imperfectly elastic demand in (10.21).

Group B fulfills the two conditions of $\partial^2 KC(c)/\partial c^2 \geq 0$ and high average demand intensity. A carrier in this group should serve perfectly elastic demand, as is true for a firm with homogeneous service technology in Group B. That is, the firm is forced to capture a demand segment on a thin catchment. This outcome is the direct consequence of the pricing formula in (10.20), which is identical to (10.13) for homogenous service technology.

Finally, Group C fulfills the two conditions of $\partial^2 KC(c)/\partial c^2 \geq 0$ and low average demand intensity. The condition of low average demand intensity implies that demand for this service is imperfectly elastic. It is also likely that service frequency $\breve{c}$ is not very large, and thereby that $\breve{c}MWT(\breve{c};\breve{\xi})$ is positive. Hence, even though carriers have non-increasing returns, their profit functions can satisfy the inequality of $\breve{c}MKC(\breve{c}) - \widehat{c}\,MWT(\breve{c};\breve{\xi}) - KC(\breve{c}) \langle 0$. Therefore, carriers in this group should choose the pricing formula for imperfectly elastic demands.

10.4 Effect of Diversified Consumer Perceptions

10.4.1 Trade-Off between Price and Service Quality

Under the user equilibrium approach, the option chosen by a consumer fulfills the revealed preference condition such that the chosen option is more economical for the consumer than are other options. This revealed preference condition leads to the equilibrium prices of all options, such that an option having higher quality usually fetches a higher price. This aspect of the revealed preference condition is explored below, using an example of a non-durable service satisfying the condition that $a_k = 1$ for all m.

To begin, we introduce the method of how the perception approach quantifies the service quality of option m in quality competition. Under this approach, the implicit price of option m for consumer i is estimated by $p_m + \xi^i_m\, t_m$. In this implicit price, the term $\xi^i_m\, t_m$ is called the net-service-time-value of service m under the random perception approach. This time value estimates the implicit monetary value for service time t_m, which is subjectively judged by consumer i. This time value is expressed as the multiple of service time t_m and net-value-of-time ξ^i_m that equals $w^i - \sum_k \hat{\varphi}^i_k \beta^i_{mk}$, where $\sum_k \hat{\varphi}^i_k \beta^i_{mk}$ represents the monetary value of all qualitative attributes perceived per unit time when receiving service from option m.

The net-service-time-value $\xi^i_m\, t_m$ becomes smaller as consumer i judges that the quality of service m is higher, as explained below. The service time t_m, including congestion delay, is an important indicator for the quality of service m; as the service time is shorter, the net-service-time-value is smaller. On the other hand, the net-value-of-time ξ^i_m reflects the monetary value of qualitative attributes packed in service m; as the value of qualitative attributes, $\sum_k \hat{\varphi}^i_k \beta^i_{km}$, is larger, the net-value-of-time is smaller. Further, a higher quality service usually causes consumers to perceive a larger $\sum_k \hat{\varphi}^i_k \beta^i_{km}$ value and, thereby, to have a smaller ξ^i_m value.

Subsequently, we present the requirement for which option m captures a positive demand at market equilibrium. Consumer i chooses option m when the consumer judges that the option satisfies the revealed preference condition such that $p_m + \xi^i_m\, t_m \langle\, p_n + \xi^i_n\, t_n$ for all $n \neq m$. Hence, we can deduce from (10.4) and (10.5) that an option m has a positive demand when equilibrium price p_m fulfills the following requirement:

$$p_m \langle\, p_n, \quad \text{if } \xi^i_m\, t_m \,\rangle\, \xi^i_n\, t_n, \text{ all } i \text{ and some } n \neq m. \tag{10.24}$$

This equation depicts that, if all consumers perceive that $\xi^i_m\, t_m \,\rangle\, \xi^i_n\, t_n$ for some $n \neq m$, it must hold that $p_m \langle\, p_n$, so that option m has a positive demand at equilibrium.

The relationship in (10.24) depicts *the trade-off relationship between price and service quality* in competitive service markets, as explained below. In this relationship, the net-service-time-value $\xi^i_m\, t_m$ represents the monetary value of service quality packed in option m. Therefore, this relationship connotes that, if the quality of option m is lower than competing options for some $n \neq m$, price p_m should be smaller than p_n, so that option m has a positive demand at market equilibrium; otherwise, option m cannot have a positive demand.

Importantly, the trade-off relationship in (10.24) is equivalent to the trade-off condition for quantitative competition in (10.4) and for qualitative competition under the identical ordering condition in (10.5). For example, if all options face quantitative competition from the others, the requirement in (10.24) becomes the trade-off condition of (10.4) under which all options can have positive demands. This aspect of the trade-off condition in (10.24) is confirmed below.

Consider, first, the case of pure quantitative competition; this is synonymous with the quantitative competition considered in Sect. 5.2. Under this type of competition, every consumer i has a net-value-of-time ξ^i common to all options. Therefore, the trade-off relationship (10.24) can be simplified to the trade-off condition under quantitative competition. Accordingly, when a service market in pure quantitative competition satisfies (10.24), every option in the market can hold some customers who will judge that this option is the least implicit price option (refer to Fig. 10.1).

One typical example of service market under pure quantitative competition is the freight market. One distinctive feature of the freight market is that no qualitative service attribute will dictate shippers' choice among available options. This means that service quality is primarily perceived through service time; thus, the freight market is an example for pure quantitative competition. Further, a faster service typically charges a higher price; hence, the freight service market follows the trade-off relationship for pure quantitative competition.

Consider, secondly, the case of pure qualitative competition under the identical ordering condition. This case refers to qualitative competition that fulfills the following two conditions: first, all services offer an identical service time, denoted by t; second, all consumers perceive that $\xi_1^i \rangle \cdots \rangle \xi_M^i$. Combining these two conditions yields the identical ordering condition in (10.5). Hence, the relationship in (10.24) is equivalent to the trade-off condition in (10.5). It is therefore certain that, when a market fulfills the requirement of (10.24), all options have positive demands at market equilibrium (refer to Fig. 10.2).

A good example of service in pure qualitative competition under the identical ordering condition is international passenger service. An international carrier typically offers three different seats: economy, business and first class seats (refer to Subsect. 2.3.3). All the three seats on the same airplane offer passengers the identical service time but are differentiated by quality. These three different seats can be regarded as options in pure qualitative competition. Therefore, a higher-quality seat should fetch a larger price that satisfies the trade-off relationship between price and service quality.

Consider, thirdly, the combined form of quantitative and qualitative competition under the identical ordering condition. This combined form is actually synonymous with qualitative competition under the identical ordering condition, a term which has been used previously. For the real service market under this competition, a higher-quality service usually has a shorter service time and a smaller service time value. Therefore, the trade-off relationship between price and service quality for this competition must be expressed as the inequality system of (10.24), which is identical to that of (10.5).

A good example that clearly illustrates the trade-off condition for the qualitative competition examined above can be seen in urban passenger markets under intermodal competition between auto and transit. In these markets, the auto mode is usually considered superior to public transit not only in travel time but also in qualitative attributes such as comfort and privacy. In turn, the auto mode usually incurs a higher monetary price.

Finally, consider the case when some consumers perceive that $\xi_m^i\, t_m \rangle \xi_n^i\, t_n$ but other consumers do not. In this case, it is possible for the remaining consumers to perceive that firm m can be the most economical option even though $p_m \rangle p_n$. This case occurs when service m does not satisfy the identical ordering condition among services in qualitative competition,

As pointed out in Subsect. 5.4.1, the identical ordering condition is not fulfilled by the option that targets a specific group of customers endowed with cultural and aesthetic tastes that differ from other groups. One example can be a Korean restaurant in a Western city. This restaurant targets a certain group of customers that has a stronger preference for Korean dishes than do the majority of consumers, who satisfies the typical identical ordering condition. The other example can be resort areas each of which has a unique climate, natural scenes, and/or entertainment facilities. The ordering of preferences these options with different types of attractiveness differs from consumer to consumer, and therefore it is infeasible to construct the representative identical ordering condition.

10.4.2 Effect of Consumer Income on Service Quality Choices

Usually, a wealthier consumer purchases a higher-quality service that incurs a higher price. One way of interpreting this consumer choice in the context of the perception approach is to apply Lemma 2.2 such that a consumer with a larger wage tolerates a larger implicit price for qualitative attributes. We first examine the implication of the lemma, and next interpret consumer choice behaviors through the application of the lemma, under the condition that $a_m = 1$ for all m.

The value-of-time of consumer i represents the marginal utility of time and is commonly equal to wage, denoted by w^i. This value-of-time satisfies the relationship with the net-value-of-time ξ^i_m, such that $\xi^i_m = w^i - \sum_k \hat{\varphi}^i_k \beta^i_{mk}$, as shown in Lemma 2.2. Such a net-value-of-time ξ^i_m is a portion of the value-of-time w^i, which can be sorted into the net cost of activities involved in consuming one unit of service m.

The net-value-of-time is a factor that delineates a consumer choice of an option from a menu of options, which usually differs from other consumer choices. For example, suppose that consumer i chooses option m. This choice satisfies the revealed preference condition such that $p_m + \xi^i_m t_m \langle p_n + \xi^i_n t_n$, for all $n \neq m$. However, the ξ^i_m and ξ^i_n values in the revealed preference condition generally differ from ξ^j_m and ξ^j_n values of other consumers, for all $j \neq i$. Therefore, it is natural that consumer i makes choices that differ from those of others.

It is important that different choices among consumers be closely related to differences in consumer incomes. To show that, we reorganize an analytical outcome of Lemma 2.2, as follows:

$$w^i \propto \xi^i_m, \quad \text{or} \quad w^i \propto \sum_k \hat{\varphi}^i_k \beta^i_{mk}, \text{ all } m. \tag{10.27}$$

This equation follows from the equality such that $\hat{\varphi}^i_k = w^i/(\partial Z^i_k/\partial t^i_k)$, for all k, in that lemma. This equation indicates that net-value-of-times for all heterogeneous services are linearly proportional to consumer wage.

From (10.27), we can deduce that there is a linear function G_m such that

$$G_m(w^i) \cong \xi^i_m \quad \text{or} \quad G_m(w^i) \cong \sum_k \hat{\varphi}^i_k \beta^i_{mk}, \text{ all } m. \tag{10.28}$$

The function G_m estimates the representative value of net-value-of-time ξ_m for consumer i with a certain wage w^i. It is obvious from (10.27) that the function G_m is linearly increasing in consumer wage w^i. However, it is also certain that the representative value, estimated by $G_m(w^i)$, differs from that the actual ξ^i_m value. This difference stems from differences among consumers in $\partial Z^i_k/\partial t^i_k$ and β^i_{mk} values that reflect differences in consumer perceptions for qualitative attributes, as can be deduced from (10.27).

Equation (10.28) depicts that a consumer with a larger wage tends to perceive larger net-value-of-times for all services, irrespective of their qualitative attributes. This relationship follows from the fact that wealthier individuals tend to assign a larger monetary value to one unit of qualitative attributes packed in all services available, as can be inferred from the implicit price $\hat{\varphi}^i_k$, which equals $w^i/(\partial Z^i_k/\partial t^i_k)$. This relationship, in turn, implies that a consumer with a larger wage chooses a higher-quality service, which generally charges a higher price according to the trade-off relationship in (10.24). This aspect of (10.28) is explored in detail next.

Consider, first, the choice of consumer i for an option under pure quantitative competition in which the net-value-of-time ξ^i is common to all options. Suppose that $t_1 \rangle \cdots \rangle t_M$ and that $m \rangle n$; option m has a higher quality than option n. Under these conditions, as the ξ^i value grows, the difference in net-service-time-values $\xi^i(t_n - t_m) \rangle 0$ increases, while the price difference $p_m - p_n \rangle 0$ is constant. Hence, as the ξ^i value grows, the possibility of $p_m + \xi^i t_m \langle p_n + \xi^i t_n$ is larger. Combining this fact and the relationship in (10.28) brings us to the conclusion that a consumer with a higher wage has greater potential to choose a higher-quality service.

Consider, secondly, the choice of consumer i for an option that faces pure qualitative competition under the identical ordering condition. Suppose that $\xi^i_1 \rangle \cdots \rangle \xi^i_M$, for all i, and that $m \rangle n$; m has a higher quality than option n. By (10.28), the inequality $\xi^i_1 \rangle \cdots \rangle \xi^i_M$ implies that $G_1(w^i) \rangle \cdots \rangle G_M(w^i)$, in which G_m for all m is linearly increasing in w^i. Hence, the difference in net-service-time-values $(\xi^i_n - \xi^i_m)t \rangle 0$ is linearly increasing in w^i. This means that, as the w^i value increases, the difference $(\xi^i_n - \xi^i_m)t \rangle 0$ increases simultaneously. However, the price difference $p_m - p_n \rangle 0$ is constant, irrespective of w^i value. Therefore, a consumer with a higher wage tends to choose a higher-quality service.

Consider, thirdly, the case of qualitative competition under the identical ordering condition such that $\xi^i_1 t_1 \rangle \cdots \rangle \xi^i_M t_M$. In this case, it can be assumed that $\xi^i_1 \rangle \cdots \rangle \xi^i_M$. Under this assumption, it can be proved that consumer i with a larger w^i value usually chooses a higher-quality option; here the proof is constructed in a manner identical to the construction for the case of pure qualitative competition.

Consider, finally, the problem of extending the relationship for non-durable service in (10.27) to durable service. In the case of durable service under competition, the implicit price of service m is estimated by $p_m - \xi^{di}_m + \xi^i_m t_m$, as shown in (4.28). In this implicit price, the term ξ^{di}_m is the sum of the monetary values for qualitative attributes packed in the durable portion of service m, whereas the term ξ^i_m is the net-value-of-time for qualitative attributes in the non-durable portion.

Moreover, the two terms ξ^{di}_m and ξ^i_m are both linearly proportional to w^i, since $\hat{\varphi}^i_k = w^i/(\partial Z^i_k/\partial t^i_k)$; that is,

$$w^i \propto \xi^{di}_m \text{ and } \xi^i_m, \text{ or } w^i \propto \sum_k \hat{\varphi}_k \beta^{di}_{mk} \text{ and } \sum_k \hat{\varphi}_k \beta^i_{mk}, \text{ all } m. \tag{10.29}$$

Therefore, we can show that a consumer with a higher wage tends to choose a higher-quality durable service in a manner identical to that used to analyze the case for non-durable service.

10.4.3 Requirement for Profitable Options

The trade-off relationship in (10.24) indicates that, if the service quality of an option is less than that of some competing options, then in order for the option to have a positive demand, the option must charge a price lower than that of those competing options. As a variant of that trade-off relationship, one can imagine the following trade-off relationship: a service with lower service quality must have a smaller marginal full cost, so as to have a positive demand. The validity of this plausible conjecture is shown next.

The forthcoming analysis targets an option that faces either quantitative competition or qualitative competition under the identical ordering condition. In order for the option to have a positive demand, the option must fulfill the trade-off relationship between price and service quality described in (10.24). To meet this requirement, with the exception of rare cases, the cost structure of the option should satisfy the following trade-off relationship: the marginal full cost of the option is lower than those of its superior substitutes that have smaller net-service-time-values.

Specifically, equation (10.24) indicates that, in order for option m to have a positive demand, the option and its closest superior substitute $m+1$ should satisfy the relationship such that

$$p_m \langle p_{m+1}, \text{ if } \xi^i_m\, t_m \rangle\ \xi^i_{m+1}\, t_{m+1}, \text{ all } i. \tag{10.30}$$

To fulfill the requirement of $p_m \langle p_{m+1}$, it should hold that

$$MFC_m \langle MFC_{m+1}, \tag{10.31}$$

unless $\partial^2 KC_{m+1}/\partial c^2_{m+1} \langle 0$. Further, even in the case $\partial^2 KC_{m+1}/\partial c^2_{m+1} \langle 0$, it is rare that the inequality $MFC_m \rangle MFC_{m+1}$ yields the outcome $p_m \langle p_{m+1}$. The proof of these assertions are presented next.

Firstly, we prove that, if $MFC_m \langle MFC_{m+1}$, the chosen price p_m always satisfies the trade-off relationship such that $p_m \langle p_{m+1}$. The proof is provided by dividing the returns-to-scale of options m into two cases.

Consider, first, the case of $\partial^2 KC_m/\partial c^2_m \geq 0$. In this case, first, the condition $\partial^2 KC_m/\partial c^2_m \geq 0$ implies that service system m exhibits non-increasing returns in throughput and, thereby, can charge the price such that (i) $p_m \cong MFC_m$, as shown in Subsect. 10.3.3. Second, price p_{m+1} should satisfy the condition that (ii) $p_{m+1} \geq MFC_{m+1}$, irrespective of the sign of $\partial^2 KC_{m+1}/\partial c^2_{m+1}$,as shown in (10.12). Under the condition $MFC_m \langle MFC_{m+1}$, the facts (i) and (ii) imply the choice of firm m can meet the requirement for positive demand, such that $p_m \langle p_{m+1}$.

Consider, next, the case of $\partial^2 KC_m/\partial c^2_m \langle 0$. In this case, first, the condition $\partial^2 KC_m/\partial c^2_m \langle 0$ implies that (iii) $p_m \rangle MFC_m$. Second, it holds that (iv) $p_{m+1} \geq MFC_{m+1}$, irrespective of the sign of $\partial^2 KC_{m+1}/\partial c^2_{m+1}$. In these circumstances, we can imagine that the sign of $p_{m+1} - p_m$ can be either positive or negative. However, the outcome $p_m \rangle p_{m+1}$ contradicts the requirement for option m to have a positive demand, as depicted in (10.30). Therefore, firm m should make the choice that fulfills the requirement of positive demand, such that $p_m \langle p_{m+1}$.

Subsequently, we prove that, if $MFC_m \rangle MFC_{m+1}$, there does not usually exist a price p_m that satisfies the trade-off relationship $p_m \langle p_{m+1}$. The proof is provided by dividing the returns-to-scale of options $m + 1$ into two cases.

Consider, first, the case of $\partial^2 KC_{m+1}/\partial c_{m+1}^2 \geq 0$. In this case, first, it holds that (i) $p_m \geq MFC_m$, irrespective of the sign of $\partial^2 KC_m/\partial c_m^2$, Second, the condition $\partial^2 KC_{m+1}/\partial c_{m+1}^2 \geq 0$ implies that (ii) $p_{m+1} \cong MFC_{m+1}$. Hence, under the condition $MFC_m \rangle MFC_{m+1}$, these two facts (i) and (ii) imply that there is no p_m value satisfying the requirement $p_m \rangle p_{m+1}$. Therefore, as long as $\partial^2 KC_{m+1}/\partial c_{m+1}^2 \geq 0$, firm m that has the production technology such that $MFC_m \rangle MFC_{m+1}$ cannot make a non-negative profit.

Consider, next, the case of $\partial^2 KC_{m+1}/\partial c_{m+1}^2 \langle 0$. In this case, first, it holds that $p_m \geq MFC_m$. Second, the condition $\partial^2 KC_{m+1}/\partial c_{m+1}^2 \langle 0$ implies that $p_{m+1} \rangle MFC_{m+1}$. Hence, under condition $MFC_m \rangle MFC_{m+1}$, it is possible that $p_m \langle p_{m+1}$. That is, if $p_{m+1} - MFC_{m+1}$ is significantly larger than $p_m - MFC_m$, it can hold that $p_m \langle p_{m+1}$. This outcome disproves that $p_m \langle p_{m+1}$ always holds.

10.5 Interpretation of Real Service Markets

10.5.1 Effect of Socioeconomic Variables on Industrial Structure

Analyses of the preceding sections have proceeded under the premise that the average demand intensity of a service firm is an exogenously given factor. In reality, this factor depends on various socioeconomic variables of consumers in a market. Among them, the most important variables may be diversity of consumer's tastes and the size of total market demand. The manner in which these two socioeconomic variables affect the industrial organization type of a particular service firm is examined below in great detail.

Socioeconomic variables are the indispensable factor to fully understand the overall industrial structure of real service markets by applying the previous analysis of this chapter. The necessity of incorporating socioeconomic variables into analyses can well be illustrated with Table 10.3, which is developed by combining Tables 10.1 and 10.2. For example, Table 10.3 shows that two different types of industrial organization, monopoly and the first case of pure oligopoly in column (1), fulfill almost identical conditions for returns-to-scale and service demand function, as depicted in columns (2)–(4).

One way of resolving this limitation of the previous analyses involves employing the two socioeconomic variables: diversity of consumer perceptions for service quality, and total population. The diversity of consumer preferences can be quantified by the range of net-value-of-times for services available to consumers;

Table 10.3 Relationship between industrial organization types and their determinants

(1) Industrial organization type	(2) Returns-to-scale in capacity	Characteristics of demand function: (3) Catchment domain	(4) Average demand intensity
Monopoly	(*A*) Increasing	Thin	No restriction
Pure oligopoly	(*A*) Increasing	Thick	No restriction
	(*C*) Non-increasing	Thick	Low
Differentiated oligopoly	(*A*) Increasing	Thick	No restriction
	(*C*) Non-increasing	Thick	Low
Perfect competition	(*B*) Non-increasing	Thin	High
Differentiated competition	(*B*) Non-increasing	Thin	High

that is, more diversified consumer perception for service quality has a wider range of net-value-of-times in constructing demand functions under the perception approach. On the other hand, the total population of a market is a decisive indicator that reflects total demand for a certain qualitative choice service.

The relevancy of these two socioeconomic variables can be ascribed to the fact that these variables play the decisive role in determining the average demand intensity adopted as a sole exogenous variable for socioeconomic characteristics in Table 10.3. To be specific, more diversified consumer perceptions for service quality have the effect of reducing the average intensity of demands for service firms; in contrast, larger values of total market demand have the opposite effect. A corollary to this rule is that, for a given demand of a particular firm, as total market demand is smaller, the average demand intensity becomes lower. Using these two socioeconomic variables, below we analyze the causality between the three cases in column (2), denoted by , , and , which come from Table 10.2, and the five industrial organization types in column (1), which are identified in Table 10.1.

Firstly, we consider Group *A*, which includes all firms in monopoly and some firms in oligopoly. These two subgroups of firms operate, in common, production systems that exhibit increasing returns in capacity and thus in throughput. In spite of this resemblance in cost structure, certain firms in this group enjoy a monopoly, but other firms face competition. The cause of this difference is analyzed below, focusing on the effect of diversified consumer tastes on the industrial structure of service markets.

Suppose, first, that all customers in a service market have almost homogeneous tastes for service quality. Then, the implicit price of services offered by a firm is naturally approximately identical across all customers. In this circumstance, theoretically, no firm can coexist with a monopolist having increasing returns. In other words, when all consumers have uniform tastes, it is logically impossible that a firm having increasing returns allows the coexistence of other firms within the same service market. Further, it can be said that, as consumer tastes are more homogeneous, a firm with increasing returns has higher potential to maintain its monopolistic position.

The fact that the monopolist usually captures inelastic demands with respect to price can well be explained by applying the random perception approach. Under this approach, consumers with nearly homogenous perceptions for service quality have service demands clustered on a thin catchment domain. Therefore, demands for a monopolist usually have a thin catchment domain. However, the thin catchment domain of demands for the service in monopoly does not usually lead to a larger value of demand elasticity. This can be deduced from the following: first, the absolute decrease in demands for service is the sole impact of price increase on demands for service in monopoly; second, in contrast, the demand shift to competing services is usually more important impact for service in competition than is the absolute decrease in demands, as considered in Chapter 5.

Suppose, next, that consumers in a market have very diverse preferences for service quality; the net-value-of-times of consumers are distributed on a wide range. If a monopolist services all these consumers, their demands for the firm certainly form a thick catchment domain. In this circumstance, it is highly probable that the monopolist invites competitors that can provide services at lower implicit prices on a certain portion of its thick catchment domain. That is, as consumer preferences become more diversified, even a firm with increasing returns has greater potential to have competitors within one market. Note also that, irrespective of number of competitors, a firm with increasing returns must capture imperfectly elastic demand, as explained in Subsect. 10.3.3; that is, the catchment domain must be thick (e.g., firm 1 in Fig. 10.1, and $M-2$ in Fig. 10.2).

Secondly, we analyze Group B, which consists of firms in perfect and differentiated competition under the user equilibrium approach. Congestion-prone service firms in this group are the counterparts of congestion-free firms in perfect and differentiated competition. We compare and contrast the characteristics of submarkets served by the firms in this group and those for their congestion-free counterparts.

Analyses of Subsects. 10.3.3 and 10.3.4 show that congestion-prone service firms in perfect and differentiated competition resemble congestion-free counterparts in the following respects. First, both congestion-prone service firms and congestion-free firms have production systems with non-increasing returns. Second, both types of firms face perfectly elastic demands, and these demands share a negligible portion of total market demand. Third, equilibrium prices for congestion-prone service firms and congestion-free counterparts are equal to marginal full and marginal costs, respectively, both of which lead to zero profit.

However, congestion-prone service firms in perfect and differentiated competition differ from their congestion-free counterparts in one important way. Each congestion-prone service firm facilitates a demand segment that does not usually overlap the others; in contrast, every congestion-free firm captures a certain portion of homogeneous market demands. For this reason, the price of a congestion-prone service firm generally differs from that of a given competitor, unless the catchment domain overlaps, while the price of congestion-free counterparts is equal to that of a competitor at market equilibrium.

This difference in prices among congestion-prone services does not mean that the prices of these services in perfect and differentiated competition significantly differ from one another, as explained below. A large group of service firms in perfect or differentiated competition usually serve a very large number of demands with identical or almost identical tastes for service quality; that is, the net-value-of-times of demands for this group are distributed on a narrow range with very high demand intensity. In this situation, by the trade-off relationship in (10.4) and (10.5), the range of prices chosen by this group of firms should also be narrow. That is, as the range of net-value-of-times in the catchment domains of firms in keen competition is smaller, the range of prices that satisfy the trade-off condition is narrower for these firms.

One example in Group B is the case where a large number of small firms compete against one another with identical and/or similar services in the submarket of huge markets for a large metropolitan area. Consumers in this submarket satisfy the following two conditions: first, they have identical or almost identical tastes for service quality; second, they generate huge demands for this group. Therefore, the demand for this group fulfills the condition for perfect elasticity under the user equilibrium approach; that is, total demands are distributed over a relatively thin range of net-value-of-times with very high demand intensity (e.g., firms $n \in \langle 2, N-1 \rangle$ in Fig. 10.1, and $m \in \langle 1, M-2 \rangle$ in Fig. 10.2).

Thirdly, we examine a firm in Group C, which exhibits non-increasing returns in throughput. The firm can make a non-negative profit by charging a price equal to their marginal full costs. Nonetheless, under the user equilibrium approach, the firm can charge a price larger than marginal full cost. The reason for this strange outcome from the standpoint of existing approaches is that the firm captures demands with low average demand intensity across a wide catchment domain.

One important cause for the low average demand intensity is the small size of population in markets. The average intensity of the demand captured by a firm usually decreases as market size become smaller, as explained previously in this subsection. This implies that a firm in small urban areas catches a demand segment with much more diversified tastes for service quality than does a firm in large urban areas, even in the case when both firms exhibit non-increasing returns.

A plausible example of a firm of the type considered above is illustrated below. Suppose that a businessman operates franchise stores of the same brand in two different urban areas. Suppose, also, that the service systems of the two urban areas have identical cost structures, and that these cost structures exhibit non-increasing returns on the relevant regions of throughputs. Suppose, further, that the population of the first area is significantly smaller than that of the second area. Suppose, however, that the demand of the first area does not significantly differ from that of the second area, due to fewer competitors in the first areas than the competitors in the second area and the decreasing returns for the service system the firm operates.

The demands of the first and second urban areas at market equilibrium could be represented by the first and second cases of Fig. 10.5, respectively. In that figure, the facilitated demands are depicted by the areas that represent the demands. By the condition that the demands of the two markets are similar, the two areas in the figure are also similar. Under this condition, the thickness of the catchment domain for the first urban area is significantly thicker than that of the second. Therefore, the optimal price in the first urban area can depart farther from the marginal full cost than can the optimal price in the second area.

Another cause of low average demand intensity is demand for a service with higher quality than offered by other competing services. Examples can be found in demand for some high-quality services that mainly target a narrow group of wealthy people, and that are provided by service systems with non-increasing returns. Considering that these demands share a negligibly small portion of total market demands, this demand can be characterized as demand with low demand intensity from the standpoint of the random perception approach.

The highest-quality service, considered above, targets consumers who usually have large incomes and thus have larger net-value-of-times, as discussed in Subsect. 10.4.2. The highest-quality service can be regarded as a service that has no superior substitutes among services while satisfying the identical ordering condition. Therefore, it is highly probable that the service has a thick catchment domain and, thus, allows a price to be charged that is greater than marginal full cost by a large margin.

The other cause of low average demand intensity is the presence of demand for a service that does not satisfy the identical ordering condition over other competing services. One example of a firm that offers such a service is a Korean restaurant in large Western cities. Customers of that service usually have a stronger preference for Korean dishes than the majority of total possible customers. Their demand can be characterized as demand with low demand intensity from the standpoint of the random perception approach. For this reason, their demand is relatively imperfectly elastic with respect to price.

10.5.2 Examples for Coexistence of Multiple Industrial Organization Types

Here we introduce two examples that illustrate the industrial structure of a service market within which multiple types of industrial organization coexist. One example examines the case of a market under quantitative competition, and the other example examines the case of qualitative competition under the identical ordering condition. With these two examples, we illustrate that the manner in which the findings described previously in this chapter can apply to the interpretation of real service markets.

Consider, first, service markets under quantitative competition. Service time is a sole service quality attribute for firms under quantitative competition. This implies that a service with a shorter service time is a higher-quality option. Therefore, a service that is faster captures consumers who have higher net-value-of-times.

All firms in quantitatively competitive markets usually fulfill the trade-off condition between price and marginal full cost, under which a firm in competition can have a demand sufficiently large to gain a non-negative profit. This trade-off condition indicates that, if the service time of a firm is greater than that of some competitors, the marginal full cost of the firm should be smaller than all such competitors. When this requirement for cost is fulfilled, the firm can choose a price that satisfies the trade-off condition between price and service quality, such that a firm that requires a larger service time must charge a lower price.

One typical example of service markets in quantitative competition is freight markets. One distinctive feature of freight markets is that qualitative attributes are not a factor consumers consider seriously when they choose service options. Using an example of freight markets, we analyze the industrial structure by applying findings from this chapter.

Consider an inland freight market where one or a few rail carriers and large numbers of truck carriers compete against one another in a certain area or corridor. In this market, it is known that the key factor determining service quality is confined to service time; shippers are less concerned about quantitative attributes. In these circumstances, generally, rail carriers facilitate demands that are highly sensitive to price but less sensitive to service time compared to the cargo captured by truck carriers.

Such a modal split between rail and truck carriers can be interpreted as below. From the standpoint of the user equilibrium approach, the customers of rail carriers perceive lower net-value-times for shipments per unit weight or volume than the value perceived by those of truck carriers. The reasoning for the difference in perceived net-value-times can be found from the fact that economic losses experienced by shippers during transportation service are usually proportional to the market value of goods in the form of freight that cannot be used for the purpose of earning revenue. Therefore, the net-value-of-time perceived by shippers is naturally increasing in the market value of freight per unit weight or volume. Hence, it can be concluded that rail carriers that offer slower service usually facilitate lower-valued freight having a smaller net-value-of-time.

On the other hand, a rail carrier is a typical example that exhibits increasing returns, due to huge initial facility investment. Moreover, the marginal full cost of rail technology is less than that of truck technology by several times. Therefore, from the standpoint of the user equilibrium approach, it can be said that the rail carrier offering slower service capture demands that have net-value-of-times less than a certain upper limit of its thick catchment domain under quantitative competition (e.g., firm 1 in Fig. 10.1). For this reason, the rail carrier can choose a price larger than marginal full cost, which is vital to ensure a non-negative profit.

On the other hand, truck carriers have constant or decreasing returns. Additionally, the market share transported by each trucker is negligible. Moreover, the immediate concern of the carrier is likely intra-competition. Hence, from the standpoint of the user equilibrium approach, it can be said that truck carriers serve perfectly elastic demand with a thin catchment domain, including a thin net catchment domain under quantitative competition. Therefore, the carriers are forced to service charges close to marginal full costs.

Consider, next, service markets under pure qualitative competition. Pure qualitative competition contrasts with quantitative competition in the following two respects: first, service quality difference in qualitative attributes is an important factor that affects the choice of consumers for service options; second, in many cases, there is no significant difference in service times among firms. Focusing on these dissimilarities, below, we analyze the industrial structure of service markets in pure qualitative competition under the identical ordering condition.

One important feature of pure qualitative competition is that an option with better qualitative attributes captures consumers who usually earn higher wages. Consumers with higher wages usually assign larger monetary values to differences in qualitative attributes among available options. Hence, consumers with higher wages commonly feel that price differences for options share a smaller portion of the implicit service prices that are the sum of price and net-service-time-value. For this reason, consumers with higher wages tend to choose a service with higher quality despite the higher price.

On the other hand, all firms in qualitative competition under the identical ordering condition usually fulfill the trade-off relationship between cost and price. The trade-off condition requires that a lower-quality service must have a smaller marginal full cost. Otherwise, the service cannot fulfill the trade-off condition between price and service quality.

One example to which the above analysis can apply is a lodging service market within which a luxurious hotel and a large number of inns are competing against one another in the same urban area. The hotel offers guest services of an abundantly better quality than do the inns, as can be perceived in terms of qualitative attributes. On the other hand, each of the inns imposes charges significantly lower than those charged by the luxury hotel, and they all offer services that can only be slightly differentiated from one another in terms of qualitative attributes.

The hotel could be sorted into the category of a firm in differentiated oligopolistic competition. The hotel has no competitor that offers superior services in terms of qualitative attributes. Therefore, the hotel typically attracts customers with higher incomes. It could also be argued that hotel customers have relatively diversified tastes for service quality, as represented by a thick catchment domain. Furthermore, the fact that the hotel has no close substitute can be ascribed to its increasing returns in capacity, which plays the role of creating a barrier to entry for newcomers. In these circumstances, the hotel can enjoy charging a price larger than its marginal full cost at market equilibrium.

On the other hand, each inn faces keen competition from other inns in the same area, which can be categorized into differentiated competition. Therefore, we can see that each inn collects the demand defined on a thin catchment domain. Further, the participation of a large number of inns is a clear indication that their service systems possess non-increasing returns in capacity. Given these circumstances, the only reasonable choice innkeepers can make is to charge a price approximately equal to their marginal full cost.

The above analyses for the two examples well illustrate the advantage of the user equilibrium approach, such that it can effectively describe the industrial structure of real service markets. The topics covered by the above analyses, all of which cannot be analyzed by applying existing approaches for industrial organization, are as follows: (i) the distinction of low- and high-quality services in markets under quantitative and qualitative competition; (ii) the difference in socioeconomic characteristics of customers between low and high-quality services; (iii) the relationship among price, marginal full cost, and service quality; and (iv) the coexistence of multiple industrial organization types within a market.

Part IV
Social Welfare Issues for Congestion-Prone Services

Chapter 11
Policies for Public Services under No Competition

11.1 Introduction

This chapter and the following chapter address pricing and investment policies for public services or facilities that possess the following two properties: first, they exhibit or have the potential to exhibit congestion; second, their users are supposed to pay direct user fees or indirect taxes to access such services or facilities. These services or facilities comprise toll roads, urban mass transit systems, airports, harbors, public museums, parking garages, and public sport and convention facilities. Toll-free highways can also be sorted into this type of public facility, since road users must pay various user charges in the form of indirect taxes such as fuel and vehicle taxes.

Economic analyses for these public services or facilities, called hereafter *congestion-prone public services*, or simply, *public services*, primarily consider the pricing and investment policies of the government. Earlier economic studies of congestion-prone public services have commonly estimated the optimal price of public services and the optimal capacity of public service systems from the Net Social Benefit Maximization Problem (NSBMP). These earlier studies, however, have in common shortcomings in that they ignore two important real-world concerns: first, they do not consider the possible shortage of government funds for the provision of public services; and second, they do not include the case when public services under analysis compete against other public or private services.

To produce more realistic economic analyses of public services, this study introduces an alternative modeling approach for the decision-making problem of public agencies. One key difference between this approach and existing approaches is the use of the consumer demand function under the random perception approach, which has the advantage of being able to accommodate competition between the analyzed public service and other public and/or private services. Further, here the decision-making problem for public service is modeled as a Social Welfare Maximization Problem (SWMP) into which, under the random perception approach, the demand function is incorporated.

D.J. Moon, *Congestion-Prone Services Under Quality Competition*,
Advances in Spatial Science, DOI 10.1007/978-3-642-20189-9_11,

In addition, the SWMP for public service is also modeled as a decision-making problem under the user equilibrium approach, so as to accommodate the effect of congestion on social welfare. For this reason, the SWMP has a formulation similar to that of the profit maximization problem, except that here the social welfare function is used as the objective function. Such a SWMP applies to economic analyses for public service, under the following two conditions: a shortage of government funds for its provision, as considered in this chapter; and the presence of other competing public and/or private services, as will be considered in the following chapter.

The objectives of this chapter for a public service under no competition are twofold. The first objective is to show that the SWMP for a public service under no competition and no financial constraint gives optimal pricing and investment rules basically identical to those of the NSBMP under the same decision-making environment. The second objective is to extend the preceding analysis under the restrictive condition to a more realistic case of insufficient government funds.

To begin, in Sect. 11.2, we develop and analyze a SWMP for the basic public service system under the condition of no competition and no binding constraint on government funds. This SWMP is modeled by applying assumptions about the governmental function that fundamentally differ from the assumptions applied when modeling the NSBMP. The SWMP postulates the following: first, the government executes two functions, the provision of for-pay public service and income distribution among consumers; second, the funds necessary to implement these functions are financed through lump sum taxes meted out to individual consumers. In contrast, the NSBMP assumes the following: first, the function of the government is confined to providing public services; second, the necessary funds come from the general revenue of the government.

The SWMP constructed under the above premise is used to estimate solutions for three different kinds of policy variables: lump sum taxes specific to individual consumers, public service price, and service capacity. The SWMP yields a set of social optimality conditions that constitute a simultaneous equation system sufficient to estimate the solution for these policy variables. These social optimality conditions are as follows: optimal income transfer conditions specific to individual consumers, and optimal pricing and investment rules. Further, these pricing and investment rules are identical to those for the NSBMP that is designed to estimate only the optimal price and capacity for public service, as will shown later.

Subsequently, in Sect. 11.3, we closely examine the economic implications of the social optimality conditions developed in the preceding section, called *first best social optimality conditions*. We first show that these optimality conditions imply the following. First, the optimal lump sum tax satisfies the condition such that social welfare increases brought by a one-unit increase in after-tax incomes are identical across all individuals. Second, if all other private goods and services are supplied efficiently, the optimal pricing and investment rules for public services achieve a Pareto-optimal resource allocation, as is true of the same rules developed from the NSBMP.

Further, we present a number of supplementary analyses helpful to the understanding of the economic implications of the first best social optimality. Firstly, we show that optimal lump sum taxes determine socially optimal after-tax incomes through analyses that characterize optimal lump sum taxes by analogy to the solution for neoclassical utility maximization problems. Secondly, we convert the optimal pricing and investment rules into the Pareto optimality condition specific to congestion-prone services, which fundamentally differs from that of congestion-free goods and service. Thirdly, we schematically illustrate the Pareto-optimal resource allocation under first best governmental policies for price and capacity.

Finally, in Sect. 11.4, we extend analyses from previous sections for the case of no binding constraint on government funds to the case of non-optimal government funds. The key concern of analyses in this section is to search for a socially optimal policy, under the constraint of an insufficient budget. Using an example of the highway sector, the analyses answer the question of how to determine a better policy alternative under the condition of insufficient governmental funds from among the two plausible options that follow. The first policy alternative is to construct highways so as to have less capacity than the first best optimum and to impose a road user charge smaller than optimum. The second alternative involves providing a capacity less than optimum, while imposing user charges larger than optimum.

The SWMP under budget constraint is constructed by adding one additional constraint on the government budget to the SWMP developed in Sect. 11.2. This amendment gives social optimality conditions, called the *second best social optimality conditions under budget constraint*, which cannot satisfy the Pareto optimality condition for the public service provision. Using these second best social optimality conditions, we thoroughly analyze the effect of non-optimal funds not only on optimal price and public service capacity but also on social welfare and resource allocation efficiency.

11.2 The Basic Form of Social Welfare Maximization Problems

11.2.1 Modeling of the Social Welfare Maximization Problem

This subsection presents the modeling approach taken in this study for the SWMP of the government. The SWMP is used to maximize social welfare through the operation of the basic service system introduced in Chap. 6 and through the execution of the income distribution function. The choice variables of the SWMP consist of two groups: one group related to the operation of the service system is comprised of price, capacity, and service time; the other group for lump sum taxation consists of lump sum taxes specific to all consumers.

Assumption 11.1. The SWMP is expressed as the following maximization problem with multiple constraints.

(a) The objective function of the SWMP is the social welfare function W such that

$$W\left(\bar{U}^1, \cdots, \bar{U}^I\right),$$

where $\bar{U}^i$ is the indirect utility of individual i. The function W is increasing, concave, and differentiable in U^i for all i.

(b) The service time of the congestion-prone service system, t, is estimated by

$$t = T(\bar{q}, c),$$

where $\bar{q}$ is the market demand function for public service under the deterministic perception approach in Assumptions 2.1 and 2.2, c the capacity of a public service system, and T the service time function defined in Assumption 6.1.

(c) The production of capacity c satisfies the constraint such that

$$c \leq F(x),$$

where $x \equiv (x_1, \cdots, x_J)$ is the vector of inputs to the production of c, and F is the production function that is increasing and differentiable in x.

(d) The decision of the government fulfills the budget constraint such that

$$\sum_i r^i + p\bar{q} - \sum_j p_j x_j \geq 0,$$

where r^i is the lump sum tax imposed on i, p the price of public services, p_j the price of input j to capacity, and x_j the quantity of input j in F. In addition, it is assumed that the price p_j equals the social cost of input j.

The SWMP specified above has an expression identical to that of the profit maximization problem for monopolists under the user equilibrium approach in Chap. 8, except for the following two differences: first, the former employs the social welfare function W as the objective function; second, the former has an additional constraint that formulates the governmental budget constraint. The structure and economic implication of this SWMP are examined in detail below.

First, the government is used to maximize the social welfare index, estimated by the function W in Assumption 11.1(a), through the execution of two functions: provisions for a for-pay public service, and the implementation of income distributions among individuals within its administrative boundary. To pursue this objective, the government provides the public service at price p, through the operation of a congestion-prone service system with capacity c. The government also executes the income distribution function through imposition of lump sum taxes $r \equiv (r^1, \cdots, r^I)$ specific to individual consumers.

Second, the SWMP is constructed under the user equilibrium approach for public service, which is synonymous with the postulate that the government is the leader and consumers are followers in leader-and-follower games. Under this approach, the government has and utilizes complete knowledge of consumer reactions to the government choice regarding its directly controllable variables: price p, capacity c, and lump sum taxes r. Specifically, the government is assumed to accurately forecast service time t at user equilibrium, through the use of the user equilibrium condition in Assumption 10.1(b), in which service time t is estimated for arbitrary values of directly controllable variables p, c and r. Further, the government is postulated to indirectly control the value of t through the choice of the directly controllable variables.

Third, the social welfare function W has a structure sensitive to the relevant control variable of the government, as explained below. The social welfare function is sensitive to changes in the indirect utilities of all consumers within the administrative boundary of the government. The indirect utility of a consumer represents the maximum utility, which is estimated from the utility maximization problem under the deterministic perception approach of Chap. 2. This utility maximization problem is structured so that the optimal choice of consumers is sensitive to the relevant control variables of the government. Accordingly, social welfare is sensitive to relevant control variables of the government.

Fourth, the service system specified in Assumption 11.1(c) is the simplest form of a congestion-prone service system, termed the basic service system. This service system does not consume variable costs in facilitating throughputs; that is, the supplier cost of this system consists only of capacity cost. Further, the use of the basic service system connotes that the random arrival of demands has a constant arrival rate throughout the whole analysis period.

Fifth, the budget constraint of Assumption 11.1(d) depicts that the government revenues necessary for the provision of public service and the execution of income distribution are collected from two sources: first, a uniform service charge imposed on all users of a public service system; second, lump sum taxes levied on all consumers. The budget constraint is formulated under the postulate that revenues collected from users have no binding relationship to expenditures consumed in the operation of the service system. That is, if service charge revenues are not sufficient to maintain optimal capacity, the government subsidizes additional expenditures; on the other hand, if revenues exceed necessary expenditures, profit is consolidated into general government revenues.

Sixth, the lump sum taxes introduced above can be regarded as surrogate variables for the aggregation of all progressive individualistic taxes such as property and income taxes, and social welfare programs that provide financial aid to the economically disadvantaged. These lump sum taxes do not need to be understood as lump sum income transfers. Note, finally, that the introduction of lump sum taxes is an indispensible device for all SWMPs, including the ones used in other studies, in order to develop social optimality conditions using simple mathematical formulas (Mohring 1970; Diamond and Mirrlees 1971; Moon and Park 2002b).

11.2.2 Sensitivities of Utility Maximization Problems

In this subsection, we cover two aspects of the indirect utilities that constitute the arguments of the social welfare function introduced in Assumption 11.1. We first present the specific formulation of the utility maximization problem under the deterministic perception approach. We next estimate the sensitivity of indirect utility functions for the developed utility maximization problem with respect to the relevant control variables of the government.

To begin, we construct the utility maximization problem. Under the condition that the government control variables are composed of r^i, p, and t, the utility maximization problem under the deterministic perception approach of Assumptions 2.1 and 2.2 can be expressed as a Lagrangian L_1^i such that

$$\begin{aligned} L_1^i(q^i,x^i,y^i,z^i,\lambda^i,\mu^i,\eta^i;\ r^i,p,t) &\equiv \max\{\ U^i(y^i,z^i)\} + \lambda^i\left(q^i - y^i\right) \\ &+ \sum_k \mu_k^i\left(Z_k^i(x_k^i) + b_k^i t q^i - z_k^i\right) \\ &+ \eta^i\left(\bar{M}^i - r^i - (p + w^i t)q^i - \sum_{kj} p_j x_{kj}^i\right). \end{aligned} \tag{11.1}$$

This utility maximization problem is identical to the problem in (2.16) except for the following: first, an innocuous assumption $a = 1$is applied; second, a lump sum tax r^i is added to the budget constraint; third, the public service is the sole service option that offers a certain congestion-prone service; fourth, the substitute production function is simplified to exclude time variable t_k.

Let $(\bar{q}^i,\bar{x}^i,\bar{y}^i,\bar{z}^i,\bar{\lambda}^i,\bar{\mu}^i,\bar{\eta}^i)$ be the solution to L_1^i. It follows from Lemma 2.2 that L_1^i gives the implicit service price $\bar{\pi}^i$ that equals $p + v^i t$, where $v^i \equiv w^i - \sum_k \bar{\varphi}_k^i b_k^i$ is the net-value-of-time for the public service. Moreover, Theorem 2.5 shows that the net-value-of-time v^i satisfies the following:

$$\frac{\partial \bar{q}^i}{\partial p} = \frac{1}{v^i}\frac{\partial \bar{q}^i}{\partial t}. \tag{11.2}$$

This net-value-of-time represents the marginal user time cost of service time for consumer i as a monetary unit.

Subsequently, we estimate the sensitivity of the indirect utility $U^i(\bar{y}^i,\bar{z}^i)$, denoted by $\bar{U}^i$, with respect to three government control variables in the utility maximization problem.

Lemma 11.1. *The sensitivities of indirect utility functions $\bar{U}^i$ with respect to r^i, p, and t are*

$$\frac{\partial \bar{U}^i}{\partial r^i} = -\bar{\eta}^i,\ \frac{\partial \bar{U}^i}{\partial p} = -\bar{\eta}^i\bar{q}^i,\ \frac{\partial \bar{U}^i}{\partial t} = -\bar{\eta}^i v^i \bar{q}^i,\ \textit{all } i.$$

Proof. The proof can readily be worked out by applying the envelop theorem for constrained optimization problems. □

Finally, we introduce two different averages for net-value-of-times. One is the social value-of-service-time, denoted by either $\hat{v}$ or $\widehat{v}$, defined by

$$\hat{v} \text{ or } \widehat{v} = \sum_i v^i \bar{q}^i \Big/ \bar{q}, \tag{11.3}$$

where $\bar{q} \equiv \sum_i \bar{q}^i$. The second is the private value-of-service-time $\breve{v}$, estimated by

$$\breve{v} = \frac{\partial \bar{q}}{\partial t} \Big/ \frac{\partial \bar{q}}{\partial p} = \sum_i v^i \frac{\partial \bar{q}^i}{\partial p} \Big/ \sum_i \frac{\partial \bar{q}^i}{\partial p}. \tag{11.4}$$

Here, the third term of this equation comes from (11.2).

The above two value-of-service-times have fundamentally different economic meanings and generally have different values. The social value-of-service-time $\hat{v}$ is equal to the mean net-value-of-time for market demand $\bar{q}$ and is equivalent to the mean user time cost for market demand per unit service time. On the other hand, the private value-of-service time $\breve{v}$ estimates the marginal revenue loss of service time for the supplier. Further. it holds that $\hat{v} \neq \breve{v}$, unless all consumers have an identical v^i value, as shown in Theorem 6.8.

11.2.3 Development of Social Optimality Conditions

We here present a set of social optimality conditions for the SWMP of Assumption 11.1, which have formulations suitable for deducing their economic implications. To develop this final output, we first formulate the SWMP into a constrained optimization problem. We next develop first order conditions for the SWMP with respect to choice variables. Finally, we develop the social optimality conditions from the first order conditions.

Firstly, we formulate the SWMP of Assumption 11.1 as a Lagrangian SW_o:

$$\begin{aligned} SW_o(r,x,p,c,t,\kappa,\tau,\omega) &= \max\left\{W(\bar{U}^1,\cdots,\bar{U}^I)\right\} + \kappa(F(x)-c) \\ &+ \tau\left(t - T(\bar{q},c)\right) + \omega\left(\sum_i r^i + p\bar{q} - \sum_j p_j x_j\right), \end{aligned} \tag{11.5}$$

where κ, τ and ω are Lagrange multipliers.

Let $(\hat{r},\hat{x},\hat{p},\hat{c},\hat{t},\hat{\kappa},\hat{\tau},\hat{\omega})$ be the solution of SW_o. Differentiating $SW_o$with respect to government control variables and substituting the sensitivities of indirect utilities in Lemma 11.1 into the outputs of the first step gives the following:

$$\frac{\partial SW_o}{\partial r^i} = -\frac{\partial \hat{W}}{\partial \hat{U}^i}\hat{\eta}^i - \hat{\tau}\frac{\partial \hat{T}}{\partial \bar{q}}\frac{\partial \hat{q}^i}{\partial r^i} + \hat{\omega}\left(1 + \hat{p}\frac{\partial \hat{q}^i}{\partial r^i}\right) = 0, \text{ all } i \tag{11.6}$$

$$\frac{\partial SW_o}{\partial p} = -\sum_i \frac{\partial \hat{W}}{\partial \hat{U}^i}\hat{\eta}^i\hat{q}^i - \hat{\tau}\frac{\partial \hat{T}}{\partial \bar{q}}\frac{\partial \hat{q}}{\partial p} + \hat{\omega}\left(\hat{q} + \hat{p}\frac{\partial \hat{q}}{\partial p}\right) = 0 \tag{11.7}$$

$$\frac{\partial SW_o}{\partial t} = -\sum_i \frac{\partial \hat{W}}{\partial \hat{U}^i}\hat{\eta}^i v^i \hat{q}^i + \hat{\tau}\left(1 - \frac{\partial \hat{T}}{\partial \bar{q}}\frac{\partial \hat{q}}{\partial t}\right) + \hat{\omega}\hat{p}\frac{\partial \hat{q}}{\partial t} = 0 \tag{11.8}$$

$$\frac{\partial SW_o}{\partial c} = -\hat{\kappa} - \hat{\tau}\frac{\partial \hat{T}}{\partial c} = 0 \tag{11.9}$$

$$\frac{\partial SW_o}{\partial x_j} = \hat{\kappa}\frac{\partial \hat{F}}{\partial x_j} - \hat{\omega} p_j = 0, \text{ all } j, \tag{11.10}$$

where $\hat{W} \equiv W(\hat{U}^1, \cdots, \hat{U}^I)$, $\hat{q} \equiv \bar{q}(\hat{r}, \hat{p}, \hat{t})$, $\hat{T} \equiv T(\hat{q}, \hat{c})$, and $\hat{F} \equiv F(\hat{x})$.

Secondly, we show that the Lagrange multiplier $\hat{\tau}$ represents the marginal social welfare loss of service time. To this end, we first estimate the specific expression of $\hat{\tau}$ below, by arranging the above first order conditions.

Lemma 11.2. *The solution to SW_o gives the marginal social welfare loss of service time, $\hat{\tau}$, estimated by $\hat{\tau} = \hat{\omega}\,\hat{v}\,\hat{q}$.*

Proof. Using the private value-of-service-time $\breve{v}$, as defined in (11.4), the first order conditions (11.7) and (11.8) can be rearranged as follows:

$$\breve{v}\frac{\partial SW}{\partial p} - \frac{\partial SW}{\partial t} = \hat{\omega}\breve{v}\hat{q} - \hat{\tau} + \delta = 0, \tag{11.11}$$

where

$$\delta = \sum_i \frac{\partial \hat{W}}{\partial \hat{U}^i}\hat{\eta}^i v^i \hat{q}^i - \breve{v}\sum_i \frac{\partial \hat{W}}{\partial \hat{U}^i}\hat{\eta}^i\hat{q}^i. \tag{11.12}$$

This implies that

$$\hat{\tau} = \hat{\omega}\breve{v}\,\hat{q} + \delta. \tag{11.13}$$

Substituting (11.13) into (11.6) and (11.7) gives

$$\frac{\partial SW}{\partial p} - \sum_i \frac{\partial SW}{\partial r^i}\hat{q}^i = \hat{\omega}\left(\hat{p} - \breve{v}\hat{q}\frac{\partial \hat{T}}{\partial \bar{q}} - \frac{\delta}{\hat{\omega}}\frac{\partial \hat{T}}{\partial \bar{q}}\right)\sum_i\left(\frac{\partial \hat{q}^i}{\partial p} - \hat{q}^i\frac{\partial \hat{q}^i}{\partial r^i}\right) = 0. \tag{11.14}$$

Here the term $\partial\bar{q}^i/\partial p - \bar{q}^i\partial\bar{q}^i/\partial r^i$ estimates the substitution effect of an increase in price, and thereby is always negative. Hence, (11.14) implies that

$$\hat{p} = \breve{v}\hat{q}\frac{\partial\hat{T}}{\partial\bar{q}} + \frac{\delta}{\hat{\omega}}\frac{\partial\hat{T}}{\partial\bar{q}}. \tag{11.15}$$

Substituting (11.13) and (11.15) into (11.6) leads to

$$\frac{\partial\hat{W}}{\partial\bar{U}^i}\hat{\eta}^i = \hat{\omega}\left(1 + \left(\hat{p} - \breve{v}\hat{q}\frac{\partial\hat{T}}{\partial\bar{q}} - \frac{\delta}{\hat{\omega}}\frac{\partial\hat{T}}{\partial\bar{q}}\right)\frac{\partial\hat{q}^i}{\partial r^i}\right) = \hat{\omega}. \tag{11.16}$$

Subsequently, substituting (11.16) and (11.3) in sequence into (11.12) gives

$$\delta = \hat{\omega}\sum_i v^i\hat{q}^i - \hat{\omega}\breve{v}\sum_i \hat{q}^i = \hat{\omega}\left(\hat{v} - \breve{v}\right)\hat{q}. \tag{11.17}$$

Substituting (11.17) into (11.13) yields the following: $\hat{\tau} = \hat{\omega}\,\hat{v}\,\hat{q}$. □

We next show that the term $\hat{\tau}$ represents the marginal social welfare loss of service time. Equation (11.16) shows that $\partial\hat{W}/\partial\bar{U}^i \times \hat{\eta}^i = \hat{\omega}$, for all i. Substituting this relationship into (11.8) gives

$$\hat{\tau} = \hat{\omega}\left(\sum_i v^i\hat{q}^i - \hat{p}\frac{\partial\hat{q}}{\partial t}\right)\Big/\left(1 - \frac{\partial\hat{T}}{\partial\bar{q}}\frac{\partial\hat{q}}{\partial t}\right). \tag{11.18}$$

In this equation, the term $\sum_i v^i\hat{q}^i \rangle\ 0$ quantifies the marginal user time cost of service time for market demand $\hat{q}$, whereas the term $-\hat{p}\partial\hat{q}/\partial t \rangle\ 0$ estimates the marginal revenue loss of service time for supplier. Therefore, the numerator of the equation estimates the total social welfare loss due to a one-unit increase in service time. On the other hand, the denominator $1 - \partial\hat{T}/\partial\bar{q} \times \partial\hat{q}/\partial t$ represents the ratio of the actual service time change under the constraint of the user equilibrium condition to the marginal service time change under no constraint, as explained in Subsect. 8.3.2. Therefore, the term $\breve{\tau}$ can be interpreted as the marginal social welfare loss of actual service time under the constraint of the user equilibrium condition.

Thirdly, we show that the term $\hat{\tau}/\hat{\omega}\times\partial\hat{T}/\partial q\ (= \hat{v}\,\hat{q}\partial\hat{T}/\partial q)$ in (11.6)~(11.8) represents the social marginal full cost of throughput for the public service system. To this end, we construct the SCMP, a dual problem of the SWMP, denoted by Z_o, by applying the marginal social welfare of service time in Lemma 11.1:

$$\begin{aligned} Z_o(x, c, t, \kappa, \tau; s, \hat{v}) \equiv \min\left\{\sum_j p_j x_j + t\hat{v}s\right\} + \kappa\left(c - F(x)\right) \\ + \tau(T(s, c) - t), \end{aligned} \tag{11.19}$$

where $s = \hat{q}$. By Theorem 6.5, this SCMP gives the social marginal full cost of throughput, $MFC(s; \hat{v})$, which satisfies the following relationship:

$$SMFC(s; \hat{v}) = \hat{v}\, s \frac{\partial T(s, c = \hat{c})}{\partial s}. \tag{11.20}$$

Fourthly, we introduce social optimality conditions for SW_o in (11.5), which have formulations suitable for deducing their economic implications. Arranging the analysis outcomes presented above gives these optimality conditions, as shown below.

Theorem 11.1. *The optimal solution to SW_o satisfies the following social optimality conditions.*

i. *The social optimality condition for income distribution:.*

$$-\frac{\partial \hat{W}}{\partial r^i} = \frac{\partial \hat{W}}{\partial(\bar{M}^i - r^i)} = \hat{\omega}\,,\ \text{all } i. \tag{11.21}$$

ii. *The optimality condition for resource allocation:.*

$$\hat{t} - T(\hat{q}, \hat{c}) = 0 \tag{11.22}$$

$$\hat{p} = \hat{v}\hat{q}\frac{\partial \hat{T}}{\partial \bar{q}} = SMFC(\hat{q}) \tag{11.23}$$

$$MKC(\hat{c}) = MUCS(\hat{c}) \equiv -\hat{v}\hat{q}\frac{\partial \hat{T}}{\partial c} \tag{11.24}$$

$$MKC(c) \equiv \frac{\partial KC(c)}{\partial c} = p_j \Big/ \frac{\partial F(\hat{x})}{\partial x_j},\ \text{all } j, \tag{11.25}$$

where MUCS stands for the marginal user time cost savings of capacity.

Proof. Equation (11.16) implies (11.21). Equation (11.22) is none other than the user equilibrium condition that should be held. Substituting (11.17) into (11.15) yields the first equality of (11.23). The equality of (11.20) implies the second equality of (11.23). Substituting $\hat{\tau} = \hat{\omega}\, \hat{v}\, \hat{q}$ in Lemma 11.2 into (11.9) yields (11.24). Finally, substituting (11.10) and $\hat{\tau} = \hat{\omega}\, \hat{v}\, \hat{q}$ in sequence into (11.10) results in (11.25). □

Theorem 11.1 presents a set of optimality conditions for the SWMP of (11.5) by dividing them two groups. The first group comprises I optimality conditions in (11.21), which characterizes the after-tax incomes of all consumers. The second group consists of $J + 3$ optimality conditions in (11.22)–(11.25), which depict socially optimal resource allocations. These two groups of optimality conditions are sufficient to estimate all the unknowns of the SWMP, without recourse to other conditions. Specifically, the total number of equations in the theorem is $I + J + 3$; additionally, the total number of unknowns is the same number. Therefore, mathematically, it is feasible to estimate all the unknowns from the social optimality conditions.

11.2.4 Differences from Net Social Benefit Maximization Problems

In this subsection we compare and contrast the SWMP of (11.5) with a NSBMP that gives optimality conditions similar to those of Theorem 11.1. This NSBMP estimates the solution of throughput s and capacity c, so as to maximize the net social benefit, denoted by NSB:

$$NSB(s, c) = \max\left\{\int_0^s MSB(w)\,dw - vsT(s, c) - KC(c)\right\}, \qquad (11.26)$$

where $MSB = p + vt$. Here, the function MSB estimates the marginal social benefit of throughput s in a unit of money. The value of MSB equals the implicit service price common to all consumers, and is the sum of price p and value of service time vt. This MSB is the inverse function of the market demand function for the public service under analysis.

The pricing and investment rules for the above NSBMP can readily be estimated from first order conditions for NSB with respect to s and c, respectively. The pricing and investment rules estimated in this manner are identical to the rules in (11.23) and (11.24), respectively, except that the uniform net-value-of-time v replaces the social value-of-service-time $\hat{v}$ in those rules. Hence, it can be said that the NSBMP gives the outcome basically identical to that of the SWMP, under the following two restrictive conditions: first, the analyzed public service has no competition; second, the government can finance the necessary funds without any binding constraint.

Next, we introduce dissimilarities between the NSBMP and the SWMP. The NSBMP of (11.26) has a simpler formulation than has the SWMP of (11.5). Further, the NSBMP requires a less complex analysis to develop social optimality conditions than is true of the SWMP. These differences between the two decision-making problems mainly stem from the method used to quantify consumer benefit. The SWMP specifies consumer benefit as the social welfare function for which arguments are consumers' indirect utilities under the perception approach. The use of the social welfare function has two unique advantages.

The first advantage of the SWMP over the NSBMP is that the former can reflect the quality of public service in estimating consumer benefit. The NSBMP is constructed under the premise that the social cost of service time equals the multiple of service time and value-of-time common to all consumers. However, the value-of-time represents the marginal utility of service time as a unit of money and is independent of service quality perceived by consumers. In contrast, the SWMP estimates user time cost by applying net-value-of-service-time under the perception approach. Importantly, net-value-of-service accounts for the effect of qualitative service attributes that should be included in consumer demand analyses and thus in analyses of consumer benefit.

The second advantage of the SWMP over the NSBMP is extendibility to other governmental decision-making problems under more realistic circumstances than the problem considered above. The NSBMP can hardly have the workable amendments of (11.26), which address policy issues in circumstances that do not satisfy the three restrictive conditions: no competition, no financial constraint, and no technical barrier to implement the optimal policy. In contrast, the SWMP of (11.5) have workable amendments for a public service under the circumstances of competition, financial constraint, and/or technical barrier. These amendments yield optimality conditions similar to those of Theorem 11.1, as will be demonstrated in Sect. 11.4 and Chap. 12 through analyses of a number of SWMPs that release one or two of the restrictive conditions.

Finally, the modeling approach of the SWMP has an additional advantage of estimating consumer benefit by applying the measure free from estimation error. The NSBMP uses consumers' surplus or similar social benefit measures that quantify consumer benefit in a unit of money.[1] However, all these surrogate measures are, at best, only good approximations of consumer benefit. On the other hand, the SWMP estimates social benefit using the social welfare function for which arguments are indirect utilities free from estimation error.

11.3 Implications of First Best Social Optimality

11.3.1 Characterization of Market Equilibrium

The SWMP of Assumption 11.1 is modeled by incorporating the user equilibrium condition. The use of the user equilibrium condition reflects the postulate such that the government is the leader of a leader-and-follower game with consumers who act as followers. It is therefore possible to assert that the social optimality conditions of

[1]Four different measures of consumer benefit for changes in utility are thoroughly explored with use of consumer indifference curves in Currie et al (1971). Consumers' surplus and compensation variation are estimated from utility maximization problem and its dual cost minimization problem, respectively, in Burns (1973). Similar analyses for compensation variation are presented in Diamond and McFadden (1974). It is illustrate in Willig (1976) that consumers' surplus is a quite accurate measure that estimates the monetary value of changes in consumer utility through numerical analyses.

Theorem 11.1 depict the equilibrium of the leader-and-follower game, at which point no player can be better off by changing its choice. From this perspective, we interpret the social optimality conditions in a manner similar to that used to characterize the optimality conditions for the profit maximization problem of a monopolist in Subsect. 8.3.3.

Firstly, the social optimality condition for income distribution in (11.21) plays the role of determining the after-tax income of all individuals, under the condition that the government has determined the value of (p, c, t). This optimality condition depicts that the marginal contribution of a one-unit increase in a consumer's after-tax income to social welfare index is identical across all consumers. The solution of lump sum taxes to this optimality condition generally differs from individual to individual, due to differences in before-tax incomes among individuals.

Importantly, the term $\hat{\omega}$ in (11.21) can be interpreted as *the marginal social welfare of money*. Under the lump sum taxation that satisfies the optimality condition of (11.21), the marginal social welfare of money is equal to the common marginal social welfare of after-tax income for all consumers. Further, this marginal social welfare of money implies that one unit of money is equivalent to a $\hat{\omega}$ unit increase to the social welfare index; a one-unit increase in money for the economy raises the social welfare index by $\hat{\omega}$ units.

Secondly, the user equilibrium condition of (11.22) characterizes the service time determined by consumers themselves. The consumers are scheduled to ensure that the greatest utility is achieved, in the circumstance that the government has already made the choice for (p, c, t) values. The service time determined by consumers is the solution to the following two simultaneous equations: $t = T(s, \hat{c})$ and $s = \bar{q}(\breve{p}, t)$. This solution $\hat{t}$ is the service time at user equilibrium. Such a service time at user equilibrium can graphically be depicted as Fig. 8.1. Further, this service time can be interpreted in a manner identical to the service time in the same optimality condition for the profit maximization problem of a monopolist in Subsect. 8.3.3.

Thirdly, the pricing formula in (11.23) estimates the optimal price $\hat{p}$ so as to maximize social welfare in the circumstance that the government has already calculated the solution of (r, c, t). This optimal price $\hat{p}$ is the intersection point of the two curves in Fig. 11.1, which is prepared in a manner analogous to Fig. 8.3 for the pricing rule of monopolists.

One curve in the figure depicts the social marginal benefit of service demand $\bar{q}^i$ as a unit of money, denoted by SMB^i, which is the function of an independent variable $\bar{q}^i$ for all i. This function SMB^i is estimated by

$$\begin{aligned} SMB^i(\bar{q}(\hat{r}, p, \hat{t})) &= \frac{1}{\hat{\omega}} \frac{\partial W}{\partial \bar{q}^i} = \frac{1}{\hat{\omega}} \frac{\partial W}{\partial \bar{U}^i} \frac{\partial \bar{U}^i}{\partial \bar{q}^i} \\ &= p + v^i \hat{t}, \quad \text{all } i. \end{aligned} \tag{11.27}$$

Further, the function $\partial W / \partial \bar{q}^i$ is monotonically decreasing in $\bar{q}^i$, since a larger value of p gives a smaller value of $\bar{q}^i$, as illustrated in the figure.

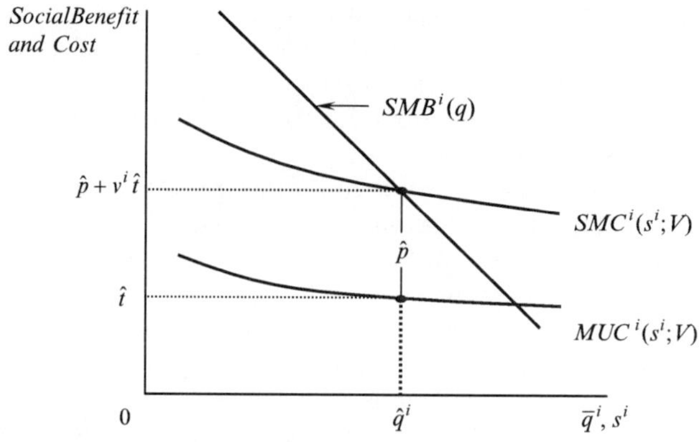

Fig. 11.1 Representation of socially optimal price

The other curve represents the social marginal cost of throughput, denoted by $SMC^i(s^i;V)$, as estimated in Theorem 6.2:

$$SMC^i(s^i;V) = SMFC(s^i;V) + MUC^i(s^i;V), \text{ all } i. \tag{11.28}$$

The slope of this curve depends on the returns-to-scale of service systems in capacity, as explained in Sect. 7.2.

The figure depicts that the demand at social optimality, denoted by $\hat{q}^i$, is the point where the two curves intersect. At that demand, the price $\hat{p}$ equals the social marginal full cost $SMFC\,(\hat{q})$, which is estimated by $SMC^i(\hat{q}) - MUC^i(\hat{q})$. Further, the figure illustrates that, if the demand for a certain value of p is smaller (or larger) than $\hat{q}^i$, the social marginal benefit of demand is greater (or smaller) than the social marginal full cost of throughput. This implies that the price $\hat{p}$ attains maximum social welfare.

Fourthly, the investment rule for capacity in (11.24) characterizes the optimal capacity $\hat{c}$ under the condition that the solution $(\hat{r}, \hat{p}, \hat{t})$ is known. This optimal capacity $\hat{c}$ is represented as the intersection point of two curves. One curve is the marginal capacity cost function $MKC(c)$. Another curve represents the function $MUCS(c)$, which estimates marginal user time cost savings for capacity as a unit of money, estimated by $-\hat{v}\hat{q}\partial T(\hat{q},c)/\partial c$. These two curves and the intersecting capacity $\hat{c}$ can be depicted in a manner identical to Fig. 8.4 for the investment rule of monopolists.

The function $-\hat{v}\hat{q}\partial T(\hat{q},c)/\partial c$ estimates user time cost savings caused by a one-unit increase in capacity, because of the following: one term $-\hat{\tau}(=-\hat{v}\hat{q})$ represents the marginal user time cost savings for a one-unit decrease in service time; the other term $\partial T/\partial c$ estimates the marginal decrease in service time by one unit expansion of capacity. Additionally, (11.24) depicts that the capacity should be increased to the point where the marginal capacity cost is equal to the marginal user time cost savings for capacity due to a decrease in service time; that is, if capacities are smaller (or greater) than the optimum $\hat{c}$, the value of $MKC(c)$ is smaller (or larger) the value of $MUCS(c)$.

Finally, (11.25) depicts the necessary conditions for the choice of inputs to capacity. These necessary conditions are identical to the necessary conditions for the cost minimization problem of (6.6), which estimates the minimum supplier cost required when constructing a certain capacity. This coincidence implies that the government should construct a congestion-prone public service system as efficiently as possible, without considering other effects such as the effect of changes in capacity on congestion or social benefit.

11.3.2 Social Optimality Conditions for Lump Sum Taxation

Here we interpret the implication of optimality conditions for lump sum taxation such that $\partial\hat{W}/\partial r^i = -\hat{\omega}$, for all i, in Theorem 11.1. The implication of these optimality conditions is deduced from the solution for a SWMP that has a formulation similar to that for neoclassical utility maximization problems.

Firstly, we introduce a SWMP for the case when the sole function of the government is to implement income distribution among consumers through lump sum taxation. This SWMP, denoted by SW_1, is used to estimate the solution of lump sum taxes r^i, for all i, so as to maximize the social welfare function W:

$$SW_1(r,\omega) \equiv \max\left\{W(\bar{U}^1,\cdots,\bar{U}^I)\right\} + \omega\sum_i r^i. \tag{11.29}$$

Here, the indirect utility $\bar{U}^i$ is estimated from the utility maximization problem, which is identical to that of (11.1), except that the congestion-prone service is not a public service but rather a private service.

The indirect utility function $\bar{U}^i$ satisfies the condition that $\partial\bar{U}^i/\partial r^i = -\bar{\eta}^i$, as shown in Lemma 11.1. Hence, it follows that

$$-\frac{\partial\hat{W}}{\partial r^i} = \frac{\partial\hat{W}}{\partial(\bar{M}^i - r^i)} = \hat{\omega}, \text{ all } i\,. \tag{11.30}$$

This optimality condition is identical to that of (11.21). Therefore, it can be concluded that this optimality condition can hold, whether or not the government participates in the production of public services.

Secondly, we restructure the SWMP of (11.29) into an optimization problem handy for simple graphical analyses of optimal lump sum taxes. As the first step, we convert the function W for the control variable of lump sum taxes r^i for all i into the social welfare function V for after-tax incomes $\bar{M}^i - r^i$ for all i:

$$W(\bar{U}^1,\cdots,\bar{U}^I) = V(\bar{M}^1 - r^1,\cdots,\bar{M}^I - r^I). \tag{11.31}$$

Further, the constraint for the total resources available in the economy can be amended as follows:

$$M_o \equiv \sum_i \bar{M}^i = \sum_i (\bar{M}^i - r^i). \tag{11.32}$$

This constraint for total available resources is actually identical to the constraint for income distribution, such that $\sum_i r^i = 0$.

Using (11.31) and (11.32), we construct an alternative formulation of SW_1 in (11.29), denoted by SW_2:

$$SW_2(\bar{M} - r, \omega) \equiv \max \{ V(\bar{M} - r)\} + \omega \left(M_o - \sum_i (\bar{M}^i - r^i) \right), \tag{11.33}$$

where $\bar{M} - r \equiv (\bar{M}^1 - r^1, \cdots, \bar{M}^I - r^I)$. This SWMP has a formulation similar to neoclassical utility maximization problems, in which the choice vector is $\bar{M} - r$ and in which the prices of all the choice variables are one.

Thirdly, we pictorially depict the optimal income redistribution in Fig. 11.2 for the case of a two-person economy: one consumer is a rich person, denoted by subscript r, and another consumer is a poor person, denoted by p. In the figure, the straight line $A - B$ represents the constraint for available resources, such that $\bar{M}^r + \bar{M}^p = (\bar{M}^r - r^r) + (\bar{M}^p - r^p)$. On the other hand, the two curves depict the indifference curves for the social welfare function V.

The figure shows that the before-tax incomes of these two persons, denoted by $C \equiv (\bar{M}^r, \bar{M}^p)$, are redistributed to the optimal after-tax incomes, denoted by $D \equiv (\bar{M}^r - \hat{r}^r, \bar{M}^p - \hat{r}^p)$, through the optimal lump sum taxes $(\hat{r}^r, \hat{r}^p)$. By (11.30), the governmental choice $(\hat{r}^r, \hat{r}^p)$ satisfies the equalitysuch that

$$\frac{\partial V(\bar{M}^r - \hat{r}^r, \bar{M}^p - \hat{r}^p)}{\partial(\bar{M}^r - r^r)} = \frac{\partial V(\bar{M}^r - \hat{r}^r, \bar{M}^p - \hat{r}^p)}{\partial(\bar{M}^p - r^p)} = \hat{\omega}. \tag{11.34}$$

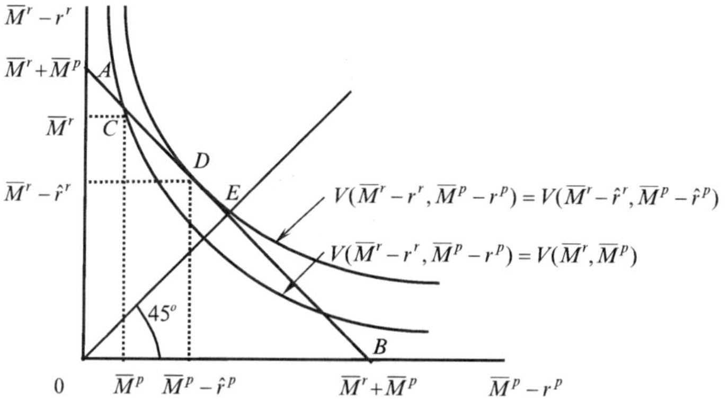

Fig. 11.2 Representation of optimal lump sum taxes

Hence, this social indifference curve is tangent with the line that depicts the total available resources of the economy at point D. Further, this indifference curve is located above the indifference curve that passes through point C.

The figure is drawn so that the resulting after-tax income D reflects the following two conditions. First, the government executes a progressive taxation program that transfers a certain portion of the wealth of the rich to the economically disadvantaged. However, second, the resulting income redistribution maintains vertical equity between the two consumers, such that the lump sum tax does not cause a different ordering of after-tax incomes from that of before-tax incomes among individuals. By the first condition, point D should be inside the interval $[B, C]$. However, by the second condition, point D should be inside the interval $[A, E]$, wherein E is the point at which the after-tax incomes of the two persons are equal. Therefore, the optimal choice D belongs to the interval $[C, E]$, as depicted in Fig. 11.2.

Fourthly, the above graphical analysis is extended to the case when the government implements not only the income distribution function but also the function of public service provision. Suppose that the optimal subsidy of the government to the provision of public service is $\hat{e}$ dollars. Then, the straight line between points A and B depicts the equation $\bar{M}^r + \bar{M}^p - \hat{e} = (\bar{M}^r - r^r) + (\bar{M}^p - r^p)$.

In this case, points C and D in Fig. 11.2 represent, respectively, the two different after-tax incomes of two persons under two different lump sum taxation plans to finance the subsidy $\hat{e}$. To be specific, point C depicts the after-tax income attained under a taxation plan other than the optimal lump sum taxation, e.g., a uniform tax on all consumers, whereas point D represents the after-tax income under the optimal taxation. Further, these two taxation plans should satisfy the two budget constraints of the government such that $\hat{r}^r + \hat{r}^p - \hat{e} = 0$ and $\hat{p}\hat{q} + \hat{e} - KC(\hat{c}) = 0$.

Fifthly, we explore the relationship between the after-tax income $\bar{M}^i - \hat{r}^i$ and the optimality condition for lump sum tax $-\partial\hat{W}/\partial r^i \; (\equiv \partial\hat{W}/\partial\bar{U}^i \times \partial\hat{U}^i/\partial\bar{M}^i) = \hat{\omega}$. For this analysis, we adopt the assumption that the marginal change in utility of the economically advantaged by a one-unit increase in after-tax income is generally less than that of the economically disadvantaged:

$$\bar{M}^i - \hat{r}^i \rangle \bar{M}^j - \hat{r}^j \Leftrightarrow \frac{\partial\hat{U}^i}{\partial(\bar{M}^i - r^i)} \langle \frac{\partial\hat{U}^j}{\partial(\bar{M}^j - r^j)}, \quad \text{all } i, j. \tag{11.35}$$

This relationship does not reflect the subjective perception of each individual, but rather the judgment of analysts who participate in determining lump sum taxes.

The term $\partial\hat{W}/\partial\bar{U}^i$ in $\partial\hat{W}/\partial U^i \times \partial\hat{U}^i/\partial\bar{M}^i$ estimates the marginal contribution of a one-unit increase in the indirect utility of consumer i to the social welfare judged by the government. Hence, under the condition of (11.35), the optimality condition that $\partial\hat{W}/\partial U^i \times \partial\hat{U}^i/\partial\bar{M}^i = \hat{\omega}$ can be interpreted as follows: the government should assign a larger weight to a one-unit increase in the indirect utility for the economically advantaged than to a one-unit increase for the economically disadvantaged. However, this difference in the marginal social welfare of consumers' indirect utilities does not in any way connote that the government assigns a larger value to the economically advantaged than to the economically disadvantaged as human beings, as explained next.

We first reconsider the social optimality condition for lump sum taxation in (11.30). Under the condition of (11.35), it follows from (11.30) that

$$\frac{\partial \hat{W}^i}{\partial \bar{U}^i} \rangle \frac{\partial \hat{W}^j}{\partial \bar{U}^j} \Leftrightarrow \bar{M}^i - \hat{r}^i \rangle \bar{M}^j - \hat{r}^j, \text{ all } i, j. \tag{11.36}$$

Therefore, it can be said that the term $\partial \hat{W} / \partial \bar{U}^i$ is none other than an indicator that reflects the relative magnitudes of after-tax incomes among taxpayers. Importantly, this interpretation of the social welfare function is judged to be free from the following ethical issue: the social welfare function reflects the inter-personal comparison of utility, as raised in Samuelson (1947).

The value of the optimal lump sum taxes estimated above hinges mainly on the geometry of social welfare functions applied in the analysis. However, in reality, there is no way to construct a social welfare indifference curve that can be universally accepted by all individuals in the economy. Instead, all individuals can imagine a socially desirable form of social indifference curves, which generally differs from one another. In this regard, the social indifference curve used in the above analysis fundamentally differs from consumers' utility functions, which, theoretically, can be objectively defined.

Then, how do we understand the above analysis for optimal lump sum taxes? For the SWMP analyzed above, the social optimality condition is realized through the social choice for lump sum taxes. This in turn is represented by the governmental choice for a certain aggregated package of all public programs related to income distribution among taxpayers, as noted in Subsect. 11.2.1. Further, in a democratic society, this social choice commonly occurs through a political decision-making mechanism, e.g., majority voting. Accordingly, this social choice can be seen as the realization of social optimality conditions for social indifference curves that reflect the collective preference of participants in the political decision-making process for the allocation of their after-tax incomes.

11.3.3 Pareto Optimality Conditions for Public Services

We here prove that any governmental choice that satisfies a set of social optimality conditions for resource allocation in Theorem 11.1 leads to a Pareto-optimal resource allocation. In this proof, we accommodate the following two peculiar aspects of congestion-prone service systems: first, the throughput of a service system is identical to the demand facilitated by the service system; second, therefore, the production of throughputs consumes the human resource of customers.

To begin, we introduce the approach taken in this study to prove the above assertion. The Pareto optimality of economies refers to the state when no one can be better off without making others worse off. This Pareto optimality can be translated into three optimality conditions: exchange, social production, and overall efficiency conditions. Therefore, we work out the proof by showing that the social optimality conditions for resource allocation in Theorem 11.1 satisfy these three Pareto optimality conditions.

In this proof, we formulate the three Pareto optimality conditions as trade-off relationships between a congestion-prone public service and congestion-free goods or services traded in markets. In other words, we do not use commodities, which are the yield of consumer production and, therefore, are not traded in markets. For example, the exchange efficiency condition of consumers is expressed as the marginal rate of substitution between $\bar{q}^i$ and $\bar{x}^i_{kj}$, for all k, j, both of which are traded in markets.

Firstly, we present the exchange efficiency condition for the utility maximization problem of (11.1), under the convention that the utility-maximizing choice of input (q,x) is $(\bar{q},\bar{x})$. The exchange efficiency condition is expressed as the marginal rate of substitution of $\bar{x}^i_{kj}$ for $\bar{q}^i$, for all k, j. To develop this efficiency condition, we first estimate the marginal utility of $\bar{q}^i$, expressed by $MU^i_{\bar{q}}$:

$$MU^i_{\bar{q}} = \frac{\partial \bar{U}^i}{\partial y^i}\frac{\partial a\bar{q}^i}{\partial q^i} = \bar{\eta}^i\bar{\pi}^i = \bar{\eta}^i(p + v^i\, t), \text{ all } i. \tag{11.37}$$

We next estimate the marginal utility of $\bar{x}^i_{kj}$, denoted by $MU^i_{\bar{x}_{kj}}$, in the same manner:

$$MU^i_{\bar{x}_{kj}} = \frac{\partial \bar{U}^i}{\partial z^i}\frac{\partial \bar{Z}^i_k}{\partial x^i_{kj}} = \bar{\eta}^i\bar{\varphi}^i\frac{\partial \bar{Z}^i_k}{\partial x^i_{kj}} = \bar{\eta}^i p_j, \text{ all } i,\ k,\ j. \tag{11.38}$$

where $\bar{Z}^i_k \equiv Z^i_k(\bar{x}^i_k)$ is the amount of commodity j in substitute production.

Combining (11.37) and (11.38) gives the marginal rate of substitution of $\bar{x}^i_{kj}$ for $\bar{q}^i$, denoted by $MRS^i_{\bar{x}_{kj}\bar{q}}$, such that

$$MRS^i_{\bar{x}_{kj}\bar{q}} = \frac{MU^i_{\bar{x}_{kj}}}{MU^i_{\bar{q}}} = \frac{p_j}{p + v^i\, t}, \text{ all } i,\ k,\ j. \tag{11.39}$$

This equation indicates that the marginal rate of substitution differs by consumer, due to the difference in net-value-of-times among consumers.

Secondly, we construct the social production efficiency condition for congestion-prone service system from the SCMP of (11.19), which a dual of the SWMP analyzed here. This SCMP gives optimality conditions identical to the social optimality conditions in (11.22), (11.24), and (11.25), except that q^i is replaced by s^i, as shown in Lemmas 6.1 and 6.3. These optimality conditions are merged into one efficiency condition compatible with the marginal rate of substitution in (11.39). Such analyses are conducted under the convention that the optimal choice of capacity c and its input x for the production of an arbitrary throughput $s(=\sum_i s^i)$ are $\widehat{c}$ and $\widehat{x}$, respectively.

The first step to construct the social production efficiency condition develops the formula that estimates the optimal amount of input j consumed in constructing capacity c under the constraint that $c \leq F(x)$. This efficiency condition can be represented by the marginal product of $\widehat{x}_j$ for $\widehat{c}$, denoted by $MP_{\widehat{x}_j \widehat{c}}$. By (11.25), this marginal product is

$$MP_{\widehat{x}_j \widehat{c}} = \frac{\partial F(\widehat{x})}{\partial x_j} = \frac{p_j}{MKC(\widehat{c})}, \text{ all } j. \tag{11.40}$$

Here price p_j equals the social cost of input j, as postulated in Assumption 11.1(d).

The second step characterizes the optimal capacity so as to minimize the total social cost necessary for the production of throughput s under the constraint that $t = T(s, c)$. The efficiency condition can be expressed as the marginal rate of technical substitution ($MRTS$) of capacity c for total service time Y ($\equiv sT(s, \widehat{c})$), denoted by $MRTS^s_{\widehat{c}Y}$. By (11.24), this marginal rate is

$$MRTS^s_{\widehat{c}Y} = -s\frac{\partial T(s, \widehat{c})}{\partial c} = \frac{MKC(\widehat{c})}{\widehat{v}}, \tag{11.41}$$

where $\widehat{v} = \sum_i v^i s^i / \sum_i s^i$.

The third step is related to the user equilibrium condition in (11.22). The market demand at user equilibrium is actually attained by the desire of consumers who are willing to maximize their utilities. Further, under the user equilibrium approach, the user equilibrium condition for this market demand is one necessary input for the decision made by the operator; that is, the user equilibrium condition must be fulfilled by the operator's optimal choice.

Such a user equilibrium condition gives the social marginal product of total service time Y for throughput s^i, denoted by SMP^i_{Ys}, such that

$$SMP^i_{Ys} = 1 \bigg/ \frac{\partial sT(s, c = \widehat{c})}{\partial s^i} = \widehat{v} \bigg/ \sum_i \frac{\partial v^i s^i T(s, c = \widehat{c})}{\partial s^i}$$

$$= \frac{\widehat{v}}{SMC^i(s^i; V)} \tag{11.42}$$

$$= \frac{\widehat{v}}{SMFC(s; \widehat{v}) + v^i T(s, \widehat{c})}, \text{ all } i. \tag{11.43}$$

Here, the social marginal product of Y for s^i is expressed by the inverse of $\partial Y / \partial s^i$. Additionally, (11.42) and (11.43) follow from Theorems 6.2 and 6.5, respectively.

Combining the above three production efficiency conditions leads to the social marginal rate of transformation of $\widehat{x}_j$ for s^i, denoted by $SMRT^i_{\widehat{x}_j s}$, such that

$$SMRT^i_{\widehat{x}_j s} = MP_{\widehat{x}_j \widehat{c}} \cdot MRTS^s_{\widehat{c}Y} \cdot SMP^i_{Ys}$$

$$= \frac{p_j}{SMFC(s; \widehat{v}) + v^i T(s, \widehat{c})}, \text{ all } i, j. \tag{11.44}$$

Thirdly, we show that the optimal price estimated in (11.23) satisfies the overall efficiency condition. The overall efficiency condition implies that the social production possibility frontier of economies is tangent to the indifference curves of all the consumers' utilities. To meet this requirement, the optimal price should equate $MRS^i_{x_{kj}q}$ to $SMRT^i_{x_js}$ for all consumers. This requirement can be fulfilled by the price estimated in (11.23), as shown below.

It follows from the user equilibrium condition in (11.22) that

$$\hat{s} = \sum_i \hat{s}^i = \hat{q}, \tag{11.45}$$

where $\hat{q} = \sum_i \bar{q}(\hat{p}, \hat{t})$. Hence, the optimal price of (11.23) equates $MRS^i_{x_{kj}q}$in (11.39) and $SMRT^i_{x_js}$ in (11.44); that is,

$$MRS^i_{\hat{x}_{kj}\hat{q}} = \frac{p_j}{\hat{p} + \hat{v}^i \hat{t}} = \frac{p_j}{SMFC(\hat{s}; \hat{v}) + \hat{v}^i \hat{t}} = SMRT^i_{\hat{x}_j \hat{s}}, \text{ all } i, k, j, \tag{11.46}$$

where $\hat{t} = T(\hat{s}, \hat{c})$, $\hat{v} = \sum_i \hat{v}^i \hat{s}^i / \sum_i \hat{s}^i$, and $\hat{c}$ is the optimal capacity for throughput $\hat{s}$. This equation implies that the resource allocation, which satisfies the four optimality conditions of Theorem11.1, fulfills the overall efficiency condition.

11.3.4 A Graphical Illustration of Pareto-Optimal Resource Allocations

Here we pictorially illustrate that the Pareto-optimal resource allocation satisfying the first best optimality conditions in Theorem 11.1 is located on the production possibility frontier. The first step of the analysis formulates the production possibility frontier of an economy in which a congestion-prone service is traded. The second step shows that the Pareto-optimal resource allocation meets the requirement that the production possibility frontier of the economy and the indifference curves of all consumers are tangent to each other.

Firstly, we specify a hypothetical market that will be analyzed in this subsection. The market is very similar to the monopoly market analyzed in Chap. 8, aside from the one major difference that the government operates a congestion-prone service system. In addition, the details have a number of differences that are introduced so as to simplify forthcoming analyses.

The market analyzed below can be described as follows. First, consumers, who follow the deterministic perception approach, have utilities that depend on two commodities: one kind of prime commodity and one kind of hedonic commodity. Second, the input to the prime commodity is a for-pay congestion-prone service supplied by the government, and the input to the substitute production of the hedonic commodity is composed only of numeraire. Third, the government provides the congestion-prone service through the employment of a service system that is homogeneous of degree zero in both throughput and capacity.

Secondly, we formulate the production possibility frontier of the economy, so that it fulfills the following three requirements. First, all points on the frontier satisfy the constraint for the total resources of the economy. Second, all points on the frontier fulfill the production efficiency conditions introduced in the previous subsections. Third, the explanatory variables of the function that estimates the frontier consist only of the choice variables of all consumers, so that it is feasible to identify the relationship between the frontier and the consumers' indifference curves using the same independent variables.

The monetary value of total resources, introduced in the first requirement, equals the sum of all consumers' full incomes. This total monetary value, denoted by $\sum_i \bar{M}^i$, is

$$\sum_i \bar{M}^i = \sum_i pq^i + \sum_i v^i q^i T(q/c) + \sum_i p_x x^i + \sum_i h^i, \tag{11.47}$$

where p_x is the price of numeraire, which is actually "1". Here, the first term on the right side estimates the total amount of service charges paid by consumers, the second term quantifies the value of total service times consumed by consumers at user equilibrium, the third term represents the total expenditure spent in purchasing numeraire for the substitute production of consumers, and the fourth term is the sum of lump sum taxes levied on consumers.

The monetary value of the total resources, as estimated above, equals the summed input costs of supplier's congestion-prone service productions and consumers' substitute productions. Hence, it follows that

$$\sum_i \bar{M}^i = p_x x_c + \sum_i p_x x^i + \sum_i v^i s^i T(s/c), \tag{11.48}$$

where x_c is the amount of numeraire inputted to the production system for capacity.

By the second requirement, the choice of the government for x_c value in (11.48) satisfies the production efficiency condition for the SWMP in (11.19). This x_c value can be estimated from the function X, defined by

$$x_c = X(s) = \bar{x}_c(\bar{c}(s)). \tag{11.49}$$

The function X is the composite function of $\bar{c}$ and $\bar{x}_c$. The function $\bar{c}$ estimates the solution of c to the optimality condition in (11.24) for an arbitrary value of s, whereas the function $\bar{x}_c$ estimates the solution of x_c to the optimality condition in (11.25) for an arbitrary value of c. Remind that (11.24) and (11.25) are identical to counterpart social optimality conditions for the SCMP of (11.19).

We are now ready to develop the function that estimates the production possibility frontier with the choice variables of consumers. This function, denoted by Z, is developed by substituting the functions X and $\bar{c}$ into (11.48); that is,

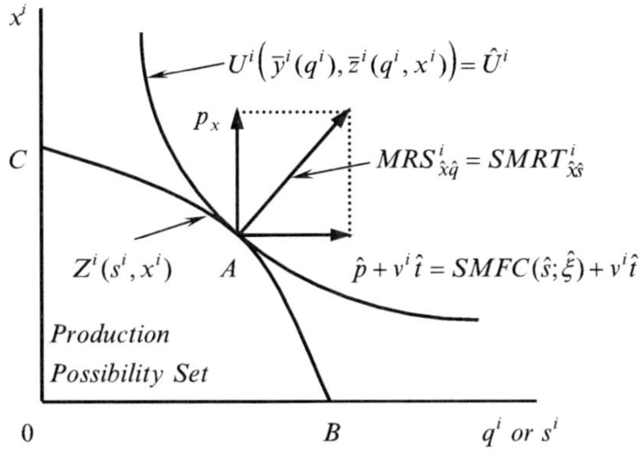

Fig. 11.3 Resource allocation at Pareto optimality

$$Z(s_o, x_o) \equiv p_x X(s) + \sum_i p_x x^i + \sum_i v^i s^i T(s/\bar{c}) - \sum_i M^i = 0, \tag{11.50}$$

where $s_o \equiv (s^1, \cdots, s^I)$ and $x_o \equiv (x^1, \cdots, x^I)$. The function Z depicts the relationship among all the components of $(s_o, x_o) \in \mathbf{R}^{2I}$ on the production possibility frontier.

Thirdly, we schematically illustrate the Pareto-optimal resource allocation as Fig. 11.3. The lower part of the figure depicts the graph of the function Z on the $s^i - x^i$ plane; in contrast, the upper part shows the indifference curve of consumer i's utility. Point A in the figure represents the resource allocation at Pareto optimality under the condition that the optimal consumption $(\hat{q}^k, \hat{x}^k)$, for all $k \neq i$, is predetermined. At that point, the choice of consumer for all i is $(\hat{q}^i, \hat{x}^i)$, and the choice of the operator is $(\hat{s}, X(\hat{s}))$. Moreover, at that point, the indifference curve of consumer i is tangent to the production possibility frontier, as will be proved later.

The production possibility frontier of Fig. 11.3 represents the set of (s^i, x^i), which satisfies the amended form of Z, denoted by Z^i, such that

$$\begin{aligned} Z^i(s^i, x^i) &\equiv p_x X(s^i + S^i) - p_x X(S^i) + p_x x^i + v^i s^i T\big((s^i + S^i)/\bar{c}(s^i + S^i)\big) - \bar{M}^i \\ &= 0, \end{aligned} \tag{11.51}$$

where $S^i \equiv \sum_{k \neq i} \hat{s}^k$. Here, point B represents the choice of consumer i such that $(\bar{M}^i/p, 0)$; in contrast, point C depicts the choice of consumer i such that $(0, \bar{M}^i/p_x)$.

Fourthly, we prove that the Pareto-optimal resource allocation meets the condition that the production possibility frontier of the economy and the indifference curve of all consumers are tangent to each other. To this end, first, we show that the optimal choice of consumer i regarding (x^i, q^i) satisfies the exchange efficiency condition in (11.39). Suppose that the choice of consumer i is $(\hat{x}^i, \hat{q}^i)$, denoted by point A. Then, the indifference curve, which should pass the point $(\hat{x}^i, \hat{q}^i)$, is expressed by

$$U^i\left(\bar{y}^i(q^i), \bar{z}^i(q^i, x^i)\right) = \hat{U}^i, \text{ all } i, \tag{11.52}$$

where $\bar{y}^i(q^i) = a^i q^i$, $\bar{z}^i(q^i, x^i) = b^i \hat{t} q^i + Z^i(x^i)$, $\hat{U}^i = U^i\left(\bar{y}^i(\hat{q}^i), \bar{z}^i(\hat{q}^i, \hat{x}^i)\right)$, and $\hat{t} = T(\hat{s}/\hat{c})$. Note that the term $\hat{t}$ in the demand function $\bar{z}^i$ is not a function of s but a constant, since the consumer is assumed to take the service time as given in making utility-maximizing choices.

The indifference curve defined in (11.52) gives the marginal rate of substitution of x^i for q^i, such that

$$\frac{MU_x^i}{MU_q^i} = \frac{\partial \bar{M}^i}{\partial x^i} \bigg/ \frac{\partial \bar{M}^i}{\partial q^i} = \frac{p_x}{\hat{p} + v^i \hat{t}}, \text{ all } i, \tag{11.53}$$

where $\bar{M}^i = (\hat{p} + v^i \hat{t})\, \hat{q}^i + p_x \hat{x}^i$. This implies that the resource allocation at point A gives the exchange efficiency condition identical to that of (11.39).

We, next, show that the (x_c, s) value at point A fulfills the social production efficiency condition in (11.44). Every point on the frontier should satisfy the social production efficiency conditions in (11.40), (11.41), and (11.43). By these conditions, it holds that

$$\begin{aligned} SMRT_{xs}^i &= \frac{\partial Z(\hat{s}_o, \hat{x}_o)}{\partial x^i} \bigg/ \frac{\partial Z(\hat{s}_o, \hat{x}_o)}{\partial s^i} \\ &= \frac{p_x}{SMFC(\hat{s}; \hat{v}) + v^i T(\hat{s}/\hat{c})}, \text{ all } i, \end{aligned} \tag{11.54}$$

where

$$\begin{aligned} \frac{\partial Z(s_o, x_o)}{\partial s^i} &= p_x \frac{\partial \bar{x}_c(\bar{c})}{\partial c} \frac{\partial \bar{c}}{\partial s^i} + v^i T(s/\bar{c}) + \sum_i v^i s^i \frac{\partial T(s/c = \bar{c})}{\partial s^i} + \sum_i v^i s^i \frac{\partial T(s/\bar{c})}{\partial c} \frac{\partial \bar{c}}{\partial s^i} \\ &= SMFC(s; \hat{v}) + v^i T(s/\bar{c}). \end{aligned}$$

Equation (11.54) implies that the resource allocation represented by point A satisfies the social production efficiency condition in (11.44).

Equations (11.53) and (11.54) show that the collective choice of $\hat{p} = MFC(\hat{s}; \hat{v})$, $\hat{c} = \bar{c}(\hat{s})$, and $\hat{x}_c = \bar{x}_c(\bar{c}(\hat{s}))$ leads to the Pareto-optimal resource allocation such that the production possibility frontier of the economy and the indifference curve of all consumers are tangent to each other. Therefore, at that resource allocation, no one can be better off without making others worse off. In other words, a point outside the production possibility set could give a larger utility to some consumers without changing the decision of others, but, of course, it is impossible to reach such a point. In contrast, a point that does belong to the production possibility set, excluding point A, is attainable, but all such points make some consumers worse off.

11.4 Second Best Choices Under Budget Constraints

11.4.1 Development of Second Best Social Optimality Conditions

Here we analyze a SWMP for the public provision of for-pay public services under the condition that predetermined government expenditures for the public provision are not socially optimal. As the first step, we construct an amendment of the SWMP in Assumption 11.1 to reflect this budget constraint. Subsequently, we develop the approximation of social optimality conditions for this amendment in a manner analogous to that which led to those conditions of Theorem 11.1.

Firstly, we construct the SWMP under budget constraints. Suppose that the government subsidy for the provision of for-pay public services is e units of money, which differ from the socially optimal value. For this case, the amendment of the SWMP in Assumption 11.1, denoted by SW_3, is

$$SW_3(r,p,c,t,\tau,\omega,\psi;e) \equiv \max\left\{W(\bar{U}^1,\cdots,\bar{U}^I)\right\} + \tau\,(t - T(\bar{q},c))$$
$$+\,\omega\Big(\sum_i r^i - e\Big) + \psi(e + p\bar{q} - KC(c)), \qquad (11.55)$$

where e is a certain portion of lump sum tax revenues, spent on public service provisions. This SWMP is analyzed below, under the convention that its solution is $(\widehat{r},\widehat{p},\widehat{c},\widehat{t},\widehat{\tau},\widehat{\omega},\widehat{\psi})$ and that $\widehat{q} \equiv (\widehat{r},\widehat{p},\widehat{t})$, $\widehat{W} \equiv W(\widehat{U}^1,\cdots,\widehat{U}^I)$, and $\widehat{U}^i \equiv U^i(\widehat{y}^i,\widehat{z}^i)$.

The above SWMP has a formulation identical to that of (11.5) except for the different specification of constraints. In this equation, the constraint $\sum_i r^i - e = 0$ depicts that the government channels e units of money from lump sum tax revenues to public service provisions. The other constraint $e + p\bar{q} - KC(c)$ shows that the total expenditure on public service production is the sum of government subsidies, e, and service charge revenues, pq, and that the sum of these two revenues are equal to service production costs, $KC(c)$. It should also be noted that the e value is negative when a certain portion of service charge revenues is used to fund income distribution.

Secondly, we introduce one simplifying assumption, which will apply to forthcoming analyses in this section:

$$v^i \cong \widehat{v}, \text{ all } i. \qquad (11.56)$$

This assumption depicts that all consumers have net-value-of-times approximately identical to one another. By Theorem 6.8, this assumption is equivalent to another assumption that $\widehat{v} \cong \breve{v}$.

Thirdly, we consider the sensitivity of indirect utilities with respect to the control variables of the government. Compared with the SWMP of (11.5), the

SWMP of (11.55) has one additional choice variable of subsidy e. This additional choice variable has no direct relationship to consumers' utility-maximizing decisions. For this reason, the sensitivity analysis of indirect utilities in Lemma 11.1 can apply to forthcoming analyses without any amendment.

Fourthly, we present the marginal social welfare of service time for SW_3 in (11.55). Proceeding with the analysis of SW_3 in a manner analogous to that which led to Lemma 11.2 gives the following.

Lemma 11.3. *Under the assumption (11.56), the solution to SW_3 gives the marginal social welfare loss of service time, $\widehat{\tau}$, such that*

$$\widehat{\tau} \cong \widehat{\psi}\,\widehat{v}\,\widehat{q} \cong \widehat{\psi}\,\breve{v}\,\widehat{q}. \tag{11.57}$$

Proof. It is shown in Appendix D.1 that the exact expression of $\widehat{\tau}$ is

$$\widehat{\tau} = \widehat{\psi}\,\breve{v}\,\widehat{q} + \sum_i \frac{\partial \widehat{W}}{\partial \bar{U}^i}\widehat{\eta}^i(v^i\widehat{q}^i - \breve{v}\widehat{q}^i) \cong \widehat{\psi}\,\widehat{v}\,\widehat{q}. \tag{11.58}$$

It is clear that substituting (11.56) into (11.58) leads to (11.57). □

Fifthly, we develop social optimality conditions for SW_3 in a format analogous to that of Theorem 11.1, through the analysis similar to that which led to that theorem.

Theorem 11.2. *Under the condition (11.56), the solution to SW_3 satisfies the following:*

i. *The optimality condition for income distribution:*

$$-\frac{\partial \widehat{W}}{\partial r^i} = \frac{\partial \widehat{W}}{\partial(\bar{M}^i - r^i)} = \widehat{\omega} + \left(\widehat{\psi} - \widehat{\omega}\right)\widehat{p}\frac{\partial \widehat{q}^i}{\partial r^i} \Big/ E_s(\widehat{q}) \cong \widehat{\omega},\ all\ i \tag{11.59}$$

where

$$E_s(\widehat{q}) = -\sum_i \left(\frac{\partial \hat{q}^i}{\partial p} - \widehat{q}^i\frac{\partial \widehat{q}^i}{\partial r^i}\right) \Big/ \frac{\widehat{q}}{\widehat{p}}. \tag{11.60}$$

ii. *The optimality condition for resource allocation:*

$$\widehat{t} = T(\widehat{q}, \widehat{c}) \tag{11.61}$$

$$\widehat{p}\left(1 - \frac{\widehat{\psi} - \widehat{\omega}}{\widehat{\psi}}\frac{1}{E_s(\widehat{q})}\right) \cong SMFC(\widehat{q}) \tag{11.62}$$

$$MKC(\widehat{c}) \cong -\widehat{v}\,\widehat{q}\frac{\partial \widehat{T}}{\partial c}. \tag{11.63}$$

Proof. The proof is presented in Appendix D.1. Note that approximation errors in (11.62) and (11.63) are introduced by replacing the term $\widehat{\tau}$ with an approximation $\widehat{\omega}\,\widehat{v}\,\widehat{q}$ in (11.57). On the other hand, the last term of (11.59) has a different kind of approximation error caused by the assumption that $\partial \widehat{q}^i / \partial r^i \cong 0$. □

Theorem 11.2 presents the approximations of social optimality conditions for the SWMP under budget constraints. These optimality conditions regarding income distribution and resource allocation are very similar to the counterpart conditions for the case of no budget constraint in Theorem 11.1, except for one major difference regarding the pricing rule. This pricing rule has an expression similar to that of a monopolist that pursues maximum profit. Implications of these optimality conditions are closely examined in the remaining part of this section.

11.4.2 Effect of Non-optimal Subsidies on Social Welfare

Raises in subsidies for the provision of a public service reduce after-tax incomes of general consumers who actually pay the subsidies. Therefore, these raises that expand public consumption reduce the private consumption of general consumers. These changes, in turn, influence resource allocation and thus social welfare. This aspect of governmental choices for the amount of subsidies is analyzed below.

Firstly, we estimate the sensitivity of maximum social welfare indexes with respect to government subsidies. By the envelop theorem for constrained optimization problems, it follows that

$$\frac{\partial SW_3}{\partial e} = -\widehat{\omega} + \widehat{\psi}. \tag{11.64}$$

To determine the economic implications of $\widehat{\omega}$ and $\widehat{\psi}$, it is necessary to distinguish between a change in social welfare indexes for one budget constraint $\sum_i r^i - e_1 = 0$ and the change for the other budget constraint $e_2 + p\,\bar{q} - KC(c) = 0$. It is also necessary to employ the two choice variables e_1 and e_2 so to as distinguish between e values for two different budget constraints, as is true of the above two formulas. Under these conventions, we estimate the sensitivity of maximum social welfare indexes with respect to government subsidies.

Theorem 11.3. *Under the condition* (11.56), *the sensitivities of the maximum social welfare index, expressed by $\widehat{W}$, with respect to e_1 and e_2 are as follows:*

$$\frac{\partial \widehat{W}}{\partial e_1} = -\widehat{\omega} \cong -\sum_i \frac{\partial \widehat{W}}{\partial \bar{U}^i} \frac{\partial \bar{U}^i}{\partial (\bar{M}^i - r^i)} \frac{\partial \widehat{r}^i}{\partial e_1} \tag{11.65}$$

$$\frac{\partial \widehat{W}}{\partial e_2} = \widehat{\psi} \cong \sum_i \frac{\partial \widehat{W}}{\partial \bar{U}^i} \frac{\partial \bar{U}^i}{\partial t} \frac{\partial \widehat{T}}{\partial c} \frac{\partial \widehat{c}}{\partial e}. \tag{11.66}$$

Proof. The second terms of (11.65) and (11.66) are obtained by applying the envelop theorem to SW_3. The third term of (11.65) omits a part of changes in $\widehat{W}$ values, which is caused by changes in $\widehat{p}$ and $\widehat{t}$ values due to a marginal increase in the e_1 value, as explained in Appendix D.2. Theorem 12.2.i indicates that the error caused by this omission for changes in $\widehat{p}$ and $\widehat{t}$ values is negligible, since $\widehat{\omega} \sum_i \partial \widehat{r}^i / \partial e_1 = 1.0$. On the other hand, the third term of (11.66) deletes a part of changes in $\widehat{W}$ value, which is caused by changes in $\widehat{r}^i$ and $\widehat{p}$ values due to a marginal increase in the e_2 value. The error caused by this deletion is also negligible, as shown in Appendix D.2. □

The term $\widehat{\omega}$ is the Lagrange multiplier for the constraint $\sum_i r^i - e_1 = 0$. This constraint depicts that the total revenue of lump sum taxes, $\sum_i r^i$, is larger than government expenditures, which are redistributed to consumers for the purpose of income distribution, by the e_1 unit of money. Therefore, a one-unit increase in e_1 value reduces the amount of government funds redistributed to consumer by one unit. This increase also brings about a one-unit decrease in the sum of general consumers' after-tax incomes. This increase is equivalent to a one-unit decrease in the sum of resources consumed in the private sector. Therefore, the Lagrange multiplier $\widehat{\omega}$ can be interpreted as *the marginal social welfare of private consumption*. Further, the third term of (11.65) indicates that the marginal social welfare loss $-\widehat{\omega}$ is approximately equal to the decrease in the social welfare index, which reflects the sum of decreases in consumer utilities due to a one-unit decrease in government expenditures for income distribution.

The other term $\widehat{\psi}$ is the Lagrange multiplier for the budget constraint $e_2 + p\bar{q} - KC(c) = 0$. This constraint reflects that a one-unit increase in government subsidies e_2 accompanies a one-unit increase in government spending on public service provision. This increase is equivalent to a one-unit increase in investments on the expansion of service system capacity. Hence, it can be said that the multiplier $\widehat{\psi}$ represents *the marginal social welfare of government expenditures for public service provision,* a synonym of *the marginal social welfare of public consumption*. Further, the third term of (11.66) shows that this marginal social welfare gain $\widehat{\psi}$ is approximately equal to increases in the social welfare index, which is brought about by reductions in service time due to an increase in service system capacity for a one-unit increase in government expenditures.

Based on the above discussion, we can interpret the term $\partial SW_3/\partial e$ in (11.64) as below. The term $-\widehat{\omega} + \widehat{\psi}$ in that equation reflects two opposite effects of increases in one unit of government subsidies for public service provision: the negative effect of a one-unit decrease in private consumption, quantified by $-\widehat{\omega}$; and the positive effect of a one-unit increase in government spending for public service provision, estimated by $\widehat{\psi}$. Therefore, the term $\partial SW_3/\partial e$ estimates *the net change in marginal social welfare,* which is brought about by the governmental choice that channelizes one unit of funds for income distribution to subsidies for public service provision.

Subsequently, we analyze the sensitivities of Lagrange multipliers $\widehat{\omega}$ and $\widehat{\psi}$ with respect to subsidy e. Among various combinations of $\widehat{\omega}$ and $\widehat{\psi}$, the sensitivities of some combinations, which have definite signs and which are used as inputs to subsequent analyses, are presented below.

Theorem 11.4. *The Lagrange multipliers $\widehat{\omega}$ and $\widehat{\psi}$ in Theorem 11.2 have sensitivities with respect to e such that*

$$\frac{\partial \widehat{\omega}}{\partial e} > 0, \qquad \textit{and} \quad \widehat{\omega} \begin{matrix} < \\ = \\ > \end{matrix} \hat{\omega}, \qquad \textit{if } e \begin{matrix} < \\ = \\ > \end{matrix} \hat{e} \tag{11.67}$$

$$\frac{\partial (\widehat{\psi} - \widehat{\omega})}{\partial e} < 0, \quad \textit{and} \quad \widehat{\omega} - \widehat{\psi} \begin{matrix} < \\ = \\ > \end{matrix} 0, \quad \textit{if } e \begin{matrix} < \\ = \\ > \end{matrix} \hat{e} \tag{11.68}$$

$$\frac{\partial}{\partial e}\left(\frac{\widehat{\omega}}{\widehat{\psi}}\right) > 0, \quad \textit{and} \quad \frac{\widehat{\omega}}{\widehat{\psi}} \begin{matrix} < \\ = \\ > \end{matrix} 1.0, \quad \textit{if } e \begin{matrix} < \\ = \\ > \end{matrix} \hat{e}. \tag{11.69}$$

Proof. Firstly, prove (11.67). The functions W and $\bar{U}^i$ are both increasing and concave, respectively, in $\bar{U}^i$ and $\bar{M}^i - r^i$. (i) This implies that the function W is increasing and concave in $-r^i$, for all i. (ii) By the second equality of (11.65), the fact (i) implies that the term $\widehat{\omega}$ is monotonically increasing in e, as depicted in the first inequality of (11.67). (iii) In addition, if $e = \hat{e}$, Theorem 11.1 indicates that $\widehat{\omega} = \hat{\omega}$. By facts ii) and (iii), the second inequalities of (11.67) follow.

Secondly, prove (11.68). (i) If $e = \hat{e}$, by Theorem 11.1, it holds that $\hat{\psi} - \hat{\omega} = 0$. (ii), If $e < \hat{e}$, the term $\widehat{\psi}$ should be greater than $\widehat{\omega}$; otherwise, increases in e would decrease the net social welfare index. (iii) The argument (ii) can be extended to changes in an arbitrary e such that $e < e_o$ and $e_o < \hat{e}$. Hence, the first inequality of (11.68) follows. Further, under condition (i), the first inequality implies the second inequality.

Thirdly, prove (11.69). (i) It is clear that $\widehat{\psi}/\widehat{\omega} = (\widehat{\psi} - \widehat{\omega})/\widehat{\omega} + 1$. (i) By the facts that $\partial\widehat{\omega}/\partial e > 0$ and $\partial(\widehat{\psi} - \widehat{\omega})/\partial e < 0$, it follows that $\partial((\widehat{\psi} - \widehat{\omega})/\widehat{\omega})/\partial e < 0$. Facts (i) and (ii) imply that $\partial(\widehat{\psi}/\widehat{\omega})/\partial e < 0$, and thus that $\partial(\widehat{\omega}/\widehat{\psi})/\partial e > 0$. □

The findings of Theorem 11.3 are graphically represented as Fig. 11.4. The figure depicts that the marginal social welfare of private consumption, $\widehat{\omega}$, always is increasing in e. It also depicts that the net marginal social welfare, $\widehat{\psi} - \widehat{\omega}$, is decreasing in e. However, it is not certain that the marginal social welfare of government consumption, $\widehat{\psi}$, is always decreasing in e, because the slope $\partial\widehat{c}/\partial e$ in (11.66) can be either positive or negative.

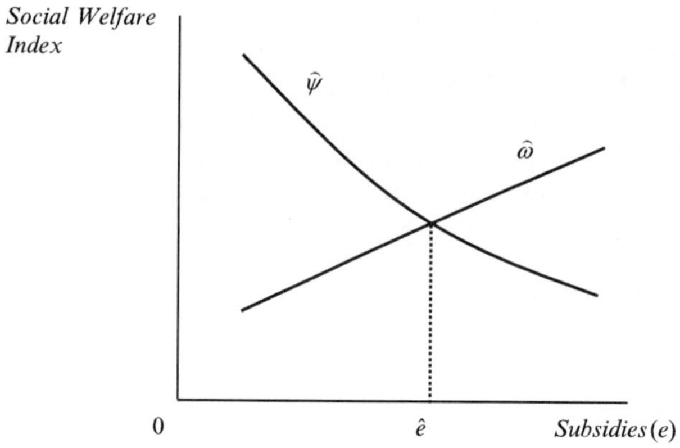

Fig. 11.4 Relationship between $\widehat{\omega}(e)$ and $\widehat{\psi}(e)$

Further, Fig. 11.4 depicts the following. First, if subsidies e are less than the optimum $\hat{e}$, the marginal social welfare of private consumptions, $\widehat{\omega}$, is smaller than that of government expenditures, $\widehat{\psi}$. This implies that social welfare can be improved by increasing public consumptions for public service provision. Second, in contrast, if subsidies e are greater than optimum, the term $\widehat{\omega}$ is larger than $\widehat{\psi}$. Therefore, reductions in public consumption improve social welfare. Third, if the subsidy equals the first best optimum $\hat{e}$, the marginal social welfare of private consumption also equals that of government consumption.

11.4.3 The Effect of Non-optimal Subsidies on Governmental Choices

Suppose that, for some reasons, the government cannot allocate sufficient funds for the provision of a public service. In this circumstance, the desirable policy is involves choosing a price larger than the first best price, while operating a capacity less than the first best. The validity and implications of this assertion are presented below.

Firstly, we introduce another simplifying assumption, in addition to that of (11.56), which will apply to forthcoming analyses:

$$\frac{\partial E_s(\widehat{q})}{\partial p} = -\frac{\partial}{\partial p}\left(\sum_i \left(\frac{\partial \hat{q}^i}{\partial p} - \hat{q}^i \frac{\partial \hat{q}^i}{\partial r^i}\right) \Big/ \frac{\widehat{q}}{\widehat{p}}\right) \cong 0. \tag{11.70}$$

This condition implies that demand elasticity for the substitution effect, $E_s(\widehat{q})$, is constant on the relevant region of p.

Secondly, we estimate the sensitivities $\partial\widehat{p}/\partial e$ and $\partial\widehat{c}/\partial e$ through analyses of the pricing rule of (11.62) and the investment rule of (11.63). To facilitate the analyses, the pricing rule in (11.62) is expressed, as below:

$$\widehat{p}G \cong SMFC(\widehat{q}), \tag{11.71}$$

where

$$G = 1 - \frac{\widehat{\psi} - \widehat{\omega}}{\widehat{\psi}} \frac{1}{E_s(\widehat{q})}. \tag{11.72}$$

Differentiating (11.71) and (11.63) with respect to e, and reorganizing the preceding outcome gives

$$\begin{pmatrix} \frac{\partial SMFC}{\partial \widehat{q}}\frac{\partial \widehat{q}}{\partial p} - G & \widehat{v}\frac{\partial SMFC}{\partial \widehat{q}}\frac{\partial \widehat{q}}{\partial p}\frac{\partial \widehat{T}}{\partial c} \\ \widehat{v}\frac{\partial \widehat{q}}{\partial p}\frac{\partial \widehat{T}}{\partial c} & \frac{\partial^2 KC}{\partial c^2} + \widehat{v}\widehat{q}\frac{\partial^2 \widehat{T}}{\partial c^2} + \widehat{v}^2\frac{\partial \widehat{q}}{\partial p}\left(\frac{\partial \widehat{T}}{\partial c}\right)^2 \end{pmatrix} \begin{pmatrix} \frac{\partial \widehat{p}}{\partial e} \\ \frac{\partial \widehat{c}}{\partial e} \end{pmatrix} = \begin{pmatrix} \widehat{p}\frac{\partial G}{\partial e} \\ 0 \end{pmatrix} \tag{11.73}$$

Note that the term $\widehat{v}\partial\widehat{q}/\partial p$ on the first raw of the left side follows from (11.4) and (11.56) such that $\partial\widehat{q}/\partial t = \breve{v}\partial\widehat{q}/\partial p \cong \widehat{v}\partial\widehat{q}/\partial p$. From this matrix equation, we deduce the following.

Theorem 11.5. *Under the assumption* (11.70), *the second best price* $\widehat{p}$ *and the second best capacity* $\widehat{c}$ *in Theorem 11.2 satisfy the following:*

$$\frac{\partial \widehat{p}}{\partial e} \langle\, 0, \quad \frac{\partial \widehat{c}}{\partial e} \rangle\, 0, \quad \frac{\partial \widehat{q}}{\partial e} \rangle\, 0, \quad if \quad \frac{\partial SMFC(\widehat{q})}{\partial \widehat{q}} \rangle\, Z,$$

where

$$Z = G\left(\frac{\partial^2 KC}{\partial c^2} + \widehat{v}\widehat{q}\frac{\partial^2 \widehat{T}}{\partial c^2} + \widehat{v}^2\frac{\partial \widehat{q}}{\partial p}\left(\frac{\partial \widehat{T}}{\partial c}\right)^2\right) \Big/ \left(\frac{\partial^2 KC}{\partial c^2} + \widehat{v}\widehat{q}\frac{\partial^2 \widehat{T}}{\partial c^2}\right)\frac{\partial \widehat{q}}{\partial p} \langle\, 0.$$

Proof. The signs of terms in (11.73) are as follows:

$$\begin{pmatrix} ? & ? \\ + & + \end{pmatrix}\begin{pmatrix} \cdot \\ \cdot \end{pmatrix} = \begin{pmatrix} + \\ 0 \end{pmatrix}, \tag{11.74}$$

as shown in Appendix D.3. Further, if $Z \langle 0$, the determinant of the matrix on the left side of (11.73) is negative, as also shown in the appendix. Hence, by Cramer's rule, (11.74) implies the inequalities in the theorem.

Note that most public services satisfy the condition that $\partial SMFC/\partial \overset{\frown}{q} \rangle Z$, since Z is negative. Note also that, if $\partial SMFC/\partial \overset{\frown}{q} = Z$, the matrix on the left side of (11.73) becomes singular. Further, if $\partial SMFC/\partial \overset{\frown}{q} \langle Z$, it follows from (11.74) that $\partial \overset{\frown}{p}/\partial e \rangle 0$, $\partial \overset{\frown}{c}/\partial e \langle 0$, and $\partial \overset{\frown}{q}/\partial e \langle 0$, all of which contradicts our economic sense. □

Theorem 11.5 shows that most public service systems have sensitivities such that $\partial \overset{\frown}{p}/\partial e \langle 0$ and $\partial \overset{\frown}{c}/\partial e \rangle 0$. These sensitivities imply that, as subsidies grow, second best prices gradually decrease, while second best capacities increase. They also imply the following:

$$\overset{\frown}{p} \underset{\langle}{\overset{\rangle}{-}} SMFC(\overset{\frown}{q}),\ \overset{\frown}{p} \underset{\langle}{\overset{\rangle}{-}} \hat{p},\ \overset{\frown}{c} \underset{\langle}{\overset{\rangle}{-}} \hat{c},\ if\ e \underset{\rangle}{\overset{\langle}{-}} \hat{e}. \tag{11.75}$$

This equation depicts that, when subsidies are less than optimum, second best prices are greater not only than the social marginal full cost for the demand at that price but also than the first best price. Moreover, when subsidies are less than optimum, second best capacities are less than the first best capacity.

Fig. 11.5 graphically illustrates the relationship between $\overset{\frown}{p}$ and $SMFC(\overset{\frown}{q})$ in the theorem. In the figure, the graph of $SMFC(\overset{\frown}{q})$ for varying e values is drawn by reflecting that the demand function $\overset{\frown}{q}\ (\equiv \bar{q}(\overset{\frown}{r}, \overset{\frown}{p}, \overset{\frown}{T}))$ is increasing in e, as shown in the theorem. The other graph for the second best price $\overset{\frown}{p}$ is developed by applying the relationship of (11.71) in which the function G is increasing in e; that is

$$\frac{\partial G}{\partial e} = \frac{\partial}{\partial e}\left(\frac{\overset{\frown}{\omega}}{\overset{\frown}{\psi}}\right)\frac{1}{E_s(\overset{\frown}{q})} \rangle 0. \tag{11.76}$$

Here, $\partial(\overset{\frown}{\omega}/\overset{\frown}{\psi}/\partial e \rangle 0$, as shown in (11.69).

The figure is drawn so that it reflects the following. First, if $e \langle \hat{e}$, the second best price $\overset{\frown}{p}$ is greater than the first best price $\hat{p}$ and the marginal cost $SMFC(\overset{\frown}{q})$; in contrast, if $e \rangle \hat{e}$, the price $\overset{\frown}{p}$ is less than $\hat{p}$ and $SMFC(\overset{\frown}{q})$, as shown in (11.75). Second, the difference $\overset{\frown}{p} - SMFC(\overset{\frown}{q})$ is usually decreasing in subsidies e, because the function G is increasing in e, as proved in (11.76). Fourth, since $G(\hat{e}) = 1$, the two functions $\overset{\frown}{p}$ and $SMFC(\overset{\frown}{q})$ intersect at $\hat{e}$. Fifth, therefore, if $e \langle \hat{e}$, the difference $\overset{\frown}{p} - SMFC(\overset{\frown}{q})$ usually is positive; in contrast, if $e \rangle \hat{e}$, this difference is negative.

Thirdly, we analyze the effect of differences in $\partial SMFC/\partial \overset{\frown}{q}$ values on the sensitivities $\partial \overset{\frown}{p}/\partial e$ and $\partial \overset{\frown}{c}/\partial e$. The term $\partial SMFC/\partial \overset{\frown}{q}$ is included on the left side of (11.73). Hence, it is possible to deduce the effect of differences in $\partial SMFC/\partial \overset{\frown}{q}$ values on the sensitivities $\partial \overset{\frown}{p}/\partial e$ and $\partial \overset{\frown}{c}/\partial e$ from (11.73). To be specific, by Cramer's rule, these two sensitivities are both inversely proportional to the determinant of the matrix on the left side of (11.73). The determinant is negative, as

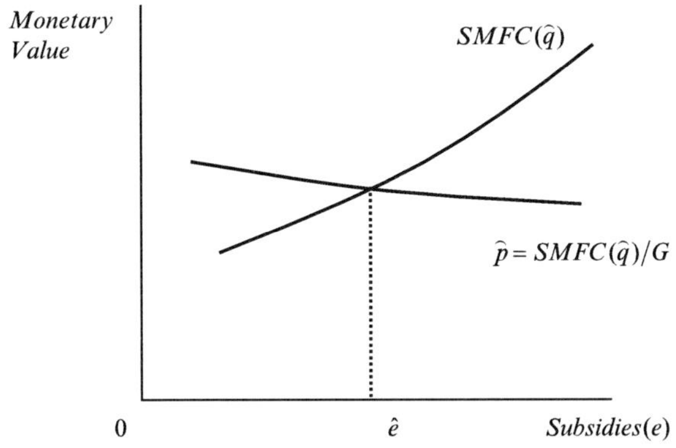

Fig. 11.5 Effect of changes in subsidies on second best prices

shown in Appendix D.3. Further, if $\partial SMFC/\partial\hat{q}$ is positive (or negative), the term $\partial^2 KC/\partial c^2$ is also positive (or negative), as proved in Sect. 7.2. Therefore, as $\partial SMFC/\partial\hat{q}$ increases, the absolute value of the determinant of the matrix becomes larger.

From these facts, we can deduce the following: as $\partial SMFC/\partial\hat{q}$ increases, the sensitivity $\partial\hat{p}/\partial e$ gradually increases and approaches zero but the term $\partial\hat{c}/\partial e$ decreases and also approaches zero. These findings for $\partial\hat{p}/\partial e$ and $\partial\hat{c}/\partial e$ are graphically illustrated in Figs. 11.5 and 11.6, respectively. In these figures, System 1 represents a public service system that exhibits increasing returns in throughput, and thus satisfies the condition that $\partial SMFC/\partial\hat{q} \langle 0$; in contrast, System 2 is a service system that has non-increasing returns, and thereby satisfies the condition that $\partial SMFC/\partial\hat{q} \rangle 0$.

Finally, we analyze the effect of the returns-to-scale of service systems on financial outcomes. Suppose that a government choice for expenditures e is less

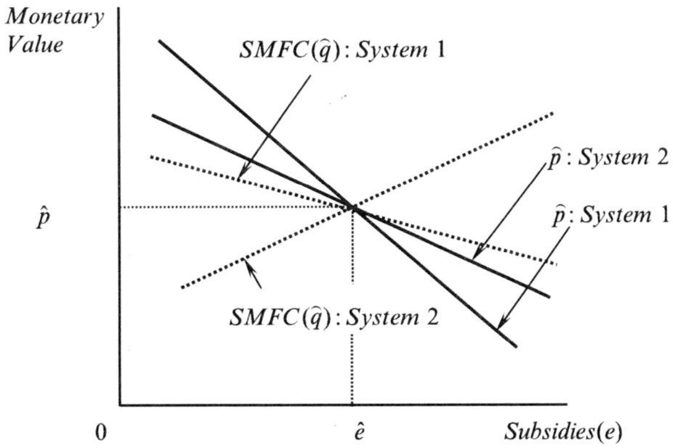

Fig. 11.6 Effect of returns-to-scale on second best prices

Fig. 11.7 Effect of returns-to-scale on second best capacities

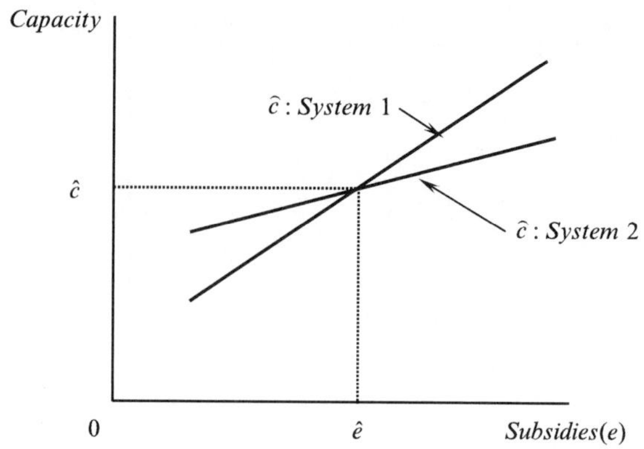

than the optimum $\hat{e}$. In this circumstance, Fig. 11.6 shows that the second best price of System 1 with increasing returns is higher than that of System 2 with decreasing returns. In contrast, Fig. 11.7 indicates the second best capacity of System 1 is smaller than the capacity of System 2. These two facts do not mean that System 1 places a financial burden on the government that is less than that imposed by System 2. Instead, System 1 calls for financial burdens larger than those required by System 2.

The reason is as follows. In the case of System 1, the price equal to social marginal full cost would result in a deficit, as shown in Subsect. 10.3.3. Therefore, the choice of expenditures e that is less than the optimum $\hat{e}$ implies that the government subsidy is less than the optimal deficit to maximize social welfare. In the case of System 2, the price equal to the social marginal full cost would yield a profit, as also pointed out in Subsect. 10.3.3. Hence, the choice of e less than $\hat{e}$ connotes that the profit channeled to funds for income distribution is greater than would be socially optimal.

Chapter 12
Policies for Public Services under Competition

12.1 Introduction

This chapter is concerned with economic analyses of a congestion-prone public service under competition, as a sequel to the previous chapter for a public service under no competition. The economic analyses of a public service under competition address public policies under decision-making environments that fundamentally differ from those for a public service under no competition. The former should account for the fact that government choices regarding the price and capacity of a public service influence demands for competing public and private services and, therefore, the resource allocation of entire markets. Further, it should reflect the reality that most public services face competition from other public and/or private services that have prices and capacities that cannot be controlled by the government.

Economic analyses of a public service in competition with other substitutes, which cannot be controlled by the government, explicitly account for the interdependency of demands between the public and its competing services in preceding studies such as Baumol and Bradford (1970) and Harberger (1971). These studies search for optimal government policies for the congestion-free public service under the following premise: the social benefit that must be considered in policy analyses is the sum of consumers' surplus for the public service and its substitute, both of which are the independent ingredients of consumer utility. Thus, these studies suggest a second best price, which differs from Pareto-optimal price, as the choice to maximize net social benefit.

This chapter also considers economic analyses for a congestion-prone public service under competition. For these analyses, this chapter applies the user equilibrium approach for the modeling of governmental decision-making problems. To be specific, this chapter formulates governmental decision-making problems as the SWMPs, all of which are extensions of the SWMP described in the previous chapter for a public service under no competition.

D.J. Moon, *Congestion-Prone Services Under Quality Competition*,
Advances in Spatial Science, DOI 10.1007/978-3-642-20189-9_12,

Importantly, some SWMPs considered in this chapter yield optimal public policies that do not account for the interdependency of demand between a public service and its competing services. Such a distinctive feature of these SWMPs stems from the use of consumer demand functions under the random perception approach. Under the random perception approach, each option captures a market demand segment that can be served most economically by the option. Further, the utility of a consumer who chooses a particular public service is independent of the presence of competing substitutes; that is, the competing services are not the ingredients of consumer utility. Therefore, it is not always necessary to consider the interdependency of demand when searching for socially optimal policies.

If optimal policies for a public service do not need to account for resource allocations for all competing services, the policies can be a first best policy, which results in a Pareto-optimal resource allocation in the submarket for the public service. In contrast, if optimal policies should consider resource allocations for competing services, the policies should be a second best one, which leads to a resource allocation that differs from the Pareto-optimal one. However, it is not straightforward to determine the condition under which optimal policies for a public service should account for the presence of competing services.

For this reason, the present study determines this condition by testing a number of SWMPs under the user equilibrium approach. The tested SWMPs are mainly differentiated from one another by types of competing services. The types of competing services considered in this study are distinguished by the three factors that influence the values of choice variables for a public service in the SWMPs: the ownership of competing services, grouped into public and private services; the feasibility of the government to control the prices and capacities of competing services; and the availability of knowledge for competing service demands to the government.

We in this chapter test a limited number of the SWMPs among from all possible SWMPs, each of which reflects a different combination of the three factors identified above. Mathematically, we can imagine a quite large number of possible SWMPs. However, economically, only a few numbers of combinations can reasonably describe real decision-making environments.

To reflect this reality, the SWMPs tested in this chapter are modeled under the following postulates. First, governmental ownership of competing services is a prerequisite for the government to control both prices and capacities of the services. Second, because of political and/or technical constraints, governmental ownership alone does not guarantee its control of competing services. Third, the government directly manages the revenues and expenditures for only competing services that the government owns. Fourth, the government knows and utilizes customer reaction only to competing services the government owns when choosing the price and capacity of a given public service.

Under these postulates, we construct four different SWMPs analyzed in Sects. 12.2 and 12.3. Analyses of these governmental decision-making problems focus on presenting answers to the following two topics. The first topic determines the condition under which the government must pursue a first best policy for a given public service without accounting for inefficient resource allocations in submarkets for competing services. The second topic compares and contrasts the second best policy of the present study and that policy suggested in the preceding studies.

Sect. 12.2 analyzes one SWMP for a government that provides multiple options for offering the same kind of qualitative choice service under the no technical and financial restriction. The economy considered in the SWMP is identical to a market in which multiple private services compete with one another, except for ownership of services. Therefore, the solution for this SWMP depicts the highest level of social welfare for a market economy under the hypothetical circumstance such that the government could completely control the prices and capacities of all private services in competition for the sake of maximum social welfare.

Sect. 12.3 tests three different SWMPs for a public service under competition so as to show the following. First, the second best policy is applicable only to a public service that competes with other public services having prices and capacities uncontrollable by the government. Second, in contrast, the first best policy for a public service in competition with private services constitutes necessary conditions for maximum social welfare in market economies, irrespective of resource allocation efficiency in submarkets for competing private services.

Finally, analyses in this chapter will be utilized as a key input to subsequent analyses in the following chapter. The main theme of the next chapter assesses marketwise resource allocation efficiency for a service market under quality competition. This theme must consider resource allocation efficiency for all submarkets constituting the entire market. In this circumstance, the SWMP can give useful guidelines to judge marketwise resource allocation efficiency, as will be discussed in the following chapter.

12.2 Multiple Public Services in Competition under Government Control

12.2.1 Sensitivities of Utility Maximization Problems

The SWMPs analyzed in this chapter consider public policies for the provision of public services that compete with other public and/or private services. To accommodate competition, it is necessary to use utility maximization problems under the random perception approach of Assumptions 4.1 and 4.2, rather than the deterministic approach adopted in the previous chapter. For this random perception approach, we here iterate sensitivity analyses for the utility-maximizing choice of consumers in a manner similar to that described in Subsect. 11.2.2.

Suppose that, under mixed competition, M options, which belong to $L\,(\leq M)$ heterogeneous service groups, offer services differentiated from one another by service quality. Suppose also that some options are provided by public agencies and others are provided by private firms. In these circumstances, consumer choices of one option from among M options are affected only by the service quality of options, irrespective of ownership. Hence, the stochastic utility maximization problem of consumer i under Assumptions 4.1 and 4.2 can be formulated as follows:

$$E\{L_1^i(q^i,x^i,y^i,z^i,\lambda^i,\mu^i,\eta^i;\ r^i,p,t)\} \equiv E\Big\{\max\ \{U^i(y^i,z^i)\}\ . \\ +\lambda^i\sum_m(a_m^i q_m^i - y^i) + \sum_k \mu_k^i(Z_k^i(x_k^i) + \beta_{km}^i t_m q_m^i - z_k^i) \\ +\eta^i\left(\bar{M}^i - r^i - \sum_m(p_m + w^i t_m)\,q_m^i - \sum_{kj} p_j x_{kj}^i\right)\Big\}. \tag{12.1}$$

This stochastic utility maximization problem is identical to that of (4.4), except for the inclusion of lump sum tax r^i and the deletion of consumer time t_k in Z_k^i.

The above utility maximization problem gives the demand function that of m, which estimates the expected value of the deterministic demand function $\bar{q}_m^i$ with respect to random net-value-of-time vector $\xi \equiv (\xi_1,\cdots,\xi_L)$, denoted by Q_m^i. For this individual demand function, the market demand function can be expressed in the following three different ways:

$$Q_m(r,p,t) = \sum_i Q_m^i(r^i,p,t) = \sum_i E\{\bar{q}_m^i\},\ \text{all } m, \tag{12.2}$$

all of which are used interchangeably in subsequent analyses.

Subsequently, we estimate the sensitivities of the expected indirect utility function, $E\{\bar{U}^i\}(\equiv E\{U^i(\bar{y}^i,\bar{z}^i)\})$, with respect to government control variables, under the assumption that option m is operated by the government. We estimate the sensitivities in a manner analogous to that used to estimate those of the deterministic indirect utility function in Lemma 11.1, and thus have the following.

Lemma 12.1. *The sensitivities of the expected indirect utility function $E\{\bar{U}^i\}$ with respect to r^i, p and t are*

$$\frac{\partial E\{\bar{U}^i\}}{\partial r^i} = -E\{\bar{\eta}^i\},\ \frac{\partial E\{\bar{U}^i\}}{\partial p_m} = -E\{\bar{\eta}^i\bar{q}_m^i\},\ \frac{\partial E\{\bar{U}^i\}}{\partial t_m} = -E\{\bar{\eta}^i\xi_m^i\bar{q}_m^i\},\ \textit{all } i.$$

Proof. We present the proof of the above three equations with an example of $\partial E\{\bar{U}^i\}/\partial r^i$. (i) It is clear that $\partial E\{\bar{U}^i\}/\partial r^i = E\{\partial\bar{U}^i/\partial r^i\}$. By point-wise Kuhn-Tucker conditions for $E\{L_o\}$ in Lemma 4.1, it follows that $\partial\bar{U}^i/\partial r^i = \bar{\eta}^i$, for all ξ. (ii) Hence, $E\{\partial\bar{U}^i/\partial r^i\} = E\{\bar{\eta}^i\}$. By (i) and (ii), the assertion follows. □

Finally, we introduce three different averages for net-value-of-times. The first is the social value-of-service-time, denoted by $\hat{\xi}_m$ or $\widehat{\xi}_m$, such that

$$\hat{\xi}_m \text{ or } \widehat{\xi}_m = \sum_i E\{\, \xi_m \bar{q}^i_m\} \Big/ \sum_i E\{\, \bar{q}^i_m\}. \tag{12.3}$$

The second is the private value-of-service-time, expressed by $\breve{\xi}_m$, such that

$$\breve{\xi}_m = \frac{\partial Q_m}{\partial t_m} \Big/ \frac{\partial Q_m}{\partial p_m}. \tag{12.4}$$

The last is the private value-of-service-time for cross partial derivatives, denoted by $\breve{\xi}_{mn}$, such that

$$\breve{\xi}_{mn} = \frac{\partial Q_m}{\partial t_n} \Big/ \frac{\partial Q_m}{\partial p_n}. \tag{12.5}$$

The formulas that estimate $\partial Q_m/\partial t_n$ and $\partial Q_m/\partial p_n$ are presented in Theorems 5.2, 5.5 and 5.11 for the cases of quantitative, qualitative competition, and mixed competition, respectively.

12.2.2 Development of Social Optimality Conditions

Here we analyze the SWMP for the special case when all service options are managed by the government. One example of this special case occurs in the case of an urban corridor where transportation service is provided by a collection of transportation systems composed of multiple highway routes and more than one public transit mode. For this case, social optimality conditions are developed below.

Firstly, we develop the SWMP analyzed here. This SWMP is identical to that of Assumption 11.1, except for the following two differences. First, the objective function of the SWMP is replaced by the expected social welfare function, defined by $W(E\{\bar{U}^1\}, \cdots, E\{\bar{U}^I\})$. Second, the government is assumed to be able to accurately forecast the effect of its decision on the marketwise user equilibrium condition such that $t_m - T_m(Q_m, c_m) = 0$, for all m.

Incorporating these two differences into the deterministic SWMP in (11.5) gives the stochastic version, denoted by SW_o, such that

$$SW_o(r, x, p, c, t, \kappa, \tau, \omega) \equiv \max\left\{ W(E\{\bar{U}^1\}, \cdots, E\{\bar{U}^I\})\right\} + \sum_m \kappa_m(F_m(x_m) - c_m)$$
$$+ \sum_m \tau_m(t_m - T_m(Q_m, c_m)) + \omega\left(\sum_i r^i + \sum_m p_m Q_m - \sum_{mj} p_j x_{mj}\right). \tag{12.6}$$

Here, each of unknowns p, c, t, κ, and τ is a vector in $\mathbf{R}^{\mathrm{M}}$, but x is a vector in $\mathbf{R}^{\mathrm{JM}}$. For example, p stands for $(p^1, \cdots, p^M)$. Let also the solution of SW_o be $(\hat{r}, \hat{x}, \hat{p}, \hat{c}, \hat{t}, \hat{\kappa}, \hat{\tau}, \hat{\omega})$.

Secondly, we introduce simplifying assumptions to be applied in forthcoming analyses of the above SWMP:

$$E\{\hat{\eta}^i \hat{q}^i_m\} \cong E\{\hat{\eta}^i\} E\{\hat{q}^i_m\}, \text{ and } E\{\hat{\eta}^i \xi^i_m \hat{q}^i_m\} \cong E\{\hat{\eta}^i\} E\{\xi^i_m \hat{q}^i_m\}. \tag{12.7}$$

These two assumptions depict the relationships between the functions $\hat{\eta}^i$ and $\hat{q}^i_m$ for the varying values of random net-value-of-times ξ^i_m. These two approximate relationships hold when the marginal utility of income $\hat{\eta}^i$, for all i, is approximately constant, irrespective of (p, t) values. This implies that the utility function $\overline{U}^i$ is not strictly concave but rather linear in income.

Thirdly, we develop first order conditions for SW_o in (12.6) with respect to government control variables. We present these first order conditions in Appendix D.4. For example, the condition for r^i is

$$\begin{aligned}\frac{\partial SW_o}{\partial r^i} &= -\frac{\partial \hat{W}}{\partial E\{\bar{U}^i\}} E\{\hat{\eta}^i\} - \sum_n \hat{\tau}_n \frac{\partial \hat{T}_n}{\partial Q_n} \frac{\partial \hat{Q}^i_n}{\partial r^i} + \hat{\omega}\left(1 + \sum_n \hat{p}_n \frac{\partial \hat{Q}^i_n}{\partial r^i}\right)\\ &= 0, \text{ all } i.\end{aligned} \tag{12.8}$$

Arranging these first order conditions in a manner analogous to that used to prove Lemma 11.2 yields the following marginal social welfare of service time.

Lemma 12.2. *Under condition* (12.7), *the solution to SW_o gives the marginal social welfare loss of service time t_m, expressed by $\hat{\tau}_m$, such that $\hat{\tau}_m = \hat{\omega}\ \hat{\bar{\xi}}_m \hat{Q}_m$, for all m.*

Proof. See Appendix D.4. □

Fourthly, we analyze the SCMP, which is a dual of SW_o in (12.6). This SCMP for service system m, denoted by Z^o_m, is

$$\begin{aligned}Z^o_m(x_m, c_m, t_m, \kappa_m, \tau_m; s_m, \bar{\xi}_m) \equiv \min &\left\{\sum_j p_j x_{mj} + t_m \sum_i \bar{\xi}^i_m s^i_m\right\}\\ &+ \kappa_m\left(c_m - F_m(x_m)\right) + \tau_m(T_m(s_m, c_m) - t_m)\end{aligned} \tag{12.9}$$

where,

$$s_m = \sum_i s^i_m = \sum_i Q^i_m(p, t) \tag{12.10}$$

$$\bar{\xi}^i_m = E\{\xi_m \bar{q}^i_m\}/E\{\bar{q}^i_m\} \tag{12.11}$$

$$\bar{\xi}_m = \sum_i \bar{\xi}^i_m s^i_m / s_m. \tag{12.12}$$

Note that the term $\bar{\xi}_m$ represents the social value-of-service-time for an arbitrary Q_m value; in contrast, the term $\hat{\xi}_m$ in (12.3) is the value for a specific demand $\hat{Q}_m$.

The above SCMP gives the social marginal full cost $SMFC_m(Q_m)$, such that

$$SMFC_m(Q_m) = \bar{\xi}_m Q_m \frac{\partial T_m(Q_m, \bar{c}_m)}{\partial Q_m}, \text{ all } m. \tag{12.13}$$

Using the above results, we develop social optimality conditions for SW_o in a manner analogous to that used to develop Theorem 11.1.

Theorem 12.1. *Under condition (12.7), the solution to SW_o simultaneously satisfies the following conditions.*

i. *The optimality condition for income distribution:*

$$-\frac{\partial \hat{W}}{\partial r^i} = \frac{\partial \hat{W}}{\partial (\bar{M}^i - r^i)} = \hat{\omega}, \text{ all } i. \tag{12.14}$$

ii. *The optimality condition for resource allocation:*

$$\hat{t}_m - T_m(\hat{Q}_m, \hat{c}_m) = 0, \textit{ all } m \tag{12.15}$$

$$\hat{p}_m = SMFC_m(\hat{Q}_m), \textit{ all } m \tag{12.16}$$

$$MKC_m(\hat{c}_m) = -\hat{\xi}_m \hat{Q}_m \frac{\partial \hat{T}_m}{\partial c_m}, \textit{ all } m \tag{12.17}$$

$$MKC_m(\hat{c}_m) = p_j \Big/ \frac{\partial F_m(\hat{x}_m)}{\partial x_{mj}}, \textit{ all } m, j. \tag{12.18}$$

Proof. See Appendix D.4. □

Social optimality conditions in Theorem 12.1 are basically identical to the same conditions for the SWMP of (11.5) in Theorem 11.1. Therefore, they can be interpreted in a manner similar to that used to interpret Theorem 11.1, as outlined below. First, a set of optimality conditions in the theorem depicts the equilibrium of a leader-and-follower game, in which no participant of the game can be better off by changing the choice that fulfills these conditions, as explained in Subsect. 11.3.1. Second, the solution of lump sum taxes must satisfy the optimality condition in (12.14), which has previously been closely examined in Subsect. 11.3.2. Third, the pricing and investment rules for all public services are identical to the same rules for a public service under no competition and, therefore, attain a Pareto-optimal resource allocation in the submarket for that service. This can be shown in a manner similar to that applied in Subsections 11.3.3 and 11.3.4, as explained separately in the following subsection.

12.2.3 Marketwise Pareto Optimality Conditions under Competition

Under the user equilibrium approach, a competitive market for a qualitative choice service can be decomposed into multiple submarkets, each of which offers a particular service option in competition. Further, resources consumed in each submarket are generally disjoint to resources traded in other submarkets. For these reasons, it is necessary to independently characterize the resource allocation efficiency of each submarket. From this prospective, the resource allocation efficiency conditions of Theorem 12.1 can be interpreted, as below.

To start, we introduce the main result of this subsection, such that the resource allocation of the entire market, which satisfies the efficiency conditions in Theorem 12.1, is Pareto-optimal. This implies that, when the government policy satisfies the optimality conditions in Theorem 21.1, the submarket for every public service has a resource allocation satisfying the Pareto optimality condition identical to the condition for a public service in monopoly in (11.46).

This finding is formulated in Theorem 12.2 by employing two different expressions of consumer service demand: deterministic and expected demands. The expression $i \in SM_m$ represents that consumer i who participates in submarket m at a certain instance. Under this convention, the expression $\bar{q}^i_m$ represents the deterministic demand of consumer i for the chosen option m at that instance. This deterministic demand $\bar{q}^i_m$ fundamentally differs from the expected demands Q^i_m, which accounts not only for the case of option m being chosen but also of the case of not chosen. However, the use of these two different demands in expressing social optimality can be justified on the following ground: under the random perception approach, the expected demand is an average of all consumer demands for a random process defined over a relatively long period.

Theorem 12.2. *The resource allocation that satisfies a set of efficiency conditions in Theorem 12.1 fulfills the following Pareto optimality condition:*

$$MRS^i_{\hat{x}_{kj}\hat{Q}_m} = \frac{p_j}{\hat{p}_m + \hat{\xi}^i_m \hat{t}_m} = SMRT^i_{\hat{x}_{mj}\hat{s}_m}, \; all\ j,\ k,\ m,\ and\ i \in SM_m,$$

where

$$MRS^i_{\hat{x}_{kj}\hat{Q}_m} = \frac{p_j}{\hat{p}_m + \hat{\xi}^i_m \hat{t}_m}, \quad and \quad SMRT^i_{\hat{x}_{mj}\hat{s}_m} = \frac{p_j}{SMFC(\hat{s}_m; \hat{\xi}^i_m) + \hat{\xi}^i_m \hat{t}_m}.$$

Proof. The proof for the SWMP of (12.6) can be provided in a manner analogous to that used to show the same relationship in (11.46) for the SWMP of (11.5). An outline of the proof is presented below.

Firstly, we develop the exchange efficiency condition of consumer i who chooses service m. Point-wise Kuhn-Tucker conditions for constrained stochastic optimization problems, as introduced in Lemma 4.3, indicate that the marginal utility of the deterministic service demand $\bar{q}^i_m$ for a certain realization of $\xi^i \in \mathrm{R}^{\mathrm{L}}$, denoted by $MU^i_{\bar{q}_m}$, can be expressed as follows:

$$MU^i_{\bar{q}_m} = \frac{\partial \bar{U}^i}{\partial y^i}\frac{\partial a\bar{q}^i_m}{\partial q^i_m} = \bar{\eta}^i(p_m + \xi^i_m t_m). \tag{12.19}$$

Hence, the marginal rate of substitution of $\bar{x}^i_{kj}$ for $\bar{Q}^i_{mn}$, denoted by $MRS^i_{\bar{x}_{kj}\bar{Q}_m}$, is

$$MRS^i_{\bar{x}_{kj}\bar{Q}_m} = \frac{MU^i_{\bar{x}_{kj}}}{MU^i_{\bar{Q}_m}} = \frac{E\{\bar{\eta}^i\}p_j}{E\left\{\bar{\eta}^i(p_m + \bar{\xi}^i_m t_m)\right\}} \tag{12.20}$$

$$\cong \frac{p_j}{p_m + \bar{\xi}^i_m t_m}, \quad \text{all} \quad k, j. \tag{12.21}$$

Here, by condition (12.7), (12.20) is simplified to (12.21).

Secondly, we estimate the social production efficiency condition for the SCMP of (12.9). This SCMP has optimality conditions that are identical to the conditions for resource allocations in (12.15), (12.17), and (12.18), with the exception that Q^i is replaced by s^i. Hence, proceeding with analyses for these optimality conditions in a manner identical to that used to estimate (11.44) gives the social marginal rate of substitution of $\bar{x}_{mj}$ for s^i_m, denoted by $SMRT^i_{x_{mj}\hat{s}_m}$, such that

$$SMRT^i_{x_{mj}\hat{s}_m} = \frac{p_j}{SMFC_m(s_m; \xi^i_m) + \hat{\xi}^i_m t_m}, \text{all} \quad m, \ j \tag{12.22}$$

Finally, under the user equilibrium condition of $\hat{Q}_m = \hat{s}_m$, the price estimated in (12.16) satisfies the overall efficiency condition such that two terms estimated in (12.21) and (12.22) have the same value. □

Theorem 12.2 characterizes the resource allocation at the state when the entire market attains maximum social welfare. This theorem depicts that the resource allocation at the state of maximum social welfare should attain Pareto optimality for all submarkets constituting the entire economy. The implication of such maximum resource allocation efficiency for the entire economy is closely examined next.

First, each customer, for all $i \in SM_m$, participates in submarket m in which the consumer can attain a higher level of utility than can be achieved in other submarkets. To be specific, the service system chosen by a consumer satisfies the revealed preference condition for the consumer, such that the implicit price of the consumer for the chosen system is lower than the implicit prices for other systems. Further, the market demand for the system is composed only of demands that satisfy such a revealed preference condition. Therefore, it can be said that a consumer who chooses a particular service system at equilibrium can achieve the maximum utility by consuming the service offered by the system.

Second, the resource allocation efficiency of each submarket is independent of the efficiency of other submarkets. Each consumer participates in only one submarket at the moment when he consumes a service offered by the government. This choice satisfies the revealed preference condition that identifies the least price option at that moment. Such a choice connotes that the utility of a consumer who chooses a certain system is not affected by the presence of competing systems that offer more expensive services. This means that the resource allocation efficiency of each submarket can be characterized in a fashion independent of those of other submarkets.

Third, the Pareto-optimal resource allocation in submarket m implies that no customer of service system m can be better off by changing the demand for the system. As shown in Theorem 12.2, the Pareto-optimal resource allocation in submarket m satisfies the condition such that the marginal rate of substitution of $\hat{x}^i_{kj}$ for $\hat{q}^i_m$ equals the social marginal rate of substitution of $\hat{x}_{mj}$ for $\hat{s}^i_m$ $(= \hat{q}^i_m)$. Hence, the indifference curves of all consumers i, who choose service system m, are tangent to the social production possibility frontier for service system m. Such a resource allocation implies that no consumer can be better off without making others worse off, as explained in Subsect. 11.3.4 using Fig. 11.3.

Fourth, Pareto optimality conditions for all service systems constitute the necessary condition for maximum social welfare. The resource allocation, which satisfies all the Pareto optimality conditions in the theorem, is none other than the solution to the governmental decision-making problem expressed as the SWMP. This decision-making problem searches for the maximum value for the social welfare index that depends on the utilities of all consumers in the economy. Accordingly, it can be argued that any resource allocation that does not fulfill the Pareto-optimality conditions cannot reach the highest level of social welfare attainable in the economy.

Fifth, it should however be noted that the optimality condition of Theorem 12.2 is not a sufficient condition to attain the highest possible level of social welfare. Rigorously speaking, Theorem 12.2 depicts social optimality under a restrictive condition such that the government has already made a decision to operate the M service systems. Therefore, we cannot exclude the possibility that another package of public service systems can reach a higher level of the social welfare as estimated by the social welfare function.

Such a limitation of Theorem 12.2 is illustrated with the example that follows. Suppose that the government plans to choose one package from among two packages of service systems: one composed of M systems, and the other one consisting of N systems. For these two packages, we can imagine two different resource allocations that satisfy the Pareto optimality conditions characterized in Theorem 12.2. However, we cannot make any conclusive judgment regarding which package will attain a higher level of social welfare.

The choice of the best package of public service systems from among all candidate packages commonly relies on an additional economic analysis, called benefit-cost analysis. A benefit-cost analysis compares net social benefits among all possible packages. The importance of benefit-cost analysis lies in the fact that this analysis overrides the optimality conditions of the theorem when choosing the best package. For example, it is possible that some service systems in the best package achieving maximum net social benefit do not fulfill the optimality conditions, while all systems in an inferior package satisfy the optimality conditions. This possibility will be thoroughly examined in the following chapter.

12.3 A Public Service in Competition with Services beyond Government Control

12.3.1 A Public Service in Competition with Private Services

We here analyze the SWMP for a public service in competition with multiple private services. The SWMP is formulated as a decision-making model, which is very similar to the PMP for a private service firm in competitive markets; the one major difference is the method used to specify the objective function. Through analyses of the SWMP, we show that the government must pursue first best pricing and investment rules for that public service, whether or not submarkets for competing private services attain Pareto optimality.

To begin, we introduce examples of a public service that competes with private services offering the identical qualitative choice service. One example of such a public service includes intercity rail lines managed by a public corporation that faces competition from private carriers operating other modes. Another example is found in convention facilities that are operated by local governments, and that compete with private facilities.

Subsequently, we model the SWMP for a public service, designated by 1, that competes with multiple private services, denoted by $m \in \langle 2, M \rangle$. The SWMP can be formulated as an optimization problem identical to that of (12.6) except that government control variables are confined to the unknowns for option 1:

$$SW_1(r, x_1, p_1, c_1, t_1, \kappa_1, \tau_1, \omega) \equiv \max\Big\{ W(E\{\overline{U}^1\}, \cdots, E\{\overline{U}^I\}) \Big\}$$
$$+ \kappa_1(F_1(x_1) - c_1) + \tau_1(t_1 - T_1(Q_1, c_1))$$
$$+ \omega\left(\sum_i r^i + p_1 Q_1 - \sum_j p_j x_{1j}\right). \tag{12.23}$$

Note that the indirect utility $\bar{U}^i$ is estimated from the utility maximization problem of (12.1) for the case when M service options are available.

The distinctive feature of the SWMP of (12.23) involves including the incomplete user equilibrium condition such that $t_1 - T_1(Q_1, c_1) = 0$. This user equilibrium condition connotes that government forecasts demand for system 1 without accounting for changes in the service quality of competing systems. Such an implication of the condition is actually identical to that of the same condition for private firms in competition.

Next, we develop social optimality conditions for the SW_1 of (12.23). Proceeding with the analysis of this SW_1 in a manner analogous to that which led from the SWMP in (12.6) to Theorem 12.1 gives social optimality conditions, as presented below.

Theorem 12.3. *Under condition (12.7), the solution to* SW_1 *has social optimality conditions identical to those for Theorem 12.1 with the exception that the optimality condition for resource allocation applies only to public service option* 1.

Proof. The proof can be worked out in a manner identical to that used to prove Lemma 12.2 and Theorem 12.1, as shown in Appendix D.4. □

Theorem 12.3 has significance in that it depicts optimal government policies for a public service in the circumstance when the government cannot control the prices and capacities of competing services. This theorem indicates that the government policy should satisfy the resource allocation efficiency conditions identical to those of Theorem 12.1. The implication of the theorem is more closely examined below.

First, optimality conditions for a public service in Theorem 12.3 are necessary conditions to attain maximum social welfare in the circumstance when the government cannot control the prices and capacities of competing private services. These optimality conditions are, by their nature, not the global optimality conditions capable of attaining the highest level of social welfare on marketwise bases. Of course, the highest level of social welfare can be attained only when all services, including private ones, satisfy resource allocation efficiency conditions, as can be deduced from Theorem 12.1.

Second, optimality conditions for a public service dictate that the government must pursue a first best policy toward a public service, irrespective of resource allocations in submarkets for private services. This first best policy leads to a Pareto-optimal resource allocation in the submarket for the public service, as can be shown in a manner identical to that used to prove Theorem 12.2. This implies that no customer of the public service can be better off, without making others worse off.

Third, the reasoning for the recommendation that the government must pursue a first best policy can be found from the following three facts. First, the utility of a consumer who chooses a particular public service is independent of the presence of competing services, as pointed out in Subsect. 12.2.3. Second, resources consumed in the submarket for a public service are disjoint to those used in competing services, as explained also in that subsection. Third, the concern of the government is confined to resource allocation efficiency for the submarket of the public service in the circumstance when it cannot control the prices and capacities of competing services.

Fourth, analyses for the SWMP of (12.23) can readily be extended to the SWMP for the case when the government operates $M(\geq 2)$ public services in competition with $N(\geq 1)$ private services. The SWMP for this more generalized case can be constructed by amending the SWMP of (12.6) through a minor change to increase the number of available services in the indirect utility functions $\bar{U}^i$ from M to $M+N$. Additionally, social optimality conditions for this amendment can readily be developed by combining analyses for the two SWMPs of (12.6) and (12.23). Further, social optimality conditions developed in this manner are identical to those of Theorem 12.1 for the SWMP of (12.6).

12.3.2 A Public Service in Competition with Public Substitutes

The SWMP analyzed in the previous subsection and the SWMP considered here are both used to estimate the optimal policy for a public service in competition with other services that have fixed prices and capacities. However, the competing services considered in the former are private services such that the government cannot participate in their management; in contrast, the competing services described in the latter are public services that the government directly manages. This difference leads to a different outcome for the latter, such that the optimal policy for the targeted public service must be a second best one that cannot attain the Pareto optimality in the submarket for the public service.

One example to which analyses of the SWMP considered here are applicable is as follows. Suppose that the government operates a public transit system in competition with highway modes. Suppose, also, that the government has no financial constraint on the expenditures necessary to pursue the optimal provision of public transit services. Suppose, further, that the government directly manages both transit and highway systems. Suppose, however, the government can optimally adjust neither road user charges nor highway capacities.

The SWMP under the conditions specified above can readily be modeled by amending the SWMP of (12.6). Let the public transit service be denoted by option 1, and multiple highway routes available to trip-makers be expressed by

$m \in \langle 2, M \rangle$. Then, this amended SWMP, denoted by SW_2, can be formulated as follows:

$$SW_2(r, p_1, c_1, t, \tau, \omega) \equiv \max \left\{ W(E\{\bar{U}^1\}, \cdots, E\{\bar{U}^I\}) \right\} + \sum_m \tau_m \left(t_m - T_m(Q_m, c_m) \right) + \omega \left(\sum_i r^i + \sum_m p_m Q_m - KC_1(c_1) \right), \tag{12.24}$$

where $t \equiv (t_1, \cdots, t_M)$ and $\tau \equiv (\tau_1, \cdots, \tau_M)$. Let also this SWMP have the solution, denoted by $(\widehat{r}, \widehat{p}_1, \widehat{c}_1, \widehat{t}, \widehat{\tau}, \widehat{\omega})$.

The above SWMP assumes that, for all $m \geq 2$, p_m and c_m are constants, but Q_m and t_m are sensitive to p_1 and t_1. In this circumstance, the inclusion of incomplete user equilibrium conditions for all m in the SWMP reflects that the government can accurately forecast the impact of changes in p_1 and c_1 on Q_m and t_m, for all m. Also, the presence of $\sum_m p_m Q_m$ in the budget constraint indicates that the government directly collects all revenues from transit and highway users.

We analyze the SWMP of (12.24), under the following three conditions for the market demand function. First, the marginal utility of money is constant; that is, (12.7) holds. Second, the income effect of the market demand function is negligible; that is,

$$\frac{\partial \widehat{Q}^i_m}{\partial r^i} \cong 0, \text{ all, } i \text{ and } m. \tag{12.25}$$

Third, the catchment domain for transit service and all highway routes has a narrow thickness; that is,[1]

$$\breve{\xi}_{m1} = \frac{\partial \widehat{Q}_m}{\partial t_1} \Big/ \frac{\partial \widehat{Q}_m}{\partial p_1} \cong \breve{\xi}_1 = \frac{\partial \widehat{Q}_1}{\partial t_1} \Big/ \frac{\partial \widehat{Q}_1}{\partial p_1}, \text{ if } \frac{\partial \widehat{Q}_m}{\partial p_1} \neq 0, \text{ all } m \neq 1. \tag{12.26}$$

The condition of thin catchment domains for all service options implies that all options have more than one close substitute in terms of implicit price. The more specific description of this condition is as follows: first, each consumer has a highway route that is a close substitute for transit service under qualitative competition satisfying the identical ordering condition; second, each highway

[1] The proof of (12.26) for thin catchment domain can be worked out in a manner identical to that used to prove (8.33). Further, the implication of (12.26) such that an option with a narrow catchment domain has close substitutes is detailed in Chapter 5; this implication for the case of quantitative, qualitative and mixed competitions is explained in Subsections 5.2.3, 5.4.3, and 5.5.3, respectively.

route has an alternative route that is a close substitute under quantitative competition. Under these conditions, proceeding with analyses of the SWMP in (12.24) gives the following.

Lemma 12.3. *Under conditions* (12.7), (12.25), *and* (12.26), *the solution to* SW_2 *satisfies the following:*

i. *The marginal social welfare loss of service time for public transit,* $\widehat{\tau}_1$, *is approximated by*

$$\widehat{\tau}_1 \cong \widehat{\omega}\widehat{\xi}_1\widehat{Q}_1. \tag{12.27}$$

ii. *The marginal social welfare loss of service time for highways,* $\widehat{\tau}_m$, *satisfies the following inequality:*

$$\frac{\widehat{\tau}_m}{\widehat{\omega}}\frac{\partial \widehat{T}_m}{\partial Q_m} \gtrless p_m, \quad \text{if} \quad \widehat{\xi}_m\widehat{Q}_m\frac{\partial \widehat{T}_m}{\partial Q_m} \gtrless p_m, \ \text{all } m \neq 1. \tag{12.28}$$

Proof. See Appendix D.5. □

Lemma 12.2 is an outcome of analyses that purport to estimate the marginal social welfare loss of service time, τ_m, for all m. Analyses for $\widehat{\tau}_1$ give a relatively concrete expression for this marginal value, which is approximately identical to the expression for other SWMPs analyzed previously. However analyses for other terms $\widehat{\tau}_m$, for all $m \geq 2$, do not yield definite expressions. For this reason, we present the relevant optimality condition for SW_2, which can be used in judging the sign of $\widehat{\tau}_m$, for all $m \geq 2$.

Subsequently, we estimate the second best policy for a public service that competes with other public services that have prices and capacities that cannot be adjusted by the government. The estimation result is as below.

Theorem 12.4. *Under the conditions* (12.7), (12.25), *and* (12.26), *the solution to* SW_2 *fulfills the optimality condition for income distribution, which is identical to that of Theorem 12.1 for* SW_0, *and the optimality condition for resource allocation, such that*

$$\widehat{p}_1 \cong SMFC_1(\widehat{Q}_1) + \sum_{m\geq 2}\frac{S_{1m}}{S_{11}}\left(\frac{\widehat{\tau}_m}{\widehat{\omega}}\frac{\partial \widehat{T}_m}{\partial Q_m} - p_m\right) \tag{12.29}$$

$$MKC_1(\widehat{c}_1) \cong -\widehat{\xi}_1\widehat{Q}_1\frac{\partial \widehat{T}}{\partial c_1}, \tag{12.30}$$

where

$$S_{1m} = \frac{\partial \hat{Q}_m}{\partial p_1} - \hat{Q}_1 \frac{\partial \hat{Q}_m}{\partial r^i}.$$

Proof. See Appendix D.5. □

The above theorem introduces pricing and investment rules that are similar to the first best ones in Theorem 12.3 except for a major difference that the pricing rule has an additional term. The implication of such a pricing rule is interpreted below, using the example of multimodal urban transportation systems introduced in the beginning of this subsection.

Firstly, we determine the economic implication of $p_m - (\widehat{\tau}_m/\widehat{\omega})\partial\widehat{T}_m/\partial Q_m$ in the pricing rule. This term equals the difference between $p_m + (\widehat{\tau}_m/\widehat{\omega})\widehat{\xi}_m t_m$ and $(\widehat{\tau}_m/\widehat{\omega})\partial\widehat{T}_m/\partial Q_m + (\widehat{\tau}_m/\widehat{\omega})\,\widehat{\xi}_m t_m$. Here, the term $\widehat{\tau}_m/\widehat{\omega}$ is the marginal social cost of service time for SW_2 as a unit of money, because of the following: $\widehat{\tau}$ is the marginal social welfare loss brought by a one-unit increase in service time; and $\widehat{\omega}$ is the marginal social welfare of money.[2] Hence, the term $p_m + (\widehat{\tau}_m/\widehat{\omega})\widehat{\xi}_m t_m$ is the marginal social benefit of service demand Q_m as a unit of money.[3] The other term $(\widehat{\tau}_m/\widehat{\omega})\partial\widehat{T}_m/\partial Q_m + (\widehat{\tau}_m/\widehat{\omega})\widehat{\xi}_m t_m$ is the marginal social cost of throughput $s_m(= \widehat{Q}_m)$ for system m with a fixed capacity as a unit of money.[4] Hence, the term $p_m - (\widehat{\tau}_m/\widehat{\omega})\partial\widehat{T}_m/\partial Q_m$ represents the net marginal social benefit of demand $\widehat{Q}_m$ for SW_2 as a unit of money.

Secondly, (12.28) implies that, in the case of congested urban corridors, the term $\widehat{p}_m - (\widehat{\tau}_m/\widehat{\omega})\partial\widehat{T}_m/\partial Q_m$ for all $m \geq 2$ is negative. The term $\widehat{\xi}_m\,\widehat{Q}_m\partial\widehat{T}_m/\partial \widehat{Q}_m$ in (12.28) is the marginal congestion cost of route m for the observed demand $\widehat{Q}_m$ that has the social value-of-service-time $\widehat{\xi}_m$. It is also known that, in the case of congested unban highways, this marginal congestion cost $\widehat{\xi}_m\,\widehat{Q}_m\partial\widehat{T}_m/\partial Q_m$ is usually larger than the actual monetary charge $\widehat{p}_m$. Hence, via (12.28), it can be concluded that the term $p_m - (\widehat{\tau}_m/\widehat{\omega})\partial\widehat{T}_m/\partial Q_m$ is negative.

Thirdly, we interpret the meaning of S_{1m}/S_{11} in the pricing rule. The term S_{11} is approximately equal to the decrease in Q_1 by a marginal increase Δp_1, denoted by ΔQ_1; on the other hand, the term S_{1m} for all $m \geq 2$ is approximately equal to the increase in Q_m due to an increase of Δp_1, as denoted by ΔQ_m. Therefore, the term S_{1m}/S_{11} is approximately equal to $\Delta Q_m/\Delta Q_1$; further, the term S_{1m}/S_{11} is approximately equal to the diversion ratio of ΔQ_1 from public transit 1 to highway route m. Finally, this ratio is always negative and satisfies the condition that $-1 \langle \sum_{m\geq 2} S_{1m}/S_{11} \langle 0$, as shown in Theorem 5.12.

---

[2] This property of $\widehat{\omega}$ is introduced in Subsect. 11.3.1. Note also that one unit of money is equivalent to $\widehat{\omega}$ units of social welfare index.

[3] The reason for this assertion is presented in the comment for (11.27).

[4] The reason for this assertion is also explained in the comment for (11.28).

Fourthly, we determine the meaning of $\sum_{m\geq 2} S_{1m}/S_{11} \times ((\tau_m/\widehat{\omega}_m)\partial\widehat{T}_m/\partial Q_m - p_m)$. The term $(\tau_m/\widehat{\omega}_m)\partial\widehat{T}_m/\partial Q_m - p_m$ can alternatively be interpreted as net marginal social cost savings in a unit of money, due to a one-unit decrease in demand for route m. Therefore, the term $S_{1m}/S_{11} \times ((\tau_m/\widehat{\omega}_m)\partial\widehat{T}_m/\partial Q_m - p_m)$ expresses the social cost savings of auto trips that continue to use route m, due to the S_{1m}/S_{11} unit diversion of demands from route m to the transit system. Hence, the term $\sum_{m\geq 2} S_{1m}/S_{11} \times ((\tau_m/\widehat{\omega}_m)\partial\widehat{T}_m/\partial Q_m - p_m)$ can be understood as the total social cost savings of trips that continue to use highways, owning to a one-unit trip that switches from auto to transit.

Therefore, we can interpret the second best pricing rule in (12.29) as follows. The optimal price $\widehat{p}_1$ is equal to the social marginal full cost of throughput for the public transit system minus an additional term. This additional term is positive and estimates the total social cost savings of trips that continue to use highways, due to a one-unit trip that switches from auto to transit. Therefore, the pricing rule implies that the optimal fare should be equal to the social marginal cost of transit passengers, which equals the social marginal full cost for the public transit system minus the marginal social cost savings one transit passenger provides highway users.

12.3.3 Relationship Between Ownership and the Scope of Knowledge for Consumer Reaction

In modeling the SWMPs analyzed in this chapter, we have applied a number of postulates, which are spelled out in Sect. 12.1. Among them, one controversial postulate is as follows: the government has and utilizes knowledge of incomplete user equilibrium conditions for competing services only when the government has ownership of competing services. Here we first explain how this postulate is accommodated in the two SWMPs previously analyzed. We next validate the postulate through analyses of a SWMP that violates this assumption.

To begin, we detail the manner in which the above postulate is incorporated into the SWMPs of (12.23) and (12.24). Both SWMPs are used to search for optimal policies for a public service in competition with other services. Moreover, both decision-making problems deal with the case when some competing services choose prices that depart from social marginal full costs. However, these two decision-making problems have the following two critical differences.

The first difference is ownership of competing services. The SWMP of (12.23) does not include the revenue of competing services in the budget constraint; in contrast, that of (12.24) does include such revenue. This difference reflects the fact that the government described in the former provides a public service in competition with private services the government does not manage; in contrast, the government considered in the latter manages not only a public service under analysis but also competing public services.

The second difference is the scope of knowledge the government has. The SWMP of (12.23) includes only one incomplete user equilibrium condition for a public service operated by the government. That formulation reflects that the government forecasts the effect of its choice for a given public service on demand for the public service, ignoring the effect of the choice on demand for competing services. In contrast, the SWMP of (12.24) contains the incomplete user equilibrium conditions for all competing public services. This formulation indicates that the government predicts the effect of its choice on demand for a given public service through an understanding of the effect on competing services.

These two differences between the two SWMPs do not violate the postulate of this study in that the government has and utilizes knowledge of demand only for services owned by the government. To be specific, the SWMP of (12.23) contains neither revenue for competing private services nor the incomplete user equilibrium condition for these private services. In contrast, the SWMP of (12.24) includes both revenue for all competing public services and the incomplete user equilibrium condition for these public services.

Subsequently, we validate the postulate applied to both the SWMPs of (12.23) and (12.24), such that ownership of competing services should coincide with the scope of knowledge. To this end, we compare the following two government choices regarding the price for a given public service: the first choice based only on the incomplete user equilibrium condition for the public service; the second choice utilizing complete knowledge of the marketwise user equilibrium condition for all services, including private services.

The first choice is none other than the solution to the SWMP in (12.23). The second choice can be characterized as the solution to the amendment of the SWMP in (12.23) for the government, which incorporates the marketwise user equilibrium condition:

$$SW_3(r,p_1,c_1,t,\tau,\omega) \equiv \max\left\{ W(E\{\bar{U}^1\},\cdots,E\{\bar{U}^I\})\right\} + \sum_m \tau_m\left(t_m - T_m(Q_m,c_m)\right) + \omega\left(\sum_i r^i + p_1 Q_1 - KC_1(c_1)\right). \tag{12.31}$$

Under the simplifying assumptions of (12.7), (12.25), and (12.26), this SWMP gives the following pricing formula:

$$\widehat{p}_1 \cong SMFC(\widehat{Q}_1) + \sum_{m\geq 2} \frac{S_{1m}}{S_{11}} \frac{\widehat{\tau}_m}{\widehat{\omega}} \frac{\partial \widehat{T}_m}{\partial Q_m}, \tag{12.32}$$

as shown Appendix D.6.

We judge that the first choice is superior to the second in several respects. First, it is unrealistic, in many cases, to postulate that a public agency would have complete knowledge of the marketwise user equilibrium condition in (12.31). Second, it is difficult to draw a plausible economic rationale explaining the introduction of the last term of (12.32). Third, the pricing rule contradicts the same rule of Theorem 12.1 for the global social optimality of a market, as explained next.

The optimal price $\widehat{p}_1$ for the SWMP of (12.31) has an additional term that is not included in the price for the SWMP of (12.23). To judge which of the two prices can achieve more efficient resource allocation, we consider a market in which all competing private services have perfectly elastic demands. For this special case, Theorem 9.3 for private firms shows that the pricing and investment rules for these private services are almost identical to those of Theorem 12.1, as will be confirmed in the subsequent chapter. Therefore, the pricing rule for the public service should be the first best in order to achieve maximum social welfare. In this regard, the optimal price for (12.23) fulfills this requirement; in contrast, the price for (12.31) does not.

Finally, we examine, under what circumstances, the three restrictive conditions of (12.7), (12.25), (12.26) that have been applied in to characterizing optimal public policies for SWMPs with simple approximate formulas. The condition of (12.7) for the marginal utility of money is applied to all SWMPs for public services under competition throughout this study. The condition of (12.25) for the income effect of service demand appears to be necessary for SWMPs that yield second best solutions, whether or not the public service under analysis faces competition. One example for a public service under no competition is the SWMP analyzed in Section 11.4, whereas one example for a public service under competition is the SWMP analyzed in this subsection. On the other hand, the condition of (12.26) for close substitutes has applied to decision-making problems that estimate the optimal price of service under competition, irrespective of service ownership. One example for private service is the PMP analyzed in Subsection 8.4.3, whereas an example for a public service is the SWMP considered above.

Chapter 13
The Resource Allocation Efficiency of Service Markets

13.1 Introduction

It is said that market economies attain the highest level of resource allocation efficiency when their resource allocations attain Pareto optimality at which no one can be better off without making others worse off. Is this well-known proposition of current welfare economics applicable to the evaluation of resource allocation efficiency in congestion-prone service markets under quality competition? We introduce here one example for which this proposition does not provide a satisfactory answer for marketwise resource allocation efficiency, as described below.

Suppose that all existing services in a market for a certain qualitative choice service offer identical or very similar services to one another. Suppose also that they face very elastic demands and, therefore, charge prices approximately equal to marginal full cost. Under these circumstances, submarkets for all these services have Pareto-optimal resource allocations. Therefore, from the standpoint of traditional approaches, the entire service market is described as attaining the highest level of resource allocation efficiency.

Suppose, further, that to the market considered above, a firm introduces an innovative service satisfying one or both of the following two conditions: first, its service production cost is significantly lower than the cost for identical or similar service; second, its quality attributes significantly differ from those of existing services. Under the user equilibrium approach, the innovative service captures a demand segment from some existing services and facilitates the captured demand segment more economically than do the existing services. Moreover the introduction of the innovative service does not decrease the elasticity of demand for other services. This means that the introduction of the new service does not cause the deterioration of the resource allocation efficiency of all the submarkets previously served by existing services. Therefore, the introduction of the innovative service contributes to improving customer well-being, without causing the deterioration of the resource allocation efficiency of submarkets for the remaining services.

D.J. Moon, *Congestion-Prone Services Under Quality Competition*, Advances in Spatial Science, DOI 10.1007/978-3-642-20189-9_13,

We next consider whether the introduction of the innovative service improves marketwise resource allocation efficiency. Under the user equilibrium approach, an innovative service generally has a thick catchment domain leading to inelastic demand, irrespective of its market share. Therefore, the profit-maximizing price of the innovative service is larger than marginal full cost. The choice of this price cannot lead to a Pareto-optimal resource allocation in the submarket for the service. This implies that the introduction of the innovative service would not be conceived of as desirable from the traditional viewpoint to assess resource allocation efficiency, despite the fact that the introduction of the new service has a positive effect on marketwise resource allocation efficiency. However, such a viewpoint based on the traditional approach is not convincing.

One plausible approach to interpreting the resource allocation efficiency of the above example could be to designate *the diversity of service quality* as another independent criterion used to assess efficiency. The diversity of service quality for a particular qualitative choice service refers to the availability of a wide spectrum of services differentiated by quality on marketwise bases. A service market that has more qualitatively diversified services gives consumers a better chance of finding a more economical service from among a larger number of services. Further, a better chance of finding a more economical service usually allows for services to be purchased at lower implicit prices and thus improves consumer well-being.

The objective of this chapter is to prove that the marketwise resource allocation efficiency of a qualitative choice service market depends on the following two independent evaluation criteria: first, the resource allocation efficiency of the submarket for each service; and second, the diversity of service quality on marketwise bases. The first criterion targets resource allocation efficiency for an individual submarket, but the second criterion covers resource allocation efficiency for the entire service market on an aggregated basis. The relevancy of these two criteria is advocated through a series of analyses briefed below.

In Sect. 13.2, we analyze the resource allocation efficiency of each submarket constituting the total service market. Firstly, we introduce the rationale for why the Pareto optimality of each submarket is a necessary condition for attaining maximum social welfare on marketwise bases, whether or not other submarkets fulfill this optimality condition. Subsequently, by applying this necessary condition, we show that services in perfect or differentiated competition fulfill this necessary condition, while services in pure and differentiated oligopolistic competition do not. Further, we show that, if a firm makes a choice that does not fulfill this efficiency condition, this choice is less beneficial to its customers than a choice that satisfies the condition.

In Sect. 13.3, we analyze how an innovative service influences the profit of a firm that introduces it and of competing firms. In the analyses, innovative efforts in the pursuit of profit are sorted into two categories: reductions of service production cost; and improvements in service quality attributes. Further, it is shown that a more innovative service usually results in a larger and more inelastic demand for the service, while decreasing the volume and elasticity of demands some competing firms.

In Sect. 13.4, we demonstrate that service quality diversity is indeed an indispensible and independent criterion to evaluate marketwise resource allocation efficiency through two different analyses. The first analysis proves that the introduction of an innovative service, which has the effect of enriching service quality diversity, increases benefit not only to the customers of the new service but also to the customers of some existing services, without having a negative effect on the consumers of the remaining services. The second analysis shows that the array of more qualitatively diversified services in a market provides a better opportunity for consumers to find a more economical option and thus increases consumer well-being.

In the final section, Sect. 13.5, we apply the preceding findings of this chapter to two topics that illustrate the advantage of the user equilibrium approach in analyses of marketwise resource allocation efficiency under quality competition. The first topic shows that the successive introduction of service innovations propels market economies to reach higher and higher levels of marketwise resource allocation efficiency. The second topic advocates that agglomeration economies of large urban areas arise from efficient resource allocations that are beneficial to consumers and play a key role in the continuous growth of service industries that, in turn, form a strong economic base.

13.2 The Resource Allocation Efficiency of Submarkets

13.2.1 Identification of Two Evaluation Criteria

In this subsection, we consider why some findings from Chap. 12 suggest that the marketwise resource allocation efficiency of a competitive service market can be properly assessed only by applying two independent criteria. Specifically, we show that the resource allocation efficiency of a submarket for each service in competition is not a sufficient condition but rather a necessary condition for marketwise resource allocation efficiency. In addition, we advocate that the diversity of service quality is an independent and indispensible criterion by which to judge marketwise efficiency.

In Sect. 12.2, it was pointed out that under the user equilibrium approach a service market is decomposed into a number of submarkets that can be characterized as below. First, each service traded in a submarket can be distinguished from other services by quantitative and/or qualitative attributes. Second, each consumer participates in one submarket in which he can attain a utility higher than he can achieve in other submarkets. Third, resources consumed in a submarket are usually disjoint to those of other submarkets.[1]

For the service market characterized above, Theorem 12.1 suggests a hint regarding marketwise resource allocation efficiency. That theorem shows that

[1]This restrictive condition for non-jointness holds only when every firm operates one single service system that offers one single service option. In other words, this condition does not holds when a service firm provides multiple services differentiated by quality.

maximum social welfare can be achieved when every service chooses a first best price and capacity so as to attain the Pareto optimality of the submarket for the service. It has also been previously explained in the comment to that theorem that the maximum social welfare attainable depends on the content of the service package available to consumers, under the condition that all the services in the package choose Pareto-optimal prices and capacities.

To be specific, a package with more diversified services is usually more beneficial to consumers with unique perceptions for service quality. Each consumer chooses the most economical service that gives a lower implicit price relative to that given by other services. Moreover, because of the diversity of perceptions, each consumer differently perceives the implicit price for a certain service. Therefore, the package with more diversified services usually provides a better opportunity for consumers to find a desired option for which a lower implicit price is charged.

However, Theorem 12.1 has a critical shortcoming in that it is developed under the unrealistic premise that the government chooses the prices and capacities of all services in competition. For this reason, it is unclear whether the theorem can apply to a public service in a realistic circumstance where the public service competes with other private services and where some private services do not choose first best prices and capacities. We therefore consider in Theorem 12.3 the socially optimal choice for a public service in this realistic circumstance.

Theorem 12.3 shows that the Pareto optimality of a submarket for a public service is a necessary condition for marketwise resource allocation efficiency, whether or not resource allocations in submarkets for some competing private services are efficient. Importantly, this theorem for a public service can apply to a private service in competition with other private ones, since service ownership is not a relevant factor in determining social optimality. Below, this theorem is reintroduced in an amended expression applicable to forthcoming analyses in this chapter.

Theorem 13.1. *Irrespective of the choice of other service firms, necessary conditions for the choice of service firm m to attain maximum marketwise resource allocation efficiency are as follows:*

$$\hat{t}_m = T_m(\hat{Q}_m, \hat{c}_m) \tag{13.1}$$

$$\hat{p}_m = SMFC_m(\hat{Q}_m) \tag{13.2}$$

$$MKC_m(\hat{c}_m) = -\hat{\xi}_m \hat{Q}_m \frac{\partial T_m(\hat{Q}_m, \hat{c}_m)}{\partial c_{mn}} \tag{13.3}$$

$$MKC_m(\hat{c}_m) = p_j \bigg/ \frac{\partial F_m(\hat{x}_m)}{\partial x_{mj}}, \ all\ j. \tag{13.4}$$

Here, all notations in the above are identical to those in Theorem 12.3.

Theorem 13.1 indicates that a Pareto-optimal resource allocation in the submarket for a service is a necessary condition for marketwise resource allocation efficiency, irrespective of resource allocations in other submarkets. This theorem applies to a private service as well as a public service when assessing the resource allocation efficiency for the service from the standpoint of marketwise efficiency. Further, the theorem indicates that, in this assessment, resource allocations in other submarkets are not a factor of consideration.

However, the social optimality conditions in Theorem 13.1 have a critical limitation in that they are not sufficient conditions but rather necessary conditions for marketwise resource allocation efficiency. This limitation stems from the fact that the optimality conditions of the theorem do not reveal the best package of service options from among all candidate packages to achieve maximum resource allocation efficiency, as can be inferred from the same previous assertion for public service in the fourth comment for Theorem 12.2. In other words, the optimality conditions do not give any clue about whether a certain service contributes to marketwise resource allocation efficiency more than does another service given that the two services have differentiated qualities.

For example, suppose that all customers of some existing services are absorbed by an innovative service. Suppose, also, that all the existing services satisfy the resource efficiency conditions of the theorem, but the innovative service does not. In these circumstances, from the fact that the existing services satisfy the resource efficiency condition and the innovative service does not, it is impossible to judge whether the introduction of the innovative service is beneficial to consumers on marketwise bases.

Finally, it is worth considering a hypothetical circumstance in which all consumers have an identical perception for service quality. In this circumstance, the net-value-of-time perceived in consuming services would be identical across all consumers. Then, all services available to consumers must have an identical price; that is, a service charging a higher price can hold no demand. Further, it is certain that Pareto optimality would be a necessary and sufficient condition for the resource allocation efficiency of a market, as is true of the traditional approach in which implicit price is equal to price.

13.2.2 Resource Allocations under Perfect and Differentiated Competition

Service firms in perfect competition and those in differentiated competition both serve very elastic demands. These two types of service firms, therefore, both charge prices equal to marginal full costs at market equilibrium, and both satisfy the zero profit condition, as shown in Sect. 10.3. Such choices satisfy social optimality conditions for resource allocation in Theorem 13.1 and thus fulfill necessary conditions for marketwise resource allocation efficiency, as shown below.

To begin, we analyze the relationship between the two different choices made by service firm m. One choice is the real choice of firm m, which fulfills the optimality conditions of Theorem 9.3 (or 9.5). Let this choice yield the demand $\breve{Q}_m$, which has a private value-of-service-time $\breve{\xi}_m$ and a social value-of-service-time $\bar{\xi}_m$. The other choice is a hypothetical choice of firm m, which satisfies social optimality conditions in Theorem 13.1. Let this choice give the demand $\hat{Q}_m$ that has a social value-of-service-time $\hat{\xi}_m$ at market equilibrium. Then, the demands and value-of-service-times introduced above satisfy the following relationships.

Theorem 13.2. *The demand function of firm m in perfect or in differentiated competition satisfies the following relationships:*

$$\breve{Q}_m \cong \hat{Q}_m, \text{ and } \breve{\xi}_m \cong \bar{\xi}_m \cong \hat{\xi}_m.$$

Proof. Demand for firm m, which is very elastic, has a thin catchment domain. Hence, it follows from Theorem 6.10 that $\breve{\xi}_m \cong \bar{\xi}_m$. Since $\breve{\xi}_m \cong \bar{\xi}_m$, the optimality conditions of Theorem 9.3 are approximately identical to those of Theorem 13.1. Hence, it holds that $\breve{Q}_m \cong \hat{Q}_m$. This implies that $\bar{\xi}_m \cong \hat{\xi}_m$. □

Theorem 13.2 indicates that, if demands for a firm are very elastic, optimality conditions for private firms in Theorem 9.3 are approximately identical to social optimality conditions in Theorem 13.1. Therefore, the profit-maximizing choice of firm m in perfect or differentiated competition leads to a Pareto-optimal resource allocation in submarket m, as shown below.

Theorem 13.3. *The choice of service firm m in perfect or differentiated competition attains a Pareto-optimal resource allocation in submarket m, which can be characterized as follows:*

$$MRS^i_{\breve{x}_{kj}\breve{Q}_m} \cong MRS^i_{\hat{x}_{kj}\hat{Q}_m} = SMRT^i_{\hat{x}_{mj}\hat{s}_m} \cong SMRT^i_{\breve{x}_{mj}\breve{s}_m}, \quad all\ i \in SM_m.$$

Proof. (i) Theorem 13.2 shows that $\breve{Q}_m \cong \hat{Q}_m$ and $\breve{\xi}_m \cong \hat{\xi}_m$. (ii) These two relationships imply that $MFC_m(\breve{s}_m; \breve{\xi}_m) \cong SMFC_m(\hat{s}_m; \hat{\xi}_m)$. (iii) The relationship (i) implies that the price $\breve{p}_m$ in Theorem 9.3 is approximately equal to the price $\hat{p}_m$ in Theorem 13.1. (iv) Hence, it follows from (i)–(iii) that $MRS^i_{\breve{x}_{kj}\breve{Q}_m} \cong MRS^i_{\hat{x}_{kj}\hat{Q}_m}$ and $SMRT^i_{\breve{x}_{mj}\breve{s}_m} \cong SMRT^i_{\hat{x}_{mj}\hat{s}_m}$. (v) Further, Theorem 12.2 shows that the choice satisfying Theorem 13.1 gives the outcome that $MRS^i_{\hat{x}_{kj}\hat{Q}_m} = SMRT^i_{\hat{x}_{mj}\hat{s}_m}$. The facts (iv) and (v) imply the theorem. □

13.2.3 Resource Allocations under Monopoly or Oligopolistic Competition

In Sect. 10.2, we identify three different types of competition in which service firms have imperfectly elastic demands: monopoly, and pure and differentiated oligopolistic competition. A service firm, which faces one of these types of competition, chooses a price larger than marginal full cost. Such a profit-maximizing choice of a firm leads to the following resource allocation in the submarket for that firm: first, the resource allocation is not Pareto-optimal and, therefore, not desirable from the standpoint of marketwise resource allocation efficiency; and second, the allocation is therefore less beneficial to consumers than is the Pareto-optimal choice. These two assertions are proved below.

To begin, we introduce the assumption applied in the proof of the above two assertions. This condition is

$$\breve{\xi}_m \cong \bar{\xi}_m \cong \hat{\xi}_m. \tag{13.7}$$

The relationship $\breve{\xi}_m \cong \bar{\xi}_m$ holds when the catchment domain D_{mn} is relatively narrow, since both $\breve{\xi}_m$ and $\bar{\xi}_m$ belong to the set $\{\xi_m \mid .\xi \in D_m(\breve{p}, \breve{t})\}$, as shown in Theorem 6.9. Also, the other relationship $\bar{\xi}_m \cong \hat{\xi}_m$ usually holds, since a large portion of $D_m(\breve{p}, \breve{t})$ and $D_m(\hat{p}_m, \breve{p}_m^o, \hat{t}_m, \breve{t}_m^o)$ overlap each other, where $\breve{p} \equiv (\breve{p}_1, \cdots, \breve{p}_m, \cdots, \breve{p}_M)$, while $(\hat{p}_m, \breve{p}_m^o) \equiv (\breve{p}_1, \cdots, \hat{p}_m, \cdots, \breve{p}_M)$.

The condition that the thickness of D_m is relatively small can apply to service firms not only in relatively keen oligopolistic competition but also in monopoly, as pointed out in Subsect 10.5.1. This assertion for relatively keen oligopolistic competition immediately follows from the fact that a firm, facing keener competition, has a relatively thin catchment domain. On the other hand, the assertion for monopoly reflects that the monopolist usually serves customers who have relatively homogeneous net service time values and thus yield a thin catchment domain; otherwise, it is highly probable that a newcomer will enter the monopoly market.

Subsequently, we introduce an approach to prove the two assertions introduced in the beginning of this subsection. It generally holds that $\breve{Q}_m \neq \hat{Q}_m$, because of the following: the profit-maximizing price $\breve{p}_m$ for imperfectly elastic demands is larger than marginal full cost, but the socially optimal price $\hat{p}_m$ is equal to marginal full cost, irrespective of the elasticity of demands. Further, the inequality $\breve{Q}_m \neq \hat{Q}_m$ implies that $SMRT^i_{\breve{x}_{mj}\breve{s}_m} \neq SMRT^i_{\hat{x}_{mj}\hat{s}_m}$, since $\breve{s} = \breve{Q}_m \neq \hat{s}_m = \hat{Q}_m$.

Therefore, it is infeasible to evaluate the efficiency of resource allocations for a firm serving inelastic demand in a manner analogous to previous analyses for a firm capturing very elastic demand. To be specific, only when $\breve{s} \cong \hat{s}_m$, is it possible to compare $MRS^i_{\breve{x}_{kj}\breve{Q}_m}$ and $SMRT^i_{\hat{x}_{mj}\hat{s}_m}$ in a manner similar to the previous analyses. However, the profit-maximizing choice for inelastic demand does not fulfill the condition that $\breve{s} \cong \hat{s}_m$. For this reason, we evaluate resource allocation efficiency for the case of inelastic demand through two-step analyses.

The first step compares relative magnitudes between $MRS^{i}_{\breve{x}_{kj}\breve{Q}_m}$ and $SMRT^{i}_{\breve{x}_{mj}\breve{s}_m}$. In this comparison, the marginal rate of substitution $MRS^{i}_{\breve{x}_{kj}\breve{Q}_m}$ is estimated by applying the profit-maximizing choice $(\breve{x}_m, \breve{c}_m, \breve{t}_m)$ that satisfies Theorem 9.3. On the other hand, the social marginal rate of transformation $SMRT^{i}_{\breve{x}_{mj}\breve{s}_m}$ is estimated using the socially optimal solution of (x_m, c_m, t_m) to the simultaneous equation system composed of (13.1), (13.3), and (13.4) for the given throughput $\breve{s}_m\ (= \breve{Q}_m)$.

By the condition $\breve{\xi}_m \cong \bar{\xi}_m$, the profit-maximizing choice for (x_m, c_m, t_m) and the socially optimal choice for the same variables satisfy the following:

$$\breve{c}_m \cong \bar{c}_m, \text{ and } \breve{t}_m \cong T_m(\breve{s}_m, \breve{c}_m) \cong \bar{t}_m = T_m(\breve{s}_m, \bar{c}_m). \tag{13.8}$$

Moreover, the condition that $\breve{\xi}_m \cong \bar{\xi}_m$ leads to an outcome such that $MFC_m(\breve{s}_m; \breve{\xi}_m) \cong MFC_m(\breve{s}_m; \bar{\xi}_m)$. Hence, it follows that

$$\breve{p}_m = MFC_m(\breve{s}_m, \breve{\xi}_m) - \breve{Q}_m \Big/ \frac{\partial \breve{Q}_m}{\partial p_m} \rangle\ MFC_m(\breve{s}_m; \bar{\xi}_m). \tag{13.9}$$

Equations (13.8) and (13.9) imply that

$$MRS^{i}_{\breve{x}_{kj}\breve{Q}_m} \ \langle\ SMRT^{i}_{\breve{x}_{mj}\breve{s}_m}, \quad \text{all } i \in SM_m, \tag{13.10}$$

as can be deduced from Fig. 11.3. Note that this inequality holds, irrespective of the returns-to-scale of service systems in throughput.

The second step compares $MRS^{i}_{\breve{x}_{kj}\breve{Q}_m}$ and $SMRT^{i}_{\hat{x}_{mj}\hat{s}_m}$ using analyses of the first step. The inequality (13.10) implies that the resource allocation for the profit-maximizing choice leads to market equilibrium at the point where the indifference curves of consumers, for all $i \in SM_m$, are not tangent to the social production possibility frontier of the service system m. In contrast, the resource allocation for the Pareto-optimal choice reaches market equilibrium at the point where all the indifference curves are tangent to the social production possibility frontier.

On the other hand, the utility function of consumers is concave and increasing in Q_m and x_{kj}. Hence, the inequality (13.10) implies that

$$MRS^{i}_{\breve{x}_{kj}\breve{Q}_m} \ \langle\ MRS^{i}_{\hat{x}_{kj}\hat{Q}_m} = SMRT^{i}_{\hat{x}_{mj}\hat{s}_m} \neq SMRT^{i}_{\breve{x}_{mj}\breve{s}_m}, \quad \text{all } i, \tag{13.11}$$

as can be deduced from Fig. 11.3. Using this relationship, we characterize the resource allocation for the profit-maximizing choice of firm m, as below.

Theorem 13.3. *Suppose that service firm m serves inelastic demands, and that this demand satisfies the condition* $\breve{\xi}_m \cong \bar{\xi}_m \cong \hat{\xi}_m$. *Then, the resource allocation in submarket m satisfies the following:*

$$\breve{Q}_m \langle \hat{Q}_m, \; and \; \breve{c}_m \langle \hat{c}_m, \tag{13.12}$$

$$\breve{p}_m \rangle \hat{p}_m \;, \; and \; \breve{p}_m + \breve{\xi}^i_m \breve{t}_m \rangle \hat{p}_m + \hat{\xi}^i_m \hat{t}_m, \; all \; i \in SM_m. \tag{13.13}$$

Proof. First, the first inequality of (13.11) implies that $\breve{Q}_m \langle \hat{Q}_m$, due to the fact the utility function of consumers for all i is concave and increasing in $\breve{Q}^i_m$. Second, under the condition of $\breve{\xi}_m \cong \hat{\xi}_{mn}$, the two inequalities $\breve{Q}_m \langle \hat{Q}_m$ and $\partial \bar{c}(s)/\partial s \rangle 0$ imply that $\breve{c}_m \langle \hat{c}_m$. Here, the inequality $\partial \bar{c}(s)/\partial s \rangle 0$ comes from (7.11) and (7.16), and the capacities $\breve{c}$ $(= \bar{c}(\breve{s}))$ and $\hat{c}$ $(= \bar{c}(\hat{s}))$ are the solutions to Theorems 9.3 and 13.1, respectively. Third, it follows from (13.9) that $\breve{p}_m \rangle \hat{p}_m$. Fourth, $\breve{Q}_m \langle \hat{Q}_m$ implies that $\breve{p}_m + \breve{\xi}^i_m \breve{t}_m \rangle \hat{p}_m + \hat{\xi}^i_m \hat{t}_m$, for all i, since Q^i_{mn} is decreasing in $p_m + \xi_m t_m$.

Note that the assumption of $\breve{\xi}_m \cong \hat{\xi}_m$ is a critical input in proving $\breve{c}_m \langle \hat{c}_m$ and $\breve{p}_m \rangle \hat{p}_m$. This does not however mean that, if $\breve{\xi}_m \neq \hat{\xi}_m$, these two inequalities do not always hold. In fact, these two inequalities do hold, unless $\breve{\xi}_m$ and $\hat{\xi}_m$ are not significantly different. Further, no claim is being made that the assumption itself is invalid in reality.

Note also that the profit-maximizing choice of firm m does not always yield the outcome $\breve{t}_m \rangle \hat{t}_m$. To be specific, if a service system exhibits non-increasing (or increasing) returns in throughput, increases in throughput cause increases (or decreases) in optimal congestion delay, as shown in Theorem 7.4. Hence, if service system m exhibits non-increasing (increasing) returns, it holds that $\breve{t}_m \langle \hat{t}_m$ (or $\breve{t}_m \rangle \hat{t}_m$). □

Theorem 13.3 implies the following. First, the inequalities $\breve{p}_m \rangle \hat{p}_m$ and $\breve{c}_{mn} \langle \hat{c}_{mn}$ indicate, respectively, that a service firm in imperfect competition chooses a price larger than the socially optimal and a service capacity less than the socially optimal. Second, the relationship $\breve{Q}_m \langle \hat{Q}_m$ implies these profit-maximizing choices result in a demand, which is less than the demand for the socially optimal choices. Third, the inequality $\breve{p}_m + \breve{\xi}^i_m \breve{t}_m \rangle \hat{p}_m + \hat{\xi}^i_m \hat{t}_m$ indicates that the profit-maximizing choice is less beneficial to the customers of service m than is the socially optimal choice synonymous with the Pareto-optimal choice.

13.3 Characterization of Innovations in Service Markets

13.3.1 Innovations from the Standpoint of Profitability

The introduction of an innovative private service is motivated by the entrepreneurs' desire to earn profit. Such an innovation made by service firms can be classified into two different types: reduction in service production cost and improvement in service quality attributes. The manner in which these two different types of innovation can contribute to profitability is analyzed below, through the application of the user equilibrium approach.

Firstly, we introduce two important inputs to subsequent analyses for the profitability of innovative service m. This first input is the following pricing formula:

$$p_m\left(1-\frac{1}{E_m(Q_m)}\right)=MFC_m(Q_m). \tag{13.14}$$

This pricing formula shows that one crucial profitability index of $p_m - MFC_m$ depends mainly on demand elasticity $E_m(Q_m)$.

The second input is the thickness of catchment domain for an innovative service. The catchment domain of service m, denoted by D_m, can be expressed as follows:

$$D_m(p,t)=\{\,\xi\mid p_m+\xi_m t_m\ \le\ p_k+\xi_k t_k,\ \text{all}\ k\neq m\}. \tag{13.15}$$

For this set D_m, its thickness is defined to be the minimum width of D_m on the axis of net-value-of-time ξ_m.

The thickness of D_m influences the profitability of service m in two different ways. First, the thickness of D_m decisively determines the volume of the multiple integral that estimates the demand Q_m. As the thickness of D_m grows, the demand Q_m increases, and therefore the potential to earn a larger profit increases. Second, a demand with a thicker catchment domain has smaller elasticity with respect to price. Hence, the catchment domain with a larger thickness allows the choice of a price greater than the marginal cost by a larger margin and thus gives a larger profit. This can be deduced from (13.14).

Secondly, we show that a reduction in service production cost generally increases the profit of the firm that introduces this innovation. To be specific, an innovation that decreases the marginal full cost of service m increases both demand Q_m and profitability index $p_m - MFC_m$. These two changes increase the value of $Q_m \times (p_m - MFC_m)$, which is an effective index of profitability for service m, as shown below.

Theorem 13.4. *An innovation of service m in production cost, which decreases $MFC(Q_m)$ on the relevant region of Q_m, increases both Q_m and $p_m - MFC_m(Q_m)$.*

Proof. Firstly, we evaluate the differential of (13.14) with respect to MFC, under the convention that MFC is an exogenous variable affected by innovation in production cost. Let x denote this exogenous variable MFC. Under this convention, the differentiation of (13.14) with respect to x is

$$\frac{\partial p_m}{\partial x}\left(1-\frac{1}{E_m(Q_m)}\right)+\frac{p_m}{E_m(Q_m)^2}\frac{\partial E_m(Q_m)}{\partial x}=1. \tag{13.16}$$

This holds, irrespective of types of competition faced by firm m.

Equation (13.16) implies the following:

$$\frac{\partial p_m}{\partial x} \langle\, 0, \text{ and } \frac{\partial E_m(Q_m)}{\partial x} \langle\, 0. \tag{13.17}$$

The proof of this equation is as below. (i) Both terms $(\cdot)$ and $p_m/(E_m)^2$ in (13.16) are positive. (ii) Increases in p_m reduce the thickness of D_m, as can be deduced from (13.15). This will be confirmed in the two subsequent subsections. (iii) Decreases in the thickness of D_m raise demand elasticity E_m, as shown in Subsect. 10.2.2. (iv) It follows from (ii) and (iii) that the signs of $\partial p_m/\partial x$ and $\partial E_m/\partial x$ are identical. By (i) and (iv), (13.17) follows.

Subsequently, we show that (13.17) implies that, as the value of MFC_m decreases, both the values of Q_m and $p_m - MFC_m$ increase. The decrease in MFC_m allows firm m to choose a lower p_m value, as can be deduced from $\partial p_m/\partial x \langle\, 0$. This decrease in p_m widens the thickness of D_m, as will be shown in the two subsequent subsections. The wider thickness of D_m, in turn, leads to increases in the demand Q_m. Moreover, the wider thickness decreases demand elasticity, as can be confirmed from $\partial E_m/\partial x \langle\, 0$. This decrease in elasticity allows the choice of price p_m to be greater than MFC_m by a larger ratio. □

Thirdly, we explain how an innovation to improve service quality attributes causes an increase in Q_m and/or $p_m - MFC_m$. The innovation that improves the quality of service m decreases the net service time value $\xi_m t_m$ that quantifies the value of service quality attributes as a unit of money. The decrease in $\xi_m t_m$ value, in turn, strengthens profitability. Such an effect of service quality improvements is closely analyzed below, by dividing the type of competition into two categories: quantitative and qualitative.

Theorem 13.5. *An innovation that improves the quality of service m has the following effects: the decrease in service time t_m increases both Q_m and $p_m - MFC_m$, whereas the decrease in net value-of-time ξ_m increases Q_m only.*

Proof. Consider, first, the case of quantitative competition in which service time is only one service quality attribute. Under this competition, it holds that the net-value-of-time ξ_m equals ξ_k, for all $k \neq m$; that is, the net-value-of-service-time perceived by consumers is identical across all service options. Hence, the innovation of firm m mainly involves shortening service time t_m. Moreover, the innovation of decreasing the service time t_m has the effect of widening the thickness D_m, as will be confirmed in the next subsection.

Consider, next, the case of qualitative competition in which qualitative attributes play the dominant role in determining service quality. In this case, it can be assumed that t_m is approximately equal to t_k, for all $k \neq m$. Therefore, the innovation of firm m in qualitative competition mainly improves qualitative attributes. This innovation reduces the net-value-of-time ξ_m, which reflects the monetary value of qualitative attributes perceived by consumers in receiving service m.

This decrease in ξ_m values increases demands for service m, without exerting an direct impact on the thickness of D_m, as will be shown in Subsect. 13.3.3. □

13.3.2 Innovations under Quantitative Competition

In the previous subsection, we showed that a thicker catchment domain resulting from service quality improvements usually gives larger and more inelastic demands. As a sequel to the previous analyses, below, we analyze two topics for strategies to improve the quality of a service under quantitative competition. One topic specifies the specific content of strategies to seize a thicker catchment domain, and the other topic analyzes the impact of these strategies on the profit not only of the corresponding service but also of competing services.

To begin, we characterize a carrier's action that introduces an innovative service into a freight market, a typical service market in quantitative competition. Suppose that the existing N services satisfy the following trade-off conditions: $p_1 \langle \cdots \langle p_N$ and $t_1 \rangle \cdots \rangle t_N$. In these circumstances, the choice of the firm introducing an innovative service, denoted by n', regarding price $p_{n'}$ and service time $t_{n'}$, can be sorted into two different categories.

One category of choices involves selecting price $p_{n'}$ so as to be smaller than p_1 or larger than p_N. These choices give the thickness of $D_{n'}$, denoted by $W_{n'}$, such that

$$W_{n'}(p,t) = \begin{cases} \dfrac{p_1 - p_{n'}}{t_{n'} - t_1} - LB, & \text{if } p_{n'} \langle p_1 \\ UB - \dfrac{p_{n'} - p_N}{t_N - t_{n'}}, & \text{if } p_{n'} \rangle p_N, \end{cases} \tag{13.18}$$

where LB and UB are the lower and upper boundaries of value-of-service-times, respectively.

The above formula indicates that, when the chosen service time $t_{n'}$ is larger than t_1, price $p_{n'}$ must be selected so as to be smaller than p_1 to ensure a positive demand. One example of an innovative service that might charge such a price is a rail service that operates a container train on a corridor served by truck carriers only. On the other hand, when service time $t_{n'}$ is shorter than t_N, the chosen price $p_{n'}$ can be larger than p_N. An example of an innovative service that might choose this different type of price is an air cargo service that is newly introduced to a certain corridor covered by truck and/or rail services only.

Another category is the choice of $p_{n'}$ and $t_{n'}$, so as to satisfy the trade-off conditions such that $p_n \langle p_{n'} \langle p_{n+1}$ and $t_n \rangle t_{n'} \rangle t_{n+1}$, for some $n \in \langle 2, N-1 \rangle$. This choice should give the positive thickness $W_{n'}$, which is estimated by

$$W_{n'}(p,t) = \frac{p_{n+1} - p_{n'}}{t_{n'} - t_{n+1}} - \frac{p_{n'} - p_n}{t_n - t_{n'}}. \tag{13.19}$$

One example of a new service that might choose the price and service time characterized above is a freight service that employs the same transportation technologies as existing ones.

Subsequently, we show that a business strategy to lower price p'_n and/or to shorten service time t'_n yields a larger value for $W_{n'}$. To show that, we differentiate the function $W_{n'}(p,t)$ in (13.18) or (13.19) with respect to p'_n and t'_n. The differentiations with respect to p'_n and t'_n are both negative, as can be shown through a trite calculation. This implies the assertion.

The strategy to lower price p'_n and/or to shorten service time t'_n can be pursued through two different types of innovations. The first is to employ a transportation system that keeps service production costs as small as possible, so that the firm can choose a lower price. The second type involves introducing transportation and/or loading/unloading technologies that provide faster services.

Finally, we describe the impact of an innovative service on the service diversity of freight markets and competing carriers. The introduction of the innovative service generally increases the diversity of services differentiated by price and service time, unless the innovative service expels some obsolete services. Further, the introduction of an innovative service simultaneously decreases the thickness of the catchment domains of some competing services, as can readily be confirmed by (13.18) and (13.19). Such an impact results in smaller and more elastic demands for the competing services, as can be deduced from previous analyses for the opposite case of an innovation to increase catchment domains.

13.3.3 Innovations under Qualitative Competition

Here we present analyses for qualitative competition in a manner similar to analyses for quantitative competition in the previous subsection. For the analyses, we estimate the thickness of the catchment domain for an innovative service in qualitative competition by dividing qualitative competition into two types. The first type involves an innovative service that fulfills the identical ordering condition with existing services. The second type is the service that does not.

Firstly, we consider a service market in qualitative competition under the identical ordering condition among existing M services. Suppose that $a_m = 1$ for all m, and thereby that the identical ordering condition among these firms is expressed by $\xi_1 t_1 \rangle \cdots \rangle \xi_M t_M$. Under this condition, existing options, which have positive demands, satisfy the trade-off condition such that $p_1 \langle \cdots \langle p_M$, as shown in Lemma 5.7.

Under the identical ordering and trade-off conditions, the catchment domain of an innovative service, denoted by m', has the thickness with respect to $\xi_{m'}$, denoted by $W_{m'}$, such that

$$W_{m'}(p,t) = \begin{cases} \dfrac{p_{m+1} - p_{m'}}{t_{m'}}, & \text{if } p_m \langle\, p_{m'} \,\langle\, p_{m+1}, \ \text{all } m+1 \le M \\[2ex] \dfrac{p_{\max} - p_{m'}}{t_{m'}}, & \text{if } p_{m'} \,\rangle\, p_M, \end{cases} \qquad (13.20)$$

where $p_{\max} = UB_{m'}/\xi_{m'}t_{m'}$ is the maximum allowable price. Note that, typically, service time $t_{m'}$ does not significantly differ from service times t_m, for all m.

For the service characterized above, one important innovation strategy is to reduce service production cost as much as possible. This strategy enables the supplier of service m' to choose a lower price $p_{m'}$. This strategy increases the thickness $W_{m'}$ and reduces the thickness W_m for closest inferior m, but does not change the thickness for other services, including closest superior $m+1$, as can be deduced from (13.20). Therefore, this strategy absorbs a certain portion of demands for the closest inferior, but does not affect demands for other substitutes, including closest superior.

However, in reality, the ordering of preferences among options is not identical across all consumers, although a large portion of consumers has identical ordering. For example, we can imagine that a certain portion of consumers follows the ordering of $\xi_m t_m \,\langle\, \xi_{m+1} t_{m+1}$, instead of the ordering $\xi_m t_m \,\rangle\, \xi_{m+1} t_{m+1}$ that the majority follows; that is, they perceive that service m is the closest superior substitute to service $m+1$.[2] Then, innovative service m' has the possibility to capture some customers of service $m+1$, who have the preference ordering of $\xi_m t_m \,\langle\, \xi_{m+1} t_{m+1}$. It can therefore be argued that, in reality, innovative service m' generally attracts the customers of close substitutes, including service $m+1$.

Another important innovation strategy is to enhance the level of various qualitative attributes. This improvement strategy does not alter the thickness of D_m, as can be deduced from (13.20). Instead, this strategy decreases the $\xi_{m'}$ value perceived by consumers. Such a strategy decreases the difference $\xi^i_{m'}t_{m'} - \xi^i_{m+1}t_{m+1} \,\rangle\, 0$ but increases the difference $\xi^i_{m'}t_{m'} - \xi^i_{m}t_{m} \,\rangle\, 0$, and thus makes more consumers perceive that service m' is the most attractive option. It can therefore be said that this strategy has the effect of increasing demands, without exerting any impact on the thickness of catchment domain.

Secondly, we consider innovative service m', which does not satisfy the identical ordering condition with existing services. This service usually targets a small group of consumers with unique perceptions differentiated from those of the majority of consumers, as pointed out in Subsect. 5.4.1. The demand for this service can be expressed as a multiple integral that has the following geometry: average demand intensity is very low, but catchment domain thickness is relatively large.

[2] One typical example can be resort areas, each of which has unique climate, natural scenes, and/or entertainment facilities, as discussed in Subsect. 5.4.1.

The two different kinds of innovation for a service that does not satisfy the identical ordering condition result in the very similar impact on profitability for the service that satisfies the identical ordering condition. To show that, we estimates the thickness for the service not satisfying the identical ordering condition, dented by $W_{m'}$ such that

$$W_{m'}(p, t;\ \xi_m) = \max\left\{0,\ \frac{p_m - p_{m'}}{t_{m'}} + \xi_m \frac{t_m}{t_{m'}}\right\},\ \text{all } m, \tag{13.21}$$

as shown in Lemma 5.5. This equation shows that the strategy to decrease price $p_{m'}$ through the reduction in marginal full costs widens the thickness of $D_{m'}$. Further, it indicates that the strategy to decrease $\xi_{m'}$ value through the improvement of qualitative attributes increases the demand $Q_{m'}$ but does not widen the thickness of $D_{m'}$.

Finally, the introduction of an innovative service generally increases the diversity of services differentiated by price and qualitative attributes, as in the case of quantitative competition. Also, the introduction of an innovative service simultaneously decreases the thickness of the catchment domains of some competing services, as can be deduced from (13.20) and (13.21). Further, when the total number of services is very large, it is highly probable that most services in competition have thin catchment domains.

13.4 Contribution of Innovations to Resource Allocation Efficiency

13.4.1 A Benefit-Cost Analysis for Innovative Services

We here prove the following. First, the introduction of an innovative service with a quality and/or a cost structure significantly superior to those of existing services generally causes an increase in social welfare. Second, this introduction increases benefit not only to the customers of the new service but also to the remaining customers of some existing services, without making the customers of other services worse off.

The proof is provided through a benefit-cost analysis conducted under the following three conditions. First, an innovative service introduced into a market satisfies one or both of the following two requirements: (i) its service quality is significantly higher than those of existing some services that lose parts of their demands or their entire demands; (ii) its service production cost is significantly lower than those of these existing services. Second, the prices and capacities of all services are the outcomes of profit-maximizing choices that are made under no restriction on capacity adjustment. Third, the introduction of the new service does not bring about significant changes in the prices and service times of existing services, unless a certain portion of demands for these services shifts to the innovative service.

The rationale behind these three conditions is as follows. The first condition defines an innovative service, which excludes a new service that captures a perfectly elastic demand by offering a service identical or very similar to those of some existing services. The second condition is incorporated so as to characterize the reaction of existing firms by applying optimality conditions for the profit-maximizing choice in Theorem 9.3. The third condition is a device to simplify analyses by ignoring the secondary impact on some existing services that are not close substitutes to the innovative service; that is, changes in the prices and capacities of existing services that have catchment domains tangent to that of the innovative service exert a negligible effect on other existing services that have catchment domains spatially separate from that of the innovative service.

Firstly, we introduce conventions used in forthcoming analyses of changes in benefit and cost. We first sort existing services into three groups by the types of impacts on demands: losing all demands; a part of demands; and no demand. These are denoted by I_1, I_2, and I_3, respectively. According to this classification scheme, we next introduce other notations that will be used in subsequent analyses.

Let the innovative service be denoted by m. Let, also, $\bar{p}$ and $\bar{t}$ be the values of vectors p and t, respectively, at original market equilibrium before the introduction of the service m. Let, further, $\hat{p}$ and $\hat{t}$ be the values of p and t, respectively, at new market equilibrium after the introduction. Let, finally, $\bar{\pi}_n \equiv \bar{p}_n + \xi_n \bar{t}_n$ and $\hat{\pi}_n \equiv \hat{p}_n + \xi_n \hat{t}_n$ be the implicit price of existing service n before and after the introduction of the service m.

Under the third condition introduced above, the relationship between the catchment domain before and after the introduction of the service m can be expressed as below. First, the relationship for the new service m is

$$D_m(\hat{p},\hat{t}) = \bigcup_{n \in I_1} D_n(\bar{p},\bar{t}) + \bigcup_{n \in I_2} \left(D_m(\hat{p},\hat{t}) \bigcap D_n(\bar{p},\bar{t}) \right), \tag{13.22}$$

where

$$D_m(\hat{p},\hat{t}) \bigcap D_n(\bar{p},\bar{t}) = \{\xi \mid \hat{\pi}_m \leq \hat{\pi}_n \text{ and } \bar{\pi}_n \leq \bar{\pi}_k, \text{ all } k \neq n\}.$$

Second, the relationship for all $n \in I_1$ is $D_n(\hat{p},\hat{t}) = \emptyset$. Third, the relationship for all $n \in I_2$ is

$$\begin{aligned} D_n(\hat{p},\hat{t}) &= D_n(\bar{p},\bar{t}) - D_m(\hat{p},\hat{t}) \bigcap D_n(\bar{p},\bar{t}) \\ &= \{\ \xi \mid \hat{\pi}_n \leq \hat{\pi}_m \text{ and } \bar{\pi}_n \leq \bar{\pi}_k, \text{ all } k \neq n\}. \end{aligned} \tag{13.23}$$

Fourth, the relationship for all $n \in I_3$ is $D_n(\hat{p},\hat{t}) = D_n(\bar{p},\bar{t})$.

The above analysis shows that, after the introduction of the new service, the catchment domains of the new service m and services for all $n \in I_2$ contain all the demands that experience changes in implicit prices. Therefore, the targets of analyses to estimate changes in consumers' surplus can be confined to submarkets m and $n \in I_2$. Based on this judgment, we estimate net social benefit for these submarkets.

Secondly, we estimate changes in consumers' surplus caused by the introduction of service m. We first estimate the change for submarket m. The demand for service m is the outcome of consumer judgment such that $\hat{\pi}_m \leq \bar{\pi}_n$, for all $n \in I_1$ and $n \in I_2$. Hence, the increase in consumers' surplus for the customers of innovative service m, denoted by CS_m, can be estimated by

$$CS_m = \sum_{n \in I_1, I_2} \int_{\hat{\pi}_n}^{\bar{\pi}_m} \int_{D_m(\hat{p},\hat{t}) \cap D_n(\bar{p},\bar{t})} f_n(\pi_n)\, h(\xi) d\mu\, d\pi_n \rangle 0. \tag{13.24}$$

Here, the first iterated integral estimates the portion of Q_n, which is switched to service m, and the second iterated integral calculates the change in consumers' surplus for the switched portion.

We next estimate changes in consumers' surplus for submarkets belonging to group I_2. Consumers who continue to choose service $n \in I_2$ perceive that $\hat{\pi}_n \leq \hat{\pi}_m$. The fact that $\hat{\pi}_n \leq \bar{\pi}_n$ can be proved by contradiction; if they judge that $\hat{\pi}_n \rangle \bar{\pi}_n$, it would hold that $\hat{\pi}_n \rangle \hat{\pi}_m$ and thus $Q_n(\hat{p}, \hat{t}) = 0$. Hence, the net change in consumers' surplus for the remaining consumers, denoted by CS_n, can be expressed by

$$CS_n = \int_{\hat{\pi}_n}^{\bar{\pi}_n} \int_{D_n(\hat{p},\hat{t})} f_n(\pi_n)\, h(\xi) d\mu\, d\pi_n \rangle 0. \tag{13.25}$$

Here, the sign that $CS_n \rangle 0$ implies that the remaining customers experience increases in consumers' surplus.

Thirdly, we introduce the formula that estimates the net social benefit accrued from the introduction of service m. The net social benefit is the sum of changes in consumers' surpluses and quasi-rents for all services. Under the three conditions identified previously, the net social benefit, denoted by NSB, is estimated by

$$\begin{aligned} NSB \cong\, & CS_m + \sum_{n \in I_2} CS_n + QR_m(\hat{Q}_m) - \sum_{n \in I_1} QR_n(\bar{Q}_n) \\ & + \sum_{n \in I_2} \left(QR_n(\hat{Q}_n) - QR_n(\bar{Q}_n) \right),^3 \end{aligned} \tag{13.26}$$

[3]One example of a benefit-cost analysis similar to this analysis can be seen in Chapter 7, Mishan (1976). Both benefit-cost analyses assess the project that introduces an innovative service. However, the details of the two benefit-cost analyses are significantly different. The benefit-cost analysis considered here explicitly accounts for user time cost; in contrast, the analysis in the reference does not.

where QR_n stands for the quasi-rent of firm n. In addition, the terms $QR_n(\bar{Q}_n)$ and $QR_n(\hat{Q}_n)$ represent, respectively, the quasi-rent of firm n before and after the entry of service m.

The main concern of forthcoming analyses is to evaluate the sign of NSB in (13.26). If the sign is positive, the introduction of innovative service m brings a net gain of social benefits in total, though some consumers and existing firms have the possibility to experience economic losses. To evaluate such a sign of NSB, we estimate specific expressions of all terms in (13.26).

We first approximate changes in consumers' surplus CS_m and CS_n for $n \in I_2$:

$$CS_m \cong \sum_{n \in I_1, I_2} (\bar{p}_n - \hat{p}_m)(Q_n^1 + 0.5\Delta Q_n^1) + \sum_{n \in I_1, I_2} (\bar{\xi}_n \bar{T}_n - \hat{\xi}_m \hat{T}_m)(Q_n^1 + 0.5\Delta Q_n^1) \rangle 0 \tag{13.27}$$

$$CS_n \cong (\bar{p}_n - \hat{p}_n) Q_n^2 + \hat{\xi}_n(\bar{T}_n - \hat{T}_n) Q_n^2 \rangle 0, \quad \text{all } n \in I_2 \tag{13.28}$$

where

$$Q_n^1 = \int_{D_m(\hat{p},\hat{t}) \cap D_n(\bar{p},\bar{t})} f_n(\bar{\pi}_n) h(\xi) d\mu$$

$$Q_n^2 = \int_{D_n(\hat{p},\hat{t})} f_n(\bar{\pi}_n) h(\xi) d\mu = \bar{Q}_n - Q_n^1$$

$$\Delta Q_n^1 = \int_{D_m(\hat{p},\hat{t}) \cap D_n(\bar{p},\bar{t})} (f_m(\hat{\pi}_m) - f_n(\bar{\pi}_n)) h(\xi) d\mu$$

$$\Delta Q_n^2 = \int_{D_n(\hat{p},\hat{t})} (f_n(\bar{\pi}_n) - f_n(\bar{\pi}_n)) h(\xi) d\mu.$$

Note that all the terms $\bar{\xi}_n$, $\hat{\xi}_m$, and $\hat{\xi}_n$ are social value-of-service-times.

We next estimate quasi-rents in (12.26). Without loss of generality, it can be assumed that all services are provided by the basic service systems. By the condition that all firms simultaneously adjust prices and capacities, their quasi-rents earned through the operation of basic service systems are estimated by

$$QR_n(\bar{Q}_n) = \bar{p}_n \bar{Q}_n - KC_n(\bar{c}_n(\bar{Q}_n)), \quad \text{all } n \in I_1,\ I_2 \tag{13.29}$$

$$QR_m(\hat{Q}_m) = \hat{p}_m \hat{Q}_m - KC_m(\hat{c}_m) \cong \hat{p}_m(\bar{Q}_m + \Delta\bar{Q}_m) - KC_m(\bar{c}_m(\bar{Q}_m)) - MKC_m(\bar{c}_m(\bar{Q}_m))(\bar{c}_m(\hat{Q}_m) - \bar{c}_m(\bar{Q}_m)) \tag{13.30}$$

$$\begin{aligned} QR_n(\hat{Q}_n) &= \hat{p}_n \hat{Q}_n - KC_n(\bar{c}_n(\hat{Q}_n)) \cong \hat{p}_n(Q_n^2 + \Delta Q_n^2) - KC_n(\bar{c}_n(Q_n^2)) \\ &\quad - MKC_n(\bar{c}_n(Q_n^2))(\bar{c}_n(\hat{Q}_n) - \bar{c}_n(Q_n^2)), \quad \text{all } n \in I_2 \end{aligned} \tag{13.31}$$

where $\bar{Q}_m = \sum_{I_1,I_2} Q_n^1$, and $\Delta\bar{Q}_m = \sum_{I_1,I_2} \Delta Q_n^1$. Note that $\hat{Q}_m = \bar{Q}_m + \Delta\bar{Q}_m$ and that $\bar{c}_m$ and $\bar{c}_n$ are the functions estimating the solution of c to the investment rule in (13.4).

Fourthly, substituting (13.27)–(13.31) into (13.26) gives

$$NSB \cong SC_a - SC_b + \Delta CS + \Delta QR_m + \Delta QR_n \rangle 0, \tag{13.32}$$

where

$$SC_b = \sum_{n\in I_1,I_2} \bar{\xi}_n \bar{T}_n \bar{Q}_n + \sum_{n\in I_1,I_2} KC_n(\bar{c}_n(\bar{Q}_n))$$

$$SC_a = \hat{\xi}_m \hat{T}_m \bar{Q}_m + KC_m(\bar{c}_m(\bar{Q}_m)) + \sum_{n\in I_2}\left(\hat{\xi}_n \hat{T}_n Q_n^2 + KC_n(\bar{c}_n(Q_n^2))\right)$$

$$\Delta CS = \sum_{n\in I_1,I_2} 0.5(\bar{\pi}_n - \hat{\pi}_m)\Delta\bar{Q}_n$$

$$\Delta QR_m = \hat{p}_m \Delta\bar{Q}_m - MKC_m(\bar{c}_m(\bar{Q}_m))(\bar{c}_m(\hat{Q}_m) - \bar{c}_m(\bar{Q}_m))$$

$$\Delta QR_n = \sum_{n\in I_2} \hat{p}_n \Delta Q_n^2 - \sum_{n\in I_2} MKC_n(\bar{c}_n(Q_n^2))(\bar{c}_n(\hat{Q}_n) - \bar{c}_n(Q_n^2)).$$

The inequality $NSB \rangle 0$ follows from that $SC_a - SC_b \rangle 0$, $\Delta CS \rangle 0$, $\Delta QR_m \rangle 0$, and $\Delta QR_2 \rangle 0$, as shown below.

Prior to the proof of $SC_a - SC_b \rangle 0$, we interpret the economic meaning of SC_b and SC_a. The term SC_b estimates the sum of social costs in submarkets for all $n \in I_1$ and $n \in I_2$, before the introduction of innovative service m; while the term SC_a represents the sum of hypothetical social costs in submarkets m and all $n \in I_2$, after the introduction. The hypothetical social cost estimated in the latter represents the social cost required to facilitate the outputs $\bar{Q}_m$ and Q_n^2, which are equal to the outputs applied in the former. It also be relevant to note that the outputs $\bar{Q}_m$ and Q_n^2 are smaller than the actual outputs $\hat{Q}_m$ and $\hat{Q}_n$, respectively.

The inequality $SC_a - SC_b \rangle 0$ follows that the first condition of the benefit-cost analysis, such that the innovative service m satisfies one or both of the following two conditions. First, the quality of service m is significantly higher than those of existing services in groups I_1 and I_2; that is,

$\hat{\xi}_m \hat{T}_m Q_m \langle \sum_{I_1,I_2} \bar{\xi}_n \bar{T}_n \bar{Q}_n - \sum_{I_2} \hat{\xi}_n \hat{T}_n \hat{Q}_n$. Second, its service production cost is significantly lower than those of the services in these two groups; that is, $KC_m(\hat{c}_m) \langle \sum_{I_1,I_2} KC_n(\bar{c}_n(\bar{Q}_n)) - \sum_{I_2} KC_n(\bar{c}_n(\hat{Q}_n))$.

The proof of three remaining inequalities is as below. The assertion that $\Delta CS \rangle 0$ is clear from $\bar{\pi}_n - \hat{\pi}_m \rangle 0$, which was shown in deriving (13.24). Subsequently, the proof of $\Delta QR_m \rangle 0$ is as follows. The innovative service m attains the maximum profit when $Q_m = \hat{Q}_m$ and $c_m = \bar{c}_m(\hat{Q}_m)$. This implies that the action to adjust Q_m and c_m from $\bar{Q}_m$ and $\bar{c}_m(\bar{Q}_m)$ to $\hat{Q}_m$ $\bar{c}_m(\hat{Q}_m)$, respectively, should increase the profit of service m. Hence, it should hold that $\Delta QR_m \rangle 0$. Further, the proof of $\Delta QR_n \rangle 0$ can be worked out a manner identical to show $\Delta QR_m \rangle 0$.

Finally, we examine economic implications of the above benefit-cost analysis. First, equation (13.24) indicates that all customers of an innovative service, who switch from existing services, experience increases in consumer benefit. Second, equation (13.25) shows that the remaining customers of some existing services that lose a part of their customers are also better off, without causing the customers of other services to be worse off. Third, these two facts imply that the introduction of an innovative service makes no consumer worse off. Fourth, equation (13.32) depicts that the benefit of consumers and the profit of the innovative service exceeds the loss of profits for existing services and, thus, results in a net increase in social benefit.

13.4.2 Consumer Benefit from Service Quality Diversity

This subsection shows following. First, a package of more qualitatively diversified services provides a better opportunity for consumers to find a more economical option and thus increases consumer well-being. Second, such consumer benefit from service quality diversity is independent of consumer benefit from efficient resource allocations due to keen competition. The validity of these assertion are illustrated through a comparison of consumer benefit between small and large markets for a particular qualitative choice service; the number of service options and the diversity of service quality in a large market is greater, respectively, than the number and diversity in a small market by very large extents.

A more efficient resource allocation must be more beneficial to consumers and, thereby, must attain a higher level of social welfare. In this regard, service quality diversity on aggregated bases together with keen competition among services is an indispensable factor determining the resource allocation efficiency of a service market. To show this, below we introduce a three different kinds of consumer benefit for a large service market in which variety of services differentiated by quality are offered by a large number of firms in competition.

The first kind of benefit for the large market is the resource allocation closer to the Pareto optimal in all submarkets. It has been pointed out in Subsects. 13.3.2 and 13.3.3 that, as the number of firms in competition increases, the thickness of the catchment domain for each firm tends to decrease. This implies that, as the number of service firms grows, the elasticity of demands for all firms in a market tends to increase. Further, increases in demand elasticity force firms to decrease price down to the point equal to marginal full cost. Therefore, a large market has the higher potential to provide the same service in terms of quality at a price lower than the price in a small market.

The second kind of consumer benefit for the large market consists in the availability of more diversified services from the standpoint of quality. A consumer in a large market has a better opportunity to purchase a service at a lower implicit price in a large market than the lowest possible implicit price in a small market. Such an advantage of a large market stems from the fact that each consumer has his own unique perception for service quality. This fact implies that, in the circumstance that multiple options are available, each consumer has a most desirable option that usually differs from that for other consumers. Further, each consumer finds a more economical option when he is able to choose from a wider array of service choices, each of which has an implicit price that differs from the others.

The third kind of consumer benefits is related to the randomness of consumer perception for service quality. Consumer perception for service quality varies widely and changes from time to time. It is therefore usual that a consumer prefers to have a sufficiently large number of options, so as to allow his choices to change as desired. In other words, a consumer achieves more satisfaction by changing options as his perception changes than he does by consistently choosing the same options. For example, one can hardly deny that the residents of a large urban area are happier with their more diversified dining options than are residents of a small town with relatively limited dining options.

Subsequently, we quantify these three different advantages of a large market over a small market. To this end, we estimate differences in implicit service price between the two markets under the following conditions. First, a small market has only one service firm that offers a certain qualitative choice service, whereas a large market has a very large number of firms in keen quality competition. Second, a large market has a service firm that employs the identical production and service technology as the firm in a small market. Third, input prices for service production are identical between the two markets.

First, we analyze the difference in implicit service price between the two markets by applying the deterministic perception approach. Let $\pi^s \ (= p^s + v\,t^s)$ be the deterministic implicit service price of the service offered in a small market, perceived by a consumer under analysis. Let also $\pi^l_m \ (= p^l_m + v_m\,t^l_m)$ be the implicit price of service m available in a large market for the same consumer. Then the implicit price for the service chosen by the consumer in a large market, denoted by π^l, is

$$\pi^l = \min_m \{p_m + v_m t_m\}. \qquad (13.31)$$

Further, the difference in implicit price between the two markets, denoted by $\Delta\pi$, is

$$\Delta\pi = \pi^s - \pi^l \rangle\, 0. \tag{13.32}$$

The difference $\Delta\pi$ is always positive for all consumers.

The proof of (13.32) is as follows. Suppose that firm o in a large market offers the identical service and has the same production technology as the sole firm in a small market. Because of keen competition, firm o faces more elastic demand than does the firm in a small market. Therefore, by (13.14), it certainly holds that $\Delta\pi_1 = \pi^s - \pi^l_o \rangle\, 0$, where $\pi^l_o = p^l_o + v\,t^l_o$. Moreover, by the definition of π^l in (13.31), it is certain that $\Delta\pi_2 = \pi^l_o - \pi^l \geq 0$. Hence it follows that

$$\Delta\pi = \Delta\pi_1 + \Delta\pi_2 \rangle\, 0. \tag{13.33}$$

Note that the inequality $\Delta\pi_2 \rangle\, 0$ holds when the consumer under consideration chooses an option other than the service of firm o.

Equation (13.33) indicates that a large market gives two different kinds of consumer benefit. The first kind is benefit caused by reduction in implicit service price due to keener competition among options, and is expressed by the term $\Delta\pi_1$. The second kind is benefit accrued by service quality diversity, and is denoted by the term $\Delta\pi_2$. This additional benefit $\Delta\pi_2$ can be larger as the services available are more diversified, and as consumer perceptions for service quality, quantified by net-value-of-times, are more widely dispersed.

Next, we extend the above analyses to a consumer with random taste. The expected value of the implicit service price, perceived by a consumer in a small market, is estimated by

$$E\left\{\pi^s(\xi)\right\} = \int_{RV} (p^s + \xi\, t^s)\, h^s(\xi)\, d\xi, \tag{13.34}$$

where E is the expectation operator, and h^s is the probability density function of the random net-value-of-time $\xi \in \mathbf{R}$. On the other hand, the expected value of the implicit service price, perceived by the same consumer in a large market, is

$$E\left\{\pi^l(\xi)\right\} = \sum_{mn} \int_{D_{mn}} (p_{mn} + \xi_m\, t_{mn})\, h^l(\xi)\, d\mu. \tag{13.35}$$

Then, the difference in the two implicit service prices in (13.34) and (13.35), denoted by $E\{\Delta\pi\}$, is

$$E\{\Delta\pi\} = E\{\pi^s(\xi)\} - E\left\{\pi^l(\xi)\right\} \rangle\, 0. \tag{13.36}$$

The proof of the above inequality is worked out below, in a manner similar to the proof for the case of deterministic value-of-service-time.

Consider a hypothetical case when firm o in a large market offers the same service in a small market without changing its price and service time in a large market. Then, the consumer considered above has the expected value of implicit service price for this hypothetical case, denoted by $E\left\{\pi^h(\xi)\right\}$:

$$E\left\{\pi^h(\xi)\right\} = \int_{RV} (p_o^l + \xi\, t_o^l)\, h^s(\xi)\, d\xi. \tag{13.37}$$

This implicit price $E\left\{\pi^h(\xi)\right\}$ is always smaller than the price $E\left\{\pi^s(\xi)\right\}$; that is,

$$\begin{aligned} E\left\{\Delta\pi_1(\xi)\right\} &= E\left\{\pi^s(\xi)\right\} - E\left\{\pi^h(\xi)\right\} \\ &= \int_{RV} \left\{ (p^s + \xi\, t^s) - (p_o^l + \xi\, t_o^l)\right\} h^s(\xi)\, d\xi \rangle\ 0, \end{aligned} \tag{13.38}$$

since the integrand in (13.38) is always positive for every ξ, as can be deduced from Theorem 13.3.

Consider another hypothetical case when only firm o serves all service demands in a large market with the actual price and service time. This hypothetical case gives the implicit service price identical to that of the hypothetical case considered above; that is,

$$\int_{RV} (p_o^l + \xi\, t_o^l)\, h^s(\xi)\, d\xi = \sum_m \int_{D_m} (p_o^l + \xi\, t_o^l)\, h^l(\xi)\, d\mu, \tag{13.39}$$

since $E\{h^s(\xi)\} = \sum_m E\left\{h^l(\xi)\right\} = 1.0$.

Hence, the difference between the implicit prices $E\left\{\pi^h(\xi)\right\}$ and $E\left\{\pi^l(\xi)\right\}$, denoted by $E\left\{\Delta\pi_2(\xi)\right\}$, is

$$\begin{aligned} E\left[\Delta\pi_2(\xi)\right] &= E\left\{\pi^h(\xi)\right\} - E\left\{\pi^l(\xi)\right\} \\ &= \sum_m \int_{D_m} \left\{ (p_o^l + \xi\, t_o^l) - (p_m + \xi_m\, t_m)\right\} h^l(\xi)\, d\mu \rangle\ 0, \end{aligned} \tag{13.40}$$

since

$$(p_o^l + \xi\, t_o^l) - (p_m + \xi_m\, t_m) \begin{cases} = 0, & \text{if } o = m \\ \rangle\ 0, & \text{otherwise.} \end{cases}$$

By (13.39) and (13.40), it follows that

$$E\left\{\Delta\pi\right\} = E\left\{\pi_1(\xi)\right\} + E\left\{\pi_2(\xi)\right\} \rangle\ 0, \tag{13.41}$$

as claimed in (13.36).

The above analysis of consumer benefit under the random perception approach identifies two different kinds of consumer benefit for large markets, as is true of the analysis under the deterministic perception approach. One kind of benefit, expressed by $E\{\Delta\pi_1(\xi)\}$, reflects the reduction in implicit service price due to keener competition among firms. The other kind, denoted by $E\{\Delta\pi_2(\xi)\}$, quantifies the reduction in implicit price due to the diversity of service quality. However, the analysis under the random perception approach differs from the analysis under the deterministic approach in that only the former can explicitly account for the consumer benefit related to the randomness of consumer perception for service quality.

13.5 Progress of Resource Allocation Efficiency in Market Economies

13.5.1 Dynamic Process of Improvements in Resource Allocation Efficiency

Service innovations contribute to marketwise resource allocation efficiency, as pointed out in Sect. 13.4. It can therefore be argued that the successive introduction of innovative services tends to gradually improve the marketwise resource allocation efficiency of market economies. This dynamic process of market economies is described in detail by reorganizing the previous findings of this study.

First, in market economies, the key cause of progress in marketwise resource allocation efficiency can be found in a desire to make larger profits. This desire of a firm can be achieved through the introduction of innovative services. Such an innovative effort by a firm can be grouped into two categories: reductions in service production costs; and improvements in service quality attributes.

Besides the entrepreneurial desire to make a profit, growth in consumer income plays a significant role in promoting the introduction of innovative services. A consumer with a larger wage tends to choose a higher-quality service, as pointed out in Subsect. 10.4.2. Therefore, growth in consumer income increases demand for high-quality services. In this circumstance, one business strategy to earn profits is to introduce a higher-quality service than the others so as to capture demand with a thick catchment domain, as can be deduced from (13.19) and (13.20). Such a business strategy, of course, usually enables the supplier of the service to charge a price larger than marginal full cost by a margin usually larger than competing services.

Second, the introduction of an innovative service triggers changes in the industrial structure of a service market within which multiple industrial organization types usually coexist. The innovative service should be able to capture a positive demand. The introduction of such an innovative service triggers the reactions of competing services to adjust prices and capacities in order to maximize profits. These reactions result in a new resource allocation at market equilibrium and thus accompany a change in the industrial structure of the entire market in the direction described subsequently.

The innovative service generally captures an inelastic demand. To be specific, as service production cost decreases by a bigger margin and as service quality improves by a large extent, the innovative service holds a thicker catchment domain that leads to a larger and more inelastic demand, as shown in Sect. 13.3. Further, as the demand for the innovative service is more inelastic, the service can choose a price larger than marginal full cost by a larger margin and, therefore can yield a larger profit, as explained also in Sect. 13.3.

Further, the introduction of an innovative service exerts three different types of impacts on existing services: completely absorbing demands; partially absorbing demands; and no significant change in demands. The impact that completely absorbs demand implies that some obsolete services disappear in markets. The impact that partially absorbs demand reduces the thickness of catchment domains for affected services, and thus forces the supplier of the affected services to choose prices closer to the Pareto-optimal.

Third, the introduction of an innovative service generally improves resource allocation efficiency on marketwise bases. The innovative service causes a net social benefit in its submarket, because of the following: first, the switch of option from existing services to the innovative service implies that the customers of the innovative service experience increases in consumers' surplus; second, the innovative service that captures an inelastic demand usually earns a positive profit synonymous with a positive quasi-rent. Moreover, the introduction of the innovative service usually increases in net social benefit in submarkets for some competing services, without affecting resource allocations efficiency in submarkets for remaining services, as detailed next.

As noted above, the introduction of the new service exerts the following three different types of impacts on existing services. The impact that completely absorbs demand for some services contributes to improving marketwise resource allocation efficiency by making obsolete services to leave markets. The impact that partially absorbs demand reduces the thickness of catchment domains for affected firms, and thus forces the affected firms to choose prices closer to the Pareto-optimal.

Fourth, the successive introduction of innovative services promotes gradual improvements in marketwise resource allocation efficiency. The introduction of each innovative service usually improves the resource allocation efficiency of submarkets for some services, and also often enriches the diversity of service quality. Therefore, the successive introduction of innovative services continuously moves marketwise resource allocations toward a higher level of efficiency.

Finally, it should be noted that the introduction of an innovative service does not always result in a non-negative profit, which is prerequisite for survival under competition. Under the user equilibrium approach, a firm is postulated to make choices regarding price and capacity based on the incomplete user equilibrium condition that reflects incomplete knowledge of consumers' and competitors' reactions to the choice of the firm. The use of the incomplete user equilibrium condition usually leads to a profit that differs from the one that the firm expected at the moment when they made its choice. The possible outcome includes a deficit that can lead to bankruptcy, which is clearly contrary to the expectation of the firm, as pointed out in Subsect. 9.2.2. This implies that the introduction of an innovative service has the possibility of causing losses in social welfare.

13.5.2 An Illustrative Example: Agglomeration Economies for Large Urban Areas

The previous analyses in this chapter can be applied to explain that agglomeration economies for large urban areas, one important research theme in urban economics, are partially caused by efficient resource allocations attained through keen service quality competition. Such analyses can also help argue that efficient resource allocations in large urban areas benefit residents and positively impact the growth of many large urban areas having an economic base consisting of service industries. Given these considerations, below, we analyze agglomeration economies for large urban areas.

Agglomeration economies bring unique advantages that are brought about by the spatial concentration that results from the scale of an entire urban area but not from the scale of a particular firm. A larger urban area usually has bigger agglomeration economies, which give larger economic benefit not only to producers but also to consumers. However, previous studies have primarily focused on identifying economic benefit that larger urban areas provide from the producers' point of view (Mills and McDonald 1992). In contrast, we here consider the consumer side. From this perspective, we conclude that agglomeration economies in large urban areas arise not only from keen competition among service firms but also from service quality diversity on marketwise bases.

The significant resource allocation efficiency of service industries is thought to allow the development of agglomeration economies in modern metropolises. Because of their larger populations, metropolises have larger aggregated demands for various types of qualitative choice services than are found in smaller urban centers. Larger demand for a certain type of qualitative choice service on marketwise bases usually attracts a larger number of service firms that are differentiated by quantitative and/or qualitative attributes. Additionally, the increase in the number of service firms commonly strengthens both competition among all firms and service quality diversification on marketwise bases.

Therefore, agglomeration of a larger number of service firms in large urban areas causes keener competition and greater diversification of service quality than is true in small urban areas. Importantly, keener competition and more diversified services in large urban areas result in more efficient resource allocations on marketwise bases than resource allocations in small areas. Further, more efficient resource allocations in large urban areas usually give larger benefit to residents than are provided by less efficient resource allocations.

Consumer benefit accrued from efficient resource allocations can be sorted into two types, both of which are analyzed in detail in the previous section. First, a metropolitan consumer has a better chance of purchasing services from a group of options that are more appropriate to his unique perceptions at lower implicit service prices. Second, consumers achieve more satisfaction by changing options to meet their changing perceptions than they do by consistently choosing the same options.

The above analysis for the agglomeration economies of services can be applicable not only to consumption services for urban residents but also to the basic industries of urban areas. Typical examples of consumption services that exhibit agglomeration economies beneficial to consumers are found in retail, restaurant, medical, recreation, transportation, telecommunication, hotel, and other industries. Equally valid examples of basic industries that provide agglomeration economies to customers can include sightseeing, entertainment, financing, fashion, and various business service industries.

Further, it can be argued that efficient resource allocation promotes growth in many metropolitan areas. It was previously pointed out that one important condition of agglomeration economies is the efficient resource allocations generated from accumulations of firms in certain industries. Such accumulations are beneficial to customers and, therefore, have the effect of attracting large numbers of customers. The attractiveness of metropolitan areas, in turn, strengthens the competitive edge as an industrial location, as explained in detail below.

The traditional theory of urban growth emphasizes the role of transportation accessibility. In the industrial age, manufacturing industries provided the main thrust for economic growth in urban areas. These industries generated a large volume of freight and passenger demands. For this reason, during the industrial age, manufacturing industries seriously assessed transportation issues when determining location. Cause and effect became intermingled over time. Naturally, locations where industrial facilities were concentrated became ever more accessible.

Today, service industries dominate the economic growth of postindustrial nations. In addition, many already large urban areas continue to grow ever larger, forming ever greater mega-metropolitan regions. These growing urban areas usually have only weak links to manufacturing industries. Instead, they have large populations and powerful knowledge-based service industries. For example, various knowledge-based service industries now constitute the basic industries of existing metropolitan areas such as New York, London, and Tokyo. The list goes on and on. Another special example of a modern, non-manufacturing economy is the entertainment industry, which serves as the backbone of the rapid growth of Las Vegas away from manufacturing.

Urban growth based on service industries is a clear indication that agglomeration economies accrue from the accumulation of various consumption and knowledge-based service industries. The increasing accumulation of service firms in certain consumption or basic service industries leads to increasingly efficient resource allocation, as noted previously. This allocation efficiency generates two different types of benefit, which support the continuous growth of some large urban areas.

The first type of benefit is received by customers of the basic service industries, which support the continuous growth of large urban areas. The accumulation of a particular basic service industry in a large urban area provides customer benefit accrued from keen competition and diversified services. Therefore, the basic service industry of the area has a strong competitive power to attract more customers. This competitive power has the effect of attracting more service firms into competition, as the demand for the industry grows, and thus increases consumer benefit from agglomeration economies.

The second type of benefit is acquired by employees of knowledge-based industries from developed consumption service industries in large urban areas. For knowledge-based industries, one important factor that delineates the competitive edge of a particular service firm is the intellectual capacity of employees. To recruit capable employees, it is necessary for firms to choose locations where employees prefer to live. In this regard, large urban areas offer efficient resource allocation enabled by the accumulation of many firms across various consumer services that delineate attractive quality of life amenities of many types.

Finally, it should also be noted that urban growth is not a simple theme that can be explained through only the resource allocation efficiency of service industries. For example, it is known that employees of knowledge-based industries consider the accumulation of professionals in the same field as an important factor when choosing work locations. However, the agglomeration economies accrued from the accumulation of professionals are not directly related to efficient resource allocation, but are mainly related to information and knowledge gathering. As another example, urban growth is cursed by agglomeration diseconomies, too. Such detriments include traffic congestion, air pollution, high housing costs, crime, etc. However, further discussion of urban growth is beyond the scope of this study.

Chapter 14
Summary and Concluding Remarks

The main theme of this study has been economic analyses of both private and public services at the final consumption stage, which can account for two unique features of the services: quality competition among service options, and congestion due to capacity shortage. To accommodate these two unique features, this study has introduced a series of modeling approaches for the decision-making problems of consumer and suppliers. These modeling approaches fundamentally differ from those used in existing studies. For this reason, this study has developed analytical outcomes that depict market equilibrium and assess resource allocation efficiency in a manner that significantly differs from that used in existing studies. Here these distinctive aspects of the present study are highlighted, as summary and concluding remarks.

The first objective of this study has been to develop the consumer demand and service cost functions that can adequately reflect quality competition and congestion and that can apply to subsequent economic analyses. To this end, this study applies the perception approach and the full cost approach to developing the demand and cost functions, respectively, that explicitly account for quality competition and congestion. These two functions are incorporated into the profit and social welfare maximization problems for private and public services, respectively, under the user equilibrium approach. Therefore, these two functions have significance in that they are key inputs that enable the accommodation of quality competition and congestion in market analyses. The distinctive features of such demand and cost functions are as below.

First, the market analysis of this study employs three different independent explanatory variables to depict market equilibrium: price, service time, and capacity. Service time is a variable that conveys consumer perception of service quality defined so as to depend on congestion delay and qualitative service attributes. On the other hand, capacity is the supplier's choice variable that controls congestion. The use of these three independent choice variables is dissimilar from that of existing studies where only one variable, typically output, is employed.

Second, the market analysis uses three different measures for service time value per unit time: net-value-of-time in consumer demand function, social value-of-

D.J. Moon, *Congestion-Prone Services Under Quality Competition*,
Advances in Spatial Science, DOI 10.1007/978-3-642-20189-9_14,

service-time in social cost function, and private value-of-service-time in cost function in cost function for private firms. These three different measures reflect, in common, not only marginal utility of time but also consumer perceptions of the magnitudes of qualitative attributes packed in an option. In contrast, existing studies for consumer demand and public project investment implicitly or explicitly specify that service time value per unit time is equal to the marginal utility of time, called value-of-time, which is free from service quality.

Third, the consumer demand function for an option is structured to reflect consumer perception for service quality through the use of net-value-of-time. The demand function of an option is incorporated with a revealed preference condition such that consumers choose an option only when the implicit price of the option is smaller than those of other options. In this condition, the implicit price of an option is the sum of price and perceived monetary value for service quality. Further, the perceived monetary value of service quality is expressed as the function of all service quality variables; the perceived value equals the multiple of service time and net-value-of-time that equals value-of-time minus perceived value for all qualitative attributes packed in the option.

Fourth, demand for an option under competition is classified into perfect and imperfect demands by applying a qualitative yardstick. The demand function for an option under the random perception approach is expressed as a multiple integral that estimates demands more economically served by the option than are facilitated by competing options. Such a demand function for an option is defined to be perfectly elastic, if the customers of the option have close substitutes such that the implicit prices of the former, as perceived by its customers, are less than those of the latter by negligible margins. In contrast, the demand function for an option is termed to be imperfectly elastic if the option does not have close substitutes.

Fifth, the cost function for both private and public services accounts for congestion by separating capacity from throughput being synonymous with demand. The cost minimization problem from which this cost function is developed is structured to find an optimal capacity so as to minimize the total cost required to facilitate a given throughput. In addition, the total cost is estimated in the following manner: first, total cost is the sum of supplier's capacity cost and time cost; second, time cost is the multiple of service time, including congestion delay, and social or private value-of-service-time; third, congestion delay is increasing in throughput but decreasing in capacity. Therefore, the cost minimization problem estimates the solution of capacity through a trade-off between capacity cost, which is increasing in capacity, and time cost, which is decreasing in capacity.

Sixth, both social and private value-of-service-times for an option reflect the monetary value of qualitative attributes packed in the option. The two different value-of-service-times are both an average for the net-value-of-times of demands facilitated by the service system of the option. However, the methods used to estimate averages for the two differ; the social value-of-service-time takes the mean for the net-value-of-time for throughputs facilitated, whereas the private value-of-service-time is the marginal revenue loss of service time.

Seventh, the cost minimization problems for public and private services yield the social marginal full cost for throughput and the marginal full cost for throughput, respectively. These social marginal full cost and marginal full cost functions for congestion-prone service systems are equivalent to social marginal cost and marginal cost for congestion-free production systems, respectively. However, the two marginal full costs fundamentally differ from the two marginal costs in that the formers reflect the monetary value of service quality attributes specific to each service system. Note also that the two marginal full costs have an identical formulation, except for the use of different value-of-service-times.

The second objective has been to realistically describe the unique features of market equilibrium for a qualitative choice service offered by multiple options by applying the user equilibrium approach. Market equilibrium refers to the state at which no consumer and no private service firm are willing to change their choices in order to increase utility and profit, respectively, as is true of other studies for market equilibrium. However, the market equilibrium characterized in this study fundamentally differs from those of other studies, as explained below.

First, the user equilibrium approach implicitly defines that a resource allocation at market equilibrium is a realization at a certain instance in the process of continuous changes in resource allocations over a long time span. To be specific, the market equilibrium at a certain moment is characterized under the following premise: all firms operate service systems that have predetermined qualitative attributes and cost structures. Under this premise, it is feasible to properly characterize market equilibrium by applying the user equilibrium approach. However, this premise connotes that the introduction of innovative services that greatly improve qualitative attributes and/or reduces service production cost forces all firms to adjust their choices for prices and capacities. Therefore, theoretically, the introduction of such innovative services leads to new resource allocations at market equilibrium, as will be separately discussed later.

Second, the profit maximization problem for a firm is formulated as the decision-making problem of firms under the combination of the following two games: a leader-and-follower game in which each firm is the leader and its customers are followers; and a non-cooperative game among competitors in which the targets of conjectural variation are price and service time. The profit maximization problem has a functional structure identical across all firms, irrespective of the industrial organization types of firms.

Third, the industrial organization type of a firm is judged from the posterior evaluation for the solution to profit maximization problem for the firm. Such an approach to determine industrial organization type connotes that the industrial organization type of a firm is not exogenously fixed but rather endogenously determined through interactions between consumers and firms. Further, under this approach, it is possible that multiple types of industrial organizations coexist within a market.

Fourth, one way to judge the industrial organization type of a firm is to evaluate the geometry of the demand function for the firm, expressed as a multiple integral with respect to a vector of random net-value-of-times. The geometry of the multiple integral for a firm contains information not only about the volume of demand for the firm but also about the type of competition faced by the firm, which is synonymous with the type of industrial organization. The candidate types of competition are pure and differentiated oligopolistic competition, both of which yield imperfectly elastic demand, and perfectly and differentiated competition, both of which result in perfectly elastic demand.

Fifth, the industrial organization type of a firm depends on two exogenous factors: returns-to-scale in throughput, and average intensity of demand for the firm. Returns-to-scale in throughput is the exogenous factor unique to each firm. This returns-to-scale has a positive relationship with the returns-to-scale in capacity. On the other hand, average demand intensity is a socioeconomic variable of consumers in the market. This exogenous variable tends to have a smaller value as the population of the market decreases and as consumer perceptions for service quality becomes more diversified. It should also be noted that, typically, other studies for industrial organization do not consider socioeconomic variables as the exogenous factor affecting the type of industrial organization.

Sixth, the solution to profit maximization is characterized by pricing and investment rules. The pricing rule shows that the optimal price should equate marginal revenue to marginal full cost. On the other hand, the investment rule indicates that the optimal capacity should equate the marginal capacity cost to the marginal revenue of capacity, which is the multiple of the marginal revenue of service time and the marginal service time of capacity.

Seventh, the pricing rule introduced above is similar to the rule suggested in existing studies for industrial organization. In the case of a service system exhibiting increasing returns in capacity, the system should capture imperfectly elastic demand. Therefore, the pricing rule takes the form basically identical to the counterpart rule for congestion-free firm with increasing returns. However, in the case of a service system having non-increasing returns, the system can serve either perfectly elastic demand, which has high demand intensity, or imperfectly elastic demand, which has low demand intensity. When the system serves perfectly elastic demand, the pricing rule takes the form basically identical to the rule for congestion-free firms serving perfectly elastic demand. In contrast, when the system facilitates imperfectly elastic, the pricing rule has the form identical to the rule for the system exhibiting increasing returns. An example of this pricing rule can be found in a firm that competes with a few competitors in a small town.

Eighth, service quality competition among firms results in the industrial structure that satisfies a number of regularities. One is that a lower-quality service should charge a lower price so as to have a positive demand. Another one is that in most cases, a lower-quality service should operate a service system that has a lower marginal full cost in order to charge a lower price. The other one is that a consumer with a larger wage tends to choose a higher-quality service.

The third objective of this study has been to introduce a new view to assess marketwise recourse allocation efficiency under the market analysis framework of the user equilibrium approach. Analytical outcomes under the user equilibrium show that the resources consumed in a submarket for a certain service option are generally disjoint to those for other options and, further, that the level of resource allocation efficiency of a submarket differs from those of other submarkets. For these reasons, we judge that the concept of Pareto optimality is not sufficient to assess marketwise resource allocation efficiency for services, and that the qualitative diversity of services, each of which forms a submarket, should be accommodated into the evaluation of marketwise resource allocation efficiency. From this perspective, below we show how service quality competition improves resource allocation efficiency in market economies.

First, marketwise resource allocation efficiency for a qualitative choice service is evaluated by applying the following two independent criteria: first, the resource allocation efficiency of the submarket for an individual option; and second, the diversity of service quality on marketwise bases. The first criterion for each submarket defines that the submarket for an option attains the most efficient resource allocation when the price and capacity chosen by the option reaches Pareto optimality for the submarket. On the other hand, the second criterion for whole service markets indicates that a wider spectrum of services differentiated by quality reaches a higher level of marketwise resource allocation efficiency.

Second, the resource allocation efficiency of the submarket for a firm depends on the elasticity of the demand served by the firm. When the demand faced by a firm is perfectly elastic, the profit-maximizing choice of the firm for price and capacity reaches Pareto optimality for the submarket of the firm. This means that a firm facing either perfect or differentiated competition chooses the price and capacity that approximately fulfill the Pareto optimality condition. In contrast, when the demand is imperfectly elastic, the profit-maximizing choice does not attain Pareto optimality. That is, a firm facing either pure or differentiated oligopolistic competition makes a choice not to satisfy the Pareto optimality condition.

Third, the assertion that service quality diversity is indeed an indispensible and independent criterion to evaluate marketwise efficiency is demonstrated through two different analyses. The first analysis proves that the introduction of an innovative service enriches service quality diversity on marketwise bases and also increases benefit to some customers without exerting a negative effect on remaining consumers. The second analysis shows that the array of more diversified services available in a market provides a better opportunity for consumers to find a more economical option and thus increases consumer well-being.

To be specific, the introduction of an innovative service forces market economy to reach a higher level of marketwise resource allocation efficiency, as explained below. An innovative service typically reduces service production cost and/or improves service quality as characterized by service time and qualitative attributes. The introduction of such an innovative service triggers changes in the choices of existing firms for prices and capacities and thus alters the industrial structure of the market. In this process, the innovative service generally captures an inelastic demand but improves the well-being of its customers who have switched from existing services. Moreover, the innovative service increases the elasticity of demands for some existing services together with reductions in demands, and thus decreases the prices for the existing firms closer to Pareto-optimal prices.

On the other hand, when diversified services are available in a market, two different types of consumer benefit accrue. One type of consumer benefit stems from different consumer perceptions for service quality. That is, each consumer who has his own particular perception finds a more economical option when he is able to choose from a wider possible array of service choices. Another type of consumer benefit is generated from the randomness of consumer perception. That is, consumers can achieve more satisfaction by changing options to meet their changing perceptions than they do by consistently choosing the same options.

Fourth, the successive introduction of innovative services promotes gradual improvements in marketwise resource allocation efficiency for market economies. As explained above, the introduction of each innovative service usually improves the resource allocation efficiency of submarkets for some services, and also often enriches the diversity of service quality. Therefore, the successive introduction of innovative services continuously propels resource allocations in a direction to reach a higher and higher level of marketwise resource allocation efficiency.

Fifth, the introduction of innovative services does not always result in a non-negative profit, which is prerequisite for survival under competition. Under the user equilibrium approach, a firm is postulated to make choices for price and capacity based on incomplete knowledge of consumer reaction to its choice. The use of the incomplete knowledge usually leads to a profit that differs from the one that the firm expected at the moment when it made its choices. The possible outcome includes a deficit that can lead to bankruptcy, which is clearly contrary to the expectation of the firm. Hence, the introduction of innovative services has the possibility of causing losses in social welfare.

The fourth objective has been to consider the applicability of analytical outcomes presented in this study to other economic studies addressing practical decision-making problems. In this regard, one important finding of the present study is as follows: the service time value per unit time, which determines the implicit price of consumers for services under quality competition, is not value-of-time but rather net-value-of-time. Contrary to this finding, most economic studies for practical decision-making problems presume that the service time value per unit time is value-of-time. The two typical study areas that commonly adopt this premise are econometric estimations of consumer choices and cost-benefit analyses of transportation investment projects. For these two study areas, we below present a method to apply analytical outcomes in this study.

First, we consider the problem of applying consumer demand analyses under the perception approach to modeling consumer choice behaviors for econometric estimations that commonly utilize logit or probit model. The perception approach identifies the best option by comparing the implicit prices of all options, each of which equals the sum of its price and its multiple of service time and net-value-of-time. Such implicit prices of available options can be statistically estimated by applying logit or probit model. Further, for statistical estimations, the implicit prices of available options for a particular qualitative choice service can be developed from a consumer cost minimization problem that realistically describes decision-making environments specific to the qualitative choice service.

A number of examples that show how to estimate implicit prices in this manner have been illustrated in Chapter 3.

Second, we consider the application of implicit prices for net-value-of-times to benefit-cost analyses of transportation investment projects. For such projects, consumer benefit consists mainly of user time cost savings. Time cost savings is very sensitive to applied service time value per unit time. Under the user equilibrium approach, the appropriate measure of service time value per unit time is net-value-of-time that reflects service quality. One example that applies net-value-of-time is illustrated through a benefit-cost analysis for the introduction of an innovative service in Section 13.4. Note also that, compared with the existing approach of using value-of-time, the approach to applying net value-of-time yields more favorable analytical outcome for public projects where high-quality service is offered.

Additionally, this study has presented optimal public policies for congestion-prone public services for a number of different decision-making environments. It is shown that, under the condition of no financial and technical barrier, the governmental decision-making problem under the user equilibrium approach yields outcomes basically identical to those developed in existing studies for congestion pricing. It is also shown that, when government funds are not sufficient, the desirable policy for a public service is to set a price larger than the first best price, while operating a capacity less than the first best.

In sum, the advantage of the new modeling approach proposed in this study can be summarized as follows. First, the modeling approach explicitly accounts for two unique features of services under competition: service quality differentiation and congestion. Second, in the circumstance when all consumers have almost identical perceptions for service quality, the analytical outcomes from the new modeling approach are basically identical to those yielded from existing studies. Third, in the circumstance when consumers have differentiated perceptions, the analytical outcomes of this study can apply to explaining many observations in real service markets, which cannot be interpreted in the context of existing modeling approaches, as demonstrated throughout this study.

Chapter 15
Appendices

Appendix A: Appendix to Part I

Appendix A.1: Proof of Lemma 2.2 and Theorem 2.2

(1) The Kuhn-Tucker conditions for Lagrangian L_2: Let $(\bar{q}, \bar{x}, \bar{\pi}, \bar{\varphi}, \bar{\gamma})$ be the saddle point of Lagrangian L_2. Then, the Kuhn-Tucker conditions for L_2 are as follows:

$$y - \sum_{mn} a_m \bar{q}_{mn} = 0 \tag{A.1}$$

$$z_k - \sum_{mn} b_{kmn} t_{mn} \bar{q}_{mn} - \bar{Z}_k = 0, \text{ all } k \tag{A.2}$$

$$\frac{\partial L_2}{\partial q_{mn}} = p_{mn} + w t_{mn} - \bar{\pi} a_m - \sum_k \bar{\varphi}_k b_{kmn} t_{mn} - \bar{\gamma}_{mn} = 0, \text{ all } mn \tag{A.3}$$

$$\frac{\partial L_2}{\partial x_{kj}} = p_j - \bar{\varphi}_k \frac{\partial \bar{Z}_k}{\partial x_{kj}} = 0, \text{ all } k,\ j, \text{ and}$$

$$\frac{\partial L_2}{\partial t_k} = w - \bar{\varphi}_k \frac{\partial \bar{Z}_k}{\partial t_k} = 0, \text{ all } k \tag{A.4}$$

$$\bar{\gamma}_{mn} \bar{q}_{mn} = 0, \quad \bar{q}_{mn} \geq 0, \quad \text{and} \quad \bar{\gamma}_{mn} \geq 0, \text{ all } mn. \tag{A.5}$$

(2) Proof of Lemma 2.2 and Theorem 2.2.i for $\bar{\varphi}_k$: The formula in Lemma 2.2, which estimates $\bar{\varphi}_k$, can be readily developed from (A.4). Also, by the three conditions in Assumption 2.1(c), the implicit price $\bar{\varphi}_k$ is a constant that depends only on the prices of inputs to the substitute production Z_k, as proved below.

D.J. Moon, *Congestion-Prone Services Under Quality Competition*,
Advances in Spatial Science, DOI 10.1007/978-3-642-20189-9_15,

The first condition, which requires that the input (x_k, t_k) be positive, excludes the outcome that the price $\bar{\varphi}_k$ depends on $\bar{q}_{mn}$; without this condition, the minimization problem L_2 should include an additional constraint $(x_k, t_k) \geq 0$, and this constraint can give the price $\bar{\varphi}_k$ that is the function of $\bar{q}_{mn}$ via (A.2) and (A.3). The second condition, which requires that the input (x_k, t_k) be non-joint to the input to other substitute productions, prevents the price $\bar{\varphi}_k$ from being dependent on the yield of other hedonic commodities. The third condition, which requires that the function $Z_k(x_k, t_k)$ for all m exhibits constant returns, leads to the outcome that the price $\bar{\varphi}_k$ is independent of the output z_k.

(3) Proof of Lemma 2.2 for π_{mn}: When only one option mn is available, the above Kuhn-Tucker conditions are simplified as follows: first, the term $\bar{\gamma}_{mn}$ in (A.3) is deleted; second, the whole equation (A.5) is deleted. Then, the simplified versions of (A.3) give the expression of π_{mn} in the lemma.

(4) Proof of Theorem 2.2.i: We estimate the implicit price $\bar{\pi}$ under the premise that option mn is chosen; that is, $\bar{q}_{mn} \rangle 0$. (i) It follows from (A.5) that $\bar{q}_{mn} \rangle 0$ implies $\bar{\gamma}_{mn} = 0$. (ii) Moreover, (A.5) implies that $\bar{\gamma}_{m'n'} \geq 0$, for all $m'n' \neq mn$. Under conditions (i) and (ii), (A.3) implies that

$$\bar{\pi} = \pi_{mn} = \min_{m'n'} \left\{ \pi_{m'n'} = \frac{1}{a_{m'}} (p_{m'n'} + v_{m'} t_{m'n'}) \right\}. \tag{A.6}$$

(5) Proof of Theorem 2.2.ii: Consider, first, the case when $\bar{\pi} = \pi_{mn} \langle \pi_{m'n'}$, for all $m'n' \neq mn$. Then, by (A.3) and (A.5), it holds that $\bar{\gamma}_{mn} = 0$ and $\bar{q}_{mn} \rangle 0$, but $\bar{\gamma}_{m'n'} \rangle 0$ and $\bar{q}_{m'n'} = 0$. Hence, by (A.1), it follows that $a_m \bar{q}_{mn} = y$. Consider, next, the case when $\bar{\pi} \langle \pi_{mn}$. Then, by (A.3) and (A.5), it is clear that $\bar{\gamma}_{mn} \rangle 0$ and $\bar{q}_{mn} = 0$. Consider, finally, the case when $\bar{\pi} = \pi_{mn} = \pi_{m'n'}$, for all $m'n' \in I_{mn}$. In this case, the equality $a_m \bar{q}_{mn} = y$ for the first case must be amended as follows: $a_m \bar{q}_{mn} \leq \sum_{m'n' \in I_{mn}} a_{m'} \bar{q}_{m'n'} = y$.

Appendix A.2: Proof of Lemma 2.3

The details of the proof are as follows:

$$C(p, t; y, z) = \sum_{mn} (p_{mn} + w t_{mn}) \bar{q}_{mn} + \sum_{kj} p_j \bar{x}_{kj} + w \sum_{k} \bar{t}_k \tag{A.7}$$

$$= \sum_{mn} \left(\bar{\pi} a_m + \sum_{k} \bar{\varphi}_k b_{km} t_{mn} + \bar{\gamma}_{mn} \right) \bar{q}_{mn}$$

$$+ \sum_{kj} \bar{\varphi}_k \bar{x}_{kj} \frac{\partial \bar{Z}_k}{\partial x_{kj}} + \sum_{k} \bar{\varphi}_k \bar{t}_k \frac{\partial \bar{Z}_k}{\partial t_k} \tag{A.8}$$

$$= \sum_{mn} \bar{\pi} a_m \bar{q}_{mn} + \sum_k \bar{\varphi}_k \left(\sum_{mn} b_{km} t_{mn} \bar{q}_{mn} + \bar{Z}_k \right) \quad \text{(A.9)}$$

$$= \bar{\pi}\, y + \sum_k \bar{\varphi}_k z_k. \quad \text{(A.10)}$$

The right side of (A.7) expresses the definition of the cost function. Equation (A.8) is given by substituting (A.3) and (A.4) into (A.7). Subsequently, (A.8) is simplified to (A.9) by substituting the following two equalities: $\bar{\gamma}_{mn}\bar{q}_{mn} = 0$ in (A.5); and $\sum_j \bar{x}_{kj} \partial \bar{Z}_k / \partial x_{kj} + \bar{t}_k \partial \bar{Z}_k / \partial t_k = \bar{Z}_k$ that comes from the constant returns of Z_k in its inputs, as stated in Assumption 2.1(c). Finally, substituting (A.1) and (A.2) into (A.9) yields (A.10).

Appendix A.3: Proof of Lemma 2.4

(1) The outline of the proof: It suffices to prove that the Kuhn-Tucker conditions for the basic choice problem L_1 are identical to the combination of the same conditions for the cost minimization problem L_2 and the reduced form L_3. The reasoning is as follows: by the strong concavity condition in Assumption 2.2(a), this assertion is equivalent to the fact that each of the two different sets of the optimality conditions yields a unique solution identical to the other. That is, under the condition that the cost minimization problem L_2 gives the choice of option mn, it follows that

$$\bar{y} = a_m \bar{q}_{mn} = \hat{y} = a_m \hat{q}_{mn}, \quad \text{and} \quad \bar{z}_k = \hat{z}_k, \ \text{all } k, \quad \text{(A.11)}$$

as claimed in the lemma.

(2) The Kuhn-Tucker conditions for L_1: Some Kuhn-Tucker conditions for L_1 in (2.16), which are utilized in forthcoming analyses, are as follows:

$$\sum_{mn} a_m \bar{q}_{mn} - \bar{y} = 0 \quad \text{(A.12)}$$

$$\frac{\partial L_1}{\partial q_{mn}} = \bar{\lambda} a_m - \bar{\eta}\,(p_{mn} + v_m t_{mn}) + \bar{\phi}_{mn} = 0, \ \text{all } mn \quad \text{(A.13)}$$

$$\frac{\partial L_1}{\partial y} = \frac{\partial U(\bar{y}, \bar{z})}{\partial y} - \bar{\lambda} = 0 \quad \text{(A.14)}$$

$$\frac{\partial L_1}{\partial z_k} = \frac{\partial U(\bar{y}, \bar{z})}{\partial z_k} - \bar{\eta}\bar{\varphi}_k = 0, \ \text{all } k \quad \text{(A.15)}$$

$$\bar{\phi}_{mn}\bar{q}_{mn} = 0, \quad \bar{\phi}_{mn} \geq 0 \quad \text{and} \quad \bar{q}_{mn} \geq 0, \text{ all } mn. \tag{A.16}$$

Here, (A.13) is obtained by substituting the first order condition for L_1 with respect to (x_k, t_k) and $v_m = w - \sum_k \bar{\varphi}_k b_{mk}$ into the first order condition for L_1 with respect to q_{mn}.

(3) The Kuhn-Tucker conditions for L_2 and L_3: Under the condition that option mn is chosen from L_2, optimality conditions for L_2 can be expressed as follows:

$$\bar{\pi} = \pi_{mn} = \min_{m'n'} \left\{ \pi_{m'n'} = \frac{1}{a_{m'}} (p_{m'n'} + v_{m'} t_{m'n'}) \right\} \tag{A.17}$$

$$y = a_m \hat{q}_{mn} \rangle\, 0 \quad \textit{and} \quad \hat{q}_{m'n'} = 0, \text{ all } m'n' \neq mn. \tag{A.18}$$

These two equations are none other than (A.6) and (A.5), respectively.

Next, under the condition that L_2 chooses option mn, the reduced form L_3 has optimality conditions such that

$$\frac{\partial L_3}{\partial y} = \frac{\partial U(\hat{y}_{mn}, \hat{z}_{mn})}{\partial y} - \hat{\eta}\,\bar{\pi} = 0 \tag{A.19}$$

$$\frac{\partial L_3}{\partial z_k} = \frac{\partial U(\hat{y}_{mn}, \hat{z}_{mn})}{\partial z_k} - \hat{\eta}\,\bar{\varphi}_k = 0, \text{ all } k. \tag{A.20}$$

(4) Proof of the equivalency between optimality conditions for L_1 and the combination of the conditions for L_2 and L_3: (A.13) can be rearranged as follows:

$$\frac{\bar{\lambda}}{\bar{\eta}} = \frac{1}{a_{m'}} \left((p_{m'n'} + v_{m'} t_{m'n'}) - \frac{\bar{\varphi}_{m'n'}}{\bar{\eta}} \right), \text{ all } m'n'. \tag{A.21}$$

Here, it holds that $\bar{\lambda} \rangle\, 0$, $\bar{\eta} \rangle\, 0$, $\bar{\phi}_{m'n'} \geq 0$.

Subsequently, under the condition that L_1 selects option mn, (A.16) can be restated as follows:

$$\bar{q}_{mn} \rangle\, 0 \quad \text{and} \quad \bar{\phi}_{mn} = 0, \quad \text{but} \quad \bar{q}_{m'n'} = 0 \quad \text{and} \quad \bar{\phi}_{m'n'} \rangle\, 0, \text{ all } m'n' \neq mn. \tag{A.22}$$

Merging (A.22) into (A.21) gives

$$\frac{\bar{\lambda}}{\bar{\eta}} = \pi_{mn} = \min_{m'n'} \left\{ \frac{1}{a_{m'}} (p_{m'n'} + v_{m'} t_{m'n'}) \right\} = \bar{\pi}. \tag{A.23}$$

Also, substituting (A.23) into (A.12) yields

$$\bar{y} = a_m \bar{q}_{mn} \quad and \quad \bar{q}_{m'n'} = 0, \text{ all } m'n' \neq mn. \tag{A.24}$$

Furthermore, substituting (A.23) into (A.14) gives

$$\frac{\partial U(\bar{y}, \bar{z})}{\partial y} = \bar{\lambda} = \bar{\eta}\pi_{mn} = \bar{\eta}\bar{\pi}. \tag{A.25}$$

Finally, we confirm that the above analysis shows the following: the two sets of Kuhn-Tucker conditions are identical. This fact can readily be conformed by checking that (A.17), (A.18), (A.19) and (A.20) are identical to (A.23), (A.24), (A.25), and (A.15), respectively. This implies (A.11), as claimed at the beginning of the proof.

Appendix A.4: Proof of Theorem 2.3

(1) Prove the following part of Theorem 2.3:

$$\bar{\pi}(p,t) = \pi_{mn}(p_{mn}, t_{mn}) \Leftrightarrow U(\bar{y}, \bar{z}) = U(\bar{y}_{mn}, \bar{z}_{mn}), \tag{A.26}$$

where

$$\bar{\pi} = \pi_{mn} = \min_{m'n'} \left\{ \pi_{m'n'} = \frac{1}{a_{m'}}(p_{m'n'} + v_{m'} t_{m'n'}) \right\}. \tag{A.27}$$

Prove, first, that the left side of (A.26) implies the right. (i) By Theorem 2.2, (A.27) implies that the cost minimization problem L_2 results in the choice of option mn; that is, $(\bar{y}, \bar{z}) = (\bar{y}_{mn}, \bar{z}_{mn})$. (ii) Then, by Lemma 2.4, the solution to L_1 satisfies the equality that $(\bar{y}, \bar{z}) = (\hat{y}, \hat{z})$ and, thereby $(\hat{y}_{mn}, \hat{z}_{mn}) = (\bar{y}_{mn}, \bar{z}_{mn})$. Hence, by (i) and (ii), it follows that $(\bar{y}, \bar{z}) = (\bar{y}_{mn}, \bar{z}_{mn})$.

Prove, next, that the right side of (A.26) implies the left. The right side of (A.26) implies that the basic choice problem L_1 selects option mn. Hence, (A.11) holds. Therefore, (A.23) holds. Also, (A.23) implies (A.27). Hence, the assertion follows.

(2) The proof of the following part of Theorem 2.3:

$$\pi_{mn} \langle \pi_{m'n'} \Rightarrow U(\bar{y}_{mn}, \bar{z}_{mn}) \rangle U(\bar{y}_{m'n'}, \bar{z}_{m'n'}), \text{ all } m'n' \neq mn. \tag{A.28}$$

By Lemma 2.4, the above relationship is equivalent to

$$\pi_{mn} \langle \pi_{m'n'} \Rightarrow U(\hat{y}_{mn}, \hat{z}_{mn}) \rangle U(\hat{y}_{m'n'}, \hat{z}_{m'n'}), \text{ all } m'n' \neq mn. \tag{A.29}$$

Therefore, the proof can be completed by showing (A.29).

To prove (A.29), we introduce the production possibility set S_{mn} defined by

$$S_{mn}(y, z; \pi_{mn}, \bar{\varphi}) = \left\{ y, z \mid \bar{M} - \pi_{mn}\, y - \sum_{k} \bar{\varphi}_k\, z_k \; \geq 0,\; (y, z) \geq 0 \right\}, \tag{A.30}$$

where $\bar{\varphi} \equiv (\bar{\varphi}_1, \cdots, \bar{\varphi}_K)$. The set S_{mn} is convex, since it is a polyhedron in $\mathbf{R}^{K+1}$. Also, as will be shown later, it holds that

$$\pi_{mn} \langle \pi_{m'n'} \Rightarrow S_{mn}(\cdot) \supset S_{m'n'}(\cdot), \text{ all } m'n' \neq mn. \tag{A.31}$$

On the other hand, the solution $(\hat{y}_{mn}, \hat{z}_{mn})$ in $\mathbf{R}^{K+1}$, for all mn, is the tangent point between the iso-indifference curve, expressed by $U(y, z) = U(\hat{y}_{mn}, \hat{z}_{mn})$, and the frontier of the production possibility set S_{mn}. Hence, it follows that

$$S_{mn}(\cdot) \supset S_{m'n'}(\cdot) \Rightarrow U(\hat{y}_{mn}, \hat{z}_{mn}) \rangle U(\hat{y}_{m'n'}, \hat{z}_{m'n'}), \text{ all } m'n' \neq mn, \tag{A.32}$$

since S_{mn} is convex, and since $U(y, z)$ is increasing and concave in (y, z). Then, by (A.31) and (A.32), it is clear that the left inequality of (A.29) implies the right. Therefore, the proof can be completed by showing (A.31).

The proof of (A.31) is as follows. Let y_{mn} be the maximum value of y, such that $(y_{mn}, z) \in S_{mn}$ for an arbitrarily given value of z. Then, by the definition of S_{mn}, the condition on the left side of (A.29) implies that

$$y_{mn} \rangle y_{m'n'}, \text{ all } z \text{ and } m'n' \neq mn. \tag{A.33}$$

Hence, it follows that $S_{mn} \supset S_{m'n'}$, as claimed.

(3) The proof of the following part of Theorem 2.3:

$$\pi_{mn} \langle \pi_{m'n'} \Leftarrow U(\bar{y}_{mn}, \bar{z}_{mn}) \rangle U(\bar{y}_{m'n'}, \bar{z}_{m'n'}), \text{ all } m'n' \neq mn. \tag{A.34}$$

By Lemma 2.4, the above relationship is equivalent to

$$\pi_{mn} \langle \pi_{m'n'} \Leftarrow U(\hat{y}_{mn}, \hat{z}_{mn}) \rangle U(\hat{y}_{m'n'}, \hat{z}_{m'n'}), \text{ all } m'n' \neq mn. \tag{A.35}$$

The proof of (A.35) is as follows. Since $U(y, z)$ is increasing and concave in (y, z), it must hold that

$$\begin{aligned} U(\hat{y}_{mn}, \hat{z}_{mn}) \rangle U(\hat{y}_{m'n'}, \hat{z}_{m'n'}) \Rightarrow \pi_{mn}\hat{y}_{mn} + \sum_{k} \bar{\varphi}_k \hat{z}_{kmn} \\ \rangle\, \pi_{mn}\, \hat{y}_{m'n'} + \sum_{k} \bar{\varphi}_k \hat{z}_{km'n'}, \end{aligned} \tag{A.36}$$

where z_{kmn} is the kth element of the vector z_{mn}. On the other hand,

$$\bar{M} - \pi_{mn}\,\hat{y}_{mn} - \sum_k \bar{\varphi}_k\,\hat{z}_{kmn} = 0, \text{ all } mn. \tag{A.37}$$

This implies that the solution $(\hat{y}_{mn}, \hat{z}_{mn})$ is located on the frontier of the set S_{mn}. Therefore, it follows that

$$\pi_{mn}\hat{y}_{mn} + \sum_k \bar{\varphi}_k\hat{z}_{kmn} \rangle\ \pi_{mn}\,\hat{y}_{m'n'} + \sum_k \bar{\varphi}_k\hat{z}_{km'n'} \Rightarrow S_{mn}(\cdot)\ \supset\ S_{m'n'}(\cdot). \tag{A.38}$$

Here, one extreme point of polyhedron S_{mn} is $(\breve{y}_{mn}, 0)$, where $\breve{y}_{mn}$ is estimated by $\bar{M}/\bar{\pi}_{mn}$. By the same token, one extreme point of $S_{m'n'}$ is $(\breve{y}_{m'n'}, 0)$, where $\breve{y}_{m'n'}$ is estimated by $\bar{M}/\bar{\pi}_{m'n'}$. On the other hand, the condition $S_{mn}(\cdot)\ \supset\ S_{m'n'}(\cdot)$ in (A.38) implies that $\breve{y}_{mn} \rangle\ \breve{y}_{m'n'}$. Hence, it follows that $\pi_{mn} \langle\ \pi_{m'n'}$, for all $m'n' \neq mn$. This implies that the converse also holds.

Appendix A.5: Proof of Theorem 2.5

(1) Proof of Theorem 2.5.i: Prove first the continuity of $\hat{y}\,(\bar{\pi}(p,t))$ in (p,t). The function $\hat{y}(\bar{\pi})$ is continuous in $\bar{\pi}$, by the strong concavity of the utility function. Also, the implicit price function $\bar{\pi}$, which is the point-wise infimum of linear functions, is concave, and therefore continuous in (p,t). Hence it follows that $\hat{y}(\bar{\pi})$ is continuous in (p,t), since the composite function of two continuous functions is also continuous.

Next evaluate the continuity of $\bar{q}_{mn}(p,t)$. Combining the continuity of $\hat{y}\,(\bar{\pi}(p,t))$ and Theorem 2.4 leads to the outcome that $\bar{q}_{mn}(p,t)$ is continuous, except at the point where $\bar{\pi}(p,t) = \pi_{mn}(p_{mn}, t_{mn}) = \pi_{m'n'}(p_{m'n'}, t_{m'n'})$, for some $m'n' \neq mn$. Note that the function $\bar{q}_{mn}(p,t)$ is not continuous at the point where $\bar{q}_{mn}(p,t)$ has a degenerate value, as depicted in the third case of Theorem 2.4.

(2) Proof of Theorem 2.5.ii: The two equations can readily be proved by differentiating $\hat{y}(\bar{\pi})$ with respect to p_{mn} and t_{mn}. That is, in the case of $\bar{q}_{mn}(p,t) \rangle\ 0$, it holds that

$$\frac{\partial\,\bar{q}_{mn}(p,t)}{\partial\,p_{mn}} = \frac{1}{a_m}\frac{\partial\hat{y}\,(\bar{\pi}(p,t))}{\partial\bar{\pi}}\frac{\partial\bar{\pi}(p,t)}{\partial p_{mn}} = \frac{\partial\,\hat{y}\,(\bar{\pi}(p,t))}{\partial\bar{\pi}} \langle\ 0. \tag{A.39}$$

Subsequently, in the case of $\bar{q}_{mn}(p,t) \rangle\ 0$, it holds that

$$\frac{\partial\bar{\pi}(p,t)}{\partial p_{m'n'}} = \frac{\partial\bar{\pi}_{mn}(p_{mn}, t_{mn})}{\partial p_{m'n'}} = 0. \tag{A.40}$$

(3) Proof of Theorem 2.5.iii: If $\pi_{mn}(p_{mn}, t_{mn}) = \pi_{m'n'}(p_{m'n'}, t_{m'n'})$, a marginal increase in p_{mn} or t_{mn} results in the inequality such that $\pi_{mn}(p_{mn}, t_{mn}) \rangle \pi_{m'n'}(p_{m'n'}, t_{m'n'})$. Therefore, this marginal change decreases the value of $\bar{q}_{mn}$ from a positive to zero. This implies the first equation of Theorem 2.5.iii. In contrast, a marginal increase in $p_{m'n'}$ or $t_{m'n'}$ leads to the inequality such that $\pi_{mn}(p_{mn}, t_{mn}) \langle \pi_{m'n'}(p_{m'n'}, t_{m'n'})$. Therefore, the second equation of the theorem follows.

Appendix A.6: Proof of Theorem 3.1 and Related Equations

(1) Proof of (3.13) for ψ: Combining first order conditions for L_2 with respect to g and q_m gives

$$\pi_m = \frac{r_o}{\alpha(\bar{g})^{\alpha-1}(\bar{q}_m)^{1-\alpha}} = \frac{r_m}{(1-\alpha)(\bar{g})^{\alpha}(\bar{q}_m)^{-\alpha}}, \tag{A.41}$$

where $r_o = p_o + v_o t_o$ and $r_m = p_m + v_m t_m$. This equation can be rearranged as follows:

$$(1-\alpha)\, r_o \bar{g} - \alpha\, r_m\, \bar{q}_m = 0. \tag{A.42}$$

Also the solutions $\bar{g}$ and $\bar{q}_m$ satisfy the constraint of L_2, such that

$$y = \bar{g}^{\alpha} \bar{q}_m{}^{1-\alpha}. \tag{A.43}$$

The Jacobian of (A.42) and (A.43) with respect to $\bar{g}$ and $\bar{q}_m$, denoted by J, is

$$J = \begin{pmatrix} (1-\alpha)\, r_o & -\alpha\, r_m \\ \alpha\, (\bar{g})^{\alpha-1} (\bar{q}_m)^{1-\alpha} & (1-\alpha)\, (\bar{g})^{\alpha} (\bar{q}_m)^{-\alpha} \end{pmatrix}. \tag{A.44}$$

The determinant of this Jacobian, $\det\{J\}$, is

$$\det\{J\} = (1-\alpha)^2 r_o (\bar{g})^{\alpha} (\bar{q}_m)^{-\alpha} + \alpha^2\, r_m\, (\bar{g})^{\alpha-1} (\bar{q}_m)^{1-\alpha} \rangle\, 0. \tag{A.45}$$

Hence, by the implicit function theorem, both $\bar{g}$ and $\bar{q}_m$ are the functions of r_o and r_m. Therefore, it follows from (A.41) that there is a function ψ such that

$$\begin{aligned} \pi_m(p_o, t_o, p_m, t_m) &= \frac{r_o}{\alpha(\bar{g}(r_o, r_m))^{\alpha-1} (\bar{q}_m(r_o, r_m))^{1-\alpha}} \\ &\equiv \psi(r_o, r_m). \end{aligned} \tag{A.46}$$

(2) Proof of (3.14) for $\partial\psi/\partial p_m$: Differentiating (A.42) and (A.43) with respect to p_m results in the following simultaneous equation system:

$$\begin{pmatrix} (1-\alpha)\,r_o & -\alpha\,r_m \\ \alpha(\bar{g})^{\alpha-1}(\bar{q}_m)^{1-\alpha} & (1-\alpha)\,(\bar{g})^{\alpha}(\bar{q}_m)^{-\alpha} \end{pmatrix} \begin{pmatrix} \dfrac{\partial \bar{g}}{\partial p_m} \\ \dfrac{\partial \bar{q}_m}{\partial p_m} \end{pmatrix} = \begin{pmatrix} \alpha \bar{q}_m \\ 0 \end{pmatrix}. \tag{A.47}$$

Solving the above equation by applying Cramer's rule gives

$$\frac{\partial \bar{g}}{\partial p_m} = \alpha(1-\alpha)\frac{(\bar{g})^{\alpha}(\bar{q}_m)^{1-\alpha}}{\det\{J\}} \rangle\ 0 \tag{A.48}$$

$$\frac{\partial \bar{q}_m}{\partial p_m} = -\alpha^2\frac{(\bar{g})^{\alpha-1}(\bar{q}_m)^{2-\alpha}}{\det\{J\}} \langle\ 0. \tag{A.49}$$

Subsequently, differentiating (A.46), with respect to p_m gives

$$\frac{\partial \pi_m}{\partial p_m} = \frac{\partial \psi(r_o, r_m)}{\partial p_m} = \frac{\partial \psi(r_o, r_m)}{\partial r_m}\frac{\partial r_m}{\partial p_m} = \frac{\partial \psi(r_o, r_m)}{\partial r_m}. \tag{A.50}$$

Here, the last equality follows from the fact that the net-value-of-time $v_m(= w - \sum_k \bar{\varphi}_k b_{km})$ in $r_m(= p_m + v_m t_m)$ satisfies the consistency condition. On the other hand, differentiating the first equality of (A.41) with respect to p_m gives

$$\frac{\partial \pi_m}{\partial p_m} = \frac{(1-\alpha)}{\alpha} r_o(\bar{g})^{-\alpha}(\bar{q}_m)^{\alpha-1}\frac{\partial \bar{g}}{\partial p_m} - \frac{(1-\alpha)}{\alpha} r_o(\bar{g})^{1-\alpha}(\bar{q}_m)^{\alpha-2}\frac{\partial \bar{q}_m}{\partial p_m} \tag{A.51}$$

$$= (1-\alpha)\frac{r_o}{\det\{J\}} \rangle\ 0. \tag{A.52}$$

Here, (A.51) is converted to (A.52) by substituting (A.48) and (A.49). Finally, (A.50) and (A.52) imply (3.14); that is.

$$\frac{\partial \psi(r_o, r_m)}{\partial r_m} = (1-\alpha)\frac{r_o}{\det\{J\}} \rangle\ 0. \tag{A.53}$$

(3) Proof of (3.20): We estimate $\partial \hat{q}_m/\partial p_m$ through analyses of (A.42) and (A.43) in a manner identical to that used to estimate $\partial \bar{q}_m/\partial p_m$ in (A.49). The only difference between this one and the former is that the function $\hat{y}(\psi)$ replaces parameter y in (A.43). Hence, the term $\partial \hat{q}_m/\partial r_m$ can be estimated from the following simultaneous equation system:

$$\begin{pmatrix} (1-\alpha)\,r_o & -\alpha\,r_m \\ \alpha\,(\hat{g})^{\alpha-1}(\hat{q}_m)^{1-\alpha} & (1-\alpha)\,(\hat{g})^{\alpha}(\hat{q}_m)^{-\alpha} \end{pmatrix} \begin{pmatrix} \dfrac{\partial \hat{g}}{\partial r_m} \\ \dfrac{\partial \hat{q}}{\partial r_m} \end{pmatrix} = \begin{pmatrix} \alpha \hat{q}_m \\ \dfrac{\partial \hat{y}(\psi)}{\partial r_m} \end{pmatrix}. \tag{A.54}$$

Solving this equation gives

$$\frac{\partial \hat{q}_m}{\partial r_m} = \frac{1}{\det\{J\}}\left((1-\alpha)\,r_o\frac{\partial \hat{y}(\psi)}{\partial r_m} - \alpha^2(\hat{g})^{\alpha-1}(\hat{q}_m)^{2-\alpha}\right) \langle\, 0. \tag{A.55}$$

Here, the first term in the parentheses is negative, since the prime commodity is normal. This gives (3.20) such that

$$\frac{\partial \hat{q}_m}{\partial p_m} = \frac{1}{v_m}\frac{\partial \hat{q}_m}{\partial t_m} = \frac{1}{\det\{J\}}\left((1-\alpha)\,r_o\frac{\partial \hat{y}(\psi)}{\partial r_m} - \alpha^2(\hat{g})^{\alpha-1}(\hat{q}_m)^{2-\alpha}\right) \langle\, 0.$$

Here, the first equality follows from the fact that the net-value-of-time v_{mn} satisfies the consistency condition.

Appendix A.7: Equations (3.35)–(3.37)

(1) The Kuhn-Tucker conditions for the cost minimization problem L_2: We first introduce some Kuhn-Tucker conditions for L_2 in (3.34). These conditions, which are utilized in forthcoming analyses, are as follows:

$$\frac{\partial L_2}{\partial q_m} = p_m - \bar{\pi}_1\delta(\bar{q}_m) - \sum_k \bar{\varphi}_k b_{km} - \bar{\gamma}_m = 0, \text{ all } m \tag{A.56}$$

$$\frac{\partial L_2}{\partial g_{lm}} = p^a_{lm} + wt^a_{lm} - \bar{\pi}_l\delta(\bar{q}_m) - \sum_k \bar{\varphi}_k b^a_k t^a_{lm} - \bar{\tau}_{lm} = 0, \text{ all } lm \tag{A.57}$$

$$\frac{\partial L_2}{\partial x_{kj}} = p_j - \bar{\varphi}_k\frac{\partial \bar{Z}_k}{\partial x_{kj}} = 0, \text{ all } kj, \quad \frac{\partial L_2}{\partial t_k} = w - \bar{\varphi}_k\frac{\partial \bar{Z}_k}{\partial t_k} = 0, \text{ all } k \tag{A.58}$$

$$\bar{\gamma}_m\bar{q}_m = 0, \quad \bar{\gamma}_m \geq 0, \quad \bar{q}_m \geq 0, \text{ all } m \tag{A.59}$$

$$\bar{\tau}_{lm}\bar{g}_{lm} = 0, \quad \bar{\tau}_{lm} \geq 0, \quad \bar{g}_{lm} \geq 0, \text{ all } lm \neq 1m. \tag{A.60}$$

(2) Proof of (3.35) and (3.36): Suppose that only one option m is available. Then, by (3.28), (A.59), and (A.60), it follows that

$$\delta_m(q_m) = 1, \quad \bar{\gamma}_m = 0, \quad \bar{\tau}_{lm} = 0. \tag{A.61}$$

Substituting (A.61) into (A.56) and (A.57) gives

$$\bar{\pi}_1 = \pi_{1m} = p_m - \sum_k \bar{\varphi}_k b_{km} = p_m - r_m, \tag{A.62}$$

$$\bar{\pi}_l = \pi_{lm} = p^a_{lm} + \left(w - \sum_k \bar{\varphi}_k b^a_k\right) t^a_{lm} = p^a_{lm} + v^a t^a_{lm}, \quad \text{all } l \geq 2. \tag{A.63}$$

(3) Proof of (3.37): The cost function C can be rearranged as follows:

$$C(\cdot) = \sum_n p_n \bar{q}_n + \sum_{ln} (p^a{}_{ln} + w t_{ln}{}^a) \bar{g}_{ln} + \sum_{kj} p_j \bar{x}_{kj} + w \sum_k \bar{t}_k \tag{A.64}$$

$$= \sum_n \left(\left(\pi_{n1} \delta(\bar{q}_n) + \sum_k \bar{\varphi}_k b_{kn} + \bar{\gamma}_n \right) \bar{q}_n + \sum_{l \geq 2} \left(\pi_{nl} \delta(\bar{q}_n) + \sum_k \bar{\varphi}_k b^a_k t^a_{ln} + \bar{\tau}_m \right) \bar{g}_{ln} \right) + \sum_k \bar{\varphi}_k \left(\bar{x}_{kj} \frac{\partial \bar{Z}_k}{\partial x_{kj}} + \bar{t}_k \frac{\partial \bar{Z}_k}{\partial t_k} \right). \tag{A.65}$$

Equation (A.64) is none other than the definition of the cost function. Substituting (A.56)–(A.58) into (A.64) yields (A.65).

Suppose now that location m is chosen. Substituting (A.61)–(A.63) into (A.65) gives

$$C(\cdot) = \left(\pi_{m1} + \sum_k \bar{\varphi}_k b_{km} \right) \bar{q}_m + \sum_{l \geq 2} \left(\pi_{ml} + \sum_k \bar{\varphi}_k b^a_k t^a_{lm} \right) \bar{g}_{lm} + \sum_k \bar{Z}_k. \tag{A.66}$$

Substituting the production function of (3.30)–(3.32) into (A.66) yields

$$C(\cdot) = \sum_l \pi_{lm} y_l + \sum_k \bar{\varphi}_k z_k. \tag{A.67}$$

Finally, prove the inequality of (3.37). Suppose that only one option m' is available. Then, the cost function, denoted by $C(p_{m'}, p^a_m, t^a_m)$ is

$$C(\cdot) = \sum_l \pi_{lm'} y_l + \sum_k \bar{\varphi}_k z_k, \tag{A.68}$$

as can be proved in a manner almost identical to that used to prove (A.67). Moreover, the assertion that the cost minimization problem L_2 results in the choice of location m implies the inequality of (3.37). Otherwise, it contradicts that location m yields the minimum cost.

Appendix A.8: Proof of Theorems 3.3 and 3.4 and Related Equations

(1) Estimation of the net wage in (3.51): Under the condition that only mode m is available, first order conditions for L_o in (3.50) with respect to q_m and x are

$$\frac{\partial L_m}{\partial q_m} = \sum_k \bar{\mu}_{km} b_{km} t_m - \bar{v}_m(t_w + t_m) + \bar{\eta}_m(wt_w - p_m) = 0 \tag{A.69}$$

$$\frac{\partial L_m}{\partial x_{kj}} = \bar{\mu}_{km} \frac{\partial \bar{Z}_k}{\partial x_{kj}} - \bar{\eta}_m p_j = 0, \text{ and } \frac{\partial L_o}{\partial t_k} = \bar{\mu}_{km} \frac{\partial \bar{Z}_k}{\partial t_k} - \bar{v}_m = 0, \text{ all } k, j. \tag{A.70}$$

It follows from (A.70) that

$$\frac{\bar{\mu}_{km}}{\bar{\eta}_m} = \bar{\varphi}_k = p_j \bigg/ \frac{\partial \bar{Z}_k}{\partial x_{kj}}, \text{ and } \frac{\bar{\mu}_{km}}{\bar{v}_m} = 1 \bigg/ \frac{\partial \bar{Z}_k}{\partial t_k}, \text{ all } k, j. \tag{A.71}$$

Substituting the above two equations into (A.69) gives

$$\bar{\eta}_m wt_w = \bar{v}_m(t_w + t_m) + \bar{\eta}_m p_m - \sum_k \bar{\eta}_m \bar{\varphi}_k b_{km} t_m. \tag{A.72}$$

Estimating $w_m \equiv \bar{v}_m / \bar{\eta}_m$ from (A.72) yields

$$w_m = \frac{\bar{v}_m}{\bar{\eta}_m} = \frac{w\, t_w - p_m + \sum_k \bar{\varphi}_k b_{km} t_m}{t_w + t_m}. \tag{A.73}$$

(2) Proof of Theorem 3.3: The proof of (3.55) is worked out by rearranging (A.72). Dividing both sides of (A.72) by $\bar{\eta}_m$ gives

$$\begin{aligned} wt_w &= w_m(t_w + t_m) + p_m - \sum_k \bar{\varphi}_k b_{km} t_m \\ &= w_m t_w + p_m + \left(w_m - \sum_k \bar{\varphi}_k b_{km} \right) t_m \\ &= w_m t_w + p_m + v_m\, t_m. \end{aligned} \tag{A.74}$$

(3) Proof of (3.56): By applying the equality $\bar{\mu}_{mk} = \bar{\varphi}_k \bar{\eta}_m$ estimated from (A.71), we merge all the constraints of L_m in (3.53). Thus, we have

$$\bar{M}_m \equiv I_o + w_m T_o = \sum_k \varphi_k \bar{z}_{km}, \text{ all } m. \quad \text{(A.75)}$$

(4) The equation system necessary for estimating the comparative statics of travel demand function: This simultaneous equation system is constructed by arranging the Kuhn-Tucker conditions for the reduced form L_3 in (3.57), under the condition that mode m is chosen.

One part of the Kuhn-Tucker conditions are first order conditions such that

$$\frac{\partial U(\hat{z})}{\partial z_k} = \bar{\eta}\bar{\varphi}_k, \text{ all } k. \quad \text{(A.76)}$$

The remaining two conditions are two different expressions of the budget constraints for the UMP:

$$\bar{M}_m \equiv I_o + w_m T_o = \sum_k \bar{\varphi}_{km} \hat{z}_k, \quad \text{(A.77)}$$

$$\bar{M} \equiv I_o + wT_o = \pi'_m \hat{y}_m + \sum_k \bar{\varphi}_k \bar{z}_m = \pi'_m t_w \bar{q}_m + \sum_k \bar{\varphi}_k \hat{z}_m, \quad \text{(A.78)}$$

where $\pi'_m(p_m, t_m) = p_m + v'_m t_m$ and $v'_m = w - \sum_k \bar{\varphi}_k b_{km}$. These $K+2$ equations can be used in estimating $K+2$ unknowns; $\bar{z}_1, \cdots, \bar{z}_K, \bar{q}_m$, and $\bar{\eta}$. Therefore, the sensitivity of $\bar{q}_m$ with respect to p_m (or t_m) can be estimated by solving the simultaneous equations obtained by differentiating the $K+2$ equations with respect to p_m (or t_m).

Appendix A.9: Proof of Lemma 4.2

(1) Outline of proof: The fact that the range of mapping $\xi = w - \hat{\varphi}\beta$ is a convex set in $\mathbf{R}^M$ is clear, since the mapping is linear, as shown in many books, e.g., §3 of Rockafellar (1970). Therefore, the proof of the lemma can be completed by showing the following: (a) there exists a uniquely defined distribution function H that satisfies the equality in Lemma 2.1; (b) the distribution function H is absolutely continuous in ξ.

(2) Existence of H: Prove that there exists a distribution function H such that

$$E\{\bar{u}(\beta) \mid \beta \in RB\} \equiv \int_{RB} \bar{u}(\beta) d\lambda_G = E\{\hat{u}(\xi) \mid \xi \in RV\} \equiv \int_{RV} \hat{u}(\xi) d\mu_H, \quad \text{(A.79)}$$

under the condition that $\xi = w - \hat{\varphi}\,\beta$.

Let $\{IB_n : n \in \mathrm{N}\}$ be a partition of RB. Then, by the absolute continuity of $\bar{u}$, it follows that

$$\sum_n E\{\,\bar{u}(\beta) \mid \beta \in IB_n\} = \inf_{IB_n} \sum_n v_n \lambda_G(IB_n), \tag{A.80}$$

where $v_n = \sup\{\,\bar{u}(\beta)|\,\beta \in IB_n\} \,\langle\, \infty$, and $\lambda_G(IB_n)$ is the probability that $\beta \in IB_n$.

Subsequently, let IV_n be a subset of RV such that

$$IV_n = \left\{\,\xi \in \mathbf{R}^{\mathrm{M}} |\, \xi = w - \hat{\varphi}\,\beta, \text{ and } \beta \in IB_n\right\}. \tag{A.81}$$

Then, it is certain that

$$\bigcup_n IV_n = RV \quad \text{and} \quad IV_n \bigcap IV_m \neq \emptyset, \text{ some } m \neq n, \tag{A.82}$$

since the function $\xi = w - \hat{\varphi}\,\beta$ maps B into Ξ.

For each n, suppose that

$$IV_n = \bigcup_{k=n_1}^{n_{nm}} KV_k, \tag{A.83}$$

where $\{\,KV\}_{k=n_1}^{n_{nm}}$ forms a partition of IV_n such that

$$KV_k = \left(\bigcap_{i \in I_k} IV_i\right) \Bigg\backslash \left(\bigcup_{i \notin I_k} IV_i\right), \tag{A.84}$$

and I_k is a set whose element includes only n, or n and some $j \neq n$. For example, the partition of IV_1 can be defined as follows:

$$KV_{I_k=(1)} = IV_1 \Bigg\backslash \left(\bigcup_{n=2}^{\infty} IV_n\right)$$

$$KV_{I_k=(1,j)} = \left(IV_1 \bigcap IV_j\right) \Bigg\backslash \left(\bigcup_{n=2}^{j-1} IV_n\right) \bigcup \left(\bigcup_{n=j+1}^{\infty} IV_n\right)$$

$$KV_{I_k=(1,\cdots,j)} = \left(\bigcap_{n=1}^{j} IV_n\right) \Bigg\backslash \left(\bigcup_{n=j+1}^{\infty} IV_n\right).$$

For each n, select k such that I_k includes n but does not include every $j \,\langle\, n$, and arrange the selected k as follows:

$$n_1 \langle \cdots \langle n_{nm} \langle (n+1)_1 \quad \text{and}$$
$$\bigcup_{n=1}^{\infty} \{n_1, \cdots, n_{nm}\} = \text{N}. \tag{A.85}$$

Then, $\{KV_k\}_{k=1}^{\infty}$ forms a partition of RV.

Let the set KB_{nk} be the subset of IB_n, which is the preimage of KV_k for the mapping $\xi = W - \hat{\varphi}\beta$. That is,

$$KB_{nk} = \{\beta \in \mathbf{R}^{\text{KM}} \mid \xi = W - \hat{\varphi}\beta, \;\; \beta \in IB_n, \text{ and } \xi \in KV_k\}. \tag{A.86}$$

Then, by the definition of I_k, it follows that

$$\bigcup_{n \in I_k} KB_{nk} = \text{the preimage of} \quad KV_k \quad \text{of the mapping} \quad \xi = W - \hat{\varphi}\beta. \tag{A.87}$$

Hence, it is certain that $\{KB_{nk}\}_{k \in I_k}$ forms a partition of IB_n for each n.

Let $w_k \equiv \max_n \{v_n \mid n \in I_k\}$. Then, it is clear

$$w_k = \sup\{\hat{u}(\xi(\beta)) | \; \xi \in KV_k\}. \tag{A.88}$$

By an argument of refinement of the partition, the absolutely continuous function $\bar{u}$ satisfies the condition such that

$$\begin{aligned}\int_{RB} \bar{u}(\beta) d\lambda_G &= \inf_{IB_n} \sum_n v_n \lambda_G(IB_n) \\ &= \inf_{IB_n} \sum_k w_k \sum_{n \in I_k} \lambda_G(KB_{nk}).\end{aligned} \tag{A.89}$$

Hence, there exists a distribution H such that

$$\sum_{n \in I_k} \lambda_G(KB_{nk}) = \mu_H(KV_k), \text{ all } k, \tag{A.90}$$

where μ_H is the probability measure for the distribution H. Therefore, it follows that

$$\int_{RB} \bar{u}(\beta) d\lambda_G = E\{\bar{u}(\beta)\} = \inf_{IB_n} \sum_k w_k \sum_{n \in I_k} \lambda_G(KB_{nk}) \tag{A.91}$$

$$= \inf_{IV_n} \sum_k \sup\{\hat{u}(\xi) \mid \; \xi \in KV_k\} \mu_H(KV_k) \tag{A.92}$$

$$= E\{\,\hat{u}(\xi) \mid \xi \in RV\} = \int_{RV} \hat{u}(\xi) d\mu_H. \tag{A.93}$$

These equalities imply (A.79) holds, as claimed previously.

(3) Absolute continuity of H: The absolute continuity of H can be proved by showing that the density function h for the distribution function H satisfies the following:

$$H(RV) = \int_{RV} h\,(\xi)\,d\mu = 1, \tag{A.94}$$

where μ is an ordinary measure in $\mathbf{R}^{\mathrm{M}}$. To this end, it suffices to show the following:

$$\begin{aligned} 1 = E\{g(\beta) \mid \beta \in RB\} &\equiv \int_{RB} g(\beta) d\lambda_G \\ = E\,\{\,h(\xi) \mid \xi \in RV\} &\equiv \int_{RV} h(\xi) d\mu_H, \end{aligned} \tag{A.95}$$

where λ is an ordinary measure in $\mathbf{R}^{\mathrm{KM}}$ (refer to Chapter 5, Feller, 1966). In addition, the proof of (A.95) can be worked out in a manner analogous to the proof of (A.79).

Appendix A.10: Proof of Theorem 5.2

We illustrate the proof of the lemma with an example of $\partial Q_n(p,t)/\partial p_n$ in (5.9). The function $Q_n(p,t))$ can be expressed as follows:

$$Q_n(p,t) = T(p_n, l_n(p_n),\ u_n(p_n)). \tag{A.96}$$

Then, by the chain rule, it follows that

$$\frac{\partial Q_n}{\partial p_n} = \frac{\partial T}{\partial p_n} + \frac{\partial T}{\partial l_n}\frac{\partial l_n}{\partial p_n} + \frac{\partial T}{\partial u_n}\frac{\partial u_n}{\partial p_n}. \tag{A.97}$$

Here, the first term of (A.97) corresponds to the first term of $\partial Q_n(p,t)/\partial p_n$ in (5.9). The second and third terms of (A.97) can be arranged, respectively, into the second and third terms of $\partial Q_n(p,t)/\partial p_n$ in (5.9), by applying the theorem for the differential of indefinite integrals in (5.6).

Appendix A.11: Proof of Theorem 5.5

(1) Proof of the following equality in (5.25):

$$\frac{\partial Q_m(p,t)}{\partial p_k} = \sum_{j \neq m} \frac{\partial SQ_{mj}(p,t)}{\partial p_k} = \frac{\partial SQ_{mk}(p,t)}{\partial p_k}. \tag{A.98}$$

The proof is as follows. The term $\partial Q_m / \partial p_k$ estimates the impact of a marginal price increase dp_k on Q_m. This effect is confined to the movement of the tangent plane $D_m \cap D_k$ in the outward direction of D_m. Also, the set D_m is composed of multiple subsets SD_{mj}, for all $j \neq m$, as defined in Lemma 5.4. However, only the subset SD_{mk} includes the tangent plane $D_m \cap D_k$. This implies (A.98).

(2) Proof of the following equality in (5.25): Here we prove the following:

$$\begin{aligned}\frac{\partial SQ_{mk}(p,t)}{\partial p_k} &= \frac{\partial}{\partial p_m} \sum_{k \neq m} \int_{SD^o_{mk}} \int_0^{g_{mk}} f_m(p'_m + \xi_m t_m)\, h(\xi)\, d\xi_m\, d\mu^o_m \\ &= \frac{1}{t_m} \int_{D_m \cap D_k} f_k(p_k + \xi_k t_k)\, h(\xi)\, d\mu^o_m \rangle\ 0,\end{aligned} \tag{A.99}$$

where p'_m has a value identical to p_m and is a constant. The proof is worked out by applying a number of simplified problems as presented below.

Firstly, consider the following iterated indefinite integral:

$$Q_1(p,t) = \int_0^{X_1} \int_0^{p+tx_1} f(x_2) dx_2 dx_1. \tag{A.100}$$

The integral domain of this integral has a geometry identical to that of D_m in Fig. 5.5, when x_1 and x_2 replace ξ_k and ξ_m, respectively. Let F be the integral of f. Then, it follows that

$$Q_1(p,t) = \int_0^{X_1} F(p + tx_1) dx_1. \tag{A.101}$$

Hence, if follows:

$$\begin{aligned}\frac{\partial Q_1(p,t)}{\partial p} &= \int_0^{X_1} \frac{dF(p+tx_1)}{d(p+tx_1)} \frac{\partial(p+tx_1)}{\partial p} dx_1 \\ &= \int_0^{X_1} f(p+tx_1) dx_1.\end{aligned} \tag{A.102}$$

Secondly, consider the following integral:

$$Q_2(p,t) = \int_0^{X_1} \int_0^{x_1} f(\pi_2) dx_2 dx_1. \tag{A.103}$$

where

$$\pi_m(x_m) = \frac{1}{a_m}(p + tx_m), \quad \text{for} \quad m = 1,\ 2.$$

The integral Q_2 can be converted as follows:

$$Q_2(p,t) = \frac{a_2}{t} \int_0^{X_1} \int_{(1/a_2)p}^{(a_1/a_2)\pi_1} f(\pi_2) d\pi_2 dx_1, \tag{A.104}$$

since

$$d\pi_2 = \frac{t}{a_2} dx_2, \quad \pi_2(0) = \frac{p}{a_2}, \quad \pi_2(x_2) = \frac{1}{a_2}(p + tx_1) = \frac{a_1}{a_2}\pi(x_1).$$

Hence, it follows that

$$Q_2(p,t) = \frac{a_2}{t} \int_0^{X_1} F\left(\frac{a_1}{a_2}\pi_1\right) dx_1 - \frac{a_2}{t} \int_0^{X_1} F\left(\frac{p}{a_2}\right) dx_1. \tag{A.105}$$

Thirdly, we consider an integral Q_3, which a simplified version of Q_m

$$Q_3(p,t) = \int_0^{U_k} \int_0^{g_{mk}(\xi_k)} f_m(\pi_m) d\xi_m d\xi_k. \tag{A.106}$$

We convert Q_3 in manner that which led from (A.103) to (A.105). Thus, we have

$$\begin{aligned} Q_3(p,t) &= \frac{a_m}{t_m} \int_0^{U_k} \int_{\pi_m(\xi_m=0)}^{\pi_m(\xi_m=g_{mk})} f_m(\pi_m) d\pi_m d\xi_k \\ &= \frac{a_m}{t_m} \int_0^{U_k} F_m(\pi_m(\xi_m = g_{mk})) d\xi_k - \frac{a_m}{t_m} \int_0^{U_k} F_m(\pi_m(\xi_m = 0)) d\xi_k. \end{aligned} \tag{A.107}$$

By the definition of g_{mk}, it holds that $\pi_m(\xi_m = g_{mk}) = \pi_k$. Hence,

$$Q_3(p,t) = \frac{a_m}{t_m}\frac{a_k}{a_m}\int_0^{U_k} F_k(\pi_k)d\xi_k - \frac{a_m}{t_m}\int_0^{U_k} F_m(\pi_m(\xi_m = 0))d\xi_k. \tag{A.108}$$

Differentiating (A.108) with respect to p_k in a manner that estimated $\partial Q_1/\partial p$ in (A.102) gives

$$\begin{aligned}\frac{\partial Q_3(p,t)}{\partial p_k} &= \frac{a_m}{t_m}\frac{a_k}{a_m}\int_0^{U_k} f_k(\pi_k)\frac{\partial \pi_k}{\partial p_k}d\xi_k \\ &= \frac{1}{t_m}\int_0^{U_k} f_k(\pi_k)d\xi_k.\end{aligned} \tag{A.109}$$

One can readily deduce from (A.109) that (A.98) holds.

(3) Proof of the following equality in (5.26):

$$\frac{\partial Q_m(p,t)}{\partial p_k} = \frac{\partial Q_k(p,t)}{\partial p_m}. \tag{A110}$$

To simplify presentation, we work out the proof for $\partial Q_3/\partial p_k$, as shown below:

$$\begin{aligned}\frac{\partial Q_3(p,t)}{\partial p_k} &= \frac{1}{t_m}\int_0^{U_k} f_k(\pi_k)d\xi_k \\ &= \frac{1}{t_m}\int_{\pi_k(0)}^{\pi_k(U_k)} f_k(\pi_k)\frac{a_k}{t_k}d\pi_k \\ &\quad - \frac{1}{t_m}\frac{a_k}{t_k}\int_{\pi_m(0)}^{\pi_m(U_m)} \frac{a_m}{a_k}f_m(\pi_m)d\pi_m \\ &= \frac{1}{t_k}\int_0^{U_m} f_m(\pi_m)d\xi_m.\end{aligned} \tag{A.111}$$

(4) The proof of (5.27): By applying the chain rule, the differentiation of (5.24) with respect to p_m can be expressed as follows:

$$\begin{aligned}\frac{\partial Q_m(p,t)}{\partial p_m} &= \sum_{k\neq m}\frac{\partial SQ_{mk}(p,t)}{\partial p_m} \\ &= \sum_{k\neq m}\int_{SD^o_{mk}}\int_0^{g_{mk}} \frac{\partial f_m(p_m + \xi_m t_m)}{\partial p_m} h(\xi)\, d\xi_m\, d\mu^o_m \qquad \text{(A.112)} \\ &\quad + \frac{\partial}{\partial p_m}\sum_{k\neq m}\int_{SD^o_{mk}}\int_0^{g_{mk}} f_m(p'_m + \xi_m t_m)\, h(\xi)\, d\xi_m\, d\mu^o_m, \qquad \text{(A.113)}\end{aligned}$$

where p'_m has the value identical to p_m, and is a constant. By Lemma 5.4, (A.112) is simplified as follows:

$$(A.112) = \int_{D_m} \frac{\partial f_m(p_m + \xi_m t_m)}{\partial p_m} h(\xi)\, d\xi_m\, d\mu_m^o. \tag{A.114}$$

By (A.98), (A.113) satisfies the following:

$$(A.113) = \sum_{k \neq m} \frac{\partial SQ_{mk}(p,t)}{\partial p_k} = \sum_{k \neq m} \frac{\partial Q_m(p,t)}{\partial p_k}. \tag{A.115}$$

Equations (A.114) and (A.115) imply (5.27).

Appendix A.12: Proof of Lemma 5.8

Firstly, estimate the range of $CD_{m(m+1)}$: The set $CD_{m(m+1)}$ is estimated from the following two inequalities:

$$\hat{\pi}_m = \frac{1}{a_m}(p_m + \xi_m t_m) \leq \hat{\pi}_{m+1} = \frac{1}{a_{m+1}}(p_{m+1} + \xi_{m+1} t_{m+1}) \tag{A.116}$$

$$\frac{\xi_m t_m}{a_m} \rangle \frac{\xi_{m+1} t_{m+1}}{a_{m+1}}. \tag{A.117}$$

Solving (A.116) and (A.117) yields the following:

$$\xi_m \leq g_{m(m+1)}(\xi_{m+1}, p, t) = \frac{a_m}{a_{m+1}} \frac{p_{m+1}}{t_m} - \frac{p_m}{t_m} + \xi_{m+1} \frac{a_m}{a_{m+1}} \frac{t_{m+1}}{t_m} \tag{A.118}$$

$$\xi_m \geq r_{m(m+1)}(\xi_{m+1}, p, t) = \xi_{m+1} \frac{a_m}{a_{m+1}} \frac{t_{m+1}}{t_m}. \tag{A.119}$$

Secondly, estimate the thickness $\psi_{m(m+1)}$. This thickness is

$$\begin{aligned} \frac{\psi_{m(m+1)}}{t_m} &= g_{m(m+1)}(0.p.t) - r_{m(m+1)}(0, p, t) \\ &= \frac{a_m}{a_{m+1}} \frac{p_{m+1}}{t_m} - \frac{p_m}{t_m}. \end{aligned} \tag{A.120}$$

Thirdly, estimate the range of CD_{mk}, for all $k \neq m,\ m+1$. The set CD_{mk} is estimated from the following three inequalities: $\hat{\pi}_m \leq \hat{\pi}_k$, $\hat{\pi}_k \leq \hat{\pi}_{m+1}$, and $\xi_m t_m / a_m \geq \xi_{m+1} t_{m+1} / a_{m+1}$. Here, the first two inequalities follow from the definition of CD_{mk}, such that $\hat{\pi}_m \leq \hat{\pi}_k \leq \hat{\pi}_{m+1}$. The first inequality gives

$$\xi_m \leq g_{mk}(\xi_k, p, t) = \frac{a_m}{a_k}\frac{p_k}{t_m} - \frac{p_m}{t_m} + \xi_k \frac{a_m}{a_k}\frac{t_k}{t_m}. \tag{A.121}$$

Combing the second and third inequalities yields

$$\frac{1}{a_k}(p_k + \xi_k t_k) \leq \frac{1}{a_{m+1}}(p_{m+1} + \xi_{m+} t_{m+1}) \leq \frac{p_{m+1}}{a_{m+1}} + \xi_m \frac{t_m}{a_m}.$$

Solving this equation gives

$$\xi_m \geq r_{mk}(\xi_k, p, t) = \frac{a_m}{a_k}\frac{p_k}{t_m} - \frac{a_m}{a_{m+1}}\frac{p_{m+1}}{t_m} + \xi_k \frac{a_m}{a_k}\frac{t_k}{t_m}. \tag{A.122}$$

Finally, estimate the thickness ψ_{mk}, for all $k \neq m,\ m+1$:

$$\begin{aligned}\frac{\psi_{mk}}{t_m} &= g_{mk}(0.p.t) - r_{mk}(0, p, t)\\ &= \frac{a_m}{a_{m+1}}\frac{p_{m+1}}{t_m} - \frac{p_m}{t_m}.\end{aligned} \tag{A.123}$$

Appendix A.13: Proof of Theorem 5.9

To begin, we introduce an alternative expression of Q_m. By Lemmas 5.6 and 5.9, it follows that

$$SD_{mk} \cong \theta_m t_m \mu(D_m \cap D_k), \qquad \text{all } m \in \langle 1, L-1 \rangle \text{ and } k \neq m. \tag{A.124}$$

Hence, by (5.36) and (A.124), it follows that

$$\begin{aligned}Q_m &\cong F_m \theta_m t_m \sum_{k \neq m} \mu(D_m \cap D_k)\\ &\equiv F_m \theta_m t_m G_m, \quad \text{all } m \in \langle 1, L-1 \rangle.\end{aligned} \tag{A.125}$$

Subsequently, by (5.40) and (A.125), it follows that

$$\begin{aligned}Q_m \Big/ \sum_{l \in \langle 1, L-1 \rangle} Q_l &= \theta_m t_m F_m G_m \Big/ \sum_{l \in \langle 1, L-1 \rangle} \theta_l t_l F_l G_l\\ &\rangle \frac{\theta_m t_m F_m G_m}{(p_L - p_1)A} = \delta_m,\end{aligned} \tag{A.126}$$

where

$$A = \sum_{l\in\langle 1,L-1\rangle} Q_l \Big/ \sum_{l\in\langle 1,L-1\rangle} \theta_l t_l = \sum_{l\in\langle 1,L-1\rangle} \theta_l t_l F_l G_l \Big/ \sum_{l\in\langle 1,L-1\rangle} \theta_l t_l \rangle 0.$$

Finally, we show that, under conditions (b)–(e), (A.126) implies that $\theta_m \cong \varepsilon$. (i) Condition (d) implies that δ_m is very small. (ii) Condition (c) implies that one or both of θ_l and $G_l F_l$, for all $l \in \langle 1, L-1\rangle$, are sufficiently larger than zero, and thereby that A is sufficiently larger than zero. (iii) Under condition (b), (5.40) implies that $p_L - p_1$ is sufficiently larger than zero. (iv) Condition (e) shows that the term F_m is significantly larger than zero. (v) The value G_m is generally larger than zero, since UB_k in (5.19), for all k, is assumed to be sufficiently larger than zero. Facts (ii)–(v) imply that all terms on the right side of (A.126), excluding θ_m, are sufficiently large. Therefore fact (i) implies that $\theta_m \cong \varepsilon$.

Appendix B: Appendix to Part II

Appendix B.1: Proof of Theorem 6.9

(1) Proof of $\bar{\xi}_{mn} \in L_{mn}$: By applying the mean value theorem for integrals (Bartle, 1976), we show that the $\bar{\xi}_{mn}$ value, estimated in (6.44), satisfies the condition such that $\bar{\xi}_{mn} \in L_{mn}$. To prove this, we reorganize the numerator of (6.44) as follows:

$$\int_{D_{mn}} \xi_m f_m(p_{mn} + \xi_m t_{mn})\, h(\xi)\, d\mu = \bar{\xi}_{mn} Q_{mn}(p,t). \tag{B.1}$$

By (5.46)–(5.50), the left side of (B.1) can be converted into the following indefinite integrals:

$$\text{Left Side of (B.1)} = \sum_{m'n' \neq mn} \int_{D^o_{m'n'}} \int_{s_{m'n'}}^{g_{m'n'}} \xi_m f_m(p_{mn} + \xi_m t_{mn})\, h(\xi)\, d\xi_m d\mu^o_m. \tag{B.2}$$

where $s_{m'n'}$ is one the following: $l_{m(n-1)}$ in (5.48), 0 in (5.49), and $r_{m'n'}$ in (5.50).

The integrand f_m in (B.2) is continuous and positive in ξ_m, as shown in Lemma 4.6. Hence, it follows from the mean value theorem for integrals that there is $\alpha_{m'n'} \in L_{mn}(p,t)$ such that

$$\begin{aligned}
&\int_{D^o_{m'n'}} \int_{s_{m'n'}}^{g_{m'n'}} \xi_m f_m(p_{mn} + \xi_m t_{mn})\, h(\xi)\, d\xi_m d\mu^o_m \\
&= \alpha_{m'n'} \int_{D^o_{m'n'}} \int_{s_{m'n'}}^{g_{m'n'}} f_m(p_{mn} + \xi_m t_{mn})\, h(\xi)\, d\xi_m d\mu^o_m \\
&= \alpha_{m'n'} SQ_{m'n'}(p,t).
\end{aligned} \tag{B.3}$$

Substituting (B.3) into (B.2) and estimating the $\bar{\xi}_{mn}$ value from the outcome of the previous step gives

$$\bar{\xi}_{mn} = \sum_{m'n' \neq mn} \alpha_{m'n'} \frac{SQ_{m'n'}(p,t)}{Q_{mn}(p,t)} \in L_{mn}(p,t).$$

Here, $\bar{\xi}_{mn} \in L_{mn}(p,t)$ follows from that $\alpha_{m'n'} \in L_{mn}(p,t)$ and $\sum SQ_{m'n'} = Q_{mn}$.

(2) Proof of $\breve{\xi}_{mn} \in L_{mn}$: It follows from Theorem 5.11 that

$$\frac{\partial Q_{mn}}{\partial p_{mn}} = \int_{D_{mn}} \frac{\partial f_m(p_{mn} + \xi_m t_{mn})}{\partial p_{mn}} h\, d\mu - \sum_{m'n' \neq mn} \frac{\partial Q_{mn}}{\partial p_{m'n'}} \tag{B.4}$$

$$\frac{\partial Q_{mn}}{\partial t_{mm}} = \int_{D_{mn}} \frac{\partial f_m(p_{mn} + \xi_m t_{mn})}{\partial_{mn}} h\, d\mu - \sum_{m'n' \neq mn} \frac{\partial Q_{mn}}{\partial t_{m'n'}}. \tag{B.5}$$

By the mean value theorem for integrals, there exists $\alpha_{mn} \in L_{mn}(p,t)$ such that

$$\int_{D_{mn}} \frac{\partial f_m}{\partial t_{mn}} h\, d\mu = \int_{D_{mn}} \xi_m \frac{\partial f_m}{\partial p_{mn}} h\, d\mu = \alpha_{mn} \int_{D_{mn}} \frac{\partial f_m}{\partial p_{mn}} h\, d\mu, \tag{B.6}$$

as can be proved in a manner analogous to the above proof of $\bar{\xi}_{mn} \in L_{mn}(p,t)$. Here, the function $\partial f_m / \partial p_{mn}$ is negative and continuous, since the utility function is twice differentiable. In addition, it will be shown that there is $\alpha_{m'n'} \in L_{mn}$ such that

$$\frac{\partial Q_{mn}}{\partial t_{m'n'}} = \alpha_{m'n'} \frac{\partial Q_{mn}}{\partial p_{m'n'}}, \quad \text{if} \quad \frac{\partial Q_{mn}}{\partial p_{m'n'}} \rangle\, 0, \quad \text{some } m'n' \neq mn. \tag{B.7}$$

On the other hand, it follows from (B.4)–(B.7) that

$$\breve{\xi}_{mn} = \left(\alpha_{mn} \int_{D_{mn}} \frac{\partial f}{\partial p_{mn}} h\, d\mu - \sum_{m'n' \neq mn} \alpha_{m'n'} \frac{\partial Q_{mn}}{\partial p_{m'n'}} \right) \Bigg/ \left(\int_{D_{mn}} \frac{\partial f}{\partial p_{mn}} h\, d\mu - \sum_{m'n' \neq mn} \frac{\partial Q_{mn}}{\partial p_{m'n'}} \right). \tag{B.8}$$

The term $\breve{\xi}_{mn}$ is the weighted average of α_{mn} and $\alpha_{m'n'}$, for all $m'n' \neq mn$. Moreover, all the terms α_{mn} and $\alpha_{m'n'}$ belong to L_{mn} and are positive, whereas all the other terms are negative. Hence, it holds that $\breve{\xi}_{mn} \in L_{mn}(p,t)$.

Subsequently, prove (B.7) for the cases of $m(n-1)$ and $m(n+1)$. The partial derivatives $\partial Q_{mn} / \partial p_{m(n\pm1)}$ and $\partial Q_{mn} / \partial t_{m(n\pm1)}$ satisfy the following relationships:

$$\frac{\partial Q_{mn}}{\partial t_{m(n-1)}} = l_{mn} \frac{\partial Q_{mn}}{\partial p_{m(n-1)}}, \quad \text{and} \quad \frac{\partial Q_{mn}}{\partial t_{m(n+1)}} = u_{mn} \frac{\partial Q_{mn}}{\partial p_{m(n-1)}}, \tag{B.9}$$

where

$$l_{mn} = \frac{p_{mn} - p_{m(n-1)}}{t_{m(n-1)} - t_{mn}}, \quad \text{and} \quad u_{mn} = \frac{p_{m(n+1)} - p_{mn}}{t_{mn} - t_{m(n+1)}}.$$

Hence, it follows that

$$\alpha_{m(n-1)} = l_{mn} \in L_{mn}, \quad \text{and} \quad \alpha_{m(n+1)} = u_{mn} \in L_{mn}. \tag{B.10}$$

Finally, prove (B.7) for all $m' \neq m$: It follows from Theorem 5.11 that

$$\frac{\partial Q_{mn}(p,t)}{\partial p_{m'n'}} = \frac{1}{t_{mn}} \int_{D_{mn} \cap D_{m'n'}} f_m(p_{mn} + g_{m'n'} t_{mn})\, h(g_{m'n'}, \xi^o_m) d\mu^o_m \geq 0 \tag{B.11}$$

$$\frac{\partial Q_{mn}(p,t)}{\partial t_{m'n'}} = \frac{1}{t_{mn}} \int_{D_{mn} \cap D_{m'n'}} f_m(p_{mn} + g_{m'n'} t_{mn})\, h(g_{m'n'}, \xi^o_m) \xi_m d\mu^o_m \geq 0\,. \tag{B.12}$$

By the mean value theorem, there is $\alpha_{m'n'} \in \{\, \xi_m |\, \xi \in D_{mn} \cap D_{m'n'}\}$, such that

$$\frac{\partial Q_{mn}(p,t)}{\partial t_{m'n'}} = \alpha_{m'n'} \frac{\partial Q_{mn}(p,t)}{\partial p_{m'n'}}. \tag{B.13}$$

Since $\{\, \xi_m |\, \xi \in D_{mn} \cap D_{m'n'}\} \subseteq L_{mn}$, it holds that $\alpha_{m'n'} \in L_{mn}(p,t)$.

Appendix B.2: Proof of Theorem 6.10

(1) The proof for the case of keen quantitative competition: The proof is worked out using the expressions $\overline{\xi}_{mn}$ and $\breve{\xi}_{mn}$ in (6.44) and (6.45), respectively.

Firstly, we extend the expressions Q_n and $\partial Q_n / \partial p_n$ under quantitative competition in (5.11) and (5.12), respectively, to mixed competition. By analogy to (5.11), the demand function Q_{mn} can be approximated as follows:

$$Q_{mn}(p,t) \cong \theta^n_{mn} f_{mn}(p_{mn} + l_{mn} t_{mn}) \Psi_{mn}, \tag{B.14}$$

where

$$\theta^n_{mn} = u_{mn} - l_{mn}$$

$$\Psi_{mn} = \frac{1}{2}\int_{D^o_{m(n-1)}} h(l_{mn}, \xi^o_m)\, d\mu^o_m + \frac{1}{2}\int_{D^o_{m(n+1)}} h(u_{mn}, \xi^o_m) d\mu^o_m$$

$$D^o_{mk}(p, t) = \{\, \xi^o_m \mid \xi \equiv (\xi_m, \xi^o_m) \in D_{mn}(p, t)\,\}.$$

Under the condition of (6.46), an approximation of $\partial Q_{mn}/\partial p_{mn}$ can be estimated by differentiating (B.14); that is,

$$\frac{\partial Q_{mn}(p,t)}{\partial p_{mn}} \cong \frac{\partial Q_{mn}(p,t)}{\partial p_{m(n-1)}} + \frac{\partial Q_{mn}(p,t)}{\partial p_{m(n+1)}} \tag{B.15}$$

$$\cong \frac{\partial \theta^n_{mn}}{\partial p_{mn}} f_{mn}(p_{mn} + l_{mn}t_{mn})\Psi_{mn}. \tag{B.16}$$

It should be noted that the right side of (B.15) can alternatively be expressed as follows:

$$\frac{\partial Q_{mn}(p,t)}{\partial p_{m(n-1)}} + \frac{\partial Q_{mn}(p,t)}{\partial p_{m(n+1)}} \cong \int_{D^c_{mn}} f_{mn}(p_{mn} + \xi_m t_{mn}) h(\xi_m, \xi^o_m)\, d\mu.$$

Also, the right side of this equation is none other than the numerator of (6.45).

Subsequently, by analogy to (B.14), the numerator of (6.44) can be expressed as follows:

$$\int_{D_{mn}} \xi_m f_m(p_{mn} + \xi_m\, t_{mn})\, h(\xi)\, d\mu \cong \theta^n_{mn} f_{mn}(p_{mn} + l_{mn}t_{mn})\Phi_{mn}, \tag{B.17}$$

where

$$\Phi_{mn} = \frac{l_{mn}}{2}\int_{D^o_{m(n-1)}} h(l_{mn}, \xi^o_m)\, d\mu^o_m + \frac{u_{mn}}{2}\int_{D^o_{m(n+1)}} h(u_{mn}, \xi^o_m) d\mu^o_m.$$

Similarly, the numerator of (6.45), $\partial Q_{mn}/\partial t_{mn}$, can be approximated as follows:

$$\begin{aligned} \frac{\partial Q_{mn}(p,t)}{\partial t_{mn}} &\cong \frac{\partial Q_{mn}(p,t)}{\partial t_{m(n-1)}} + \frac{\partial Q_{mn}(p,t)}{\partial t_{m(n+1)}} \\ &\cong \frac{\partial \theta^n_{mn}}{\partial t_{mn}} f_{mn}(p_{mn} + l_{mn}t_{mn})\psi_{mn} \\ &= \frac{\partial \theta^n_{mn}}{\partial p_{mn}} f_{mn}(p_{mn} + l_{mn}t_{mn})\Phi_{mn}. \end{aligned} \tag{B.18}$$

Hence, it follows that

$$\frac{\breve{\xi}_{mn}}{\bar{\xi}_{mn}} = \frac{(6.45)}{(6.44)} \cong \frac{(\text{B}.18)}{(\text{B}.16)} \Big/ \frac{(\text{B}.17)}{(\text{B}.14)} = 1.0. \tag{B.19}$$

This confirms that $\breve{\xi}_{mn} \cong \bar{\xi}_{mn}$.

(2) The proof for the case of qualitative competition: Without loss of generality, the proof can be worked out through analyses for a special case of qualitative competition under the identical ordering condition, considered in Section 5.4.

Firstly, we introduce an approximation of $\partial Q_m/\partial p_m$ in Theorem 5.7. Under the condition of (6.46), the term $\partial Q_m/\partial p_k$ in the theorem can be simplified as the following approximation:

$$\frac{\partial Q_m(p,t)}{\partial p_m} \cong -\sum_{k\neq m} \frac{\partial SQ_{mk}(p,t)}{\partial p_k} = -\sum_{k\neq m} \frac{\partial Q_m(p,t)}{\partial p_k}. \tag{B.20}$$

By (5.25), the term $\partial Q_m/\partial p_k$ can be expressed as follows:

$$\frac{\partial Q_m(p,t)}{\partial p_k} = \frac{1}{t_m} \int_{D_m\cap D_k} f_k(p_k + \xi_k t_k)\, h(\xi) d\mu_m^o, \quad \text{all } k \neq m. \tag{B.21}$$

Substituting (B.21) into (B.20) gives

$$\frac{\partial Q_m(p,t)}{\partial p_m} \cong -\frac{1}{t_m} \sum_{k\neq m} \int_{D_m\cap D_k} f_k(p_k + \xi_k t_k) h(\xi) d\mu_m^o. \tag{B.22}$$

It should be noted that this equation expresses the numerator of (6.45)

Secondly, we convert the function Q_{mn} into an expression similar to (B.22). Substituting Lemma 5.9 and (B.22) into (5.28) gives

$$\begin{aligned} Q_m(p,t) &\cong -\theta_m t_m \sum_{k\neq m} \frac{\partial Q_m(p,t)}{\partial p_k} \\ &= \theta_m \sum_{k\neq m} \int_{D_m\cap D_k} f_k(p_k + \xi_k t_k) h(\xi) d\mu_m^o. \end{aligned} \tag{B.23}$$

Thirdly, we introduce an approximation of $\partial Q_m/\partial t_k$ in Theorem 5.7. Equation (5.25) shows the following:

$$\frac{\partial Q_m(p,t)}{\partial t_k} = \frac{t_k}{t_m} \int_{D_m\cap D_k} \xi_k f_k(p_k + \xi_k t_k)\, h(\xi) d\mu_m^o. \tag{B.24}$$

Under the condition (6.46), the term $\partial Q_m/\partial t_m$ can be simplified as follows:

$$\frac{\partial Q_m(p,t)}{\partial t_m} \cong \frac{t_k}{t_m}\sum_{k\neq m}\int_{D_m\cap D_k} \xi_k f_k(p_k+\xi_k t_k)\, h(\xi)d\mu_m^o. \tag{B.25}$$

Fourthly, we convert the numerator of (6.44) into an expression similar to (B.25). To this end, we first introduce the equality such that

$$\int_{D_{mn}} \xi_m f_m(p_m+\xi_m t_m)h(\xi)d\mu = \frac{t_k}{t_m}\int_{D_{mn}} \xi_k f_k(p_k+\xi_k t_k)h(\xi)d\mu, \tag{B.26}$$

This equation follows from that $f_m = (a_k/a_m)f_k$ and $d\xi_m = (a_m t_k/a_k t_m)d\xi_k$. Hence, it holds that

$$\int_{D_{mn}} \xi_m f(p_m+\xi_m t_m)h(\xi)d\mu \cong \theta_m \sum_{k\neq m}\frac{t_k}{t_m}\int_{D_m\cap D_k} \xi_k f(p_k+\xi_k t_k)h(\xi)d\mu_m^o. \tag{B.27}$$

Combining the above analyses leads to

$$\frac{\breve{\xi}_{mn}}{\bar{\xi}_{mn}} \cong \frac{(\text{B.25})}{(\text{B.22})}\Big/\frac{(\text{B.27})}{(\text{B.23})} = 1.0. \tag{B.28}$$

This shows that $\breve{\xi}_{mn} \cong \bar{\xi}_{mn}$.

Appendix B.3: Proof of Equations (7.10) and (7.11)

(1) Proof of (7.10): For homogeneous service time function, the differentiation of $MCC(= MFC)$ with respect to s yields is

$$\begin{aligned}\frac{\partial MFC(s;\breve{v})}{\partial s} &= \frac{\partial}{\partial s}\left(\breve{v}s\frac{\partial T^d}{\partial s}\right)\\ &= \breve{v}\frac{\partial T^d}{\partial s} + \breve{v}s\frac{\partial^2 T^d}{\partial s^2} + \breve{v}s\frac{\partial^2 T^d}{\partial s\partial c}\frac{\partial \bar{c}}{\partial s}\\ &= \frac{1}{s}MFC + \breve{v}s\frac{\partial^2 T^d}{\partial s^2} - \frac{1}{c}MFC\frac{\partial \bar{c}}{\partial s} - \breve{v}s\frac{s}{c}\frac{\partial^2 T^d}{\partial s^2}\frac{\partial \bar{c}}{\partial s} \qquad (\text{B.29})\\ &= \left(\frac{1}{s}MFC + \breve{v}s\frac{\partial^2 T^d}{\partial s^2}\right)\left(1 - \frac{s}{c}\frac{\partial \bar{c}}{\partial s}\right), \qquad (\text{B.30})\end{aligned}$$

since

$$\breve{v}\, s \frac{\partial^2 T}{\partial s \partial c} = -\breve{v}\, s \frac{\partial}{\partial s}\left(-\frac{\partial T}{\partial c}\right) - \breve{v}\, s \frac{\partial}{\partial s}\left(\frac{s}{\bar{c}} \frac{\partial T}{\partial s}\right) \tag{B.31}$$

$$= -\frac{1}{c} MFC - \breve{v} \frac{s^2}{\bar{c}} \frac{\partial^2 T}{\partial s^2}. \tag{B.32}$$

Here, (B.32) is obtained by substituting (6.1) and Lemma 6.6 into the second and third terms of (B.31) sequentially.

(2) Proof of (7.11): For homogenous service time function, the differentiation of the optimality condition in Lemma 6.6 with respect to s is

$$\frac{\partial^2 KC(\bar{c})}{\partial c^2} \frac{\partial \bar{c}}{\partial s} = \frac{\partial}{\partial s}\left(-\breve{v} s \frac{\partial T}{\partial c}\right) + \frac{\partial}{\partial c}\left(-\breve{v} s \frac{\partial T}{\partial c}\right) \frac{\partial \bar{c}}{\partial s}, \tag{B.33}$$

where $\bar{T} \equiv T(s/\bar{c})$. Estimating $\partial \bar{c}/\partial s$ from (B.33) gives

$$\frac{s}{\bar{c}} \frac{\partial \bar{c}}{\partial s} = -s \frac{\partial}{\partial s}\left(\breve{v} s \frac{\partial T}{\partial c}\right) \Big/ \bar{c} \frac{\partial}{\partial c}\left(\frac{\partial KC(\bar{c})}{\partial c} + \breve{v} s \frac{\partial T}{\partial c}\right). \tag{B.34}$$

Note that the denominator of (B.34) is not zero, since the capacity $\bar{c}$ is the intersection of the two graphs depicting the following two functions: $\partial KC(\bar{c})/\partial c$ and $-\breve{v} s \partial T/\partial c$.

We, next, show that the numerator of (B.34) equals that of (7.11). The former satisfies the following equalities:

$$\frac{\partial}{\partial s}\left(\breve{v} s \frac{\partial T}{\partial c}\right) = \breve{v} \frac{\partial T}{\partial c} + \breve{v}\, s \frac{\partial^2 T}{\partial s \partial c}. \tag{B.35}$$

By Lemma 6.6, the second term of (B.35) is converted to the following:

$$-\breve{v} \frac{\partial T}{\partial c} = \frac{1}{s} \frac{\partial KC(\bar{c})}{\partial c}. \tag{B.36}$$

Substituting equations (B.36) and (B.32) into (B.35) gives the result identical to the numerator of (7.11).

We, finally, show that the denominator of (B.34) equals that of (7.11). Substituting (6.1), Lemma 6.6 and (B.36) into the second term of the denominator sequentially gives

$$\breve{v}s\frac{\partial^2 T}{\partial c^2} = \breve{v}s\frac{\partial}{\partial c}\left(-\frac{s}{\bar{c}}\frac{\partial T}{\partial s}\right)$$
$$= \breve{v}s\frac{s}{c^2}\frac{\partial T}{\partial s} - \breve{v}s\frac{s}{c}\frac{\partial}{\partial c}\frac{\partial T}{\partial s \partial c}$$
$$= \frac{2}{\bar{c}}\frac{\partial KC(\bar{c})}{\partial c} + \breve{v}\frac{s^3}{\bar{c}^2}\frac{\partial^2 T}{\partial s^2}. \tag{B.37}$$

This result implies that the denominator of (B.34) equals the denominator of (7.11).

(3) The proof of $\partial\bar{c}/\partial s \rangle 0$: It suffices to show that the right side of (B.33) has a denominator and numerator, both of which are positive. It follows from (B.35) and (B.36) that the numerator of (B.33) is positive. The fact that the denominator is always positive can be deduced from the following:

$$\frac{\partial}{\partial c}\left(\frac{\partial KC(\bar{c})}{\partial c} + \breve{v}s\frac{\partial \bar{T}}{\partial c}\right) = \left.\frac{\partial^2 Z^7(c; s+e, \breve{v})}{\partial c^2}\right|_{e=s}, \tag{B.38}$$

where Z^7 is the QCMP in (6.40). This minimization problem Z^7, from which the marginal full cost is developed, must be convex at $\bar{c}$. Thereby, the denominator must be positive at $\bar{c}$.

Appendix B.4: Proof of Equations (7.15) and (7.16)

(1) Proof of (7.15): For non-homogeneous service time function, the differentiation of $MCC(= MFC)$ with respect to s is as follows:

$$\frac{\partial MFC(s;\breve{v})}{\partial s} = \frac{\partial}{\partial s}\left(\frac{1}{2y}\right) \times \breve{v}s\frac{\partial T^d}{\partial s} + \frac{1}{2y} \times \frac{\partial}{\partial s}\left(\breve{v}s\frac{\partial T^d}{\partial s}\right)$$
$$= -\frac{1}{y} \times \frac{\breve{v}s}{2y}\frac{\partial T^d}{\partial s}\frac{\partial \bar{c}}{\partial s} + \frac{1}{s}\frac{\breve{v}s}{2y}\frac{\partial T^d}{\partial s} + \frac{\breve{v}s}{2y}\frac{\partial^2 T^d}{\partial s^2} + \frac{\breve{v}s}{2y}\frac{\partial^2 T^d}{\partial s \partial c}\frac{\partial \bar{c}}{\partial s}$$
$$= -\frac{1}{y}MFC(s;\breve{v})\frac{\partial \bar{c}}{\partial s} + \left(\frac{1}{s}MFC(s;\breve{v}) + \frac{\breve{v}s}{2y}\frac{\partial^2 T^d}{\partial s^2}\right)\left(1 - \frac{s}{c}\frac{\partial \bar{c}}{\partial s}\right). \tag{B.39}$$

(2) Proof of (7.16): Differentiating the optimality condition of Lemma 6.6 with respect to s and arranging the result of the previous step yields an outcome similar to (B.33); that is,

$$\frac{s}{\bar{c}}\frac{\partial \bar{c}}{\partial s} = -s\frac{\partial}{\partial s}\left(\breve{v}s\frac{\partial}{\partial c}\left(\frac{T^d}{2\bar{y}}\right)\right) \Big/ \bar{c}\frac{\partial}{\partial c}\left(\frac{\partial KC(\bar{c})}{\partial c} + \breve{v}s\frac{\partial}{\partial c}\left(\frac{T^d}{2\bar{y}}\right)\right). \tag{B.40}$$

Arranging the numerator on the right side of (B.40) gives

$$
\begin{aligned}
-s\frac{\partial}{\partial s}\left(\breve{v}s\frac{\partial}{\partial c}\left(\frac{T^d}{2y}\right)\right) &= s\frac{\partial}{\partial s}\left(\frac{\breve{v}s}{2y^2}T^d - \frac{\breve{v}s}{2y}\frac{\partial T^d}{\partial c}\right)\\
&= \frac{s}{y}\left(\frac{\breve{v}}{2y}T^d - \breve{v}s\frac{\partial}{\partial s}\left(\frac{T^d}{2y}\right)\right) - \frac{\breve{v}s}{2y}\frac{\partial T^d}{\partial c} - \frac{\breve{v}s^2}{2y}\frac{\partial}{\partial s}\left(\frac{\partial T^d}{\partial c}\right)\\
&= -\frac{s}{y}MFC + \frac{\partial KC(c)}{\partial c} - \frac{\breve{v}s^2}{2y}\frac{\partial}{\partial s}\left(-\frac{s}{c}\frac{\partial T^d}{\partial s}\right)\\
&= \left(\frac{s}{c} - \frac{s}{y}\right)MFC + \frac{\partial KC(c)}{\partial c} + \frac{\breve{v}s^3}{2yc}\frac{\partial^2 T^d}{\partial s^2}.
\end{aligned}
\tag{B.41}
$$

Reorganizing the denominator of (B.40) results in the following:

$$
\begin{aligned}
c\frac{\partial}{\partial c}\left(\frac{\partial KC(c)}{\partial c} + \breve{v}s\frac{\partial}{\partial c}\left(\frac{T^d}{2y}\right)\right) &= c\frac{\partial^2 KC(c)}{\partial^2 c} - c\frac{\partial}{\partial c}\left(\frac{\breve{v}s}{2y^2}T^d - \frac{\breve{v}s}{2y}\frac{\partial T^d}{\partial c}\right)\\
= c\frac{\partial^2 KC(c)}{\partial^2 c} + c\frac{\breve{v}s}{y^3}T^d - c\frac{\breve{v}s}{2y^2}\frac{\partial T^d}{\partial c} &- c\frac{\breve{v}s}{2y^2}\frac{\partial T^d}{\partial c} + c\frac{\breve{v}s}{2y}\frac{\partial^2 T^d}{\partial c^2}\\
= c\frac{\partial^2 KC(c)}{\partial^2 c} + 2\left(\frac{c}{y} + 1\right)\frac{\partial KC(c)}{\partial c} &+ \frac{\breve{v}s^3}{2yc}\frac{\partial^2 T^d}{\partial s^2}.
\end{aligned}
\tag{B.42}
$$

Substituting (B.41) and (B.42) into (B.40) gives

$$
\begin{aligned}
\frac{s}{\bar{c}}\frac{\partial \bar{c}}{\partial s} = \left(\left(\frac{s}{c} - \frac{s}{y}\right)MFC(s;\breve{v}) + \frac{\partial KC(c)}{\partial c} + \frac{\breve{v}s^3}{2yc}\frac{\partial^2 T^d}{\partial s^2}\right)\Bigg/\left(c\frac{\partial^2 KC(c)}{\partial^2 c}\right.\\
\left.+2\left(1 + \frac{c}{y}\right)\frac{\partial KC(c)}{\partial c} + \frac{\breve{v}s^3}{2yc}\frac{\partial^2 T^d}{\partial s^2}\right).
\end{aligned}
\tag{B.43}
$$

Equation (B.43) is none other than (7.16).

Appendix B.5: Proof of Equations (7.75)–(7.78)

(1) Proof of (7.75): The proof is worked out by solving the differential equation (7.72). One special solution to this differential equation applicable to the case when s approaches zero from the right is

$$
\bar{c}(s) = \left(\frac{\bar{v}}{2\beta}\right)^{1/2} s^{1/2} \equiv \alpha s^{1/2}. \tag{B.44}
$$

Using this special solution, the value of $\lim_{s\to\infty} MUC(s)$ is estimated below:

$$\lim_{s\to+0} MUC(s) = \lim_{s\to+0} \bar{v}\left(t_o + \frac{1}{2\bar{c}} + \frac{1}{2\bar{c}}\frac{Js/\bar{c}}{1-s/\bar{c}}\right)$$

$$= \lim_{s\to+0} \bar{v}\left(t_o + \frac{1}{2\alpha\, s^{1/2}} + \frac{1}{2\alpha\, s^{1/2}}\frac{Js/\tau\alpha\, s^{1/2}}{1-s/\tau\alpha\, s^{1/2}}\right) = \infty. \tag{B.45}$$

Subsequently, the value of $\lim_{s\to+0} SMFC(s)$ is

$$\lim_{s\to+0} SMFC(s) = \lim_{s\to+0} \frac{\bar{v}s}{2\bar{c}}\frac{\partial \bar{T}^d}{\partial s} = -\lim_{s\to+0} \frac{\bar{v}}{2}\frac{\partial \bar{T}^d}{\partial c}$$

$$= \lim_{s\to+0} \frac{\bar{v}}{2}\frac{J\tau s}{(\tau\bar{c}-s)^2}$$

$$= \lim_{s\to0} \frac{\bar{v}}{2}\frac{J\tau}{(\tau\alpha - s^{1/2})^2} = \frac{J\beta}{\tau}. \tag{B.46}$$

(2) Proof of (7.76): The proof is worked out using the following special solution to the differential equation (7.72), which is applicable to the case when s approaches ∞:

$$\widehat{c}(s) = \frac{s}{\tau} + \left(\frac{\bar{v}J}{2\beta}\right)^{1/2} s^{1/2} \equiv \frac{s}{\tau} + \alpha s^{1/2}. \tag{B.47}$$

Using this special solution, the value of $\lim_{s\to\infty} MUC(s)$ is estimated below:

$$\lim_{s\to\infty} MUC(s) = \lim_{s\to\infty} \bar{v}\left(t_o + \frac{1}{2}\frac{1}{s/\tau + \alpha\, s^{1/2}} + \frac{1}{2}\frac{1}{s/\tau + \alpha\, s^{1/2}}\frac{Js/\tau(s/\tau + \alpha\, s^{1/2})}{1 - s/\tau(s/\tau + \alpha\, s^{1/2})}\right)$$

$$= \lim_{s\to\infty} \bar{v}\left(t_o + \frac{1}{2}\frac{Js}{\alpha\tau\, s^{1/2}(s/\tau + \alpha\, s^{1/2})}\right) = \bar{v}t_o. \tag{B.48}$$

On the other hand, the value of $\lim_{s\to\infty} SMFC(s)$ is

$$\lim_{s\to\infty} SMFC(s) = \lim_{s\to\infty} \frac{\bar{v}}{2}\frac{2\beta}{\bar{v}J}\frac{J\tau s}{\tau^2 s} = \frac{\beta}{\tau}. \tag{B.49}$$

(3) Proof of (7.77) and (7.78): Equations (B.45) and (B.48) imply that MUC is decreasing in s. Substituting $\partial^2 KC/\partial c^2 = 0$ into (7.17) gives

$$\frac{\partial MFC(s;\breve{v})}{\partial s} = -\frac{1}{s}MFC(s;\breve{v})\left(1 - \frac{s}{\bar{c}}\frac{\partial \bar{c}}{\partial s}\right) - \frac{\breve{c}}{s}\frac{\partial MWT(s,\bar{c};\breve{v})}{\partial c}\frac{\partial \bar{c}}{\partial s}. \tag{B.50}$$

If s is sufficiently larger than 1.0, the sign of $\partial SMFC/\partial s$ mainly depends on the sign of $-\partial MWT/\partial c$. In this circumstance, it holds that $-\partial MWT/\partial c \geq 0$. Hence, it follows that $\partial SMFC/\partial s \geq 0$. In addition, this assertion coincides with the *SMFC* values estimated in (B.46) and (B.49).

Appendix C: Appendix to Part III

Appendix C.1: Proof of Theorem 8.4

(1) The approach to prove Theorem 8.4: We estimate the sensitivities of $\tilde{p}$, $\tilde{t}$, and $\tilde{q}$ with respect to c. These sensitivities are estimated from the following simultaneous equation systems:

$$\tilde{t} = T(\bar{q}(\tilde{p},\tilde{t}), c) \tag{C.1}$$

$$MR(\tilde{q}) = \breve{v}\tilde{q}\frac{\partial T(\tilde{q},c)}{\partial \bar{q}}. \tag{C.2}$$

Here, (C.1) expresses the user equilibrium condition, and (C.2) is the pricing formula in (8.20).

By the implicit function theorem, there exist functions $\tilde{p}(c)$ and $\tilde{t}(c)$, which satisfy (C.1) and (C.2) simultaneously. Also, we can introduce the function $\tilde{q}$ such that $\tilde{q}(c) \equiv \bar{q}(\tilde{p}(c), \tilde{t}(c))$. Using these functions, we below estimate the signs of $\tilde{t}(c)/\partial c$ and $\tilde{p}(c)/\partial c$ for homogeneous and non-homogeneous service technologies, respectively.

(2) The proof for the case of homogeneous service technology: Firstly, it follows from (C.1) that

$$\frac{\partial \tilde{t}}{\partial c} = \frac{\partial T(\tilde{q},c)}{\partial q}\left(\frac{\partial \tilde{q}}{\partial c} - \frac{\tilde{q}}{c}\right). \tag{C.3}$$

Also, it follows from Assumption 6.1 that $\partial T/\partial q \rangle\ 0$. Hence, the sign of $\partial \tilde{t}/\partial c$ is positive (or negative), if the sign of $\partial \tilde{q}/\partial c - \tilde{q}/c$ is positive (or negative).

Subsequently, the differentiation of (C.2) is

$$\begin{aligned}\frac{\partial MR(\tilde{q})}{\partial c} &= \breve{v}\frac{\partial \tilde{q}}{\partial c}\frac{\partial T(\tilde{q},c)}{\partial \bar{q}} + \breve{v}\tilde{q}\frac{\partial T^2(\tilde{q},c)}{\partial \bar{q}^2}\frac{\partial \tilde{q}}{\partial c} + \breve{v}\tilde{q}\,\frac{\partial T^2(q=\tilde{q},c)}{\partial \bar{q}\partial c} \\ &= \left(\breve{v}\frac{\partial T(\tilde{q},c)}{\partial \bar{q}} + \breve{v}\tilde{q}\frac{\partial T^2(\tilde{q},c)}{\partial \bar{q}^2}\right)\left(\frac{\partial \tilde{q}}{\partial c} - \frac{\tilde{q}}{c}\right).\end{aligned} \tag{C.4}$$

Here, it holds that $\partial T/\partial q \rangle 0$ and $\partial^2 T/\partial q^2 \rangle 0$. Hence, the sign of $\partial MR(\tilde{q})/\partial c$ entirely depends on the sign of $\partial\tilde{q}/\partial c - \tilde{q}/c$, as in the case of $\partial\tilde{t}/\partial c$.

On the other hand, under the condition that $\partial E(\bar{q})/\partial p \cong 0$, it holds that

$$\tilde{p} \mathrel{\substack{\langle \\ - \\ \rangle}} \breve{p}, \quad \mathit{if} \quad MR(\tilde{q}) \mathrel{\substack{\langle \\ - \\ \rangle}} MR(\breve{q}). \tag{C.5}$$

This implies that

$$\tilde{q} \mathrel{\substack{\langle \\ - \\ \rangle}} \breve{q}, \quad \tilde{p} \mathrel{\substack{\rangle \\ - \\ \langle}} \breve{p} \quad \mathit{and} \quad \tilde{t} \mathrel{\substack{\rangle \\ - \\ \langle}} \breve{t}, \quad \mathit{if} \quad c_o \mathrel{\substack{\langle \\ - \\ \rangle}} \breve{c}. \tag{C.6}$$

The proof of (C.6) is worked out by contradiction. It follows from (C.3)–(C.5) that, if $\partial\tilde{q}/\partial c - \tilde{q}/c \rangle 0$, the inequality $\tilde{c} \langle \breve{c}$ implies that $\tilde{t} \langle \breve{t}$ and $\tilde{p} \langle \breve{p}$, and thus that $\tilde{q} \rangle \breve{q}$. These results imply that a service system with increasing returns satisfies the inequality $MR(\tilde{q}) \rangle MR(\breve{q})$ if $\partial E(\bar{q})/\partial p \cong 0$, as can be deduced from Fig. 8.5. This contradicts (C.5) that shows $\tilde{p} \rangle \breve{p}$. Hence, (C.6) follows.

(3) The proof for the case of non-homogeneous service technology defined in Assumption 6.1: In this case, (C.3) is amended as follows:

$$\frac{\partial\tilde{t}}{\partial c} = \frac{\partial T(\tilde{q},c)}{\partial q}\left(\frac{\partial\tilde{q}}{\partial c} - \frac{\tilde{q}}{c}\right) - \frac{1}{2c^2}T^d(\tilde{q}/c). \tag{C.7}$$

On the other hand, (C.4) becomes

$$\frac{\partial MR(\tilde{q})}{\partial c} = \left(\tilde{v}\frac{\partial T(\tilde{q},c)}{\partial\tilde{q}} + \tilde{v}\tilde{q}\frac{\partial T^2(\tilde{q},c)}{\partial\tilde{q}^2}\right)\left(\frac{\partial\tilde{q}}{\partial c} - \frac{\tilde{q}}{c}\right) - \frac{\tilde{v}}{2c^2}T^d(\tilde{q}/c). \tag{C.8}$$

Also, the inequality $\partial MR(\tilde{q})/\partial c \langle 0$ implies that $\partial\tilde{t}/\partial c \langle 0$, although the converse does not always hold. This implies (C.6), as can be proved in a manner identical to the proof for homogenous service technology.

Appendix C.2: Proof of Theorem 9.1

The uniqueness of the marketwise user equilibrium is proved through analyses of the following mapping $\Gamma^t{:}t \to t$, which denotes the simultaneous equation system in (9.19). The proof is worked out by applying the following univalence theorem: *the mapping such that* $f_n(x_1,\cdots,x_N) = p_n$, *for all* $n \in \langle 1,N\rangle$, *has the unique solution of* $x \in X$, *where* X *is a rectangle in* $\mathbf{R}^{\mathrm{N}}$, *if Jacobian* $J(x)$ *is everywhere the positive definite matrix (or P-matrix) in* X (Theorem 20.4 in Nikaido,1968).

To start, we estimate the Jacobian of the mapping $\Gamma^t(t;p,c)$:

$$\frac{\partial \Gamma^t(t;p,c)}{\partial t} = \begin{pmatrix} 1-a_{11}^{11} & \cdots & -a_{ml}^{11} & \cdots & -a_{ML}^{11} \\ \vdots & \ddots & \vdots & \ddots & \vdots \\ -a_{11}^{ml} & \cdots & -a_{ml}^{ml} & \cdots & -a_{ML}^{ml} \\ \vdots & \ddots & \vdots & \ddots & \vdots \\ -a_{11}^{ML} & \cdots & -a_{ml}^{ML} & \cdots & -a_{ML}^{ML} \end{pmatrix} \tag{C.9}$$

where

$$1-a_{ml}^{ml} \equiv 1-\frac{\partial T_{ml}}{\partial t_{ml}} = \frac{\partial T_{ml}}{\partial s_{ml}}\frac{\Phi_{ml}}{Q_{ml}}\left(\frac{\partial Q_{ml}}{\partial t_{ml}} - \sum_{mn\in I_{ml}}\frac{\partial \Phi_{mn}}{\partial t_{ml}}\right) \langle\ 0 \tag{C.10}$$

$$-a_{ij}^{ml} \equiv -\frac{\partial T_{ml}}{\partial t_{ij}} = -\sum_{mn\in I_{ml}}\frac{\partial T_{ml}}{\partial s_{ml}}\frac{\Phi_{ml}}{Q_{ml}}\frac{\partial Q_{mn}}{\partial t_{ij}}\ \rangle\ 0, \quad \text{all } ij \neq ml \tag{C.11}$$

$$Q_{ml} = \int_{D_{mn}} f_m(p_{ml}+\xi_m \bar{t}_{ml})\,h(\xi)d\mu = \sum_{mn\in I_{ml}}\Phi_{mn}. \tag{C.12}$$

In the above, the signs of (C.10) and (C.11) are estimated by applying $\partial Q_{ml}/\partial t_{ml}\ \langle\ 0$ and $\partial Q_{ml}/\partial t_{ij}\ \rangle\ 0$ from Theorem 5.11. In addition, the last equality of (C.10) comes from the following:

$$\begin{aligned} 1-a_{ml}^{ml} = 1 - \frac{\partial T_{ml}}{\partial s_{ml}}\Bigg(&\frac{\partial Q_{ml}}{\partial t_{ml}}\frac{\Phi_{ml}}{\sum_{mn\in I_{ml}}\Phi_{mn}} \\ &+Q_{ml}\left(\sum_{mn\in I_{ml}}\Phi_{mn}\right)^{-2}\left(\frac{\partial \Phi_{ml}}{\partial t_{ml}}\sum_{mn\in I_{ml}}\Phi_{mn} - \sum_{mn\in I_{ml}}\frac{\partial \Phi_{mn}}{\partial t_{ml}}\Phi_{ml}\right)\Bigg) \end{aligned} \tag{C.13}$$

$$= 1-\frac{\partial T_{ml}}{\partial s_{ml}}\left(\frac{\partial Q_{ml}}{\partial t_{ml}}\frac{\Phi_{ml}}{Q_{ml}} + \frac{\partial \Phi_{ml}}{\partial t_{ml}} - \sum_{mn\in I_{ml}}\frac{\partial \Phi_{mn}}{\partial t_{ml}}\frac{\Phi_{ml}}{Q_{ml}}\right) \tag{C.14}$$

$$= \frac{\partial T_{ml}}{\partial s_{ml}}\frac{\Phi_{ml}}{Q_{ml}}\left(-\frac{\partial Q_{ml}}{\partial t_{mn'}} + \sum_{mn\in I_{ml}}\frac{\partial \Phi_{mn}}{\partial t_{ml}}\right). \tag{C.15}$$

Here substituting (C.12) into (C.13) yields (C.14), and substituting the equation in Lemma 9.2 into (C.14) gives (C.15).

Subsequently, we reorganize the Jacobian of Γ^t as follows:

$$\frac{\partial \Gamma^t(t;p,c)}{\partial t} = YX = \begin{pmatrix} y^{11} \\ \vdots \\ y^{ml} \\ \vdots \\ y^{ML} \end{pmatrix}^T \begin{pmatrix} x_{11}^{11} & \cdots & x_{ml}^{11} & \cdots & x_{ML}^{11} \\ \vdots & \ddots & \vdots & \ddots & \vdots \\ x_{11}^{ml} & \cdots & x_{ml}^{ml} & \cdots & x_{ML}^{ml} \\ \vdots & \ddots & \vdots & \ddots & \vdots \\ x_{11}^{ML} & \cdots & x_{ml}^{ML} & \cdots & x_{ML}^{ML} \end{pmatrix} \tag{C.16}$$

where

$$x_{ml}^{ml} = -\frac{\partial Q_{ml}}{\partial t_{ml}} + \sum_{mn \in I_{ml}} \frac{\partial \Phi_{mn}}{\partial t_{ml}} \rangle\, 0 \tag{C.17}$$

$$x_{ij}^{ml} = -\frac{\partial Q_{ml}}{\partial t_{ij}} \langle\, 0, \quad \text{all } ij \neq ml \tag{C.18}$$

$$y^{yl} = \sum_{mn \in I_{ml}} \frac{\partial T_{ml}}{\partial s_{ml}} \frac{\Phi_{ml}}{Q_{ml}}. \tag{C.19}$$

The matrix X defined above satisfies the diagonal dominance condition. That is, by the diagonal dominance condition of Q_{mn} in Theorem 5.12 and the inequality of $\partial \Phi_{ml}/\partial t_{ml} \rangle\, 0$ in (9.13), it holds that

$$x_{ml}^{ml} \rangle\, 0, \quad \text{and} \quad x_{ml}^{ml} \rangle \sum_{ij \neq ml} \left| x_{ij}^{ml} \right| \rangle\, 0. \tag{C.20}$$

Hence, the matrix X is positive definite. Therefore, by the univalence theorem, it is clear that the user equilibrium is unique, as claimed.

Appendix C.3: Proof of Lemma 9.7

(1) The outline of the proof: In this appendix, we prove the continuity of Γ^u at the point such that $p_{mn} = p_{mn'}$, for some $n' \neq n$. The mapping $\Gamma^u \equiv (\Gamma_{11}^u, \cdots, \Gamma_{MN}^u)$ is used to estimate the solution to the following simultaneous equation system:

$$\Gamma_{mn}^u(p,c) - T_{mn}(Q_{mn}(p, \Gamma^u(p,c)), c_{mn}) = 0, \quad \text{all } mn. \tag{C.21}$$

This function Γ_{mn}^u differs from T_{mn}^{ue} considered in Lemma 9.5 in that the former is the function of (p,c), whereas the latter is the function of (p_{mn}, c_{mn}).

Without loss of generality, the proof can be worked out under the following condition:

$$p_{m1} \langle \cdots \langle p_{m(n-1)} \langle p_{m(m+1)} \langle \cdots \langle p_{mN_m}, \quad \text{all } m. \tag{C.22}$$

If $Q_{mn}(p,t) \rangle 0$ for all mn, by Lemma 5.1, the inequality in (C.22) leads to the following inequality:

$$\Gamma^u_{m1}(p,c) \rangle \cdots \rangle \Gamma^u_{m(n-1)}(p,c) \rangle \Gamma^u_{m(n+1)}(p,c) \cdots \rangle \Gamma^u_{mN_m}(p,c). \tag{C.23}$$

Moreover, the sign of $\Gamma^u_{mn}/\partial p_{mn}$ at the point such that $p_{mn} \neq p_{m(n\pm 1)}$ is

$$\frac{\partial \Gamma^u_{mn}(p,c)}{\partial p_{mn}} \langle 0, \tag{C.24}$$

as will be shown later in this appendix. Hence, the proof of the continuity of Γ^u_{mn} at the point $p_{mn} = p_{m(n+1)}$ can be worked out in a manner analogous to that used to show the continuity of T^{ue}_{mn} through the use of Fig.9.1 in the proof of Lemma 9.6.

(2) Proof of (C.24). The proof is worked out by applying the following property of the P-matrix: *If a matrix A is a P-matrix, the relationship* $Ax = u \rangle 0$ *implies that* $x \rangle 0$, *where* $A \in \mathbf{R}^n \times \mathbf{R}^n$, $x \in \mathbf{R}^n$, *and* $u \in \mathbf{R}^n$ (Corollary 1 to Theorem 20.4 in Nikaido,1968).

We estimate the specific expression of $\partial \Gamma^u_{mn}/\partial p_{mn}$ from (C.21). Differentiating the NT simultaneous equations in (C.21) with respect to p_{mn} gives

$$\begin{pmatrix} 1 - x^{11}_{11} & \cdots & -x^{11}_{mn} & \cdots & x^{11}_{MN} \\ \vdots & \ddots & \vdots & \ddots & \vdots \\ -x^{mn}_{11} & \cdots & 1 - x^{mn}_{mn} & \cdots & x^{mn}_{MN} \\ \vdots & \ddots & \vdots & \ddots & \vdots \\ -x^{MN}_{11} & \cdots & -x^{MN}_{mn} & \cdots & 1 - x^{MN}_{MN} \end{pmatrix} \begin{pmatrix} \partial \Gamma^u_{11}/\partial p_{mn} \\ \vdots \\ \partial \Gamma^u_{mn}/\partial p_{mn} \\ \vdots \\ \partial \Gamma^u_{MN}/\partial p_{mn} \end{pmatrix} = \begin{pmatrix} y^{11}_{mn} \\ \vdots \\ y^{mn}_{mn} \\ \vdots \\ y^{MN}_{mn} \end{pmatrix} \tag{C.25}$$

where

$$x^{m'n'}_{m''n''} = \frac{\partial T_{m'n'}}{\partial Q_{m'n'}} \frac{\partial Q_{m'n'}}{\partial t_{m''n''}} \quad \text{and} \quad y^{m'n'}_{mn} = \frac{\partial T_{m'n'}}{\partial Q_{m'n'}} \frac{\partial Q_{m'n'}}{\partial p_{mn}}. \tag{C.26}$$

Let the matrix equation in (C.25) be expressed by

$$Xu = y. \tag{C.27}$$

Here, it holds that $y \langle 0$. Hence, if X is a P-matrix, it follows that $u \langle 0$, as can be deduced from the P-matrix property introduced above. Therefore, the proof of

(C.24) can be completed by showing that X is a P-matrix. Also, the fact that X is a P-matrix can be proved by showing that X satisfies the diagonal dominance condition, in a manner analogous to that used to show that the matrix in (C.9) satisfies this condition.

Appendix C.4: Proof of Theorem 9.6

(1) We here analyze the PMP without constraints, X_{mn}, in (9.58). It is shown here that the first order conditions for X_{mn} with respect to p_{mn} and c_{mn} can be converted to the optimality conditions in (9.41) and (9.42), respectively, under the condition that X_{mn} is differentiable at $(\breve{p}_{mn}, \breve{c}_{mn})$.

The first order conditions for X_{mn} with respect to p_{mn} and c_{mn} are

$$\frac{\partial X_{mn}}{\partial p_{mn}} = \breve{Q}^{ue}_{mn} + \breve{p}_{mn}\frac{\partial \breve{Q}^{ue}_{mn}}{\partial p_{mn}} = 0 \tag{C.28}$$

$$\frac{\partial X_{mn}}{\partial c_{mn}} = \breve{p}_{mn}\frac{\partial \breve{Q}^{ue}_{mn}}{\partial c_{mn}} - MKC_{mn}(\breve{c}_{mn}) = 0. \tag{C.29}$$

Moreover, the demand function Q^{ue}_{mn} satisfies the relationship in (9.23). Differentiating (9.23) with respect to p_{mn} and c_{mn}, and arranging the results of the previous step gives

$$\frac{\partial \breve{Q}^{ue}_{mn}}{\partial p_{mn}} = \frac{\partial \breve{Q}^{s}_{mn}}{\partial p_{mn}} \bigg/ \left(1 - \frac{\partial \breve{Q}^{s}_{mn}}{\partial t_{mn}}\frac{\partial \breve{T}_{mn}}{\partial Q_{mn}}\right) \tag{C.30}$$

$$\frac{\partial \breve{Q}^{ue}_{mn}}{\partial c_{mn}} = \frac{\partial \breve{Q}^{s}_{mn}}{\partial t_{mn}}\frac{\partial \breve{T}_{mn}}{\partial c_{mn}} \bigg/ \left(1 - \frac{\partial \breve{Q}^{s}_{mn}}{\partial t_{mn}}\frac{\partial \breve{T}_{mn}}{\partial Q^{s}_{mn}}\right). \tag{C.31}$$

In addition, the private value-of-service-time $\breve{\xi}_{mn}$ is estimated by

$$\breve{\xi}_{mn} = \frac{\partial \breve{Q}^{s}_{mn}}{\partial t_{mn}} \bigg/ \frac{\partial \breve{Q}^{s}_{mn}}{\partial p_{mn}}. \tag{C.32}$$

Substituting (C.30) and (C.32) into (C.28) gives the pricing rule of (9.41):

$$\breve{Q}^{ue}_{mn} + \breve{p}_{mn}\frac{\partial \breve{Q}^{s}_{mn}}{\partial p_{mn}} - \breve{\xi}_{mn}\breve{Q}^{s}_{mn}\frac{\partial \breve{T}_{mn}}{\partial Q_{mn}}\frac{\partial \breve{Q}^{s}_{mn}}{\partial p_{mn}} = 0. \tag{C.33}$$

Subsequently, substituting (C.31) and (C.32) into (C.29) yields

$$\breve{\xi}_{mn}\frac{\partial \breve{T}_{mn}}{\partial c_{mn}}\left(\breve{p}_{mn}\frac{\partial \breve{Q}^{s}_{mn}}{\partial p_{mn}}\bigg/\left(1-\breve{\xi}_{mn}\frac{\partial \breve{Q}^{s}_{mn}}{\partial p_{mn}}\frac{\partial \breve{T}_{mn}}{\partial Q_{mn}}\right)\right)-MKC_{mn}(\breve{c}_{mn})=0. \tag{C.34}$$

Substituting (C.33) into (C.34) gives the investment rule of (9.42).

(2) The proof of the case when X_{mn} is not differentiable at $(\breve{p}_{mn}, \breve{c}_{mn})$: In this case, the first order conditions of X_{mn} with respect to (p_{mn}, c_{mn}) are

$$\frac{\partial X_{mn}}{\partial p_{mn}}=\breve{\Phi}_{mn}+\breve{p}_{mn}Y(\breve{p}_{mn})=0 \tag{C.35}$$

$$\frac{\partial X_{mn}}{\partial c_{mn}}=\breve{p}_{mn}\frac{\partial \breve{\Phi}_{mn}}{\partial c_{mn}}-MKC_{mn}(\breve{c}_{mn})=0. \tag{C.36}$$

where $Y(\breve{p}_{mn})$ is the sub-differential of $\breve{Q}^{s}_{mn}$ with respect to p_{mn} in (9.46).

The proof can be completed by showing that (C.35) and (C.36) imply the following:

$$\breve{\Phi}_{mn}+\breve{p}_{mn}Y(\breve{p}_{mn})-\breve{\xi}_{mn}\breve{\Phi}_{mn}\frac{\partial \breve{T}_{mn}}{\partial \Phi_{mn}}Y(\breve{p}_{mn})=0 \tag{C.37}$$

$$\breve{\xi}_{mn}\frac{\partial \breve{T}_{mn}}{\partial c_{mn}}\left(\breve{p}_{mn}Y(\breve{p}_{mn})\bigg/\left(1-\breve{\xi}_{mn}Y(\breve{p}_{mn})\frac{\partial \breve{T}_{mn}}{\partial Q_{mn}}\right)\right)-MKC_{mn}(\breve{c}_{mn})=0. \tag{C.38}$$

where $\breve{\xi}_{mn}=Y(\breve{t}_{mn})/Y(\breve{p}_{mn})$. Here, (C.37) and (C.38) are the counterparts of (C.33) and (C.34) for the case when X_{mn} is differentiable at $(\breve{p}_{mn}, \breve{c}_{mn})$. Also the proof can be worked out in a manner identical to the proof for the case when X_{mn} is differentiable at $(\breve{p}_{mn}, \breve{c}_{mn})$.

Appendix D: Appendix to Part IV

Appendix D.1: Proof of Lemma 11.3 and Theorem 11.2

(1) The development of the first order conditions for SW_3 of (11.55): Differentiating SW_3 with respect to government control variables, and substituting Lemma 11.1 into the preceding outcome gives

$$\frac{\partial SW_3}{\partial r^i} = -\frac{\partial \widehat{W}}{\partial \bar{U}^i}\eta^i - \widehat{\tau}\frac{\partial \widehat{T}}{\partial \bar{q}}\frac{\partial \hat{q}^i}{\partial r^i} + \widehat{\omega} + \widehat{\psi}\widehat{p}\frac{\partial \widehat{q}^i}{\partial r^i} = 0, \quad \text{all} \quad i \tag{D.1}$$

$$\frac{\partial SW_3}{\partial p} = -\sum_i \frac{\partial \widehat{W}}{\partial \bar{U}^i}\widehat{\eta}^i\widehat{q}^i - \widehat{\tau}\frac{\partial \widehat{T}}{\partial \bar{q}}\frac{\partial \widehat{q}}{\partial p} + \widehat{\psi}\left(\widehat{q} + \widehat{p}\frac{\partial \widehat{q}}{\partial p}\right) = 0 \tag{D.2}$$

$$\frac{\partial SW_3}{\partial t} = -\sum_i \frac{\partial \widehat{W}}{\partial \bar{U}^i}\widehat{\eta}^i v^i \widehat{q}^{\,i} + \widehat{\tau}\left(1 - \frac{\partial \widehat{T}}{\partial \bar{q}}\frac{\partial \widehat{q}}{\partial t}\right) + \widehat{\psi}\widehat{p}\frac{\partial \widehat{q}}{\partial t} = 0 \tag{D.3}$$

$$\frac{\partial SW_3}{\partial c} = -\widehat{\tau}\frac{\partial \widehat{T}}{\partial c} - \widehat{\psi}\, MKC(\widehat{c}) = 0. \tag{D.4}$$

(2) Estimation of (11.57) for $\widehat{\tau}$: Arranging (D.2) and (D.3) gives

$$\breve{v}\frac{\partial SW_3}{\partial p} - \frac{\partial SW_3}{\partial t} = \widehat{\psi}\breve{v}\widehat{q} - \widehat{\tau} + \delta = 0, \tag{D.5}$$

where

$$\delta = \sum_i \frac{\partial \widehat{W}}{\partial \bar{U}^i}\widehat{\eta}^i v^i \widehat{q}^i - \breve{v}\sum_i \frac{\partial \widehat{W}}{\partial \bar{U}^i}\widehat{\eta}^i \widehat{q}^i.$$

By (11.56), (D.5) is simplified as follows:

$$\widehat{\tau} = \widehat{\psi}\breve{v}\widehat{q} + \delta \cong \widehat{\psi}\breve{v}\widehat{q}, \tag{D.6}$$

since

$$\delta = \sum_i \frac{\partial \widehat{W}}{\partial \bar{U}^i}\widehat{\eta}^i (v^i \widehat{q}^i - \breve{v}\widehat{q}^i) \cong 0. \tag{D.7}$$

(3) Estimation of (11.62) for $\widehat{p}$: Reorganizing (D.1) and (D.2) yields

$$\begin{aligned}\frac{\partial SW_3}{\partial p} - \sum_i \frac{\partial SW_3}{\partial r^i}\widehat{q}^i &= \left(\widehat{\psi}\widehat{p} - \widehat{\tau}\frac{\partial \widehat{T}}{\partial q}\right)\sum_i \left(\frac{\partial \widehat{q}^i}{\partial p} - \hat{q}^i\frac{\partial \widehat{q}^i}{\partial r^i}\right) + \left(\widehat{\psi} - \widehat{\omega}\right)\widehat{q} \\ &= 0.\end{aligned} \tag{D.8}$$

Substituting (D.5) into (D.8) and reorganizing this outcome gives

$$\widehat{p} \cong \breve{v}\widehat{q}\frac{\partial \widehat{T}}{\partial \bar{q}} + \frac{\widehat{\psi} - \widehat{\omega}}{\widehat{\psi}}\widehat{p}\Big/E_s(\widehat{q}). \tag{D.9}$$

(4) Proof of (11.59) for $\widehat{\omega}$: Substituting (D.5) and (D.9) into (D.1) gives

$$\frac{\partial \widehat{W}}{\partial \bar{U}^i}\widehat{\eta}^i = -\widehat{\tau}\frac{\partial \widehat{T}}{\partial \bar{q}}\frac{\partial \hat{q}^i}{\partial r^i} + \widehat{\omega} + \widehat{\psi}\widehat{p}\frac{\partial \widehat{q}^i}{\partial r^i}$$

$$= \widehat{\omega} + \left(\widehat{\psi} - \widehat{\omega}\right)\widehat{p}\frac{\partial \widehat{q}^i}{\partial r^i}\Big/E_s(\widehat{q}) \cong \widehat{\omega}. \tag{D.10}$$

(5) Proof of (11.63) for *MKC*: It follows from (D.4) and (D.6) that

$$MKC(\widehat{c}) = -\frac{\widehat{\tau}}{\widehat{\psi}}\frac{\partial \widehat{T}}{\partial c} \cong -\widehat{v}\widehat{q}\frac{\partial \widehat{T}}{\partial c}. \tag{D.11}$$

Appendix D.2: Proof of Theorem 11.3

(1) Proof of (11.65): A marginal change in e_1 values accompanies changes in all government control variables: r, p, and t. Hence, it is clear that

$$\frac{\partial \widehat{W}}{\partial e_1} = -\widehat{\omega} = -\sum_i \frac{\partial \widehat{W}}{\partial \bar{U}^i}\frac{\partial \bar{U}^i}{\partial(\bar{M}^i - r^i)}\frac{\partial \widehat{r}^i}{\partial e_1} + \sum_i \frac{\partial \widehat{W}}{\partial \bar{U}^i}\frac{\partial \bar{U}^i}{\partial p}\frac{\partial \widehat{p}}{\partial e_1}$$
$$+\sum_i \frac{\partial \widehat{W}}{\partial \bar{U}^i}\frac{\partial \bar{U}^i}{\partial t}\frac{\partial \widehat{t}}{\partial e_1}. \tag{D.12}$$

Here, the third term reflects the direct effect of changes in e_1 on consumer utilities and thus on social welfare, whereas the fourth and fifth terms represent the secondary effect of changes in e_1 Specifically, the fourth and fifth terms estimate the change in social welfare, which is caused by changes in p and t due to changes in q and c for a marginal increase in e_1.

On neglecting the secondary effect of a marginal increase in e1, equation (D.12) is simplified as follows:

$$\frac{\partial \widehat{W}}{\partial e_1} \cong -\sum_i \frac{\partial \widehat{W}}{\partial \bar{U}^i}\frac{\partial \bar{U}^i}{\partial(\bar{M}^i - r^i)}\frac{\partial \widehat{r}^i}{\partial e_1}$$
$$\cong -\widehat{\omega}\sum_i \frac{\partial \widehat{r}^i}{\partial e_1} = -\widehat{\omega}. \tag{D.13}$$

This equation indicates that the error caused by the deletion of the second and third terms on the right side of (D.12) is negligible.

(2) Proof of (11.66): As in the case of $\partial \widehat{W}/\partial e_1$, the sensitivity $\partial \widehat{W}/\partial e_2$ can be expressed as follows:

$$\frac{\partial \widehat{W}}{\partial e_2} = \widehat{\psi} = -\sum_i \frac{\partial \widehat{W}}{\partial \bar{U}^i} \frac{\partial \bar{U}^i}{\partial(\bar{M}^i - r^i)} \frac{\partial \widehat{r}^i}{\partial e_2} + \sum_i \frac{\partial \widehat{W}}{\partial \bar{U}^i} \frac{\partial \bar{U}^i}{\partial p} \frac{\partial \widehat{p}}{\partial e_e}$$
$$+ \sum_i \frac{\partial \widehat{W}}{\partial \bar{U}^i} \frac{\partial \bar{U}^i}{\partial t} \frac{\partial \widehat{T}}{\partial e_2}. \tag{D.14}$$

On neglecting the first and second terms on the right side, the above equation is simplified as follows:

$$\frac{\partial \widehat{W}}{\partial e_2} \cong \sum_i \frac{\partial \widehat{W}}{\partial \bar{U}^i} \frac{\partial \bar{U}^i}{\partial t} \frac{\partial \widehat{T}}{\partial c} \frac{\partial \widehat{c}}{\partial e}. \tag{D.15}$$

Substituting (D.3), (D.9), and (D.4) into (D.15) sequentially yields:

$$\begin{aligned}
\frac{\partial \widehat{W}}{\partial e_2} &\cong -\widehat{\tau}\frac{\partial \widehat{T}}{\partial c}\left(1-\frac{\partial \widehat{T}}{\partial \bar{q}}\frac{\partial \widehat{q}}{\partial t}\right)\frac{\partial \widehat{c}}{\partial e} - \widehat{\psi}\frac{\partial \widehat{T}}{\partial c}\widehat{p}\frac{\partial \widehat{q}}{\partial t}\frac{\partial \widehat{c}}{\partial e} \\
&= -\widehat{\tau}\frac{\partial \widehat{T}}{\partial c}\left(1-\frac{\partial \widehat{T}}{\partial \bar{q}}\frac{\partial \widehat{q}}{\partial t}\right)\frac{\partial \widehat{c}}{\partial e} - \widehat{\psi}\frac{\partial \widehat{T}}{\partial c}\frac{\partial \widehat{q}}{\partial t}\frac{\partial \widehat{c}}{\partial e}\left(\widehat{v}\widehat{q}\frac{\partial \widehat{T}}{\partial \bar{q}} + \frac{\widehat{\omega}-\widehat{\psi}}{\widehat{\psi}}\widehat{p}\Big/E_s(\widehat{q})\right) \\
&= \left(\widehat{\psi} + (\widehat{\psi}-\widehat{\omega})\widehat{p}E_s(\widehat{q})\frac{\partial \widehat{q}}{\partial t}\right) MKC(\widehat{c})\frac{\partial \widehat{c}}{\partial e} \\
&= \widehat{\psi} + (\widehat{\psi}-\widehat{\omega})\widehat{p}E_s(\widehat{q})\frac{\partial \widehat{q}}{\partial t} \cong \widehat{\psi}.
\end{aligned} \tag{D.16}$$

The last equation indicates that the error caused by the deletion of the first and second terms on the right side of (D.14) is negligible.

Appendix D.3: Proof of Theorem 11.5

(1) Analyses for the sign of all elements in (11.73). Let (11.73) be expressed by

$$\begin{pmatrix} a_{11} & a_{12} \\ a_{21} & a_{22} \end{pmatrix} \begin{pmatrix} \cdot \\ \cdot \end{pmatrix} = \begin{pmatrix} b_1 \\ 0 \end{pmatrix}. \tag{D.17}$$

First, it is clear that

$$a_{21} = \widehat{v}\frac{\partial \widehat{q}}{\partial p}\frac{\partial \widehat{T}}{\partial c} \rangle\ 0. \tag{D.18}$$

Second, by Theorem 11.4, it follows that

$$b_1 \equiv \widehat{p}\frac{\partial G}{\partial e} = \frac{\widehat{p}}{E_s}\frac{\partial}{\partial e}\left(\frac{\widehat{\omega}}{\widehat{\psi}}\right) \rangle\ 0. \tag{D.19}$$

Third, by the concavity of SW_3 with respect to c, it follows that

$$a_{22} = \frac{\partial}{\partial c}\left(\widehat{v}\widehat{q}\frac{\partial \widehat{T}}{\partial c} + \frac{\partial KC(\cdot)}{\partial c}\right) = \widehat{v}\widehat{q}\frac{\partial^2 \widehat{T}}{\partial c^2} + \widehat{v}^2\frac{\partial \widehat{q}}{\partial p}\left(\frac{\partial \widehat{T}}{\partial c}\right)^2 + \frac{\partial^2 KC(\cdot)}{\partial c^2} \rangle\ 0. \tag{D.20}$$

Here the parenthesis of the second term represents $-\partial SW_3/\partial c$. This term depicts that " – *marginal benefit* + *marginal cost*". Therefore, the sign of a_{22} should be positive, since SW_3 is concave in c.

The above analyses can be summarized as follows:

$$\begin{pmatrix} ? & ? \\ + & + \end{pmatrix}\begin{pmatrix} \cdot \\ \cdot \end{pmatrix} = \begin{pmatrix} + \\ 0 \end{pmatrix}. \tag{D.21}$$

(2) Estimation of the sign of $\partial\widehat{q}/.\partial e$: Differentiating the investment rule in (D.11) with respect to e and substituting (B.32) into the result of the previous step gives

$$\begin{aligned}\left(\frac{\partial^2 KC(\cdot)}{\partial c^2} + \widehat{v}\,\widehat{q}\frac{\partial^2 \widehat{T}}{\partial c^2}\right)\frac{\partial \widehat{c}}{\partial e} &= -\widehat{v}\frac{\partial \widehat{q}}{\partial e}\frac{\partial \widehat{T}}{\partial c} - \widehat{v}\widehat{q}\frac{\partial^2 \widehat{T}}{\partial c \partial q}\frac{\partial \widehat{q}}{\partial e} \\ &= \left(\frac{2}{\widehat{c}}MFC\left(\widehat{q}\right) + \widehat{v}\frac{\widehat{q}^2}{\widehat{c}}\frac{\partial^2 \widehat{T}}{\partial q^2}\right)\frac{\partial \widehat{q}}{\partial e}.\end{aligned} \tag{D.22}$$

The parenthesis on the first formula is greater than a_{22} and, therefore, is positive. Also, the parenthesis on the third formula is positive. Hence, it follows that

$$\frac{\partial \widehat{q}}{\partial e} \begin{matrix} \rangle \\ \langle \end{matrix} 0, \quad \text{if} \quad \frac{\partial \widehat{c}}{\partial e} \begin{matrix} \rangle \\ \langle \end{matrix} 0. \tag{D.23}$$

(3) Estimation of the signs of $\partial\widehat{p}/\partial e$ and $\partial\widehat{c}/\partial e$: The sign of $\partial\widehat{p}/\partial e$ and $\partial\widehat{c}/\partial e$ is estimated by applying Cramer's rule to (11.73). The estimation shows that

$$\frac{\partial \widehat{p}}{\partial e} \begin{matrix} \langle \\ \rangle \end{matrix} 0, \frac{\partial \widehat{c}}{\partial e} \begin{matrix} \rangle \\ \langle \end{matrix} 0, \quad \text{if} \quad \det\{A\} \begin{matrix} \langle \\ \rangle \end{matrix} 0, \tag{D.24}$$

where $\det[A]$ stands for the determinant of matrix A on the left of (11.73).

On the other hand, the value of $\det\{A\}$ is

$$\det\{A\} = \frac{\partial MFC(\cdot)}{\partial \widehat{q}} \frac{\partial \widehat{q}}{\partial p} \alpha - G\beta. \tag{D.25}$$

where

$$\alpha = \frac{\partial^2 KC(\cdot)}{\partial c^2} + \widehat{v}\,\widehat{q}\frac{\partial^2 \widehat{T}}{\partial c^2} \rangle\, 0 \text{ and } \beta = \frac{\partial^2 KC(\cdot)}{\partial c^2} + \widehat{v}\,\widehat{q}\frac{\partial^2 \widehat{T}}{\partial c^2} + \widehat{v}^2 \frac{\partial \widehat{q}}{\partial p}\left(\frac{\partial \widehat{T}}{\partial c}\right)^2 \rangle\, 0.$$

This equation implies that

$$\frac{\partial MFC(\cdot)}{\partial \widehat{q}} \underset{\langle}{\overset{\rangle}{-}} Z, \text{ if } \det\{A\} \underset{\rangle}{\overset{\langle}{-}} 0, \tag{D.26}$$

where

$$Z = G\left(\frac{\partial^2 KC(\cdot)}{\partial c^2} + \widehat{v}\,\widehat{q}\frac{\partial^2 \widehat{T}}{\partial c^2} + \widehat{v}^2 \frac{\partial \widehat{q}}{\partial p}\left(\frac{\partial \widehat{T}}{\partial c}\right)^2\right) \Big/ \left(\frac{\partial^2 KC(\cdot)}{\partial c^2} + \widehat{v}\,\widehat{q}\frac{\partial^2 \widehat{T}}{\partial c^2}\right)\frac{\partial \widehat{q}}{\partial p} \,\langle\, 0.$$

From (D.24)-(D.26), it follows that

$$\frac{\partial \widehat{p}}{\partial e} \underset{\rangle}{\overset{\langle}{-}} 0,\ \frac{\partial \widehat{c}}{\partial e} \underset{\langle}{\overset{\rangle}{-}} 0,\ \frac{\partial \widehat{q}}{\partial e} \underset{\langle}{\overset{\rangle}{-}} 0 \text{ if } \frac{\partial MFC\left(\widehat{q};\widehat{v}\right)}{\partial \widehat{q}} \underset{\langle}{\overset{\rangle}{-}} Z. \tag{D.27}$$

However, the outcome of $\partial\widehat{c}/\partial e \,\langle\, 0$ and $\partial\widehat{q}/\partial e \,\langle\, 0$ contradicts the reality. This argument can apply to the outcome $\partial\widehat{p}/\partial e \,\rangle\, 0$. Therefore, it is judged to be economically unacceptable that $\partial MFC/\partial q$ is smaller than a negative value significantly larger than zero, represented by Z.

Appendix D.4: Proof of Lemma 12.2 and Theorem 12.1

(1) Development of first order conditions for SW_o: Differentiating the Lagrangian SW_o in (12.6) with respect to control variables gives

$$\begin{aligned}\frac{\partial SW_o}{\partial r^i} &= -\frac{\partial \hat{W}}{\partial E\{\bar{U}^i\}}E\{\hat{\eta}^i\} - \sum_n \hat{\tau}_n \frac{\partial \hat{T}_n}{\partial Q_n}\frac{\partial \hat{Q}_n^i}{\partial r^i} + \hat{\omega}\left(1 + \sum_n \hat{p}_n \frac{\partial \hat{Q}_n^i}{\partial r^i}\right) \\ &= 0, \quad \text{all } i\end{aligned} \tag{D.28}$$

$$\frac{\partial SW_o}{\partial p_m} = -\sum_i \frac{\partial \hat{W}}{\partial E\{\bar{U}^i\}} E\{\hat{\eta}^i \hat{q}_m^i\} - \sum_n \hat{\tau}_n \frac{\partial \hat{T}_n}{\partial Q_n}\frac{\partial \hat{Q}_n}{\partial p_m}$$
$$+ \hat{\omega}\left(\hat{Q}_m + \sum_n \hat{p}_n \frac{\partial \hat{Q}_n}{\partial p_m}\right) = 0, \quad \text{all} \quad m \tag{D.29}$$

$$\frac{\partial SW_o}{\partial t_m} = -\sum_i \frac{\partial \hat{W}}{\partial E\{\bar{U}^i\}} E\{\hat{\eta}^i \xi_m^i \hat{q}_m^i\} + \hat{\tau}_m - \sum_n \hat{\tau}_n \frac{\partial \hat{T}_n}{\partial Q_n}\frac{\partial \hat{Q}_n}{\partial t_m}$$
$$+ \hat{\omega}\sum_n \hat{p}_n \frac{\partial \hat{Q}_n}{\partial t_m} = 0, \quad \text{all } m \tag{D.30}$$

$$\frac{\partial SW_o}{\partial c_m} = -\hat{\kappa}_m - \hat{\tau}_m \frac{\partial \hat{T}_m}{\partial c_m} = 0, \quad \text{all } m \tag{D.31}$$

$$\frac{\partial SW_o}{\partial x_{mj}} = \hat{\kappa}_m \frac{\partial \hat{F}_m}{\partial x_{mj}} - \hat{\omega} p_j = 0, \quad \text{all} \quad m, j. \tag{D.32}$$

(2) Estimation of $\hat{\tau}_m$: Using (12.7), (D.29) and (D.30) are arranged as follows:

$$\breve{\xi}_m \frac{\partial SW_o}{\partial p_m} - \frac{\partial SW_o}{\partial t_m} = \hat{\omega}\breve{\xi}_m \hat{Q}_m - \hat{\tau}_m + \delta_m - \sum_n \hat{\tau}_n \varepsilon_{mn} \frac{\partial \hat{T}_n}{\partial Q_n} + \hat{\omega}\sum_n \varepsilon_{mn}\hat{p}_n$$
$$= 0, \tag{D.33}$$

where

$$\delta_m = \frac{\partial \hat{W}}{\partial E\{\bar{U}^i\}} E\{\hat{\eta}^i \xi_m^i \hat{q}_m^i\} - \breve{\xi}_m \sum_i \frac{\partial \hat{W}}{\partial E\{\bar{U}^i\}} E\{\hat{\eta}^i \hat{q}_m^i\} \tag{D.34}$$

$$\varepsilon_{mn} = (\breve{\xi}_m - \breve{\xi}_{mn})\frac{\partial \hat{Q}_n}{\partial p_m}. \tag{D.35}$$

Equation (D.33) gives

$$\hat{\tau}_m = \hat{\omega}\breve{\xi}_m \hat{Q}_m + \delta_m - \sum_n \hat{\tau}_n \varepsilon_{mn} \frac{\partial \hat{T}_n}{\partial Q_n} + \hat{\omega}\sum_n \varepsilon_{mn}\hat{p}_n, \quad \text{all } m. \tag{D.36}$$

Here note that $\breve{\xi}_{mm} = \breve{\xi}_m$.

(3) Estimation of $\widehat{p}_m$: Reorganizing (D.28) and (D.29) yields

$$\left\{(12.42) - \sum_i \hat{Q}^i_m \times (12.41)\right\} = \begin{pmatrix} S_{11} & \cdots & S_{1M} \\ \vdots & \ddots & \vdots \\ S_{M1} & \cdots & S_{MM} \end{pmatrix} \begin{pmatrix} R_1 \\ \vdots \\ R_M \end{pmatrix} = \begin{pmatrix} 0 \\ \vdots \\ 0 \end{pmatrix} \quad \text{(D.37)}$$

where

$$S_{mn} = \frac{\partial \hat{Q}_n}{\partial p_m} - \sum_i \hat{Q}^i_m \frac{\partial \hat{Q}^i_n}{\partial r^i}$$

$$R_m = \hat{\omega}\hat{p}_m - \hat{\tau}_m \frac{\partial \hat{T}_m}{\partial Q_1}.$$

The matrix $\{S_{mn}\}$ is negative definite, as proved below. By Theorem 5.12, it follows that

$$\left|\frac{\partial Q_m}{\partial p_m}\right| \rangle \sum_{n \neq m} \frac{\partial Q_m}{\partial p_n}. \quad \text{(D.38)}$$

In addition, it holds that

$$S_{mm} \geq \left|\frac{\partial Q_m}{\partial\, p_m}\right|, \quad \text{and} \quad S_{mn} \leq \frac{\partial Q_m}{\partial p_n}, \quad \text{(D.39)}$$

since the prime commodity of services is non-inferior. It follows from (D.38) and (D.39) that the matrix $\{S_{mn}\}$ satisfies the diagonal dominance condition and therefore is negative definite.

The fact that $\{S_{mn}\}$ is negative definite implies that the term R_m, for all m, in (D.39) should be zero. Hence,

$$\hat{p}_m = \frac{1}{\hat{\omega}} \hat{\tau}_m \frac{\partial \hat{T}_m}{\partial Q_m}, \quad \text{all } m. \quad \text{(D.40)}$$

(4) Proof of (12.14): Substituting (D.40) into (D.28) gives

$$\frac{\partial \hat{W}}{\partial E\{\bar{U}^i\}} E\{\hat{\eta}^i\} = \hat{\omega} + \sum_n \hat{\omega}\left(\hat{p}_n - \frac{\hat{\tau}_n}{\hat{\omega}} \frac{\partial \hat{T}_n}{\partial Q_n}\right) \frac{\partial \hat{Q}^i_n}{\partial r^i} = \hat{\omega}. \quad \text{(D.41)}$$

(5) Proof of Lemma 12.2: Substituting (12.7) and (D.41) into (D.34) gives

$$\begin{aligned} \delta_m &= \hat{\omega} E\{\xi_m \hat{q}^i_m\} - \hat{\omega}\breve{\xi}_m \sum_i \hat{Q}^i_m \\ &= \hat{\omega}(\hat{\xi}_m - \breve{\xi}_m)\hat{Q}_m, \quad \text{all } m. \end{aligned} \quad \text{(D.42)}$$

Substituting (D.40) and (D.42) into (D.36) leads to

$$\hat{\tau}_m = \hat{\omega}\hat{\xi}_m \hat{Q}_m, \quad \text{all } m. \tag{D.43}$$

(6) Proof of (12.16)–(12.18): Substituting (D.43) into (D.40) yields (12.16). From (D.32) it follows that

$$MKC_m(\hat{c}_m) = p_j \Big/ \frac{\partial \hat{F}_m}{\partial x_{mj}} \tag{D.44}$$

$$= \frac{\hat{\kappa}_m}{\hat{\omega}} \frac{\partial \hat{F}_m}{\partial x_{mj}}, \quad \text{all } m. \tag{D.45}$$

Third, (D.44) implies (12.18). Fourth, substituting (D.43) and (D.45) into (D.31) yields (12.17).

Appendix D.5: Proof of Lemma 12.3 and Theorem 12.4

(1) Development of first order conditions for SW_2: Differentiating the Lagrangian SW_2 with respect to control variables gives

$$\frac{\partial SW_2}{\partial r^i} = -\frac{\partial \widehat{W}}{\partial E\{\bar{U}^i\}} E\{\widehat{\eta}^i\} - \sum_n \widehat{\tau}_n \frac{\partial \widehat{T}_n}{\partial Q_n} \frac{\partial \widehat{Q}^i_n}{\partial r^i} + \widehat{\omega}\left(1 + \sum_n \widehat{p}_n \frac{\partial \widehat{Q}^i_n}{\partial r^i}\right) = 0, \text{ all } i \tag{D.46}$$

$$\frac{\partial SW_2}{\partial p_1} = -\sum_i \frac{\partial \widehat{W}}{\partial E\{\bar{U}^i\}} E\left\{\widehat{\eta}^i \widehat{q}^i_1\right\} - \sum_n \widehat{\tau}_n \frac{\partial \widehat{T}_n}{\partial Q_n} \frac{\partial \widehat{Q}_n}{\partial p_1} + \widehat{\omega}\left(\widehat{Q}_1 + \sum_n \widehat{p}_n \frac{\partial \widehat{Q}_n}{\partial p_1}\right) = 0 \tag{D.47}$$

$$\frac{\partial SW_2}{\partial t_m} = -\sum_i \frac{\partial \widehat{W}}{\partial E\{\bar{U}^i\}} E\left\{\widehat{\eta}^i \xi^i_m \widehat{q}^i_m\right\} + \widehat{\tau}_m - \sum_n \widehat{\tau}_n \frac{\partial \widehat{T}_n}{\partial Q_n} \frac{\partial \widehat{Q}_n}{\partial t_m} + \widehat{\omega} \sum_n \widehat{p}_n \frac{\partial \widehat{Q}_n}{\partial t_m} = 0, \quad \text{all } m \tag{D.48}$$

$$\frac{\partial SW_4}{\partial c_1} = -\widehat{\tau}_1 \frac{\partial \widehat{T}_1}{\partial c_1} - \widehat{\omega} MKC\,(\widehat{c}_1) = 0. \tag{D.49}$$

Note that, in the above, the prices of competing public services are expressed as $\widehat{p}_m$, for all $m \geq 2$, instead of the correct expression p_m, in order to simplify expressions.

(2) Proof of the inequality in (12.28): Arranging (D.46) and (D.48) gives

$$\frac{\partial SW_2}{\partial t_m} - \sum_i \breve{\xi}_m^i \widehat{Q}_m^i \frac{\partial SW_2}{\partial r^i} = -\delta_m + \widehat{\tau}_m - \widehat{\omega}\breve{\xi}_m \widehat{Q}_m$$
$$- \sum_n \breve{\xi}_{mn} S_{mn} \left(\widehat{\tau}_n \frac{\partial \widehat{T}_n}{\partial Q_n} - \widehat{\omega}\widehat{p}_n \right) = 0, \quad \text{(D.50)}$$

where δ_m and S_{mn} are equal to the terms defined in (D.34) and (D.38), respectively.

Subsequently, we simplify (D.50) by applying (12.7) and (12.25). Under the condition of (12.25), (D.46) is simplified as follows:

$$\frac{\partial \widehat{W}}{\partial E\{\bar{U}^i\}} E\{\widehat{\eta}^i\} \cong \widehat{\omega}. \quad \text{(D.51)}$$

Substituting (12.7) and (D.51) into (D.34) gives

$$\delta_m \cong \widehat{\omega}(\xi_m - \breve{\xi}_m)\widehat{Q}_m, \quad \text{all } m. \quad \text{(D.52)}$$

Substituting (D.52) into (D.50) yields

$$\widehat{\tau}_m - \widehat{\omega}\breve{\xi}_m \widehat{Q}_m + \sum_n \breve{\xi}_{mn} S_{mn} \left(\widehat{\omega}\widehat{p}_n - \widehat{\tau}_n \frac{\partial \widehat{T}_n}{\partial Q_n} \right) \cong 0, \quad \text{all} \quad m. \quad \text{(D.53)}$$

Equation (D.53) is reorganized as follows:

$$\begin{pmatrix} \breve{\xi}_{11} S_{11} & \cdots & \breve{\xi}_{1M} S_{1M} \\ \vdots & \ddots & \vdots \\ \breve{\xi}_{M1} S_{M1} & \cdots & \breve{\xi}_{MM} S_{MM} \end{pmatrix} \begin{pmatrix} R_1 \\ \vdots \\ R_M \end{pmatrix} \cong \begin{pmatrix} \widehat{\omega}_1 \breve{\xi}_1 \widehat{Q}_1 - \widehat{\tau}_1 \\ \vdots \\ \widehat{\omega}_M \breve{\xi}_M \widehat{Q}_M - \widehat{\tau}_M \end{pmatrix}, \quad \text{(D.54)}$$

where S_{mn} and R_m are defined in (D.38) and (D.39), respectively.

The matrix $\{\breve{\xi}_{mn} S_{mn}\}$ in (D.54) negative definite, as proved below. By the assumption of (12.25), each element of the matrix in (D.54) is simplified as follows:

$$\breve{\xi}_{mn} S_{mn} \cong \breve{\xi}_{mn} \frac{\partial \widehat{Q}_n}{\partial p_m} = \frac{\partial \widehat{Q}_n}{\partial t_m}. \quad \text{(D.55)}$$

Hence, by the diagonal dominance condition of demand functions for the case of mixed competition in Theorem 5.12, the matrix $\{\breve{\xi}_{mn} S_{mn}\}$ is negative definite.

Since the matrix $\{\breve{\xi}_{mn} S_{mn}\}$ is negative definite, it holds that

$$X \geq 0, \quad \text{if} \quad -\{S_{mn}\}X \geq 0, \quad \text{(D.56)}$$

where X is a column vector (refer to the theorem introduced in Appendix C.3). This implies that

$$p_m - \frac{\widehat{\tau}_m}{\widehat{\omega}}\frac{\partial \widehat{T}_m}{\partial Q_m} \geq 0, \quad \text{if} \quad \widehat{\omega}\widehat{\xi}_m \widehat{Q}_m - \widehat{\tau}_m \geq 0, \quad \text{all} \quad m. \tag{D.57}$$

Multiplying $\widehat{\omega}^{-1}\partial \widehat{T}_m/\partial Q_m$ to the condition $\widehat{\omega}\widehat{\xi}_m \widehat{Q}_m - \widehat{\tau}_m \geq 0$ gives

$$\widehat{\xi}_m \widehat{Q}_m \frac{\partial \widehat{T}_m}{\partial Q_m} - \frac{\widehat{\tau}_m}{\widehat{\omega}}\frac{\partial \widehat{T}_m}{\partial Q_m} \geq \widehat{\xi}_m \widehat{Q}_m \frac{\partial \widehat{T}_m}{\partial Q_m} - p_m \geq 0, \quad \text{all} \quad m. \tag{D.58}$$

Hence, it follows that

$$\widehat{p}_m - \frac{\widehat{\tau}_m}{\widehat{\omega}}\frac{\partial \widehat{T}_m}{\partial Q_m} \geq 0, \quad \text{if} \quad \widehat{p}_m - \widehat{\xi}_m \widehat{Q}_m \frac{\partial \widehat{T}_m}{\partial Q_m} \geq 0, \quad \text{all} \quad m. \tag{D.59}$$

(3) Estimation of $\widehat{\tau}_1$ in (12.27): Arranging (D.47) and (D.48) gives

$$\begin{aligned}\breve{\xi}_1 \frac{\partial SW_2}{\partial p_1} - \frac{\partial SW_2}{\partial t_1} &= \widehat{\omega}\breve{\xi}_1 \widehat{Q}_1 - \widehat{\tau}_1 + \delta_1 + \sum_n (\breve{\xi}_{1n} - \breve{\xi}_1)\left(\widehat{\tau}_n \frac{\partial \widehat{T}_n}{\partial Q_n} - \widehat{\omega}\widehat{p}_n\right)\frac{\partial \widehat{Q}_n}{\partial p_1} \\ &= 0. \end{aligned} \tag{D.60}$$

Substituting (12.26) into (D.60) gives

$$\begin{aligned}\widehat{\tau}_1 &\cong \widehat{\omega}\breve{\xi}_1 \widehat{Q}_1 + \delta_1 \\ &= \widehat{\omega}\widehat{\xi}_1 \widehat{Q}_1. \end{aligned} \tag{D.61}$$

(4) Proof of (12.29) and (12.30): Reorganizing (D.46) and (D.47) yields

$$\frac{\partial SW_2}{\partial p_1} - \sum_i \frac{\partial SW_2}{\partial r^i}\widehat{Q}_1^i = \sum_n S_{1n}\left(\widehat{\omega}\widehat{p}_n - \widehat{\tau}_n \frac{\partial \widehat{T}_n}{\partial Q_n}\right) = 0. \tag{D.62}$$

Substituting (D.61) into (D.62) gives the pricing rule in (12.29). Substituting (D.61) into (D.49) yields (12.30).

Appendix D.6: Proof of Equation 12.32

(1) Development of first order conditions for SW_2: Differentiating SW_2 in (12.31) with respect to control variables, and simplifying the preceding outcomes using (12.25) gives

$$\frac{\partial SW_3}{\partial r^i} = 0 \cong -\frac{\partial \widehat{W}}{\partial E\{\bar{U}^i\}} E\left\{\widehat{\eta}^i\right\} + \widehat{\omega}, \quad \text{all} \quad i \tag{D.63}$$

$$\frac{\partial SW_3}{\partial p_1} = 0 \cong -\sum_n \widehat{\tau}_n \frac{\partial \widehat{T}_n}{\partial Q_n} \frac{\partial \widehat{Q}_n}{\partial p_1} + \widehat{\omega} \widehat{p}_1 \frac{\partial \widehat{Q}_1}{\partial p_1} \tag{D.64}$$

$$\frac{\partial SW_3}{\partial t_m} = 0 \cong -\widehat{\omega} \sum_i E\left\{\xi^i_m \widehat{q}^i_m\right\} + \widehat{\tau}_m - \sum_n \widehat{\tau}_n \frac{\partial \widehat{T}_n}{\partial Q_n} \frac{\partial \widehat{Q}_n}{\partial t_m}$$

$$+\widehat{\omega} \widehat{p}_1 \frac{\partial \widehat{Q}_1}{\partial t_m}, \quad \text{all} \quad m. \tag{D.65}$$

(2) Estimation of $\widehat{\tau}_1$: Using (12.4) and (12.5), arranging (D.64) and (D.65) gives

$$\breve{\xi}_1 \frac{\partial SW_3}{\partial p_1} - \frac{\partial SW_3}{\partial t_1} = 0 \cong \widehat{\omega} \breve{\xi}_1 \widehat{Q}_1 - \widehat{\tau}_1 + \sum_n \widehat{\tau}_n (\breve{\xi}_{1n} - \breve{\xi}_1) \frac{\partial \widehat{T}_n}{\partial Q_n} \frac{\partial \widehat{Q}_n}{\partial p_1}.$$

$$+ \widehat{\omega} (\breve{\xi}_1 - \breve{\xi}_{1n}) \widehat{p}_1 \frac{\partial \widehat{Q}_1}{\partial p_1}. \tag{D.66}$$

Under the condition of (12.26), it follows from (D.66) that

$$\widehat{\tau}_1 \cong \widehat{\omega} \breve{\xi}_1 \widehat{Q}_1. \tag{D.67}$$

(3) Estimation of $\widehat{p}_1$: Reorganizing (D.63) and (D.64) yields

$$\frac{\partial SW_3}{\partial p_1} - \sum_i \frac{\partial SW_3}{\partial r^i} \widehat{Q}^i_1 = \widehat{\omega} S_{11} \widehat{p}_1 - \sum_n \widehat{\tau}_n S_{1n} \frac{\partial \widehat{T}_n}{\partial Q_n} = 0. \tag{D.68}$$

Substituting (D.67) into (D.68) gives the final result of (12.32).

References

Bartle RG (1976) The elements of real analysis, 2nd edn. Wiley, New York
Baumol WJ, Bradford DF (1970) Optimal departure from marginal cost pricing. Am Econ Rev 60:265–83
Becker GS (1965) A theory of the allocation of time. Econ J 75:493–517
Beckmann M, McGuire CB, Winston CB (1955) Studies in the economics of transportation. Yale University Press, New Haven
Ben-Akiva M (1974) Structure of passenger travel demand models. Trans Res Rec 526:26–42
Berge C (1963) Topological spaces, (trans: Patterson EM). The Macmillan Company, New York
Bertrand J (1883) Review of Walras's théorie mathématique de la richesse sociale and Cournot's recherches sur les principes mathématiques de la théorie des richesses. Journal des Savants. In: Daughety AF (eds) (1988) Cournot oligopoly: characterization and applications. Cambridge University Press, Cambridge
Boadway RW (1979) Public sector economics. Winthrop Publishers, Inc., Cambridge
Boudreau PE, Griffin JS, Kac M (1962) An elementary queuing problem. Am Math Mon 69:713–724
Boyce DE (1984) Urban transportation network-equilibrium and design models: recent achievements and future prospects. Environ Plan A-16:1445–1474
Boyce DE (1987) Integration of supply and demand models in transportation and location. Environ Plan 18:485–489
Burns ME (1973) A note on the concept and measure of consumer's surplus. Am Econ Rev 63:335–338
Chamberlin EH (1933) The theory of monopolistic competition. Harvard University Press, Cambridge
Cinlar E (1975) Introduction to stochastic processes. Prentice-Hall, Inc., Englewood Cliffs
Cournot A (1838) Of the competition of producers (Chapter 7, Review of Walras's théorie mathématique de la richesse sociale and Cournot's recherches sur les principes mathématiques de la théorie des richesses. L. Hachette, Paris) In: Daughty AF (eds) (1988) Cournot oligopoly: characterization and applications. Cambridge University Press, Cambridge
Currie JM, Murphy JA, Schmitz A (1971) The concept of economic surplus and its use in economic analysis. Econ J 81(324):741–765
De Palma A, Meyers GM, Papageorgiou YY (1994) Rational choice under imperfect ability to choose. Am Econ Rev 84:419–440
DeVany AS, Saving TR (1980) Competition and highway pricing for stochastic traffic. J Bus 53:45–60
Diamond PA, McFadden DL (1974) Some uses of the expenditure function in public finance. J Pub Econ 3:3–21

D.J. Moon, *Congestion-Prone Services Under Quality Competition*,
Advances in Spatial Science, DOI 10.1007/978-3-642-20189-9,

Diamond PA, Mirrlees JA (1971) Optimal taxation and public production. Am Econ Rev 62 (8–27):261–78
Domencich T, McFadden D (1975) Urban travel demand: a behavioral analysis. North-Holland, Amsterdam
Douglas GW, Miller JC III (1974) Quality competition, industry equilibrium, and efficiency in the price-constrained airline market. Am Econ Rev 64:657–669
Feller W (1966) An Introduction to probability theory and its application, vol II. Wiley, New York
Frieman JW (1983) Oligopoly theory. Cambridge University Press, Cambridge
Hall RE (1973) The specification of technology with several kinds of output. J Polit Econ 81 (4):878–892
Harberger AC (1971) Three basic postulates for applied economics: an interpretive essay. J Econ Lit 9:785–97
Jara-Diaz SR, Videla J (1989) Detection of income effect in mode choice: theory and application. Trans Res B 23(6):393–400
Keeler TE, Small KA (1977) Optimal peak-load pricing, investment, and service levels on urban expressways. J Polit Econ 85(1):1–25
Kockelman KM (2001) A model for time- and budget-constrained activity demand analysis. Trans Res B 35:255–269
Kolmogorov AN, Fomin SV (1970) Introductory real analysis. Dover Publication, Inc., New York
Lancaster KJ (1966) A new approach to consumer theory. J Polit Econ 74:132–156
Lancaster KJ (1975) Optimal product differentiation. Am Econ Rev 65(65):567–585
Luenberger DG (1969) Optimization by vector space method. Wiley, New York
Manheim ML (1979) Fundamentals of transportation systems analysis. The MIT press, Cambridge
Manski C (1977) The structure of random utility models. Theor Decis 8:229–254
McFadden D (1973) Conditional logit analysis of qualitative choice behaviors. In: Zarembka P (ed) Frontiers in econometrics. Academic, New York, pp 105–142
McFadden D (1998) Measuring willingness-to-pay for transportation improvements. In: Gärling T et al (eds) Theoretical foundation of travel choice modeling. Elsevier Science, Oxford
Meyer JR, Kain JF, Wohl M (1965) The urban transportation problem. Harvard University Press, Cambridge
Mills DE (1981) Ownership arrangements and congestion-prone facilities. Am Econ Rev 71 (3):493–502
Mills E, McDonald J (eds) (1992) Sources of metropolitan growth and development. Rutgers University, Center of Urban Policy Research, New Brunswick
Mishan EJ (1976) Cost benefit analysis. Praeger Publishers, New York
Mohring H (1970) The peak load problem with increasing returns and pricing constraints. Am Econ Rev 60:693–705
Mohring H (1972) Optimization and scale economies in urban bus transportation. Am Econ Rev 62:591–604
Mohring H, Harwitz M (1962) Highway benefits: an analytical framework. Northwestern University, Evanston
Moon DJ, Kim TJ (2002) Assessment of travel choice decisions under household production theory, presented at the 49th annual North American meetings of the Regional Science Association International, San Juan
Moon DJ, Park CH (2002a) Cost functions for multiple transportation modes in the presence of congestion. Ann Reg Sci 36:315–346
Moon DJ, Park CH (2002b) Congestion pricing of multi-modal transportation systems. Ann Reg Sci 36:455–481
Moses LN, Williamson HF (1963) Value of time, choice of mode, and the subsidy issue in urban transportation. J Polit Econ 71:247–264
Muellbauer J (1974) Household production theory, quality, and the "hedonic technique". Am Econ Rev 64(6):977–993
Nikaido H (1968) Convex structures and economic theory. Academic, New York

Pollak RA, Wachter ML (1975) The relevance of the household production function and its implications for the allocation of time. J Polit Econ 83(2):255–277
Rockafellar RT (1970) Convex analysis. Princeton University Press, Princeton
Rockafellar RT, Wets RJ-B (1978) The optimal recourse problem in discrete time L^1-multipliers for inequality constraints. SIAM J Control Optim 16(1):16–35
Roth RD (1977) An approach to measurement of modal advantages. American Trucking Association, Washington, DC
Samuelson PA (1947) Foundations of economic analysis. Harvard University Press, Cambridge
Samuelson PA (1956) Social indifference curves. Q J Econ 70:1–22
Sandmo A (1973) Public goods and the technology of consumption. Rev Econ Stud 40:517–528
Sheffi Y (1985) Urban transportation networks: equilibrium analysis with mathematical programming methods. Prentice-Hall, Inc., Englewood Cliffs
Silberberg E (1981) The structure of economics: a mathematical analysis. McGraw-Hill Book Company, New York
Small KA (1992) Urban transportation economics. Harwood Academic Publishers, Luxembourg
Sweezy PM (1939) Demand under condition of oligopoly. J Polit Econ 47:568–573
Transportation Research Board (1999) Highway capacity manual, special report 209. National Research Council, Washington, DC
Vickrey WS (1963) Pricing in urban and suburban transport. Am Econ Rev Pap Proc 53:452–465
Willig RD (1976) Consumer's surplus without apology. Am Econ Rev 66:589–597
Wohl M (1972) Transportation investment planning. Lexington Books, Lexington

Index

D.J. Moon, *Congestion-Prone Services Under Quality Competition*,
Advances in Spatial Science, DOI 10.1007/978-3-642-20189-9,

O

P

Q

R

S